To. Thad
Best Wishes for Xmas.
1985.
LES.

An attractive border of tulips and grape hyacinths.

EVERYDAY GARDENING

EVERYDAY GARDENING

Edited by C. E. PEARSON, O.B.E., N.D.A.

Contributors: F. A BUSH, W. G. FRY,
J. C. GOUGH, C. E. PEARSON,
R. C. M. WRIGHT

TREASURE PRESS

First published in Great Britain by Ward Lock Ltd
This edition published in 1983 by Treasure Press
59 Grosvenor Street
London W1

Revised 1971
Reprinted 1985
ISBN 0 907812 32 5
Printed in Czechoslovakia
50521/2

Contents

CHAPTER ONE

Garden Tools and Equipment

THAT good tools and equipment pay is a principle which should be accepted by all gardeners. Well-made tools outlast poor ones and are generally less fatiguing to use.

In this chapter it is not intended to give descriptions of spades, forks, rakes and hoes—these are the four chief tools needed for the cultivation of any small piece of garden land—because they are well known and can be easily obtained from any good ironmonger or garden supplies shop. Such stores also display many other useful items of equipment; for example, trowels of many shapes for small plantings, weeding tools to clean between rows or among border plants, others to take weeds out of lawns, barrows, sieves, watering cans and innumerable other tools and gadgets. Although the general form of garden tools does not change, different designs are occasionally introduced by manufacturers.

The increasing use of rust-resisting finishes is one of the notable advances of recent years, and tools made of such material are well worth their slight extra cost. Rusty tools and any which are put away without being cleaned do not make for clean and well finished work; besides they need more effort to use than clean, bright ones.

Sundry cutting tools will be wanted in most gardens in addition to cultivating equipment. Long-handled shears are needed to keep edges and corners of lawns tidy; lawn shears are those with a horizontal cut, while border shears with a vertical cut are used for edging. Special edge trimmers can be used instead of border shears. They can be pushed along and cut faster than shears, but to ensure a good finish with a trimmer the lawn's edges must be firm and stand well above the border or path.

Short-handled shears are used for a multitude of jobs, notably for hedge trimming, and the size chosen depends upon the type of work. If a lot of hedge cutting of mixed growth has to be done then a robust tool with a 9- or 10-in. blade should be purchased, and the blade should be a 'notched' blade if the growth is unusually strong. On the other hand, if the work is likely to be only the trimming of soft growth or perhaps the tidying up of unwanted growth in the herbaceous border, then a small size will be more suitable and certainly lighter to use. For this kind of work a blade 6 or 7 in. long should be large enough.

When buying tools it is as well to remember that one which feels light is likely to be the more comfortable to use, but it must not be so small that an unnecessary number of strokes are needed to cover the work, for that will defeat the object which, of course, is to get over the work with the minimum of effort. So, when choosing insist on handling tools of differing weights, and lengths, before deciding. A handle, especially of a digging tool, if it is too long is uncomfortable to use and makes for slow work, whereas too short a handle or shaft is apt to produce a backache! Beginners are advised to start with good quality tools of conventional design. Patented or special types can wait until experience shows where, or how, these special kinds can be really helpful.

Thanks to the ingenuity of horticultural engineers in the application of mechanical power to gardening operations it is now true to say that the backache can be taken out of most garden jobs.

Grass cutting and digging are two operations which take a lot of physical effort and time, but both these heavy jobs, as well as many others, can be eased and speeded up if done by powered tools. Before considering the type and capabilities of various machines it is well to look at some fundamentals.

Petrol engines

Most garden power tools are equipped with petrol engines although a few designs are driven by electric motors. Petrol engines are of two types, the 'four-stroke' and 'two-stroke'.

When petrol engines were first introduced to drive small mowers and other garden tools two-stroke engines were used because they were then the only truly efficient small petrol engine. Subsequent developments have resulted in the production of equally efficient small four-stroke engines and these are to a large extent replacing the two-stroke, although the simplicity of the two-stroke with its smaller number of moving parts still appeals to those who wish to do the necessary maintenance themselves. Two-strokes are slightly cheaper than four-strokes with a corresponding power output and this, of course, is reflected in the price of the machine. The purring note of a two-stroke engine, in good order, is somewhat less distracting than is the sharper bark of the four-stroke. On the other hand, some two-strokes are difficult to re-start when they are warm and are apt to soot up the sparking plug. A sooted plug makes for difficult starting from cold and for inefficient running, and owners of two-strokes will be well advised to keep a clean sparking plug on hand to put in if their engine does not start quickly or runs erratically. The plug that is taken out can be cleaned and kept on hand for future use.

The changing of a sparking plug is not difficult, and the choice of a machine need not be influenced by this factor. The choice should be based on the suitability of the machine itself for the work required of it, taking into account the views of the person who will use it most often. Having acquired a machine, keep it, and particularly its engine, in good order and follow implicitly the maintenance routine given in the maker's instruction book. Proper attention as laid down should result in many seasons of useful service. *Most complaints and trouble arise from not carrying out the maker's instructions.*

Most small engines are started by a 'recoil starter', a device by which an engine can be made to turn over (revolve) quickly several times when a cord, attached to the engine's crankshaft, is pulled outwards. A handle is fitted to the cord for easy use and on the recoil the cord rewinds itself after each pull and so is instantly ready for use. This is a simple and trouble-free method of starting, but another type, best described as an 'impulse starter', is in use and may prove popular. An impulse starter as seen on some of the newer machines is perhaps one that calls for less exertion than does a recoil starter but it is more complicated. In some designs a small handle on the top of the engine is turned and in turning winds up a spring which, when released by a suitable device, causes the engine to turn over quickly and start. Bigger machines and those that are almost outside the garden range, are started by a conventional 'kick starter'.

Engine controls

The majority of garden grass cutting or cultivating machines driven by small petrol engines have only two controls. One is the throttle by means of which the power of the engine, and so the speed of the machine, can be controlled, and the other is the clutch, the engagement or withdrawal of which causes the machine to move or stop. A few of the biggest machines may have a variable-speed gear providing more than one forward speed or even a reverse but these are not common; the detail of their operation is described in the handbooks issued with them.

A variant of the simple clutch and throttle controls which is sometimes used might puzzle those coming across it for the first time. It is known by various names; 'automatic', 'automotive', 'centrifugal' or 'self-energizing' clutch being those most commonly used. This is a device which makes the usual hand clutch control unnecessary because an automatic clutch engages itself as the opening of the throttle allows the engine speed to increase. At a predetermined engine speed the clutch engages and the machine moves off. Similarly, as the engine speed is decreased, by closing the throttle, the machine will come to rest. This simplicity of control appeals strongly to some users, whilst others hold that real delicacy of control is lost in a centrifugal clutch. Centrifugal clutches are, of necessity, more complex than the hand-controlled variety, and users must realize that any action, a stumble perhaps, that inadvertently causes the throttle to be opened wider makes the machine travel forward faster and that it will not stop travelling until the throttle is closed. A machine with the two usual controls can be stopped by disengaging the clutch, so leaving the engine running, or by closing the throttle and so stopping both engine and machine.

Electric motors

The outstanding advantage which might be expected from the use of an electrically driven tool is silence. Unfortunately some designs produce a high-pitched hum or whine, but the absence of the noise and fumes from the exhaust of a petrol engine is often more than welcome. The great disadvantage of any electric motor supplied by current from the mains is that the supply must be brought to it through a trailing cable. While this is not a disadvantage to a stationary machine, such as a saw bench, a cable that has to be pulled around can be a nuisance to anyone using a moving machine. It frequently happens that the only socket to which a cable's plug can be connected is within the house and this in itself is an inconvenience. A special socket can be provided out of doors, but if this is done it *must* be of the special weatherproof kind and *be put in by an expert, otherwise it can become very dangerous in wet or damp weather.*

If a trailing cable is accidentally cut and the current it carries is being taken direct from the mains the user of the machine runs the risk of receiving a very severe electric shock, which could be, and sometimes is, fatal. It is common sense and sound practice to insist, if a mains-powered tool is to be selected, that it is one with a motor designed to operate on a reduced voltage of not more than 110 volts. Then the mains current must come through a transformer which the maker of the machine will probably supply with safety instructions. This method is one of the safest because the danger of a shock at mains voltage is absent.

Lawn mowers are also made with a battery-operated electric motor. This method retains the great advantage of silent operation and is more mobile than the mains-operated type because there is no need for a cumbersome trailing cable. On the other hand the battery must be kept charged and topped up in the same way as a car battery, and during winter months must not be allowed to spoil from lack of care. These are not such great difficulties as they may first seem. A battery charger is now incorporated in the machine so all that is needed to keep the battery in good order is to plug it in to the house mains from time to time. After charging, it should be topped up with distilled water as necessary. Battery-driven machines are a new departure but they have so much to commend them that they may well become one of the commonest types of power mowers. As they operate from a 12-volt battery the danger of a severe shock is entirely absent.

Power-take-off points

The versatility of several of the grass cutting and the cultivating machines is increased by the use of a 'power-take-off', a device, as its name suggests, whereby the power of the engine can be transmitted, usually by a flexible shaft, but sometimes by a belt, to some stationary machine, with the parent machine acting for the time being merely as a frame to hold the engine.

Lawn mowers and grass cutters

The ordinary type of lawn mower in which a cylinder of five or six blades is made to revolve over a fixed knife, is so well known as to need no description here. Of the two varieties of cylinder mower, that is, roller or side-wheel machines, roller models are those most commonly supplied with power drive. They may be had in various widths, from a 12-in. cut upwards. A favourite size for use in gardens is a 14-in., but for large areas of grass cuts of greater width are more suitable. If the amount of grass to be covered warrants the expense, a machine with a 36-in. cut and trailing seat will be very suitable. Side-wheel machines, usually with a cut of about 20 in., are available too, with power drive, but the smaller sizes of this type are not mechanically driven. The great merit of the roller models is that they are solid machines which in use have the effect of rolling the grass while cutting. They are the most suitable for use on grass that is used as a playing court.

When choosing a cylinder mower the number of blades comprising the cutting cylinder should be examined. The popular 12- and 14-in. power-driven machines usually have cylinders of five or six blades; a few may have more. Really big machines with cuts of 20 in. upwards may have ten or twelve blades. Hand-pushed machines usually have cylinders composed of five or six blades. The number of blades comprising the cylinder and the speed at which it revolves affect the number of cuts the machine makes in a given length of travel and so it will be seen that the mowers having cutting cylinders with the greater number of blades will leave a better finish than machines with a much smaller number. On the other hand, the higher the number of cuts the greater the energy needed to drive the machine. But the experience of many years is reflected in the machines now made and prospective buyers can rest content that mowers by reputable makers are designed to do good work whatever the source of power used.

Rotary cutters

In recent years rotary mowers or grass cutters have come into use and their popularity seems to be increasing. They are simple and generally cheaper than roller mowers of equal width. The popular sizes, with cutting widths of 18 in. or 21 in., have to be pushed but as the machines are mounted on four wheels they travel easily over lawn turf. On long grass the effort needed to push them may be considerable. The rotating cutting blade is driven by the engine and the largest machines, which deal easily with long grass as well as short, are propelled by the engine too.

In this sort of machine the cutter revolves in a horizontal plane and may be a disc to the periphery of which cutting knives are attached, or a knife mounted at its central point so that both ends are used for cutting. There is little to choose between the two types; the knives of the first mentioned type can be renewed easily and the two-ended knife of the other is generally so made that when it becomes blunt it can be reversed and two fresh edges be presented for work before re-sharpening is needed. The rotaries are powered by small petrol engines. No clutch is provided on the small hand-pushed machines, the engine thus having a direct drive to the cutting blade, so that when the engine is running the cutter must be revolving at high speed. Alteration to the height of cut is commonly made by adjusting the wheel carriage whereby the whole machine is raised or lowered as needed. It will be appreciated that this kind of adjustment means that the distance between the ground and the bottom edge of the machine gets greater as the length of cut is increased. Users must always be careful not to get a foot or hand under a rotary cutter or serious injury may result, and fingers or toes may be lost! Rotaries make a most useful addition to labour-saving garden tools and there are thousands in use, but the possibility of injury must never be forgotten.

Although rotary machines are efficient they do not cut as closely as cylinder mowers. For lawns which are not to be played on they are excellent, but it must be remembered that they have to be pushed and that they are light and do not roll the grass. Many of them have no provision for collecting the cut grass but often this is so cut up that it is discharged in a fine state and acts as a mulch, to the benefit of the lawn. A few, however, have collectors to receive the cut grass. Rotary cutters show to the greatest advantage when used on large expanses of grass.

Motor cultivators

There are many designs of garden cultivators available as a glance in the windows of garden shops or ironmongers will show. They are sometimes called 'garden tractors', but whatever their name they are designed to do a variety of jobs and to take different kinds of tools. For a small garden most of the work can be done with one machine and its numerous attachments, which is an economy in that only one engine is bought. Since it will be used for so many jobs the running cost per hour will be smaller and the capital outlay on equipment reduced.

It is a matter of opinion, and often for heated discussion during winter evenings, at what point it is more economical to equip a garden with separate engine-driven tools, such as a lawn mower, a cultivator and, possibly, a sprayer, instead of getting all these facilities from one all-purpose machine with a suitable range of attachments and fittings.

An attachment for rotary cultivation is available with most motor cultivators and will be needed by many who wish to avoid the labour of digging. These attachments are either front or rear mounted and both will do good work within their range. Some users hold that machines with rear-mounted rotors are easier to keep on a line of work than those in which the rotor is in front, but much depends upon the operator, the sort of job and the kind of land on which the machine is to be used. If the going is very hard and the land rough, a front mounting may cause the tool to jump about and deviate from a straight line more than one with a rear-mounted rotor. The designs are different and machines with rear-mounted tools are usually the more costly, but this question of ability to hold the machine on a required line is one of prime importance, for much of the hardest work it will have to do will be with the rotor in place. It is wise to make a preliminary examination of a range of machines at a stockists' premises and select one or two from the range for demonstration and trial on the purchaser's own land. At such a demonstration all the attachments that will be needed should be tried out, and the method by which they are attached to and detached from the machine's main frame should be examined. It is essential that the operator should know how to fit the various tools properly *and safely*. The methods used by manufacturers vary. A good design will be one in which the attachments or linkages are simple and robust. Complicated linkages are time-wasting nuisances while thin and flimsy ones must be regarded with suspicion because they may break, bend or sag in use and prove expensive to replace.

In addition to a rotary cultivator most of these machines may be equipped with tools for cultivating, harrowing, ridging and the like. Grass-cutting attachments are generally available too, so that the machines can be converted to a cylinder mower, rotary cutter or power scythe (with a reciprocating knife) at will. It is becoming general practice to provide a power-take-off point on these general purpose machines, as well as on some mowers, and a power-take-off extends the usefulness of the machine to still more kinds of work. Flexible shaft-driven tools, such as hedge cutters, can be worked from a power-take-off, and drives for small saw benches, dynamos, pumps and sprayers can also be arranged by means of a flexible shaft or belt and pulley drives. Some of these versatile machines can be supplied with a small bulldozer blade which could be of great value for pushing soil on, or from, banks when making a garden. Specially designed trailers are offered by some makers so that transport of materials to and from the site is added to the list of useful work that can be got from a carefully selected motor 'cultivator'.

Naturally the bigger and heavier machines with the more powerful engines will tackle hard rough work better than less powerful and lighter ones, but it is surprising what the smaller ones will accomplish if users are content to take a narrow, or shallow, cut in accordance with the engine's capability and so not force the machine, but it will be necessary to repeat the operation a number of times until the desired result is achieved. It is bad practice and a waste of time to attempt to force a low-powered machine beyond its capability; damage to the engine and the tool in use may well result. 'Gently and with patience' must be the motto if a rough job is to be attempted with a small machine.

The lower-powered lighter machines should be regarded as essentially garden cultivation and general aid tools. They can be bought at prices ranging from about £40 to £100 or so. The bigger machines with engines of about 5 h.p. or 7 h.p. costing somewhere about £200 according to the tools chosen to go with them can be used successfully for rough work in the first preparation of a new garden site and later for much of the continuing cultivations but by reason of their size they are of little use in ornamental gardens, except for grass cutting. If really large areas have to be dealt with there are one or two machines which are miniature tractors that may be worth considering. Grass cutting, cultivating, harrowing and other tools are made specially for them and they are powered by 8–9 h.p. engines. They are expensive, and when equipped with a modest range of tools might cost up to £500. They are useful machines for large garden estates, but are outside the range of the small garden enthusiast. The direct opposite to the miniature tractor is the tiny electrically driven hoe/tiller. Driven by a motor taking its current through a trailing cable from the nearest mains point this tiny tool will hoe or cultivate, according to the blades in use. It is about 6 in. in width and can be useful in rose beds or herbaceous borders.

Hedge cutters

For keeping a length of hedge in good order mechanical cutters will prove to be a labour- and time-saving boon. They are reliable, easy to manipulate and not expensive. There are two kinds in use; in the one the knife is actuated by power transmitted from a power-take-off point on a garden cultivator or mower through a flexible shaft, in the other the knife is driven by a small electric motor which is an integral part of the tool. In the latter case the motor gets its current through a trailing cable and so has all the disadvantages arising from this. The lack of mobility can be overcome if a cutter working on 110 volts is chosen and the current is provided by a dynamo which is itself driven from the power-take-off of a motor cultivator or mower. Battery-operated cutters are also available. A trailing cable is still necessary with both types, but it need not be so long since a battery or dynamo as the source of power can be moved about to convenient points. Besides mobility the low-voltage method avoids the danger of the operator receiving a severe, and perhaps fatal, shock if the cable is inadvertently cut through.

Flame guns

Flame guns produce a forced and very hot flame for killing weeds on drives and paths or cleaning the joints in crazy paving. They burn paraffin and work on the same principle as pressure stoves and lamps. Small ones are tubular in form and can be used and carried in the hand quite easily but larger ones are mounted on a light wheeled frame and the flame is covered by a metal hood so that it is directed downwards. They face strong competition from modern weed-killers.

Sprayers

The choice of a suitable sprayer depends, as with other equipment, on the sort of garden it is to be used in and the kind of plants grown. If there is a fruit section a good machine which will deliver spray fluid at a pressure of 80 lb. per sq. in. is likely to be the most suitable. There are a number of these and, as has been mentioned earlier, many of the motor cultivating machines have also a spraying attachment which may be suitable. For effective spraying of fruit trees in large plantations pressure is important if the top branches are to be reached and time is not to be wasted, and if a choice of machines is available the one which will give a pressure up to 100 lb. per sq. in. is preferable to one in which the maximum pressure is lower.

The very small pneumatic sprayers, holding about a quart of fluid, are very useful for the small garden. Larger sprayers holding from 1–4 gal. are available in several makes and different models of each make. Many of these machines are supplied with carrying straps and a few are available on wheels. The commonest form of pneumatic sprayers is one in which the spray fluid is put into the machine's tank and air is pumped in until a sufficient pressure is obtained when the machine is ready for use. Development in spraying techniques and machines is continuous and a gardener with a lot of spraying to get over ought to consider the latest ideas before deciding what kind of equipment is best suited to his purpose.

We have been accustomed to spray fluids composed of an active chemical agent dissolved or suspended in a large volume of water. Recent developments are towards low-volume spraying in which new chemicals are used. These are effective in minute quantities carried in quite small volumes of water. Such concentrated material needs to be applied in a special form of spray. Air-blast machines are used in which a small quantity of fluid is fed into a blast of air from a high-speed fan. The result is an extremely fine mist which can be thrown to the tops of orchard trees or directed downwards for ground crops. These machines are expensive but very efficient; at least one model is available in knapsack form.

Garden sheds and stores

A place to keep tools and equipment is essential. From the many designs of sectional sheds available it should be easy to find something suitable, unless it is decided to build a shed to blend in with the surroundings of the chosen site. A common fault is to put up a shed that is soon found to be too small. Always allow plenty of floor space to begin with; it is difficult to enlarge after the building is up and in use. Before building or buying, it must be decided if the shed is to be merely a place to hold tools and equipment. If so the door must be wide enough to enable mowers or cultivators to be put inside and parked in their proper places without other things having to be moved, and double doors may be the most convenient. Arrangements should be made for hand tools and items of small equipment to be hung up rather than left standing on the floor, and for hooks, nails or racks to keep things where they can be found quickly and put away easily. If possible the floor should be concrete.

But many garden sheds have to serve more than one purpose. As well as providing space for tools it may be necessary to accommodate a potting bench or storage trays or bins. If so, and particularly if it is likely that much time will be spent at the bench, a wooden floor for that part of the shed will be found more comfortable for standing on. If, however, the floor is made throughout of concrete a platform of wooden slats may serve instead, although it can cause the unwary to trip, especially when carrying a load. A dark shed is never satisfactory. It should be light even if it is supposed to be merely a tool store; sooner or later some other job

PLATE I
Left ALYSSUM. Two species make good border plants, the others are mostly suited to the rock garden.
Below ALTHAEA (Hollyhock). Make most attractive plants in a "cottage" type border.

PLATE 2
Left ANTHEMIS (Chamomile). There are a few species suitable for the rock garden or border.
Below ANTIRRHINUM (Snapdragon). Shown here in a border backed with a row of stately hollyhocks.

will have to be done in it. At least one window in a potting shed should be placed to direct good light on to the bench.

If a potting bench is to be put in, a good type is one with a high back to which divisions can be fixed to make bins for various compost mixtures. This is convenient but takes up a lot of space and the alternative is to make up bins under the bench. Cleaned pots and trays should be kept handy to the bench to be ready for use and in the dry. It is a waste of time to clean dirty pots and then leave them outside where they get wet and may become contaminated with disease.

Produce stores

Stores for fruit and vegetables have certain requirements which are common to both. They need to be frost proof and to remain at a steady temperature, about 4·4 deg. C. or 40 deg. F. They should be dry and are better if they are dark. The common kind of garden shed is not suitable for prolonged storage because its thin walls and roof allow far too great a variation of the inside temperature. A garden store must be well insulated, usually by using double walls and packing the intervening space with an insulating material, while the roof can be constructed in the same way or it may be thatched. A thatch roof is attractive and has the double merit of providing good insulation as well. If it is given a good thick cover, 18 in. or more, no other roof insulation should be needed. An earth floor is very suitable so long as the site is dry or outside drainage is arranged to take off surface water. A wet floor is useless.

A more elaborate store can be made by excavating the site and putting the store below, or partially below, ground level. It is easier to maintain a steady temperature in this way. The walls should be of brick, preferably cavity, and treated with damp-proof material. A thatch roof is the most suitable, but if this cannot be provided then a double roof well insulated must be used. Drainage in a below-ground store is very important and will depend on the type of soil and the slope of the land. It may be essential to drain the site first and to provide valley gutters around the building to take off surface drainage water. Given a good below-ground store, apples and other produce can be kept in good condition. If large quantities of apples are to be kept for long periods then a refrigerated store might be worth considering. It would be expensive and for the private grower might be thought a luxury.

Watering systems

Every gardener knows that plants use water quickly in hot weather and that to replenish what has been used can be a slow, laborious job, but today it is not necessary to stand and hold a hose for long periods. The advent of the plastic hose and couplings has got rid of the old weighty rubber and canvas hose, and those wretched brass couplings which always seemed to leak and so easily got damaged have gone too and been replaced by simple plastic fittings.

It is not a very expensive matter to run a plastic hose around those parts of the garden which are likely to need frequent water, which means to practically every part except to established shrubs, and to cut the hose at convenient places and insert 'plug-in' fittings. Then a sprinkler with its own shorter hose can easily be connected up and after its set time be moved on to another of the connectors. Sprinklers which can be set to differing positions to give different spray patterns can be used. The revolving or oscillating kind are popular but in some places a 'sprinkler hose' might be the best thing to have. There are many varieties to choose from. Shut-off valves are available too, and will shut off the water from a hose after it has been running for a given time or after it has delivered a given volume. These are adjustable so that the amount of water used can be altered to suit different crops or conditions.

A most clever device for watering large areas is a travelling spray. This consists of a hose which is first laid out along the path that the spray is to cover. When the water is turned on the sprinkler gradually travels back along the laid out hose line and some types will even pick up the hose as they go. Automatic shut-off can be arranged either by a cut-off valve which will turn off the supply from the hose line when the travelling sprinkler reaches it, or a water-timing valve can be used instead and set to give a required quantity of water. For those who have a large kitchen garden to keep up a semi-permanent spray line might be worth while considering. These are specially made of light-alloy metal pipes which are mounted about 2 ft. from the ground. Spray nozzles or rainers as they are sometimes called, are fitted at equal intervals along the pipes and a length of garden can be watered from them. The pipes can be turned from side to side so that a really big area is covered. The turning, in the simplest form, is done by means of a hand lever, but it has the disadvantage of requiring constant attention. More elaborate installations are provided with an automatic fitment to make the required changes of direction.

The accurate estimation of the amount of water required over an area of land for a given crop is a somewhat complicated business. The amount is usually expressed in terms of 'inches per acre', and it may be interesting to note that 1 in. of rain amounts to some 23,000 gallons of water on 1 acre of land. A recent aid to more accurate watering is the soil-moisture meter, or moisture indicator, a simple instrument which shows on a dial whether the soil is 'wet', 'moist' or 'dry' when a probe at its lower end is thrust into the soil to be tested. These meters are most useful and not expensive. They are somewhat like a more elaborate instrument known as a 'tensiometer' which indicates the soil-moisture tension on a dial from which, with other data available, accurate calculations of soil moisture requirements can be made.

New designs and fresh ideas in these labour-saving appliances are constantly coming along and by careful selection of those that are best to suit his particular needs a gardener can make sure that his plants are well watered, but not damaged by excessive force, and that in the meantime he is free to attend to other jobs, or perhaps sit back and enjoy his garden.

CHAPTER TWO

Basic Operations

THE tending of a garden involves a whole series of operations, some specific to certain crops or kinds of crops, others of more general application. Those which are concerned with specific crops such as, for example, the pruning of fruit trees and shrubs, or the sowing and edging of lawns, are dealt with under their respective headings. This chapter is concerned only with those operations which are of basic and general application.

DIGGING

This is the basic operation in the garden, and on it largely depends the results which will be obtained. In order to give the young roots a nice loose open soil into which they can easily penetrate, the top 'spit', the top layer of 9 to 12 in., has to be loosened up, and the easiest and best way of doing this is to invert it. This is what 'digging' really means as compared with 'forking', which simply leaves the soil in its same relative position. Digging also enables any weeds to be buried, and organic manure to be dug in below the surface. Where the sub-soil is hard and compacted, it can be loosened with a fork as the work proceeds, but where it is open and friable there is little to be gained by going deeper than one spit. In the past, under the more Spartan approach to gardening, it was usual to use the trenching method; that is, of digging three spits deep, but there are, in practice, very few occasions which justify this operation, unless it is to break up a solid layer of soil laying at the third spit, or to grow exhibition parsnips.

Once plants have got established, it is surprising how their roots will penetrate into a quite firm sub-soil, and it is much easier to let the plant do the opening up. It is unwise to bring the sub-soil to the surface unless it has been deeply cultivated previously, for the lower soil may not be fertile and it would be in this that the young seedlings would have to grow when they were in their most tender stage.

The technique of digging

Digging is such an important operation that some detailed description of it is warranted. The question of whether a spade or a fork should be used puzzles many people. Where the work can be done satisfactorily with a digging fork, that is one with flattened tines, the fork should be used, as it makes for very much easier work than does a spade. This will generally be on stiff loams or on still heavier soils. On lighter soils much of the 'crumb' would fall between the tines, and it would be impossible to make a good job of the digging; on such a soil a spade must be used.

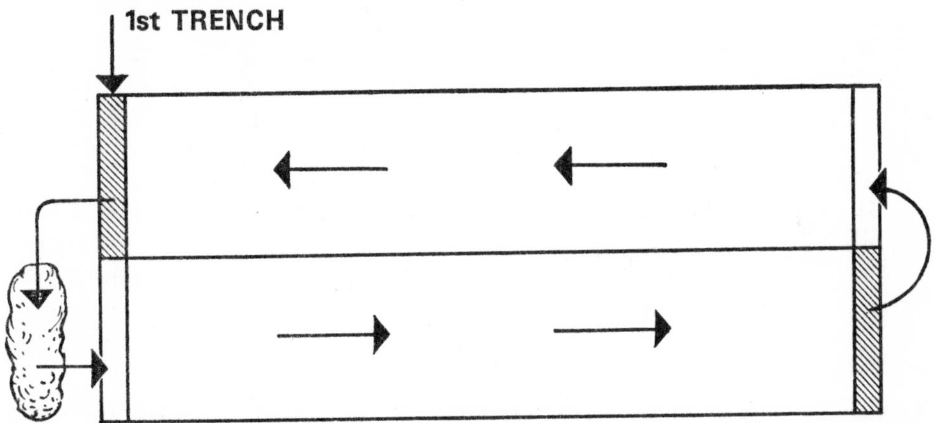

Fig. 1 When a plot is more than 20 ft. wide it saves a long haul to divide the area up the centre, and to open the trench across one half only.

If a spade is used on heavy soil, the soil will continually stick to it, which will make really hard work. Even when a fork is used on such soils it helps a lot to have a wedge-shaped piece of wood about 2 in. wide, with which to scrape off any clay which sticks to the fork's tines.

The essentials of good digging are that it should be done slowly and rhythmically. When done in this style it is not nearly so tiring, even on heavy land. In starting the work, a trench must be taken out a spit deep and 12 in. wide across the plot, taking the excavated soil to the far end, where it will be available to fill in the last trench. Where the plot is 20 ft. or more wide, however, it saves this long haul, if the plot is divided up the centre, and the trench opened across only one half. When the far end is reached, the last trench is filled in with soil from the first trench of the second half (see Fig. 1). The trench having been taken out, stand behind the line B–C, shown in Fig. 2. Then push the spade into the ground for 2 or 3 in. at a spade's width from the last 'dig', that is along the line A, D, B. This

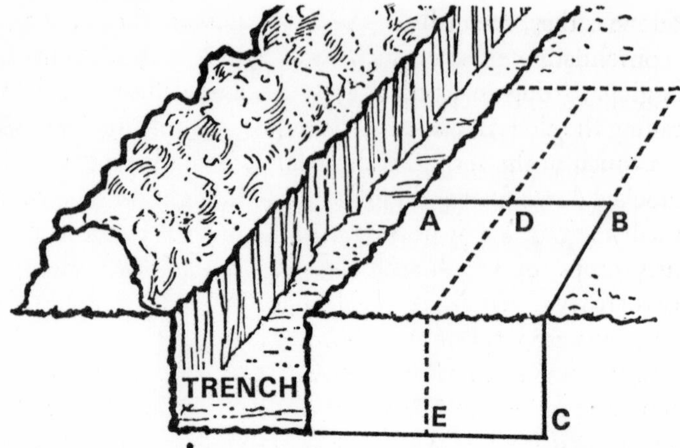

Fig. 2 This diagram shows the lines along which the spade should be inserted.

is to ensure that the top layer is severed along that line, so that the block of soil being moved comes away cleanly. Next insert the spade vertically along the line BC, press it in with the foot to its full depth, bend the back, and at the same time slide the left hand (or the right-hand for left-handed diggers) along to the bottom of the shaft, lift the soil and with a turn of the wrist invert it as it is put forward into the trench in front. Do not lift the soil high in the air before turning it over; it is completely wasted effort. Lift it just high enough to be able to turn it over tidily. After a little practice a steady rhythmic movement will develop which takes most of the effort out of it. Where it is desired to make lighter work of it, this should not be achieved by putting the spade in at an angle, since it is impossible to make a good job if that is done, but by reducing the size of the block of soil from back to front; that is, by putting the spade in at DE, or any other position in front of BC. Most people find it difficult to work both from left to right and right to left along the trench, so that it is best to work in one direction only, usually from left to right for right-handed people. Keep a good open trench in front of you and into which a layer of manure can be placed if such is to be added. Try to make the dug land as level as possible, and to do this it is sometimes necessary to put a spadeful of soil in a low spot to one side rather than immediately in front, but with practice this is done automatically. Once the knack of digging is mastered, there is no garden operation that gives more pleasant exercise or more satisfaction when surveying the completed job.

The time for digging

Heavy soils should be dug sufficiently early for them to be exposed to most of the winter frost after digging, and the best time is late November or December.

If done earlier, especially in the wetter parts of the country, the autumn rains have a consolidating effect on such a soil, which may undo much of the good effect of digging. If dug in good time, the surface should be left as rough as possible, leaving the clods unbroken. The frosts will work on them and make them crumble at a touch in the spring. If done later, when little frost is in prospect, it must be knocked down finer as digging proceeds. Light soils can be dug at any time, but are usually left as late as possible consistent with being ready for the sowing of the early crops for which such soils are particularly suitable. If dug too early, and particularly if manure is added, much of the plant food may be washed out before the plants are large enough to use it.

Any creeping rootstocks of perennial weeds, such as couch-grass or bindweed, should be forked out. Where pieces have to be pulled out, a gentle pull will often get the whole piece, whereas a snatch will merely break it off. Docks and dandelions also should be dug out for burning, but most other weeds can usefully be buried. With good digging, not a piece of green weed should be visible on the completed plot, and that is easily achieved if a good open trench is maintained the whole time. When digging between fruit trees do not dig to any depth over the area beneath the branches, or over a wider area if any roots are encountered. The lightest forking up is all that is needed. In the few cases where trenching would be justified, the method of doing it is shown in Fig. 3.

Mechanical digging

While digging is the best method of preparing soil, larger areas must be done by mechanical means, either by ploughing or by rotary cultivation. There is no doubt

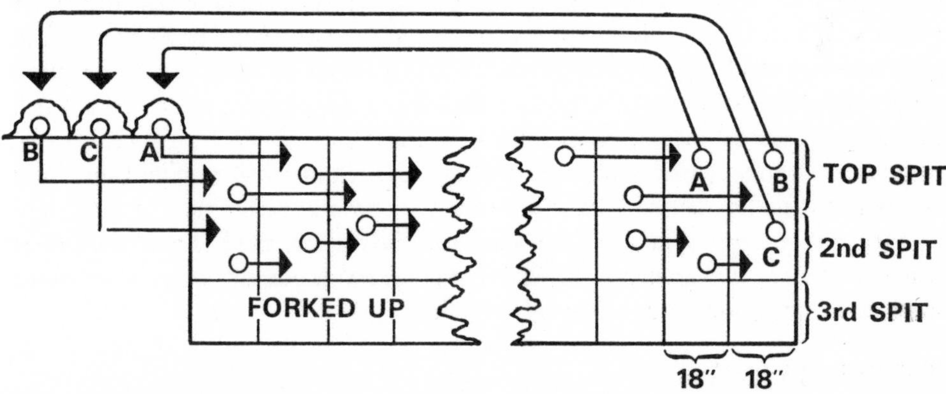

Fig. 3 The method of trenching shown here may be a bit old-fashioned but it is an effective way of preparing the sub-soil for deep-rooting plants.

that for this initial preparation, ploughing is preferable. Unfortunately most of the small garden ploughs are not sufficiently strong to do a good job on any but the lighter soils, and on heavier land it is better to employ a contractor who can use a bigger plough. But this is not possible in confined spaces, because such equipment needs a fair amount of turning space, and in such circumstances rotary cultivation is the best alternative. This method is not ideal, however, since it makes too fine a tilth which is liable to compact badly, particularly on heavy soils, but it is often the only practicable one. It is important to do the job when the soil is reasonably dry, but unfortunately it is often impossible to arrange for a contractor to do it then, as he wants to be using his machine at all times, so there is a lot to be said for buying a machine (see Chapter 1).

PREPARING A SEED BED

While an established plant is a reasonably tough organism, seedlings can be very frail, and if not given congenial conditions will easily perish. The first thing, therefore, is to ensure that soil conditions are right when the seed is sown; that is, that the soil shall break down to a nice friable crumbly condition when worked with a fork. This should give a moderately moist and moderately open soil of even texture. It is what the gardener calls a good 'tilth'. The most important factor in obtaining this tilth, is in choosing the right time to carry out the operation. On the lighter soils there are quite long spells when the soil will work down well, but on heavy land, striking the right day for the job calls for continuous watching. It generally occurs when the soil is drying out after a spell of wet weather, and when it is at the right stage just a slight knock with a rake or fork will make the clods crumble to pieces. For this seed-bed preparation the rotary cultivator is ideal, and if one is available it should be used. If the work has to be done by hand the first thing is to level out the clods roughly with a cultivator, fork, or whichever tool makes it easiest, to give a reasonably level surface.

The site for the actual seed sowing should then be marked out, and should be firmed by treading. This treading should be a forward shuffling movement, with both feet together, which fractures the remaining lumps rather than treads them downwards. The treading at the same time presses in any cavities which were formed below ground when the soil was rough dug. It should be realized that it is imperative that a heavy soil is reasonably dry when this work is carried out, otherwise the treading will seriously compact it and should then be avoided. Or it may be as well to loosen the top 3 in. or so of a heavy soil with a fork or cultivator after the treading has been done. After this it should be raked to get as level a surface as possible, all the stones being raked off. The rake should be pressed into the soil as it is pulled to and fro, so that the soil is brought into fine condition to a depth of an inch or two, and the seedlings will have suitable soil all round them. In raking, the art of getting a level surface is to keep the rake as near horizontal as possible, with no part more than 18 in. from the ground. It should then be used with a light swinging action.

HOEING

The main objects of hoeing are to keep down weeds and to break the crust on the surface of bare land. Doubt is now being expressed as to the merits of the latter, but most practical gardeners feel sure that it is beneficial to the plants and until some convincing evidence to the contrary is forthcoming, it is a practice which should be encouraged. For loose soil in which the hoe will run easily, the dutch hoe is best, working backward so that the hoed soil is not trodden on. It takes very little effort or time, so that it can be done frequently, ensuring that the weeds are killed immediately they germinate. For harder soil, or for larger and more firmly embedded weeds, the draw hoe should be used, and it may be necessary to use a chopping action to dislodge some of the weeds. Wherever hoeing is being done over the roots of plants, care must be taken not to go too deeply, or the roots will be damaged. Many plants are made to suffer badly in the interest of weed-free appearance.

MULCHING

During very hot or very dry weather the roots of plants, especially those near the surface, are liable to become hot and dry, conditions very unsuitable for healthy growth. This is particularly harmful with transplanted shrubs and similar plants, where the deeper roots will have been unavoidably damaged, so that the plant is relying on those lying nearer the surface. Relief can be given by frequent watering, but a better method is to mulch the plants; that is, to spread a layer of material over the surface of the soil, which will prevent rapid evaporation of the soil moisture and so keep the roots cool and moist. It will also prevent most weed growth and is therefore particularly useful with plants which have most of their roots near the surface, as it is unsafe to hoe near such plants.

The material used for the mulch should be of a spongy nature so that it retains moisture, yet at the same time allows plenty of air to pass through so that the roots can breathe. Suitable materials are straw, peat, half-decayed stable manure or compost, leaf-mould, coconut fibre, hop-manure, sawdust or any similar material. A layer of at least 2 in. thick is necessary for it to be really effective, but this will last for a season. In the case of straw or sawdust, however, about 2 oz. per sq. yd. of a nitrogenous fertilizer should be spread over the surface of the mulch to help its decomposition, and prevent the plants suffering from nitrogen shortage in their early stages. If farmyard manure is used, it should have plenty of straw in it, as the solid dung part alone either lays cold, or cakes together and keeps out air. It may also be slightly caustic, which will burn surface roots, or damage the stems if placed in contact with them. Pine needles should not be used, as the resin in them has a harmful effect, neither should undecomposed large leaves like chestnut or sycamore because they lie close and flat and so exclude air. As the main object of the mulch is to conserve moisture, the soil must obviously be moist when it is applied, and if it is dry it should be thoroughly watered first. If the water is cold it is best to allow 2 or 3 days for the soil to warm up again before mulching. Similarly, the mulch should not be applied too early in the year, when the soil is still cold, since a mulch also prevents the sun's heat getting through to the soil to warm it. On the other hand it needs to be applied before the really dry weather sets in. From mid-May to the end of June is generally the best time. Polythene is also useful as a mulch, and the black polythene of 150 gauge is best as it has a longer life than the clear kind, and also prevents weed growth which the clear kind does not. The foliage of the plants must of course be above the polythene, so that if it is put over a row of garden plants, cuts must be made in it for the plants to grow through. Polythene allows air to pass through it, but not moisture, so that the whole area must not be covered completely or the plants will get no water.

WATERING AND IRRIGATING

While rain-water is best for plants, any water supplied for household purposes is generally suitable, except that really hard water should not be used for rhododendrons and other lime-hating plants. The frequency of watering depends partly on the kind of soil, a sandy porous soil requiring watering much more often than a heavy one, although very heavy soils can lose moisture rapidly through the cracks which develop in them. It also depends on the depth to which the roots of the plants go. The roots of young seedlings will all be within the top inch or two of soil, and as that would dry out rapidly, especially on sandy soil, watering every other day may be needed in hot weather. Once plants have got established they send down their roots to a remarkable depth, and can call on unsuspected reserves of moisture. If frequent surface waterings are given to such plants, they send out surface roots to take up the water, their deeper roots ceasing to grow or even becoming atrophied, with the result that if for any reason the surface watering ceases, the plant suffers seriously. Nevertheless it is unwise to let plants actually wilt before watering them, and in a dry spell a check should be made by digging to about 4 in. at random spots, and if the soil there is practically devoid of moisture, watering should be done.

The general approach to watering is to leave the water running for an hour or two, and to turn it off when one feels so inclined, but it is much better to give a measured amount so that you know that it is getting well down into the soil. To moisten thoroughly a soil that is dry down to 4 in. below the surface, ½ in. of water is necessary, that is about 2½ gal. per sq. yd., and to penetrate 9 in. deep will need 1 in. of water. The amount per minute being obtained from a tap at a fixed setting can easily be found by using a receptacle of known capacity, and from that the time needed to give the required amount from the area being covered can be easily reckoned. Sprinklers with as fine a spray as possible should be used, because a heavy spray 'cakes' the soil surface. While most plants will come to no harm from being watered overhead in bright sunshine, a few, notably hearted lettuce and cauliflower, may be damaged, so that it is best to avoid watering during the heat of the day if possible (see also Chapter 1).

CONTROLLING WEEDS

Weeds compete with the garden plants for sun, air, soil, moisture and nutriment. They also harbour pests and diseases. Being much more numerous than the garden plants, and in most cases much more vigorous, it is only a short time before they completely smother them, unless they are removed. Action must be taken early. Indeed it must never cease, for some weeds such as groundsel will grow, flower and seed during a mild spell even in the shortest days of winter. The smothering effect of weeds among a sown crop starts immediately the seeds are up, so that weeding those crops as early as possible is imperative. It should be done when the soil is moist, otherwise the weeds are liable to break off instead of coming out by the root, when they will grow again, and in dry soil the roots of the crop seedlings are more likely to be damaged in the process of weeding.

Where the soil is not moist enough it should be watered the day before the weeding is to be done, rather than postpone the operation until rain comes. Where it has not been possible to do the weeding in good time, and tall weeds have smothered a low-growing crop, such as anemones, it is usually better just to cut off the weeds, as pulling them out would pull the crop out as well. Between vegetable crops or between herbaceous plants or shrubs, the hoe is the most effective tool. If used early in the season and kept in constant use the weeds will have little opportunity to multiply. Even the perennial weeds will be so weakened by this process of attrition that most of them will die, but it is best to fork them out, getting up as much as possible of the whole rootstock. The hoeing must of course be done in dry weather, preferably when it is hot or windy, so that the weeds get dried up quickly, otherwise many of them will re-root. Mulches are also effective in controlling weeds. Most weeds spread by seed, and it is important to see that there are no waste patches where weeds can flourish and spread their seeds to the cultivated land. Gravel paths can be hoed or hand-weeded but chemical control is much less laborious.

Chemical control of weeds

This method of weed control is very much in the news but great care must be taken in applying chemical weedkillers and the makers' instructions must be followed carefully. Many specialised products are available for the wide range of plants grown by amateurs, and as often only a small number of each are grown, their purchase is not always economic. In addition, in many cases, their application requires precision timing, and considerable knowledge of secondary factors which come into the picture. There are, however, a few 'contact herbicides' which scorch up the parts on which they actually fall, which are comparatively safe, and can on occasion be used. Their use is generally restricted to slow-germinating crops like onions, parsnips or anemones, where a big proportion of the weeds come up before the crop does. If the herbicide is applied just before the crop comes through, the weeds which have developed will be killed, while the crop will be protected by the soil covering. The chief substances used in this type of herbicide are pentachlorphenol, (P.G.P.) cresylic acid and vaporizing oils. Such herbicides can also be used on bulbs, or on asparagus beds, before any growth comes above ground, and there are others, based on paraquat or diquat, that can safely be used under trees and shrubs. In a neglected garden, where the object is to kill all vegetation completely, this can be done by applying sodium chlorate in the early autumn, but in that case it will be late spring before it is safe to sow or plant any crops. Sodium chlorate needs storing and handling with care, and any absorbent material which is wetted by it, becomes inflammable on drying. Deep-rooted perennials like bindweed or docks can be sprayed with a hormone weed-killer, which will travel through the plant and kill it, but this again can only be done when the land is free of garden plants. On drives and paths, many substances like salt, copper sulphate and caustic soda, will give reasonably good results if applied in strong concentrations, but much better results will be obtained with sodium chlorate, or with simazin. Simazin is particularly useful in that being only very slightly soluble, it stays in the top 2 in. or so of the soil, and there is no danger of damage to deeper roots of adjacent plants. Sodium chlorate tends to spread laterally so should not be used right up to the edge of the path where it adjoins growing plants.

STAKING AND TYING

Most flowering plants are grown because they are aesthetically attractive. When stakes are inserted to support such plants, the stakes become part and parcel of the picture, and they can mar it just as effectively as defects in the plants themselves. Yet how often do we see herbaceous borders, shrubs or pot-plants, beautiful in themselves, made to look hideous by nondescript stakes of all sizes and shapes, stuck in at all angles. A plant can only be as beautiful as its supporting stakes will allow it to be.

For annuals and taller plants with fine branching stems, twiggy branches of hazel or birch, of the kind usually employed for supporting peas, give the most natural effect, as the lateral shoots grow through them, and plant and stakes merge together. The sticks must be pointed, and placed so that they enclose what will be the natural outline of the plant. They should reach only to the necks of the stems, so that no sticks obtrude when the flowers are being admired. Where these branches are not available, support can be given by placing four or more stakes around the plant at a sufficient distance from the centre not to constrict it, and stretching string from stake to stake to enclose it. Additional tiers of string can be added as the plant grows. For plants with up to six strong stems, one central stake is often enough. The string, or raffia, should first be tied round the stake, and then looped round a stem at a distance leaving it in its natural position. It looks neater if the tie is crossed over between stake and stem. This method can be extended by looping smaller stems on the outside of the plant to those stems already tied to the central stake, in which case of course the main stem must be left on till the smaller stems have finished flowering.

For special plants such as chrysanthemums which are to be disbudded, it is wise to give one stake to each of the main stems, but when this is done bamboo or similar canes should be used. These are less rigid than wooden stakes, and since they give with the wind to a certain extent, they reduce damage to the plant. Apart from appearance, it is important that the stakes do not reach flower level, or the flower heads will rub against them and be spoilt. For rows of plants, stakes of appropriate height can be placed on each side at 6 to 10 ft. intervals, and string or wire stretched from stake to stake at the height at which it will best support the plants, adding additional strands as the plants grow. String should also be placed from stake to stake across the row, and in exposed positions, additional cross-strands may be needed between the stakes. For chrysanthemums and similar plants grown in beds for cutting, it is often possible to rig up a skeleton framework on which 6- to 8-in. mesh netting can be fixed. The plants grow through this, and as they increase in height, the netting can be raised. A method of keeping the netting taut as it is raised is shown in Fig. 4.

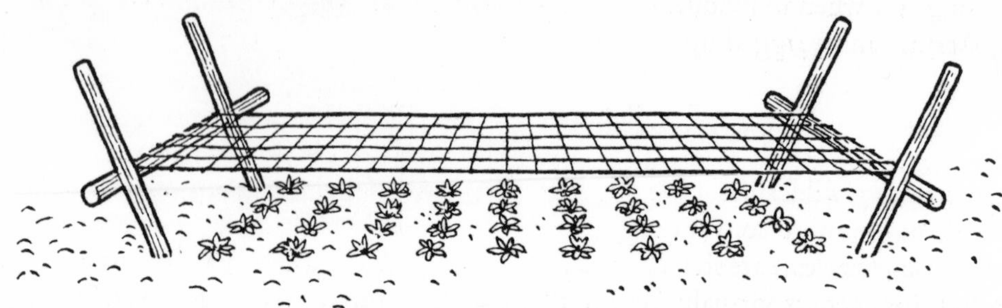

Fig. 4 A simple method of keeping the strings or wires taut.

A good range of stakes should be kept in stock, otherwise there is always the temptation to use ones which are unsightly. The material used for tying should be appropriate to the size of the plant and the length of time it has to function. For shrubs and trees, moderately thick tarred twine is best, but for most tying that only has to last one season, raffia or soft string is the most suitable. For staking taller trees specially made 'tree-ties' are available.

IMPROVISED PROTECTION

The main method of protecting plants is by covering them with glass or plastic materials in the form of a greenhouse, frame or cloche, and these are dealt with in Chapter 8. It is, however, often necessary to improvise some protection to tide an outdoor plant over difficult conditions, of which frost is the most serious. Dry frost, unless severe, does comparatively little harm; it is the combination of wet with cold that is the most damaging. For herbaceous plants and shrubs of doubtful hardiness, it is a good plan to cover the crowns with a layer of straw or other loose material at the onset of severe weather, putting some soil or ashes on top to keep the loose material in position. It must be removed about late February, especially if slugs are troublesome. Where there is hope of saving the tops of tender shrubs, they can be wrapped around with straw or bracken in the same way that roses are packed for transport. It is best to let the leaves fall off first if possible. The sweet verbena (*Lippia*) can often be preserved in cold districts in this way. Mats can also be used. Dwarf plants liable to frost damage such as the earliest broad beans, can be given some protection by placing straw or bracken between them. Some of the branches which are to be used for staking later can be spread over an early crop in the case of a snap frost in the spring, and will keep off 3 or 4 deg. Later in the year it may be necessary to prevent show blooms being bleached by strong sun when individual covers about 9 in. across can be used, or cheap calico or scrim can be rigged up over the plants.

SWEEPING AND TIDYING UP

Even in the 'wilderness' type of garden, some unobtrusive tidying up is necessary, while in the more conventional garden considerably more time must be devoted to it. Nevertheless care should be taken to see that this does not become too onerous a task for there is virtually no limit to the time that can be spent on it. If every piece of rubbish was picked up every morning, and every dead leaf or petal removed, tending a garden of 400 sq. yds. could become a full-time job. With a little experience, however, it is possible to arrive at a standard that keeps the garden basically tidy and attractive without making the task too exacting. For example, there is no need to spend time plaiting the dying narcissus leaves when in 10 days they will be dead and can be removed altogether. It is impossible to say how often tidying up should be done, because it depends so much on varying circumstances, but once weekly in the summer and once monthly in winter, could be a starting schedule. Apart from making the garden look more attractive, this tidying up also helps to keep pests and diseases in check, for many of them harbour in the debris which is removed. Sweeping of lawns and drives is best done with a 'besom' or birch broom. These brooms should not be used with a heavy action, but the leaves and material being swept up should be flicked along with a light surface touch. Always work with the wind, or the effort will be largely wasted. Where heavy or substantial rubbish is to be removed, a rake, an ordinary broom or a worn-down besom should be used.

CHAPTER THREE

Soils—Their Nature and Care

It might be felt that from the practical point of view all that a gardener needs to know about soils is enough for him to tell the difference between a soil that will grow crops successfully and one that will not, and that he can leave the more technical whys and wherefores to the experts. But some deeper understanding of soils will make for better judgment and better practical use. To look on the soil as a mass of dead matter, devoid of interest and of use solely as an anchorage for plants, is to have a completely false conception of it. It is, in fact, an extremely complex substance, showing a wide range of structural features and teeming with minute organisms which in a highly organized manner ensure adequate food for the plants which grow in it and feed us or give us visual pleasure.

What is soil?

Until fairly recently one could have said that soil was the medium in which plants grow, but with the development of soil-less cultivation, a method by which plants can be brought to maturity without the use of any 'soil', that description is hardly valid. A better description would probably be that it is the surface layer of the earth modified in such a way that plants can grow in it.

The main bulk of the earth's soil is derived from the breaking down of mineral rocks, and the basic differences in soils correspond very largely with the basic differences in the rocks from which they were formed. The greatest factor in the breakdown of rock is the weathering process in which rain, snow, frost and wind persistently fracture and erode it, and in the process break it up into the small particles which form the bulk of any soil. A secondary factor is a chemical one in which the carbon dioxide of the air dissolves in the rain-water to form a weak acid, and this slowly but inexorably eats into the hard rock. With the rock reduced to a state in which the plant nutrients are liberated, the lower forms of vegetable life appear. They die and their residue sustains a higher form of vegetation, which in turn dies, to provide residues for an even higher standard of plant life. Eventually there is enough food and organic matter in it for the crops of the demanding gardener to be brought to maturity, and we have a 'good garden soil'.

Sub-soil

The top layer of soil, from 9 in. to 12 in., of an established garden usually shows a distinct difference from the soil below it. It is generally darker and of more open texture. This is because organic matter from decayed plant roots and from surface material taken down by worms is generally restricted to that depth, and it is the organic matter which has such beneficial effect. It also benefits from weathering, which does not affect the deeper soil below which is known as the 'sub-soil'. Quite apart from this surface effect on 'one-type' soils, it often happens that the sub-soil is of a type basically different to the top soil, the latter probably having been deposited on the sub-soil by river or ice action many centuries ago. Such sub-soils can often be very useful. For instance a clay sub-soil under sand will prevent a too rapid drying out of the top, gravel under clay will ensure good drainage, or chalk under an acid soil gives a ready supply to be used for correcting the top acidity, for it is possible for a top soil overlying solid chalk to be acid. On the other hand, gravel under sand will give a dry hungry soil and deep clay will be cold and wet.

Humus

All living organisms, both plants and animals, are stages in a process of continual building up and breaking down. In the soil, bacteria bring about the decomposition of organic substances or take in nitrogen from the soil-air to help build up their bodies, and after a short life they die and the nitrogen from their bodies is taken up by plants. These plants combine the nitrogen with other materials obtained from the soil and the air and build them into complex substances. The plants die, or are eaten by animals which in turn die, and the plant or animal tissues form the food material for other soil organisms, and so the process goes on continuously. As the breakdown of the organic material proceeds, it gradually loses its form until eventually it becomes dark in colour and completely formless, in which state it is known as humus. The fact that plant and animal substances are in such complex forms, with cell-walls toughened and hardened, and with a large proportion of their chemical substances in forms highly resistant to change, is an advantage to the plants which are eventually to utilize their residues. If all the substances were readily changed to forms in which other plants could use them, there would be a large but short-lived supply of such food material, much of which would be washed out of the soil and lost before the plant could make use of it.

Plant foods

The plant food occurring in the largest amount in this organic matter is nitrogen, and its supply to growing plants depends upon the various organisms living within the soil. By their action, a small but steady supply of ammonia and nitrate, the only two forms in which the higher plants can take up nitrogen, are assured. Humus has another manurial advantage in that phosphorus, another important plant food, remains in a soluble form in it, whereas in a mineral soil it quickly changes into an insoluble form and so is not available to the plant. Humus also contains a steady supply of 'minor elements', those foods needed only in very small quantities by plants, but essential to their well-being. There is another circumstance which very conveniently fits the amount of food material supplied to the needs of the growing plant. This is the fact that the conditions which favour the action of the bacteria in breaking down the organic matter and so supplying food, also favour the growth of the plant needing that food, so that the two run in unison. It is, in fact, a foolproof process. The basic conditions for the two processes are a moist environment and a temperature of between 50 and 70 deg. F. though activity continues to a lesser degree outside that range. The breakdown of the organic matter results in the formation of acids, and as an acid condition is unsuitable for most of the plants we want to grow in our gardens, and as it tends to check the breaking-down process itself, this acidity must be counteracted by the addition of lime in some form. (More detailed information on liming is given in Chapter 4.) In addition to the advantages already stated, the supply of humus or other organic matter to the soil is of tremendous benefit in improving the physical condition of clay or sandy soils. On clay it gives a 'crumbly' texture instead of the soapy sticky condition which it usually has, while on sands it gives bulk and so increases the water-holding capacity.

Soil populations

In addition to the many kinds of bacteria always present, the soil swarms with other competing organisms, fungi, protozoa, actinomycetes, and many others all ready to devour and in turn to be devoured. It is a veritable microscopic jungle.

The fungi form a group of organisms more easily seen, especially those like the toadstools that have aerial parts. All start from spores, but they later produce masses of thin threads called mycelium, which forms the foraging part of the plant. As the fungus extends, the older mycelium dies and is decomposed by bacteria which liberate nitrogen to become available for plant roots in the area. This is often seen in 'fairy rings' on lawns. As the fungus spreads outwards from a central spot, the dying mycelium adds fresh vigour to the grass for so long as the additional nitrogen lasts. Unfortunately many of the fungi are parasitic and cause plant diseases.

The soil also swarms with pests such as slugs, snails, wireworms and cutworms, and these have to be controlled if good crops are to be obtained. Worms abound in a fertile soil, and except in lawns, where they cause unsightly wormcasts, their effect is wholly beneficial. Their tunnels aerate the soil and the large amount of dead leaves and similar material which they pull down from the surface and pass through their bodies, adds considerably to its fertility.

Types of soil

The kind of soil in a given area can often be told by the kind of plants growing on it. Nettles indicate a good fertile soil, as do strong-growing hedges and woodlands devoid of birch trees and conifers. Cowslips usually thrive on a clay soil, and beech trees and wild scabious on chalk. Birch trees and conifers usually indicate a poor and hungry soil, heather a poor and acid one, and sphagnum moss, sedges or cotton-grass a wet, badly-drained one. A further check on the soil can be made by an examination of it. A loose open soil shifts beneath the feet, and does not adhere to the boots; a clay, or heavy soil, especially when wet, has a greasy or soapy feel and can be moulded in the hand; a loose sandy soil is gritty and will pass through the fingers. The basic kinds of soils and their characteristics are given below.

Sandy soil. The 'light' or sandy soil is a very open and well-drained one, because the particles of which it is formed are large and irregular in shape, so that it is impossible for them to fit in closely together or become compacted. The advantages of such a soil are (1) since it contains a large proportion of air it is an easy soil to work and calls for little effort in cultivation; (2) no artificial drainage is needed, saving considerable trouble and expense; (3) it is workable at practically any time, indeed on a really sandy soil it is possible to go on to the land almost immediately after heavy and prolonged rain, and no harm will be done; (4) the open texture enables roots to penetrate easily, so that on such soils a large fibrous root system is quickly developed; (5) as it holds comparatively little water, it warms up quickly in spring, and is thus very suitable for early crops. There are, however, two main disadvantages to sandy soil; it is very 'hungry' and it is liable to suffer from drought. As water runs through it quickly, it means that the dissolved plant foods are more easily washed out, so that artificial fertilizers must be applied 'little and often' to maintain a constant supply of plant food. It also means that very little water is stored in it to carry it through a dry period, and crops are liable to suffer. This is best counteracted by irrigation and by the addition of liberal amounts of organic matter such as farmyard manure, compost or peat which acts as a sponge and retains the water. Unfortunately this must be added regularly because with the plentiful supply of air present in such soil, decomposition of the organic material is rapid and little of any additive will be left after a year. The maintenance of the supply is essential, however, if fertility is to be maintained.

Clay soil. The 'heavy' or clay soil has almost the opposite characteristics and defects of the sandy soil. Its main advantage is that it is rich in plant foods and in that respect is capable of giving good crops for many years without the addition of very much fertilizer. Unfortunately that is about its only real merit. Since the particles are so small and regular in shape, they fit closely together leaving little space between them, with the result that the soil is a heavy compact mass. Even the spaces which do exist are largely filled with water, being held there by the surface pull of the tiny particles. It has been estimated that the total surface area of the particles in 1 oz. of pure clay is about 1 acre. This means (1) that the cultivation of such soil is hard work; (2) that drainage will almost certainly have to be put in; (3) that it is only possible to get on to the land after it has appreciably dried out and this is a slow process; if it is trodden on while still wet it compacts almost like cement and the texture may be spoilt for a very long time; (4) being a wet soil it is slow in warming up in the spring and consequently it is useless for early crops. Being of such close texture it might be thought that it would have the redeeming feature of retaining moisture in dry periods, but unfortunately this is not the case since during periods of drought large cracks or fissures appear in it, and these result in a very rapid drying out and breaking of roots. However, in spite of the obvious drawbacks of such a soil good results can be obtained from a moderately heavy soil by treating it skilfully, particularly by keeping off it when it is saturated. It is of course difficult soil for young seedlings to cope with, and on such a soil it is better to confine one's interest to reasonably tough and deep-rooting subjects, of which roses are an outstanding example. Even so, for really happy gardening the very heavy soil is best avoided.

Chalk soil. The 'calcareous' or chalky soil is derived from a mass of calcium carbonate and the soil consists of the impurities which were in it, and which were left behind as the calcium carbonate was dissolved and washed away over the course of centuries. As the impurities were generally small in proportion to the bulk, the resulting layer of soil is usually thin. Like sandy soil, it is very hungry and at the slightest suggestion of drought it will quickly dry up. Most plants will grow quite well on it if this 'poverty' factor can be overcome, but achieving this can be a formidable task and as a general rule chalky soils severely restrict the amount of growth which plants will make. The most serious effect is felt with vegetables where lush growth is generally required, but there is the compensation that some vegetables are of much better flavour from such soils, as instanced by the well-known 'limestone Edwards', which are King Edward potatoes grown on such a soil, and which are acknowledged as being of superior quality. Flowering plants too, while being of smaller stature than on normal soils, will usually flower profusely, while the majority of shrubs do quite well on chalk as they send their roots well deep down and get their sustenance that way. There are a few plants which definitely prefer such chalky conditions; the way in which the wild clematis thrives in almost pure chalk is an example, while members of the clover and scabious families are particularly happy on it. But obviously the acid-loving plants such as heathers and rhododendrons will not find it at all congenial.

Peaty soils. These usually occur in patches, and are found in areas where drainage has been bad over a long period and consequently there was insufficient air in the soil to cause decomposition of the accumulating vegetable matter, with the result that it becomes built up into thick compressed mats. In low-lying areas where there is a good deal of dissolved calcium carbonate in the water, the peat formed is only moderately acid, and is reasonably fertile. In the wetter areas, however, where the water runs off the hard rocks, there was nothing to neutralize the acidity and these peat soils remain very acid and are of little use for the general run of plants. Even the more fertile peat soils, however, have insufficient 'body' for the successful cultivation of most plants which tend to become too soft and sappy, with insufficient anchorage. Root vegetables grow large but generally lack flavour, while shrubs and trees are liable to be loosened by strong winds, and flowering plants generally run to leaf rather than to flower. With crops such as lettuce and celery, where quick tender growth is all-important, the fertile peats form the ideal soil. There is also a range of plants, particularly shrubs, which will only give really good results on a moderately acid peat soil, and it is obviously better to concentrate on those plants, than to achieve only mediocre results with plants which do not like the conditions. The heathers and rhododendrons are the outstanding peat-lovers.

Garden soils. The above are the four basic types of soil, but the best garden soils are a mixture of them and contain sand, clay, chalk and humus (of which peat is a form) in varying proportions. The predominant ingredient determines the nature of the soil. The ideal-textured soil for the garden is one in which sand figures prominently, for as already explained, it has many advantages, but with sufficient clay in it to counteract the excessive hungriness and open-ness of the sand. Such a mixture is called a loam, and one with about 50% to 60% of sand and around 30%

of clay is a 'medium loam', and is best for general gardening purposes. 'Light loams' or 'heavy loams' are soils with higher proportions of sand or clay respectively, but without so much as to be of inferior texture. It takes much less clay than sand for it to be the dominating factor in the soil, although in both cases the remaining bulk of the loam will consist mainly of organic matter in the form of humus with lime. Ideally there should be about twice as much organic matter as there is lime, but unfortunately that seldom occurs in practice because where lime occurs in any quantity rapid decomposition of the organic matter takes place, leaving the lime as the predominating constituent, after the sand and clay. Regular manuring is therefore essential. Where lime is absent or is present in only small quantities the organic matter will persist longer, but the soil is likely to be acid. This is no real disadvantage, as the humus will be extremely valuable in improving the physical condition of the soil, and the acidity can easily be corrected by the addition of lime.

Marl. A mixture of clay and chalk is known as marl, and this is very useful to add to excessively open soils like sands and peats, particularly if they are acid. Unfortunately really heavy dressings are needed to give a lasting effect, around 1 ton to every 50 sq. yd., so that it is only practicable in some of the fenland areas where marl underlies the peat.

Silt. Obviously there is not a sharp division between the large-particled sands and the small-particled clays, and there are some soils in which the particle size comes between the two, and these are known as 'silts'. The silts have none of the virtues of a loam because while they have ample plant food in them, their physical condition is poor. They are particularly prone to 'capping', that is, to form a surface crust after rain has fallen on to a fine seed bed, and this crust is often so hard that seedlings find it difficult or impossible to penetrate it. In a bad season it may be necessary to sow up to three times on such a soil. Once established, however, plants growing on silt will grow away quite happily, and will do well.

Stones. These are usually looked upon with disfavour, but in a heavy soil they can be useful in assisting drainage. Their main disadvantage is that they make it very difficult to prepare a nice level seedbed for the sowing of the smaller seeds, but the theory that they encourage fungus disease in crops like lettuce has now been discarded. They are mainly a negative factor in soil, in that they occupy space which could better be occupied by fertile soil, but unless they are very numerous, and so occupy a large proportion of the space, they are no serious disadvantage.

Improving soils

Many of the normal processes of gardening effect an improvement in the soil either by adding to its food content, or by giving it a better texture. These include draining, rolling, cultivating, manuring, mulching, controlling soil pests and diseases, controlling weeds, and other measures which are dealt with in detail in the relevant chapters of this book. Other operations aimed more specifically at soil improvement include 'grassing down', green manuring, adding soil of different texture, liming and preparing and adding compost.

Grassing down. This is done frequently by commercial growers, especially in orchards, and where opportunity offers, their example can profitably be followed by amateur gardeners. It merely involves sowing grass and clover, which is left to grow for four or more years, but is kept cut reasonably short, the cut grass being left on the surface to rot. The best mixture is one of timothy grass and clover, sown at the rate of 1 oz. per sq. yd., but if timothy cannot be easily obtained, then ryegrass, which can be had from all seedsmen, can be substituted. It is obviously impossible to do this in any part of the garden which is in full use, but it often happens that the kitchen garden, or some other cultivated area, is rather larger than can be conveniently dealt with, and if some part of it is grassed down, the amount of work is reduced, and at the same time that area of soil will be tremendously improved. The grass develops a mass of fibrous roots, which open up the soil and in some unknown way produce a more friable condition when the land comes into cultivation again. The clover will go deeper than the grass, and so will help improve the sub-soil, and being a legume will build up the nitrogen supply in the soil. The clover is particularly useful on chalk soils because it helps to keep the iron in the soil in soluble form and so prevents the pale sickly foliage caused by a deficiency of that element.

Balancing soils. The texture of a soil can obviously be improved by adding soil of the opposite texture, such as adding clay to peaty or sandy soil, or peat or sand to a heavy clay soil. Unfortunately quite appreciable amounts are necessary to produce any worthwhile effect, so that it is only practicable and economic on small areas, or when the two different kinds of soil are adjacent to each other. This sometimes happens with a top soil and the sub-soil beneath it. Marl is particularly useful for boosting the more sandy soils.

Water effects. On heavy soils care must be taken not to walk on them when they are wet. It is a great temptation to ignore this precept when jobs need doing and the time is available to do them, but it should be resisted, for it seriously spoils the texture for that season, and is reflected in the crops that are grown. Even when such soils have dried out sufficiently for planting or sowing to be done but are still on the wet side, boards should be used to walk on while the operations are carried out, so that the weight is distributed over a wider area. A good 'tilth', that is, a good workable condition, can be obtained on heavy soil by leaving the soil in as large lumps as possible when dug in the autumn or early winter. The frost acts on them so beneficially that in the spring even heavy clay will fall to pieces with a touch when surface cultivation is carried out.

Liming. While calcium, the active element in chalk or lime, is necessary in small quantities as a food for plants, it is mainly as a soil conditioner that chalk or lime is applied. Liming is particularly valuable on heavy soils, because it flocculates such a soil, that is, it makes the very small particles go together into larger aggregates, and so increases the size of the pore spaces and aerates the soil, making it warmer and drier. It is equally valuable on acid soils because it neutralizes the acidity, and so makes conditions more suitable for the majority of plants grown in gardens, and for the soil bacteria which break down the organic compounds and liberate foods for the use of plants. Even on soils which are neither heavy nor acid, liming is necessary, though at a much lower rate, because on these soils, plant foods are likely to be in insoluble form, and so unavailable to plants unless some lime is present. It also discourages certain fungus diseases, such as 'club root' of brassicas. Lime should never be applied in direct contact with organic manure, or much plant food will be lost. It is best applied to the surface of the soil and not dug in as it is washed downwards fairly quickly, or it may be put on in late winter or early spring, to land that has been dug. On heavy land slaked or hydrated lime is best. (See Chapter 4 under heading 'Lime'.)

Composting. Building a compost heap takes less time than burning a lot of green vegetation, and the resulting material is far more valuable. All plant refuse and kitchen waste can be used, but the shorter material like lawn-mowings and leaves should be mixed with the longer material otherwise it may pack too tightly for the air to get to it. Material which is badly affected by soil pests or disease, like clubroot of brassicas, or eelworm of potatoes, must be burned, but most leaf or stem troubles, like potato blight or leaf mildews, will do little harm and such material can be safely included in the heap. Paper, and any material tainted with oil, creosote or other preservative should be excluded, as should woody material, particularly rose prunings. Weeds with creeping rootstocks like bindweed and couch-grass are best excluded, unless care can be taken to fork out all surviving roots when the compost is used, but other perennial weeds will generally be killed.

The heap is best placed in a position sheltered from strong wind, to avoid excessive drying and loss of heat. It should be at least 4 ft. wide, with vertical sides, and up to 5 ft. high, and made in layers: first a layer of refuse about 9 in. thick, seeing that it is moist, then either a 2-in. layer of any sort of animal manure, or a handful per sq. yd. of sulphate of ammonia or other nitrogenous fertilizer, or one of the proprietary chemicals sold for the purpose. These materials accelerate decomposition and add to the nutrient content of the heap. Then add another layer of refuse and then a sprinkling of chalk or lime at about two handfuls per sq. yd. Where only small amounts of refuse become available, the heap should be built up in a short length at a time to its full height so that decomposition can be proceeding in that part. Decomposition is helped if the heap is turned about 4 to 6 weeks after making, starting at one end and turning the unrotted part on the outside to the centre. Water can be added if needed, but while the heap should be moist all through, it should not be saturated. In the summer a heap may be ready for use 3 months after making, but during the cooler part of the year it may be 6 months or more before it is ready. On heavy soil compost is best added in the course of digging the land in the autumn, at which time some of it is likely to be only partly decomposed, but this does not matter as it will help to open up heavy land. On lighter land fully decomposed compost is best and should be worked into the top 3–4 in. of soil in spring or early summer.

CHAPTER FOUR

The Nutrition and Growth of Plants

THE art of gardening is directly concerned with the care and cultivation of plants. Hence for the gardener it is a great advantage to have some knowledge of how plants live, grow and secure their food. If we examine an ordinary plant, such as a snapdragon or wallflower, we can see at a glance that it consists of three distinct parts, namely the root, the stem with branches attached and the leaves. Such plants will also at a certain time of the year produce brightly coloured flowers which are normally the forerunners of fruits and seeds.

Role of root, stem and leaves

Each of these parts has a special role to play in the life of a plant. Thus the root serves to anchor the plant in the soil and to hold it in its normal position; that is, upright or vertical for most plants. The root is also the means whereby water and nutrients are absorbed from the soil to feed the plant. The stem with its branches bears the leaves, flowers and fruits and, in addition, provides internal channels through which water and nutrients may pass from one part of the plant to another.

The leaves have three main functions. Firstly, they act as the plant's lungs, in other words they are responsible for respiration, which is the equivalent of breathing in animals. Secondly, leaves provide the plant with the means of getting rid of surplus moisture, an operation which is termed transpiration. Lastly, the leaves actually co-operate with the roots in feeding the plant by means of the process known as photosynthesis.

The plant's internal structure

Obviously the internal structure of the different plant parts has considerable bearing on their vital functions. Here, however, it is possible only to deal very briefly with this aspect. Most people are aware that all living things are composed of millions of tiny cells, and that it is mainly due to the constant division of the innumerable cells and the formation of new ones that growth or increase in size occurs.

In the early growth stages of a seedling all the cells are of similar type, but as development proceeds a considerable degree of what is called cell differentiation occurs. This means in effect that groups of cells become specialized to form tissues adapted for particular purposes; such as, for example, food storage. Other groups of cells in the root and stem form strengthening tissues which enable them to withstand the strains and stresses they have to endure. Again, many cells inside the root and stems are arranged in such a way as to form continuous tiny channels or special conducting tissues, through which nutrient solutions may pass.

Absorption of water and nutrients from the soil

As already stated, the taking up of water from the soil is an important function of plant roots. Only the finer fibrous roots are involved. These are normally present in large numbers and spread through the soil in all directions. Near the tips of such young rootlets are the root hairs. These pass between the minute grains or particles of which a soil is composed and come in close contact with a film of moisture which usually surrounds the soil grains.

Soil water is in fact normally a weak solution of various chemicals and is absorbed into the root by the process called osmosis. This occurs because of the fact that when two solutions are separated by a membrane through which water and the chemicals dissolved in it can pass, the stronger solution attracts the weaker. Indeed in such cases the latter passes through the membrane and will continue to do so provided the difference in solution strengths is maintained. Consequently as the root hairs contain the stronger solution (cell sap) the weak dilution of chemicals in the soil is attracted and absorbed into them. From the root hairs it passes from cell to cell and soon reaches the roots' conducting channels. As this process of absorption continues and the volume of solution inside the root increases, an internal pressure is built up. This root pressure, as it is called, in turn forces the solution upwards through the stems' conducting channels and finally into the leaves.

Transpiration

An interesting feature of a leaf's interior is the rather large intercellular spaces. These spaces are in direct contact with the atmosphere because of numerous tiny openings or pores in the leaf's protective cover. Thus air passes readily into the leaf's interior while the same openings allow water vapour to escape. The transmission of water from the leaves is called transpiration and goes on continually.

Hence we have a picture of water being absorbed by the roots and moving in a steady current or stream through the plant's conducting channels and thence into the leaves from which the surplus is transpired into the air. This water stream not only provides the plant's water requirements, but also carries (in solution) the basic chemical nutrients from the soil to all the plant's organs.

Another part played by transpiration is to lower the temperature around the leaves when necessary. Indeed without this cooling effect the foliage would probably be scorched by the sun's rays during hot weather.

Photosynthesis

The soil is not by any means the only source of a plant's foods. Indeed by far the greater part of its dry matter is secured from the air. The capacity to undertake this is the most important of all plant processes and is called photosynthesis. Briefly it consists of the absorption of carbon dioxide (contained in the air to the extent of only 0·03%) by the leaves. This gas is then broken down into its component parts, namely oxygen and carbon, and while the latter unites with water to form the foods we call carbohydrates, such as sugar and starch, the oxygen is released into the air.

Photosynthesis occurs only in green plants because their green colouring matter, called chlorophyll, found chiefly in the leaves, is essential for its operation. Hence this process never occurs in non-green plants such as mushrooms. In addition, photosynthesis cannot take place in the absence of light, but this will be discussed further when the general effect of light on plants is considered.

Glucose sugar is the first product of photosynthesis, but other forms of sugar as well as starch are produced. In addition nitrogen absorbed by the roots combines with some of the carbohydrates to form proteins. Thus from simple raw materials secured from the soil and air, complex organic foods are manufactured within the plant. Food so made must be transferred from one part of the plant to another as required for growth. Furthermore many plants have special organs where surplus food is stored. Examples are the roots of carrots and parsnips, potato tubers, onion bulbs and the fruits of apples and pears.

Respiration

In common with animals, all living plants breathe or respire. The effects of respiration are largely the opposite of photosynthesis. Thus instead of building up carbohydrates, respiration breaks them down with the release of carbon dioxide and during the process oxygen is absorbed. The main object of respiration is to release energy for the plant's vital processes.

Also, unlike photosynthesis, respiration is not affected by light, and in growing plants goes on day and night. Apart from the leaves, which are the main respiratory organs, all living parts of the plant also respire to some extent. It is important to remember this in relation to the roots which must, for this reason, have adequate soil aeration.

Respiration takes place most rapidly in actively growing plants, such as seedlings, provided the environment is favourable. On the other hand its rate is at a minimum with dormant plants, such as deciduous trees in winter.

Factors which influence growth

The factors which directly affect a plant are temperature, light and the supply of moisture and nutrients. If one of these is low or deficient this acts as a limiting factor and growth is affected. Sometimes the gardener can alter and improve a plant's environment, as when he grows them in heated glasshouses, augments the natural water supply by irrigation or supplies extra nutrients to the soil. He can also select plants which are most suited for a particular environment. Thus he can grow hardy plants in cold areas and shade loving species where the light is of a low intensity.

Temperature

Strictly speaking every kind of plant has an optimum temperature at which it will grow and develop most successfully. In practice, however, a degree of compromise is necessary and all plant species may be placed in broad temperature groups such as tropical, sub-tropical and temperate. Gardeners have their own system of classification which is also of an approximate nature and may be defined as follows:

(*a*) Plants which require the protection of a glasshouse (heated in winter) all the year round. Examples are gloxinias and crotons.

(*b*) Half-hardy plants which may be grown in the open when there is no risk of frost. Examples are vegetable marrows and tuberous-rooted begonias.

(*c*) Hardy plants which thrive in a temperate climate unprotected throughout the year. Some hardy plants of course, such as annuals, complete their growth during the warmer months of the year.

Hardy plants show considerable adaptation to seasonal changes of temperature. Thus deciduous trees lose their foliage in the autumn while herbaceous perennials die down with the onset of winter and only their roots remain, protected by the soil. Many other plants form special structures such as bulbs and corms which are resistant to low temperatures. The seed of annuals can also be regarded as a means of enabling the plant to survive the cold of winter.

Changes in temperature are largely responsible for the growth pattern during the growing season. Thus growth usually commences in spring, reaches its maximum in summer, declines thereafter and ceases altogether in winter. Sometimes the gardener forces certain plants (rhubarb and seakale) into early growth by placing the rootstocks in heated glasshouses. Bulbous plants too, like tulips, are forced in this way and the object of course is to secure early vegetables or flowers.

In general and within limits, an increase in temperature starts or steps up growth. But temperature can be too high as well as too low. This rarely occurs in temperate climates in the open, although in glasshouses excessive heat may cause damage or, in the case of tomatoes, cause vegetative growth at the expense of the fruit. For glasshouse culture, therefore, it is essential to have some knowledge of the temperature requirements of particular plants.

Light

The necessity of light for the vital process of photosynthesis has already been stated. But it is the intensity of the light that determines the rate of photosynthesis, and the rate on a sunny day may be reduced by about two-thirds on a dull cloudy day. Exceptionally brilliant sunshine, however, at the height of summer may also retard photosynthesis or, by destroying the chlorophyll, stop it altogether.

Another effect of light is that it tends to dwarf plants and promote sturdy growth. Hence plants grown in shade or deprived of light because they are crowded together often make tall, weak, spindly growth. Some plants, however, such as various species of ferns, have adapted themselves to shade conditions and do not succeed if fully exposed to the sun. On the other hand plants such as many alpines prefer the maximum of sunshine.

When light is excluded entirely from green plants they assume a white or yellowish appearance and are said to be blanched or etiolated. If this is continued for any length of time the plant will die, but for a period lack of light may be advantageous in the forcing of some plants such as rhubarb and is a practice used by gardeners. In this case the growth of the stems without light is accelerated but occurs at the expense of nutrients stored in the root. Light is sometimes excluded from part of a plant, as with celery which is earthed up to cause blanching of the lower portions of the stems and to improve flavour.

Photoperiodism

The daily duration of light in relation to the flowering period of a plant has a remarkable effect which is covered by the term photoperiodism. Thus some plants (*Sedum spectabile*) will flower only after they have been subjected to more than 12 hours of light daily. Such plants are called long-day plants. On the other hand poinsettia (*Euphorbia pulcherrima*), blooms around Christmas in a heated glasshouse because it is a short-day plant. A third group of plants is indifferent to the daily light duration and other things being equal will bloom at any time of the year. Good examples are perpetual flowering carnations, the African Violet (*Saintpaulia ionantha*) and tomatoes.

Long-day plants can be made to flower when the days are short by supplementing the natural light with artificial light so as to lengthen the light period every day. Light of a much lower intensity than that required for photosynthesis will serve for this purpose. Lengthening the daily light period will also delay or prevent short-day plants, such as certain varieties of chrysanthemums, from coming into flower at their normal time, and conversely the flowering period of such plants can be brought forward by excluding light from them for a period every day. The careful and controlled use of these factors has resulted in the development of the modern all-the-year-round chrysanthemum trade.

Apart from controlling the time of flowering, photoperiodism affects the formation of storage organs in some plants. Thus dahlias form tubers only under short-day conditions. On the other hand the onion must have a day length exceeding 12 hours in order to produce bulbs, the process being accelerated when the day length is 16 hours or more.

Water

Ninety per cent or even more of an ordinary green plant may consist of water, and it is water which keeps the soft young cells in the leaves and stems turgid or plump and extended. But if water is in short supply this cell turgidity is lost so that the leaves droop and wilt while the stems of herbaceous plants become limp and often sag. Should water shortage be prolonged the plant may wither and die.

Just as plants vary in their light and temperature requirements there are also wide differences in their water needs. Moreover, plant adaptations in relation to water supply are most pronounced. Thus most plants growing near or in water have large leaves and are called 'hydrophytes', the water-lily being an example.

At the other extreme a large number of species, called 'xerophytes', have adapted their form and structure to conditions of water shortage. This usually takes the form of a reduced leaf area as with broom and gorse. Under desert conditions a plant may have to go without water for months or even years. Some plants (species of cactus) may dispense with leaves altogether, but their fleshy stems are not only very suitable for water storage but also act as leaves.

Intermediate between the hydrophytes and the xerophytes are the great majority of ordinary plants called 'mesophytes'. These also, however, have developed various means to restrict water loss. Thus verbascums produce a mass of hairs on their leaves for this purpose, and various evergreens, such as laurel, have thick leaves with a waxy surface designed to limit transpiration.

Unless plants receive adequate water their growth may be checked or prevented. Too much water in the soil can also be bad for plants because the excess water replaces air, and the roots being unable to breathe properly are seriously handicapped. Consequently the growth of the whole plant suffers and prolonged waterlogging may cause its death.

Plant nutrients

A plant derives its nutrients or food from both the air and the soil, as we have already seen. Experiments have shown that there are ten chemical elements all of which are essential for healthy growth; carbon, hydrogen, oxygen, nitrogen, sulphur, phosphorus, magnesium, potassium, calcium and iron. Carbon we know is secured from the air and by photosynthesis is combined with water, consisting of hydrogen and oxygen, to form carbohydrates. The remaining seven elements are taken from the soil although it is known that some of them may to a limited extent be assimilated when sprayed on the leaves. Within recent years it has been proved that there are still a number of other elements required by plants but in minute quantities. These are known as minor or trace elements and include manganese, copper, zinc, molybdenum and boron.

As already mentioned plant nutrients must be dissolved in water before they can be absorbed by the root. When a plant is growing naturally in the soil two factors control the amount of each element absorbed. They are (*a*) the quantity of soluble material available in each case and (*b*) whether the particular substance is transformed, utilized and removed from the root cells. Plants are able to exercise some degree of selective absorption in relation to particular elements, and two species growing side by side will absorb and accumulate different amounts of the same element.

PLATE 3
AQUILEGIA (Columbine). Available in a wide range of colours.

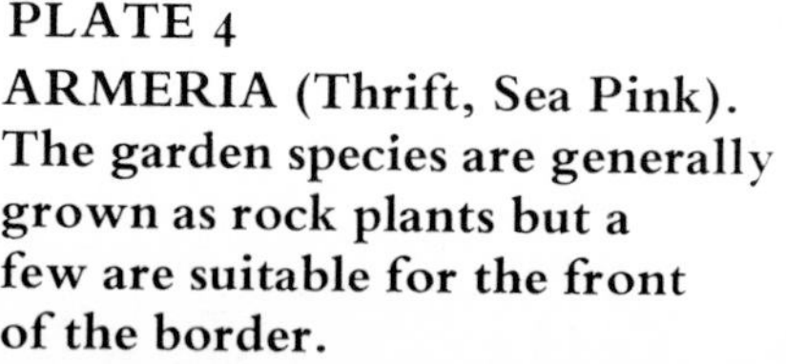

PLATE 4
ARMERIA (Thrift, Sea Pink). The garden species are generally grown as rock plants but a few are suitable for the front of the border.

Nutrition and manuring

The gardener's role in plant feeding is largely concerned with the addition of manures and fertilizers to the soil. There are two objects in manuring: (1) to improve the soil's texture or physical condition; (2) to supplement plant nutrients already present.

The first is achieved by the use of bulky organic materials, such as farmyard manure or compost, and this aspect will be discussed later. Such manures also contain plant nutrients but in relatively small amounts.

Plant nutrients are mainly provided by fertilizers. Those nutrients most likely to be low are nitrogen, phosphorus (phosphate) and potassium (potash). All soils contain these in varying amounts but they are constantly being removed by the growing and removal of crops and by the leaching or washing out effect of rain. Moreover, as a rule, a large proportion of the substances mentioned is in an insoluble form and therefore cannot be used by plants. Herein lies a difficulty for the gardener. How can he tell whether the supply of nutrients in his soil is adequate for the needs of the crops he wishes to grow?

The best answer to this problem is to have samples of the soil tested. Once the samples have been taken and chemically analysed a report on the result is supplied. This normally shows the quantities of phosphate and potash present and states the approximate amount of each which should be applied to make good any deficiency.

Advice on the need for lime or otherwise is also included. The soil report does not usually refer to nitrogen because, for reasons which will be given later, it is possible to make a fair estimate of nitrogen needs from general observations on the growth of the previous or current crop. Furthermore the supply of available nitrogen in any soil tends to vary over a period and an assessment based on soil analysis may not be very accurate for any length of time. The report on glasshouse soil samples includes particulars of the soluble salt concentration which is discussed later in this section.

Concentrated fertilizers are classified according to the plant nutrient supplied, and are (*a*) nitrogenous, (*b*) phosphatic and (*c*) potassic. In addition there are also compound fertilizers which contain these three nutrients in varying proportions. These are very convenient to use but a basic knowledge of the 'straight' fertilizers as classified above and the effect of the nutrients is of first importance to all gardeners.

Nitrogen

Most soils, and especially the lighter types, benefit from applications of nitrogen. The effect of nitrogen on plant growth is far more obvious than that of any other nutrient because it promotes rapid growth, darkens the foliage and frequently increases crop yield. It is of particular benefit to crops grown for their leaves or stems, such as cabbage, spinach or rhubarb, while being quick acting it is valuable as a top dressing for most growing crops. Plants which are short of nitrogen are usually a pale green colour and growth becomes stunted. On the other hand excess nitrogen causes soft growth, makes the plant more liable to disease, hinders fruiting in certain plants and delays ripening, but these effects can to some extent be counterbalanced by the use of adequate phosphate and potash. Nitrogenous fertilizers include both organic and inorganic forms. The most important of these are described below, together with their percentage of nitrogen (N).

Sulphate of Ammonia (21% N). This is a very popular fertilizer and usually available at a reasonable price. It is slower in action than the nitrate fertilizers, taking 10 to 17 days after application to become available to the plants. This fertilizer uses up lime in the soil and tends to cause acidity. Particular care should be taken that adequate lime is present where sulphate of ammonia is being used. The average rate of application is ½ to 1 oz. per sq. yd.

Nitrate of Soda (15·5% N). One of the first fertilizers to be widely used. It is obtained from natural salt deposits in Chile. It is available to plants immediately on application and is recommended as a top dressing. It should never be used on heavy clay soil as it tends to make such soils more intractable. It may be applied at rates similar to sulphate of ammonia.

Nitro-chalk (21% N). Manufactured by granulating ammonium nitrate with calcium carbonate (ground limestone) this fertilizer is easy to handle and quick in action. It is a good fertilizer for acid or sour soils and is also used at the same rate as sulphate of ammonia.

Hoof and Horn (13–15% N plus 10% phosphoric acid). This is probably the best of the organic fertilizers. It is slow in action and therefore valuable for supplying nitrogen over a long period. This fertilizer is widely used for making pot-plant composts such as the 'John Innes' compost and for glasshouse work in general. Average application is 2 to 4 oz. per sq. yd.

Dried blood is another nitrogenous fertilizer with about the same percentage nitrogen as hoof and horn. It is sometimes used for feeding tomatoes but is too expensive for general use.

Phosphate

The effect of phosphate on plants is to encourage root development in the early stages of growth. It also forwards maturity in certain plants. Soils in wet districts respond best, but under acid conditions this substance does not become available to plants. To get the best results from phosphate, acidity must be anticipated and prevented by liming.

Phosphate fertilizers such as bone meal were the first to be applied to the soil and in the past have been used extensively. Their value is based on the percentage of phosphoric acid (P_2O_5) contained.

Superphosphate (18% P_2O_5). This is the most popular of these fertilizers and is manufactured from rock phosphate treated with sulphuric acid. It is water soluble and readily available to plants. Average application is 1–2 oz. per sq. yd.

Triple superphosphate (48% P_2O_5). This is much more highly concentrated than superphosphate and while the effect is similar about one-third the rate recommended for superphosphate is adequate.

Bone meal (20–24% P_2O_5 and 3–4% N). This consists of ground bones and, unlike superphosphate, is of organic origin. It is more expensive and less effective but supplies some nitrogen. The rate of application is about the same as superphosphate.

There are a number of other phosphatic fertilizers, such as basic slag, which are quite reliable. Those mentioned, however, should prove adequate for all garden work and superphosphate is particularly recommended.

Potash

The effect of potash is largely complementary to that of nitrogen. For just as nitrogen promotes vegetative growth, potash aids the production of flowers and fruits. Moreover, the tendency of nitrogen to develop rather soft lush growth is balanced by the uptake of potash. In this way a plant supplied with this nutrient is less liable to disease or the effects of unfavourable conditions, such as drought in summer or frost in winter. Potash is of particular value for plants which are grown for their fruits, such as tomatoes and apples. When plants are not getting enough potash the leaves often have a marginal scorching or browning.

Potash is obtained from underground deposits and from lakes. The principal European sources are Germany, Alsace, Spain, Poland and Russia. The value of any potassic fertilizer is based on its potash (K_2O) content.

Sulphate of Potash (50% K_2O). This fertilizer is manufactured from muriate of potash. It is considered to be the best of its class for many horticultural crops, particularly tomatoes and soft fruits. Average application is ½ to 1 oz. per sq. yd.

Muriate of Potash (50% and 60% K_2O). This is a cheaper form of potash than sulphate but if used too freely or too frequently on the same soil an accumulation of chlorides may have a harmful effect on such crops as soft fruit and tomatoes. It is generally suitable, however, for vegetable crops and especially celery, beetroot and asparagus. The rate of application is similar to the sulphate form.

Nitrate of Potash (44% K_2O and 13% N). This fertilizer supplies both potash and nitrogen. It is quick acting and is excellent for feeding high-quality crops, such as tomatoes, although it is rather expensive. It should be used in small quantities.

Compounds

Nitrogen, phosphate and potash may be applied separately to the soil in the form of one or other of the straight fertilizers mentioned. It is much more convenient, however, to apply all three together. To make this possible, compound fertilizers are manufactured by many firms, and are often made to suit the requirements of particular crops. Thus there are compound tomato fertilizers and chrysanthemum fertilizers. Apart from these there are several compound fertilizers produced for general garden use. An example of such a compound contains 9% N, 9% P_2O_5 and 15% K_2O. This may simply be expressed as 9 : 9 : 15, it being understood that the figures refer to percentages and always in the order of N : P : K. An even better compound for general use is one with an analysis of 10 : 10 : 18.

Home-made compound fertilizers can be prepared by simply mixing straight fertilizers of different types together. An example of such a mixture is:

4 parts sulphate of ammonia
4 ,, superphosphate
2 ,, sulphate of potash

This mixture has an approximate analysis of 10 : 8 : 12.

Home-made fertilizer mixtures should be applied shortly after they are mixed and not stored. Mixing should be done very thoroughly. Certain fertilizers should not be mixed together because of a chemical reaction between the components. This applies in particular to sulphate of ammonia which should not be mixed with any fertilizer containing free lime, such as basic slag.

Other major elements

Magnesium. This element although essential and used by plants in appreciable quantities is, unlike nitrogen, phosphate and potash, usually present in most soils in sufficient quantity. Routine applications are rarely necessary. Magnesium deficiency can occur and is most frequently seen on light soils and in wet seasons. Sometimes, too, magnesium may be rendered unavailable to plants by the excessive use of potash or lime. Deficiency rarely occurs where farmyard manure is used freely.

A symptom of magnesium deficiency is the presence of white or pale green areas between the veins of the leaves. This is called 'intervenal chlorosis' and often occurs with tomatoes grown in glasshouses. The leaves of affected apple trees may assume a similar appearance followed by premature defoliation while if the deficiency is severe the fruits may fail to ripen. The remedy for magnesium deficiency is to apply Epsom salts (magnesium sulphate) to the soil at the rate of 1/[illegible] lb. per sq. yd. When applying lime for horticultural crops it is a good idea to use ground magnesium limestone which supplies magnesium as well as lime. Spraying tomatoes or apples with a weak solution of Epsom salts (2 oz. in 5 pints water) has an immediate remedial effect.

Sulphur is another major element but a deficiency is highly improbable.

Iron. In some areas iron deficiency is a widespread and serious problem. It is found only in soils with a high lime or chalk content, usually called calcareous soils. Under such conditions iron, although present, is not available to plants because of excessive calcium. Iron deficiency causes the leaves of plants to lose their healthy green colour and to become white or yellowish. This condition is called 'chlorosis' and retards or prevents the process of photosynthesis. The plant's constitution is thus weakened and its productive capacity is reduced. Fruit trees and bushes, particularly plums and raspberries, are susceptible to chlorosis and in severe cases may die. Rose bushes and other ornamental plants are also liable to this complaint.

On land containing excessive lime, control of iron deficiency is very difficult. Within the last few years, however, some success has been achieved by spraying the affected plants, when in full growth, with soluble iron compounds known as sequestrenes or chelates. This is a greenish-yellow powder which is added to water at 1½ oz. to 1 gal. A chemical wetter or spreader should also be added. The spray should be applied to the foliage as a fine mist. The sequestrene solution may also be used to water the soil around the plant but the effect is slower than spraying.

Manganese. A deficiency of this element in beetroot causes a typical leaf yellowing, known as 'speckled yellows'. Various other plants, such as roses and fruit trees, may be affected. Deficiency of manganese is most likely to occur on light land well supplied with organic matter and containing excess lime. Affected crops may be sprayed with a weak solution of manganese sulphate. There is available a manganese sequestrene which is used in the same manner as the iron sequestrene. Excessive manganese is sometimes present in acid soils and may be toxic to plants.

Boron. A deficiency of this element may occur in light soils with a high lime content, particularly under dry conditions. Affected crops of beetroot develop heart or crown rot, while swedes, turnips and cauliflowers show typical signs of this trouble. Cracked stems of celery have also been attributed to this cause. Boron deficiency is controlled by applying 15 to 20 lb. borax per acre to the soil. Excess boron is very harmful to plants.

Molybdenum. Deficiency of this element is comparatively rare in the general run of plants, except in the case of brassicas, particularly cauliflowers, where it is frequently observed. Affected plants develop peculiar narrow and sometimes twisted leaf-blades, this condition being known as 'whiptail'. Acid soils are the most liable to give rise to symptoms of molybdenum deficiency. The application of lime is usually an effective remedy. The complaint may also be prevented by spraying the plants in the seed bed before setting out with a solution of sodium molybdate (1 oz. in 10 gal.).

Lime

Lime can hardly be regarded as an ordinary fertilizer but it has been described as one of the basic factors of soil fertility. It has the following important effects:

(1) The calcium which it contains is an essential plant food. When it is deficient the leaves tend to curl inwards, while their edges become jagged and brown.

(2) Lime induces the very minute grains of a clay soil to form aggregates, that is, numbers of the grains hang together to produce larger particles called soil crumbs. This makes a clay soil coarser, thereby improving its texture and promoting drainage and aeration. In sandy soils it cements the particles together thus giving cohesion.

(3) The most important effect of lime is the neutralizing of acidity so that a sour or acid soil becomes sweet. This condition aids the life of bacteria by means of which organic matter is broken down in the soil and valuable plant nutrients are made available to plants. The majority of fruit and vegetable crops will not succeed under acid conditions, those which are particularly sensitive being beetroot, lettuce, peas and beans. Certain crops, such as potatoes, celery and tomatoes, will tolerate moderate acidity. With the cabbage family the serious root disease known as club root is likely to appear if the soil is sour. Phosphate becomes fixed or unavailable in acid soils and in such conditions plants may suffer from phosphate deficiency. Other plant foods, including nitrogen and potash, are more freely available where there is adequate lime.

Soil pH. A scale for measuring the degree of soil acidity is called the pH. This scale operates from 0 to 14 and a pH of 7·0 is neutral. Figures below 7·0 indicate acidity and above 7·0 alkalinity. Most plants succeed where the pH is between 6·0 and 7·0. Exceptions are heathers, rhododendrons and similar plants which call for acid conditions. From the pH shown by soil analysis, a soil chemist can give a fair estimate of a soil's lime requirement (if any) in accordance with the type of plants being grown. In practice, however, it is found that clay soils and those with a high humus content need larger amounts to increase their pH by a given figure than do sandy soils low in humus.

The presence of certain weeds, such as bracken, foxglove, sheep's sorrel, spurrey and corn marigold, often indicate soil acidity. Certain chemical indicators are available for testing a soil in the field as to its approximate pH. The degree of acidity or alkalinity is shown by a change in colour when the chemical is added to the soil.

Overliming may induce certain diseases in crops, such as scab in potatoes, while excess lime may render certain nutrients, such as boron, iron and manganese, unavailable to plants.

Lime application. Lime is applied in various forms as follows:

(1) *Ground limestone and chalk (calcium carbonate).* With ground limestone fineness of grinding is important otherwise it will not be very effective. Chalk is soft and need not be ground. In some areas limestone contains impurities such as magnesium carbonate, which increases its value on magnesium-deficient soils.

(2) *Burnt lime or quicklime (calcium oxide).* When limestone is burnt in a kiln quicklime is produced. This is usually available in the form of large lumps which if placed on the soil absorb moisture and fall to powder. It is then easy to spread.

(3) *Hydrated or slaked lime (calcium hydroxide).* This is burnt lime which has been slaked down with added water. It is fine, easy to handle and popular with gardeners. Slaked lime if exposed to the air absorbs carbon dioxide and soon reverts to the carbonate form, in other words, limestone.

These three forms of lime are valued according to their calcium oxide (CaO_2) content apart from other considerations such as ease of handling. Thus burnt lime is almost pure calcium oxide and 1 ton of it is equivalent to about 27 cwt. of hydrated lime or 35 cwt. limestone or chalk.

Lime is usually applied in the winter or early spring after digging. It is then worked in lightly. The amount to apply should be determined by soil analysis. Subsequently most soils can be kept in good condition by application of 4 oz. ground limestone or its equivalent per sq. yd. every year or so.

Bulky organic manures

Organic matter plays an important part in making soils fertile and can be regarded as indispensable. The following are its more important effects:

(1) It modifies the condition of both clays and sands; the former are opened

up and aerated by its addition while it binds the particles of a sandy soil together. Thus the texture of both soils is improved, cultivation is made easier and there is no caking.

(2) Most substances of this type, especially farmyard manure, are sources of valuable plant foods, particularly nitrogen, and these although somewhat slow in action have a gradual effect on plant growth.

(3) Partly decomposed organic matter or humus provides vital foods for bacteria and other beneficial soil organisms and forms a medium in which they may flourish.

(4) Humus has great water-holding properties and enables plants to resist drought. It also assists in holding soluble plant foods.

(5) Organic matter on decomposing produces weak acids which render certain plant foods soluble and thus available to plants. Should the soil become too acid this condition must be corrected by the addition of lime.

Farmyard manure. The quality of this material depends largely on (*a*) the kind of animal producing it, (*b*) the food on which the animal was fed and (*c*) the kind of litter used for bedding. Stable or horse manure from straw-bedded animals is probably the best, and is particularly good for heavy soils. Cow and pig manure are colder materials but when well rotted give good results, especially on light soils. An average sample of farmyard manure contains 0·5% N, 0·3% P_2O_5 and 0·6% K_2O. On this basis 10 tons will supply the equivalent of 5 cwt. sulphate of ammonia, 3 cwt. superphosphate and 2–2½ cwt. muriate of potash. Thus it is relatively low in phosphates. Application may range from ½ cwt. to 2 cwt. per 10 sq. yd.

Liquid manure. This is usually derived from farmyard manure. Because of its relatively high nitrogen content and fairly rapid action it may be used for feeding growing plants, but only as a weak solution.

Poultry manure. This substance is richer in plant foods than farmyard manure, particularly in phosphates and nitrogen, but its physical effect is inferior. It is sometimes used for leafy market-garden crops at the rate of about 5 lb. per sq. yd.

Sewage sludge. This substance also contains much more nitrogen and phosphates than farmyard manure, but it is not nearly so good for soil texture. It contains practically no potash and should be supplemented by a special potash dressing. In industrial districts it sometimes contains substances that are harmful to plants. Average application may be ¼ cwt. to ½ cwt. per 10 sq. yd.

Seaweed. This contains about the same amount of nitrogen as farmyard manure, much more potash, but very little phosphate. Seaweed decomposes rapidly, and is not so long lasting as farmyard manure. It is popular with growers near the sea. Average application per 10 sq. yd. is 1 cwt.

Shoddy. This is waste material from wool factories. It is a useful source of organic matter for light soils but is applied mainly for its nitrogen content which in a good sample is up to 15%. Average application per 10 sq. yd. is around 20 lb.

Spent hops. This material supplies small quantities of organic matter. It also contains 3–4% nitrogen, and 1–2% phosphate. Average per 10 sq. yd. is 5 lb.

Compost. Composting is a method of making various waste materials and garden rubbish into manure. Straw is often used for this purpose and the resulting compost may be equal to farmyard manure.

Green manuring. This is a method of supplying organic matter to the soil by growing a crop and then digging it in. Quick-growing crops capable of providing a good bulk of readily decomposable greenstuff are preferred, and such crops as mustard, turnip and rape fall into this category. Mustard for green manuring may be sown as late as Aug. and by Nov. is usually ready for digging in which should be done before heavy frosts set in. The application of a nitrogeneous fertilizer to the crop before digging it in hastens decomposition. While growing, green crops absorb and hold soil nitrates, thus preventing loss of nitrogen by leaching. If leguminous plants (annual lupins) are used for this purpose, they also add to the soil's nitrogen by their association with the 'nodule' bacteria which fix air nitrogen in the soil. Lupins are somewhat slower in growth than mustard and should be sown from Apr. to July.

Soil fertility

Maximum production from the soil depends upon a high level of fertility. This means good aeration with an adequate water supply and balanced proportions of the different plant nutrients in available form. How can the gardener secure such conditions? Firstly he must make sure that drainage and cultivation are properly done, otherwise his efforts will go for nothing. The importance of pH and the addition of lime according to crop or plant needs has been explained and the role of bulky organic matter and the part it plays especially in the form of humus in promoting a balance between water and air in the soil has been pointed out.

Fertilizers require special consideration and although soil analysis does give a guide to deficiencies or excesses it is only of an approximate nature. There are other factors in relation to every site and its cropping which should be considered. Thus if a vegetable garden has been well supplied with farmyard manure over a number of years it is probable that a reserve of both phosphate and potash will build up. Such a soil may give excellent crops for one or two years at any rate without the application of the nutrients mentioned, especially if lime is applied to make these substances available.

Apart from the instance mentioned above there has often been a tendency in the past to be over generous with phosphate fertilizers. Thus bone meal is sometimes applied and not nitrogenous or potassic fertilizers. Again, most compound fertilizers contain an unduly high proportion of phosphate in relation to plant requirements. In general, therefore, gardeners should avoid the excessive use of such fertilizers as bone meal and superphosphate while a compound with a comparatively high percentage of nitrogen and potash should be preferred. Alternatively a home-made mixture might be more suitable.

The use of nitrogen in the garden deserves special consideration. The organic forms of nitrogen, such as hoof and horn, are slow acting and are therefore available to plants over a long period. On the other hand the quicker acting nitrate fertilizers (nitro-chalk) are excellent for top or side dressings of growing plants to stimulate them into rapid growth. This type of fertilizer could be used more widely in many gardens to bring forward crops which are backward and generally to accelerate growth when this is considered desirable. Heavy doses of nitrogen should be avoided, 'little and often' being the rule. Moreover, it is best to apply nitrogen early in the season. It gives good results in the late spring and early summer.

Liquid fertilizers

The application of nutrients in liquid form is not by any means a new idea, for this has been done since time immemorial by using liquid animal manure. In the past, however, artificial fertilizers have usually been applied to the soil in solid form. Then, in the presence of water, they were dissolved and absorbed by plant roots as a solution. More recently chemical solutions have been prepared for the feeding of growing plants. This method is now used extensively in glasshouses for tomatoes and various pot plants. Normally these preparations contain the three important nutrients N, P and K as well as trace elements. They are sold in concentrated form and must be diluted according to instructions. Artificial liquid fertilizers give excellent results and can be recommended for feeding most growing plants.

Excess salts in the soil

Generous helpings of natural or artificial manures if continued over a number of years usually result in the build up of soluble salts in the soil which are not needed by the plants. These salts naturally increase the concentration of the soil solution and, depending on the quantities present, this may seriously interfere with the uptake of nutrients, for plant roots can absorb a weak solution only. These conditions are more likely to occur in glasshouse soils where intensive cropping needs the free use of manures and fertilizers. For this reason glasshouse crops, particularly tomatoes, are sometimes retarded in growth and the yield of fruit reduced.

Fortunately the soluble salt concentration in a soil can be easily measured by the electrical conductivity of the soil water solution. The result so obtained is indicated by what is called the CF (conductivity factor) scale. This scale is 1 to 36, the higher figures indicating the greater salt concentration. Thus a reading of 1 to 10 is low and quite safe, while a reading of 25 and above is too high for most plants. The CF of soil samples taken from glasshouses for chemical analysis is normally included in a report together with an indication from the soil chemist of its significance.

Soil-less cultivation of plants

Soil is not included among a plant's essential requirements and is best defined as a convenient medium in which to grow plants. Indeed it is so convenient that its substitution on a large scale would be impracticable. Nevertheless soil is not a perfect medium and its principal disadvantages are:

(1) It harbours pests and diseases which attack plants above and below ground level necessitating expensive control measures.

(2) Weeds present in most soils compete with cultivated plants and to keep them in check involves time and expense.

(3) Some soils, such as heavy clays, are difficult to cultivate and expensive to maintain in good physical condition.

For one or more of these reasons it may be best to grow particularly valuable crops such as carnations and tomatoes without soil, but this method is restricted to glasshouse culture. Botanists have been familiar since the middle of the last century with the growing of plants in weak chemical solutions, and various adaptations of this method were first tried on a commercial scale in America. Originally this type of culture was called 'hydroponics' and consisted in stretching a wire mesh over a tank of solution. This support was then covered with a layer of such material as peat or wood shavings in which the seed or seedlings were planted. Air was usually pumped into the solution. This system, however, has been largely superseded by using an aggregate of sand or gravel as a root anchorage. A clean sterile lime-free sand is preferable and experience has shown that the size of the grains is not critical although rather coarse sand having particles $\frac{1}{8}$ to $\frac{3}{8}$ in. in diameter can be recommended.

On a small scale various types of containers may be used to hold the medium ranging from clay pots of suitable size to wooden or concrete boxes or troughs. These must be sufficiently deep to allow ample root room for the particular kind of plants to be grown. On a larger scale beds about 1 ft. deep may be constructed with concrete. Four feet wide is convenient for easy working, and to allow drainage the bottom should be dished towards the centre where a row of 2-in. drain pipes will remove surplus water. Alternatively holes can be made at intervals centrally along the bottom. The beds or other containers should be filled to within an inch or so of the top with the sand which is then thoroughly hosed and allowed to drain.

Nutrient solutions

Obviously a solution must include all the essential elements required by plants. So long as this rule is observed a wide range of chemicals may be used, avoiding of course any injurious substances. Over the years many formulae have been tried and one which has given good results for one of the most popular soil-less crops, namely tomatoes, is given below. The substances listed are in the form of crude salts.

Potassium chloride	2 oz.
Sodium nitrate	28 oz.
Superphosphate of lime (18% P_2O_5)	14 oz.
Magnesium sulphate	9 oz.
Ammonium sulphate	2 oz.
Water	100 gal.

Two groups of trace elements should be added as separate solutions. They are:

(*a*) Boric acid	$\frac{1}{4}$ oz.
Manganese sulphate	$\frac{1}{4}$ oz.
Zinc sulphate	$\frac{1}{28}$ oz.
Water	1 pt.
(*b*) Iron citrate	$\frac{1}{2}$ oz.
Water	1 pt.

Another formula devised by the Ohio State University, U.S.A., is suitable for a wide variety of plants.

Potassium nitrate	11½ oz.
Ammonium sulphate	1¾ oz.
Magnesium sulphate	8½ oz.
Monocalcium phosphate	4½ oz.
Calcium sulphate	20 oz.
Water	100 gal.

In addition a solution of:

Boric acid	1 oz.
Manganese sulphate	1 oz.
Water	1 gal.

should be made and a pint of this added to the main solution at monthly intervals. ½ oz. ferrous sulphate should also be added at weekly intervals.

The pH of the above solutions should be kept at about 6·5. To lower the pH apply a solution of 2 oz. sulphuric acid in 1 gal. water and to raise the pH use 2 oz. sodium hydroxide per gal. water. Should any sign of chlorosis (leaf yellowing) appear, iron solutions should be given more frequently.

There are various methods of applying the solutions, the simplest being with a watering can fitted with a coarse rose. Another method is by means of a raised tank to which a hose is fitted. Automatic supply of the solution can also be arranged when required by placing perforated pipes along the beds (two pipes to a 4-ft. bed). These pipes may be attached to a tank containing the solution. Alternatively they may be fitted to the mains water supply and when the water is turned on a concentrated solution previously prepared can be injected into the flow at any given dilution by a special machine.

A wide range of crops can be grown by soil-less culture but two of the most popular are tomatoes and carnations. Plants for this method should be raised in a medium similar to that used for cropping. In their early stages of growth, however, they should be supplied with a solution whose strength is only one-quarter of the standard. The concentration of this is gradually increased as the plants grow, until just before planting out it is at the normal dilution. In transplanting it is best to lift each plant with some surrounding sand and drop the lot into prepared holes in the bed or other container. Very little firming is required.

At first the nutrient solution should be applied once or twice per week but as the plants develop, more frequent applications are necessary. Eventually robust plants like tomatoes in full growth may require daily applications. The strength of the solution may also sometimes be increased with advantage in the later stages. Every 3 or 4 weeks the sand should be thoroughly hosed with clean water.

CHAPTER FIVE

Plant Propagation

THE successful raising of new plants is one of the most fascinating of all garden operations and one which every gardener is bound to be involved in to a greater or lesser extent. Obviously the period of a plant's early development is its most vulnerable, and then it requires greater safeguards and protective measures than for established specimens. In spite of this quite a large number of plants of different kinds may be increased from seed or cuttings in the open ground.

Of course if one wants to extend the range and scope of propagation a glass-house is essential. If artificially heated it is better still and allows one to garden practically all the year round, and a source of heat immediately below the propagation medium (compost, sand, etc.), usually termed 'bottom heat', is of great value. There are various methods of arranging this, such as fixing a propagating frame over hot-water pipes or inserting special electrical heating cables beneath the propagating frame. A temperature of 55 deg. F. to 60 deg. F. is suitable for this bottom heat. Frames of various types, usually unheated, and cloches are other useful propagation aids.

Plants may be increased by two quite distinct methods. These are by seed and vegetatively. Seed being the result of the pollination of flowers has a sexual origin. Vegetative propagation consists in the use of portions, usually called cuttings, of the plant's vegetative organs, roots, stems and leaves, and is described as asexual. Both these methods have their advantages and disadvantages and the use of one or other depends on circumstances.

Seed propagation

Seed is often a cheap and easy method of raising large numbers of plants which are often more vigorous and healthy than those raised from cuttings. The main disadvantage of seed propagation is the probable variation among the seedlings. This applies when the parents are of mixed ancestry and rules out seed increase for innumerable garden hybrids, such as varieties of apples, pears, plums and many named ornamental plants. However, a great many other plants, including most varieties of vegetables, do grow reasonably true from seed because over many generations true-breeding types have been developed by careful selection. Sometimes seed is the only possible method of increase, as with all true annuals and biennials. Seed is also the means of raising new varieties of plants.

When the gardener sows seed in the soil he expects it to germinate and produce seedlings. Germination, however, depends on three basic conditions, the presence of adequate moisture, air and warmth. The first is an obvious requirement and the absorption of water and its effect on seeds like broad beans is familiar to most people. Therefore drying out of the soil after sowing may retard or prevent germination. Excessive moisture on the other hand, by excluding air from the breathing seed, may also prove bad for germination, while burying the seed too deeply may have the same effect.

The temperature required for germination varies with different species, but few will grow when it is below 40 deg. F. Obviously the seed of hot-house plants needs a higher temperature than that of hardy species which grow in the open.

Even when seed is sown under perfect conditions it is rare to secure 100% germination because, for various reasons, a number of seeds die even before sowing. It is important, however, to keep the number of losses to a minimum, and as a lot depends on handling, storage and age, seed should always be purchased from a reliable source. With most vegetable seeds the gardener has some legal protection for these must conform by law to certain specified standards of purity and germination.

Certain types of seed however, although alive and quite sound, fail to germinate or may take a long time to do so even under normal conditions. This is called 'delayed germination' and is frequently found among species of trees and shrubs, bulbous plants and alpines. These seeds usually respond to special treatment as described below.

Hard seed coats. This is a common reason for delayed germination because water cannot be taken in. Many trees and shrubs have seeds of this type, and it is a common feature of both woody and herbaceous members of the pea and bean family (Leguminosae). Various methods to rupture hard seed coats before sowing have been tried. These include filing and soaking such seeds in acid or hot water. A more natural method is to bury them in damp peat or compost, preferably under warm conditions. There the seed coats will gradually decompose by the action of bacteria and fungi. Seeds which benefit from this method include the snowdrop tree (*Halesia carolina*), cotoneasters, most palms and the hazel nut (*Corylus*).

Stratification. Under natural conditions the seeds of many trees and shrubs fall to the ground in the autumn and after lying half-buried in moist leaf-mould over the winter they may germinate in the warmth of spring. This cold treatment is indeed essential for the germination of the seeds of many woody species, and is called stratification. The gardener may copy nature by burying such seed in moist sand or peat in containers which are left outside over winter. In spring these seeds may be sown. Autumn sowing is an alternative method and is preferable for many alpines which also require stratification. In this case the seed is sown in pots or pans which are left outside over winter and are brought indoors in the spring to germinate.

Some seeds having hard seed coats may also require statification. These require, (*a*) warm, moist conditions and (*b*) cold, moist conditions. This may be achieved naturally by summer sowing when conditions will be warm at first followed by the cold of winter. Seeds which respond to this treatment include cotoneasters, *Cornus* and some species of *Berberis*. Similar conditions are necessary for the seed of such lilies as *L. auratum*, *L. rubellum* and *L. canadense*. In this case the seed germinates in the warmth of summer but further development then ceases until the seedlings are subjected to a period of low temperature.

Fortunately seed from many species germinates without pre-treatment and for these spring sowing is most convenient. When dealing with seed from species whose germination requirements are unknown, the plant's natural habitat should be considered. Thus the seed of plants from warm climates is not likely to benefit from stratification. But if spring-sown seed fails to germinate during the season it may be wise to retain and subject it to low temperature conditions during the succeeding winter. Germination may then be brought on by heat the following spring. When dealing with pots or boxes containing seed whose germination has been delayed, always keep the compost reasonably moist.

Seed sowing in the open

Quite a large proportion of our garden plants are raised by sowing seeds in the open. Examples are most vegetables, annual and biennial flowering plants and many perennials such as hardy trees and shrubs. Sometimes the seed is sown where the crop will remain and mature, as with many vegetable crops, but here we are mainly concerned with the raising of plants for transplanting elsewhere.

For this purpose the seed bed should be situated in a warm sheltered position while the soil should be light and well drained. Unless the soil is deficient in humus, farmyard manure or similar material may not be necessary. A general purpose fertilizer, not too high in nitrogen, applied at the rate of 2 oz. per sq. yd.

PLATE 5

Above dwarf varieties of ASTER. Below tuberous BEGONIA, which has richly-coloured flowers and striking foliage.

PLATE 6

CALLISTEPHUS (China Aster). There are garden varieties available in a wide range of colours, many with double flowers.

PLATE I

Leaf cuttings

Some plants, such as certain types of begonia, can be propagated by leaf-cuttings taken in spring or early summer. Cut off a well-grown leaf and cut the main veins in three or four places. Pin the leaf down in a pan filled with a mixture of peat and sand. Shade the pan with a sheet of glass and put in a greenhouse or frame. Rooting takes 6 to 8 weeks when the plants should be potted up singly.

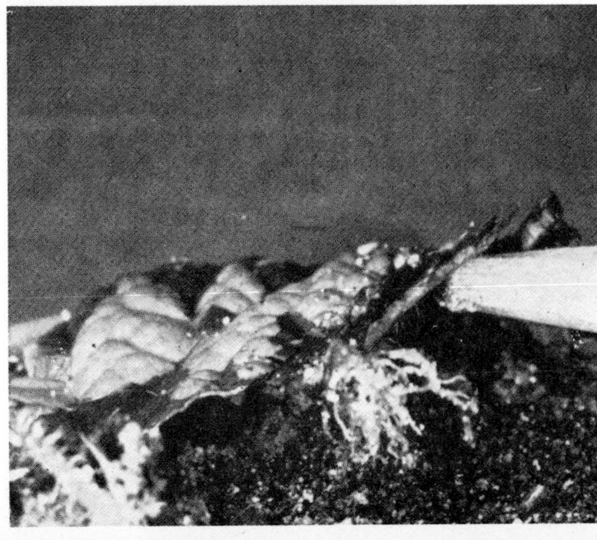

PLATE 2
Layering carnations

Above, **select a healthy well-grown shoot. Remove a few of the leaves.** *Right*, **make a cut on the underside of the stem starting just below a joint and running upwards to the centre.**

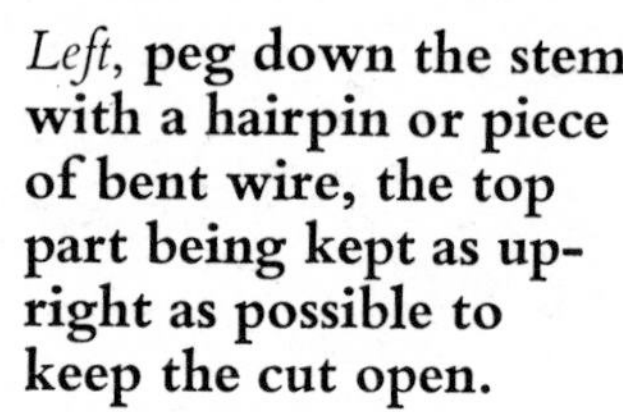

Left, **peg down the stem with a hairpin or piece of bent wire, the top part being kept as upright as possible to keep the cut open.**

Right, **sprinkle with coarse sand and cover to form a mound and water. It takes about 6 weeks to root when the layers should be severed and potted up or transplanted.**

PLATE 3

Pelargonium cuttings. The cuttings should be healthy side shoots from a mature plant and cut straight across below a joint. Make a hole in the side of the pot with a stick and put in the cutting. Make sure that the soil is well firmed in. The number of cuttings depend on the size of the pot, but they must not be overcrowded. The arrangement shown here is ideal.

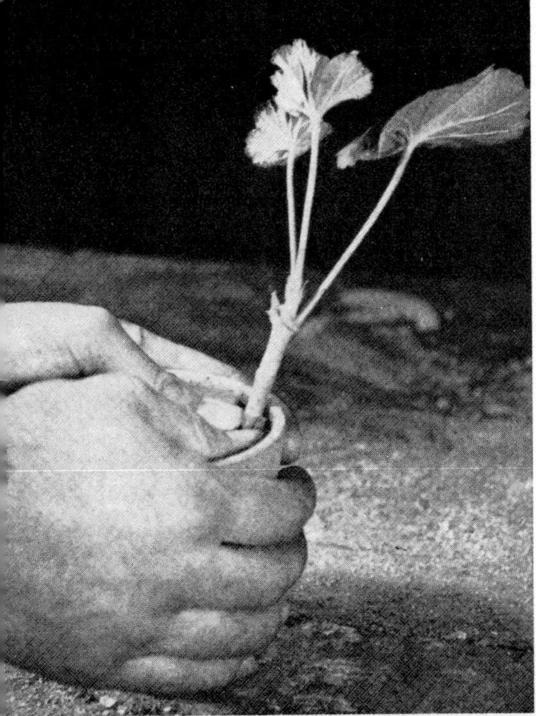

1

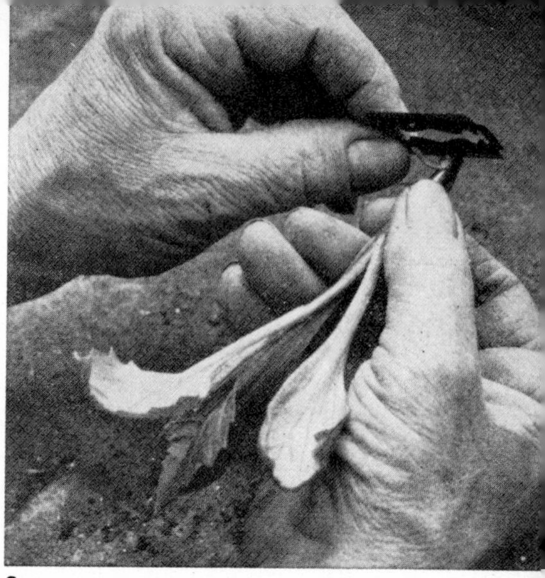

2

PLATE 4

Dahlia cuttings. **The cuttings are new shoots taken when the stored roots start into growth again. Remove the lower leaves and trim neatly just below the joint. Dip the end of the cutting into a reliable rooting compound. Place and firm in round the rim of the pot, 3 or 4 to a 4-in. pot. Keep in a close temperature and shaded from the sun. Rooting takes 6–8 weeks.**

4

3

PLATE 5
Disbudding chrysanthemums
To obtain choice large blooms the number of flower buds must be reduced to one on each stem. This is called 'disbudding'.

Above, **head of the plant before disbudding.** *Right*, **after disbudding. This operation must be done carefully with the fingers; a small pen-knife may be used to cut out the side shoots.**

PLATE 6
Planting out tomatoes
When planted in the open the soil should not be too rich nor freshly manured and watering should be light.

Above, **making a hole to take the plant which must be sturdy and well-rooted.**

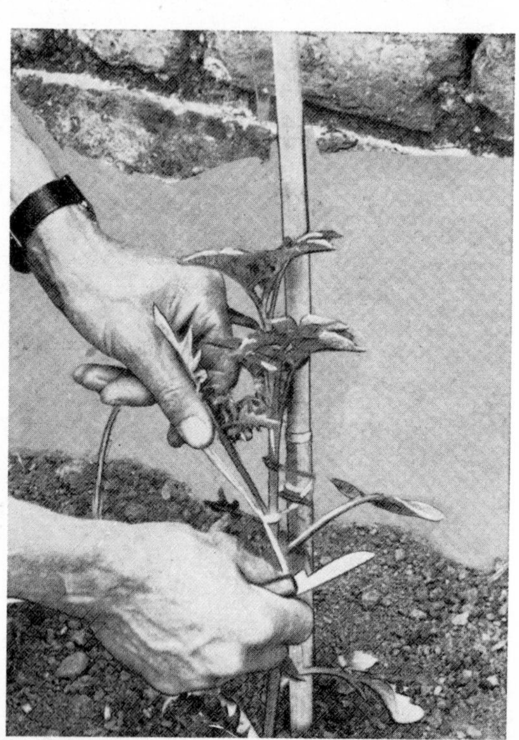

Above, **gently firm in the soil. The plants should be set level or slightly lower.** *Left*, **staking the plant to a cane (4 ft.). The plant must be supported as it grows.**

PLATE 7

Training tomatoes

It is important that tomato plants be kept tied to the stakes as they grow. The growing point should be pinched out at the second leaf above the fourth truss or at a height of about 3 ft. The lower leaves should be removed to allow air to circulate.

Above, **plant after side shoots have been removed.**

Right, **plant before removal of side shoots.**

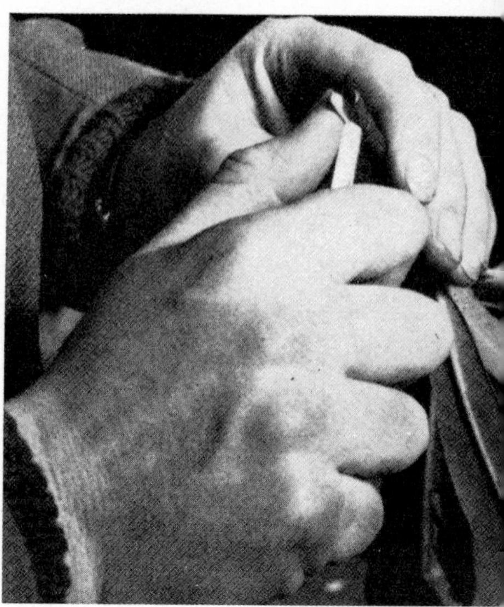

PLATE 8
Saddle grafting. **This form of grafting is used for propagating such shrubs as rhododendrons. First cut a wedge at the head of the stock and then cut the scion to match; one side should have a bud. Marry the scion to the stock and tie firmly with raffia. Protect the union with wax.**

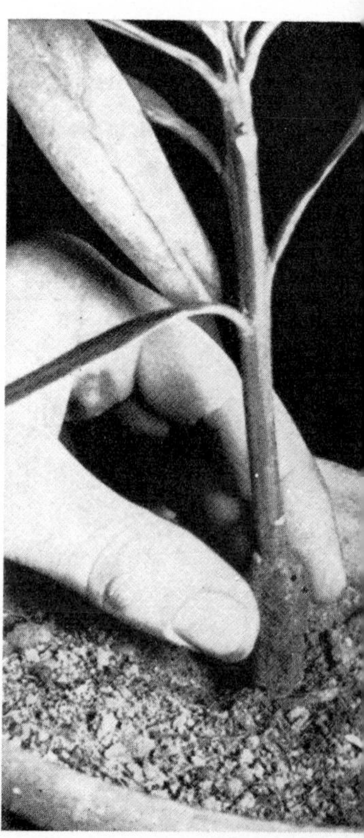

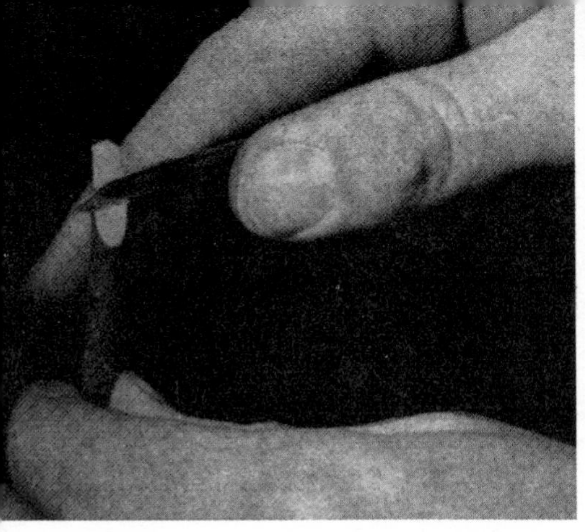

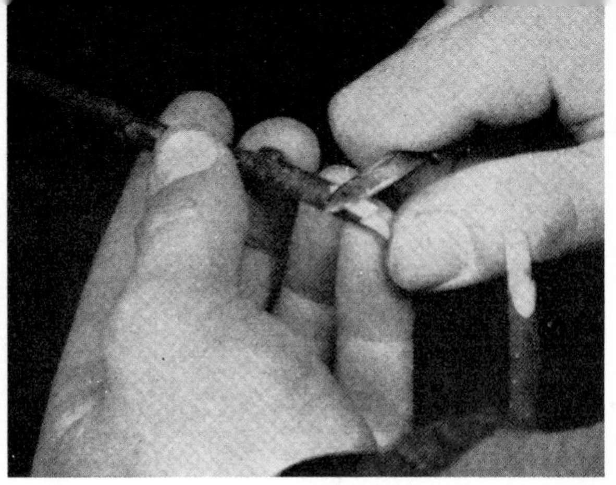

PLATE 9

Splice grafting. **In this form of grafting the stock is cut at the slope, as shown, and the scion cut to fit. The two are secured together with raffia and waxed. On plants growing out-of-doors, the scion should be made more secure by slitting a tongue in the cut with a corresponding slit in the stock.**

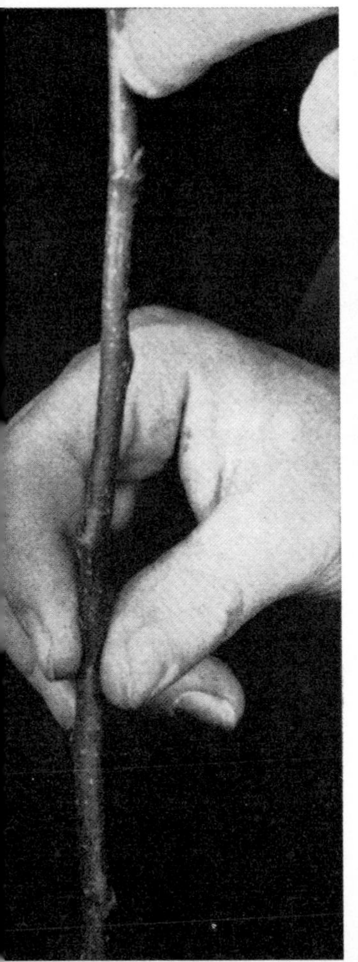

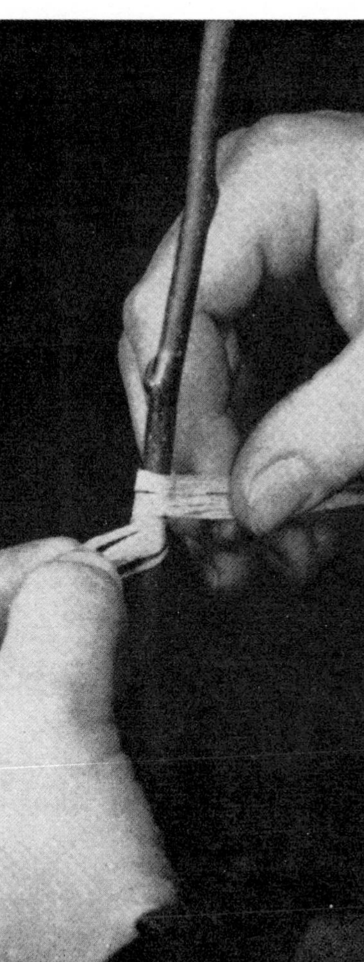

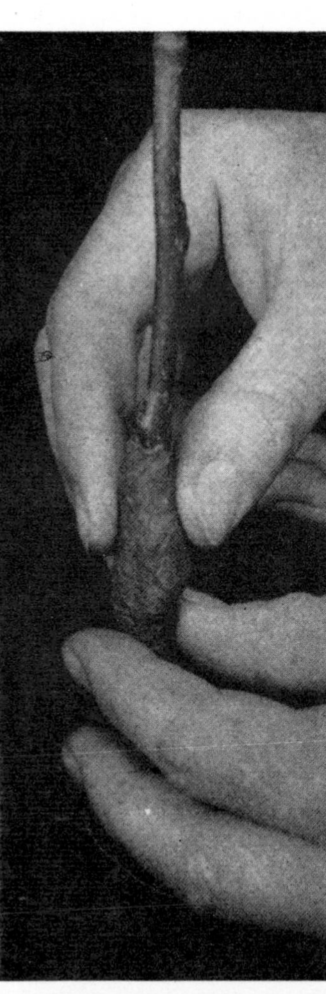

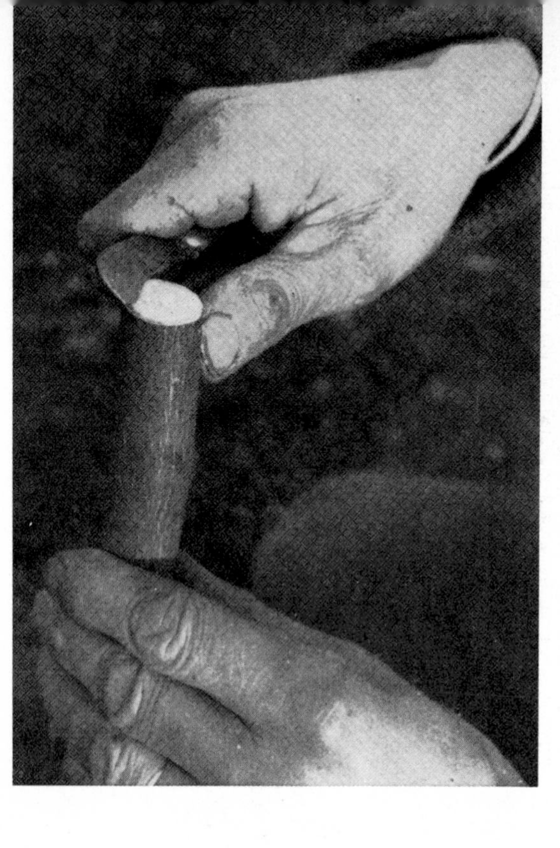
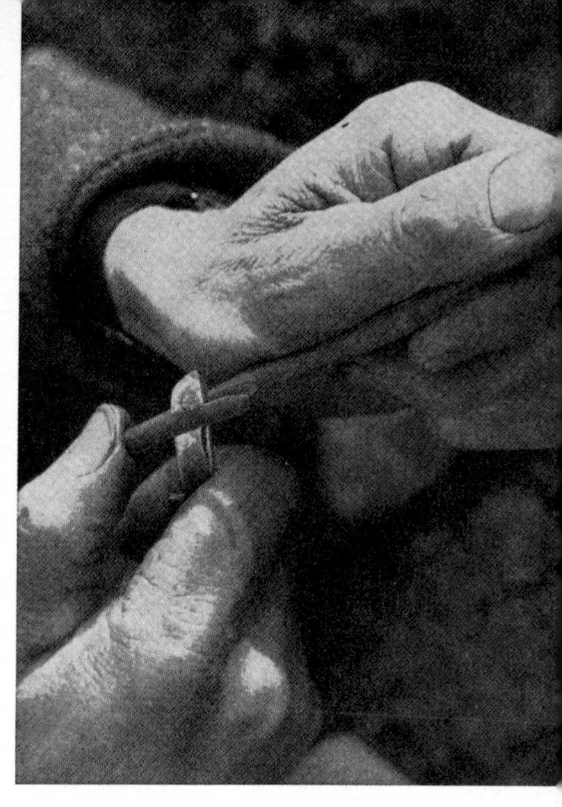

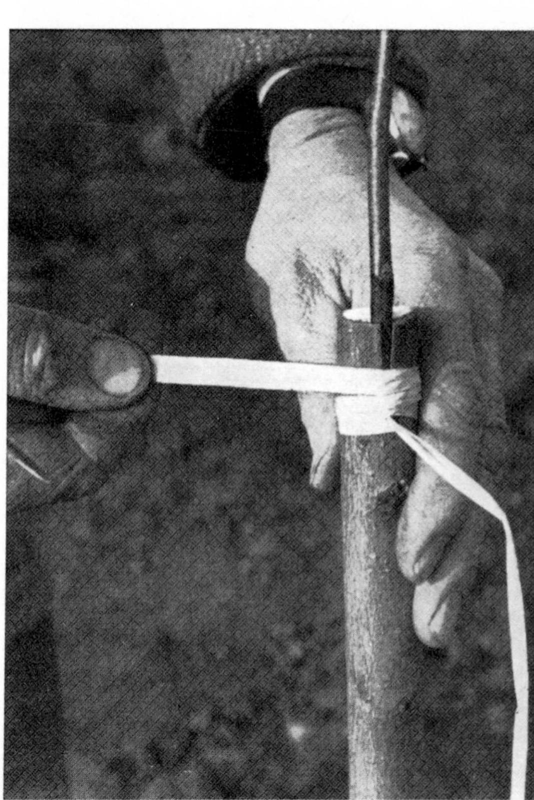

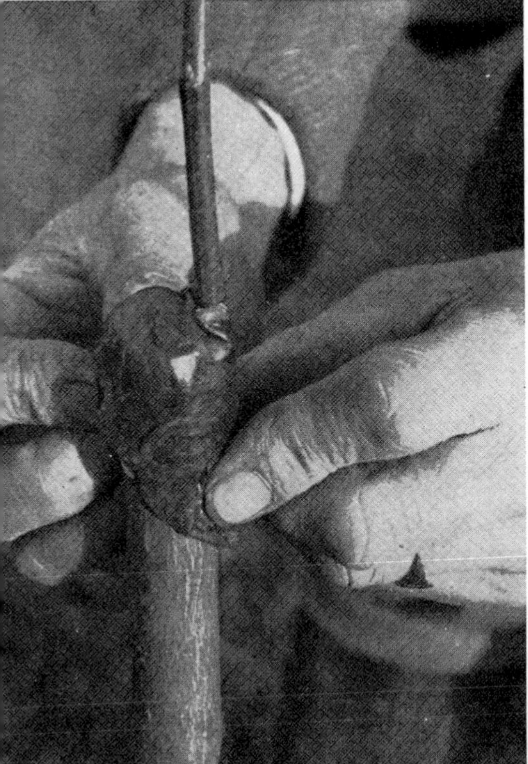

PLATE 10

Crown grafting

This form of grafting is valuable for renovating old but healthy trees, for changing an unsuitable variety or adding another to a part of a fruit tree to improve pollination. This is done in spring when the sap is rising. Cut and trim the stock and, according to the size of the stock, make a vertical slit 2–3 in. long through the bark but not into the wood. Carefully prise open the slit and insert the scion which should be cut to a thinly-tapering wedge about 2 in. long. The lowest bud on the scion should be a little above the wedge. Tie securely with raffia and wax the joint.

PLATE 11

Bridge grafting

When the bark of a tree is seriously damaged this form of grafting can be used to preserve a tree which would otherwise die. The object is to provide a bridge along which the sap may flow. Trim off the damaged bark as shown. (One or more bridges may be required depending on the size of the stem and the extent of the damage.) Cut shoots to span the damage, each end being shaped into a wedge to fit into the slits in the bark. Secure firmly, but not tightly, with raffia and cover with wax. Rub out the buds on the bridges. When the bridges are seen to be carrying the sap, the ties should be slit but need not be removed.

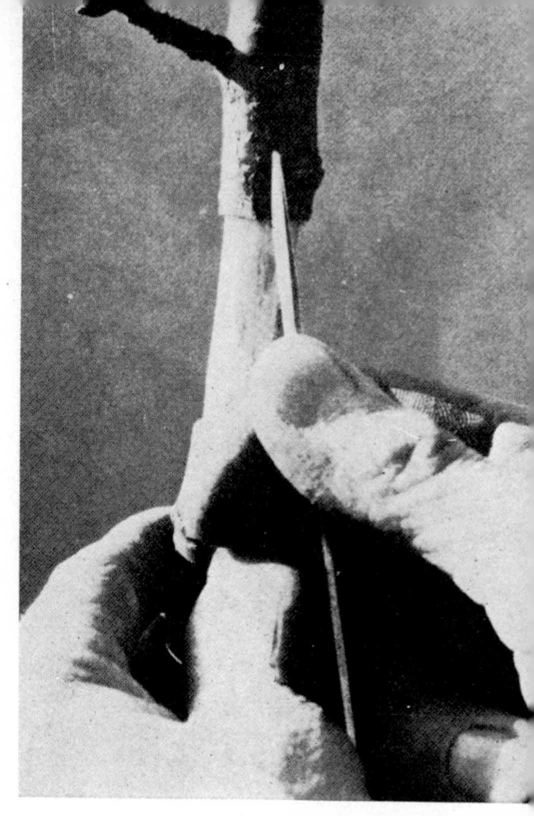

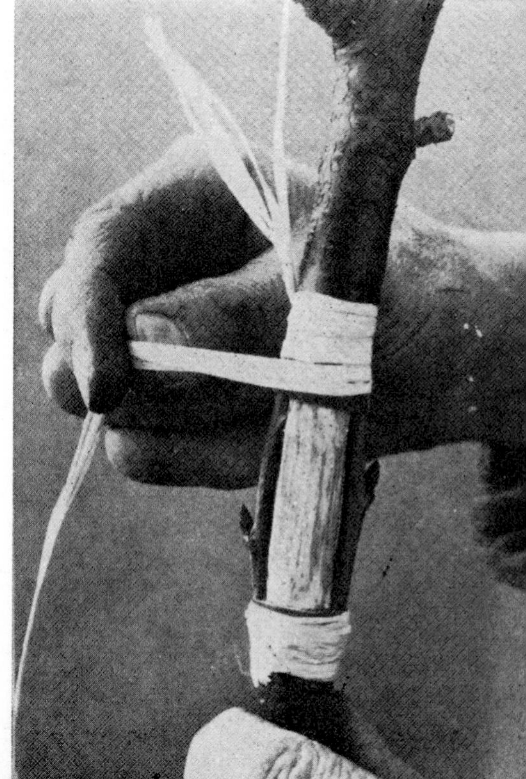

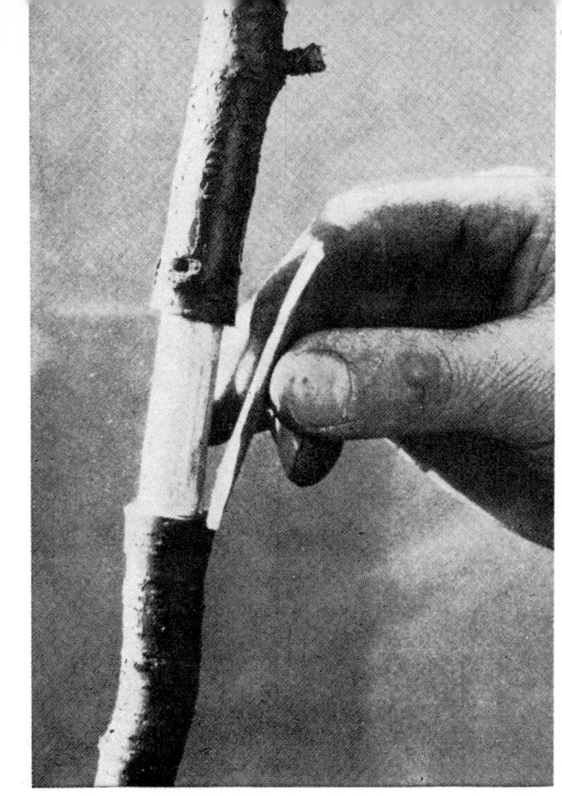
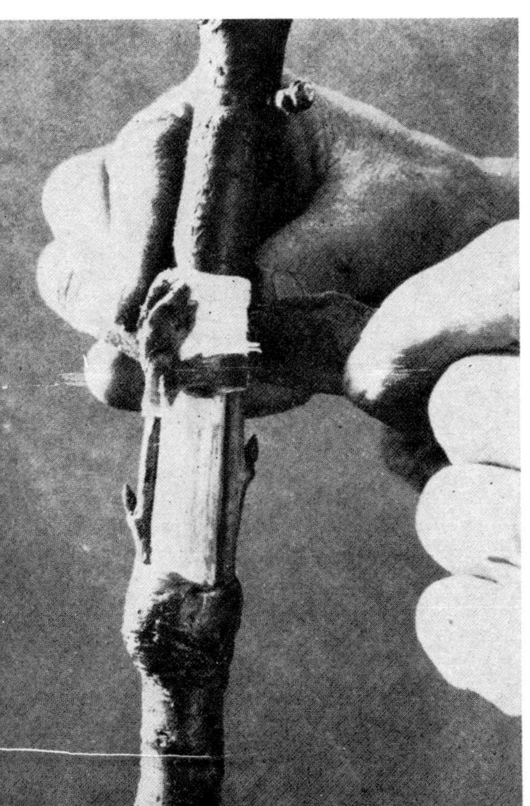
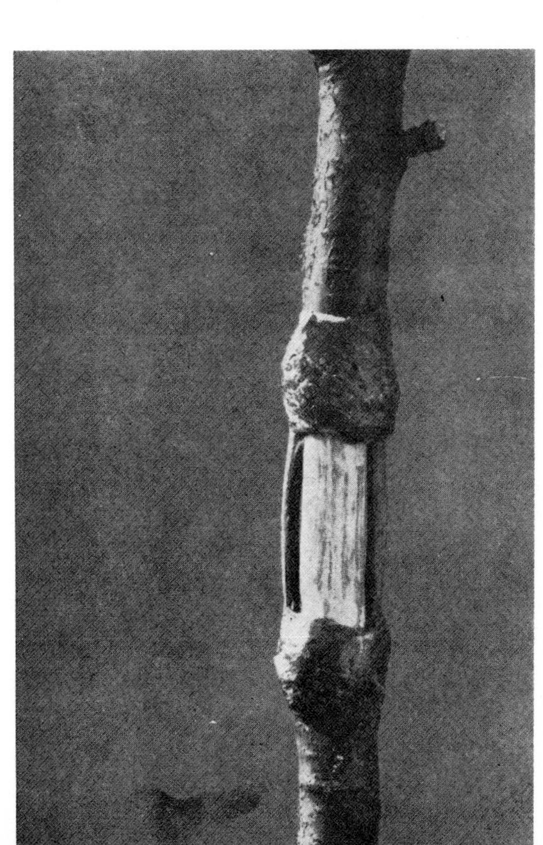

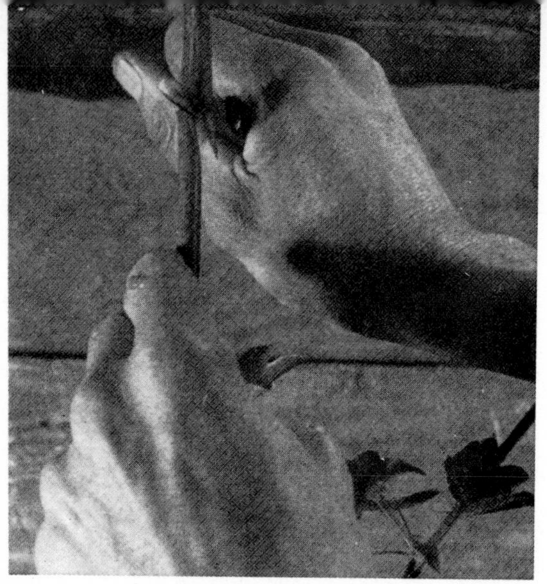

PLATE 12

Air layering. Certain shrubs, magnolias for example, are difficult to propagate by ordinary methods, but may be increased by air-layering. This work is best done in Apr. when the sap is flowing and is most successful on one-year old growth. Cut the stem upwards, as shown, to the centre of the stem level with a leaf bud. Place a twist of well-soaked sphagnum moss into the slit to keep it open and bunch more round the stem and protect with a sheath (plastic film) tied at the top and bottom. When the roots have formed they can be seen through the transparent sheet. Cut the stem off below the tie and unwrap the film. The rooted stem should be potted up in a suitable compost, well watered and placed in a frame or greenhouse.

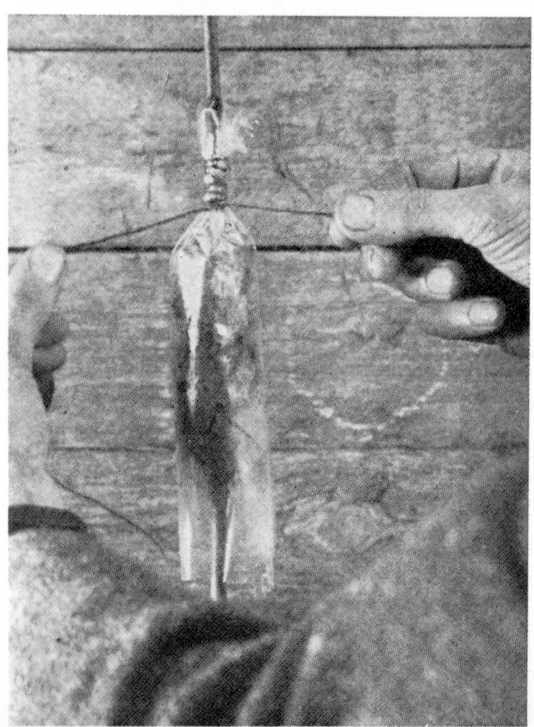

PLATE 13

Planting a rose bush

Roses do best in an open situation, protected from strong winds and in a good heavy loam or clay soil. Planting may be done from Nov. to Mar.; the earlier the better. Dig a hole large and deep enough to take the roots and give a dressing of bone meal. Place the roots in the hole and sprinkle fine soil around them and shake the bush gently to help the soil fill in closely. Put more soil over the roots and firm down. Bush roses in beds should be set out 2–2½ ft. apart. Finally, attach the label giving planting time and variety.

A bud is cut out from the middle of the shoot in a shallow slice, beginning $\frac{1}{2}$ in. below and finishing $\frac{1}{2}$–1 in. above the bud.

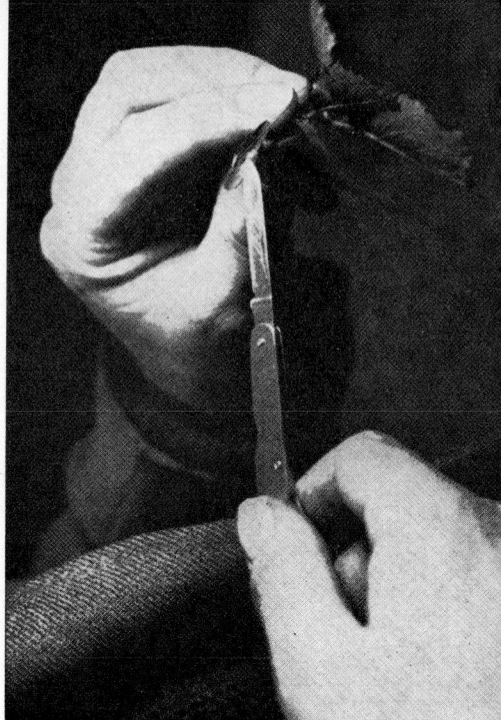

Using the leaf stem as a handle, the small piece of hard wood immediately under the bud is prised out with a knife. This is a delicate job and needs some practice.

Carefully open up the 'T' cut with the budding knife.

PLATE 14
Budding roses
The usual method of propagating roses is budding which is best done between June and Sept. Various stocks are used, the most common being the Dog Rose.

Make a vertical cut 1–$1\frac{1}{2}$ in. long through the bark but not into the hard wood.

Across the cut make another cut to form a 'T' cut.

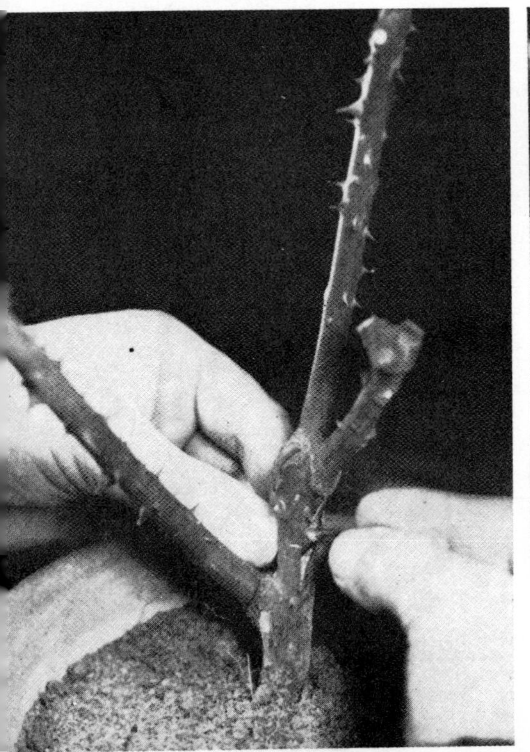

Slip the bud under the bark down to the bottom of the slit. Tie in the bud with raffia. When the bud has 'taken' the tie can be released.

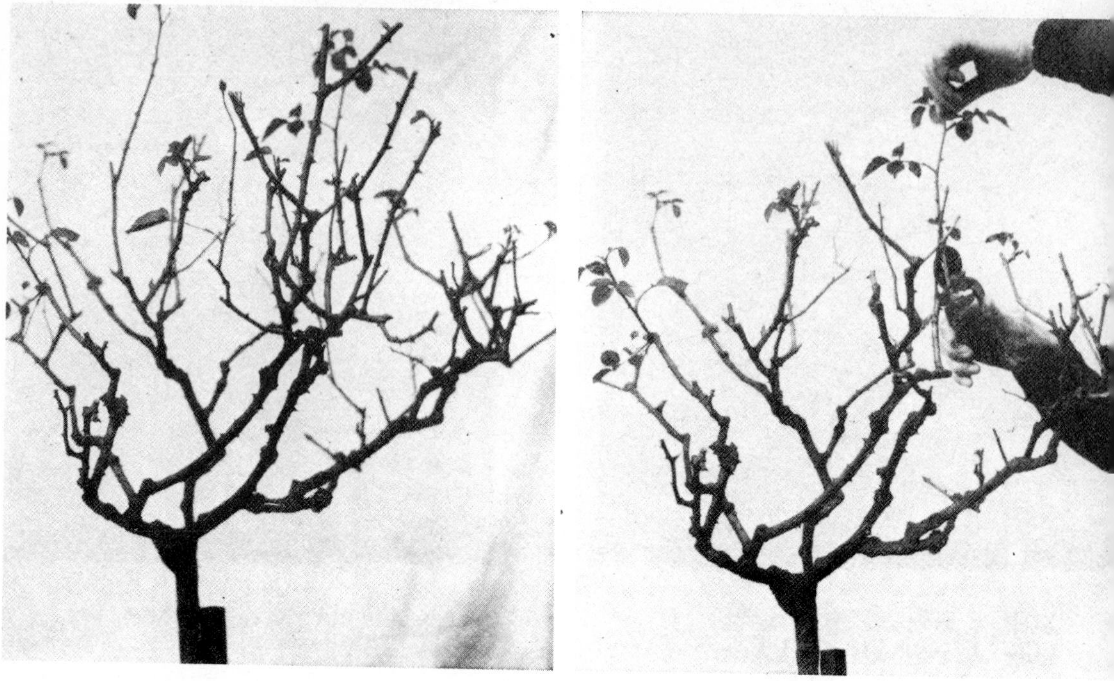

PLATE 15

Pruning standard roses. **Established roses should be pruned every year. All badly-placed, weak or dead wood should be cut out and the tree kept in shape. All suckers growing up must be cut away.**

PLATE 16

Training. Above, **fan-trained fruit tree and,** *below,* **an oblique cordon fruit tree. These two styles of training enable the growth of the trees to be controlled, improves the fruit yield and facilitates the picking of the crop.**

PLATE 17

Pruning (Leveller gooseberry). The purpose of pruning this form of bush is to keep the centre of the bush open (clearly shown in the lower photograph), remove the crossing and in-growing branches and shorten the new growth so as to improve the fruiting wood and increase the fruit yield.

PLATE 18

Pruning gooseberries (stool)

The main aims in pruning gooseberry bushes are to encourage the branches to grow as evenly spaced as possible and to keep the centre open so that light and air can enter freely and also enable the fruit to be picked that much easier.

PLATE 19

Pruning an apple tree

Apple trees should be pruned in late winter and before the buds begin to swell. With established trees the aim should be to keep the centre open, remove any crossing or in-growing branches and shorten the long growths of the previous year in order to encourage the production of fruiting wood.

Left, **taking a cutting from a mature plant.** *Above*, **making a hole with a pointed stick.** *Bottom left*, **inserting the cutting and firming down.** *Bottom right*, **finished and labelled plant.**

PLATE 20

Cacti cuttings

Cacti are generally increased from cuttings taken with a sharp knife and laid on a shelf for a few days to dry out some of the moisture in the plant.

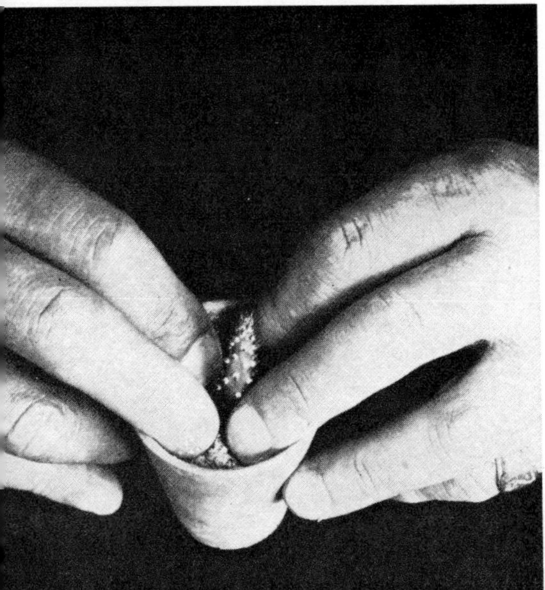

PLATE 21

Above, a well-designed rock garden which can quite readily be scaled down for the average garden. *Below*, small outcrops of rocks which can enhance the attractiveness of a garden, especially on a sloping site.

A formal garden pool.

PLATE 22

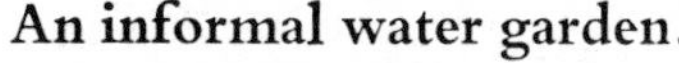

An informal water garden.

PLATE 23

Above, **a dry wall covered with cushions of flowering plants.** *Below*, **an attractive and well-matured pergola with flower borders.**

PLATE 24

Pergolas

Pergola of brick pillars faced with concrete and with garden seats in the spaces.

Pergola constructed of stout rustic poles and ideal for climbers.

Modern style pergola constructed of light timbers.

PLATE 26

Steps

Above, **steps constructed of stone slabs.** *Right*, **recessed steps of stone with brick risers and bounded by a ved wall.** *Below*, **graduated stone steps.**

Right, **crazy paving steps set between formal pillars.**

PLATE 25

Left, **paved path with lavender border.**

PLATE 27
Crazy paving. Above, **centre feature around a pool.** *Right,* **terrace area planted with well-placed flowering plants.**

PLATE 28
Garden furniture

A cushioned reclining chair.

Wooden three-tiered table and bench table or seat.

PLATE 29
Garden furniture

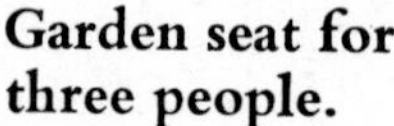

Garden seat for three people.

A wooden table for outdoor meals.

Garden seat for two people.

should prove beneficial. Lime, too, may be necessary to ensure freedom from acidity.

Normally the fertilizer and lime (if used) should be applied separately on dug land. The soil surface should then be thoroughly cultivated by a rotovator or by hand tools and finished off by good raking to ensure a fine level surface, while all rough material such as large stones should be removed.

It is usual to sow the seed in drills spaced from 9 to 12 in. apart. Depth of sowing depends on the size of the seed. Thus for fine seed (columbines) the drills should be as shallow as it is possible to draw them, whereas larger seed, like that of many trees, should be sown 1–2 in. below the soil surface. Commence by stretching a strong line tightly across the plot. Alongside this, draw the drills by the use of a triangular hoe or the corner of an ordinary draw hoe. Measuring rods should be provided at either end of the plot and the line moved forward at equal distances to draw new drills as the work proceeds.

The seed may be sown as a trickle from the open end of the packet. Some prefer to hold a small quantity in the hand and allow it to fall through the fingers in an even stream. Another method is to drop a few seeds in groups at intervals along the rows which will save seed and may simplify thinning later, if this is necessary. In any case always avoid sowing too thickly. Subsequently, the seed is covered in by careful raking along the line of the drills to prevent seed being drawn across from one drill to the next, and the plot left neat and level.

A simpler and more accurate method of sowing is to use a small hand-pushed seed drill. This implement makes the drills, sows the seed and covers it in, all in one operation, but its use is only justified if there are fair quantities of seed to sow. Seeds of a considerable size range may be sown by drill, the outlet being adjusted to suit different sized seeds. In sowing by seed drill a line should be used for the first row but the position of subsequent rows will be shown by a marker fixed to the drill, which is adjustable for different spacings.

After sowing, a light rolling or firming with the back of the spade will prove beneficial if the soil is not wet. In dry weather watering after sowing is rarely advisable as it may wash the soil off the seed or cause surface caking. If necessary, it is best to give a good soaking a day or two before sowing. When the seedlings are through, water may be applied again if necessary.

As soon as the emerging seedlings indicate the rows, the soil spaces between should be loosened with the hoe and weeds removed as soon as possible. Chemical weed control is sometimes possible. Any necessary thinning of seedlings should be done early to avoid over-crowding and the easiest way is to kneel between the rows and use one hand to pull out the thinnings and the other to hold the selected plant in place. Transplanting should not be delayed unduly, and in dry weather a good soaking of the seed bed with water a day or so in advance of lifting is beneficial. Ease the seedlings up with a fork and then remove them carefully from the soil.

Transplanting seedlings. Replanting is normally done with a dibber but for seedlings with a mass of fibrous roots a trowel may be better. A line is necessary to plant in straight rows and spacing should conform to the size to which the plants are expected to grow in that position. To plant with a dibber, make a hole the depth of the root system. Insert the plant to the bottom with the minimum of root bending. Then drive the dibber in again about 1 in. from the plant and push it towards the stem so as to firm the soil near the plant.

Trowel planting involves the driving of this tool vertically into the ground and pulling the soil out towards the planter. Then place the plant against the back of the hole and replace the soil firmly over the roots. Transplanted seedlings should be watered in if the soil is dry and a light spray in the evenings may prove beneficial.

Sowing under glass

Raising plants from seed in glasshouses or frames allows a much greater degree of control than is possible outside. Thus a higher and more uniform temperature can be maintained, the water supply accurately regulated and damage from pests more easily prevented.

This practice enables the gardener to propagate a much wider range of plants from seed than can be attempted outside. These include the more delicate or half-hardy species, such as begonias, gloxinias, tomatoes and many half-hardy annual flowers. In addition hardy plants may be raised under glass for planting out later, with the object of securing earlier or heavier crops.

Seed composts. Outside the seed is usually sown in ordinary soil but under glass it is well worth while to use special composts both for seed sowing and potting. Composts made to the John Innes formula are now considered best and are widely used for this purpose.

John Innes Seed Compost (JIS)
2 parts sterilized loam
1 ,, moss peat
1 ,, coarse sand ($\frac{1}{16}$–$\frac{1}{8}$ in. grit)

To each bushel of this mixture add 1½ oz. superphosphate (18% P_2O_5) and ¾ oz. ground limestone or chalk.

John Innes Potting Compost (JIP)
7 parts sterilized loam
3 ,, moss peat
2 ,, coarse sand

To each bushel of this mixture add ¼ lb. John Innes base and ¾ oz. ground limestone or chalk.

The JI base consists of:

2 parts by weight superphosphate (18% P_2O_5)
2 ,, ,, ,, hoof and horn finely ground
1 ,, ,, ,, sulphate of potash (50% K_2O)

The majority of plants may be grown in the above mixtures but for some (tomatoes) in pots the fertilizers recommended for the potting compost may be doubled or even trebled. Other plants, such as certain alpines or cactus plants, require a higher proportion of sand while no lime or chalk should be added for lime-haters such as most of the Ericaceae family.

The ingredients of the compost, loam, sand and peat, should all be of first-class quality. Normally the loam is chopped up finely and sterilized before mixing with the other materials. Sterilization may be done by a steam or electric sterilizer. The latter is very convenient for small lots of soil and simply involves placing the soil in the container provided. There it is heated electrically to a temperature of at least 180 deg. F. and this heat maintained for about 10 minutes.

The sterilized loam when cool should be thoroughly mixed with the sand, peat, fertilizers and lime or chalk. Afterwards the mixture is sifted through a ⅛-in. sieve and allowed to stand for a few days before use. The strictest hygiene should be observed in the mixing operations otherwise the soil sterilization will prove a waste of time and disease will be reintroduced. For the same reason a high standard of cleanliness is necessary in storage. Ready-prepared John Innes composts can be bought at most horticultural shops.

Seed sowing. All receptacles such as boxes or pots unless new should be washed thoroughly clean, and sterilized with steam or formaldehyde before use. The containers should be firmly filled with the compost and the surface left absolutely smooth and level, and the compost should then be soaked with clean water and left to drain.

Sowing is done thinly on the damp surface and the seed covered carefully with fine compost. The containers are then placed on the glasshouse staging and covered with sheets of glass and paper to retain moisture. Most seeds germinate readily in a temperature of 55 deg.–60 deg. F. and immediately the seedlings appear they should be exposed to the light but shaded from bright sunshine which may scorch them. The compost must never be allowed to dry out, but water should be given as a fine moist spray or better still, the containers should be stood in water and allowed to soak it up. Water for this purpose should preferably be taken direct from the mains supply to ensure that it is free from disease.

The seedlings should be exposed to light of moderate intensity to ensure sturdy growth and when they are large enough to handle they should be transplanted (pricked off) into other containers an inch or two apart. Later they may be potted into small pots from which they are planted outside or potted-on into larger pots as they develop. Sometimes pricked-off seedlings (antirrhinums or asters) are planted direct from the boxes outside. Soil blocks which are made in different sizes by a special tool can be used for seedlings instead of pots.

Boxes or pots in which seed has been sown may be stood in a frame if a glasshouse is not available. Alternatively seed is often sown directly on the soil in the frame. Many vegetable plants, such as brassicas, lettuce or onions, are raised in this way for transplanting outside to give early crops. Cloches may also be used to start seedlings. In the absence of artificial heat, however, sowing should be delayed to await the increase of natural warmth.

Seedlings which are raised in heated glasshouses or frames should be gradually hardened off before planting out. This can be done by reducing the heat supply and by increasing ventilation. An intermediate move from a heated glasshouse to a cold frame before final transfer outside is usually beneficial.

Artificial irradiation of seedlings

Light, as we have seen, supplies the energy which enables plants to manufacture complex foods from the raw materials present in the soil and air. Even when plants are grown in heated glasshouses their growth may be restricted during the winter months because of poor light conditions. Experiments have been done on the advantages of subjecting plants to artificial irradiation. For mature plants in general the procedure is uneconomic but it has been shown to have some value in forwarding the growth of certain seedlings raised in winter, tomatoes being a good example.

For this purpose high-pressure mercury-vapour lamps are used with reflectors. For tomatoes irradiation commences immediately the seedlings are pricked out and is continued for 3 to 4 weeks. In this case the lamps are suspended about 3 ft. above the bench and are placed 4 ft. apart. Irradiation should be done for at least 12 hours per day so that if the lamps are kept on continuously they can be used to irradiate two lots of plants. Irradiation must be arranged so that the seedlings have at least 6 hours darkness per day, otherwise they become chlorotic. Cucumber seedlings also benefit from irradiation from the point when the first leaf has developed until planted out. Cucumbers do not require light of such high intensity as tomatoes and the lamps are therefore hung 4 to 5 ft. above the seedlings.

Various bulbs, such as tulips, daffodils, hyacinths and irises, may be forced in heated buildings by the use of artificial light. For this purpose light of a much lower intensity is adequate, and 100-watt tungsten-filament lamps are used, each lamp illuminating about 9 sq. ft. The lamps are kept switched on for about 9 hours per day. Illumination is improved by whitewashing the walls of the building.

Vegetative Propagation

This practice simply involves taking portions of the vegetative parts of a plant, roots, stems or leaves, and inducing each to grow into a new plant. The advantage of this method is that every plant so raised will be exactly like its parent plant in all respects. Hence many hybrids of garden origin which would not grow true from seed can be increased and perpetuated indefinitely. Thousands of garden varieties, such as varieties of fruit, roses and innumerable other ornamental plants, have been propagated in this way, each having originated as a single hybrid seedling. Each such plant group is called a 'clone'.

Another advantage of vegetative propagation is that individuals so raised usually reach maturity much more quickly than seedlings. Thus apple trees, budded or grafted, bear fruit within a few years, but a seedling apple would probably require at least a dozen years before it produced a single fruit. Again there are certain plants (Jerusalem artichokes) which never produce seed and must therefore be increased vegetatively.

A major disadvantage of vegetative propagation is that disease may be carried from the parent plant to the new individuals. This often occurs with certain plants which are susceptible to virus diseases (strawberries and potatoes). Vegetative increase of diseased plants is to be avoided.

Natural increase

The various methods of vegetative propagation can be conveniently divided into two types which may be described as natural and artificial. Natural methods are familiar to everyone and although nature initiates the means the gardener's participation is usually essential. Common natural methods of increase are described below.

Division. Plants such as erigerons and Michaelmas daisies produce masses of stems at ground level each provided with roots at its base. Such plants only require lifting and splitting up into individuals. A great many herbaceous perennials may be increased in this way, preferably in the spring, just before growth commences. The younger outside portions of such plants are best for this purpose. Alpines like *Aubreta* and various campanulas lend themselves to this method as do a number of shrubs such as varieties of *Spiraea*, *Hypericum*, *Veronica* and *Erica*.

Bulbous plants. Bulbs and corms are one of nature's favourite methods of increase, but the plants are usually crowded together and must be lifted, divided and replanted by the gardener. Bulbs and corms have the added advantage that they may be dried and stored for quite long periods. Spring-flowering bulbs such as daffodils, tulips and hyacinths are usually planted in the autumn, whereas those that bloom in the summer and autumn (gladioli) are planted in spring. Some species of lilies produce tiny bulbs, called 'bulbils', in their leaf axils which if planted will develop into bulbs. Quite a number of other plants produce similar structures for increase, examples are the fern *Asplenium bulbiferum* and *Begonia evansiana*.

Tubers. These serve a similar purpose to bulbs and corms, the best-known example being the potato. Some species of *Begonia* also possess tubers which, unlike potatoes, do not increase naturally in numbers and therefore serve more as a means of perpetuation rather than increase.

Runners. These are one of nature's most ingenious methods of propagation; for not only do they accomplish an increase in numbers but also enable the new individuals to space themselves out at intervals. Strawberries are the best example, but with these the gardener usually assists the process by pegging down the runners and transplanting them to where required when rooted. Several plants produce offsets or 'rosettes' which have a similar function to runners, examples being various saxifrages and sempervivums. Rhizomes, possessed by the German iris and the lily-of-the-valley, are a kind of underground runner also designed for natural increase.

Suckers. Plants such as raspberries and certain species of plums have the capacity to produce new stems from their roots. These soon develop healthy roots and may then be dug up and transplanted.

Artificial methods

Although some of the so-called artificial methods of propagation such as cutting and layering are not unknown in nature, they are used or adapted by the gardener and nurseryman, and in general involve varying degrees of skill and experience.

Stem cuttings. This method is extensively used in plant propagation being next to seed propagation in importance. There are two types of stem cuttings, softwood or herbaceous cuttings and those made from hardwood stems. Intermediate between these two types a third group may be recognized. This is the semi-hardwood type. Softwood cuttings may be taken from herbaceous plants such as violas or penstemons during the growing season and also from the immature stems of woody plants including a wide range of shrubs in summer. Hardwood cuttings are available only from the ripened or mature stems of trees and shrubs.

Hardwood stem cuttings. These are normally made from stems of the current year's growth when mature, but plants such as *Tamarix* and willows grow readily from stems 2 to 3 years old. The length varies from 4 to about 12 in. but with a few species, including the mulberry and willow, stems up to 3 to 4 ft. long may be used. In preparing hardwood cuttings it is usual to cut them off just below a node and at their upper end just above a node. Some species, however, such as privet (*Ligustrum*) root so easily from hardwood cuttings that it is immaterial where the cuts are made. Again, hardwood cuttings for some species of conifers and several evergreen shrubs (including *Berberis darwinii*) should be taken with a 'heel' attached.

A great many hardwood cuttings may be inserted in the open ground, but they root best in light well-drained soil. The usual method is to dig a trench not quite so deep as the cutting length. Against the back of this the cuttings are inserted a few inches apart so that only 1 to 2 in. of their tips show above the surface. The soil is then replaced and trodden firm.

Hardwood cuttings may be taken in the autumn and planted immediately. Another method which can be recommended is to prepare them in the autumn, tie in bundles and bury these in sand in a sheltered position, until planting time in the spring. Alternatively, the bundles may be stored in a frame surrounded by damp moss during the winter.

A wide range of woody plants may be raised in this manner, including gooseberries and black currants, various deciduous shrubs such as red-stemmed dogwood (*Cornus*), flowering currants (*Ribes*), *Forsythia* and poplars (*Populus*). Evergreens so increased include common and Portugal laurels (*Prunus*), *Aucuba japonica* and the popular hedging plant *Lonicera nitida*.

For quite a number of kinds of hardwood cuttings the protection of a cold frame or cloche of the bell-glass type is desirable. They should be inserted in sandy compost placed over light well-drained soil, and covered with glass. Shrubs rooted in this way include *Berberis*, *Cotoneaster*, *Cytisus*, *Pyracantha*, evergreen *Ceanothus*, *Escallonia* and most conifers which can be rooted from cuttings such as *Chamaecyparis* (cypress), *Thuya* and *Cryptomeria*. Certain other species which root best in a cold frame need a compost with a high peat content. These are mostly members of the Ericaceae family such as *Ericas*, *Pernettya*, *Vacciniums*, *Gautherias*, some rhododendrons and evergreen azaleas. The smaller species of these are best rooted in pots stood in a frame or cold glasshouse.

Softwood stem cuttings. These can be divided into two distinct groups: (*a*) cuttings from herbaceous plants such as delphiniums, lupins, phlox and various other non-woody plants including violas, pelargoniums, penstemons, dahlias, chrysanthemums and a great many alpines, and (*b*) the immature tips of woody plants which include a wide range of ornamental shrubs.

In the first group the herbaceous perennials such as delphiniums produce young basal shoots which make ideal cuttings and are usually best taken with a 'heel' below ground level before they become too large. When inserted in boxes, pots or directly into a cold frame they root quickly and by the autumn are worthwhile plants. Practically all cuttings in this group root readily in cold frames.

Cuttings in group (*b*) are normally available from May until July, but may be produced earlier in the season by forcing certain shrubs into growth in heated glasshouses. Cuttings of this type root readily in cold frames, although rooting is accelerated by a little bottom heat. This has the added advantage of encouraging rooting to begin before top growth, a sequence which is desirable.

Softwood cuttings should be cut off just below a node and should have their bottom leaves removed. Always avoid flowering shoots and select firm terminals. They should be inserted with their leaves close to the rooting medium but not touching it. Afterwards they are kept in a close, moist atmosphere to slow down transpiration, and shaded from bright sunshine. With mist propagation, however (which is discussed later), close-shaded conditions are unnecessary.

Semi-hardwood cuttings. This definition is rather a loose one but applies in general to cuttings secured from woody plants after they have passed the softwood stage but before they are mature. With many shrubs this stage occurs during July and Aug. and when taken then speedier rooting results. Examples of shrubs easily rooted in this way are lilacs (*Syringa*), best taken in July, hydrangeas, and jasmine.

The rooting media. While a wide range of plant cuttings will root in ordinary light soil a large number of species succeed best in special rooting media or composts. A good rooting medium should be well aerated but also retain moisture. Slight acidity is an advantage. A mixture of equal parts sharp sand and good moss peat have these qualities and usually gives excellent results. An alternative mixture is 1 part loam, 2 parts peat and 3 parts sand. Either sharp sand or vermiculite may be used alone, but as such media contain practically no nutrients the cuttings should be moved from it as soon as the roots are formed. With difficult species a common practice is to insert them around the edge of a pot or pan which allows good aeration.

Hormone or growth substances. These are valuable artificial aids in the rooting of stem cuttings. Their advantage is that they promote more rapid development of the callus resulting in earlier rooting and fewer losses. Use of such substances is advised for the more difficult species and although success is not always achieved, prospects are definitely improved. Growth substances are most effective for softwood leafy cuttings and give best results in a fairly high temperature. One of these rooting aids is applied as a powder and the instructions should be carefully observed.

Mist propagation

Mist propagation is a very successful method of promoting the rooting of softwood leafy cuttings. It consists in keeping the leaves continuously wet by means of an overhead mist spray. This allows the cuttings to be exposed to light of a high intensity with little risk of damage from scorch. Thus the normal close-shaded conditions are unnecessary while the combination of high humidity and good light intensity speeds up rooting.

Experience with this method has shown the need to keep the amount of water sprayed over the cuttings to a minimum. This is best done by a series of short sharp bursts of spray rather than continuous spraying. Such intermittent spraying can be done automatically with the aid of a time switch. This is set to come on for a given period at predetermined intervals. The disadvantage of the time switch is that it continues to operate at the same rate without regard to external conditions. Thus on a dull cloudy day too much water may be applied whereas on a dry sunny day too little may be given.

The so-called 'electronic leaf' is a more ingenious mechanical device. It is placed among the cuttings and when they and it become almost dry, the electronic leaf cuts in and turns on the water in a series of short bursts, which ceases when the mist applied is adequate. This means that the amount of water applied is varied according to external conditions.

Mist propagation may be done in specially prepared beds in the open and is found to be successful during the summer months. Wind may cause the mist to drift, but this can be overcome by providing shelter around the beds with glass or plastic sheets. Azaleas and magnolias have been propagated successfully in the open under mist. Frames covered with lights may also be used for this purpose, but they must be deep enough to give sufficient space between the cuttings and the glass for the apparatus to be installed. Plastic sheets suspended on a wire frame can also be used successfully.

Well lighted airy glasshouses are, however, generally the best for mist propagation. Here beds may be made on the staging, and the nozzles, suitably spaced, suspended above them. In very hot weather some shade may be necessary as well as good ventilation.

Various rooting media have been used for mist propagation and one essential is good drainage to get rid of surplus water. Two suitable composts are 1 part peat and 3 parts sand, or 1 part soil, 1 part peat and 2 parts sand. Vermiculite used alone is also very successful.

Cuttings rooted under mist tend to produce thick fleshy roots which are not ideal for providing the new plant with water when the overhead mist ceases. Hence rooted cuttings should be gradually weaned off. Thus the mist spray may first be stopped at night and then for periods during the day which are gradually increased until finally the mist is not used at all.

A great many difficult species have been successfully raised by the aid of mist. Examples are acers, apples, azaleas, *Callistemon*, *Camellia*, *Chimonanthus*, *Daphne*, *Elaeagnus*, *Ginkgo*, *Hibiscus*, *Magnolia*, *Pieris*, rhododendrons, *Rhus cotinus* and *Viburnum burkwoodii*.

Other types of plant cuttings

Leaf cuttings. Plants like *Begonia rex*, *Gloxinia* and *Saintpaulia* are capable of producing new plants from their leaves. The usual method is to make cuts in the leaf veins in several places and then peg the leaf down over moist compost. Another method is to slit the leaves in strips tapering towards their bases and these pieces are then inserted vertically in the compost. For such plants a close warm humid atmosphere promotes rooting. Some rock plants may be increased by inserting their leaves vertically; examples are, *Ramonda*, *Haberlea* and *Sedum spectabile*. A few shrubs such as *Viburnum rhytidophyllum* and *Eriobotrya japonica* may also be increased from leaves.

Leaf-bud cuttings. This method has been used effectively for certain *Rubus* species including loganberries, boysenberries and blackberries. Briefly it consists in removing the buds with leaves attached from the canes in July with about ½ in. rind on either side of them. Keep the buds moist and insert in cold frames just beneath the compost surface in rows 5 in. apart allowing 2 in. from bud to bud. Shade and reasonably moist conditions are essential.

Camellias may also be increased from leaf-bud cuttings in Oct. inserted in a compost of peat and sand around the edge of a 3-in. pot. Each bud is pegged down with a piece of wire bent like a hairpin. Camellias may also be increased from short stem pieces having a bud and leaf attached near the tip. About ½ in.

below the bud a nick is made approximately halfway through the stem. These cuttings are taken in late summer and inserted in light compost near the side of a 3-in. pot. Small stem cuttings of this type are rather similar to the so-called eye cuttings used in the propagation of vines and other species of *Vitis*. These are really mature stem cuttings only about 2 in. long with a node at the centre of each. Usually they are inserted singly in small pots placed in a glasshouse or frame.

Root cuttings. Quite a number of plants can be raised in this manner and young roots of average thickness should be used. They should be cut into pieces 2 to 4 in. long and to make sure they are planted the right way up a straight cut is made at the upper end and a slanting cut at the lower end. Root cuttings from hardy plants may be secured during the dormant season, tied in bundles and stored in moist sand. In the spring they are planted in light well-drained soil in the open with the top of the cutting just above surface level. In cold districts they should be planted in frames. Hardy plants so increased include *Anemone japonica*, *Anchusa azurea*, perennial verbascums, Oriental poppies (*Papaver*), *Rubus* species, *Ailanthus glandulosa*, *Buddleia alternifolia*, *Daphne genkwa* and the vegetables horseradish and seakale. Less hardy species best planted in sandy compost and started in heat include *Romneya*, *Celastrus* and *Bouvardia*.

Layering

This method is designed to produce roots from stems while still attached to the plant. When this is achieved the rooted pieces are later cut off and transplanted. Layering is mainly used for the propagation of trees and shrubs which are difficult by other methods. Although very few herbaceous plants are raised in this way it is a popular method for increasing border carnations.

Ordinary layering. This may amount to nothing more than pegging flexible stems down on the ground and covering parts of them with soil. Usually, however, other means are used to promote rooting such as slitting, notching, bending or twisting the layered stems or tying wire tightly around them. In general the layered shoots should stand as nearly as possible at a right angle to the soil. In nurseries it is customary to have special stock plants of the kinds to be layered. These are encouraged to produce basal growths for periodic layering, by cutting back the top shoots.

Layering should be done in the spring or autumn. It is an advantage to spread a layer of rooting compost such as a mixture of sand and peat around the plants to be layered which can also be used to cover the shoots. Woody plants propagated in this way include *Garrya*, *Magnolia*, *Mespilus*, lilacs (*Syringa*) *Leucothoë*, *Nothofagus*, *Plagianthus*, *Photinia*, rhododendrons and lime trees (*Tilia*).

Layering

Border carnations are layered in summer. This involves cutting slits in the young stems which are then firmly pegged down into sandy compost at the point of slitting.

Continuous layering. This is a popular method for increasing several kinds of fruit tree rootstocks. It involves planting a row of the stocks to be layered each having a single stem. When the plants are established the stems are pegged down flat in autumn or winter to form a continuous line. Young shoots arise from the buds on these stems and are gradually earthed up with fine soil eventually to a depth of 6 to 8 in. as they grow. Plum stocks may be covered with soil when the buds begin to burst but apple, pear, cherry and quince stocks are left uncovered until the new shoots have developed. Shrubs with a similar habit of growth may also be increased by rooting in this way. Examples are *Hydrangea aborescens, H. paniculata* and *Rhus cotinus*.

Mound layering. This method is also used extensively in the propagation of fruit tree rootstocks. The plants are set out in rows and when established are cut down almost to ground level. The young shoots which arise from the base are earthed up as they grow on either side of the row eventually forming a mound 6 to 8 in. high. The rooted shoots are removed in winter, annually. Shrubs with stiff upright stems such as deutzias may be increased in this way.

Tip layering. Blackberries and loganberries can be increased by bending down firm young shoots in summer and covering their tips with 4 to 6 in. of soil. Rooting occurs in a matter of weeks.

Serpentine layering. Plants with long slender shoots such as *Lapageria* and *Clematis* may be layered by covering several parts of the stems alternating with portions uncovered.

Air layering. Some plants with stiff rigid stems which cannot be bent down to soil level are air layered. This involves surrounding the part of the stem to be rooted with damp sphagnum moss which is then covered over with polythene film tied in position to prevent drying out. Before applying the moss the stem should be slit or notched. Dracaenas are sometimes rooted in this way and other examples are *Hibiscus* and *Acer*.

Grafting

This is one of the most highly skilled gardening crafts. It involves the union of a part of one plant, usually termed the 'scion', with another plant normally called the 'stock'. The result is a composite plant whose roots and top growth are of different origin and both continue to maintain their individual characteristics. Roots or stems may be grafted together or stems grafted on to roots.

Grafting is a good method of propagating plants such as fruit trees which are difficult to increase by other means, but its main advantage is that it allows the substitution of one part of a plant for another. Thus a great many plants and varieties are grown on roots which are not their own and the branches of a particular variety of fruit may be grafted with another variety. One disadvantage of grafting is that it may be an expensive and lengthy process because rootstocks have to be provided before the desired variety can be grafted. Again the production of suckers from certain rootstocks such as some rosestocks can be a nuisance. Sometimes, too, the union between a stock and scion is imperfect and results in breakages or poor nutrition.

There are two important rules for success in grafting. The first is that species grafted together must be related botanically. Moreover most species have particular preferences. For instance the evergreen *Daphnes* should be grafted on *D. laureola* whereas deciduous types grow best on *D. mezereum*. Secondly when fitting the stock and scion together the cambium layer of both, which lies just beneath the rind, must come in contact. It is at this point only that the growing union occurs. For this reason monocotyledons, such as grasses, which possess no cambium tissue cannot be grafted.

The grafting of scions of various kinds on to appropriate stocks is usually done in spring just when the growth of the particular species is commencing. The scions, however, should be in dormant condition, and to achieve this they are severed from the 'parent' plant during the winter months when fully dormant. They may then be tied in bundles and laid in sand or soil in a shady place where growth will be held back. Scions of most species are usually made 4 to 8 in. long and must have at least one sound bud. The most important methods of grafting are as follows.

Inlaying. In this case the stock must be thicker than the scion and the latter is prepared by making two equal cuts at its base to form a long sideways wedge. A similar shaped piece of wood is removed from the stock and into this cavity the shaped portion of the scion is inserted. Inlaying is frequently used for herbaceous plants because if the fitting is exact by this method there is no need for tight tying.

Veneer grafting. This method is similar to inlaying except that the rind only is removed from the stock which should be much thicker than the scion. Sometimes a narrow strip of rind is removed from the stock and into this the complete scion, after shaving well down on one side, is inserted.

Side grafting. With most methods of grafting the scions are inserted at the apex of the cut-back stock but with side grafting this is unnecessary. In this case the scion which is shaved off on both sides at its base is simply inserted for an inch or two under the rind on one side of the stock. There are various methods of preparing the stock such as making a T-shaped cut on the rind as for budding, or driving a thin chisel or knife obliquely into the bark. Side grafting is often used for grafting established fruit trees with a new variety, and it is a popular method for increasing certain dwarf conifers.

Splice or whip grafting. This simply involves making a long slanting cut at the base of the scion and a corresponding one at the apex of a stock of similar thickness. The stems are then fitted and tied together with string or raffia.

Whip and tongue grafting. This represents an improvement on the previous method and is widely used in the raising of young fruit trees. Rootstocks established in nursery rows are cut down to within a few inches of the soil and the stock and scion prepared as for whip grafting. An extra cut is then made downwards about the middle of the slanting cut on the stock. This forms a kind of tongue and a corresponding slit on the scion enables the stock and scion to 'grip' each other firmly giving good cambium contact. If the stock is thicker than the scion then it is possible to secure contact of the cambium tissue on one side only of the graft.

Rind grafting. For this type of graft the stock must be comparatively thick and it is cut off transversely where one or more grafts are inserted. From its apex a downward slit a few inches long is made in the rind. An equal length of the scion base is prepared by a sloping cut on one side, this portion then being forced beneath the stock rind where it was slit. This method is popular for top grafting established fruit trees.

Saddle grafting. In this case the stock and scion must be about the same thickness. First, the stock apex is shaped like an inverted 'V' while the scion base is prepared to fit on it like a saddle. This method is chiefly used for rhododendrons and the softwood scions needed are secured from growing plants indoors. These are grafted in the spring on to stocks established in pots.

Tying and sealing grafts. When the graft is fixed in position it should be tied firmly to the stock with raffia. Instead of tying, one or two small nails are sometimes used to fix the scion to the stock. Finally the graft is usually covered with some kind of wax to exclude air and water from the union. Grafting wax may be bought at most horticultural shops or made up at home. There are various recipes for making grafting wax such as the following: Heat 10 lb. of resin and 2 lb. beeswax and mix together. While the mixture is still hot stir in 1 lb. talc. This wax is applied hot with a brush, but not so hot as to damage the tissues. Certain waxes may be used cold and petroleum jelly can be used successfully for this purpose. The most convenient way of binding grafts is to use horticultural adhesive tape which secures and seals them, thus serving the object of both raffia and grafting wax.

Grafting under glass. Herbaceous grafting is usually done in glasshouses under conditions of controlled humidity and temperature. The young shoots for grafting are secured by forcing 'parent' plants under glass in winter or early spring. Practically any semi-succulent plant can be grafted, examples being coleus and chrysanthemums. Certain valuable woody plants such as roses and certain shrubs can be conveniently grafted under glass where waxing is unnecessary. The stocks are usually grown in pots and are grafted during the winter months. Examples are daphnes, hibiscus, wisterias and rhododendrons while named varieties of clematis may be grafted on the roots of wild clematis. After grafting the plants are kept in a close case until the union is effected.

Bud grafting or budding

Budding as it is usually called is really a form of grafting. The scion, however, consists of a piece of rind with a single bud attached. It is this bud which produces the new plant. Budding is usually done from June to August when plants are in full growth. During this period the rind separates easily from the wood thus facilitating the operation. Budding is the most popular method in the propagation of roses and is also readily used for the increase of various other ornamental plants and of fruit trees. It is usually performed in the open on suitable stocks grown for the purpose. Before commencing to bud it is usual to trim off all side shoots near the stock base thus leaving a clean stem for insertion of the bud. There are several methods.

Shield or T budding. This, the most popular method, involves taking buds preferably from the central portions of current year's shoots. These are cut out in each case by inserting a sharp knife below the bud and bringing it out above the bud. The attached leaf should be cut off but the petiole is left to serve as a handle to the bud. The thin strip of wood beneath the rind is usually removed although this is not essential. Great care should be taken that the buds do not dry out before insertion. The stock, preferably not more than 2 to 3 years old, is prepared by making a T-shaped incision in the rind which is raised on either side of the downward slit. The bud with its attached rind and base of leaf-stem is then inserted and the stem bound firmly with raffia above and below the bud.

Patch budding. In this case a piece of rind is cut clean out from the stock and replaced by a portion of equal size from the selected variety with a bud attached. The substitute rind is tied in position and may be sealed over with a little grafting wax.

After-care of grafts and buds

The buds on successful grafts soon commence to grow, and in the case of fruit trees when the strongest or most suitably placed shoot can be distinguished, all the others should be removed. Early staking is important to prevent the grafts being blown out.

Buds inserted in June or July often produce shoots in the same season, but may remain dormant until the following spring. A few weeks after budding the raffia should be cut to allow swelling of the buds. In the spring budded plants are usually cut back close to the bud but in the case of fruit trees and some flowering shrubs a common practice is to leave a few inches of stem to which the young shoot from the bud can be tied in its early stages. This snag is cut back later.

CHAPTER SIX

Planning and Designing

THE first things to decide before getting down to the actual planning of a garden are what branches of gardening are to be included. Although the main object of the garden will almost certainly be as an amenity with flowers and other decorative features forming the major part of it, it is probable that fruit and vegetables will also be included in a provisional plan. These crops call for special consideration. The really keen gardener will, of course, grow all that he has room for since to him they hold an irresistible appeal. There is in some ways a greater degree of achievement in growing good-quality apples, strawberries or marrows than in having a good herbaceous border or rose bed, and if the gardener takes an interest in the local show, he will have something to put in the ever-popular fruit and vegetable classes. In addition, these crops, especially fruit, have their own attraction while growing. A vigorous row of strawberries in full flower, a row of raspberries with its hanging masses of ripe fruit or a small orchard in full blossom or bearing a crop of gold and red apples, are as pleasing as any of the accepted floral features of the garden. Alternating rows of carrot and beetroot being grown for successional cropping in the kitchen garden, are the modern counterpart of the 'sub-tropical' beds of Victorian days, in which, incidentally, both crops were often included.

Profitable crops

There is, however, another aspect of food crops which should be considered, and that is whether the growing of them is financially worth while. Apples, pears and plums are usually well worth growing. Such fruits are nowadays an expensive item in the household budget, and a real saving can be made by growing them. It is, however, very difficult for the amateur to obtain the unblemished apples of the commercial grower, for such fruit is only obtained by expensive and intricate spraying programmes generally impracticable in a small mixed garden. Plums are less exacting in that direction.

EG

Garden freshness

Soft fruits such as currants, raspberries and strawberries should be included if only for their freshness. Often there is no comparison between the strawberries bought at a shop, and the firm full flavour of fruits gathered fresh from the garden. Besides, they are in no way difficult to grow, the biggest problem in many districts being damage by birds. Where vegetables are grown to meet the needs of two or three people only it is doubtful if they can be produced very much more cheaply than they can be bought, and freshness, too, is of less importance with the dormant type of vegetable such as potatoes, parsnips and leeks, while modern hydro-cooling methods enable commercial crops of cabbage, Brussels sprouts and similar crops to reach the buyer in a much fresher condition than was previously the case. Garden freshness is of real importance with the more perishable crops such as lettuce, spinach and tender early carrots and beetroot, and for small households the best solution is probably to grow only those vegetables and salads where freshness is all-important and to leave the bulkier coarse crops to commercial growers. Catering for larger needs which would warrant the use of a quarter of an acre upwards, would make most vegetable crops worth while, for on that area some form of mechanical cultivation could be justified. Even so the kitchen garden would generally be the 'adjustable' section and if calls on space or time become particularly insistent it is this section which is likely to be reduced or even done away with altogether.

'Gardens in the air'

Having decided in general outline what is to be included, it is well worth while, as a preliminary to the down-to-earth procedure of planning, to try to recall features in other gardens which have seemed attractive. Planning a garden is essentially a matter of individual taste, but by recalling gardens and garden features which have appealed in the past, it is so often possible to develop one's own ideas to the best advantage. But no one example should be copied slavishly, nor should the garden be a hotchpotch of other people's ideas, however good they may appear to be. A garden should be a living expression of the owner's personality, with his enthusiasms, his moods, and, if appropriate, a little of his waywardness. That cannot be obtained secondhand. And do not worry whether the ideas for the garden happen to be fashionable or not, because fashions in gardening change quickly, whereas the garden itself is a lasting thing.

Principles of garden design

It is, however, highly probable that the mental picture of the garden-to-be will be partly or largely impracticable, even if the necessary money, space and time were available. So the next step is to see how much of what is considered desirable is capable of being put into practice, and to do this one must look at the main principles governing garden design. These may at first appear a little forbidding, but as with most reasonable rules, they are largely a matter of common sense and good taste.

The garden should fit in with, and make the most of the natural characteristics of the site. It should combine with the site and not over-ride it. It may be, for instance, that a small garden tapers off to an irregular corner with a damp patch of land. In such a case, instead of levelling it out to conform with the general rule that small gardens should be formal, it would be much better to leave the natural contours, and make a small 'bog' garden with moisture-loving plants such as primulas and astilbes. Or it may be that the garden backs on to a type of scenery that provides the perfect setting for a small orchard, whereas ordinarily an orchard would not be contemplated. In this case, a small orchard, of possibly only half a dozen trees, could be added.

There should be a unity of house and garden, so that the whole blends and merges, even though several quite distinct features are incorporated. Generally the garden will be more formal near the house where flower beds have to harmonize with the straight lines of the building. Hard and fast partitioning of different sections should be avoided, except for the kitchen garden, which may be screened off with a pergola, low hedge or row of cordons. Shrubs form a useful transition from one section to another.

The layout should be as simple as possible, consistent with achieving the desired effect. A complicated layout may look attractive on paper, but when the plants start developing and when tending the garden has become a reality, results are likely to be disappointing, particularly if the plants become overcrowded. It is impossible to include all the desirable features, so right at the start the decision should be made to include only those that can be adequately spaced and that fit in with the general conditions.

Formality or informality?

It is difficult to make a successful informal garden on an area of less than a quarter of an acre. Moderately good informal results can be obtained on a smaller area, and anyone to whom formality is anathema, will prefer that moderate success to a greater success achieved by a more formal and conventional layout. Generally speaking, informality needs space, but this does not mean that all smaller gardens must consist of lots of small beds in a set pattern, with individual plants regimented in straight rows. Even a formal garden must be free of rigidity, its different features must merge, and in spite of the formality there must be a pleasing softness of outline of the garden as a whole. Formality also calls for a level site or for the levelling of a sloping one, whereas slopes and undulations in a larger informal garden add to its attractiveness. On very heavy soil, levelling may add to drainage problems, and on such soils this practical consideration must be weighed against that of aesthetic appeal.

Vistas and views

There should be good views from the windows of the house, including the kitchen window, a position from which the garden is frequently viewed, particularly by housewives, and if there is sufficient length, a vista effect adds considerably to the attractiveness of a garden. Flower beds at the foot of the walls should be avoided; they cannot be seen when looking out, and get damaged when the windows are cleaned or the house is painted.

Avoid flatness

Flatness and concavity must be avoided. Generally speaking there will be taller plants around the outside of the garden to form a background for the inside features, to give shelter and privacy and possibly to hide objectionable features outside the garden. If the rest of the garden is planted with low plants, or if plants are gradually tiered down from this tall outside to give a bowl effect, a lifeless impression is almost inevitable. This can be avoided by the use of arches and pergolas for climbing plants, but these should be placed so that they form an integral part of the layout. A short length of pergola going from nowhere to nowhere certainly breaks the contour, but it jars the eye, whereas a wisely placed herbaceous border backed by a rose trellis can be very effective in breaking a flat area. The flatness can also be broken by the planting of individual specimen trees, particularly evergreens, of which there are many kinds growing to varying heights. Their symmetrical shape makes them particularly suitable for this purpose, but they need careful placing. Planting them near the house should be avoided, as they need to be seen from a distance, and if planted too near they can make the house dark and sombre when they are fully grown.

Where shrubs are used in the open and distinct from the background, they are best placed in groups of the same kind, either individually in small gardens or in groups of three to six in larger ones according to the space available. When used as a background they should not be planted with too much regularity and there should be no suggestion of straight-line planting. In all cases they should have enough room to develop their natural growth, since generally this is their main attraction.

Paths

In all but the largest gardens paths should lead somewhere. In a 5-acre garden there is room for them to meander through a woodland back to where they started, but in a smaller garden it is an anticlimax to find that the path ends up in nothing at all. It should be to a seat, or a summerhouse set at a vantage point facing the rose garden or pool, or some other attractive feature.

Labour and time

Labour needs must be taken into account, and it is wise to keep well within the estimated time available. It is no good having a large rock garden or a lot of intricate mowing and edging to attend to if all the work has got to be done by the occupier in very limited spare time. In such circumstances features demanding little attention should be chosen. The most labour-saving of all is paving or rustic brickwork let into the ground and either planted as a paved garden, or with a small number of flower beds carefully placed. This must not be overdone or the garden will take on an arid appearance, but by judicious planning up to a third of the total area can be treated in this way. In any case a paved area in a sunny position adjoining the house is extremely useful for putting out a small table and chairs, when the lawns and paths are still wet and the more exposed parts of the garden are too chilly. Lawns, if straightforward and without a lot of fancy shapes, call for comparatively little labour. Where children will be using the garden frequently, such unobstructed lawns are particularly useful for playing and reducing the harm done to the flowers. It should be remembered that balls and children often get on to the surrounding flower beds, so that the choicest plants should not be put in that position.

Plant positions

So far as is possible plants should be given the position in the garden that suits them best. The kitchen garden for instance should be in the open and unshaded by any trees. Ferns on the other hand should be in a shady position, sheltered from strong winds and direct sun, and also since they grow best if left in a natural state with their old fronds protecting them, they should not be in a prominent position where this untidyness is too easily seen. Fruit should not be put in a low-lying position where air drainage is likely to be poorest and the danger of frost greatest, but should have shelter from north and east winds, which often do much damage in spring. Full sun is needed to give the fruit colour and flavour and ripen the wood in the autumn to ensure a crop the following year. Herbaceous borders need shelter from the back or the taller subjects will be blown down, while the rock garden needs an open position away from the shade of trees. Quite obviously the water garden will have to be in a naturally low-lying depression, and even small pools which structurally could be placed anywhere, give their most natural effect in such a position.

Colour harmony

There must be colour harmony of plants that bloom at the same time; this is an important consideration in the case of trees and shrubs at the time of making the garden. Harmony in the flower beds and herbaceous borders is considered in the chapter on herbaceous borders.

Drawing the plan

A rough freehand plan with the boundaries of the plot, the house and any other permanent features plainly marked on it should first be prepared. The intended general layout should then be sketched in, bearing in mind the foregoing points, but disregarding detail at this stage. In doing this it should be borne in mind that if the land has to be levelled and the garden is a long one, it may be necessary to have several tiers with a drop in level between each, and the plan must be such that it will fit in with this.

It is always advisable to have a levelled terrace where one can sit or sunbathe, and this should be at least 12 ft. wide. The rest of the garden can then be at one lower level as in Fig. 8 (1) or it can be further terraced as in Fig. 8 (2). It is a good idea to 'walk the site' of the rough plan, and to view it from a bedroom window, which gives a semi-plan view. From this it is possible to get a fair idea as to what is practicable, and the plan can then be adjusted as necessary.

After further consideration a final general layout can be decided on and a scale plan, at not less than 1 in. to 10 ft. and preferably 1 in. to 5 ft. should then be prepared. This involves accurate measurement of the site. Where the sides of the house are parallel with the boundaries, all that is needed is to measure the external line, keeping in line with the house-sides. Where there is an irregular boundary or where other outlines have to be included, in-between measurements will have to be taken off a survey line as in A–B of Fig. 5. For these plans it is better to use plain paper as squared paper detracts from the clearness of the design, and to make sure that the paper is large enough: it is annoying, with the plan partly completed to find that it is going over the edge. When the existing features have all been clearly marked, the survey lines should be erased to leave the field clear for the features which are to be added. It is quite a good idea to make several copies of this outline plan and then to fill in each in successively greater detail, until the final one will show all detail as in Fig. 7.

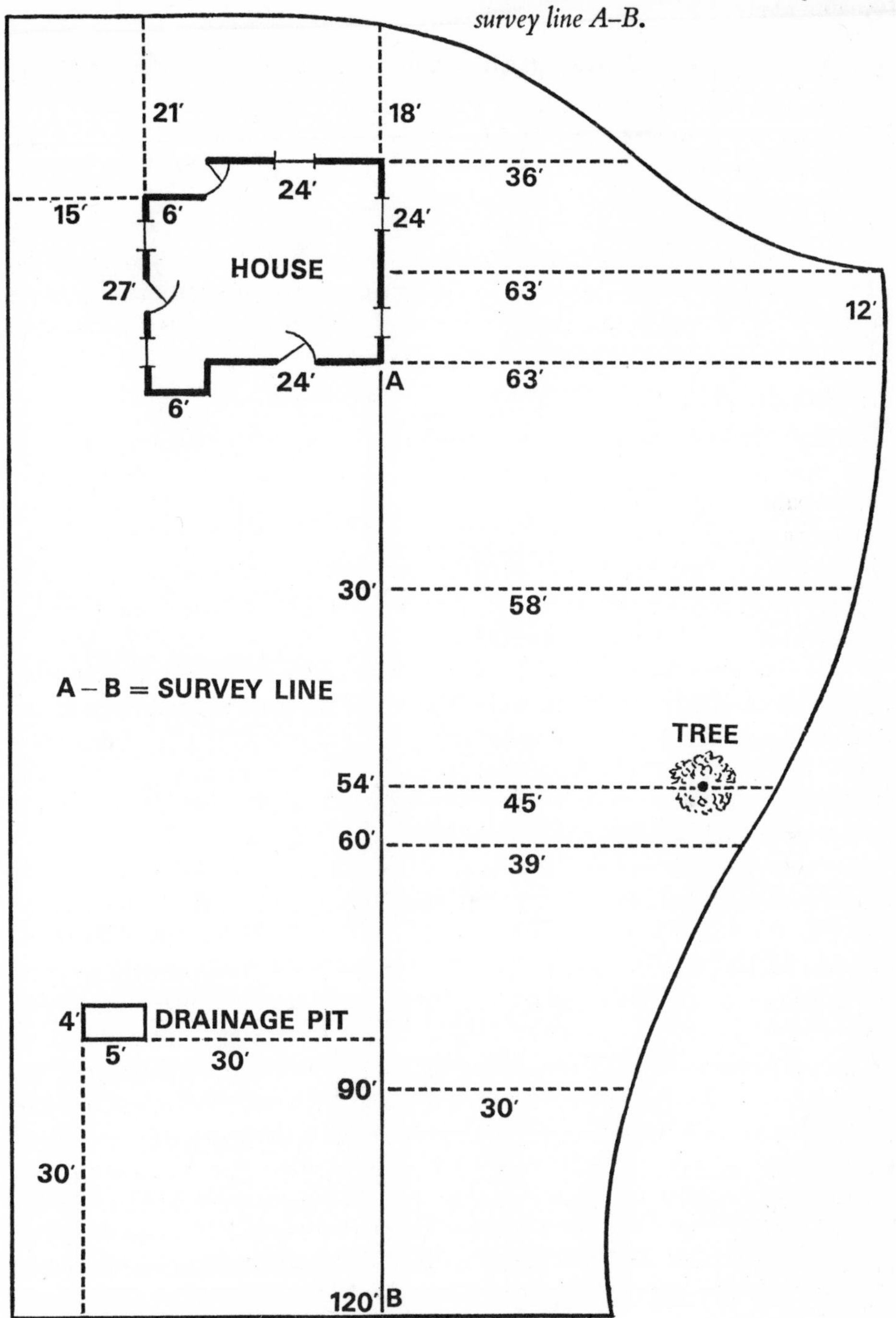

Fig. 5 First stage scale plan of a garden. All the measurements are taken from the survey line A–B.

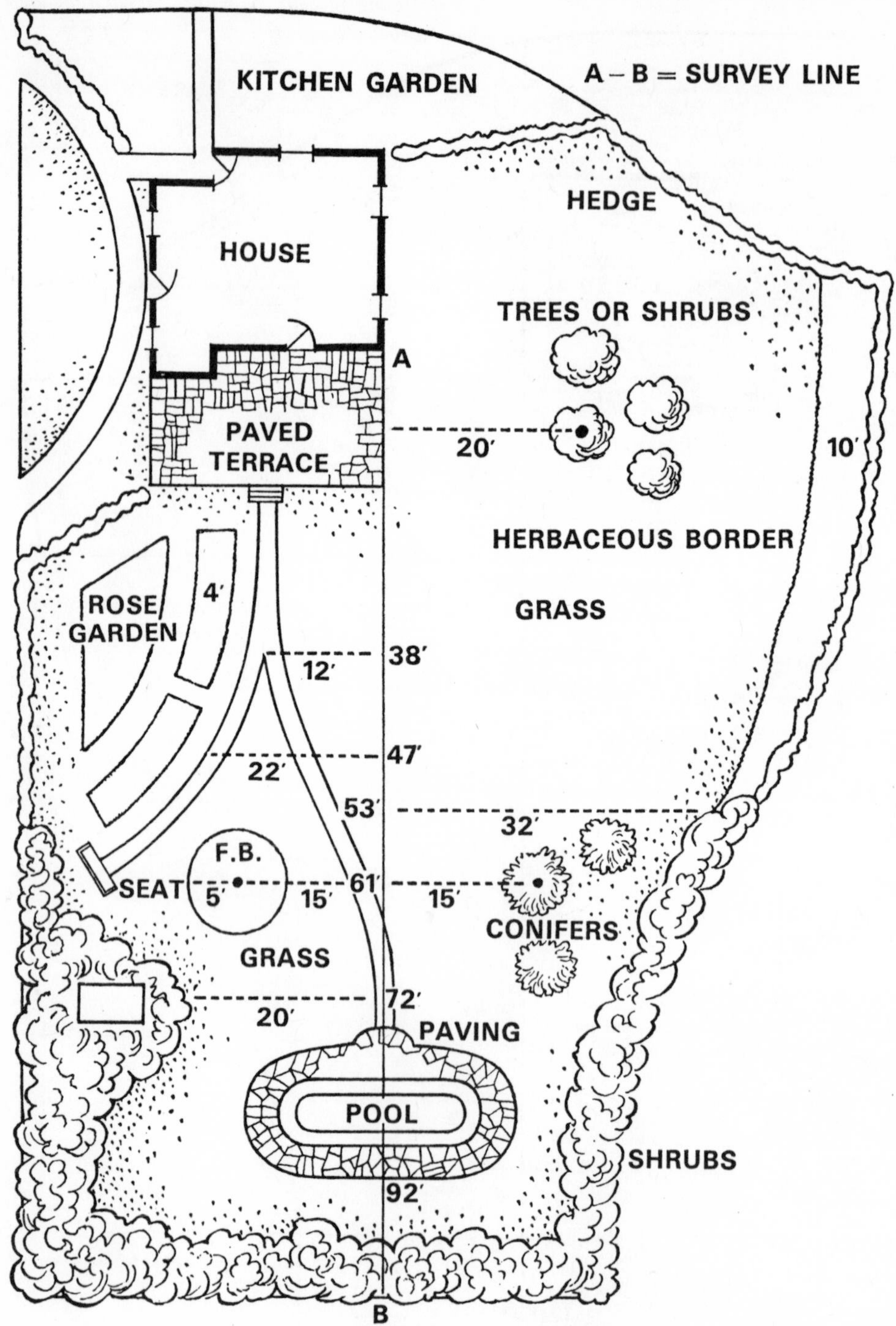

Fig. 6. Second stage scale plan.

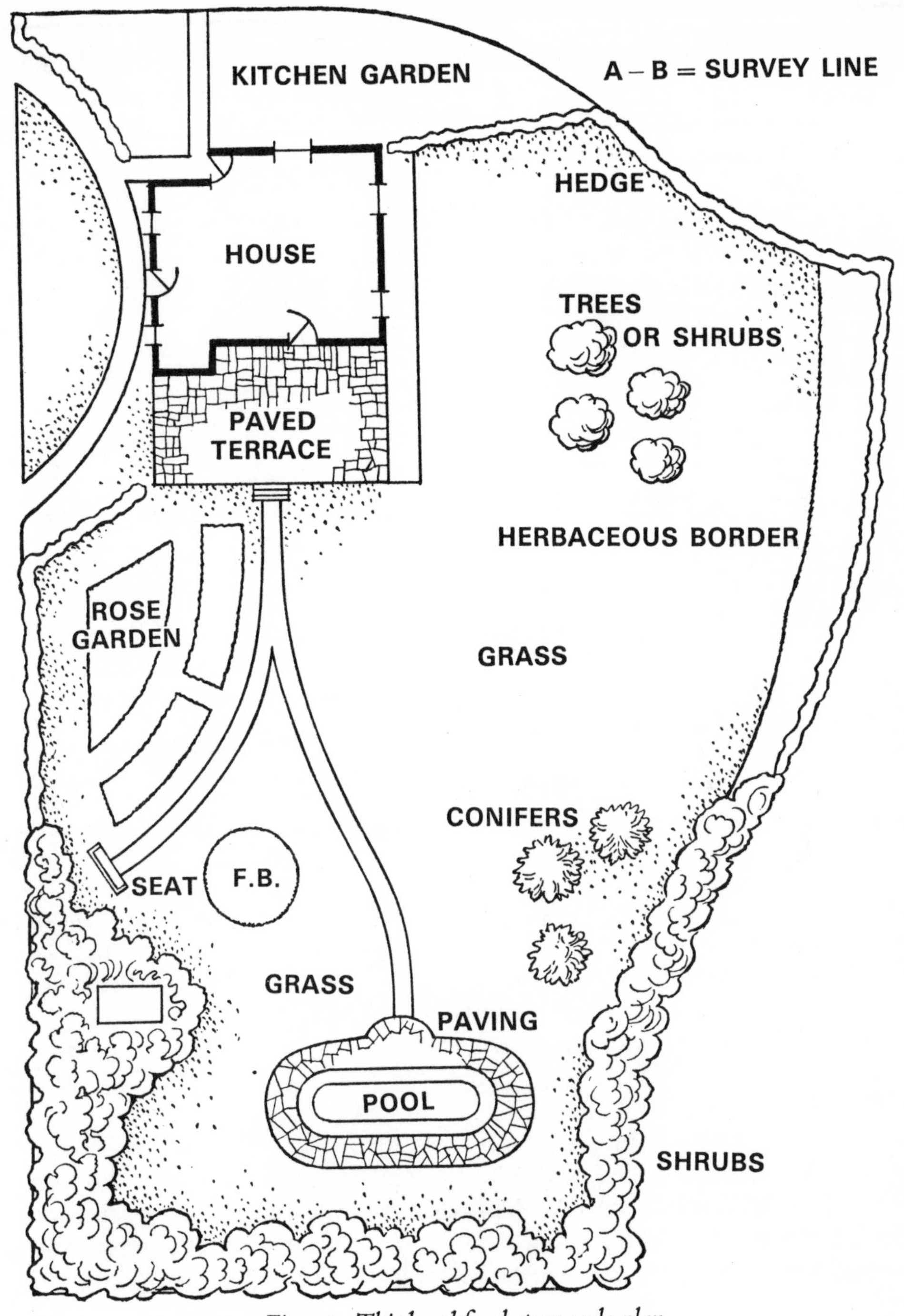

Fig. 7 Third and final stage scale plan.

All matters have to be attended to in full detail at this stage, giving the finishing touches to flower-bed shape, to deciding the actual position for a specimen tree and similar items. With flower beds, angled corners and intricate designs should be avoided, and where they are on lawns they should have the longer sides parallel with the sides of the lawn, with at least 2 ft. of grass between to allow easy mowing. Grass paths should be at least that width, and preferably between 5 and 10 ft. Herbaceous borders should have a graceful swinging curve at the front rather than a series of small serrations, and should be at least 6 ft. deep. With all the new

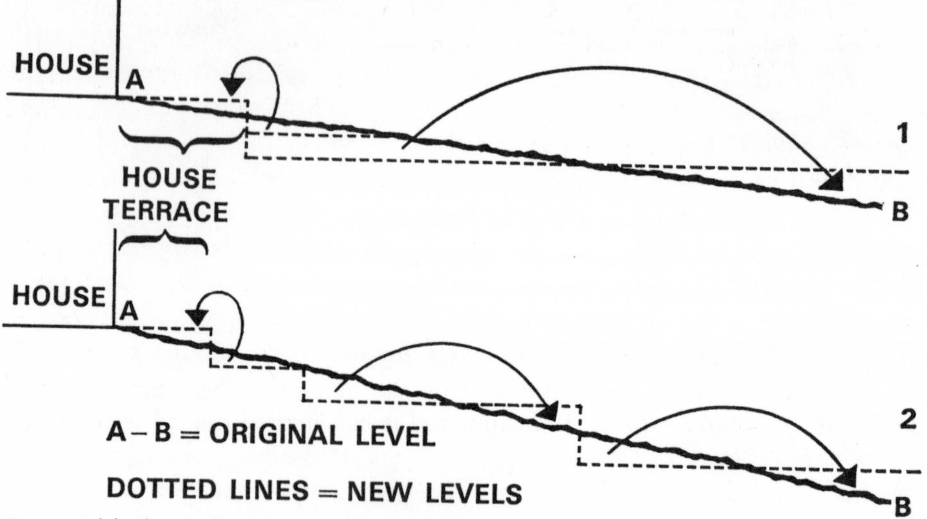

Fig. 8 (1) shows the side view for the excavation of a single terrace and (2) a series of four descending terraces.

features marked in position on the plan, the dimensions of each, together with measurements to enable them to be correctly placed on the ground, must be inserted using survey lines if necessary. Where circles or parts of circles occur either by themselves or as parts of another shape, the distances to the centre of the circles should be given with the radii added.

Levelling

It has to be admitted that levelling is fairly strenuous work although if taken steadily in the slacker period of the year it need not be very much harder than double-digging. It is wise, however, to keep all work to a minimum by adequate planning. If the whole garden is to be made up to the level of the highest point soil will have to be bought, or if to the lowest level, all the upper soil will have to be removed, and these methods can involve a great deal of work and expense. The method generally adopted is the 'take and put' or 'cut and fill' one, in which soil is taken from the higher places on the site, and put in the lower places so that the new garden is at the mean level of the old. If the garden is to be terraced, each terrace will have to be treated as a separate plot for levelling, whatever the method adopted. By the 'cut and fill' method the difference in level between tiers is bound to be in direct proportion to the depth from back to front of the lower tier, and is generally perfectly satisfactory. It is possible to alter the relative heights by taking soil from one tier to another, but this adds considerably to the work involved and in most cases there is nothing to be gained by it.

Before the actual work of moving the soil can be started, it is necessary to know the total fall in the plot to be levelled, and this can be found by two methods. The first method needs a piece of straight and rigid timber of even width and not less than 8 ft. long, but the longer the better as fewer pegs will then be needed. This will be used as a straight-edge. Also needed are a small spirit-level, and a pointed peg at least 2 ft. long for each 8 ft. length of garden. Place one end of the straight-edge at the highest position, and at the other end of the straight-edge knock in a peg progressively deeper, until the spirit-level placed on the straight-edge, shows level. The height of the lower peg out of the ground is the fall in that distance. Continue this to the end of the plot as in Fig. 9. The second method is by boning rods or T-squares, and is best carried out by two people. The boning rods must all be of the same length, about 3 ft. long with 2 ft. T-pieces. The first is placed at the highest point, and the second on a level with it by means of the straight-edge and spirit-level. The third is then placed at the lowest point at a height which brings all the T-pieces at the same level when viewed. This gives the total fall and the mean level will of course be half that

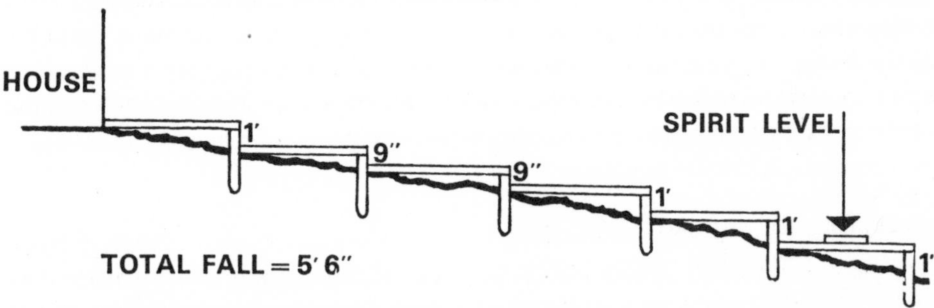

Fig. 9 Method of laying out a plot for a total fall of 5 ft. 6 in. A similar method can be used for falls of level of any reasonable distance.

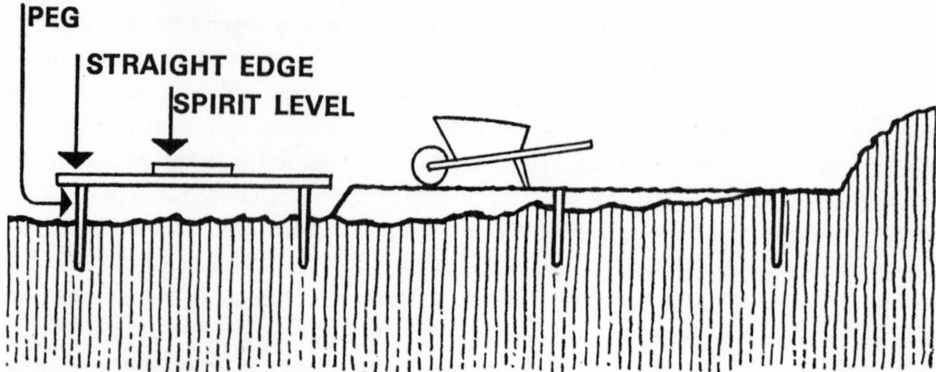

Fig. 10 This diagram shows the method of setting pegs in a plot and checking their level with a straight-edge and spirit-level.

distance below the highest point. Where the land slopes both lengthwise and across, the procedure is a little more involved. The difference in level between the highest corner and each of the other corners is found, and the total of the differences divided by four, which includes the 'o' reading of the highest corner. The distance below the highest corner is the mean level. In a case where the fall to the other corners was 2 ft., 1 ft. and 2 ft., the new level would be 15 in. below the highest corner. On a large area where the land is undulating, the highest point must be found and readings taken from that at evenly spaced intervals, and the total divided by the number of readings, including the highest point and any other 'o' readings. This will give the distance below the highest point at which the mean level lies.

Pegging out

The first actual process of levelling is to place pegs in the land, with their tops at the height to which it is to be levelled; that is, at the mean level of the plot. They are best placed at the lower end of the slope first, working up until the tops of the pegs and the existing soil level coincide. Pegs will be placed in the higher positions as excavation proceeds.

Retaining the top soil

There is, however, one complication with all these methods and that is that unless there is a considerable depth of fertile soil, the top soil must be kept on top. This is particularly important when the sub-soil is a heavy clay, for it will be practically impossible to get young plants to grow in it. This means that the top soil must be moved separately and the depth to which it should be dug out will depend partly on what depth of good top soil there is, and partly on what kind of planting is to be done. For lawns, about 6 in. of top soil is adequate depth, whereas for flower beds 12 in. is much better. It is, however, generally impracticable to cater for small areas at different depths as the work proceeds, so the overall planting for the piece of land being dealt with must be taken as the guide. There is no doubt that the best way is to remove the top soil from the whole area at the outset, and then to bring it back when the levelling has been done. In doing this it must be remembered that pegging has been done to top-soil level so the removal of the top soil exposes the pegs to that additional depth, and new sub-levels must be to that depth. The replacing of the top soil will again bring the level up to the top of the pegs: see Figs. 11 and 12.

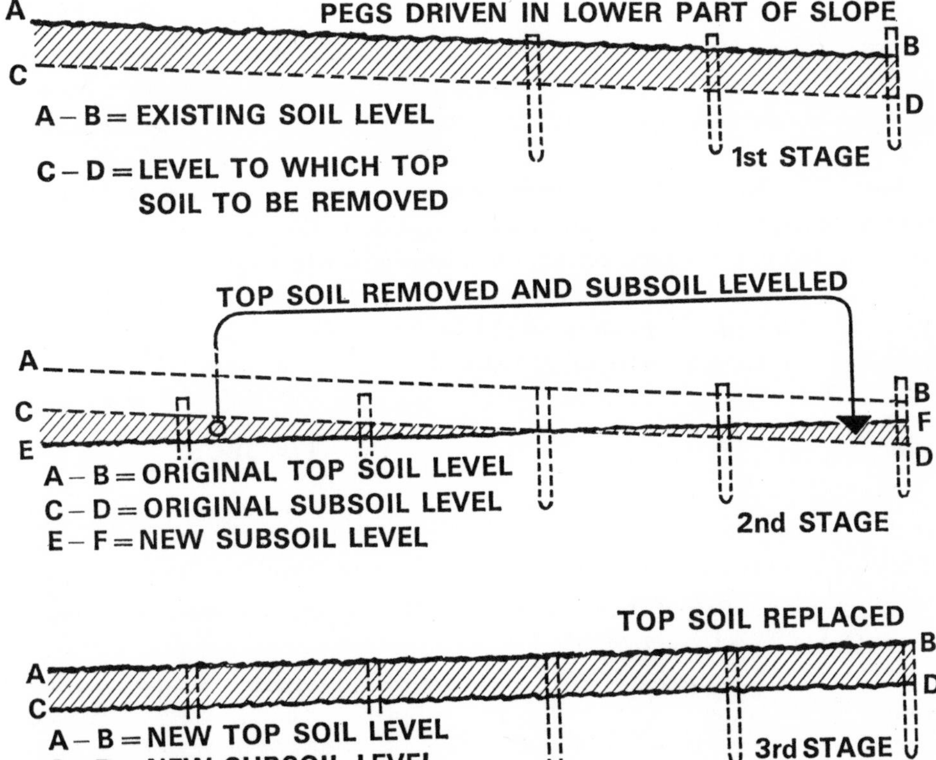

Fig. 11. The diagrams above show the three stages in levelling a sloping site in order to retain the original top soil.

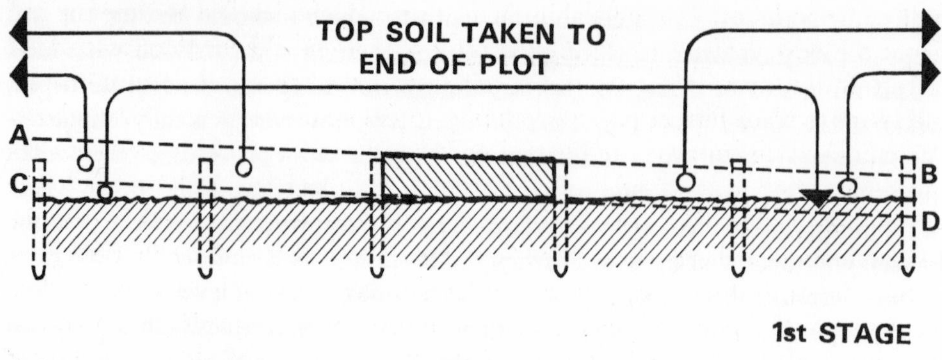

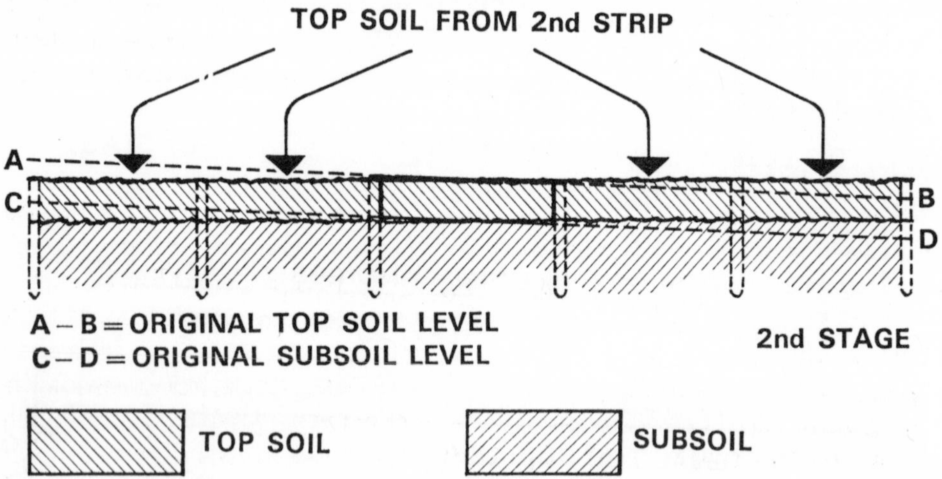

Fig. 12 A two-stage excavating operation to level a sloping site and retain the original top soil.

When the moving of the soil has to be done by hand the work involved can be considerably reduced by the following method. To start, after pegging out the plot to be levelled, mark out a strip 1 yd. wide from the top to the bottom of the slope. Then remove the top soil from the upper and lower parts of this strip, and take it to the far end of the plot. Near the centre of the slope the top soil can be left in position for such a width as there will be fertile top soil remaining at the new level, see Fig. 12. A thin layer of sub-soil on top, or a slightly reduced depth of top soil, will soon be adjusted in the ordinary process of cultivation, and will cause no harm. The sub-soil in the first strip is then levelled and the top soil from the next yard-wide strip placed on top of it and the whole plot worked across in this manner. As the soil is excavated from the higher level it will be necessary to place further pegs periodically to ensure the same level throughout. Variations of this method can be used with mechanical equipment to effect considerable saving in time and work. In moving soil from the higher to the lower levels, a start should be made by placing it in a line along the lower end to act as a containing wall, and then fill in behind it. A few stakes can be knocked in to secure the earth if necessary. It will be found that there tends to be more than enough soil at the section being filled in, and that it overtops the pegs, but this is only a temporary position due to the excavated soil being loose and so taking up more space, and this will rectify itself as the soil settles. Where small areas are to be more deeply cultivated than the general area surrounding them, such as flower beds in a lawn and the sub-soil is an impervious clay, these small areas are liable to act as sumps and take the water from the surrounding area to the detriment of the plants in them. This will necessitate draining and the pipes can be laid as the work proceeds.

Marking out the beds

The soil having been levelled, the next job is the marking out of the planned features. The requirements for this are few. A garden line long enough to reach the longest distances involved, a measuring tape, a set-square and an ample supply of canes or sticks. A set-square can easily be made with three pieces of wood fixed together in triangular form with the outside measurements in the proportion 3 : 4 : 5. The shortest side should not be less than 3 ft. in length. For long distances being taken at right angles on the site, it is best not to rely on the set-square, but to form a 3 : 4 : 5 triangle with the tape measure, as shown in Figs. 13(1) and 13(2). Any slight error in a set-square can become a serious discrepancy when extended a long distance. Transferring the plan from the paper to the site is a perfectly straightforward matter, merely a case of measuring from established points and marking the positions with canes. Where survey lines are being used these must be set out in the same way as when the original plan was drawn up, and the offset distances marked with canes. When the salient points of an irregularly shaped feature have been marked with canes, the outline should be marked, either by limewash, or better still by nicking it out with a spade, see Fig. 13(5). Where there is a lot of detail in the plan it is best not to mark out everything at once, or it becomes a forest of canes and very confusing. The salient features can be marked and made first, followed by less important ones, grouping those together which are

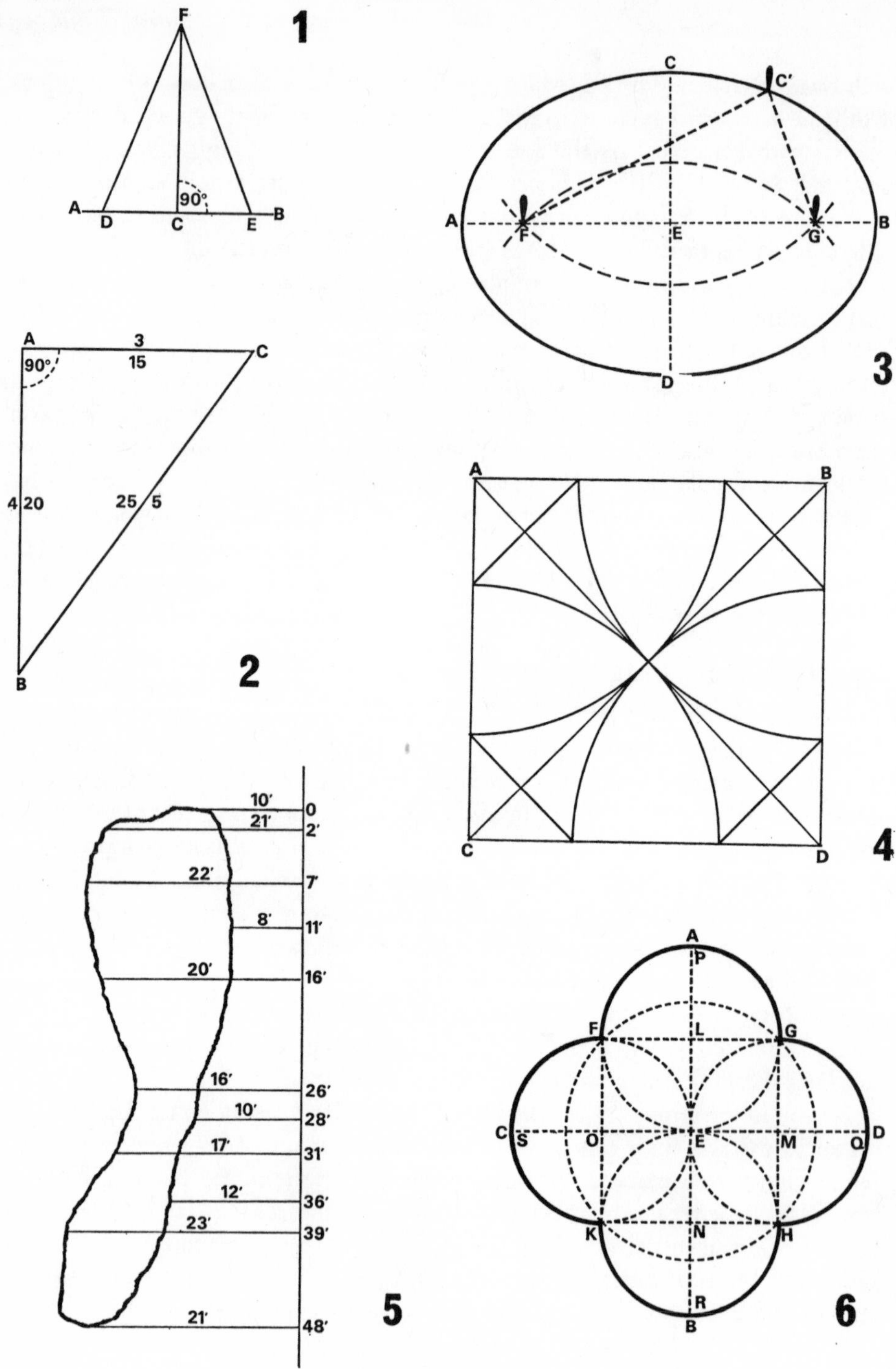

Fig. 13 Laying out and designing flower beds.

most conveniently done at the same time. With the plan to refer to, the work can be extended over any period of time.

Flower-bed design

The various designs of flower beds will generally be based on rectangles or circles. The setting out of a rectangle only involves marking out one side in the required position and of the required length, and setting out the remaining sides at right angles as already described. A circle can be marked by having a length of string equal to the radius of the circle, looping one end loosely over a cane placed in the centre, and rotating the taut string to describe the circle. A pointed stick at the outer end of the string will enable a clear mark to be made. This method can also be used for sections of a circle, built into a curved outline. To mark out an oval the following method is best. Mark out a line of the given length, as AB (Fig. 13(3)), and another at CD, of the given breadth, at right angles to it. Next take a distance of half the length of the base line AB, and with this as a radius, from points C and D describe the dotted arcs shown, which bisect each other and the line AB, at points at F and G. Place two canes firmly at F and G, and take a loop of string long enough to extend over canes F and G to point B. Then with a piece of stick C1, placed inside the looped string, trace the outline of the oval. The method of marking out an octagonal bed is shown in Fig. 13(4). First set out a square the size of the octagon ABCD, and mark the centre at the point where the diagonals cross. Then from each corner describe arcs passing through the centre, and the point where these meet the boundaries of the square will be the corners of the octagon. To form a bulged square as Fig. 13(6), first mark out a square as FGHK, and from the centre of each side of the square, describe a circle, the outer halves of the circles giving the outline of the plot. If a larger circle is drawn from the centre of the square E, and touching the corners of the square FGHK, then crescents are formed on the outside, and several other designs can be extracted from this diagram.

CHAPTER SEVEN

Construction of Garden Features

THE main purpose of a drive or path is to provide easy and pleasant passage for persons or vehicles. Nevertheless their appearance cannot be ignored because they are an important part of the garden layout. For drives the choice generally lies between gravel, tarmacadam, asphalt and concrete. For paths, which are even more a built-in feature of a garden than a drive, more attention must be paid to their appearance. For this reason concrete, tarmacadam and asphalt are less frequently used, and there is a general preference for gravel, bricks, paving-stones, crazy-paving or grass.

Gravel drives

Gravel gives the most natural effect, and when properly constructed is most satisfactory for normal day-to-day use. When, however, it is used by heavy traffic, or by drivers addicted to race-track standards of stopping and starting, it does tend to break up rather quickly. It is also true that weeds will grow in gravel, but while this can be a nuisance, it is not a great problem with the effective weed-killers now available. A gravel drive must have adequate foundations to prevent it sinking and going into pot-holes, and it must be well drained, or it will be soft and soggy, and the loose gravel will tread into the house in all but the driest weather.

The depth to be excavated will depend on the nature of the soil. On most kinds of soil, the natural drainage will be adequate and excavating to a depth of 8 in. will be sufficient to give a good foundation, and the fertile top soil can be removed and used in another part of the garden. On heavy or wet land a generous drainage layer will be needed in addition, and this will necessitate the soil being taken out to a depth of another 4–6 in. On really badly drained land it is essential to lay a pipe drain below this drainage layer, and this is best placed on a firm base along the centre of the drive. The base of the excavated area should slope down to the pipe from the edges so that the water drains down to the pipe and clear away. Where there is no natural slope to the land it will of course be necessary to give the pipe a slope by making it slightly deeper at the outfall end and to lead the pipe to an outlet where the water can run or soak away. The pipe should then be covered with a layer of large stones or similar material, topped by slightly smaller material to the total depth of about 6 in. Since this layer should be kept as open as possible, for the water must be able to percolate through it, it should be worked over with a fork to ensure that the constituent stones settle down to firm positions, otherwise considerable settling may take place some time after construction. On top of this, or at the bottom of the excavated area, if no drainage layer has been put in, coarse gravel should be put to within about 3 in. of the top, firming it well as the work proceeds. While this coarse gravel will consist mostly of large material, it must have some smaller material in with it to enable it to bind, and if none is present it must be added—usually from the original sub-soil. 'Hoggin', a mixture of gravel and clay, is often used. There should be a slight crown to the drive, about 3 in. for an 8-ft.-wide drive, and the under-layer should be raised correspondingly. The levels can be marked by wooden pegs. The top 3 in. should be filled in with finer gravel, from which all the large stones have been removed, but with the small material remaining in it for binding. This top layer must be raked and rolled until a firm level surface is obtained, and for this the gravel needs to be moderately moist, but not too wet or it will stick to the roller. Gravel is usually sold by the yard, that is, a cubic yard, but if bought by weight, a ton may be taken as being equivalent to about 20 cu. ft. Beach gravel is not generally suitable for the making of drives, as it does not bind, but some success can be achieved with it by adding 1 part of dried clay to 4 parts of shingle.

In spite of all precautions pot-holes may develop after a while and in filling them in the hole should be deepened into firm material over the full area, and the sides made vertical, before filling in with more gravel.

Tarmacadam and asphalt

Instead of the top layer of fine gravel, a layer of tarmacadam can be used. The foundation layer is needed as for a gravel finish, but except on a site which is subject to actual waterlogging, no drainage layer or pipe is needed, as after a while the surface will only drain water through it very slowly. When new gravel or other foundation is being covered it is unlikely that there will be many weed seeds in it but if the tarmac is being added to an existing drive where small weeds and weed seeds are likely to be present, it is best to treat the surface with a persistent weed-killer such as 'Simazin', otherwise weeds may later force themselves through. On the foundation layer an inch or two of coarse tarmacadam should first be spread, and this should be rolled with a roller weighing at least 5 cwt. getting a true surface with the slightly higher crown in the centre. On top of this should be laid a layer, 1 in. thick, of ¼ in. graded tarmacadam, and this also should be rolled with a heavy roller. With a material like this, which allows only slow percolation of rain, it is important that the surface should be evenly rounded so that water runs to the sides without leaving puddles, and that there should be either porous soil or turf at the side for it to soak into. Where this is not the case, outlets must be made for it every 20 ft. or so, and these can be channels which guide the water to permeable soil, or sump-holes covered by gratings. The tarmacadam can be bought from depots in most towns, and while the laying of it is a perfectly straightforward job, the rolling of it is a fairly strenuous process, and generally it is better to hire a power-driven roller from a contractor. Contractor's charges for rolling or for doing the whole of the work are not generally excessive, but care should be taken to see that adequate material is used, as described above.

Asphalt is somewhat similar material, but it is laid hot, and so needs special equipment and consequently is usually laid by contractors. It gives a more solid and impenetrable surface than tarmacadam, but is more expensive. It can be made more attractive by having white or coloured chippings scattered over the top surface and rolled in. The asphalt should be of a minimum thickness of 1 in.

Concrete

Concrete drives are very serviceable, though they are rather expensive to lay. Many people object to their appearance largely because of the glaring white of untreated concrete, but other and more attractive finishes are now available. A 4-in. layer of concrete is necessary for a drive, and it should have a layer of about 1 in. of ashes or similar material below it, so that the soil will need to be excavated to a depth of 5 in. As concrete sets quite rigid it is only on the most unstable soils that more foundation material is needed below it.

Before excavating, the level should be marked with pegs driven in to the required depth at the sides of the drive, and when the soil has been removed boards should be placed inside these pegs and at the same height, to contain the concrete. After making sure that the base of the excavated area is firm and moist, the layer of ashes should be laid, and on top of that the concrete. It should then be levelled with a rake, working it well to get rid of any air cavities, and then consolidating it either by light rolling or tamping with a rammer. This firming must be done when the concrete is thick enough in consistency to carry the weight of the roller or rammer, but still fluid enough to be consolidated. It is important that concrete should dry slowly, so it should be protected from strong sun or wind for up to 2 or 3 days by means of damp sacks, and it should not be laid in frosty weather. The amount of concrete used is appreciable for all but the smallest drives, and mixing it by hand is fairly hard work, so that where ready-mixed concrete is available it is a well worthwhile economy of effort to buy it. Care must be taken to know the time at which it will be delivered and to have arrangements laid on for laying it, as it should be laid within an hour or so of delivery. This will probably involve moving it by wheelbarrow from the drive gate, as the concrete delivery vehicles are often too large to go up a private driveway.

Ready-mixed concrete will only be available in full loads, so that smaller amounts will have to be mixed on the spot. The mixture should consist of 1 part cement, 2 parts sand and 4 parts shingle or other comparable material such as broken stone, which is usually referred to as 'aggregate', and should not include material larger than about 1 in. Both sand and shingle must be clean and free from soil. The amounts needed will be about ½ cwt. of cement, 1¼ cu. ft. of sand and 2½ cu. ft. of shingle, per sq. yd. at 4 in. deep. Thorough mixing is essential. First spread out the required amount of sand on a hard base, and put the measured amount of cement on top of it, and then mix in the dry state until it is all the same colour and free from streaks of brown or grey. Then add the measured aggregate and mix thoroughly, which will usually need three turnings, and slowly add the water, which will be about one-twelfth of the volume of the dry materials. Meddle the material as the water is being added so that it quickly soaks into it, then turn it several times until the whole has become a 'porridgy' mass of even consistency. It is better to be sparing with the water at first, adding more if needed later, as the drier the mix, so long as it is workable, the better the concrete.

It is of course much more economical to have the wheel tracks only cemented, leaving the soil between and on each side of them. The tracks should be at least 18 in. wide, and the soil between can later be planted with plants of prostrate habit. It is probably easier, however, to make these tracks of pre-cast concrete slabs, making sure that the soil below is well firmed.

Paths

A path should never be less than 3 ft. wide, and it is very much better at 4 ft. if sufficient space can be spared. This allows easy passage for a wheelbarrow and other implements, and for the temporary intrusion of pathside plants such as shrubs or creeping ground plants. It is a very unhappy task to have to cut back a mass of flower just at its best because it is jutting on to a too-narrow path. Except in very large gardens there is little object in making paths wider than 4 ft.: it makes their construction that much more expensive and except in the case of grass can give too bare an appearance to the garden. While it is important that paths should always be firm and dry, they generally look better if they are not above the level of the adjoining land, but whether they are level with it or sunk an inch or two below is largely a matter of personal preference. They should generally be flat, as this makes for more pleasant walking, but if over 4 ft. wide should be slightly raised in the centre to allow rain to run off easily.

Where the soil is of medium or light texture and where it will not get a great deal of use in the winter, ordinary earth paths are quite satisfactory, and being of the parent material generally look right. The surface can be bound together better by adding sifted ashes or brickdust and covering it with a thin layer of earth if necessary to give it a natural finish. Such paths must break the general rule and be given a rather higher rise in the centre to ensure adequate surface run-off and drainage.

The principles of constructing paths are the same as for drives, but since they are narrower, lesser depths of foundation and drainage materials are needed. For gravel paths a foundation of 3 in. to 4 in. should be adequate on soils of light or medium texture and of 4–6 in. on heavy land, with a 3-in. pipe drain below on really badly drained soils where the water cannot soak away at the sides of the paths. A 2-in. layer of top gravel will be enough.

Brick paths. These are particularly attractive when an old-established effect is being aimed at. Weathered bricks are preferable, but they must be sound and hard, or the path will be quickly broken up by frost. The foundations are made in the same way as for a gravel path, except that the top 4 in. will consist of a layer of bricks embedded in a 1-in. layer of fine ashes, gravel or similar material. So long as the bricks are fitted close together and are below ground level, there is no need to cement them in. They should always be 'bonded'; that is, so arranged that the cross-joints are not continuous, and a variety of patterns can be made by different arrangements.

Concrete paths. Plain concrete paths are a little harsh in appearance particularly in the main part of the garden, and discretion must be used in including them. Two in. of concrete is sufficient depth for a path. To ensure reasonable levels pegs and boards should be used as described for drives, and levelling of the surface of the concrete can then be done by having a board about a foot longer than the width of the path, so that it can rest on the two side boards which form the mould into which the concrete is placed. If this board is drawn forward diagonally, the concrete is levelled out with the least effort. A more pleasing effect than that given by the flat surface can be obtained by marking out a pattern of crazy paving on the cement. It is as well to take note of some real crazy paving before attempting this, otherwise the result is apt to be unrealistic. The marking should be done several hours after laying the concrete, but before it solidifies, and the artificial crevices should be about ½ in. deep.

Paving stones. These should be 2–2½ in. thick, and may be either natural stone flags or made of concrete with a surface of finer-textured material. Both make very serviceable paths, but concrete is not particularly attractive in some settings. They can be obtained in several sizes, or in the case of concrete can be made by using a suitable wooden mould of 2-in. deep timber of the required dimensions. The stones should be laid on a 1-in.-thick layer of sifted ashes or similar material, topped with a thin layer of sand, and sand should be worked in between any open joints. Alternatively the joints can be cemented, which will prevent weeds growing there.

Crazy paving. There is no doubt that the most attractive kind of stone path is that formed with crazy paving, but its siting needs choosing with discretion. It is not at home alongside an ultra-modern house, but is for the quieter and more subdued part of the garden. Nor is it the ideal design for really heavy wear, and should not be used as a service path, though with sound construction it will stand average use as long as most other types of path. It needs careful laying in mortar and is consequently rather more expensive than other paths. Crazy paving stones are usually sold by the ton in two grades, thin, which are from ¾ in. to 1½ in. in thickness, and a ton of which will cover about 15 sq. yd., and thick which are from 1½–2½ in. and will cover about 9 sq. yd. to the ton. The foundation should consist of 4–6 in. of large gravel, brick rubble or similar material, with 1 in. or so of fine ashes or sand on top in which the paving is set. It should all be well firmed as it is placed in position. The paving itself should be bedded in a 1-in.-thick layer formed of 6 parts of sand to 1 of cement. It is important that crazy paving is laid level, so pegs should be placed at about every 9 ft., alternately on each side of the path, with their tops at the required level. Stones should first be placed adjacent to the pegs and on a level with them, and the level of the intermediate stones should then be checked by means of a straight-edge, with its two ends resting on the peg-stones. The joints between the stones should be between ¼–½ in. wide, and should be filled in with mortar to a little below the surface level. There are various local stones which are suitable for crazy paving but the best have a mellowed appearance. The use of a lot of small pieces should be avoided. Generally speaking the majority should not be less than 9 in. across, and there should be no suggestion of symmetry or regular pattern in the arrangement of the stones.

The paved garden

Where a path is not used too frequently it is possible to put plants between the stones to give what is in effect a 'paved garden', and this can be a very attractive feature. Indeed, if such a path is not available, the construction of a special paved garden is well worth while. In nature many plants have to endure conditions far from conducive to vigorous growth, but they survive these adverse conditions, often blooming the more freely because of them. And no more natural setting can be obtained for such plants than in a paved garden, where their triumph over apparent adversity usually calls forth a still greater degree of affection for them.

Whether it be a special paved garden or a planted-up path, the preparation should be as for an ordinary pathway, for there must be good drainage for the plants. On top of the foundation material, however, must be placed a layer of about 4 in. of soil, preferably on the light side, and on that the stones must be placed with spaces between them of between ½–1 in. It is, however, best to defer laying the stones for 2 or 3 weeks to give the soil time to settle. If the path or paved area is raised, or if there is no feature adjoining which will keep the side stones firmly in position, they should be cemented in as described earlier. The spaces between the stones should be filled with good soil with a little bone meal added, to give the plants a good start.

Planting must be done with discretion, and the aim should be to give an impression of naturalness suggesting that the plants have come there by seed or by intrusion from neighbouring colonies. Overplanting must be avoided, for in nature many of the seeds that fall on stony ground perish, and there will be many bare spaces, so that complete filling of all the crevices will give a result never seen in nature, and will have less appeal. Too many paved gardens are spoiled by excessive planting. Quite obviously only certain plants are suitable for such a position. They must be dwarf, and particularly when used on a path, must be capable of surviving a certain amount of wear and tear from shoes of varying sizes and weight. It is surprising, however, how many plants will survive such treatment and if over-planting is avoided it will always be possible to avoid treading on plants when in flower, for even the most clumsy visitors will want to do that.

Suitable plants are:

**Acaena buchananii, A. microphylla* and *A. myriophylla*
Achillea rupestris and *A. argentea*
**Ajuga reptans atropurpurea* and *A. r. mettalica crispa*
Alyssum montanum

Antennaria dioica and *A. d. tomentosa*
Arabis bellidifolia
★*Arenaria balearica*
Armeria maritima
Aubrieta varieties
Bellium minutum
Calamintha alpina
Campanula caespitosa, *C. cochlearifolia*, *C. garganica*, *C. portenschlagiana*
Dianthus deltoides and *D. caesius*
Dryas octopetala
★*Erinus alpinus* varieties
Erodium chamaedryoides
Geranium pylzowianum
Globularia cordifolia
Gypsophila cerastioides and *G. repens*
Helianthemum glaucum
Herniaria glabra
Hutchinsia alpina
Hypericum nummularium and *H. reptans*
★*Linaria alpina* and *L. repens*
Lippia nodiflora
★*Mazus pumilio* and *M. radicans*
★*Mentha requienii*
Minuartia laricifolia
Morisia monantha (*hypogaea*)
Oxalis corniculata var. *atropurpurea*
Paronychia argentea and *P. serpyllifolia*
Penstemon menziesii
Saponaria ocymoides
Saxifraga species and varieties
Sedum acre, *S. album* and *S. anglicum*
Sempervivum montanum and *S. tectorum*
Silene acaulis
Thymus serpyllum
Tunica saxifraga
Veronica alpina and *V. repens*
★*Viola cornuta*

Those plants suitable for growing in the shade are marked ★

Grass paths

While a hard surface is essential for a path which is to have a lot of wear or which it is desired shall be usable in all weathers, a very attractive effect can be obtained with grass paths, provided summer strolling is the hardest wear that they are likely to get. In such paths there are often short stretches which get much more wear than the rest, and these can be reinforced by flags or groups of two or three bricks placed with their surfaces a little below ground level, and at about every 2 ft. to give a stepping stone effect. They must be set carefully, just below ground level so that the mower can pass over safely. They must not be set too far below soil level or the surface will be too uneven for mowing.

Generally speaking grass paths are best made from turves, or cut out of the existing turf when a new garden is made. Turf gives a good cover of grass on an already established root system, which is capable of withstanding a fair amount of wear right from the initial stages. Where seed is to be sown to form the path, an appreciable proportion of brown-top *Agrostis tenuis* should be included. It is a hard-wearing grass giving a high quality turf.

Steps

When a path goes from one level to another it will be necessary to construct steps, which should as far as possible be faced with material similar to the paths themselves. Concrete steps are easily constructed by using boards to form a mould to hold the concrete until it is set, while plywood can be used for moulding curved steps. Where gravel or earth are to be used, the material must be kept in position at the front by stout boards nailed on to strong pegs. Steps should not be made of grass, as it can be dangerously slippery when wet, and since it dries out very quickly may disintegrate in the first hot spell of the year.

Formal edgings

Fortunately the craze to have formal edgings to all paths has passed, and no longer do we find every boundary or anything remotely resembling a boundary lined with a row of diagonally placed bricks, tiles, or a line of box edging. And there is no doubt that gardens have gained in beauty as a result, for formal edgings should be kept to a minimum. Nevertheless, there are places where an edging is desirable, as for instance where a flower border adjoins a gravel path or drive, and it is important to see that such edging is well constructed for there are few things more unsightly in a garden than tiles or bricks reclining at all angles, as a result of inadequate fixing. The best formal edgings are of the following materials:

Bricks. These must be of a good hard type because softer bricks if exposed to frost when saturated with water, will quickly crumble. The bricks should be laid on edge and buried to half their depth, after the soil has been well firmed. When the soil is loose so that they are likely to be dislodged they are best set in a 2-in. layer of mortar, in which case only one third of the brick need be below the surface level. They can also be set on edge, but at an angle of 45 deg., to give a serrated finish to the edging. Where the edge is to be a straight one a line must be used and pegs driven in every 9 ft. or so, with their tops at the required level, so that the bricks can be kept at the same height by means of a straight-edge.

Tiles. These are an alternative to bricks, but greater care is needed in their alignment. The best way is to dig out a narrow trench with one side as vertical as possible, and along that side to place a long and straight board, against which the tiles are set. The earth is then filled in on the other side of the tiles, and rammed very firm, after which the board is removed, the space filled in, and that side securely rammed in turn.

Concrete. This makes a good serviceable edging, and so long as a nice rounded top edge is given, is not unattractive. A length of plain rectangular concrete edging, however, is not very pleasing to the eye. Precast concrete edging blocks in 4 ft. or 5 ft. lengths, with nicely rounded edges are obtainable, and probably offer the best way of getting a good serviceable edge with the least trouble. If loose concrete is to be laid to form the edge, it is necessary to make a mould with a board placed along each side of a narrow trench to give a thickness of 3 in. of concrete, and protruding above soil level to the height the edge is needed, usually from 2–3 in. The depth below soil level should be double that above, normally from 4–6 in.

Wood edgings. These are attractive in that they are not so harsh in appearance. Unless the wood is treated with preservative they are nothing like so durable, and really effective preservative treatment can only be done under pressure, and must be carried out by the manufacturer before purchase. The edging should be made of planks 1 in. × 6 in. buried to half their width in the soil. To ensure that the edge keeps in position, pegs of about 1–1½ in. square, and about 2 ft. long, should be driven in on the inner side of the edge at every 6 ft. and the board nailed to it with galvanized nails.

Grass verges

In addition to these artificial edgings it is possible to use living plants for the purpose, the commonest being grass in the form of a grass verge, which is particularly attractive in front of a flower border. It must be wide enough, at least 2 ft., for the mower to work efficiently on it. A grass verge calls for a good deal of attention in that it needs to be mown and edged regularly to keep it neat and tidy, and if it is unlikely that this attention can be given then use another form.

Informal edgings

An informal edging can be made to the front of a border by using an irregular and broken line of crazy paving stones, just placed on the soil or sunk very slightly below soil level. Between them are planted plants of prostrate habit, and these grow over the stones and on to the path to give an informal but quite attractive edging.

Suitable plants are:

Achillea tomentosa and *A. umbellata*
Alyssum saxatile var. *compactum*
Arabis caucasica var. fl. pl.
Aubrieta deltoides varieties
Bellis perennis varieties
Brunnera macrophylla
Campanula, all dwarf species
Cheiranthus allionii
Dianthus deltoides, *D. squarrosus*, etc.
Dryas octopetala
Erica carnea
Genista pilosa
Geranium farreri and *G. sanguineum*
Gypsophila repens

Terraces

Helianthemum nummularium varieties
Hypericum olympicum
Iberis sempervirens
Linum salsoloides
Lithospermum diffusum varieties
Lysimachia nummularia
Nepeta faassenii
Phlox subulata varieties
Polyanthus varieties
Primula vulgaris varieties
Saponaria ocymoides
Saxifraga dwarf varieties
Zephyranthes candida

These are all hardy perennials, and can be added to in the summer with half-hardy annuals and perennials.

Terraces

While a terrace can be made at any level in the garden it is best just in front of the house, where it can provide a view over the whole garden and in addition, form a natural link between the two. If practicable it should be made 18 in. or so above the level of the rest of the garden, and can be fronted either by a small retaining wall or a bank. It need not be regular in outline, neither need the steps be in the centre, but as it will often be a place for sitting out when the weather is fine, it should have ample space and be in a position that will get most sun. So that surface water will drain away from the house there should be a slight slope of about 1 in 60 in that direction. It is best for the main part of it to be paved, but before doing this it should be decided whether any small flower beds are to be included in the design or whether any climbing plants are to be planted against the house walls. If so the soil for those areas must be prepared to a depth of about 18 in., adding bone meal or other slow-acting fertilizer, and doing a sufficiently wide area to give the climbing plants a good root-run. If soil has to be added to give the extra height to the terrace it should be well firmed before the top material, usually bricks or paving, is added. It is very important that the whole shall be below the damp course of the house.

Flower beds and borders

As beds and borders will be heavily cropped with a wide range of flowers, some robust and some of much weaker constitution, the conditions must be good enough to enable even the poorest plants to put up a really good show. It is well worth while giving a good deal of attention to the preparation of the beds and borders. There must be no suggestion of bad drainage because the beds, being more deeply cultivated than the surrounding soil, tend to collect water, and if it cannot get away, the plants will quickly suffer. On really heavy and wet soil a pipe drain should be put in, but on most heavy land a 6-in. layer of broken bricks or similar builders' material, placed at 2 ft. below the surface, will generally prove adequate. There must also be a good depth of fertile soil for the plants to root into. For bedding plants and similar intensive planting it should be at least 2 ft. deep, and if the sub-soil is very heavy or otherwise unsatisfactory, it should be taken out to that depth and replaced with good top soil. Roses are rather more accommodating, and so long as there are 12 in. of good-textured soil and the sub-soil is well broken up, they will generally root freely into it. Where the soil is satisfactory, it should be double-dug, burying the turf under the second spit if it is not wanted for turfing elsewhere, incorporating a good dressing of farmyard manure in the top spit, and giving a dressing of about 8 oz. per sq. yd. of hydrated lime to the surface when planting is complete. The addition of new soil, manure and drainage material will raise the bed above its original level, but this will assist drainage and if it is sloped off from the centre to the sides, will show the plants off to the best advantage. It is a common mistake to overdo this banking up, however, with the result that rain runs off the bed instead of sinking in, and the plants very quicky suffer from drought. A bed 4 ft. wide should only be about 4 in. higher in the centre than at the sides, and narrower beds in proportion.

Hedges

A garden will benefit from having at least one length of hedge, either to give shelter from strong winds, to ensure privacy, to form a background for a floral display or as an attractive feature in its own right. Anyone who has had experience of modern housing estates, with their open, wind-swept and chain-linked gardens, will realize how valuable a hedge can be. In a small garden, however, hedges must not be overdone, or they will take up an unduly large proportion of the space and nourishment available. In a very small garden an attractive fence, possibly clothed with ivy, honeysuckle or some similar climber, may be a preferable alternative. In no case should there be any idea of partitioning off all the different sections of the garden by tall evergreen hedges, because they rob the other plants of much sun and air. Where such planting is considered desirable from the design point of view, it is much better to use more open shrubs that will give a good floral display as well as make the required break in the planting scheme.

General purpose hedges. Most hedges are planted to fulfil the combined functions of marking a boundary and of ensuring some degree of privacy, but their most important function, that of checking the force of the wind, is often overlooked. Gardening is a constant struggle against adversity, and not the least adverse factors are the periodic strong winds and gales to which exposed positions are subject.

Few plants can grow to their best if they are continually buffeted about, and the establishment of good substantial hedges should be the first concern of anyone making a garden in an exposed position. For this purpose plants must be chosen which will grow quickly, survive close planting and, as with all plants, are hardy for the district and suitable for the local soil. For the utility garden hedge the best plants are privet, holly, beech, hornbeam, cupressus and yew. For a large boundary hedge the thorn has a lot to recommend it, but it is out of character in a smaller and more formal garden. Most people prefer a hedge of one kind of plant only, but for others the mixed hedge has considerable attraction, and a hedge formed of a mixture of thorn, holly and beech certainly has its appeal. Obviously all the plants used in a mixed hedge must be of similar habit.

Privet. Privet tends to be despised as a hedge plant because its virtues have caused it to be so much planted in the past that it was difficult to get away from it. But it is cheap to buy, grows quickly, withstands wind and unlimited clipping and will thrive in practically any soil or situation, smoky or otherwise. Its main disadvantages are that it can lay no claim to social distinction, that it needs clipping at least twice in a season, and that in severe winters it will lose most of its leaves, particularly on poor soils or if clipping has been neglected. It is also a greedy-rooting plant, and will rob plants growing alongside it. The golden privet is also useful for hedges, and is less avaricious than the green type, but is even more despised by those who prefer plants of social standing. Nevertheless it is bright and cheerful, and with the other kinds of privet must be considered as the best choice for planting under the most adverse conditions, even if it cannot claim to make a quality hedge.

Beech and Hornbeam. The most popular hedge plant at present is probably the beech, and its popularity is fully justified. It will thrive in all soils, including chalk, will stand close clipping, and is a good wind-break in that the leaves, although turning to a rich russet brown in the autumn, are retained throughout the winter. Admittedly a few people find these dead leaves unattractive, but most consider them to be a pleasing feature of the plant, although they involve a second round of leaf gathering in the spring. The purple beech can also be used to form a hedge, or the two sorts can be mixed, though this mixture is not attractive to all eyes. Hornbeam closely resembles beech, and many so-called beech hedges are in fact hornbeam.

Holly. There is no doubt that the most attractive evergreen hedge is holly, particularly if it can be allowed to grow to good dimensions, say 10–12 ft. high, and 4–6 ft. thick. It makes an impenetrable wall of foliage, will keep out all intruders and reduce the strongest of winds. Unfortunately plants must be put in when quite small, which makes the growing of the hedge a long process, or plants which have been frequently transplanted in order to develop a fibrous root system must be used, and these are naturally expensive. Even after planting it will take its time in growing. There are many varieties of the common holly with silver or golden foliage, which will make perfectly good hedges of up to 5–6 ft. in height, but most of them have not the same vigour as the green type. The varieties which are variegated around the margins are best, as those with a central blotch are more likely to revert to the ordinary green type.

Conifers. The conifers are rather different in habit to other 'general purpose' plants in that adjoining plants do not intertwine to form a continuous mass of twigs, but the individual plants lie closely alongside their neighbours to make a wall of foliage. The nett result is the same, however, and several conifers are useful subjects for this work. They make good growth quickly, but the plants are rather expensive to buy. They also have the disadvantage that when the hedge gets old, say 15 to 20 years, even the best of them tend to become bare at the base. Nevertheless they do make attractive hedges up to that age. The best are *Chamaecyparis lawsoniana, Thuya lobbii, T. occidentalis, Cryptomeria japonica elegans* and the hybrid *Cupresso-cyparis leylandii. Cupressus macrocarpa*, although often recommended, should not be used because it often dies back suddenly and for no apparent reason after many years of satisfactory growth. It may however be useful near the sea, as it is more tolerant to salt spray than most conifers, but it has no other advantages. *Chamaecyparis lawsoniana* is very variable, so that if seedlings are used, those of similar habit must be chosen. Nurserymen have now selected particularly suitable strains and propagated them vegetatively so that they come true to type, and these form the best planting material; 'Green Hedger' is one such selected strain. There are also good silver and golden kinds which can be used successfully. *Cupresso-cyparis leylandii* is very hardy, will stand coastal conditions and strong winds, and can be trimmed to form a hedge of almost any height. The thuyas make neat, compact and solid hedges on good soils, but do not thrive on poor soils. Large plants do not transplant well and 2-year-old seedlings should be used. The plants should not be stopped until they reach the height to which the hedge is to go, though quite close trimming of the base can be done before this.

Yew is not favoured in this impatient age, because of the slowness of its growth, and the fact that the same hedge may be just as attractive in 100, or even 200, years' time is of little consequence today. Yew will grow on practically any soil, including chalk, and is extremely hardy; it is the ideal plant to clip into fancy shapes, and for topiary work generally. It will make a first-class hedge of any height from

2–20 ft. and while it has to be admitted that under town conditions it is a little sombre in appearance, under brighter country conditions, the deep green neatly clipped yew hedge is a very attractive feature, and gives the perfect background for a floral display. While cows wander along our roads much less frequently than they used to do, it must still be borne in mind that yew, either green in the hedge or as dried clippings, is extremely poisonous to these animals, so that yew hedges must not be put in positions where they are likely to be grazed.

Cotoneaster. Some species of this shrub make very good hedges, and will stand close clipping. *Cotoneaster simonsii* is particularly suited where a narrow hedge is wanted, as it can be had 5 ft. high and not more than 1 ft. through. *C. lactea* is also good, and will make a close-clipped hedge of 5–6 ft. or a tall 8 ft. hedge of looser form. The closely allied *Pyracantha rogersiana* and *P. yunnanensis* will also stand clipping, or can be left to grow more freely to produce a better show of flowers and fruit. *P. coccinia* var. *lalandii* is also good similarly treated.

Pittosporum. This genus consists of tender shrubs which will only flourish in a mild climate, and is useless in colder parts. *P. tenuifolium* is probably the best species and makes quite a good hedge, at the same time providing excellent foliage for cutting.

Large boundary hedges. While thorn hedges are usually associated with farms, they are ideal as boundaries for the larger garden, being attractive and almost impenetrable. The seedlings are easily raised or cheap to buy, transplant well when young and the hedge stands any amount of close clipping, even if roughly carried out. If allowed to grow to around 8 ft. high it will have a mass of blossom in the late spring, with a comparable mass of berries in the autumn, all bringing to the garden some of the atmosphere of the country scene. Laurels, both the Cherry and Portugal types, are sometimes used for boundary hedges, but they have the disadvantage that they cannot be kept in shape by clipping, but must be trimmed with a knife or secateurs. With experience, however, this need not be a particularly time-consuming task, and a vigorous laurel hedge so trimmed is very attractive, is cheap to plant and is quick-growing. The Portugal laurel is the hardier of the two, but both will grow well in all but the coldest parts. Most nurserymen have forms of both which are specially suitable for hedges. The yellow-spotted aucubas are very similar to the laurel in appearance, but are more suitable for planting in shady positions. The double-flowered gorse is particularly useful for forming a rough boundary hedge to give shelter on poor sandy soils and in exposed situations. It will stand quite close clipping, but to get the benefit of its excellent floral display it must not be too closely trimmed. Gorse transplants badly so that young plants need to be grown in pots, or seed can be sown direct on the hedge-site.

PLATE 7

CELOSIA (Cockscomb, Prince of Wales' Feathers). These striking plants can, with care and protection, be grown in a warm border.

PLATE 8

Above, CHAENOMELES JAPONICA (Japanese Quince).
Below, CLEMATIS JACKMANII, an attractive climber.

PLATE 9
CHRYSANTHEMUM

Large-flowered reflex 'Zenith'.

Large-flowered incurving 'Dallas'.

PLATE 10
CHRYSANTHEMUM. The species illustrated above is C. maxium, the Shasta Daisy. A number of excellent varieties are available.

PLATE 11

COREOPSIS (Tickseed). The shorter species are suitable for the dry wall as illustrated in the above photo.

PLATE 12

COSMOS. There are a number of named varieties of this annual for the border; single and double strains are available.

PLATE 13
CROCUS. The spring varieties bloom as early as Feb., but there are winter forms which flower Dec. to Jan.

PLATE 14

CYNOGLOSSUM (Hound's Tongue). Only three species are sufficiently hardy for general use, even so they are usually short-lived.

Small hedges. There are often positions in which a small internal hedge of say 2–3 ft. adds to the attractiveness of a garden, though at that height it obviously gives few of the benefits which a taller hedge would give. Yew is an excellent subject for such a hedge, as also is *Lonicera nitida*, a plant often recommended for taller hedges, for which, in fact, it is totally unsuited, having insufficiently rigid stems. It needs moderately good soil and must be kept closely trimmed or it will quickly become bare and ragged at the base. *L. pileata*, often wrongly sold as *L. yunnanensis*, is also good for low hedges and is of rather more rigid and more dwarf habit than *L. nitida*. The old-fashioned box, particularly the Handsworth variety, makes a good hedge of up to 6 ft. in height, but it is the variety *suffruticosa* which is mainly used for low hedges or hedges of from 6 in. to 3 ft. high. It will stand very close trimming, and will grow in practically any soil and in shady positions. Other low hedges can be formed by planting fairly closely such plants as lavender, the medium height heathers, such as *Erica darleyensis*, or the silver-leaved *Santolina incana*. All will stand clipping, which is best done in each case after the plants have flowered. The common lavender will make a hedge 3–4 ft. high, while dwarfer varieties will not exceed 2 ft.

Informal flowering hedges. Most of the flowering shrubs, if planted fairly close and given only the minimum of pruning, form loose informal banks of foliage and flowers, and make very attractive features, though in view of the fact that they cannot be hard clipped, they are bound to occupy more space than the hedge-plants proper.

Berberis is particularly suited for the purpose. Practically all species and varieties can be used, choosing for preference an evergreen and one that will grow to the height desired. *B. stenophylla* and *B. darwinii* are probably the best hedges of 5–6 ft. high and *B. coccinea* and *B.* × *irwinii* for dwarfer hedges. Of the deciduous species, *B. thunbergii* and *B. wilsonae* make excellent hedges up to 3 ft. high. *Elaeagnus macrophylla* and *E. pungens* make good large hedges. The variegated form of *E. pungens* is one of the most attractive of variegated shrubs and will make the more compact hedge.

The heaths (*Erica*) generally are not rigid enough to form hedges in exposed positions, but in more sheltered spots *E. mediterranea alba* will make a good hedge of 4–5 ft., while *E. darleyensis* will make a good dwarf hedge of around 2 ft. *E. lusitanica* will only thrive in the south and west, but in those areas it will make an attractive hedge up to 8 ft. high with long flowering sprays up to 2 ft. long.

Escallonia macrantha is the equal of many hedging plants, but it is not hardy enough for cold regions. It will stand up to any wind, even near the sea, and with its glossy leaves and pink flowers makes a very attractive hedge. Some of its varieties, most of which have red flowers, are equally as good and include 'Crimson Spire', 'Red Hedger', 'C. F. Ball' and 'Red Guard'.

Other flowering shrubs suitable for the informal hedge are given below, and information about them will be found in Chapter 14.

Atriplex halimus E S T
Ceanothus dentatus E T
Choisya ternata E S
Forsythia intermedia spectabilis
Garrya elliptica E T
Griselinia littoralis E T
Olearia haastii E T
Osmanthus delavayii E
Osmarea burkwoodii E
Philadelphus varieties
Rhododendron ponticum, and varieties E
Ribes sanguineum
Rosemarinus officinalis E
Rosa vigorous H.T.s, and floribundas, and briars
Tamarix anglica E S
Syringa vulgaris varieties
Veronica (*Hebe*) *speciosa* 'Autumn Glory' E S
Viburnum tinus E T

E = evergreen S = particularly suitable for seaside planting
T = tender, only suitable for the warmer parts of the country

Preparing the site for hedges

Plants forming a hedge should be planted much closer than they would be for any other purpose. They may be there for anything up to 50 years, and during that time they will have to find sustenance to maintain themselves in spite of the pruning or frequent clippings to which they will be subject. So the site for a hedge should be a reasonably congenial one and should be well prepared. A strip of ground 3 ft. wide should be dug two spits deep, and a moderate dressing of farmyard manure or compost added, mainly to the bottom spit. The aim with a hedge is to keep it bushy at the base, and excessive manuring in the early stages tends to make it form a few very strong shoots, at the expense of lateral growth. It must be assured of adequate plant food later on and this is best achieved by making sure that conditions are right for it to send its roots well down, and to add a slow-acting fertilizer, such as coarse bone meal or shoddy. Deep preparation has the added advantage that the hedge is encouraged to root deeply and is less likely to send out many lateral roots to rob the plants growing alongside it. It is best to prepare the land several weeks before planting, but it is unwise to let good planting conditions pass by if they occur before that period has elapsed.

Practically all deciduous hedges are best planted in Oct. or Nov., and it does not matter if some of the leaves are still on the plants, so long as all the shoots are firm and well ripened. Good planting weather should be chosen if possible, the ideal being a mild damp spell with very little wind. Frosty weather and cold drying winds should be avoided. The soil too must be moist but not saturated. If the plants arrive under bad planting conditions they should be temporarily heeled in a sheltered position until conditions improve. Planting can continue up to Mar., but plants put in in the autumn have the advantage of a warm soil into which they can immediately send out new roots, whereas later plantings have to wait for the soil to warm up in the spring. Evergreens require much more care in planting, because the leaves are giving off water the whole time, however damaged the root system may be. Generally speaking they should be planted between the middle of Sept. and the middle of Oct., or if that is not possible, then in Apr. or early May. If conditions remain good, it is possible to plant them with success during the winter, but if adverse conditions set in they are likely to suffer. As with all planting material, sturdy plants with a good root system are preferable to plants with big tops and few roots. This is best achieved with some plants by transplanting them during their early life, and good nurserymen do this as necessary, though it does mean of course that such plants will be slightly dearer. The plants should also be well furnished with shoots from the base, as once they have become bare and leggy, it is often impossible to get them to break afresh. Any long tap-roots should be shortened before planting, and the tops of evergreens may also be cut back to reduce the amount of water given off. Plants generally should be about 18 in. high, and be planted 18 in. apart in the row, with dwarf-growing plants somewhat closer, around 12 in. Vigorous-growing plants should be given up to 24 in. between them. Where a wide or dense hedge is needed, two rows, about 18 in. apart, can be planted, alternating the plants so that they are not opposite each other. In all cases the plants should be put in a little deeper than they were before (as shown by the 'soil' line) and well firmed. So long as the soil is only moderately moist treading them in will not be too drastic.

With autumn planting it is unlikely that watering will be needed, but plants put in in spring, particularly evergreens, may need water. If they can be shaded as well this will help them, while a mulch put around their roots after the soil has warmed up will help to conserve the soil moisture. An overhead spray in the evenings of hot days will also help considerably.

To ensure a good foundation for a hedge the shoots arising from the base in the early stages must be stopped when they are about 9–12 in. long, and successive shoots must be cut back to a similar length. This ensures that a series of lateral shoots are sent out up the whole height of the hedge, and that it is well furnished at the base, and not gappy. In a good growing season two, and possibly three, stoppings will be needed. At an early stage the shape the hedge is to take will have to be decided. Where hedges occur near buildings it is usual to clip them to a square top to fit in with the straight line of the building, but conifers do not lend themselves to such square shaping and they are best grown in a pyramidal form resembling their natural pyramidal shape. While it is often desired to have the hedge as narrow as possible, especially in small gardens, it is generally difficult to get a thick hedge with good faces to it, unless it is allowed to grow about half as wide as its height.

Most hedges need trimming twice a year, in May and again in late Aug. or Sept., the second trimming keeping them tidy for the winter, as little growth takes place after that. The smaller-leaved sorts such as privet, beech, box, etc., can be clipped with shears, but the large-leaved ones like laurel should have the shoots cut back individually with a knife or secateurs. When trimming with shears the secret of getting a straight and level face to the hedge is to stand close to the hedge and behind the shears so as to be able to look along the line of cut. A moderately heavy pair of shears is better than a very light pair, because the cutting is then done by the weight of the blades. Informal hedges formed of flowering shrubs require quite different treatment since the object with these is to keep them in bounds without sacrificing too much blossom in the process. This involves rather harder pruning than they would get if they were growing as 'free' shrubs, but the principles are exactly the same. With those that flower on the current year's growth, as is the case with fuchsia or ceanothus, the cutting back should be done not later than Mar., but those that flower on the previous season's wood, as is the case with most of our flowering shrubs, should be cut back as soon as they have finished flowering, so that plenty of time is left for them to make new wood to provide flowers the following year, and for it to get well ripened. There are a few kinds like *Syringa* (lilac) which do not require regular cutting back at all, but just the removal of weak or crowded shoots.

Once established, the routine treatment of the hedge, apart from clipping, consists in keeping it free of pests, diseases and weeds, and if there is any sign of lack of vigour, giving it a mulch with farmyard manure. If other plants are grown too close to a hedge, they are bound to spoil the face of it and so detract from its appearance when they die down. There should therefore be a space of at least 1–2 ft. between the foliage of adjoining plants and the hedge.

Fences

Fences are essentially utilitarian, but nevertheless they should be as attractive as possible, and this can sometimes be achieved by training plants on them. Their main purpose is usually to mark a boundary, and for this they can be of the simplest kind, merely consisting of 6-ft. posts driven into the ground at every 10 ft. with 4 strands of wire beginning at 9 in. from the ground, and then at 1-ft. intervals. The posts should be at least 3 in. in diameter, or 3 in. square, with corner posts and straining posts of 4-in. dimensions. Every tenth post should be a straining post. The wire should be fastened securely to one end post by means of strong staples, and pulled tight on to adjoining posts, similarly fastened. It is very difficult to get it really taut by hand pulling, and a wire strainer, a sufficiently large version of which can be bought for a few shillings, is a good investment. The tightening should not be done in very cold weather, or the expansion in the wire occurring when the weather turns warmer will cause it to go slack. Such a fence is no protection against wandering dogs or other animals, and for these chain-link fencing can be used. This is made in various sizes of mesh, but generally speaking that with 2-in. mesh or less is best. Wire netting is about half the cost of chain-link fencing, and while it is not so durable, it is quite satisfactory as a short-term measure. It will also keep out rabbits, and when this is the object it should be buried 9 in. below soil level, and turned outward at the bottom to prevent burrowing. An alternative to the open wire fence is split chestnut fencing, in which the palings are wired together with strong strands of wire so that there is an interval of 1 to 3 in. between each. This makes an efficient and cheap fence, although it affords no shelter or privacy, but it can be a useful boundary fence of a temporary nature and provide good protection to a newly planted hedge. Iron palings were at one time very popular, but are now little in favour. They are very durable, but very expensive and need rather frequent painting to maintain them in good condition.

Complete screening

Where the object is to give privacy or to hide some objectionable feature, close-boarded oak fencing, or interwoven fencing should be used. The close-boarded fence is the more durable and will last for a lifetime, but it is considerably more expensive than the interwoven type. Split oak is more durable than sawn oak. Where softer woods such as fir, larch, pine or deal are used, they should be treated with a preservative but even so they will not be as long-lasting as oak. The interwoven fencing is normally prefabricated in 6-ft. lengths, and is supplied with posts and fittings appropriate to the height of the fence, usually from 2–7 ft.

High mortared brick walls are generally very expensive to erect, and there are few cases where the expense would be justified from the horticultural point of view. Their erection is also a job which calls for a good deal of skill. Walls up to 2–3 ft. high can well be built by the amateur, and information on this can be found in any 'do-it-yourself' building handbook.

Dry walls

Dry walls, with suitable plants in the crevices between the stones and trailing down the face of the walls, have become increasingly popular. They are usually retaining walls; often only one side of them is exposed, the other side being laid against the vertical or near-vertical surface between two different levels of land (see Fig. 14 B and C).

The best time to construct a dry wall is in Mar. or Apr., because it is best to plant the walls as construction proceeds, and at this time root action is most vigorous. Plants to go in the wall should have their roots thoroughly moistened before lifting, and the roots should be well spread out in the soil between the stones forming the wall, keeping them central so that they have a good layer of soil both above and below them. This will enable them to get established quickly in the soil in the wall, after which the roots will penetrate into the soil behind, and that will then form their main source of sustenance. The best position for a plant is near the base of a vertical 'joint', where it is likely to keep more moist than higher up in the joint.

As no mortar is used in the construction of the dry wall, the space between the stones has to be filled with earth, and as this earth will in the early stages have to support the plants, it must be of fairly open texture and have an adequate amount of nutrient in it. It must not have a large amount of bulky manure in it, however, or this will quickly decompose and so leave gaps in the soil which will loosen the whole structure of the wall. A better mixture is of medium texture loam, lightened if necessary by the addition of coarse sand, with 4 oz. of either bone meal or John Innes base fertilizer added to every bushel and thoroughly mixed in. The amount of soil needed will be approximately a quarter of the total space that the wall will occupy.

The dry wall is usually made of natural stones, either sandstone or limestone, roughly rectangular, between 2 in. and 8 in. in thickness, and with a minimum width of 6 in. The less they are trimmed the more natural will the wall appear. The first thing to do is to prepare the soil face which will provide the backing for the wall. Where it will be $2\frac{1}{2}$ ft. or less high it can be vertical, but for higher walls a slope of 1 in 6 is advisable. The next thing is to ensure that there is a firm foundation for the wall, by taking out a trench about 6 in. deep and slightly wider than the stones which will form the base of the wall. There is no need to put in a concrete foundation, but the soil should be well rammed to give a solid base, but sloping slightly towards the back so that the stones are slightly tilted in that direction. On this sound footing place the first layer of stones, using the largest available, and keeping their upper surfaces at one horizontal level, making adjustments with the soil underneath to achieve this. If the stones are of moderate size, the vertical gaps between them should be about 3 in. wide, but with smaller stones, proportionately smaller gaps should be left. The horizontal gaps should be about 1 in. wide. These gaps should be firmly packed with the prepared soil and care must be taken to see that any crevices between the back of the wall and the vertical soil face are also filled in and firmed. Any air-pockets left there will not only weaken the wall structurally, but will cause rapid drying out of the plants' root systems.

Care must be taken in the planting, for while good solid 'joints' must be made, the plants obviously cannot be rammed too hard. With a little practice it is soon possible to achieve a happy mean which meets both needs. When the first layer

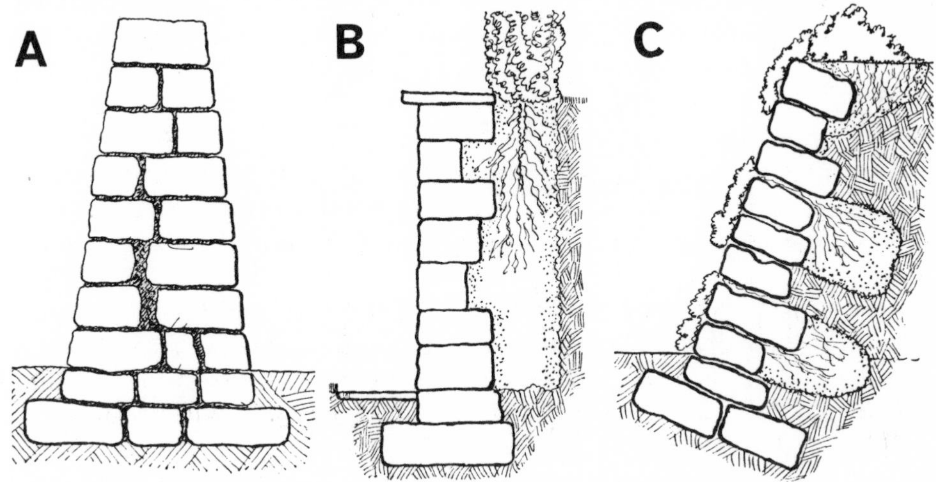

Fig. 14 Three types of construction for a dry wall.

or 'course' has been completed, succeeding courses should be added, but the stones should be bonded, so that any vertical crevice will be as near as possible to the centre of the stone below it. Unless this is done a wall will very quickly collapse. The top of the wall is best left flat, so that the rain may soak in, but a 6-in. layer of soil should be made firm on the top and in this, at intervals, large stones can be placed. These will help to keep the soil in place and will supply a moist root-run for plants like rock-roses and saxifrages which can be planted there. It is possible to plant the wall itself after it has been constructed, but generally it is not so satisfactory as planting as construction proceeds.

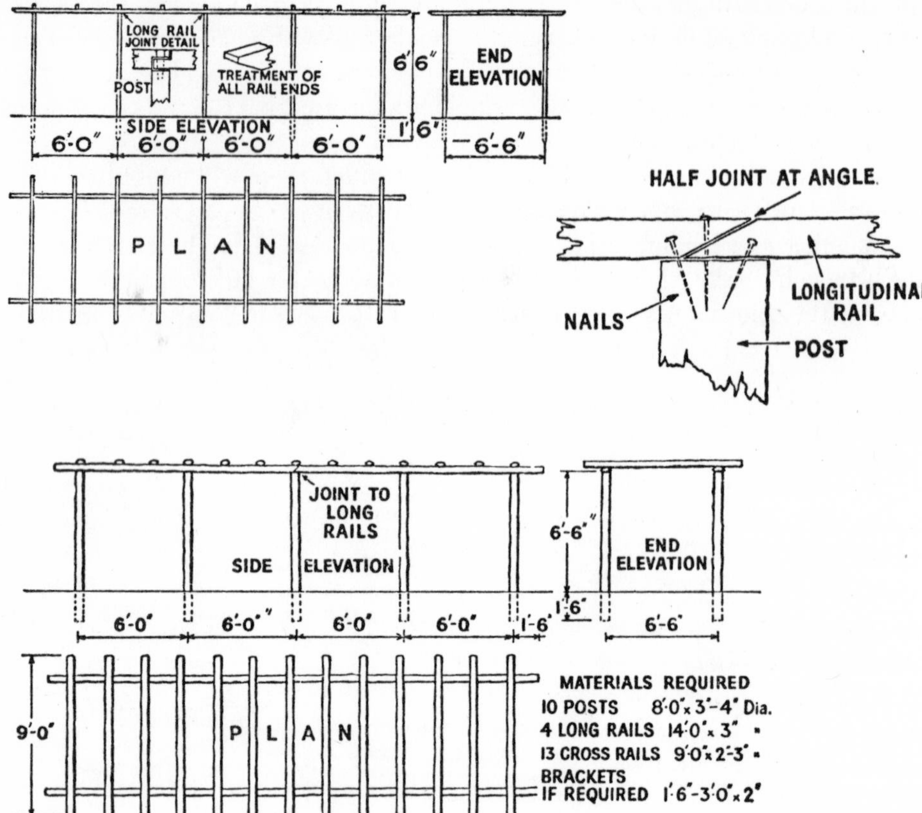

Fig. 15 Top, *constructional drawings of a pergola of sawn wood with details of the joint and rail ends.* Bottom, *constructional drawings of a pergola in unpeeled timber.* Top right, *detail showing how the joint at the top post should be made.*

Pergolas

Against a wall or on a fence plants develop with only one exposed face, but when trained on a pergola they will develop upon all sides and give horizontal as well as vertical growth. A pergola may be simple or elaborate, single or double, the double being usually placed over a path to give an arched view through which the plants are seen to good advantage, as well as providing an effect on the sides. Usual construction consists of main uprights upon which are supported the longitudinal rails and cross-rails to provide an open roof over which the climbing plants can be trained. There may be elaborations of this construction, with additional cross-rails fixed first to the post tops upon which the longitudinal rails rest; or additional longitudinal rails may be added, together with brackets on the length—and the width if high enough.

Alternatively, the pergola may be constructed as a roofed recess at the end of a garden, with the posts and roof timbers combined with a screen.

For good proportion the width of a pergola should be about equal to its height, although this may not be practicable where space is limited, as the height should be such that the growth trained on the roof will not interfere with access. Where space permits, a height of 8 ft. and a corresponding width is usual, but 6 ft. to 7 ft. height will support the climbers to give sufficient head room if fresh growths are regularly tied in. Should it not be desirable to make a path below the pergola to the full width, then side borders can be formed in which the main posts are placed, and these side borders would also accommodate the climbing plants and any other flowers.

A constructional plan of a pergola in unpeeled, unwrought timber, such as larch, is illustrated in Fig. 15.. A drawing of this kind should be prepared first to provide the information necessary for the purchase of the timber sizes and also for use during construction and erection. Larch poles are probably the most simple to erect and can be purchased in lengths ready for use. The poles should be as even in girth as possible although there will be some degree of taper in the length, but sharply tapering pieces do not look well. Pairs of posts should be erected opposite each other and for preference concrete should be placed at the bottom of the hole for a few inches and around the posts. These should be peeled for the portion to go below ground level and should be treated with a wood preservative to a minimum depth of 18 in. below ground. When the posts are set and firm, with all the tops level, the longitudinal rails are fitted. These rails should be obtained to provide a joint at every other post as shown and a half joint is made at an angle, the rails being nailed into the post tops (Fig. 15). Finally, the cross-rails are fitted and spaced at about 2 ft. apart evenly between the posts. The appearance is better if all rails overhang 12 in. to 18 in. and allowance should be made for this when ordering the lengths of poles.

The drawing (Fig. 15) shows the requirements for a pergola 24 ft. in length with a girth and height of 6 ft. 6 in. constructed in sawn timber, 2 in. or 3 in. square in section. Although of light construction it will last for many years, especially if the timber fixed below ground is first treated with wood preservative and the posts protected with concrete or bitumen.

The joints of the longitudinal rails should be arranged over the posts as shown and be a horizontal half joint. The cross-rails can be secured with a single nail either side of the long rails to keep them in position. The drawing shows the cross-rails placed 3 ft. apart, but with an additional rail to each bay this spacing could be reduced to 2 ft. The quantity mentioned on the drawing allows for the necessary lengths for an overhang to the rails, and these look best if finished with a shaped end. The timber can be left as it comes from the saw; it is not necessary to buy wood which has been finished with a plane.

Posts set in low walls of brick, and with additional longitudinal rails provide a more enclosed roof. In hot summers a charming effect is obtained by standing out pot plants on such walls. The timbering is usually of heavy section with this form of pergola, the posts, if in wood, being from 4 in. to 6 in. square, the longitudinal rails 3 in. thick and the same width as the posts, with cross-rails 2 in. to 3 in. thick. Combined brick and tile piers, with a lighter section of roof timbers spaced fairly close together, are also attractive.

The water garden

To be successful with a water garden, an adequate water supply must be assured, for aquatic plants will not survive being dried up for any length of time. While a stream gives the most natural setting for a water garden of the larger informal type, many streams dry up completely in a warm summer, and care must be taken that reliance is not placed on such a stream. Where only a small water capacity is involved, circulating it by means of a fractional h.p. electric pump is often cheaper than paying for replacement water, and the installation can usually be so arranged that, to all appearances, the supply is a constant one.

The best position for the water garden depends very largely on what form it takes. Where it consists solely of a formal pool, it is best to treat it as a main feature in its own right, and to place it in a conspicuous spot. It should not be under trees, as this not only detracts from its appeal as a centre-piece, but the water becomes fouled by the falling leaves, while water-lilies in the pool are deprived of much of the sunshine that they need. The tree-roots can also damage the structure of the pool. For the more informal pool, a low-lying piece of land should be chosen.

The formal pool. For most gardens the choice will be for the formal pool made of concrete, with or without a surround for the growing of marsh plants. Having the pool at ground level saves considerable expense, though it does make it more dangerous for young children, and precautions will have to be taken to prevent them falling in. To construct it the shape should be marked out on the ground, and the soil excavated to the required depth, from 18 in. to 3 ft. according to the size of the pool, plus the thickness of the concrete base. Where there is to be a surround

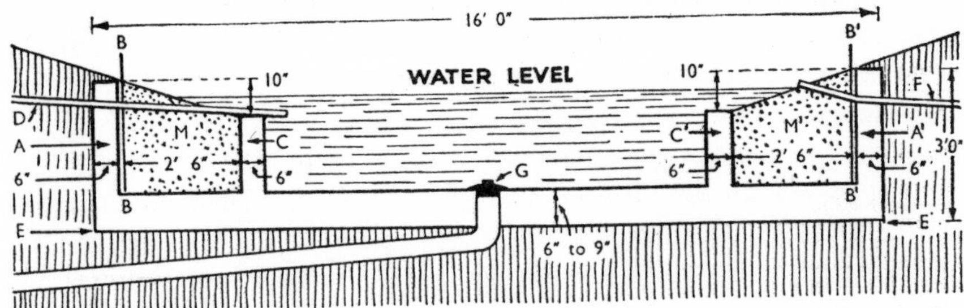

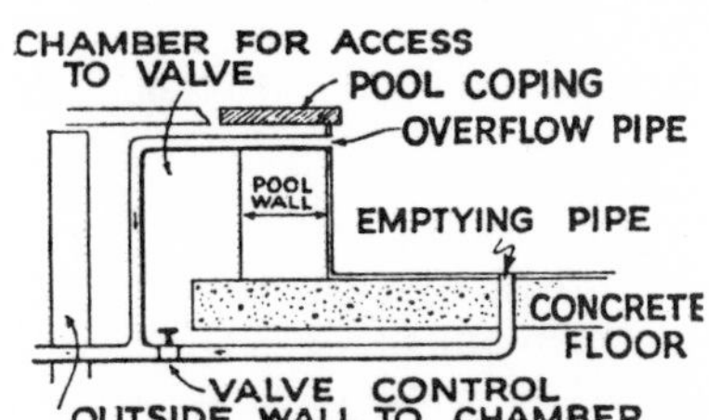

Fig. 16 Top, *cross-section drawing of a formal type water garden.*

Left, *a satisfactory system of controlled emptying pipe combined with an overflow. This system is quite cheap and easy to install.*

for an aquatic border (see Fig. 16) this should be included in the excavated areas, as this border will be inside the pool structure. When the excavation is complete, all loose soil must be shovelled out and the bottom made thoroughly firm. The weight of the concrete and the water is considerable, and if the base is not really firm there is a danger of the concrete cracking. Before any concreting is done, the pipes for supplying the water and for draining the pool must be put in position, and there should be an overflow pipe. The local plumber will give advice on this. The concrete should be made of 4 parts of aggregate not larger than $\frac{3}{4}$ in., 2 parts sand and 1 part cement. A 6-in. layer of this concrete should be placed over the bottom of the excavated area and should be 'worked' with a shovel to ensure that no air-spaces or 'voids' are left in it, after which it should be firmed and levelled, but not made too smooth or the cement lining which is to be applied later, will not grip. Next erect a layer of temporary boards 4 in. from the vertical sides, so that with the soil it forms a mould into which the concrete to form the sides A and A′ will be poured. If possible this side concrete should be put in position while the base concrete is still wet and unset, as the two will then bind together and there will be no joint in the construction. To achieve this the boarding should be prefabricated, so that it can be dropped into position without delay. When the concrete has well set, the pool should be made completely watertight by lining it with a cement, consisting of 1 part of cement to 3 of sand, plus a waterproofing material in the recommended proportion. This should be applied from ½ to 1 in. thick, and is best put on in 2 coats, giving the second coat while the first is still fresh but firm. Care should be taken to see that the corners EE are completely watertight. Where a surround for plants is to be included, the inner walls C and C′ can be constructed after the concrete has set. They should be from 12 in. to 30 in. from the edge of the pool proper, in proportion to its size, and from 8 in. to 10 in. lower than the sides. Apertures must be left in the bottom of the wall to allow for the passage of water, when the pool is emptied. When the concrete is thoroughly dry, the spaces M and M′ between the retaining walls A and C and A′ and C′ are filled with a compost of loam and peat, or loam and leaf-mould. The soil may then be banked up so that the tops of the walls A and A′ are covered with soil and hidden from sight.

The informal pool. For larger and less formal gardens, a pool to match these conditions will be needed. Its actual shape will of course depend on the contours of the land, and of the general landscaping of the area in which it is to be situated. Its design should in all cases be simple. Curves and water are complementary and the beauty of one is appreciably lessened by the absence of the other, but the curves must be sweeping and graceful and they must flow as naturally as does the water which they bound. And the softness and serenity of the scene is much enhanced if grass grows down the sloping banks to the water's edge, and further interest is added to the scene if marsh-loving plants are planted along limited stretches of the banks. These larger pools or ponds are seldom concreted as the thickness needed to ensure freedom from cracking over the comparatively large area would make the cost prohibitive. The most practicable method for these pools is 'puddling', but this needs a 9-in. layer of clay which must either be present as sub-soil, or must be easily available from elsewhere. This puddling consists of pummelling the moist clay with a rammer, until it takes on the consistency of dough and is impermeable to water, after which it must not be allowed to become at all dry, or serious cracking will take place.

Plastic pools. Prefabricated pools of various shapes are now available and are perfectly satisfactory for use on a small scale. The soil should be excavated to make a good fit, particularly along the bottom so that there are no spaces where, in time, stretching may occur. For more informal pools plastic sheeting may be used and here again the excavation must be neatly finished off so that the sheeting will lie closely along the bottom and the sides which should be gently sloping. In both cases the edges of the pools may be concealed with rocks or paving which, with a sheeted pool, must be heavy enough to hold the edges in position.

The bog or marsh garden

A pond is not an essential part of the bog garden, although if there is one its overflow can be used to feed the marsh. What is important, however, is that the soil of the marsh garden be kept in a moist, swampy state throughout the whole year. The site of the bog garden must be low-lying and where the surface drainage will collect naturally. If the sub-soil is of sticky clay, a mere trickle of water will keep the ground in a sufficiently moist condition. Should the sub-soil be light and well drained, a certain amount of excavation will be necessary before the bog garden can be made.

Dig out about 2 ft. of the top soil and introduce a little clay to form a basis, over this spread a 5-in. bed of rubble or large stones, and then a layer of coarse soil. Now fill the hollow, almost to the level of the surrounding land, with a compost of half loam and half leaf-mould or peat. Unless a natural flow of water is available, an artificial trickle, just sufficient to keep the bog swampy, must be introduced. Because bog plants should never suffer from drought, the marsh garden should be kept quite moist, but on the other hand must not become stagnant, and it is for this reason that slight bottom drainage is introduced. The bog should never be more than 2 ft. in depth; its extent, of course, will depend on the space available and upon individual need.

Paths of rough stones or bricks should be made through the bog, and over these should be placed flat stepping-stones, so that one can get to every part of the bog. If these paths are made at varying heights, they may be used to divide the bog into shelving beds, the higher and better-drained of which will accommodate plants not requiring overmuch moisture, while in the lower-lying sites can be grown the real moisture-lovers.

Almost any moisture-loving plant may be grown, as can all the subjects that are usually to be found at the margins of streams and ponds, even some of those which at times have 6 in. or more of water over their crowns. All plants growing freely in shallow water may also be grown in the bog garden. Be careful not to over-crowd plants, rather group together three to five plants of the same kind, leave a space, and again plant a clump of subjects of different colour, type and height. This irregularity and variety will please the eye, which would otherwise tend to become overdone by a mass of the same colour, size and form.

The actual marsh plants selected will, of course, depend upon the layout and size of the garden; the natural surroundings must also be very carefully considered. If the area is restricted, greater variety and beauty can be obtained by the use of dwarf-growing species, while among extensive surroundings full rein may be given to the freer-growing plants, many of which are invaluable as a background where space permits. It is always necessary, however, to bear in mind the size to which the plants will grow in from 2 to 3 years, and to arrange them accordingly. The most usual fault is overcrowding, and it is wise to avoid this at any cost. Also, study the plants in their native haunts, and then, when planting them, endeavour to give them as natural a site as possible.

The rock garden

A well-made and well-managed rock garden can provide a deep interest in a small space and its main purpose is to grow certain plants that require conditions different from those provided by the usual kind of garden bed or border. These plants should be called rock-garden plants rather than alpines because the true alpines are mountain plants growing between the snow-line and the conifer-line where they enjoy conditions of soil, sun, light, moisture and temperature that cannot possibly be reproduced in the British climate with its winter damp and low sunshine. Many true alpines have stems, leaves or roots that are specially designed for their native surroundings and they cannot adapt themselves, even in an alpine house, to moist and temperate conditions. This means that a large number, including most of the choicest, must be ruled out. But there are plenty of others that are more adaptable or come from the lower mountain regions and if some of the more usual garden plants such as bulbs, dwarf shrubs or even annuals are added, the rock garden can be made into a special feature with a long flowering period.

The aim should be to imitate as many of the mountain conditions as possible. The first essentials are a good free-draining soil, preferably a light to medium loam, and an open position in full sun, free from shade and the drip of overhanging trees. If there is any doubt about the drainage it must be attended to, and if the soil is on the heavy side, a generous quantity of manure, compost and broken stone or coarse grit must be added.

The site chosen should blend in with the general garden design yet make a special feature of its own, with the rocks appearing as natural outcrops on the land. The ideal is to incorporate a stream trickling down to a pool, but where this cannot be done, a grass frontage makes a good second best. A scale plan is essential. It should show where the miniature ranges and accompanying valleys are to run and where there are to be steps or paths. Steps should be made to look as though they have been worn out of the rock and paths should wind and slope in a natural way. To reduce labour in excavating or adding soil, the peaks and the troughs should be planned on a 'cut and fill' basis, and all features should be clearly marked on the site before setting any rocks in position.

The most suitable stone to use is the kind that occurs in the district unless it is so porous that it breaks up in frost or is so hard as to be impermeable, like granite. Limestone is the general favourite because it has a natural weather-worn appearance and retains a certain amount of moisture. Individual pieces should be two or more feet in length and a few key pieces should be as large as can be handled. Without going to the expense of hiring lifting tackle it is surprising what can be moved with the aid of two stout crow-bars. Each piece should be set firmly in the soil with no air pockets underneath or around the sides, and must be buried sufficiently to slope backwards yet show its best face as near perpendicular as possible. All should slope in the same general direction. The spaces and crevices between individual rocks should be of ample size in order to give plenty of root space for the plants, which will soon cover them over, and to allow the filling in of special composts of peat, sand or chippings suitable for particular kinds of plants.

Planting is generally best done in the spring but pot plants may be planted at any time up to late autumn. Firm planting is essential and any necessary watering should be given by running the water over the rock into the soil in the same way as the rain naturally runs in. One or two dwarf evergreens should be added as key plants together with a few Japanese azaleas or other dwarf flowering shrubs. Here and there bulbs such as crocuses, scillas or dwarf narcissi should be included. After-care consists mainly of weeding, trimming back all straggling growths that have flowered and protecting the more delicate plants from excessive wet in winter.

CHAPTER EIGHT

Greenhouses and Frames

WITH the help of glass the range of plants grown in a garden can be considerably extended. Even a cold frame makes a noticeable difference; seeds of flowers and vegetables may be sown earlier and the seedlings brought on quicker, cuttings of many kinds may be rooted successfully, and appreciable winter protection given to plants that are not quite hardy or to others such as hardy bulbs that need early root growth if they are to flower ahead of their normal season. A cold greenhouse extends the range much farther, from early-flowering plants to alpines or tomatoes and autumn chrysanthemums, makes propagation of many half-hardy plants easier and quicker, and allows certain others to be kept safely through all but the most severe winters. But the addition of heat opens an entirely new field: flowers through the winter, forced flowers in the spring, 'luxury' fruits and vegetables and a vast selection of warmth-loving or even tropical plants, shrubs and climbers.

But there are limits in most gardens and unless they are recognized at the beginning disappointments will follow. The days when every sizeable garden had more than one greenhouse and often a range of several are gone. Few can afford to run a 'stove' house for tropical plants at 70 deg. F. in winter and an 'intermediate' or warm house at 50–60 deg. F. as well as one or more general or 'cool' houses at 40–50 deg. F. Most people have to be content with one, which, under proper management, will accommodate a surprising range of plants, particularly now that it has been proved that many of the so-called stove plants will grow successfully at cool-house temperatures. And unless it is decided to specialize in one particular kind or group of plants when the house must obviously be designed, managed and heated accordingly, the best plan is to aim at a general purpose house which, however, may be partitioned to give two different temperatures and growing conditions. But in all cases there are a number of limiting factors which have to be carefully considered, particularly the site, space, heating, cost, choice of plants and time available.

Position

The greenhouse must be placed in an open position where it will get the most sun and be free from shade or long shadows cast by near-by buildings or tall trees. Some protection on the north side will be beneficial and it may be necessary to guard against strong cold wind currents that may be channelled round a building, such as for example a garage. The house may run north to south in order to provide equal distribution of the mid-day light and sun and reduce glare, or east to west in order to catch the low sun during winter when the plants, particularly early-season plants, will need all the light they can get. It should never be built close to a boundary fence because there is always the chance of trees growing up in the adjoining garden, nor close to a road or footpath because of the damage that is likely. It should be near the house to provide for easy attention and the supply of water and electricity. The size of the greenhouse will depend upon the space available and the kinds of plants that are to be grown in it, but since most kinds of modern houses are made in units of fixed widths and variable length, it may not be possible to decide the precise size until the type of construction has been selected.

Types of houses

There are many different kinds of greenhouses to choose from and most of them can be seen at the larger horticultural shows, where manufacturers are always pleased to discuss the types most suited to particular requirements. Apart from the general soundness of construction all houses should give the maximum of light, with large panes of glass and few but sufficient tie-bars, brackets or gussets in the roof so as to reduce the amount of top-shadow. Doors should be wide enough to take a barrow and should preferably open outwards, ventilation in the roof and the sides should be ample and the fixing of staging, heating equipment and training wires should be easy and well provided for by stout construction, or in metal and concrete houses by conveniently placed slots or holes. Maintenance should be easy; painting is generally straightforward but in some metal and concrete houses the replacement of broken panes is not always a simple matter.

There are two main forms of design, the span roof and the lean-to. Either kind may be built on a low wall of brick or wood or be glazed to ground level. Those with a wall are mainly used for growing plants, particularly flowering plants on staging, and those with glass to the ground are more suitable for plants grown in the soil, such as carnations, tomatoes and chrysanthemums. Some designs combine both features, with a wall on one side but not on the other. A convenient width is 9–10 ft. which gives room for a centre path with a 3–4 ft. wide bed or staging on either side. If a centre staging is also desired, making what is often called a 'show house', the width must be at least 16 ft. The most convenient height for working is one that gives not less than 5 ft. at the eaves and not less than 7 ft. at the ridge or the approximate equivalents in the case of the various types of dome-shaped construction.

Lean-to houses are now comparatively rare in gardens because they require a wall to form the tall side. They are particularly suitable for climbing plants, grapes or peaches, are cheaper to build and heat, but are not so good for the general run of flowering plants because it is difficult to reduce peak-summer temperatures if the wall faces south, or to get sufficient light if the wall faces other directions when the choice of plants may have to be restricted to ferns or other shade-loving plants.

Houses may be made of wood, aluminium, steel or concrete. Wood requires regular maintenance and, except when certain hardwoods or Western red cedar are used, regular painting, but it is easy to repair and to add any supports or brackets to suit individual requirements. Aluminium or alloy requires little maintenance and no painting, and offers the least obstruction to light, but the first cost is comparatively high. Steel is generally cheaper and if rust-proofed requires no painting. Concrete needs no maintenance but in many makes the members are substantial with the result that some light is excluded. All are available in prefabricated units for easy erection on the site.

Heating

Whatever form of heating is installed, it must be adequate for the job and for the most severe weather. Hot water is probably still the best since it provides an even warmth without drying the atmosphere. Solid fuel is economical but involves daily attention to stoking and raking morning and evening. Oil-fired boilers are cleaner, more efficient and labour saving but are more costly to install and run and are economic only in large houses. Oil heaters are suitable for small houses, particularly where high temperatures are not required, and provided they are kept clean and given proper attention daily there is little risk of danger from the fumes. Some makes are provided with an external flue. Electricity is the cleanest and easiest form of heating and can be used also for automatic ventilation and watering, but it is costly to run and must therefore be combined with thermostatic control. Initially it may involve additional expense in installation if the greenhouse is some distance from the nearest supply.

The size and positioning of water pipes, the capacity of oil heaters and the number and type of electric heaters, whether tubular, strip or convector, will be determined by the size of the house and the types of plants to be grown and all these points should be discussed with the manufacturers before the final order.

Fittings

Staging may be made of 1-in. wooden slats which allow air to circulate freely around the pots or provide a base for sheets of asbestos or corrugated iron on which shingle or gravel can be spread to keep the base of the pots moist. Shelves may also be used provided they do not obstruct the light and can be reached easily. Training and roof wires will also be needed if climbing plants or tomatoes are to be grown and for most decorative plants some form of shading must be provided. Roller or cane blinds are best because they can be quickly adjusted as required, and are therefore better than a colour wash but they require more attention. If a number of cuttings require a close atmosphere, a propagating frame will be essential.

Propagating frames range from a box with a sheet of glass put on top to the automatically controlled mist-propagating units. For most gardens something between the two is adequate, for while seeds and cuttings of most of the commonly-grown greenhouse or tender plants can be raised in pots, pans or boxes on the staging, there are generally some that require special treatment, particularly the addition of bottom heat. A suitable frame may be in the form of a box with a gauze or small-mesh base made to fit over an area of the hot-water pipes or it may be a portable electric propagator, or a bed made up on the staging and laid over soil-heating cables. The rooting medium should be a compost of peat and sand or vermiculite and after inserting the cuttings the frame should be closed or covered with glass. It must be kept moist until rooting takes place when the individual plants can be potted up in the usual way.

Potting-shed

The potting-shed of tradition which was usually heated and adjacent to the greenhouse is a comparatively rare luxury today, yet it is still necessary to have somewhere to keep the tools of the trade and carry out the work. Part of the tool shed may be made to serve, particularly if it has a window and a good stout bench can be built there, but such an arrangement entails a good deal of carrying backwards and forwards to the greenhouse and in the process tender plants may be harmed by exposure to the cold air. Alternatively a corner of the greenhouse may be used but this takes up valuable space. Generally a compromise is best, with the main stock of pots, canes, crocks and composts being kept in the tool shed where big potting jobs can be undertaken, and a smaller stock kept in the greenhouse where with the aid of a portable bench, the little jobs can be carried out conveniently and comfortably. In any case the essential is to arrange for all the materials to be conveniently at hand in both places. Composts should be stored in bins or lidded boxes so that they do not become contaminated with bits of dead leaves or rubbish that may be carrying disease, and the washing and sterilizing of pots, seed-boxes, etc., should always be done in the open or the shed, never in the greenhouse.

The old types of clay pots are steadily being replaced by porous and non-porous plastic pots which are far lighter and do not break so easily. The large sizes of clay pots are still preferable for large plants, particularly those that may be called permanent since they do not need annual re-potting. But whichever kind is used there is no need to stock every size available. For most purposes those with an internal top diameter of 3 or 3½ in., 5 in., 7 in. and 9 or 10 in. will serve, but for alpines and cacti a smaller size, 2 or 2½ in., will be required. Pots made of fibre are suitable only for plants being raised in the greenhouse for planting out later on. Seed pans and seed boxes will also be needed, and these too may now be obtained in plastic. The boxes should be of uniform size 14 in. by 8½ in., and 2–2½ in. deep. In addition a number of small items are essential: labels, dibbers, potting sticks, blocks of wood for pressing soil evenly in pans and boxes, a large and a small short-spouted can, a syringe, trowel, etc.

Composts

Research at the John Innes Horticultural Institution has taken much of the labour and all the old mystique out of making composts. Except for a few specialist plants such as orchids, the general run of greenhouse plants will thrive in the standardized and sterilized 'J.I. Composts' which can now be bought at most horticultural shops. The enthusiast who wishes to mix his own should follow the J.I. formulae:

Seed Compost 'J.I.S.'

2 parts (by volume) sterilized loam (through ⅜-in. sieve)
1 ,, peat
1 ,, coarse sand
with 1½ oz. superphosphate of lime and ¾ oz. chalk to every bushel.

Potting Compost 'J.I.P$_1$'

7 parts sterilized loam (through ⅜-in. sieve)
3 ,, peat
2 ,, coarse sand
with 4 oz. 'J.I. Base' and ¾ oz. chalk to every bushel.

J.I. Base

2 parts (by weight) hoof and horn ($\frac{1}{8}$ in.)
2 „ „ „ superphosphate of lime
1 „ „ „ sulphate of potash

J.I.P_2 and J.I.P_3 are similar but, having double and treble the amount of base, are for older and stronger-growing plants particularly when re-potting.

A J.I. Acid compost is also available. It is lime-free and made especially for lime-hating plants such as rhododendrons.

Soil-less composts, often called U.C. composts since they were formulated at the University of California, are also available, and for striking cuttings it is common to use Vermiculite or a straight compost of half peat and half coarse sand.

Management

For a single house the first essential is to grow only compatible plants. It is quite impossible to manage a house containing, say, cucumbers that require a hot moist atmosphere and carnations that require far drier and cooler conditions. If it is desired to grow such plants then there must be two houses or one house must be permanently and satisfactorily divided. Generally, however, the desire is to grow early flowers and winter flowers, giving full space to a number of summer-flowering plants or perhaps filling up with tomatoes, or the main interest may be in all-the-year-round decoratives, including indoor plants with only a small space for early-flowering kinds. With all these the choice is large and continues to increase as plant-breeders raise new and more suitable varieties, so that it becomes yearly more easy to grow a wide range of compatible plants.

The two main problems, particularly for the gardener who is away from home throughout the day, are watering and ventilation. There are no precise rules because different kinds of plants and even individual plants vary in their need, and in a changeable climate requirements inevitably change widely from day to day, or even during the day. The only general advice that can be given is never to over-water and never under-ventilate. During the winter plants need very little water, but during warm bright weather or when in full growth, daily watering is essential and it should be done thoroughly. Then if the weather turns cold and dull the plant will have a sufficient supply to see it through and will not need any more until the second or third day after. Watering lightly is bad practice and is misleading because it makes the surface look moist when the lower part of the pot where the roots are may be dangerously dry. Some guidance is given by feeling the weight of the pot or by tapping a clay pot, but tapping is no use on plastic pots. The best time for watering is the morning, particularly in the winter when it is important to keep the night moisture down as low as possible. In the summer a second watering at mid-day may be needed and on hot days over-head syringing and damping down of the paths and staging will be necessary to reduce temperatures and add moisture to the atmosphere. Tap water is generally suitable; the old custom of having tanks and tubs inside the house is unnecessary and at times objectionable.

Ventilation aims at providing fresh air, allowing excess humidity to be driven off and maintaining a constant temperature. Except on foggy days some ventilation to change the air should always be given even if it is no more than the proverbial crack and for a few minutes only. But generally, from early spring to early winter, the lee-side ventilators should be opened every morning, the amount depending on the weather outside. In the winter they should be closed in the early afternoon and in summer in the early evening. On hot summer nights some ventilation should be given all the time and on hot days the door as well as the ventilators should be opened wide. But full opening should be done by stages; if it is done suddenly the more tender plants may be severely chilled. For those who can afford the cost of installation, automatic ventilation and overhead irrigation systems are available.

For the control of pests and diseases see Chapter 18.

The alpine house

Many attractive alpines cannot be cultivated to the best advantage in the open, not because they require warm conditions, but because their blooms are apt to be spoilt by bad weather. If protection is given while they are in bloom it will also prolong their season of flowering. Most of the plants can be brought on during the summer in pans sunk to their rims in ashes in the open, or in cold uncovered frames, until they are about to flower, when they should be transferred to the alpine house, to be removed again to the open after flowering. The choicest, such as some of the saxifrages, however, are usually kept in the house the whole year through, as their neat and compact foliage is pleasing and interesting even after the flowers are over, and does not get ragged and untidy.

The plants, excepting bulbs, which should be replanted each year, require little attention, and only need re-potting every second or third year; this is generally best carried out in July or the early part of Aug.

The best design for an alpine house is the span-roof type, 10–12 ft. wide, about 6 ft. to the eaves and 9 ft. to the ridge. It should run north to south and have a centre path and a wooden-slatted staging down the sides, about 3 ft. from the floor and not more than 4 ft. wide, so that the plants will then be easily accessible. The stagings should be covered with a ½-in. layer of shingle, ashes, small breeze or coke. Heating is not essential, but it is valuable to have means of drying the air on damp or foggy days and for this electricity is the most convenient.

Ample provision must be made for ventilation, both in the sides and the roof of the house, for the plants require a fresh, cool atmosphere and plenty of air, but no cold draughts. Upon this much of the success of the alpine house depends, and it is particularly important to avoid the high temperatures that may build up in a poorly-ventilated house when the sun shines.

Some means of shading will be required. No definite dates or hours when shading should be commenced can be given, as everything depends on the prevailing weather, but some shading may be needed from about the end of Apr., as soon as the direct rays of the sun fall on the house. If constant attention can be given, roller blinds are the best, as the amount of light can be better regulated, and the blinds may be left up on dull and sunless days. Where blinds are not possible, however, and the alpine house must of necessity be left to look after itself for a good part of the day, the simplest, and the most satisfactory, method is to wash the glass over with a proprietary shading or a mixture of flour and water, which is easily washed off when necessary. Shading is rarely necessary after the end of Sept.

Most alpines thrive in gritty, well-drained soil. Two-thirds fibrous loam and peat with one-third coarse, gritty sand makes an excellent compost for most of them. Many of the finer saxifrages like also a little splintered limestone or some old lime-rubble, similar to that used in carnation culture.

Alpines require ample water during their growing period and while in bloom, but care must be taken to see that the drainage is adequate, for a stale, stagnant soil is the alpine's greatest enemy. Plants will need most water in the spring and summer, generally once a day but sometimes twice. Dormant plants and those freshly potted are best kept rather dry until growth begins. A watering once a week, or even less frequently, will suffice for most plants in winter time, but the soil must be prevented from becoming dust-dry. In the summer the watering should be done when the sun's heat is at its lowest, early in the morning or in the early evening, but in spring, late autumn and in winter it is essential to water in the morning, so that excessive moisture may have drained off before the evening, otherwise there is great liability to 'damping-off'. The more tender alpines should be stood in a shallow tray with 1–2 in. of water in the bottom, so that the water may be drawn up without damping the foliage; this is especially necessary in the case of those plants with dense, downy or waxy foliage which nestles close to the soil.

Plants should never be allowed to become so dry as to droop, for this may cause severe damage, but if it occurs the whole plant, pan as well, should be stood in water deep enough to reach the top of the pan. When thoroughly soaked, it should not at once be replaced on the staging, but should be put in the shade for an hour or two to drain. Many plants, especially those that have not recently been re-potted, will be the better for a watering with liquid manure every 10 days while the buds are forming. This must be discontinued as soon as the flowers are out.

Cleanliness inside the house is most essential. Aphids, thrips, red spiders, mealy bugs, scale insects and woodlice are the chief pests, and damping off and certain kinds of mould the principal diseases. (See Chapter 18, Diseases and Pests.)

Frames

Frames can be used cold or heated, the heat being supplied by fermenting manure when the frame is more properly called a hot-bed, or hot water, or electricity can be used. Cold frames are chiefly protective, for although they can also obtain considerable heat from the sun, unlike hot-beds they cannot maintain a high temperature throughout the night. Both kinds may be permanent with walls made of brick or concrete, or movable with walls of 1-in. wood, light metal, interlocking blocks of concrete or banked-up soil. They can be set up singly or in a row of 2, 3 or 4 built as one unit, or may be attached to the side of a greenhouse. They are covered with a 'light' which should have a slope of from 4 to 9 in. from head to foot and face south. The light consists of a wooden or metal surround with several panes of glass set in rows as in the English or French light or with only one sheet of glass as in the Dutch light. Various sizes are obtainable, the English and French types being mostly about 4 ft. wide and from 4 ft. to 6 ft. (occasionally 7 ft.) long. Some of these are fairly heavy to move about but their main disadvantage is that dirt and condensation often collect where the panes overlap each other. On the other hand they are easy and quick to repair in case of breakage. The Dutch light is easier to handle, remains cleaner and suffers less from condensation, but is expensive to repair since the whole sheet has to be renewed in the event of breakage. Here again the size may vary, but most makes conform to a British Standard which specifies overall dimensions of 4 ft. 11 in. by 2 ft. 6¾ in. In recent years manufacturers have shown great ingenuity in designing all sorts of adaptations of the English and Dutch types, some of them resembling miniature greenhouses, and the gardener now has a very wide choice and would be well advised to visit one of the horticultural shows to see all the different kinds before making his final decision. In addition to the frames themselves certain accessories are required; wooden blocks for inserting between the lights and the frames to give ventilation, wire or cord loops to prevent the lights being lifted or blown away by strong winds and straw or reed mats for covering on very cold nights. (Heavy sacking may also be used but it should be laid on canes or laths placed across the light so as to form a space that will act as an insulator.) The ventilating block should be a piece of wood from 6 to 8 in. long, 2 to 3 in. wide and 1 in. thick. This enables a small, medium or large amount of ventilation to be given according to the way in which the block is inserted. All woodwork should be painted regularly with two coats of paint or treated with a preservative guaranteed to be harmless to plant life. Creosote for example must not be used.

Management is not difficult, but there are times in the season when daily attention, morning and evening, becomes essential. It may be for only a few minutes, perhaps five at the most, but these few can determine success or failure. Before deciding to go in for frame cultivation, the gardener must therefore be sure that he will be able to find this time when necessary.

Hot-beds

Heated frames are used mainly for striking cuttings, and for growing seedlings and early vegetables. Those heated by water or electricity are more convenient and provide for better regulation of temperature, but the traditional hot-bed scores by preserving moisture in the atmosphere and the soil. Hot-beds should be made up in Feb. or early Mar., with good quality fresh farmyard manure. Stable manure is best but whatever kind is used it should first be mixed with an equal volume of compost, peat or leaf-mould for the purpose of reducing the first fierce heat of the manure and making a steadier heat last longer. The beds should be 18 in. to 2 ft. larger all round than the size of the frame and the manure well trodden down to give a final depth of 2 ft. The bed is generally made on the surface but on light, well-drained soils it may be partly or wholly sunk in a pit. When complete, the light is put on and a thermometer put inside. The first rank steam must be allowed to pass off until the temperature steadies at around 70 deg. when a layer of 4–6 in. of well-sifted soil should be placed over the manure leaving 12–15 in. between the soil and the glass at the head of the frame and 8–9 in. at the foot. Such a bed will last for 2 or 3 months but the temperature will of course gradually decline. If this happens too quickly, or more heat is required for any purpose, fresh manure can be stacked around the outside of the frame.

With a hot-bed a wide range of early out-of-season vegetables can be obtained, and with experience, many ingenious cropping plans can be devised. But it is most important to choose varieties that have been specially raised for forcing, since many that grow well in the open will not tolerate hot-bed conditions. If the light is covered to make the interior dark, rhubarb, seakale or chicory can be forced from roots lifted in Nov. and put in the bed at intervals to ensure successional production. No watering will generally be needed for the first month or so, but as growth becomes quicker the soil must be kept moist though never over-watered. Ventilation is essential and must be given during daytime in all but the severest weather, increasing the amount weekly until, in Apr. or on those occasional hot days which come in Mar., the light can be removed altogether. Ventilation should never be given by sliding the light down, because this creates a draught which may have disastrous effects.

By the end of May the frame will be empty and no heat will be coming from the manure. The bed should then be forked over, well watered and planted up with other vegetables such as self-blanching celery or summer lettuce, or with seedling flowers, rooted cuttings, etc. No covering light is needed.

Cold frames

Cold frames are used and managed in very much the same way as hot-beds, but the time of production will of course be later, although still in advance of ordinary outdoor culture. The few crops which require a minimum temperature cannot be grown with success. Cropping may follow the plan advocated for a hot-bed, but here again the choice of variety is important. Many other crops can also be grown to be ready up to 4 weeks before the normal time for outdoor crops and the frame can also be used for raising seedlings of flowers, for hardening off half-hardy bedding plants, for 'resting' certain greenhouse plants or growing them on through the summer before bringing them back under glass in the early autumn.

Cloches

Many types are available, from the simple two-piece 'tent' to larger and taller ones resembling frames or miniature greenhouses and often classed as frames. They are useful for bringing along early seedlings, flowering bulbs, certain vegetables, particularly salads, for ripening strawberries, melons or tomatoes and also for covering rock plants that dislike excessive wet in the winter or for protecting doubtfully hardy plants. As a rule neither rows of plants nor individuals need any watering while covered by the cloches because sufficient rain runs into the soil along the sides. If weeding is necessary the cloche at one end of the row should be taken up and carried to the other end, so that the others can be moved along a space, one at a time. When not in use cloches should be stacked on end on a perfectly level floor or piece of ground and fitted into each other. A strong cord or rope should then be tied round the stack.

CHAPTER NINE

The Culture of Bulbs and Corms

FROM the practical gardener's point of view there is little to distinguish between a corm and a bulb, and both will be dealt with in this chapter. Such differences as exist are mainly botanical or structural, but a brief explanation of these differences will be useful.

A true bulb consists of a mass of scales or scale-leaf structures, developed on a much shortened and flattened axis which forms the base of the bulb. Where a bulb is formed of a series of scales in a close mass, such as the tulip, hyacinth or daffodil, it is said to be 'tunicated' whereas the lily bulb with its separate fleshy scales is termed 'imbricate'.

The most important thing which concerns the grower is the method of propagation. In the case of the tunicated bulb this takes place naturally by means of a lateral bud growing out from the flattened base to form a small bulb, whereas in the case of the lily, propagation is effected by placing the bulb leaf-scales singly in small pots or boxes of sandy soil.

The corm is much more solid than the bulb, and in the case of the crocus and gladiolus it is the swollen base of the stem or axis which is terminated by a bud. Each season this bud grows upward to a flowering stem, the new corm being annually formed at the base of the stem and on top of the old one. Both bulbs and corms serve the same purpose. They are subterranean storehouses of reserve food material which has been accumulated for use during the next flowering period. Old bulb scales shrivel and give their substance to younger parts, likewise the old corm dies as the new corm develops and may generally be found as a hardened, shrivelled mass at the base of the new corm. Distinct from the two forms mentioned are those, such as cyclamen, gloxinia and begonia, which, instead of producing new corms in the manner described, yearly grow in size until they become hardened and worthless. In fact, cyclamen is best raised annually from seed.

Outdoor culture

The growing of bulbs in the garden presents no great difficulty and provided drainage is satisfactory they will thrive in almost any type of soil. For annual planting in beds or borders, it is advisable that heavy soils should be lightened by the addition of such opening material as leaf mould or coarse sand around the bulbs at planting time. With some bulbs, notably choice liliums, it is a good plan to provide a layer of sand at the base of the hole on which to rest the bulb, and it must be emphasized that of all the bulbs grown outside, the liliums have distinct soil preferences; their culture is dealt with below.

For most bulbs autumn is the main planting season and the earlier they are planted the better. They can then make root and become established before the winter—and will certainly flower better in the spring. As a general rule bulbs should be planted at about twice their own depth and as uniformly as possible. Care should be taken to make sure that the base of the bulb rests firmly on the bottom of the hole and for this reason a dibber, if used, should be blunt-ended, such as the unsharpened, sawn off fork or spade handle. In most cases, however, a trowel will be found the most convenient tool for planting in prepared soil.

For a spring display in beds or borders hyacinths and tulips are the most popular. Narcissi too are used to a reasonable extent, but they are best suited to large borders. By careful selection of varieties narcissi may be had in flower from early Mar. to May, and tulips, which commence flowering a little later, will carry on the display until late May. For a striking massed effect in large beds or borders, there is no doubt that pride of place must be given to the tulip. Those to open first are the early-flowering single varieties which are of an average height of from 10 to 15 in. The early flowering doubles follow them closely and are of rather shorter growth. In succession come the best of all bedding tulips, the 'Triumph' or early-flowering Darwins, having an almost uniform height range of 18 to 22 in. and, to finish the season, the late Darwins and Cottage varieties growing up to 28–30 in. high. There is a wide colour range in all sections.

Although much less grown than formerly, the Parrot tulips must not be omitted. They bloom in early May and are distinct from all other types with their curiously curled and twisted petals, their chief failing being a weakness of the stem which, despite prolonged efforts, breeders have so far been unable to overcome. When making a selection attention should be paid to this point. A comparatively new section is that known as 'lily flowered'. This group is becoming increasingly popular, new varieties being frequently introduced. Their average height ranges from 18 to 25 in. and there is a good selection of colours available.

Three varieties specially recommended are 'Mariette', pink, very large, 'Maytime', dark red-violet, and 'Philemon', sulphur-yellow, of perfect shape.

Hyacinths are recommended for formal planting in small beds. One of the chief objections to their wider use is the fact that they often become top-heavy and require staking to keep them erect, but on a small scale their deep intense colours and pastel shades make them well worth the trouble. As something of an insurance against 'toppling' the varieties with the heaviest spikes should be avoided for bedding purposes. When preparing the beds for planting, give a dressing of bone meal at about 6 oz. per sq. yd. and firm the soil sufficiently to provide a good hold for the bulbs which should be planted to a minimum depth of 3 in. The best effect from bulbs grown in beds is undoubtedly obtained by keeping to one colour. This not only creates a more harmonious picture, but also ensures an even blooming period and uniform height. As a backdrop for bulbs, *myosotis*, *aubrieta*, *arabis* and *polyanthus* may be used.

The planting of bulbs in borders should be done as informally as possible, arranging them in irregular groups. The size of the groups will depend on the length and width of the border. For the larger border, groups of thirty or so of such bulbs as tulips, narcissi and hyacinths will be suitable, varying this to twelve or so for the smaller border. In a general way hyacinths will be most effective if kept towards the front of the border but here and there groups of the other bulbs may also be well forward, particularly the early-flowering dwarf tulips.

The use of bulbs, however, is not confined to beds and borders. By making a suitable selection they can also be planted in the rock garden, in thin woodland, among shrubs, under large spreading trees or naturalized in the grass. Of value for the rock garden are many crocus species and varieties such as *C. biflorus*, white with blue and purple veining, and its variety *argenteus*, lilac with purple stripes; *C. imperati*, a large blooming sp. of variable colour, and *C. tomasinianus*, free flowering, lavender coloured. The golden yellow winter aconite, snowdrops and scillas, thrive well in sheltered nooks, as also do the miniature narcissus, *N. triandrus* (Angels' tears), creamy white, *N. bulbocodium conspicuus* (Yellow-hoop petticoat), *N. cyclamineus* (cyclamen-flowered daffodil) and, smallest of all, *minimus* some 3 in. in height only. These narcissus species are also admirably adapted for naturalizing in a close-kept grass sward.

In a woodland or among shrubs where cultivation is not usually undertaken various bulbs may be planted, such as *Scilla campanulata* and *sibirica*, snowdrops, *Anemone nemorosa* and *Ornithogalum umbellatum*. The ground under a large, spreading tree such as a beech may be quite attractive in spring by being planted with scillas, *Leucojum vernum* and *L. muscari*. When planting bulbs among shrubs or under trees it is advisable to give them a start by digging or loosening up the ground. When established they will require little attention.

Narcissi and daffodils naturalized in grass make a glorious picture in the spring and an orchard or meadow where the grass can be left uncut until the bulb foliage dies down can be used in this way. Cheap mixtures of all types of bulbs suitable for naturalizing, including the trumpet daffodils and the large and small cupped narcissi, are frequently offered for sale late in the season and afford a cheap way of planting such sites even if they do not bloom the first year. Bulbs lifted from the beds or borders can also be used for the same purpose. Informality must be the keynote of all such planting and it is a good plan to throw out the bulbs in drifts in the selected areas, planting them where they fall. A bulb planter is the most convenient tool to use for planting in the grass, but, failing this, a spade or even a trowel may be used. Once planted, naturalized bulbs can remain undisturbed for a number of years but should be lifted and replanted if they become too thick or if worn out patches develop.

In addition to the bulbs already mentioned there are a number of others which are sometimes grown in the open garden and a few deserve special mention. The hardy cyclamen are particularly interesting for their small, richly coloured flowers and glossy or marbled foliage and repay the trouble needed to grow them. They prefer a cool lightly shaded position such as can be found in the rock garden and with an ample supply of lime in the soil. It should be remembered that they will not usually flower until the second year after planting. *Cyclamen coum* bears crimson flowers with curiously twisted petals from Feb. to Mar., while *C. neapolitanum* with its marbled leaves and pink flowers and *C. europaeum*, reddish-pink, bloom during Sept. and Oct. The best planting time is Aug. or Sept. and the corms should not be buried more than 1 in. below the surface.

The bulbous irises of the English, Dutch and Spanish sections are not altogether suitable for garden decoration because the foliage becomes untidy after flowering. They are none the less valuable as cut flowers. They prefer a light sandy soil and may be planted 3–4 in. apart and at the same depth. The Dutch varieties are the earliest to flower (May), the pale blue Wedgewood being the most popular. Gladioli may be planted 4–6 in. deep from early to late Apr. for successional flowering either as clumps in the mixed border or set out in lines for cutting.

Anemones of the 'de Caen' and 'St. Brigid' types are favourites, but unfortunately not everyone can grow them to perfection. It is noticeable that the best anemone flowers are grown on a heavier rather than a light soil, but since good drainage is essential they usually do best on raised beds. In districts of low rainfall and light soil it is difficult to grow them successfully. There are two methods of growing, either from seed or from corms. The seed is sown in Mar. and Apr. and before sowing the woolly masses should be separated by lightly rubbing in sand. Germination is slow but this can be hastened by mixing the seed with moist sand and keeping it in a warm place for about a fortnight when it can be sown, sand and all, in beds or single rows. Should the weather be dry the young seedlings will require to be kept moist by watering and a surface mulch of fine peat will be beneficial. The planting of corms, which is perhaps the most satisfactory method to adopt, is best done in June or July, the larger corms being used for later plantings. The ground must be well prepared and firmed down before planting. The corms should be set in rows 12 in. apart allowing 6 in. between each corm and planted at a depth of 3 in. Anemones once planted object to root disturbance, therefore all weeds should be removed while quite small. Large weeds in the rows should not be pulled out but cut off just below ground level.

The lilies are a large family, some being easy to grow and others requiring a full knowledge of their likes and dislikes if they are to be grown successfully. The first need is that the soil should be fertile and well drained, and the next that the roots should be shaded from direct sun. Most good garden soils will meet the first requirement and the second may be met by selecting suitable planting sites such as may be found in the thin woodland, the shrub border or the perennial flower border. Rather deep planting is advised with 4–6 in. of soil above the bulbs, as this will assist in keeping the roots cool. Once planted and thriving well in a particular spot, they should not be disturbed without some good reason. To maintain fertility, some well-rotted manure may be worked around and above them each spring. A few that are recommended for the average garden are: *L. auratum*, white, striped and spotted with red (the var. *platyphyllum* is an improvement on the type); *L. dauricum*, scarlet with yellow at the base of the petals; *L. hansonii*, orange-yellow with brown specks; *L. maximowiczii*, orange-red; *L. pardalinum*, orange with black spots; *L. pyrenaicum*, yellow with black spots, and *L. regale*, white with purple stripes.

Lifting and storing bulbs

Usually bulbs in beds or borders in the garden will have to be lifted after flowering to make way for summer plants, but if this is not necessary then narcissi in particular are best left undisturbed for 3 years when a considerable increase of good bulbs will have taken place. The time for lifting is indicated by the dying down of the foliage. If it is necessary to lift earlier, the bulbs must be immediately laid in again, preferably in a cool shady place and without damaging the foliage, until the natural dying down is complete; that is, when the ripened foliage parts easily from the bulb by gentle pulling. When lifting mature bulbs they should not be laid out to dry in the sun, as this will dry them too quickly and may also render them liable to attack by the small narcissus fly. Trays with netting or open slatted bottoms are most suited for ripening and storing, which should take place under cover of an open, airy shed. Bulbs such as narcissi, which multiply by offsets, should be graded as they are put into store, the large single- and double-nosed bulbs and offsets being planted in a nursery bed to grow on to flowering size which will take 1–3 years according to their size.

Bulbs for pot culture

Growing bulbs in pots or bowls is extremely popular for indoor decoration. There are no great difficulties involved in the process but the first and most important point is to purchase good bulbs. They may be grown in either soil or fibre. Of the latter method little need be said except that the fibre as purchased is in a dry condition and should be soaked and squeezed out before use. Cultural details are as indicated below, but it may be mentioned that it is generally accepted that bulbs grown in fibre take a week longer to come into flower than those grown in soil. For growing in soil either pots or boxes may be used; where large quantities are handled pots are the most convenient. Hyacinths are generally the most popular, perhaps because they are easiest to grow and have a wide range of attractive colours. They come into flower from Christmas onwards, but for the earliest flowers 'prepared' bulbs are necessary.

This 'preparation' is carried out by the bulb grower or bulb merchant and means that the bulbs have been treated in a modern temperature-controlled store. The process consists of warming and cooling within strict limits of temperature, time and humidity, the precise treatment varying with the type of bulb. The object of the treatment is to complete the formation of the flower bud so that it responds readily when placed in suitable growing conditions and comes into flower far more quickly.

With large bulbs it is best to place only one in a pot but the medium and smaller types can be grown three to five in a pot of suitable size. The soil for bulb growing need be of no special mixture provided it is open and allows the free passage of water. When planted the pots should be well watered and, after allowing time for draining, placed in a dark cool place until the growth is 2 in. or so high, when they may be gradually introduced to lighter and warmer conditions. The object of keeping bulbs in the dark for a period after potting is to induce root action before top growth. Where more bulbs are grown than can be accommodated inside, it is usual to stand the pots outside in a sheltered position and cover them over with a layer of well-weathered ashes to a depth of 4 in. for some weeks, afterwards standing them in a cold frame, covered over for a few days. They may then be brought indoors as required or put into the greenhouse where they should be kept cool at first, the temperature being increased by easy stages. At no time during growth must any bulbs be allowed to become dry, otherwise both growth and flowers will suffer.

Tulips require more detailed attention than hyacinths. Watering should always be done early in the day because if watered too late and cool night conditions prevail, glassy spots may appear on the flower stems causing them to collapse. This is caused by the water uptake collecting in the stems instead of being dispersed as it is in daylight. For the same reason, tulips should not be allowed to remain on window sills at night as this too can result in chilling. Prepared tulips are not recommended for house cultivation but should be reserved for those who can give them the more congenial conditions of the greenhouse. The following varieties are recommended both for forcing and for growing indoors: Early varieties, 'Brilliant Star', scarlet; 'Prince of Austria', orange-scarlet; 'Sunburst', yellow, and 'Proserpine', rose. Early Darwins for later flowering, 'Kansas', white; 'Glory of Noordwijk', rose-pink, and 'Elmus', cherry-red edged white.

If narcissi are required for early flowering prepared bulbs must be obtained, as forcing of unprepared bulbs cannot be successfully commenced before Feb. The old favourites for early flowering are the polyanthus varieties 'Paper White' and 'Grand Soleil d'Or' which may be had in flower for Christmas. Many other varieties of narcissi and daffodils are well suited to pot culture provided they are not forced into flower too early. Crocuses also are most adaptable for growing in pots or pans, the blue varieties being the most easily managed. For early flowering they should be planted in Aug. or early Sept., the earliest variety being 'Vernus Vanguard', a beautiful blue colour. As a novelty, pots with holes in the sides may be used and are very attractive when in flower. The pots should be filled with soil as far as the first holes, a bulb placed opposite each hole, then more soil added and more bulbs planted, the top ones being planted on the surface in the ordinary way.

To conclude this section on bulbs for pot culture a few notes on the growing of the hippeastrum, or amaryllis as it is popularly known, may be welcomed by those to whom this glorious flower has a special appeal. Commencing with new bulbs, they should be potted up as soon as received, which is generally in the early winter. The bulb is large and will require a pot of 5–6 in. diameter. The soil used should consist of good loam to which some well-rotted manure, peat and sand have been added or John Innes potting compost can be used. The bulbs when potted should be about one-third above the soil surface. To grow to full maturity hippeastrums like a warm, moist atmosphere and as soon as root action is active top growth will commence. Frequently the flower bud is seen pushing from the side of the bulb at the same time as the leaves develop from the centre and they should then be kept growing by affording ample moisture at the root and a warm temperature. The flower stem will grow to a height of 18 in. or more and frequently carries three to four large, open bell-shaped flowers. While these are developing, liquid manure may be given twice a week and after the flowers fade, foliage growth must be encouraged by regular watering and feeding until signs of ripening are apparent, when the bulb is gradually allowed to go dormant by decreasing the water supply and giving more airy conditions. The following spring, carefully turn the plant out of the pot to ensure the drainage is satisfactory, remove a little of the top soil, replace the pot and top dress with good, rich soil. Complete re-potting is only necessary every 4–5 years. The magnificent flowers of this aristocrat of bulbs are in almost every shade of colour from white to rich, dark red.

CHAPTER TEN

The Rose Garden

The majority of roses propagated annually are raised by budding. This is a vegetative method because it involves the use of a portion of the plant's stem, and stems including buds are vegetative organs. So are also the roots and the leaves. An important aspect of vegetative propagation is that the new plants are almost always identical to the one from which they were increased, and are said to be true to type. But certain roses will reproduce almost exact replicas of themselves from seed provided they are not pollinated by a different kind. Roses in this category are the wild roses, such as the dog rose (*Rosa canina*) of the hedgerows and other true species collected from various parts of the world. Several of these may be successfully raised from seed. Apart from this, seed is an essential means of raising new varieties.

Budding is used extensively in preference to other vegetative methods for several reasons. The most important is that budding enables various kinds of roses to be grown on roots other than their own. Experience shows that with a great many roses, such as the hybrid teas, this is a distinct advantage. For when a suitable rootstock is used the bushes are more robust and healthy, they flower earlier in their lives, produce more blooms and last longer than if they were growing on their own roots. Moreover certain rootstocks are better than others for special purposes and different soil conditions. Another advantage of budding is that it is quick to perform. In addition this method allows a very rapid rate of increase. For instance, one rose bush may provide twelve or more buds, each of which is capable of giving rise to a sizeable flowering plant after only one season's growth.

Even when roses are raised from seed, as with new varieties, it is essential to take buds from the seedlings, and work them on a suitable rootstock so that a speedy and accurate assessment may be made of their worth. Indeed a seedling left on its own roots may not flower for several years; when it does the blooms may be imperfect and the seedling often dies after flowering. Seedlings, however, which are budded, normally produce characteristic blooms the following season.

The main disadvantage of growing roses on substitute roots is that shoots are sometimes produced below the point of budding from the rootstock. Not only do these compete with the stems of the true rose, but they look unsightly. The unwanted shoots are called suckers and must be removed. Some rootstocks are more prone to suckering than others, and this factor must be taken into account when weighing up the good and bad points of different stocks.

The desirable qualities of a rose stock may be summarized as follows:

(1) Readily propagated from seed or cuttings.

(2) Easy to bud and compatible with most rose varieties.

(3) Imparting moderate vigour, free and continuous flowering and long life to roses budded on it.

(4) Possessing adaptability for diverse soils and conditions.

(5) Not prone to suckering.

(6) Resistant to disease and hardy enough to withstand severe frost.

(7) Freedom from prickles or thorns is desirable.

While one may have difficulty in finding a stock with all these good qualities, yet their consideration enables one to weigh up the merits and inadequacies of any given specimen.

Rose canina (dog rose or briar) is found growing wild in various European countries. It was first tried as a stock about 1824, and since then has been extensively used in practically every land where roses are cultivated. In Britain probably 90% of all budded roses are worked on this stock. Unfortunately as *R. canina* is often raised from seed it is subject to great variability in vigour and other characters, and there are several inferior strains in existence. In spite of this variability, seedling caninas are extensively used, and are claimed to be the best general purpose stock for roses. Indeed, seedlings are usually preferred to plants raised from cuttings. *R. canina* is a very suitable stock for the hybrid teas and closely related roses. It produces bushes of moderate vigour and long-lasting qualities. It is also widely used for polyanthas, floribundas and rambling roses. It is found, however, that some of the weaker growing hybrid teas, such as, 'Picture', 'Golden Melody' and 'Ulster Monarch', are best budded on a more vigorous stock, such as multiflora. Good strains of the briar stock are not prone to suckering, but this is a serious fault with some inferior strains. This stock can be recommended to the amateur who wishes to try his hand at budding, and he has the option of buying them from a nurseryman or attempting to raise them himself. There are two methods of increase, namely, by seed and by cuttings.

Seed may be collected in the autumn from wild roses, making sure that the hips are well ripened. It is preferable to stratify the seed before sowing. This is done by laying the hips in a box of moist sand or peat and storing them in the open for a year. Rub out the seed the following autumn and sow it thickly in drills outside. Small quantities may be sown in boxes or in a cold frame. Probably only about 10% of the seed will germinate the first year. Weeds must be kept down, and the seedlings dusted with sulphur at the first sign of mildew. After a season's growth the strongest seedlings may be transplanted for budding the following summer.

The raising of canina stocks from cuttings is a better and more certain method for the average gardener. Cuttings may be secured from wild roses in the autumn, selecting plants with large leaves and few prickles. Firm young shoots of the current season's growth should be cut into lengths of 9–10 in. Coarse, soft or pithy stems should be rejected and also thin, weak growths. It is important to cut just below an eye and immediately above one. All the buds with the exception of two or three at the top of the cutting are then trimmed off with a sharp knife. The prepared cuttings may be planted at once or alternatively tied in bundles and laid in damp sand for the winter. There they will callus and are planted in spring. Firmly plant the cuttings about 2 in. apart in rows 12 in. asunder. Depth should be such that only about 2 in. of the cuttings appear above the ground. If the soil is inclined to be heavy some sharp sand should be placed at the base of the cuttings. Rooting is promoted by dipping the stem bases in growth-promoting powder before planting. The following autumn the cuttings are lifted and all roots except those produced at the base of the cutting are trimmed off the stems. At the same time top growths of the current season's growth should be cut back hard. The stocks are then replanted for budding the following summer.

Briar stems suitable for standards are usually collected from the hedgerows in Oct. or Nov. Select fairly young green stems, rejecting those which have turned a dark colour with age or which are coarse and thick. They should obviously be reasonably straight. Before lifting cut away the side growth with a pair of strong secateurs. Then dig out the stock with as much root as possible. For ordinary standards the stems should be left about 3 ft. long, but if the stocks are intended for weeping standards stems 5–6 ft. in length are required. After cutting back any long coarse roots plant the stocks in the garden 18 in. apart for budding in the following season. Another method for which considerable success has been claimed, and a much easier one, is to cut the briars off above the ground with secateurs. For this purpose very young plants are not recommended; those between 3 and 6 years old and from ½–1 in. in diameter have given the best results. Sever the stem about ¼ in. below a bud and then pare the cut surface smoothly with a sharp knife. To prevent suckering from the base cut out three or four of the lower eyes. These stems without roots are first treated with hormone powder and are then laid in ordinary soil in the garden. Here they form a callus and are planted in Mar. 9 in. deep and about 12 in. apart. Afterwards they are staked and are said to form roots quickly.

R. multiflora is a native of Japan, and was first introduced to Britain in 1883. It is one of the parents of the popular polyantha roses. It is a vigorous stock, induces strong growth, forms a mass of fibrous roots and transplants readily. It is recommended for poor sandy soils, and also succeeds under acid conditions. While being suitable for most bush roses it has given the best results with polyanthas and floribundas. For weak growing hybrid teas it has proved successful because of its vigour. If budded between the highest rootlet and the lowest branch suckers are not common. There are two types of this stock: one with thorns or prickles, and a thornless type called *polyantha simplex*. The latter is inferior and should not be used. *R. multiflora* is much easier to propagate than the briar stock. Thus cuttings planted in the autumn may be sufficiently rooted for spring transplanting and budding the following July. Seed also germinates readily when sown in the open in spring.

R. rugosa is also a species of Japanese origin. It was first tried as a stock about 1885. It is of vigorous habit, shallow rooted and prone to suckering. Roses budded on it are short lived, and it is rarely used for bush roses except on light poor soils. On chalky land it fails completely. As a stock for standard roses *R. rugosa* is often preferred to the briar, despite the fact of its poorer lasting qualities. This is because nurserymen find that while it is easy to bud it quickly forms a well-balanced saleable tree. All classes of roses succeed on it, but it is a poor stock on heavy soil. *R. rugosa* is easily propagated from cuttings, and its fibrous root system allows easy transplanting. Stock with long stems for standards are sometimes raised in this country, but the majority are imported from the continent.

R. manettii (*R. indica manetti*) is a stock of Italian origin which was extensively used in the last century for the hybrid perpetuals and bourbon roses. This stock produces deep, coarse, brittle roots. It is considered to be suitable only for the hybrid perpetuals, wichuraianas and a few of the stronger growing hybrid teas and polyanthas. Tea roses and most hybrid teas do not last well on *R. manettii*, but it gives fair results on light soil.

R. laxa is popular with budders because it is thornless, and its thin bark is easy to bud. Another characteristic is that it is ready for budding early in the season, in fact as early as May. Roses on this stock commence to flower early in the summer but do not give a good autumn display. It is said to suit the pernetiana roses best, but is inclined to sucker freely. Another serious fault is its susceptibility to rust, which is probably the principal reason why it is not much used. It is easily raised from seed and this method is preferred to cuttings.

The most important of the other rose stocks is *R. moschata floribunda* which is very vigorous, and therefore suitable for poor land and also for pot plants. 'De la Grifferaie' is easily raised from cuttings and is suitable for strong growing climbers, vigorous China and tea roses. The sweet briar (*R. eglanteria* syn. *R. rubiginosa*) is another rootstock with a limited use.

Budding roses

Stocks for budding may be planted in spring or autumn 9–12 in. apart and 24–30 in. between the rows. Do not make the mistake of planting in a weedy corner or close to a hedge. Instead choose an open position where the plants can be kept as free from weeds as any other garden crop. Over-manuring, however, should be avoided as buds do not take so well on soft, sappy growth. Frequent hoeing is usually necessary during the growing season but particularly up to the time of budding. Any time from June to Aug. if it is found that the sap is flowing freely and the bark can be easily separated from the wood, budding may commence.

A good budding knife is essential and should be sharpened to razor-edge keenness. Another requisite is raffia cut into 18-in. lengths which handles better if it is slightly moist. Secure a number of shoots from the variety to be budded and to facilitate handling trim off the prickles. Do not allow the shoots to wilt, standing them in water if necessary until you are ready for them.

So that the bud can be conveniently inserted below the point of branching, remove some soil from the base of each stock with a hand-fork. Make an upright cut in a smooth part of the stem right down to the wood but no deeper. Another clean crosswise cut forms the typical T incision. Now lift up the bark carefully on either side of the upright cut with the wedge-like knife handle, and the stock is ready. To take a bud hold the shoot in the left hand, lower end towards you. Cut off the leaf at the selected bud, but leave its stalk about ½ in. long to act as the 'bud handle'. Insert the knife ½ in. above the bud and cut the bark thinly until the blade is the same distance below the bud. Snap off the cut bark with a downward pull and by lifting the thin strip at the lower end the wood is exposed and can be pulled out. Take care, however, not to damage the bud when doing this, Now trim off the bark ½ in. below the bud with two cuts so that the piece of bark with bud attached is wedge-shaped at its lower end. Using the leaf-stalk as a handle push the bud down as far as possible and trim off the top of the bark level with the cross-cut on the T. Bind in neatly and firmly with raffia to exclude the air.

The best buds are secured from firm young shoots, preference being given to those nearest the shoot's centre but avoiding buds at the tip.

For standard roses the briar or *rugosa* stocks are also planted in the autumn or spring. With briar stocks two or three shoots are allowed to grow near the top, the others being removed. In each of these a bud is inserted close to the shoot's base. Shield budding is also used, but experience indicates that in this case it is best not to make the cross-cut. Without this it is more difficult to insert the bud but it can be worked in sideways and results in less risk of the buds being knocked out after they commence to grow. *Rugosa* stocks should have two or three buds inserted on the main stem just below the top growths.

Usually after a few weeks it is possible to say whether or not the bud has taken. Buds which are still green and plump indicate success, but failures soon assume a brown and shrivelled appearance. At this stage the raffia may be cut, and although this is not essential for bush roses it is advisable with standards. Sometimes the buds commence to grow the same season and may have produced quite strong shoots by the autumn.

The following Jan. or Feb. head the stocks back, but not during severe frost. It should be done, however, preferably before the sap begins to rise. Do not cut too closely to the bud as this may cause injury. If a snag is left it must be trimmed off later. Stake the young shoots early in summer to prevent their being blown out by the wind. Suckers should be removed immediately they are seen, and the soil kept cultivated and free from weeds. Good growth is usually made the first season and the bushes may be planted in their permanent positions in the autumn.

Grafting roses

Grafting is an alternative to budding and is used mainly to propagate roses for growing in glasshouses, and for this purpose grafted roses are considered to be superior. It is claimed that they live longer and are less susceptible to disease than budded roses, and that they bloom more freely during the winter. The *R. manettii* stock is favoured for growing under glass but *canina* is also used.

Grafting is always done indoors, the stocks being potted in the autumn into 3½-in. pots. The pots are afterwards stood outside or in a cold frame plunged up to their rims in ashes. The stocks should not, however, be exposed to frost as this retards them for grafting, which is done any time between Jan. and Mar.

Two or three weeks before the stocks are required they should be brought into a heated glasshouse with a temperature of 60 deg. to 65 deg. F. When the buds begin to swell this indicates that root action is taking place and the stocks are ready for grafting. To confirm this, however, it is advisable to knock out a few plants and examine their roots. If these are producing a number of young white rootlets the stocks are ready, otherwise they should be left for a further period.

Cleft grafting is the usual method and is not difficult. It involves beheading the stocks about 2 in. above soil level. An oblique upward cut about $\frac{3}{4}$ in. long is then made on one side of the stem and terminating about the centre of the top. Scions are usually secured from the previous season's growth, but for Mar. grafting, shoots of the current season from forced bushes may be used. A scion should be about 4 in. long and about the same thickness as the stock. Make a slanting cut at its lower end to correspond with the prepared stock, fit both neatly together and secure firmly with raffia.

No waxing is necessary, but the grafted plants are kept in a close propagating frame with a temperature of about 70 deg. F. The plants should be syringed daily, and if necessary shaded from bright sunlight. In 2 to 3 weeks' time the scions should commence growing. A little ventilation may then be given, this being gradually increased while the temperature is steadily lowered. When growth is free and the union appears effective, stand the pots on the staging in a temperature of 55 deg. to 60 deg. F. After 5 or 6 weeks new shoots from the scions will be 8 to 12 in. long. These may be cut back to three or four buds and the plants kept in an unheated house or hardened off for standing outside.

Own rootstocks

The great advantage of having roses on their own roots is that the risk of suckers is eliminated. Moreover, if plants are killed above ground by severe frost the roots may throw up new shoots and the bushes recover. There is also no artificial union of different parts where disease may enter, and it is probable that such plants live longer. On the other hand the rooting of certain roses is often difficult, and the bushes are much slower to establish themselves and come into flowering than budded roses. Hybrid teas are probably the least successful on their own roots, but ramblers, vigorous floribunda varieties, strong climbers and some species, and certain old-fashioned roses, do reasonably well.

Cuttings is a simple method of increase and has always considerable appeal to the amateur. Unfortunately some of our best hybrid teas do not root readily, often fail to make strong growth and are slow in flowering when raised in this way. The usual time to take cuttings is in the autumn before leaf-fall. Firm young shoots should be cut into lengths of about 9 in., avoiding those with a large pith.

Cuttings may be made with or without a heel. No buds should be cut out but the leaves should be trimmed off with the exception of a few at the top which are best left. Before planting it is advisable to insert the base of the cuttings in a growth-promoting powder after dipping them in water. Light sandy soil is best for rooting cuttings and in medium or heavy land the free use of sharp sand is recommended. A warm sheltered position is also advantageous. Plant 2–3 in. apart in rows 12–15 in. apart, and deep enough to allow only about 2 in. of the shoot tips with their attached leaves to appear above the soil. After a period of frost the soil around the cuttings should be well firmed. A more certain method of rooting cuttings is to plant them in cold frames using a sandy compost. The lights should be kept on during the winter. Cloches placed over cuttings in the garden also promote rooting. Another method is to plant cuttings in 6-in. pots filled with a mixture of equal parts peat and sand. As a rule cuttings are ready for transplanting the following autumn, but sometimes it is necessary to leave them for a second year. Leafy soft-wood cuttings taken in summer usually root quickly. These consist of firm shoot tips with two or three eyes, cut off just below a bud. Trim off the basal leaves neatly and insert the cuttings in a mixture of equal parts moss peat and sand in a close case. They should afterwards be kept moist and shaded and a little bottom heat promotes rooting. When rooted they should be potted into 3-in. pots and kept indoors until established. Afterwards they are hardened off for planting outside in the autumn.

Layering

Propagation by layering aims to secure roots on stems before they are severed from the parent plant. This is, therefore, a sure method of increase. Any rose may be layered where the shoots can be brought to the ground. For this purpose young shoots of the current season's growth are preferable and may be layered from July until Oct. Ramblers and climbers are particularly suitable for layering, but bush varieties including polyanthas, floribundas and hybrid perpetuals may be rooted by this method. Prepare the part of the stem to be layered by cutting away the leaves and making a slit or tongue there. This portion is then bent to the ground and firmly inserted, being covered over with about 6 in. of light compost. If well rooted by the autumn the layer should be severed and planted in its permanent position. Otherwise it should be left for another year.

Seed

As already explained, seed has only a limited use in the propagation of roses. It may be used, however, for increasing certain rose species, provided bushes from which the seed is saved are sufficiently isolated to prevent cross-pollination by another species. Several species are catalogued by seedsmen, such as *R. damascena* (damask rose), *R. davidii*, *R. hugonis*, *R. moyesii*, *R. nitida* and *R. spinosissima* (Scots rose). When such seed is received in the spring it is safer to sow it in boxes or pots kept indoors. If, however, it fails to germinate the first season the receptacles should be stood in the open the following winter and brought indoors in the spring. The seedlings should be potted before being planted outside. Home-saved seed from species should be treated in the same manner as recommended for germinating the seed of new varieties.

Planting roses

Experience has shown that late Oct. or early Nov. is a good time to plant roses. Normally the soil is still warm enough to allow the bushes to become established before the onset of severe weather. Sometimes, however, it may be inconvenient to plant in the autumn or the soil may be too wet owing to heavy rainfall. In such circumstances, when the roses arrive, they should be unpacked and after untying the bundles lay the plants in singly in a shallow trench, carefully covering the roots with soil. Planting should be done at the first opportunity, and may be quite successful any time during the dormant season up to the end of Mar. When roses arrive during a period of severe frost it is best to leave the package intact, simply keeping it well covered with sacking or other material in an unheated building.

Sometimes, owing to delay in transit, or for other reasons, when the bushes are unpacked their stems appear dry and shrivelled. If the condition is severe it is advisable to steep the whole plant in water for about 24 hours. In any case it is usually sound practice to soak the roots for a period before planting. Moreover, immediately rose bushes are unpacked their roots must be kept covered until they are again beneath the soil.

Roses which are lifted in the autumn will still have most of their foliage attached. As this is a ready means of drying out the stems by transpiration it is an advantage to trim off the leaves with a pair of secateurs before planting. At the same time broken roots should be cut off and any long coarse ones suitably shortened back. If the nurseryman has failed to prune off the snag above the point of budding this should also be done now.

Planting distances for roses vary according to the class and variety. Sometimes you may be tempted to plant rather thickly with a view to securing a good display as soon as possible. It should be remembered, however, that a year or two is a relatively short period in the life of the average rose plantation. Consequently it is better to plan for the years ahead, and to space the bushes far enough apart to allow them to grow as naturally as moderate pruning now preferred will allow.

Vigorous bush roses are usually planted 24–30 in. apart. For roses which do not grow so strongly a spacing of 18–24 in. is normally adequate. The dwarf polyanthas may be grown 15–18 in. apart. Planting of bush roses in beds or borders should generally be done zig-zag fashion; avoiding if possible straight lines and keeping at least 12 in. from the edge. The planting distance for other types of roses varies greatly according to the purpose for which they are being used. Standards, however, should not be spaced closer than 30 in. apart, and the minimum distance for climbers is about 8 ft. The various rose species which are termed shrub roses should be allowed at least 8 ft. each way.

Before you commence planting mark the positions for the bushes with pieces of cane or sticks. The first hole is taken out about 12 in. square and 8–9 in. deep so that the stake is left standing at the centre of one side, close to the hole's edge. At the bottom of the hole arrange some fine soil in the form of a slight mound. On this the rose is planted with its stem against the marking stick and its roots well spread out. The soil is then filled in, using fine material over the roots and treading it down firmly. It is generally recommended that the point where the stock was budded should be about 1 in. below soil level, but over-deep planting should be avoided. If, at the time of planting, the soil is wet or intractable it is advisable to prepare a compost of equal parts loam and peat in moist condition to work around the roots.

Staking roses

Standard roses require staking, and it is better to have the stake in position before planting the rose. If staking is done after planting it means probably driving the stake through the roots with the risk of injuring them. Furthermore, it is easier to site the tree correctly when the stake is driven in first. Oak or ash stakes 1¼ to 1½ in. square are ideal, and should be well sharpened at one end so that they can be easily driven into the ground. Each stake should be long enough to reach within an inch or so of the standard's head when driven about 12 in. into the soil.

Standards are often budded on *rugosa*, and this stock usually produces a mass of fibrous roots. It thoroughly resents deep planting and this is a common cause of failure. As a rule the topmost roots should not be more than 3–4 in. from the surface. When planting always use fine soil to work among the fibrous roots. Afterwards the stem is tied firmly to the stake close to the head, but to prevent injury a piece of sacking should be wrapped around it first, at the point of tying.

After planting the soil should be forked over lightly to loosen the surface. At the same time level the beds and finish them off to give a neat appearance. If planting has been done in the autumn each bush or standard should be carefully examined in spring, and should any plants have worked loose, due to frost and wind, the soil should be trodden in firmly around them again.

Pruning roses

The rose bears its flowers on shoots of the current season which arise from older stems. With bush roses pruning consists in cutting back portions of the stems usually of the previous year's growth. This reduces the total amount of older wood, and consequently the number of young flowering shoots which can be produced. A pruned bush will, therefore, have fewer flowers than one that is unpruned, but they will be larger and of better quality. No pruning even for one year has considerable influence on growth and the production of blooms, but if a rose is left untouched for several years the bush finally becomes a congested and tangled mass of weak, straggly shoots while the flowers, although numerous, are small and inferior. On the other hand severe pruning, as well as resulting in few blooms, also weakens the bush and if continued over a number of years shortens its life.

The purpose of pruning is to secure a shapely bush with a reasonable number of vigorous, sturdy stems, evenly spaced and all capable of producing first-rate blooms. Moreover you have to bear in mind not only the effect of pruning on the next season's growth and flowers, but also its influence on the lasting qualities of the bushes. There are other considerations in relation to pruning, such as the purpose for which the roses are being grown and the position they occupy. Thus it is usually desirable to keep roses in small beds within bounds, and these are usually pruned harder than the same varieties growing in a wide border. Also, when a bush rose is trained against a wall an annual increase in its size may be required. In such circumstances light pruning should be adopted.

General growing conditions also affect pruning. If these result in poor growth then little or no pruning may be necessary, other than the removal of dead or diseased shoots. If poor growth is due to the condition of the soil this should be corrected if at all possible. Atmospheric pollution which occurs in industrial areas may also affect the growth of roses, and sometimes in cold districts or during a hard winter the youngest shoots are killed back by frost.

Whether or not you should prune the first year after planting has given rise to much discussion. Some contend that it is best not to prune in the first season thus giving the bushes a chance to become established. It should be remembered, however, that when a rose is transplanted there is necessarily considerable root pruning. Therefore, to promote balance between top growth and the roots hard pruning in the first year appears to be advisable. This practice is indeed widely adopted with consistently good results.

The correct time to prune rose bushes is another aspect which is sometimes in dispute. Traditionally pruning should be done when the sap is rising and growth just commencing. This may occur from early Mar. until the end of that month, depending on the district. Undoubtedly there is a lot to be said for this practice, for if pruning is done in autumn or winter, which is sometimes advocated, the buds are induced to grow during mild weather. Should hard frosts occur afterwards these soft growths are liable to be killed or damaged, and consequently the bush is weakened. If, however, pruning is done later the new shoots normally grow away unchecked. Quite apart from this argument there does not appear to be any advantage in early pruning.

Pruners are always advised to make a clean cut. This can be consistently achieved by the use of a good sharp knife. Secateurs, however, are much easier to handle, and can be recommended as the most suitable tool for the amateur rose grower. Always make a slanting cut just above a bud or eye. Sometimes the position of the bud is difficult to detect so it is necessary, especially for the beginner, to proceed with caution. It is also advisable to prune to buds on the outside of the stem.

Newly planted bushes are easy to deal with. The bush roses, including hybrid perpetuals, hybrid teas and floribundas, are treated alike. Each stem is cut back to within three or four buds of its base. Standards, however, of this type are not cut quite so hard and each stem should have five or six buds left.

Hard cutting back is never advisable for the climbing hybrid teas because such treatment may induce some of them to revert to their dwarf form. Pruning roses of this type, after planting, should be restricted to shortening back the shoot tips in Mar. Ordinary climbers and ramblers should have their stems reduced by about half in the Feb. after planting. Weeping standards are treated similarly.

Pruning established types and classes

In tackling roses which have had one or more seasons of growth since planting, the pruner should first of all cut out all dead wood, weak or worn out shoots, and any soft unripened growths which have been produced late the previous season. When this is done consideration must be given to the type or class to which the rose belongs.

Hybrid teas are a most important class of rose and, as already mentioned, in common with the other bush roses they should be pruned from early to late Mar., depending on the district. Some authorities recommend light pruning for the strong growing varieties and harder cutting back for those of moderate vigour.

Experience, however, indicates that moderate pruning suits most varieties and gives good results. This consists in cutting back the main shoots to about half their length from the point of origin. When this method is adopted for several years the bushes of course gain in height which may not always be desirable. There is also a tendency for bushes to become rather bare at the base after a number of years. To avoid or limit either of these conditions it is advisable to cut back an occasional stem right into the old wood. This practice induces the production of shoots from below the point of pruning, and ensures a succession of young growths from the base of the plants.

Hybrid perpetuals are generally of vigorous habit, but may be pruned similarly to the hybrid teas. Several varieties are excellent for growing into large bushes trained against walls or in sheltered borders. In such circumstances light pruning is the rule, and may consist of nothing more than thinning out congested growths, removing weak shoots and shortening back unripened tips. An interesting and very effective method of dealing with this class is to select a few strong growths, cut off their soft tips in Mar. and then peg them down in a horizontal position about 9–12 in. above ground level. Blooms are produced freely all along these stems and after flowering they are cut away to be replaced the following season by 1-year-old stems.

Floribunda roses. Hard pruning is very detrimental and not only limits the life of the bush, but also results in poor growth and few flowers. On the other hand bushes which are lightly pruned often become very large and develop a mass of weak shoots. Neither of these methods can, therefore, be recommended, but the following procedure has proved successful. In the second year after planting, pruning should be very light and consist in cutting back the shoots just to the first or second eye below the old flowering head. All weak growths should be removed and laterals shortened to two or three buds. In subsequent years all young shoots of the current year are treated similarly, but stems of the previous year's growth are pruned to within three or four buds of the base. This method results in a longer flowering season because the 1-year-old lightly pruned shoots flower early and the current season's growths produce autumn blooms.

Dwarf polyantha roses. Normally these are pruned fairly hard, cutting back the young shoots to three or four buds. Old wood which is not producing new growths should be cut out completely.

Rambler roses. These are pruned after flowering in the autumn, and for this purpose may be placed in two groups. The first includes such well-known varieties as 'Dorothy Perkins', 'Excelsa' and 'Minnehaha'. These normally produce an annual crop of young shoots from the base and pruning simply consists in removing the older stems. However, if insufficient young growths arise it is feasible to leave the 1-year-old stems for a second year, but the old flowering laterals on these should be trimmed off. The second group is represented by 'Paul's Scarlet Climber', 'American Pillar' and 'Chaplin's Pink'. These produce fewer young shoots from the base and the older wood must be left until there are sufficient new stems to take its place. When a strong young growth arises on an older stem, the latter should be cut back to that point. All laterals which have borne flowers should be trimmed off. With other varieties such as 'Alberic Barbier', which are very vigorous, pruning is simply a matter of thinning out the older stems. Weeping standards in the varieties mentioned are pruned in like manner.

Climbing hybrid teas. Moderate pruning is essential for this group, and is also done in the autumn. It consists in cutting out weak growths, worn out shoots and laterals which have flowered. These roses are inclined to become bare at the base, but this tendency can be counteracted by occasionally cutting back hard one or two of the old stems.

Rose species. Pruning is a simple matter for the various rose species and similar so-called shrub roses. All that is necessary is to maintain shape and thin out side shoots. No harm will be done by cutting back an occasional old stem to encourage new growths from the base. Roses like the hybrid musks, moss roses and Provence roses, require only the removal of old and weak growths. Roses left unpruned for several years can often be improved and rejuvenated by hard cutting back. This includes neglected hybrid tea and such-like roses which are normally pruned annually. Cutting into old wood usually induces the production of new shoots, and bushes and standards after being left alone for several years when treated in this way have given excellent results.

Summer pruning

The cutting of blooms with a piece of stem attached is a form of summer pruning, and should not be overdone. In the first year after planting flowers should be cut with very little stem so as to conserve the energy of the bush. Flowers on established bushes are often cut with long stems; vigorous bushes respond to this treatment, and cutting appears to promote continuity of flowering. After a time, however, persistent flower cutting on these lines weakens the bushes and can be very injurious. Flowers which are allowed to fade on the bushes should be removed to prevent seed pods forming and to get rid of dead unsightly blooms. In doing this it is best to cut the stems back to a strong bud to induce the production of further flowering shoots.

CHAPTER ELEVEN

The Herbaceous Border

THE term 'herbaceous plants' is applied to those plants that do not have a persistent woody stem. They may be annual, biennial or perennial, but all of them, with the few exceptions, die down at the end of the season, the roots of biennials remaining alive to provide a second year's growth while those of perennials last longer and under favourable conditions may continue for many seasons.

They comprise a vast group of plants of such widely differing types and characteristics that they are found in all the gardening countries of the world. In many gardens they are the main source of colour from spring to autumn, and with reasonable care and not too much work, they can be the most outstanding feature.

Site

Some of the finest and most attractive herbaceous borders may be seen in old-established country gardens where the soil is deep and fertile and the position is open, yet warm and protected. There may even be a mellowed brick wall or old yew hedge for a background and a wide terrace of flags or patterned brick in front. Very few gardens can offer such ideal conditions; most of us have to make the best of the piece of land that goes with a house, accepting the garden as it is or planning to change it if that is possible or starting from scratch when the builders have gone. But whatever the circumstances, herbaceous plants should have a place, for among their vast range are plants that will suit widely varying situations and thrive in most kinds of soil and climate. They may be grown in small beds or massed in large borders, along the sides of a path, in a wild garden or in association with shrubs, around a pool or in a set, formal arrangement.

In most gardens some sort of protection is desirable, not only to shelter the plants from extreme winter conditions, but also to prevent high winds damaging the stems and flowers. A house or a wall is not always the best, for sometimes cutting winds will strike round a corner or pour over the wall, and while a belt of trees often serves admirably it should be some distance away and not so near as to cast heavy shade. Generally, a sound hedge that will filter the wind is the best and most suitable choice.

Soil

Any reasonably good garden soil is suitable for the general run of herbaceous perennials, but a deep, free-working loam is best. Soils that are characteristically sand, chalk, gravel or clay are not generally suitable, but often they can be made to serve by thorough cultivation and heavy dressings of farmyard manure, compost or peat. If the proportion of sand or gravel is so high that the soil is always dry and hungry or there is so much clay that the soil is always cold and wet, improvement may be considered out of the question. But even then the enthusiast may add clay to the sand or sand to the clay, buy in large quantities of organic manure or undertake a full drainage scheme and over the years build up a suitable soil. But the cost will be heavy and a good deal of hard work and patience will be required.

Preparing the soil

One of the great advantages of herbaceous perennials is that once planted, they remain where they are for several years. There is none of the annual digging, sowing or planting and lifting that has to be done for other flowers. But for this reason, all the preparatory work must obviously be done well, for it is difficult to correct mistakes afterwards or to make up for skimping a job that should have been done right at the beginning.

Whether preparing a piece of ground for a new border or remaking an old one, double digging is always worth while and on the heavier soils is essential. It is best done in early autumn so as to give time for the frost and rains of winter to break the soil down naturally to a fine tilth, and consists simply of turning over the first spit and breaking up the second spit but leaving it where it is.

If the site chosen for the border is in grass, as it often is when making a new garden or replanning an old one, the same method of digging should be adopted, the turf being buried in the bottom of the trench, grass-side down. Often the job is made easier if the grass is skimmed off first, particularly when it is tough and rough. If it is long, old and matted, the best way of dealing with it is to cut the top off roughly with a hook and add it to the compost heap. In all cases, before digging in old grass it should be treated with a proprietary preparation containing BHC (benzene hexachloride) to control wireworms.

Size of site

Borders for mixed plants should never be less than 5 ft. wide and 15 ft. long. If these measurements cannot be satisfied then it will probably be better to plan for a bed containing not more than six different kinds of plants, all of short to medium height, with foliage that is tidy and green both before and after flowering, choosing for example, pinks, pyrethrums, erigeron, phlox, liatris and the shorter heleniums or rudbeckias, or it may even be better to have a specialist bed, growing only one kind of plant such as bearded irises. A border of the traditional type is not essential, for there are many other ways in which herbaceous plants may form part of the garden design, yet occupy only a comparatively small area, and occasionally they may find places as individuals. Plants that enjoy or tolerate shade often look well when grown with shrubs, either as a foreground or in the form of irregularly-shaped drifts running up to the shrubs, while those that prefer moist conditions may be associated with a pool either to soften or cover the edges (particularly if they are obviously artificial) or to make a bed around a part of it and perhaps lead on to a larger bed or mixed border. The more colourful or long-flowering plants may be grown in narrow beds along the sides of a main path or planted away from the principal part of the garden, solely for use as cut flowers.

But for the usual type of mixed border, and where space is available, the best width is generally about 8 ft. The maximum should be 12 ft. because anything wider tends to make working more difficult. The length should generally be not less than four times the width. But this does not mean that the border must be severely rectangular. It may be planned on a curve, or one end may curve out farther than the other and the varying widths obtained will often add to the attraction.

Backgrounds

A background is not essential. A border may be deliberately planned in a lawn or it may have grass walks or broad paths around it so that it can be viewed from all sides or it may have a path on one side and the vegetable or fruit garden on the other. But such arrangements usually restrict the choice of plants, particularly the tall-growing kinds, and tend to look lone and bare in winter. For a full-sized border designed to contain a wide range of plants, a suitable background acts as a windbreak and undoubtedly helps the general display, although it may involve additional work in keeping it in condition.

Walls and fences

A wall is generally accepted as the ideal although it is usually wise to avoid the wall of the house because some damage is inevitable when the windows have to be cleaned or the house painted. In any event much depends on the kind of wall.

Mellowed brick or stone offers few problems and the claim so commonly made that it harbours pests is too often exaggerated, for snails are generally the main danger and they can be tackled easily enough with a suitable bait. New red brick is not so attractive because it kills the reds and related colours, while painted brick or concrete slab swamps the paler colours and looks unsightly. The best way to deal with these difficulties is to cover the offending colours with climbing plants such as clematis, polygonum, roses, solanum and wisteria, which may also be used if the background is wooden fencing. In such cases the climbers should be trained to horizontal wires firmly fixed to the wall or fence and due allowance should be made for the additional work involved in maintenance.

Shrubs and hedges

The advantage of shrubs and hedges, particularly the evergreens, is that they provide a living background of a natural blending colour. But it is essential for the choice to be limited to those that do not push out their roots to rob the soil of more than their share of plant-food nor spread so far that they overhang and smother the plants at the back of the border. If they are not already in the garden their planting may be a big job in itself, and depending upon choice, the initial outlay may be considerable. In any event they must be kept in good order and particularly with hedges this requires regular attention and additional work. If they once get out of hand, a great deal of work may be involved to get them back under control and in the meantime, the appearance of the border may be spoilt.

If there is plenty of space available, shrubs make the better choice, because they may then be planted to a varying width, the herbaceous plants merging with them instead of starting along a straight line as is inevitable when a hedge forms the background. But in most cases it is essential to choose those shrubs that grow slowly or can easily be kept within bounds and will not push forward to smother the plants. If there is room two or three flowering trees of medium height and spread may even be used at the back with one or two evergreens of a similar maximum size. But generally the smaller shrubs will be the most suitable and a careful choice to include some evergreens will not only provide an attractive background but will also add colour in the early and late months of the year when it is particularly valuable. If planted to a well-planned design with plenty of room, shrubs will help to break up the rectangular appearance that often seems so inevitable with many borders.

Hedges too require careful choosing, and perhaps it is fortunate that the choice is limited. But it must be admitted at the outset that the ideal of an evergreen that will grow quickly yet never get out of bounds and never require more than a light clipping once a year is unattainable. (Yew, beech, hornbeam, *Thuja compacta* and *Chamaecyparis lawsoniana* are the most suitable. See Chap. 7.)

Foreground

An attractive frontage is perhaps even more important than a good background because that is the part which must fit in with the rest of the garden design, and it is from the front that the plants will be viewed. Moreover the immediate foreground will also be the main service area for most of the work that has to be done and it should therefore be wide enough to give room and strong enough to carry a barrow.

A lawn or a broad grass path is generally suitable because it provides a good foreground colour and if well kept, with the edges firm and neatly trimmed, always gives a tidy appearance. It must however be treated carefully in wet weather and damage from heavy barrows must be avoided. A grass path dividing the border from another part of the garden must always be wide enough to mark the division clearly and give a proper sense of space. It should never be less than 6 ft. across or if the border is a long one 10 ft. will not be too much.

Stone or brick

Terraces or paths of flags, paving or brick are perhaps the best, but again they must be of a suitable width and the initial outlay may then be considerable. But they have many advantages over grass; they provide a firm clean walk at all times of the year, will stand hard use and heavy weights and, if properly made, will last for years with little or no maintenance (see Chap. 7).

Choice of plants

The main purpose of a herbaceous border is to provide the garden with colour throughout the summer and early autumn, but it is impossible to have a mass of flowers for the whole of that period. It is easy enough to have a grand display in June and Sept. with little in between, but with a careful choice it is possible to have sufficient bloom all the time and yet take advantage of the flush periods without letting them rule the scene.

Flowering period

The first thing to decide is what length of flowering period is desired. If early or late flowers are being grown in other parts of the garden there is generally little point in giving them space in the herbaceous border unless it is a very large one. In most gardens it is far better that in early spring the border should show only the fresh growth of the year and that in autumn it should be tidied up in good time than to have a few early flowers and a few late Michaelmas daisies or chrysanthemums all looking rather lonely and making little show on their own. Generally too, space will be limited, and it is therefore better to provide for the main flowering periods than to try to extend these periods by taking up room with plants that flower at times when, in the English climate, there is little encouragement to walk round the garden and stop to admire particular plants. For the same reason it is essential to choose only those plants that suit the particular soil and district and by growing happily will justify the space given to them.

Listing the plants

It is a good plan to start by making a list and to check that they span the flowering period desired and then by asking neighbours and seeing what grows well and what grows poorly in the district, cross out those that will obviously be unsuitable. This may mean discarding some old favourites but the sacrifice is generally better than setting out to spend time and trouble coaxing them along in unsuitable conditions, only to find after two or three years that the results are disappointing. The choice of unsuitable plants has too often resulted in borders failing to hold the gardener's interest and then the end is not far off.

Height

The next step is to consider height. If the border is wide, plants of all heights may be chosen provided the necessary time and trouble can be given to the proper staking of the tallest. If the border is narrow or is double-sided, the maximum height should generally be kept to about 4 ft. Such restriction does not necessarily mean crossing more names off the list; it is more likely to mean selecting particular varieties.

Colour

There are two views, each strongly held by roughly equal numbers of gardeners. One claims that great care must be taken in the planting design so that each colour blends correctly, with light shades leading to dark shades and dark shades back to light shades, while the other claims that nature never clashes. Both may be equally right or equally wrong because a herbaceous border is in itself an artificial arrangement of plants, and while it is obvious that purple and pink or deep red and pale blue will not look well with each other, too strict attention to colour gradation will look equally unnatural. Meticulous colour blending is a relic of older and more spacious days when the largest gardens had their blue borders and yellow borders or pink, mauve, red and even white borders. Today, few gardens can go in for luxuries of this kind, but where there is sufficient space, such arrangements are well worth considering, or as an alternative there may be a mixed border and a separate border for Michaelmas daisies which can make a wonderful display for the autumn and is most effective when it forms a 'surprise view'. But the average garden can usually have only one border and it is generally not large enough for a full scheme of colour blending. As long as the extreme contrasts are avoided a mixture of colours invariably looks well because always there is the green of the foliage to make a break and provide relief.

But for those who have large borders or who wish to specialize in particular groups of plants or colours, much extra care in selection and placing is essential. Blues join happily with pink or yellow which in turn may lead on to rose, red and crimson on the one side and orange, bronze, red and crimson on the other. The deeper blues may run into the lilacs, mauves or purples which should then be reduced by running back to the blues again, since purple does not go well with red or pink. In the one-colour border the shades should run lengthwise but the changes should be gradual otherwise the pale colours will be drowned by the deep ones. White is useful for breaking between contrasting colours but it should generally be used sparingly since it tends to catch the eye too easily.

Grouping

With the exception of the whites all herbaceous perennials look best when planted in bold groups, three or four together in the average size border and four or five in a large border. These numbers should not be exceeded, particularly with robust growers, otherwise there will be dull patches when flowering is over and they will be too big to hide with other plants. The groups should be planted in irregularly shaped drifts rather than round clumps, and except for edging plants any semblance of straight or regular lines must be avoided. While there must obviously be gradation in height away from the front of the border, this should be broken up here and there by planning a drift of short or medium height plants to run well in towards the tallest plants at the back or by placing a drift of taller but slender plants towards the front. The shape and exact positions of the groups should also take account of the times of flowering so that early-flowering groups and particularly those such as poppies, that look untidy when their blooms are over, may be hidden by later-flowering groups.

The planting plan

Having settled the list of plants and decided on their relative positions and grouping, a working plan must be made ready for the planting. It is essential for this plan to be drawn to scale and the scale should be not less than 1 in. to 1 ft. which will generally entail joining two or more sheets of paper together to make something like a scroll. The plants should be marked in with light pencil to begin with, because several changes will generally have to be made before the final positions are decided. Each name as marked in should be followed by the number of plants it represents and ringed with a line showing the approximate shape and size of the drift to be occupied. As a general guide dwarf plants require 9 in. between each other, medium plants 12 to 18 in. and tall plants 2 to 2½ ft.

When the general arrangement has been provisionally decided, the plan should be taken out to the site of the border to picture in imagination how it will look, using pegs and canes of the same height as the plants they represent to mark the shapes and positions of the different groups. Then having made the final changes the plan may be inked in or preferably copied on to thick, strong paper. A refinement, guaranteed to occupy many wintry hours, is to cut pieces of thick paper into the approximate shape of the drifts planned and to mark on each the name of the plant, its colour and height and juggle them round each time a visit is made to the site. Then when the last decisions have been taken the pieces can be glued down in position. But however the plan is made up the final version must be sufficiently strong and clear to take out to the garden when planting begins, and a suitable method is to fix it to a piece of hardboard and cover with polythene or a coat of clear varnish. If when planting begins any further significant change is made, a second look must be given to the whole plan because any change at this stage may involve a consequential change in some other part of the border.

Complementary and 'filler' plants

For those who wish to have some early bloom in the border there is a choice between the earliest of the flowering border plants or others such as bulbs or certain rock plants. Daffodils are probably the most suitable but they should be planted towards the back of the border where they may be left undisturbed and their leaves allowed to mature naturally, hidden by the growing foliage of the other plants around them. If planted too near the front the dying leaves look unsightly even if the extra work of tying and cutting is carried out. Rock plants in the front are most effective when the border faces a brick or stone walk and the plants are allowed to run on to the surface.

In many borders spaces are left for filling with annuals or bedding-out plants including begonias, dahlias and chrysanthemums, with the object of providing bold patches of colour at those times when the border would otherwise be short of bloom. With careful selection some striking displays can be produced, but extra work is involved, sometimes a considerable amount, and the practice defeats the main object of a herbaceous border which is to save hard work, not to make it.

Annuals and bedding-out plants may well be used in the first year or two of a new border's life, because the spaces between the young plants will not be filled up in the first season and there may even be a few casualties. The main thing to guard against is overdoing the filling in, for it is the border plants that are the main crop and they must have plenty of room and light if they are to grow successfully and fill their allotted spaces later on. Generally it is better to treat the open spaces with patience, for sometimes the chosen perennial will not make much growth early in its first year but may begin to grow away towards the autumn, or it may not get into its stride until the second year begins. In either case it will be handicapped if the space around it is filled with competing plants and it may then be condemned unjustly.

Planting

On most soils planting may be done either in the early autumn when some new root-growth will be made before winter sets in, or in the spring, the latter being preferable on the heavier or wetter soils. If the weather turns before the job is finished the plants should be kept in their pots or wrappings and heeled in in a sheltered part of the garden or put in an open frame with peat sprinkled around them. Slug pellets should be scattered about because slugs seem very happy working around paper wraps or fibre pots.

The plants should be set at the same level as they were when growing in the nursery, as shown by the 'soil-line'. Small plants may be set with a trowel, large ones with a spade, but in all cases the hole must be large enough to take all the roots comfortably without any cramping. Damaged roots should be trimmed off cleanly with a sharp knife. Often it is helpful to make the hole slightly higher in the centre and spread the roots outwards and downwards. A little soil should first be filled in and the plant shaken gently to let this soil fall around the roots. The hole should then be filled up and firmed down by pressing hard with the hands or treading fairly firmly with the feet. Each plant should be marked with a label and ticked off on the plan.

If the weather is dry, water may be given before or at the time of planting; if the soil is on the wet side, damage to its structure may be avoided by standing on planks, preferably long enough to span the border. When the planting is finished, the border should be freshened up with a Dutch hoe. Later management, staking, tying, watering, mulching and tidying-up should follow on the lines set out in Chapter 2.

CHAPTER TWELVE

Alphabetical List of Flowering Plants

AARON'S BEARD. See *Saxifraga stolonifera*

AARON'S ROD. See *Verbascum thapsus*

ABRONIA
Small, half-hardy annual or perennial trailing plants native to California, thriving in light sandy soil and suitable in sunny borders, rock gardens or as hanging-basket plants. Propagation is by seed sown in pots under glass in the autumn for planting-out the following Apr. or May. Perennial species may also be increased by cuttings taken in spring and rooted in gentle heat.
A. umbellata. Oval leaves. Pink flowers in dense clusters, May–June. Up to 24 in.

ACAENA (*New Zealand Burr*)
A genus of dwarf perennial plants native to S. America, S. Pacific and New Zealand, with flowers in close heads or short spikes. They are useful for carpeting a rock garden or growing under trees. Propagate by sowing under glass in Mar., by division in Apr. or by cuttings in a cold frame in sand in Aug. Plant out in spring or early autumn.
A. adscendens. Long, oval leaves. Purple flowers, June–Aug. 6–8 in.
A. buchanannii. Long, hairy leaves. Bright red flowers, June–Aug. 5–7 in.
A. microphylla. Greyish leaves. Showy crimson flowers, July–Aug. 2 in.

ACANTHOLIMON (*Prickly Thrift*)
Some species of these small, evergreen, perennial desert plants native to Middle East are sufficiently hardy to make useful rock plants. They like dry, sunny positions in a gritty, well-drained loam. Propagation is slow, whether by seed, by cuttings with a heel in July and placed in a cold frame or by layering in late summer.
A. glumaceum. Pointed, densely packed leaves. Flowers in rose or pale pink spikes, July–Aug. 5–7 in. Best propagated by division of roots in late summer.
A. venustum. Similar to **A. glumaceum,** but less easy to propagate. 6–8 in.

ACANTHUS (*Bear's Breeches*)
These are vigorous perennial plants native to the Mediterranean, having large attractive leaves and flowers in spikes up to 18 in. long and requiring a good well-drained soil and sunny position. Propagation is by division or by seed sown in spring, preferably in gentle heat.
A. caroli-alexandri. Leaves large. Flowers white, tinged pink, July. 1–1½ ft.
A. mollis. Leaves large, heart-shaped, up to 2 ft. long. Flowers white, pink or purplish white, in long spikes, July–Aug. 3–4 ft.
A. spinosus. Leaves dark green, hairy, deeply cut and spiny. Flowers purplish, July–Aug. 3½–4 ft.

ACHILLEA (*Milfoil, Yarrow, Double Sneezewort*)
Natives of the temperate parts of Europe, N. Asia and America, the species range from alpine plants a few inches high to border plants up to 5 ft., most of them having attractive foliage with flowers forming flat heads. They prefer full sun and grow well in most kinds of soil provided the drainage is good. Most of the large-flowered species are suitable for drying for winter decoration. Propagation is by division or by seed sown in spring.
A. ageratifolia. Leaves in close rosettes. Flowers white, July–Aug. 2–4 in.
A. clavenae. Leaves long, white. Flowers white, June–Oct. 6 in.
A. clypeolata. Leaves finely cut, hairy, mat-forming. Flowers bright yellow in dense heads, July. 2½ ft.
A. decolorans. Leaves sharply toothed. Flowers yellowish-white, July–Sept. 1½ ft.
A. filipendulina. Leaves numerous, toothed, hairy. Flowers yellow, June–Aug. Varieties vary widely in size of flower and height of plant, 2½–5 ft.
A. grandifolia. Large toothed leaves. White flowers, July–Sept. Up to 6 ft.
A. millefolium (*Yarrow*). Leaves deeply cut, mat-forming. Flowers white, pink to crimson, July–Aug. 1½–3 ft. 'Cerise Queen' (rose-cerise), 'Fire King' (crimson).
A. ptarmica (*Sneezewort*). Leaves narrow, toothed. Flowers white, June–Sept. 2 ft. 'The Pearl' is a popular double-flowered variety, good for cutting.

A. taygetea. Leaves silvery, 6–8 in. long. Flowers pale yellow, up to 4 in. across, June–Sept. 2 ft.
A. tomentosa. Similar in growth to **A. millefolium** but more compact. Flowers yellow, July–Sept. 9 in.
A. umbellata. Similar to **A. clavenae** but with silvery leaves. 4 in.

ACHIMENES

A group of perennials native to S. America. Suitable for indoors or greenhouse, and for growing in hanging baskets. Propagate by offsets in Feb. or cuttings under glass in May. Use a compost of equal parts of peat, loam and silver sand and plant five or six offsets 1 in. deep in a 5- or 6-in. pot in Feb. and place in a house at 55 deg. F. to 60 deg. F. Shade from the hot sun and feed with liquid manure. The stems should be tied to prevent their falling over. After flowering the plants should be lifted, dried off and stored.
A. coccinea (*Dazzler*). Ovate, slender pointed leaves. Flowers scarlet, July–Sept. Up to 18 in.
A. grandiflora. Ovate leaves. Flowers crimson or purple, July–Sept. Up to 18 in.
A. longiflora. Ovate toothed leaves. Flowers blue, white or rose according to variety, July–Sept. Up to 12 in.

ACONITUM (*Monk's Hood, Wolf's Bane*)

Natives of Europe, Asia and N. America, all the species contain varying amounts of aconitine, a poisonous alkaloid, mainly in the roots which are generally tuberous and dark or even black in colour. The leaves are usually lobed and the helmet-shaped flowers are borne in loose sprays in shades of blue, purple, yellow or white. Aconites require a fairly good soil that does not dry out easily and, while tolerant of shade, do best in sunny positions. They should not be moved unnecessarily. Propagation is by division or seed sown in spring.
A. carmichaelii. Leaves dark green, deeply divided. Flowers blue-purple, July–Aug. 2–3 ft. Also known as **A. fischeri.**
A. lycoctonum (*Wolf's Bane*). Leaves broadly-lobed. Roots fibrous. Flowers white to yellow, July–Aug. 4–5 ft.
A. napellus. The best-known species, comprising many varieties. Leaves finely cut and divided. Flowers with well-developed hoods, blue, purple, pink or white, July–Aug. 4–5 ft. 'Newry Blue' (deep blue), 'Sparks Variety' (violet-blue, branching).
A. wilsonii. Deeply cut leaves. Blue flowers, Sept.–Oct. 6 ft.
For *Winter Aconite* see *Eranthis.*

ACORUS (*Sweet Flag, Sweet Sedge, Myrtle Grass*)

Two species of hardy moisture-loving perennials with creeping roots, excellent for marsh or water garden. Propagate by division in spring.
A. calamus. Long, erect leaves. Yellow flowers, July–Aug. 30 in.
A. gramineus. Dwarf, tufted, suitable for the edges of pools. 10 in.
Both species have varieties with striped leaves.

ACTAEA (*Baneberry*)

Perennial plants, native to Europe, N. America and Japan, with leaves resembling those of elder, and small white flowers producing attractive ornamental berries in the autumn. They require a moist, rich leafy soil and will grow well in shade under trees. Propagation is by division, preferably in spring, or by seed.
A. alba. Flowers white, June. Berries white, tinged red, 1 ft.
A. rubra. Flowers white, May–June. Berries red, 1 ft.
A. spicata. Flowers white, tinged yellow, July. Berries black, shining. 18 in.

ACTINELLA

These perennial plants, native to N. America and somewhat resembling heleniums, need well-drained positions and are therefore suitable only for the alpine house or rock garden. Propagation is by seed or division.
A. grandiflora. Leaves woolly. Flowers yellow, July–Aug. 9 in.
A. scaposa. Leaves hairy, dotted, 2–3 in. Flowers yellow, July–Aug. 3–9 in.

ACTINOMERIS (*N. American Sunflower*)

Perennial plants, native to N. America, resembling *Helianthus* but with smaller flowers.

They require a reasonably good soil and grow well in sun or partial shade. Propagation, preferably in spring, is by division or seed.

A. helianthoides. Leaves silky and hairy. Flowers yellow, 2 in. across, July–Sept. 3–4 ft.

A. squarrosa. Leaves pointed, coarsely toothed. Flowers yellow, 1–2 in. across, in loose sprays, July–Aug. 4–8 ft.

ADDER'S TONGUE. See *Erythronium*

ADENOPHORA (*Ladybell*)

Hardy perennial plants of Eastern origin and resembling the better-known campanulas, having broad, pointed or toothed leaves of varying shape and blue flowers. They prefer a moist but well-drained soil and while they do best in full sun, will also grow reasonably well in partial shade. They do not like being disturbed. Propagation by seed sown in autumn or spring.

A. bulleyana. Lower leaves narrow and toothed, upper leaves oval to oblong. Flowers pale blue in loose spikes, July–Aug. 3 ft.

A. coelestis. Leaves narrow, toothed, on lower part of stem only. Flowers few, bright blue, Aug. 1½ ft.

A. coronopifolia. Leaves rounded, toothed. Flowers large, blue to violet, June. 1½ ft.

A. denticulata. Leaves much toothed. Flowers small, blue, June. 1½ ft.

A. lilifolia. Lower leaves round to heart-shaped, upper leaves oval, toothed. Flowers blue, scented, in loose sprays, Aug. 1½ ft.

A. potaninii. Leaves ovate, pointed. Flowers large, pale blue, Aug. 2–3 ft.

A. stylosa. Leaves ovate, smooth. Flowers blue, May. 1–2 ft.

A. verticillata. Leaves in whorls. Flowers small, pale blue, June–July. 2½ ft.

ADENOSTYLES

Spreading perennials, native to Europe, and suitable only for the wild garden with moist, cool soil. Propagation is by seed or division.

A. albifrons. Leaves large, coarsely toothed, downy beneath. Flowers mauve-pink in loose panicles, July–Aug. 2–3 ft.

ADIANTUM (*Maidenhair*). See *Ferns*

ADONIS (*Pheasant's Eye*)

Dwarf or short annual and perennial plants, natives of Europe and temperate Asia with showy but solitary flowers. They will grow in most kinds of reasonably good soil, in sun or partial shade. Propagation of annuals by seed and perennials by division or seed.

A. aestivalis (annual). Feathery foliage with deep crimson flowers, June. 12 in.

A. amurensis (perennial). Leaves finely cut. Flowers large, up to 2 in. in diameter, single or double, white, yellow, pink or striped according to variety, Feb.–Mar. 9–18 in.

A. autumnalis (annual). Blood red flowers with a black eye, May–June. 1 ft.

A. vernalis (perennial). Flowers large, bright yellow or white, Apr. 1 ft.

AETHIONEMA (*Burnt Candytuft*)

A genus of dwarf shrubby plants, of which a few perennials are excellent for rock gardens and dry walls as they thrive in gritty or sandy loam. Sow under glass in Mar. or take cuttings in autumn and put in cold frames.

A. coridifolium. Erect stems from branching base. Leaves crowded. Large rose-coloured flowers, June–July. 6 in. 'Warley Rose' has deep pink flowers, May–June. About 9 in.

A. grandiflorum. Loosely branching with blunt ovate leaves. Rose-coloured flowers, May–July. 12 in.

A. schistosum. Leaves narrow, pointed. Flowers pink, June. 6 in.

AFRICAN CORN LILY. See *Ixia*

AFRICAN HAREBELL. See *Roella*

AFRICAN LILY. See *Agapanthus*

AFRICAN MARIGOLD. See *Tagetes*

AFRICAN VIOLET. See *Saintpaulia*

AGAPANTHUS (*African Lily*)

A genus of perennial plants native to South Africa, most of the species require winter protection. Planted in rich soil they give a striking show of blooms, particularly when grown in a cool greenhouse. Propagate from seed under glass or by offsets or division in spring. During the summer the plants should be well watered and liquid manured.

A. africanus. Long, leathery leaves. Deep violet-blue flowers borne in large heads, Aug.–Sept. About 18 in.

A. campanulatus. Short, narrow leaves. Powder-blue flowers, July–Aug. 18 in.

A. orientalis (hardy). Long arching leaves. Blue or white flowers, Aug.–Sept. 18–30 in.

AGASTACHE (*Mexican Bergamot*)

A genus of half-hardy perennials of which only one species is suitable for temperate conditions and even then requires winter protection. Propagation is by seed or division.

A. mexicana. Leaves nettle-like, toothed, aromatic. Flowers rose-crimson. July. 2 ft.

AGAVE (*American Aloe*)

Although an interesting genus, the plants are of little use in the average garden because they are not hardy and take up far too much room in a greenhouse. Native to C. and S. America. The plants are slow growers, having a number of broad, leathery, pointed leaves which form a rosette several feet across, and flowers borne on a long spike at infrequent intervals. Some species flower about every 8 years, others only every 30–40 years. It used to be said that they flowered only once every 100 years, hence the popular name Century Plant. Propagate from seed in a heated greenhouse in early spring, or from offsets in summer. The plants should be repotted every 4–5 years.

A. americana. Leaves up to 3 ft. long, grey-green. Flowers white, tinted with a yellowish-green colour on a stem about 30 in. high, sometimes far taller, Aug.

A. parviflora. One of the smallest species with leaves 3 in. long. Flower stems up to 5 ft.

AGERATUM (*Floss Flower*)

A genus of half-hardy annuals and perennials native to America, some species making useful plants for rock gardens and edgings for beds and borders. Propagation is by soft cuttings in heat or by seed which, however, does not come true to type.

A. houstonianum (annual). Most commonly grown. It has heart-shaped leaves and blue, rose or white flowers, May–Sept. according to variety. 6–18 in. Of the named varieties the best are: 'Blue Ball' (deep blue), 'Fairy Pink' (rose), 'Imperial Dwarf' (blue or white), 'Little Dorrit' (azure-blue or white), 'Mauve Beauty' (mauve-blue). All 6–9 in.

AJUGA (*Bugle*)

Natives of many parts of Europe, the species are mainly dwarf plants, some of them perennial and suitable for carpeting on moist heavy soils or in shaded positions. The leaves are generally oval or oblong and toothed, and the flowers borne in whorls. Propagation is by division.

A. genevensis. Leaves dark green, coarsely toothed. Flowers blue, pale pink or white, borne in short spikes, June–July. 9 in.

A. pyramidalis. Leaves ovate. Flowers deep blue, May–June. 9 in.

A. reptans. Leaves marked with dark red, purple or yellow. Flowers small, sky blue, June–July. 9 in.

ALCHEMILLA (*Lady's Mantle*)

A genus of low-growing perennial herbs natives of temperate mountainous regions, with some species suitable for a paved or rock garden. They like a sunny, open position on a well-drained gritty soil with a little lime in it. Propagate by seed or division in spring or autumn.

A. alpina. Leaves silvery-green, greenish flowers, June–Aug. 6 in.

A. pentaphylla. Tiny white flowers, June–Aug. 6–7 in. high.

A. vulgaris. Commonly called 'Lady's Mantle'. Leaves hairy. Tiny yellowish-green flowers, June–Aug. 6 in. high.

ALISMA

A small genus of water plants of which **A. plantago-aquatica**, the Great Water Plantain, is suitable for the edges of bogs or water gardens, preferably in a sunny position. Flowers pale rose, June–Aug. 2–3 ft. Propagation is by seed or division. **A. natans** and **A. ranunculoides** are smaller, the former having white flowers, the latter mauve flowers.

ALKANNA (*Alkanet*)
A genus of perennial herbs native to the Mediterranean, containing only one suitable species, chiefly for rock gardens. Propagation is by seed or division.
A. tinctoria. Hairy oblong leaves. Deep blue flowers, June–July. 6 in.

ALL-HEAL. See *Valerian*

ALLIUM
A genus of hardy bulbous plants native to northern temperate regions. The plants like a sunny situation preferably on light sandy loam and some species are suitable for rock gardens or for potting. It should be noted that they have a distinct garlic smell, especially when stems or leaves are broken. Propagation of these hardy plants is by means of seed sown in spring or offsets in autumn. For plants grown in pots, pot-up in Oct., about six bulbs to a 6-inch pot, in a compost of $\frac{2}{3}$ loam and $\frac{1}{3}$ peat and sand, and stand the pots, covered with fibre or ashes, in the open or a cold frame. When about 1 in. of growth has been made, transfer to a greenhouse, gradually expose to the light, and raise the heat gently to 60 deg. F. Well water until flowering.
A. albopilosum. A striking species. Long lance-shaped leaves. Flowers deep lilac with heads up to 6 in. diameter, May to July. 18 in.
A. caeruleum. A good border plant. Sky blue flowers, May to July. 18 in.
A. descendens. Compact heads of purple flowers, July–Aug. 24 in.
A. moly. A plant very suitable for rock gardens or borders or potting. Blue-green leaves. Yellow flowers, May–July. 8–12 in.
A. narcissiflorum. Leaves narrow, flat. Flowers rose, bell-shaped, July. 6–12 in.
A. neapolitanum. Leaves narrow, keeled. White flowers, Mar.–May. 12–18 in. Excellent for potting.
A. roseum. A suitable plant for rock gardens and borders. Lilac-rose flowers, May–July. 12–15 in.
A. schoenoprasum (*Chives*). Although more commonly grown for salads and flavouring, the species also makes a useful edging plant, with flowers varying from rosy-violet to purplish-red, June–Aug. 4–12 in.
A. ursinum. White flowers, May–July. 6–12 in. Plant is strongly scented and should be avoided.

ALONSOA (*Mask Flower*)
Native to the Andes, the genus contains half-hardy shrubby and herbaceous plants suitable for sunny beds or pot culture in a greenhouse. Propagation is by seed sown in spring in a little heat; the herbaceous species being planted out in May. If stopped back during the summer, some plants can be lifted and potted in Sept. for flowering indoors in late autumn or winter, but it is better to grow greenhouse plants for the purpose.
A. acutifolia and **A. warscewiczii** are suitable both for borders and greenhouses. Flowers red or white.
A. cauliata and **A. linifolia** make good border plants. Both have scarlet flowers, July–Aug. 18 in.
A. incisifolia and **A. mathewsii** are for greenhouse only. Flowers red.

ALPINE COMFREY. See *Onosma*

ALSTROEMERIA (*Peruvian Lily, Herb Lily*)
Natives of S. America, few of the species are fully hardy, and all should be given a sunny but sheltered position. Planting may be done in the autumn or early spring, the roots being set not less than 12 in. and preferably 15 in. deep, and some protection should be given for the first two winters. The plants should be disturbed as little as possible. Propagation is by division or by seed, preferably under glass.
Among the hardier species are:
A. aurantiaca. Long, leafy stems. Flowers lily-like, orange or yellow, tinged or spotted with red or brown, according to variety, July–Aug. 3 ft.
A. ligtu. Hybrids with flowers in varying shades of pink, orange or yellow, the petals being generally veined with red or brown, June–July, $1\frac{1}{2}$–3 ft.
A. pulchella. Flowers red, tipped with green,

PLATE 15
DAHLIA

Giant decorative 'Satan'.

Medium cactus 'Miss Belgium'.

PLATE 16
DELPHINIUM. These perennials make stately plants for the border. Many named garden varieties are available.

PLATE 17
DEUTZIA. A deciduous flowering shrub with a profusion of blossom in May and June. Named varieties are available.

PLATE 18

DIANTHUS (Pink). The variety illustrated above is dwarf and suitable for the rock garden or the front of borders.

PLATE 19

DIANTHUS (Sweet William). This is the species D. barbatus. There are a number of attractive named varieties available.

PLATE 20

Above DORONICUM (Leopard's Bane). Is among the earliest-flowering perennials. Below GLADIOLUS (Sword Lily, Corn Flag). There are innumerable named varieties of this beautiful flower.

PLATE 21

FORSYTHIA (Golden Bell Tree). This shrub is one of the earliest to flower (Feb. to April).

PLATE 22

HEMEROCALLIS (Day Lily). A large number of hybrids have been obtained from which most of the garden varieties have been developed.

the petals often spotted with reddish brown, June–Sept. 2–3 ft.
A. brasiliensis with reddish-yellow and chocolate-spotted flowers, **A. chilensis** with pink or red flowers and **A. violacea** with lilac flowers require winter protection.

ALTHAEA (*Hollyhock*) PLATE I
Of the several species, all native to Europe and the more temperate parts of Asia, the most popular is the hollyhock, which is particularly suitable as a background in the 'cottage' type of border. Although the plants will sometimes last for many years, even when growing in what appears to be a poor unsuitable spot, the majority become infected with rust as they grow older. If, therefore, they are to form a permanent feature, a stock should be raised every year, sowing seed in the open in Apr. or May, and transplanting the seedlings to their permanent positions in autumn. They will grow in most soils but prefer the lighter kinds and require a sunny position. Staking is essential. Propagation is by seed or if a particular colour or variety is to be multiplied by basal cuttings or suckers.
A. rosea. Flowers single or double, white, cream and shades of yellow, pink or red according to variety, July–Sept. 6–8 ft. 'Palling Belle' (pink, double), 'Queen of Sheba' (primrose, double), 'Chater's Hybrids' in various shades.

ALYSSUM (*Madwort*) PLATE I
A genus of annual and perennial species mostly suited to the rock garden, two making good border plants with their masses of yellow flowers and silvery-green leaves. All prefer light, well-drained soils. Propagate from seed, or from early summer cuttings (2–3 in.) set in sand and put in a shady position.
A. argenteum (perennial). Flowers deep yellow, borne in loose, wide clusters, June–Aug. 1–1½ ft.
A. corsicum (perennial). Flowers yellow-golden, June–July. 3 ft.
A. maritimum (*Sweet Alyssum*) (annual) is a synonym of **Lobularia maritima** and has white or lilac flowers, May–July. 4–6 in.

A. saxatile (perennial). Shrubby base. Hairy, lance-like leaves. Numerous rich yellow flowers, Apr.–June. 1 ft.

AMARANTHUS (*Love-lies-bleeding, The Prince's Feather*)
A genus of half-hardy annuals which thrive in sunny beds or borders in light, rich soil. They also do well in a cool greenhouse or conservatory. Propagate from seed sown in heat in spring and plant out 4–6 weeks later. When used as a pot plant they need plenty of room, good light and ample watering.
A. caudatus. Flowers red, white or yellow, drooping or in spikes, July–Sept. Up to 36 in.
A. gangeticus. Leaves and flowers in striking colours, July–Sept. 1–3 ft.
A. hypochondriacus. A striking plant with green, red or purple leaves and deep crimson flowers, July–Oct. Up to 48 in.

AMARYLLIS
This genus of plants, native to S. Africa, contains only one species, **Amaryllis belladonna,** the Belladonna Lily, but there are several varieties with flowers varying from white to rose-red. It requires a good, well-drained soil and a warm position, preferably at the foot of a wall. The bulbs should be planted in June 6–8 in. deep and left undisturbed for several years. Under glass large-sized pots should be used. Propagate from seed sown in spring or summer. The leaves grow in winter and spring and the flowers appear Aug.–Sept. but are not formed freely. 18–30 in. See also *Hippeastrum*.

AMERICAN ALOE. See *Agave*

AMERICAN COWSLIP. See *Dodecatheon*

AMMOBIUM (*Everlasting Sunflower*)
A small genus of half-hardy annuals native to Australia, of which one species, **A. alatum,** produces 'everlasting' flowers, white with yellow, 1–2 in. across, July–Aug. Propagate from seed sown in heat in Mar. or in Sept. when the seedlings must be wintered in a cool greenhouse.

ANAGALLIS (*Pimpernel, Poor Man's Weather Glass*)
A genus of hardy annuals widely distributed. Suitable for a rock garden or cool greenhouse. Propagate from seed sown in spring, transplant about 9 in. apart.
A. arvensis. Leaves ovate, spreading. Flowers variable, pink or blue, summer. 6 in.
A. linifolia. Flowers blue above, red below, July. 8–16 in.
A. tenella (*Bog Pimpernel*). Soft pink flowers, July. 3 in. Excellent for bog garden.

ANCHUSA (*Bugloss*)
Native to Europe and Africa the genus includes annuals, biennials and perennials, but it is the perennials that can make a striking display in a border in early summer. But they must be well grown otherwise they become untidy and produce poor foliage and sparse flowers. Most soils are suitable but the lighter kinds and a sunny position are best. The leaves are dark green, rough or shiny. The flowers, in various shades of blue, are attractive to bees. The best method of propagation is to take root cuttings in the autumn, but the plants may also be divided or raised from seed.
A. azurea. Basal leaves large. Flowers in varying shades of blue, June–Aug. 3–5 ft. 'Dropmore' and 'Morning Glory' (deep blue), 'Opal' (pale blue), 'Royal Blue' (royal blue).
A. barrelieri. A compact bushy plant with oblong, toothed leaves. Flowers deep blue, May. 1–2 ft.
A. sempervirens. Suitable for partial shade. Flowers deep blue or variegated with yellow, May. 1½–2 ft.

ANDROSACE (*Rock Jasmine*)
A genus of attractive and typical alpine plants comprising both annuals and perennials. They can be divided into two groups: those of rapid growth that thrive in a sunny site in gritty, sandy loam with good drainage, and those that demand true alpine conditions and are therefore extremely difficult to maintain in this country. The species listed below are perennials and belong to the first group. Most of them have woolly leaves which need some protection from rain in the winter, Propagate from seed sown under glass in Mar., from cuttings taken in Sept. and set in sandy soil under glass, by means of division in Apr., or layering in July. Plant out in the open in spring or early autumn.
A. carnea. Bright rose or white flowers with a yellow throat, Spring. 3 in.
A. foliosa. Rose-pink flowers with yellow throat, Summer. 6 in.
A. lanuginosa. Leaves silvery. Flowers white or pink, June–Oct. 4 in.
A. obtusifolia. White or reddish flowers with yellow eye, May. 2–4 in.
A. sarmentosa. Rose flowers, May. 4 in.
A. villosa. White or rose flowers with yellowish eye, May. 3 in.
Of the more difficult species the least demanding are perhaps **A. helvetica** and **A. pyrenaica,** both have white flowers.

ANEMONE (*Windflower*)
This genus contains a number of widely differing species most of them hardy, being natives of the northern hemisphere, some with tuberous and others with fibrous roots. The majority are particularly suitable for the rock garden, but a few make good border plants and do well in shaded positions. The leaves are attractively divided or lobed. The flowers are beautiful in their delicate form and shades of colour. The border species do best in deep, moist, peaty loams and resent being disturbed. The tuberous species may be planted in Oct. 3 in. deep and 5 in. apart and given a change of position every 2–3 years. Most species may be propagated by seed and the border species also by division or root cuttings. (Some of the species listed below properly belong to the genus **Hepatica** and **Pulsatilla** but are commonly included under **Anemone.**)
A. alpina (*Pulsatilla alpina*). Flowers white or yellow, generally flushed violet or red, May. Up to 12 in.
A. apennina. Tuberous. Flowers white, rose or blue, Mar.–Apr. 6 in.
A. blanda. Tuberous. Flowers blue, white, Mar. 6 in.
A. coronaria. Tuberous. Flowers red, blue, violet, yellow and various shades, May–June.

12 in. The 'St. Brigid' (double) and 'de Caen' (single) anemones.

A. halleri (*Pulsatilla halleri*). Flowers purplish, Apr. 12 in.

A. hepatica (*Hepatica triloba*). Flowers blue, white or pink, Feb.–Mar. 6 in.

A. hupehensis. Leaves lobed, toothed. Flowers up to 2 in. across, borne on tall branching stems, white, pink, red, mauve or purple according to variety, Aug.–Oct. 2–3 ft. 'Alice' (pink, 3½ ft.), 'Honorine Jobert' (white, 3–4 ft.), 'Margarete' (pink, double, 3½ ft.), 'Mont Rosie' (pink, double, 2½ ft.), 'Whirlwind' (white, 3½ ft.).

A. narcissiflora. Leaves lobed and deeply toothed. Flowers white or cream, May. 1–1½ ft.

A. nemorasa (*Wood Anemone*). Flowers various, Mar. 6 in.

A. pavonia (*St. Bavo Anemone*) (Tuberous). Large flowers ranging from white, red to shades of purple, Mar.–May. 12 in.

A. pulsatilla (*Pulsatilla vulgaris*) (*Pasque Flower*). Flowers white to violet, Apr. 6 in.

A. sylvestris. Satin-white flowers, Apr. 8–16 in.

ANTENNARIA

A genus of low-growing perennial plants which may be used for carpeting, particularly in parts of the rock garden that are not suitable for better plants. They have silvery, tufted foliage and masses of tiny flowers in summer, and spread rapidly in a sandy, gritty loam in the sun. Propagation is by seed or division.

A. chilensis. Mat-forming with many stems and white or rose flowers. 3–6 in.

A. dioica. Woolly leaves. Light greenish-brown flowers with pink or white tips, June. Up to 12 in.

ANTHEMIS (*Chamomile*) PLATE 2

A large genus of annual, biennial and perennial plants, containing a few worth-while species. Natives of Europe and N. Africa, most of them have dainty, finely cut leaves, generally with some scent and daisy-like flowers. They will grow in most kinds of soil, preferring the lighter types and full sun. Propagation is by division, cuttings or seed.

A. cupaniana. Tufted plants with silvery, green-grey foliage. Large white flowers, June–Sept. 6–9 in.

A. montana. Tufted with branching shoots. Flowers white or pinkish, June–Aug. 12 in.

A. nobilis is the Common Chamomile used medicinally or for making Chamomile lawns. Flowers white, single or double, June–Sept. 3 in.

A. sancti-johannis. A branching, tufted plant with toothed leaves. Flowers large, up to 2 in. across, yellow to gold, July–Aug. 1½ ft.

A. tinctoria. Leaves finely cut. Flowers pale yellow to gold according to variety, June–Sept. 2–3 ft. 'Beauty of Grallagh' (deep golden yellow), 'Mrs. H. T. Brooks' (creamy yellow), 'E. C. Buxton' (canary yellow), 'Loddon' (gold, early), 'Perry's var' (golden yellow).

ANTHERICUM

Hardy tuberous-rooted perennials native to Europe, Africa and America. Grow well in a sunny border in light, rich soil, or in 12-in. pots in a cold greenhouse. Propagate from seed sown in a cold frame as soon as they have ripened, or by division.

A. liliago (*St. Bernard's Lily*). Leaves narrow, channelled. Flowers white, lily-like, borne in tall spikes, May–June. 1½ ft.

A. ramosum is similar but with smaller flowers, June. 2 ft.

A. algeriense and **A. echeandioides** are half-hardy and suitable for growing in a greenhouse.

ANTHURIUM

A genus of tropical American perennials with attractive leaves of various shapes and beautiful flowers in a wide range of striking colours backed by a coloured bract. They require a temperature of 60–70 deg. F., plenty of moisture, well-drained pots; a sphagnum compost and considerable care and attention. For these reasons they are not suitable for the ordinary heated greenhouse which is used for other plants requiring other conditions, but treated as a speciality they can make a wonderful show. Propagation is by seed or division in Jan.

Although several species are recognized, most of

the plants in general use are hybrids of which the parentage is not precisely known.

ANTHYLLIS

A genus comprising shrubs and shrubby plants, natives of C. and S. Europe. Two species make good rock plants. They like gritty soil and a sunny situation. Propagation is by seed, division or cuttings.

A. montana. Mat-forming. Purple-pink or rose flowers, June. 2–4 in.

A. vulneraria (*Ladies' Fingers*). Tufted. Flowers yellow, white or reddish, June–July. 6–15 in.

ANTIRRHINUM (*Snapdragon*) PLATE 2

Although most of the species are perennials, those that are best known as attractive border plants are invariably treated as annuals and sometimes biennials. Native to northern hemisphere, they do best in dry, well-drained loams in a sunny position and are also excellent in a cool greenhouse. Propagation is by seed or cuttings, the latter taken in Sept. and rooted in a cold frame. Cuttings can also be rooted in spring but need a gentle heat.

A. asarina. A useful plant for a sheltered rock garden but doubtfully hardy. Flowers yellow, June–Sept. 6 in.

A. majus. The snapdragons of the garden. The large number of varieties are divided into three groups: tall (30–48 in.), intermediate (16–30 in.) and dwarf (6–15 in.) All come into flower between Apr. and Oct. and provide a wide range of most attractive colours and shades. A large number of named varieties are available, and catalogues should be consulted for up-to-date selections.

APONOGETON (*Cape Pond-weed, Water Hawthorn*)

A genus of water plants, native to Africa, Asia and Australia, with two hardy species suitable for temperate conditions and having floating leaves and flowers growing above water. The tubers should be planted in pots or weighted baskets or in mud at the bottom of the pool. Propagation is by division.

A. distachyus. Leaves oblong, bright green. Flowers white, rose or tinged purple, scented, Apr.–Oct. Depth of water 6–24 in. in sun or shade.

A. krauseanus. Flowers cream or yellowish, scented, Apr.–Oct. Depth of water 4–9 in. in sun.

AQUILEGIA (*Columbine*) PLATE 3

Native to the northern hemisphere many of the species have given rise to a number of excellent border plants with graceful growth, attractive foliage and striking flowers, carried singly or in branching sprays. They will grow in most soils, but prefer the lighter kinds provided they do not dry out. They grow best in partial shade but will also do well in full sun, although the flowers do not then last as long. Their liking for cool positions and their neat form of growth and the ease with which they can be tidied up after flowering make them particularly valuable for growing near or among taller plants or those that flower later on. The modern varieties have flowers in a wide range of colours with attractive long spurs. Propagation is usually by seed sown in spring but it is important to buy from a reputable source where safeguards are taken against cross-pollination which occurs easily with the result that the seed does not then come true to type. Home-saved seed is rarely reliable and chance seedlings should always be removed. Named varieties or particular plants should be propagated by division.

A. alpina. A dwarf species suitable for the rock garden or front of the border. Leaves deeply divided into lobes. Flowers up to 3 in. across, with straight spurs, blue or blue and white, May–June. 1½ ft.

A. caerulea. Leaves large. Flowers 2–3 in. across with long straight spurs, white or white tinged blue, Apr.–July. 1½ ft.

A. canadensis. Leaves dark green. Flowers several on a stem, 1½ in. across, pale yellow, tinged red, May–June. 1½ ft.

A. chrysantha. Flowers large, yellow or yellow tinged pink, with long slender spurs, May–July. 3 ft.

A. flabellata. Flowers white, tinged rose, nodding, May–June. 6–9 in.

A. formosa. Flowers white, yellow or red, spurs generally long, May–Aug. 2 ft.
A. glandulosa. Flowers blue, nodding, spurs incurved, May–June. 8–12 in.
A. × hybrida. Comprises a number of attractive strains in a wide range of colours, those with long spurs being derived from crosses between **A. canadensis, A. chrysantha** and **A. formosa,** and those with short spurs from **A. vulgaris.** The Mrs. Scott-Elliott's strain is among the best, May–June. From 1½–3 ft.
A. longissima. Leaves deeply lobed. Flowers yellow, with spurs up to 4 in. long, July–Sept. 2–3 ft.
A. pyrenaica. Similar to **A. alpina** but a little smaller and earlier, Apr.–May. 9–12 in.
A. vulgaris. The common columbine or Granny's bonnet, Flowers small, variable, white, blue, yellow, frequently double with short, incurved spurs, May–June. 2 ft.

ARABIS (*Rock Cress*)

The annuals of this genus are of no garden value, but the perennials contain a few good rock plants. Being native to the northern hemisphere, all are hardy but prefer a sunny position in well-drained sandy loam. As they are rapid growers it is as well to keep them well away from more valuable plants which may otherwise be smothered. Propagation is by division or cuttings or seed (except for double varieties).
A. albida. Flowers white or soft pink, single or double, Apr.–Mar. 6–9 in.
A. alpina. More compact. Flowers white, Apr.–May. 6 in.
A. androsacea. Flowers white, June–July. 2 in.
A. muralis. Rosy-purple flowers, May–June. 10 in.
A. procurrens. Large white flowers, Apr.–June. 12 in.

ARCTOTIS

A genus of half-hardy annuals and perennials native to S. Africa, the annuals having attractive flowers in a wide range of colours, generally blooming for a long period from Aug. onwards, sometimes until the first frosts. Propagation is by seed and for perennials by cuttings.
A. decurrens (perennial). Leaves long, up to 12 in. Flowers solitary, 2–3 in. across, white, tinged purple. Grows well outside in summer. 2–3 ft.
A. grandis (annual). Flowers white with blue-mauve centres, cream, primrose, buff or orange, Aug.–Oct. 2–3 ft.
(See also *Venidium.*)

ARENARIA (*Sandwort*)

A genus of dwarf creeping plants widely distributed, especially in northern hemisphere, with some of the perennials making attractive plants for the rock and paved garden. They readily propagate from seed or division, and may need checking.
A. balearica. Suitable for shade. White flowers, Mar.–Aug. 3 in.
A. montana. Suitable for shade or sun. White flowers, May–July. 3 in.
A. purpurascens. Reddish-purple flowers, June–July. 3 in.

ARMERIA (*Thrift, Sea Pink, Cushion Pink, etc.*) PLATE 4

Most of the species are of European origin and have narrow, grass-like leaves and grow in a compact, tufted habit. They are generally grown as rock plants but a few are suitable for the front of a border. They prefer a light soil and sunny position. Propagation is by division or seed.
A. caespitosa. Flowers pale lilac, June–July. 2 in. Specially suitable for alpine house.
A. maritima. Flowers pink or white, June–July. 6–12 in.
A. pseudoarmeria. Flowers pink to red, July–Aug. 1½ ft.

ARNEBIA (*Prophet Flower*)

A genus of hardy annual and perennial plants native to the Middle and Far East. They thrive in sandy loam in a sunny position and are excellent for walls or rock gardens. Propagate from seed or cuttings taken with a heel in autumn and set in sand in a cool greenhouse or by root cuttings in a gentle heat.
A. cornuta (annual). Dark, hairy green leaves. Yellow flowers with dark spots, June–Aug. 18 in.
A. echioides (perennial). Narrow, hairy

green leaves. Primrose yellow flowers, with black spots, May. 9–12 in.

ARROWHEAD. See *Sagittaria*

ARTEMISIA (*Southernwood, Wormwood, Old Man, Lad's Love*)

Of the many species in this genus of annuals, shrubs and herbaceous perennials a few are suitable for garden use, mainly on account of their attractive foliage which varies widely and may be feathery or downy, grey or silvery-white and often aromatic, particularly when crushed. With few exceptions the flowers are small or insignificant. They will grow in most soils, in sun or partial shade, and since they can withstand dry conditions are suitable for banks or the tops of dry walls. Propagation of the herbaceous perennials is by division.

A. dracunculus (*Tarragon*). Flowers whitish-green in loose sprays, July. 2 ft. Leaves used for flavouring.

A. lactiflora. The best species for flowering, with white flowers in graceful spikes, Aug.–Oct. 4 ft.

A. palmeri. Leaves silvery-grey. Flowers white, in dense spikes, Aug.–Sept. 2½ ft.

A. purshiana. Leaves long and narrow, downy on both sides. Flowers white, in slender spikes up to 1 ft. long, Aug.–Oct. 2½ ft.

A. stelleriana. Leaves finely cut, with soft white down. Flowers yellow, in slender sprays, Aug.–Sept. 2½ ft.

ARUM LILY. See *Zantedeschia*

ARUNCUS (*Goat's Beard*)

The genus comprises two species of hardy herbaceous perennials, requiring moist positions and tolerant of shade. Propagation is by seed or division.

A. sylvester. Leaves finely cut. Flowers creamy-white, in slender spikes, June. 4 ft.

ARUNDO (*Great Reed*)

Perennials native to the warmer regions of Asia and Europe, one species being sufficiently hardy for a sheltered position in the water or bog garden. Propagate from seed or division in May or by inducing growth of shoots from a stem set in water.

A. donax. Stem grows to about 12 ft. Leaves 1½–2 in. broad.

ASARUM

The genus contains a few hardy species of herbaceous perennials sometimes grown in woodland areas or shady places in a rock garden. The leaves are generally heart- or kidney-shaped and the flowers scented. Propagation is by division in spring.

A. canadense. Flowers brown, bell-shaped, May–June. 8–12 in.

A. caudatum. Flowers brownish-red, July. 6 in.

A. europaeum. Flowers brown, nodding, June–July. 12 in.

ASCLEPIAS (*Milkweed*)

A genus of shrubs and herbaceous perennials, natives of America, Australasia or S. Africa, a few of the herbs being sufficiently hardy for use in a border. They grow vigorously and prefer moist, peaty soils. Flowers generally in handsome heads, 1–3 in. across. Propagation is by division of seed.

A. decumbens. Leaves up to 6 in. long, hairy beneath. Flowers bright orange, July–Sept. 2½ ft.

A. hallii. Leaves stout, up to 5 in. long. Flowers pink, Aug. 3 ft.

A. incarnata. Leaves ovate, up to 6 in. long. Flowers white or flesh-colour, tinged red, July–Aug. 2–4 ft.

A. purpurascens. Leaves up to 6 in. long, downy beneath. Flowers reddish-purple, July. 2–4 ft.

A. speciosa. Leaves greyish, up to 7 in. long. Flowers purplish, June–Aug. 2½ ft.

A. syriaca. Leaves up to 9 in. long, downy beneath. Flowers slender and drooping, purple, July–Aug. 4 ft.

A. tuberosa. Leaves up to 9 in. long, hairy. Flowers bright orange, July–Sept. 2–2½ ft. (Similar to **A. decumbens.**)

ASPARAGUS

A genus of erect, climbing or trailing plants,

native to the Old World with several species grown under glass or in the open for their decorative foliage. The flowers are inconspicuous. A rich sandy loam or good potting mixture is essential, and in greenhouses a medium temperature, some shade, plenty of moisture and good ventilation. Propagation is by seed or division or, for certain species, by cuttings.
A. madagascariensis. Erect, branching. Flowers white, berries red in winter. 12 in. Greenhouse.
A. medeoloides (*Smilax*). A climbing species suitable for training to provide long decorative growths.
A. plumosus (*Asparagus Fern*). This species and its many varieties also needs training.
A. officinalis (*Edible Asparagus*). See page 448.
A. scandens and **A. sprengeri** make excellent basket plants.
A. verticillatus is hardy and makes a slender-branched plant of 8–16 ft.

ASPERULA (*Woodruff*)

A genus comprising small shrubs, annuals and dwarf-growing perennials native to Europe, Asia and Australia, with a few species suitable for rock gardens or the front of the border. The annuals like a semi-shaded position in gritty soil, the perennials a sunny site. Propagate the annuals by seed and the perennials by division in spring.
A. hirta (perennial). Flowers white or pink, July–Sept. 3 in.
A. nitida (perennial). Flowers rose, July–Aug. 4–6 in.
A. odorata (perennial). White flowers, fragrant, May–June. 6 in. Prefers semi-shade.
A. orientalis (annual). Delicate blue flowers, fragrant, June–Sept. Up to 12 in.

ASPHODELINE

This genus of herbaceous perennials comprises only a few species, all natives of the Mediterranean, having narrow leaves and lily-like flowers. Most soils are suitable. Propagation is by division.
A. imperialis. Leaves arranged in rosettes. Flowers large, reddish-white, July. Grows up to 8 ft. high and is therefore suitable only for the back of wide borders.
A. lutea. Leaves tufted at base. Flowers yellow, fragrant, single or double according to variety, June–July. 3–4 ft.

ASPHODELUS (*Asphodel*)

A small genus of annual and perennial species, the latter similar to Asphodeline and suitable for growing best in deep sandy or light loams. Propagation is by division.
A. albus. Smooth keeled leaves. White flowers in clusters, May–July. Up to 36 in.
A. cerasiferus. Leaves stiff and sword-shaped. Flowers large, white, borne in long, dense spikes, July. 4½ ft.
A. microcarpus. Leaves flat and thick. Flowers white with a reddish stripe in the middle, in branches up to 1 ft. long, Apr.–May. 3 ft.

ASPLENIUM (*Spleenwort*). See *Ferns*

ASTER PLATE 5

Although the genus contains a few species of annuals and shrubs, its main contribution to the garden is its herbaceous perennials or Michaelmas daisies. They need little introduction, for the great progress made during the past 30 years or so in raising a large number of new and beautiful varieties has firmly established them among the most popular and useful border perennials. In many gardens they are grown in beds by themselves and can make a most striking display in late summer and autumn. The genus is a large one, most of the species being native to N. America with a number from Europe and some from S. Africa. Of those that have become garden plants three are outstanding and from them have sprung most of the best varieties that are seen in the gardens of today. Breeding and selection have produced varieties that flower profusely from late July to the end of Oct. in a wide range of brilliant colours and shades of pink, red, blue, mauve and purple, many with double flowers and varying in height from 6 in. to about 5 ft. They grow well in most kinds of soil and prefer full sun. Propagation is by division. All tall-growing varieties require staking.

The most important and valuable species are:

A. amellus. Flowers single, large, up to 2½ in. across, Aug.–Oct. 2 ft. Selected varieties:

Violet blue: 'Advance', 'Bessie Chapman', 'King George', 'Moerheim Gem', 'Ultramarine'.

Pink: 'Lady Hindlip', 'Mrs. R. Wood', 'Sonia'.

Mauve: 'Mauve Beauty', 'Queen Mary'.

A. novae-angliae. Flowers clustered in heads at the ends of the branches up to 2 in. across, rays numerous, 40–50, Sept.–Oct. 3–6 ft. Selected varieties:

Blue-purple: 'Barr's Blue', 3½ ft.; 'Incomparabilis', 3 ft.

Pink: 'Barr's Pink', 3½ ft.; 'Harrington's Pink', 4 ft.

Rosy Pink: 'Red Cloud', 4 ft.; 'September Ruby', 3½ ft.

White: 'Snow Queen', 3½ ft.

A. novi-belgii. This is the largest section, the plants being generally more branched than **A. novae-angliae** with smoother leaves and flatter flower-heads, containing fewer rays (15–25), Sept.–Oct. 6 in.–5 ft., the shortest being particularly suitable for the rock garden. All are excellent for cutting. The following varieties are selected for colour and height:

Blue: 2½ ft.—'Blue Radiance', 'Little Boy Blue', 'Royal Velvet'.
3–3½ ft.—'Blue Bonnet', 'Eventide', 'Harrison's Blue', 'Marie Ballard', 'Plenty', 'The Sexton'. 4–5 ft.—'Blue Gown', 'Gayborder Blue'.

Mauve-Blue: 3–3½ ft.—'Ada Ballard', the 'Archbishop'.

Purple: 2–2½ ft.—'Chequers', 'Pride of Colwall'.
3 ft.—'Gayborder Royal', 'Thundercloud'.

Mauve: 2½ ft.—'Sarah Ballard'.
3–3½ ft.— 'Peace', 'Peerless'.

Heliotrope: 4 ft.—'Melbourne Magnet'.

Pink: 2½ ft.—'Little Pink Lady', 'Malvern', 'Tapestry'. 3–3½ ft.—'Dawn', 'Desert Song', 'Ernest Ballard', 'Janet McMullen', 'Karen', 'Mrs. J. Sangster', 'Pink Cascade', 'Rosy Wings', 'Sylvia Grey', 'Tudor Rose'.

Red: 2½ ft.—'Freda Ballard', 'Little Red Boy', 'Rufus', 'Winston S. Churchill'.
3 ft.—'Crimson Brocade', 'Red Rover', 'Red Sunset'.

White: 2½ ft.—'Choristers'.
3½ ft.—'Apple Blossom', 'White Wings'.
4 ft.—'Blandie'.

Among the dwarf section the following grow about 1 ft. high and are suitable for the front of borders or for growing as a special feature on their own:

Blue: 'Blue Lagoon', 'Lady in Blue'.

Lavender: 'Audrey', 'Autumn Princess'.

Pink: 'Countess of Dudley', 'Little Pink Boy', 'Margaret Rose', 'Peter Harrison', 'Pink Lace', 'Venus'.

White: 'Snowcap', 'Snow Sprite'.

Of the many other species the following are the most suitable:

For borders

A. acris. Leaves small, bright green. Flowers blue, white or pink, in clusters, Aug. 2 ft.

A. cordifolius. Leaves heart-shaped, hairy, up to 5 in. long. Flowers small but numerous and forming graceful sprays, blue or silvery-white, Aug.–Oct. 2–5 ft.

A. ericoides. Leaves light, narrow, toothed, 1–3 in. long. Flowers small but numerous in long sprays, Sept.–Oct. Selected varieties:

Lavender: 'Perfection', 'Ringdove', 3½ ft.

White: 'Chastity', 2½ ft.; 'Delight', 3 ft.; 'White Heather', 3 ft.

Yellow: 'Brimstone', 2½ ft.; 'Golden Spray', 3 ft.

A. × frikartii. These hybrids of **A. amellus × thomsonii** flower profusely from July–Sept., generally pale blue, 2–2½ ft. 'Wonder of Staffa' is deep blue.

A. thomsonii. Leaves ovate, coarsely-toothed, up to 4 in. long. Flowers few but large, up to 2½ in. across, pale lilac, Aug.–Oct. 1–3 ft.

For rock gardens

A. alpinus. Spreading. Flowers large, solitary, red or purple, July. 6–9 in.

A. stracheyi. Flowers about 1 in. across, May. 3–5 in.

A. subcaeruleus. Mat-forming. Flowers large, up to 2 in. across, solitary, June. 6 in.

For China Aster see *Callistephus*.

ASTILBE (*Goat's Beard*)

Although there are few species in this genus of herbaceous perennials, crossing has resulted in a large number of named hybrids that are well worthy of a place in any garden. All are neat-growing plants with attractive divided leaves and numerous small flowers arranged in erect feathery plumes. They will grow well in most soils provided sufficient moisture is available throughout the summer, and while they prefer partial shade, will also tolerate full sun. Propagation is by division or by seed, but since most of the garden varieties are hybrids, seed is unlikely to come true and cannot be recommended. The best garden varieties are from the following hybrids:

A. × arendsii. Flowers white, pink, red, crimson or rosy-lilac, June–Aug. 1½–3 ft. There are a large number of named varieties, many differing only in small degree. Catalogues should be consulted.

A. × rosea. Excellent in damp soils, by the side of pool or in a marsh garden. Flowers in varying shades of pink, July–Aug. 2½ ft.

Other suitable species are:

A. astilboides. Leaves much toothed and hairy. Flowers white, June, 2½ ft.

A. davidi. Leaves toothed, bronzy-green. Flowers magenta, in long spikes up to 2 ft. long, July. 6–7 ft. Excellent for the back of the border, especially in partial shade. Moisture essential.

A. japonica. Suitable for forcing in a heated greenhouse. Flowers white in dense spikes, May. 1–2 ft.

A. simplicifolia. Tufted, much-toothed leaves. Small white or pink flowers, June–July. 6–7 in.

ASTRAGALUS (*Milk Vetch*)

A large genus of annuals and perennials widely distributed in the northern temperate regions. It contains only a few species suitable for garden use in borders or rock gardens. They thrive in sunny positions in well-drained soil, but dislike disturbance and do not divide easily. They should therefore be propagated from seed.

A. alopecuroides. Leaves silky, hairy. Flowers small, yellow, in spikes. June. 3½ ft.

A. alpinus. Trailing plant with bluish-purple flowers, July–Aug. Up to 8 in.

ASTRANTIA (*Masterwort*)

Natives of Europe and Asia, these are mainly dwarf perennial plants, suitable only for moist soils in shaded positions. Leaves lobed. Flowers borne in stalked heads. Propagate by division or seed.

A. carniolica. Leaves lobed, toothed and pointed. Flowers white, blush-pink or reddish, June. 1 ft.

A. major. Leaves lobed and toothed. Flowers pinkish, July–Aug. 1–2 ft.

AUBRIETA (*Rock Cress*)

A group of evergreen perennial trailing plants native to mountainous areas of Near East. The garden varieties, popularly known as Aubrietias, have been derived mainly from one species, **A. deltoidea,** although some no doubt have originated from crossing with other species and for this reason do not usually come true from seed, but can be reproduced by cuttings taken in Apr. or May. They grow well in most soils but prefer light, sandy loams and full sun, and while they are particularly suitable in a rock garden, they also look well along the edges of paths or in front of a border. The flowers show a wide range of colours, mainly blue to purple, rose to red, Apr.–June. 4 in.

AURICULA

The garden auriculas are divided into two classes, Show Auriculas (probably derived from *Primula auricula*) and Alpine Auriculas (probably from hybrids of *P. pubescens*), the latter being more hardy and easier to grow. Show auriculas can be grown out of doors but rain spoils the beautiful velvety covering of the flowers. They are therefore regarded as greenhouse plants.

Show auriculas are grouped according to the colours of the edges of the flowers, 'white-edged', 'green-edged' and 'grey-edged'. If there is no distinctive edge, the plant is known as a 'self'. They require careful watering, cool conditions and good ventilation, and grow best in a compost of equal parts of fairly heavy fibrous loam, well-rotted manure and peat with a liberal addition of silver sand. Propagation is by offsets or seed. The offsets should be taken in June or July, planted round the edge of a 3-in. pot containing a compost of loam, peat and coarse sand and potted on as required. Seed which does not often come true and is slow to germinate, should be sown in Feb. or Mar. in a pan of sandy loam, lightly covered and given gentle heat if possible. The seedlings should be pricked out, then potted into thumb pots and potted on as necessary. Some shading may be required in bright weather.

Alpine auriculas do not have a velvety covering but provide similar beautiful colours. They grow best in fairly heavy soil, moist but well drained, and prefer partial shade. Propagation is as for Show auriculas except that after pricking out, seedlings must be hardened off ready for planting outside.

There are a large number of named varieties in both classes, some of the most attractive dating back for as much as 80 years or more. Catalogues should be consulted.

AUSTRALIAN BEAN FLOWER. See *Kennedya*

AUSTRALIAN BLUE-BELL CREEPER. See *Sollya*

AUTUMN CROCUS. See *Colchicum*

AVENS. See *Geum*

BABIANA (*Baboon-root*)

A genus of half-hardy bulbous annuals native to S. Africa. Although better suited to the greenhouse they can be grown in warm, sheltered positions in the open but will then require protection or lifting for the winter. In the open the corms should be planted in spring 5 or 6 in. deep and 4 in. apart. Under glass three or four may be set in a 4–5-in. pot containing a compost of sandy loam, peat and a little manure. When the new growth appears water should be given in steadily increasing quantities, with liquid manure when the flower spikes show. After flowering the plants should be dried off or lifted if growing outside. Propagate from seeds sown in gentle heat, or by offsets.

B. stricta. Leaves spear-shaped, obtuse, occasionally downy. Flowers blue with white or pink, cream, pale yellow or red, generally with blotches of blue, May–June. 12 in.

BABOON-ROOT. See *Babiana*

BALSAM. See *Impatiens*

BANEBERRY. See *Actaea*

BAPTISIA (*False Indigo*)

Natives of N. America, the species are generally shy bloomers and the few that are suitable for garden use require good soil and sunny positions if they are to grow well. Propagation is by division or by seed.

B. alba. Leaves shaped like those of peas. Flowers white, June, 2–4 ft. Does best on sandy soil.

B. australis. Leaves stalked, with wedge-shaped leaflets. Flowers blue, in long sprays, June. 4–5 ft. Requires a moist soil.

B. tinctoria. Flowers yellow, borne in short sprays up to 3 in. long, July. 2–3 ft. Does best on sandy soil.

BARTONIA. See *Mentzelia*

BEAD PLANT. See *Nertera*

BEARD TONGUE. See *Penstemon*

BEAR'S BREECHES. See *Acanthus*

BEAR'S EAR. See *Cortusa*

BEE BALM. See *Monarda*

BEGONIA PLATE 5

There are many species and varieties of these plants grown for the beauty of their foliage or flowers. They are useful alike for the greenhouse and garden and several make good houseplants. They are conveniently classified in two main sections, 'tuberous-rooted' and 'fibrous-rooted'.

Tuberous-rooted species. To raise from seed, sow in a heated greenhouse in Feb. The seed is extremely fine and requires great care in the preparation of the seed pans and sowing. The compost must be finely sifted and consist of two-thirds loam and one-third peat and sand. Water the pans and allow to drain before sowing the seed. Sow thinly and do not cover the seed.

To keep the compost moist and obviate watering, cover the pans with glass and paper and watch carefully for germination when light must be admitted. Using a thin, notched stick gently lift the seedlings and carefully transfer to shallow boxes of fine sandy soil an inch or two apart at an early stage. Pot-off singly as soon as large enough, keep near the roof glass, shade from hot sun and give an occasional overhead spray in favourable weather. If intended for the greenhouse, pot-on as required into 5- or 6-in. pots using an open compost containing peat and sand. For outdoor bedding the plants may be grown on in shallow boxes or pots, gradually hardened off and planted out in early June. Plants raised from seed will not usually flower outdoors until the late summer. All outdoor corms should be lifted in Oct. or when slight frost has blackened the foliage. After drying, carefully remove the tops, shake the corms quite free from soil and store in boxes with some dry soil in a cool, frost-proof place. Pot-grown corms should be treated in much the same way by allowing to dry off gradually and storing throughout the winter. To start corms into growth they should be placed hollow side uppermost in shallow boxes on a little rich soil in Feb. or Mar., the corms being barely covered with sandy soil. Water sparingly until growth is evident and either pot for greenhouse use or harden off for early June planting-out.

If it is required to increase a particular variety this may be done in the spring by means of leaf-cuttings. Proceed by selecting a mature leaf, cut cleanly across the underside of the main veins and lay the leaf on a bed of sand or coconut fibre in a propagating frame or a suitable box covered with glass, holding the leaf in place by means of small pieces of broken pot. When small bulblets are seen to form where the veins have been cut, these when large enough should be taken off and potted singly.

Fibrous-rooted species. Included under this heading is a large and varied number of species and varieties. They embrace both foliage and flowering types useful for summer bedding, flowering in the greenhouse both in summer and winter and for providing attractive foliage plants for the glasshouse and dwelling house all the year round. There are two sections of winter-flowering types requiring separate treatment, a group of cultivars obtained by crossing the species *B. socotrana* with the tuberous-rooted varieties and the section represented by 'Gloire de Lorraine' and its varieties. The former group is not of the easiest culture but well worth any trouble expended on them. During the summer growing season they require a shaded house with a close, moist atmosphere and an average temperature of 60 to 65 deg. F. After flowering maintain a temperature of 55 to 60 deg. F. and reduce the water supply giving sufficient only to keep the foliage and stems in a fresh condition until young shoots are thrown up from the base in May. Increased water may then be given and when the young shoots are about 3 in. long they may be taken off and inserted as cuttings in small pots of sandy compost. A propagating case placed over a bottom heat of 70 deg. F. will afford good rooting conditions. Pot-on as necessary to 5- or 6-in. pots using an open compost through which water passes readily. Regular fumigation will be necessary to keep down insect pests. 'Gloire de Lorraine' and its varieties are the easiest to grow. They are propagated during Mar. by cuttings of young basal shoots taken from flowered plants. The production of cuttings is induced as follows. After flowering lightly cut back the plants and rest them for a few weeks. Start them into growth in a temperature raised to 65 deg. F., at the same time slightly increase the water supply. Rooting and growing-on is on much the same lines as that outlined above. If the young plants do not break out freely from the stem the growing tip may be pinched out. While the plants are growing take out any flower buds which may appear until a good plant is built up.

Tuberous-rooted varieties:

'Aurora' (salmon-orange)
'Blithe Spirit' (pale pink)
'Diana Wynyard' (pure white)
'Festiva' (yellow)
'Jamboree' (yellow ground overlaid orange)
'Kismet' (apricot and rose)
'Margaret Collins' (pink)

Hanging Baskets:
'Bettina' (salmon-pink)
'Mrs. Bilkey' (salmon-orange)
'Roberta' (scarlet)
'Yellow Sweetie'
Winter-flowering hybrids:
(*B. socotrana* × tuberous-rooted)
'Britannia' (scarlet)
'Altrincham Pink'
'Exquisite' (pink and white)
'Emita' (orange-scarlet)
'Fascination' (orange-salmon)
'Optima' (pink)
'Pink Perfection'
'Scarlet Beauty'

The crossing of the two species *B. dregei* and *B. socotrana* has given us the winter flowering 'Gloire de Lorraine' (reddish-pink) and from thence arise the cultivars 'Turnford Hall' (blush-white), 'Mrs. Leopold de Rothschild' (soft pink), 'Glory of Cincinnati' (pink), 'Mrs. Petersen' (dark foliage, rosy-red flowers), 'Ege's Favourite' (red).

Ornamental-leaved species and varieties:
B. maculata (silver and green)
B. masoniana (crinkled green leaves marked with a black cross)
B. mazae (dark copper)
B. Gloire de Sceaux (dark foliage)
B. serratifolia (reddish leaves, undersides spotted pink and red)
B. imperialis (olive and greyish-green)
'President Carnot' (leaves spotted white)
Begonia Rex in many named varieties

Fibrous-rooted for bedding and greenhouse: B. semperflorens. Of many varieties, the following are some of the best.
'Carmen' (rose, bronze foliage)
'Brightness' (carmine-pink)
'Purity' (white)
'Gustave Knaaka' (carmine)
'Indian Maid' (scarlet in bud, open flowers deep bronze)
'Loveliness' (rose-pink)

BELL FLOWER. See *Nierembergia*

BELLADONNA LILY. See *Amaryllis*

BELLFLOWER. See *Campanula*

BELLIS (*Daisy*)
A small genus of low-growing, hardy, herbaceous perennials, growing well in most soils, preferably in sun. Propagation is by seed sown in spring, or by division after flowering. Useful for edging or in the rock garden.
B. perennis. Flowers white, pink, red or mixtures, usually with yellow centres, single or semi-double, some with quilled petals, May–June. There are several named varieties. 6–10 in.

BELLIUM
A small genus of daisy-like perennials, resembling **Bellis** but shorter and containing one species **B. minutum,** suitable for the rock garden. Propagation is by division in spring. The flowers have a whitish disc and purple on the reverse, May–Sept. 3 in.

BELLWORT. See *Uvularia*

BERGAMOT. See *Monarda*

BERGENIA (*Megasea*)
A small genus of hardy herbaceous perennials native to India and the East and having distinctive thick large leaves, the bergenias are suitable for the front of a border or the rock garden, and grow in most soils. Propagation is by division.
B. ligulata. Leaves roundish, heart-shaped. Flowers pale pink or red, Mar.–May. 1 ft. Requires a sheltered position for protection in winter.
B. purpurascens. Leaves roundish, heart-shaped. Flowers purple, nodding, June. 3–9 in.
B. stracheyi. Leaves up to 6 in. long. Flowers pink or white, up to 1 in. across, borne in open drooping spikes, Mar.–Apr. 9 in. Requires a sheltered position for protection in winter.

BERKHEYA
Native to S. Africa, the genus contains a few good border plants which resemble thistles in their growth. They grow well in most soils preferring sunny positions. Propagation is by division.
B. adlamii. Leaves large, up to 18 in. long at the base of the stem. Flowers yellow, up to 3 in. across, July. 5 ft.
B. purpurea. Leaves large, dark green above,

greyish beneath. Flowers up to 3 in. across, purple, July. 3 ft.

BETONICA (*Betony*). See *Stachys*

BINDWEED. See *Convolvulus*

BIRD OF PARADISE FLOWER. See *Strelitzia*

BIRTH-ROOT. See *Trillium*

BITTER CRESS. See *Cardamine*

BLANKET FLOWER. See *Gaillardia*

BLAZING STAR. See *Liatris*

BLEEDING HEART. See *Dicentra*

BLETILLA
A small genus of half-hardy orchid-like plants, with one species, **B. striata,** suitable for a sheltered position or a cool greenhouse where it should be grown in pots in a compost of loam and peat with some sand. Flowers pink or white, 1 in. across. 12 in.

BLOODROOT. See *Sanguinaria*

BLOOMERIA
A small genus of half-hardy bulbous plants native to California, suitable for a rock garden if sheltered, otherwise they should be grown under glass. Do well in a mixture of loam, peat and sand. Plant in Sept.–Oct. 2–3 in. deep and 3 in. apart. Propagate from offsets in Sept.
B. aurea. Long narrow leaves. Golden-yellow flowers, May–June. 10–14 in.
B. clevelandii. Similar to above but smaller.

BLUE DAISY. See *Felicia*

BLUE MARGUERITE. See *Felicia*

BOG ARUM. See *Calla*

BOG PIMPERNEL. See *Anagallis*

BOG VIOLET. See *Pinguicala*

BOLTONIA (*False Chamomile* or *Starwort*)
Natives of N. America and Asia, these plants resemble Michaelmas Daisies in growth and are as easily grown in most kinds of soil and position. Propagation is by division or seed.
B. asteroides. Leaves narrow. Flowers white, pink or purple, borne in large heads, Aug.–Sept. 5–6 ft.
B. latisquamata. Leaves narrow. Flowers blue to violet, Aug.–Sept. 5 ft.

BOUVARDIA (*Jasmine Plant*)
A winter-flowering evergreen shrub native to C. America. Requires a mixture of fibrous loam, peat, sand and manure. Pot-up in Mar. in 5- to 8-in. pots and keep in frame from June–Sept.; water liberally. In Sept. return to greenhouse and apply liquid manure as soon as the young shoots appear. Cut hard back after flowering, and stop-back young shoots until Aug. (50–60 deg. F. in winter and 60–65 deg. F. in summer). Propagate from cuttings of young shoots or root-cuttings in Feb.–Mar. in heat of about 70 deg. F.
B. humboldtii. Dark green leaves. Large white flowers, autumn–winter. 24 in.
B. leiantha. Slender hairy leaves. Scarlet flowers, July–Nov. 24 in.
B. triphylla. Scarlet flowers, autumn–winter. 24–36 in.

BOWER PLANT. See *Pandorea*

BRACHYCOME (*Swan River Daisy*)
A small genus of half-hardy annuals and perennials native to Australia, of which one species **B. iberidifolia** is suitable for growing in the open or a greenhouse. Seed should be sown thinly in Mar.–Apr. in gentle heat or in Apr. out of doors where it is intended to grow and thinned to about 9 in. apart. Flowers blue, white or rose, July–Sept. 1 ft.

BRAVOA (*Twin Flower*)
A small genus of half-hardy bulbous plants native to Mexico, of which one species **B. geminiflora** is suitable for a cool greenhouse or may succeed in a position in rich light soil, where it can have winter protection. Propagate from seeds sown as soon as ripe or offsets in the autumn. Flowers rich orange-red colour, July–Aug. 18–24 in.

BRIDAL WREATH. See *Francoa*

BRODIAEA (*California* or *Missouri Hyacinth*)
A genus of hardy and near-hardy bulbous plants native to S. and N. America, needing a well-drained rich sandy soil and sunny position, and requiring winter protection in exposed positions only. The corms should be planted 3 in. deep, 6 in. apart and lifted every fourth year. Propagate from offsets in the autumn. Also suitable for a cool greenhouse.
B. coronaria. Violet-blue flowers, June–July. 10–20 in.
B. hendersonii. Salmon-pink flowers with purple midribs, summer, 8–18 in.
B. ixioides. Yellow flowers tinged with purple, summer. Up to 18 in. with a dwarf form growing about 9 in.

BROWALLIA
A small genus of shrubby herbs and annuals suitable for growing in a cool greenhouse, with the annuals sometimes grown for planting out in the open. Propagation is by seed sown in gentle heat.
B. demissa (annual). Leaves ovate or variable. Flowers blue or white, June–July. Up to 18 in.
B. speciosa (perennial). Leaves ovate, slender. Flowers blue, white or violet up to 2 in. across, blooming over a long period. Up to 2 ft. For greenhouse.

BRUNNERA
A small genus native to the Near East, with one species, **B. macrophylla,** suitable for moist but well-drained soils in partial shade. Leaves broad, heart-shaped. Flowers resemble Forget-me-nots, May–June. $1\frac{1}{2}$ ft.

BUCK-BEAN. See *Menyanthes*

BUGLE. See *Ajuga*

BUGLOSS. See *Anchusa*

BULBINELLA
A small genus of Australasian plants providing one species, **B. rossii,** which makes a fine perennial for a sheltered position on peaty soil and preferably in partial shade. Leaves up to 1 ft. long. Flowers, male and female, orange, in dense sprays, June. 2–3 ft.

BULBOCODIUM (*Spring Meadow Saffron*)
A genus of a single species **(B. vernum)** from the European Alps, resembling a crocus, and liking a well-drained, sandy soil in a sunny position. The corms should be planted in Aug. 3 in. deep and 4 in. apart, or potted-up for indoors. Lift every second year to separate the offsets which may be used for propagation. Flowers purple-red, Jan.–Mar. 4–6 in.

BULRUSH. See *Scirpus*

BUPHTHALMUM (*Yellow Ox-eye*)
A small genus of showy herbaceous perennials native to Europe with large, yellow, daisy-like flowers but rather coarse foliage. They will grow in most soils provided the position is sunny. Propagation is by division.
B. salicifolium. Leaves large, heart-shaped, generally hairy. Flowers yellow, borne singly, June–July. $1\frac{1}{2}$–2 ft.
B. speciosum. Leaves large, toothed, scented. Flowers large, yellow, July–Aug. 4–5 ft. Grows especially well on moist soils or around a pool but may then need checking.

BURNING BUSH. See *Dictamnus*

BURNT CANDYTUFT. See *Aethionema*

BUSH POPPY. See *Romneya*

BUTOMUS (*Flowering Rush*)
This genus contains only one species, **B. umbellatus,** a hardy aquatic perennial native to Europe and Asia, and requiring a sunny position in a bog or muddy bank. Propagation is by division in spring. Leaves basal, tuft-forming, purplish when young. Flowers rose, June–Aug. $2\frac{1}{2}$ ft.

BUTTERCUP. See *Ranunculus*

BUTTERFLY FLOWER. See *Schizanthus*

BUTTERFLY LILY. See *Hedychium*

BUTTERWORT. See *Pinguicula*

CACTI

These plants can be grown by anyone having a small greenhouse. They are diverse in form from the miniature *Mammillarias* of about a thimble size to the large *Opuntias* growing 7 or 8 ft. high. They like a compost of one-half fibrous loam and one-half a mixture of sand, broken brick and lime-rubble, through which water passes readily. *Epiphyllums*, *Rhipsalis* and *Zygocactus* appreciate a little peat in the soil mixture and also a shaded position, whilst most other species enjoy full sun. Small growers such as many of the *Echinopsis* and *Mammillarias* which have very sparse roots should have the pots three parts filled with drainage material. Potting, when necessary, should always be done in the spring and it is a good policy not to interfere with any plant which is doing well. Pot firmly so that the plants are well anchored and for several weeks after potting give the minimum of water. From the end of Apr. to mid-Aug. moderate supplies of water may be given and twice weekly inspections should be made for this purpose. *Epiphyllums* and *Rhipsalis* should never become dust dry but during the winter a little only is required. *Phyllocactus* may be watered liberally during active growth.

Hardy Cacti: This is a relative term as no cacti are completely hardy. Some however, such as *Aporocactus*, *Notocactus* and *Mammillaria*, may be planted in the spring in a well-drained, sunny, sheltered site on the rock garden in a mixture of light loam, brick rubble, sand and gravel. If left for the winter they must be protected from overhead moisture with a sheet of glass. On the whole it must be said that they are more suitable for the cold greenhouse or dwelling house.

Hardy Species:

- *Cereus engelmannii* (purple, June, 18 in.)
- *Ferocactus acanthodes* (greenish-yellow, summer, 12–30 in.)
- *Mammillaria setispina* (pink, summer, 9 in.)
- *Opuntia pulchella* (purple, summer, 10 in.)
- *Opuntia rafinesqui* (sulphur-yellow, June–Sept. 10 in.)

Greenhouse species:

- *Aporocactus flagelliformis* (Whip or Rat-tail cactus) (pink, June, 12–30 in.)
- *A. peruvianus* (white, May–July, 20–100 in.)
- *Cephalocereus senilis* (Old Man Cactus) (purple-red, summer, 15–100 in.)
- *Echinopsis cristata purpurea* (rose, July, 10 in.)
- *E. multiplex* (pale pink, fragrant)
- *Epiphyllum ackermannii* (rich rose, summer, 18 in.)
- *E. aurora boreale* (orange, June, 18–24 in.)
- *E. edwardsii* (red, summer, 24 in.)
- *E. oxypetalum* (creamy-white, June–Sept., 20–30 in.)
- *Ferocactus lecontei* (lemon-yellow, summer, 10–30 in.)
- *Mammillaria applanta* (white tinged red, July–Aug., 4–6 in.)
- *M. fuscata* (purple, summer, 6 in.)
- *M. sulphurea* (yellow, summer, 3 in.)
- *Melocactus communis* (Turk's Cap Cactus) (red, June, 12–30 in.)
- *Notocactus haselbergii* (red and yellow, Apr.–May, 12 in.)
- *Opuntia aurantiaca* (orange, June, 30 in.)
- *Ficus indica* (Prickly Pear) (yellow, June, 30 in.)
- *Pediocactus simpsonii* (Hedgehog Cactus) (red, June, 5 in.)
- *Rhipsalis cassutha* (Mistletoe Cactus) (white, Apr., 15 in.)
- *Schlumbergera russelliana* (Leaf-flowering Cactus) (pink, Nov., 10–24 in.)

CALANDRINIA (*Rock Purslane*)

A genus of annual and perennial plants native to Australasia and America, with brightly coloured flowers which, however, close in dull weather. All are best treated as half-hardy annuals, grown from seed sown in gentle heat and planted out into sandy soil in a sunny position.

C. discolor. Bright light purple flowers, up to 2 in. across, Aug. 12–18 in.

C. grandiflora. Similar to above, with slightly smaller flowers but growing to 3 ft.

C. umbellata. Bright crimson flowers, summer. 6–9 in.

CALCEOLARIA (*Slipper Flower*)

This genus contains over 100 species only a few of which are in cultivation and these chiefly in botanic gardens. Those usually found in present-day gardens can be classified under three distinct types—the 'herbaceous' (*C. herbeohybrida*), the 'shrubby' (*C. fruticohybrida*) and the hardy perennials and annuals.

Herbaceous calceolarias are beautiful plants with large, tender leaves and masses of showy, blotched flowers produced in May. A well-grown plant will be 2 ft. or more across. They are easy to grow provided the following points are noted. Sow seeds in pots or pans of light, sandy soil in June. The soil should be watered before sowing, the seed sown very thinly and pressed gently into the surface or very lightly covered. Cover the pan with a sheet of glass and stand in a shady part of the greenhouse. Germination takes about ten days and while still quite small prick out the seedlings into other pans. Keep shaded and pot singly in about three weeks. In Sept. re-pot into 4-in. pots and keep in a cool greenhouse using the minimum of fire heat throughout the winter and being careful not to overwater. In late Feb. or early Mar. pot finally into 7- or 8-in. pots using an open compost such as two parts good loam, one part granulated peat with sufficient sand and/or crushed oyster-shell to give good aeration. Grow-on in a cool shaded greenhouse, stake out the flower spikes in good time and feed gently at fortnightly intervals as growth develops. Fumigate as required to keep down greenfly.

Shrubby calceolarias may be raised from seed, old rootstocks may be split up during May or cuttings inserted in sandy soil in a propagating frame in the late summer and autumn. This latter method is usually preferred when grown for bedding. Protect the cuttings from frost throughout the winter and about the middle of Feb. pinch out the growing point to induce a bushy habit. To ensure good plants for planting-out at the end of May, potting singly into 4-in. pots in Mar. or Apr. is recommended. Seeds are sown in gentle warmth in Mar., the seedlings being pricked out into boxes as soon as large enough to handle. From the boxes, pot up the young plants to 3-in. pots, transfer to a cold frame in late Apr., from whence they may be hardened off for planting-out in early June or, if required for the greenhouse, pot-on into 6- or 7-in. pots before the roots become pot-bound. Calceolarias dislike a dry soil and provided the drainage is good should be copiously watered during dry spells.

Hardy herbaceous calceolarias are good subjects for the rock garden growing from 2 to 12 in. in height. Most varieties are readily increased by division of the rootstock during Apr. or May; cuttings inserted in pure sand in a propagating frame during the autumn will root by the spring; seeds may be sown as soon as ripe or in pots during Mar., and germinated in a cold frame. Prick out the seedlings into boxes or pans, grow-on in a closed frame until established, when gradually increase air and harden off for planting-out in a sunny position in the rock garden in the late spring.

Species and varieties:

(Shrubby types for Borders or Bedding)
C. amplexicaulis (pale yellow)
C. burbidgei (yellow)
C. clibranii (deep yellow)
C. veitchii (creamy-white)
The flowering season of all the above is from May to Sept., the height ranges from 1 to 4 ft.

Perennial species:

C. acutifolia (yellow, 6–12 in.)
C. biflora (yellow, 9–12 in.)
C. tenella (golden-yellow, marked red lines or spots, 1–2 in.)
C. uniflora (bronze-yellow, 2–4 in.)
(Annual) *C. mexicana* (yellow, 12 in.)
These all flower during late summer and autumn.

CALENDULA

A genus of hardy annuals and half-hardy shrubs native to C. and S. Europe and the M. East, known mainly for the species **C. officinalis,** the Common or Pot Marigold. Marigolds grow in most soils and prefer full sun. Propagation is by seed sown in Mar. or Apr. Flowers yellow to orange, June onwards. There are a number of named varieties growing from 1–3 ft. Seed may be sown in late Aug. for flowering in a cool greenhouse in the early part of the year.

CALIFORNIA BLUEBELL. See *Phacelia* and *Nemophila*

CALIFORNIA HYACINTH. See *Brodiaea*

CALIFORNIAN POPPY. See *Eschscholzia* and *Platystemon*

CALLA (*Bog Arum*)
A genus containing one species only, **C. palustris,** an aquatic plant of the northern temperate regions. It has creeping or floating stems and thrives in firm soil in the margins of ponds and likes the sun. Plant in Mar. in not more than 12 in. of water. Propagate by division. Flowers small, white, followed by red berries. (For *Callas* or *Calla Lilies* see *Zantedeschia.*)

CALLIOPSIS. See *Coreopsis*

CALLIRHOE (*Poppy Mallow*)
A small genus containing both annuals and perennials, native to N. America. They prefer a sunny site in well-drained light sandy soil. Propagation is by seed or cuttings. Striking crimson flowers, July–Aug. 6 in.
C. involucrata (perennial). Flowers up to 2 in. across in loose sprays, white, lilac or crimson, July–Aug. 6 in. Rock garden.
C. papaver (perennial). Long trailing stems. Flowers violet-red, July–Aug. 4–9 in. Suitable for dry sandy places.

CALLISTEPHUS CHINENSIS (*China Aster*) PLATE 6
This single species, a half-hardy annual native to China, has given rise to the popular garden asters of which there are several recognized types such as China asters (single) 'Comet' and 'Ostrich Plume' (single and double), chrysanthemum-flowered asters and paeony-flowered asters. They grow in most soils but do best in rich loams and also make good pot plants. Propagation is by seed sown under glass in Mar. or Apr. or outside in late Apr. Flowers in a wide range of colours, from 3 to 5 in. across, Aug.–Oct. Height varies from 9 in. to 2 ft. There are a number of named varieties and catalogues should be consulted.

CALTHA (*Marsh Marigold*)
A genus of hardy perennials native to the northern hemisphere. One species, **C. palustris,** thrives in a moist soil and is a showy water- or bog-garden plant. Propagate from seeds or division. Rich yellow flowers from May–July. 12 in. There are several varieties.

CAMASSIA (*Quamash*)
Hardy bulbous plants native to N. America, requiring a moist soil and sunny position. Plant in Oct. 4–5 in. deep and 6 in. apart, and leave undisturbed. Propagation is by seed sown when ripe or by offsets which are, however, rare and generally produced only if the bulbs are lifted and 'nicked' to cause a wound.
C. leichtlinii. Flowers white, cream, blue or purple, May–June. 3 ft.
C. quamash. Flowers blue or white, May–June. 2–3 ft.

CAMPANULA (*Bellflower*)
This large genus contains many popular annuals, biennials and perennials, mostly natives of Europe and W. Asia, and suitable for the border, rock garden or greenhouse. They range from a few inches to several feet high and grow well in most kinds of soil provided drainage is good. Some require plenty of moisture, others will grow in drier conditions and while the majority prefer sunny positions, a number will do well in partial shade. The leaves vary widely with the species and the bell-shaped flowers may be borne in spikes, clusters or sprays. Propagation is by seed or division or with certain of the rock garden and greenhouse species by cuttings taken in Mar.

Perennials
Of the many perennial species suitable for border plants, the following are generally the most successful:
C. bononiensis. Leaves ovate, toothed. Flowers small, up to $\frac{3}{4}$ in. across, bluish-violet or white, borne in long spikes, July. $2\frac{1}{2}$ ft.
C. carpatica. Lower leaves round to ovate, stalked and toothed. Flowers blue, up to 2 in. across, June–Aug. 1 ft. There are a number of varieties and hybrids with flowers varying from white to pale blue and purple-blue.

C. glomerata. Leaves hairy, up to 3 in. long. Flowers variable in shape and size up to 3 in. across, white to purple, May–Sept. 1–2 ft.
C. lactiflora. Leaves ovate, toothed. Flowers up to 1½ in. across in large loose sprays, white to pale blue, July–Sept. 4–6 ft. Prefers a good moist soil and will grow in partial shade, but resents being disturbed.
C. latifolia. Leaves toothed, lower large and heart-shaped, upper leaves ovate. Flowers white, deep blue or purple, July–Sept. 4–5 ft. Most varieties do best in moist, shaded positions.
C. latiloba. Leaves narrow, toothed. Flowers large, up to 2 in. across, white to blue, June–July. 1–3 ft.
C. persicifolia. Leaves tough, bluntly toothed. Flowers 1 in. across, white to deep blue, single or double according to variety, July–Aug. 1–3 ft. 'Beechwood' (pale blue), 'Fair Mile' (deep blue), 'Snowdrift' (white).
C. pyramidalis. A fine species, usually treated as a biennial although it will persist longer. Flowers blue or white, borne on pyramidial spikes, July. 4–5 ft.
C. rhomboidalis. Leaves ovate, toothed. Flowers blue to violet, borne in long spikes, July–Sept. 3–4 ft.
For rock gardens some of the species listed above, notably **C. carpatica,** provide varieties growing 6–9 in. high and others are **C. cochlearifolia** (4–6 in.), **C. portenschlagiana** (4–9 in.) and **C. × stansfieldii** (4 in.), all flowering between June and Aug., in white, purple or varying shades of blue, according to variety.

For growing in greenhouses the trailing species such as **C. isophylla** (blue or white) or **C. fragilis** (blue) make good basket plants and **C. portenschlagiana** and **C. pyramidalis** are excellent for pots, the latter making stately, erect displays.

Of the biennials the most important is the well-known Canterbury Bell (**C. medium,** growing 1–3 ft.) with flowers ranging from white, yellow, pink to various shades of blue and purple. Seed should be sown in June for planting out in autumn or the following spring. **C. michauxioides** is taller, up to 4 ft., and makes a good biennial for a border but has not such a wide range of colour in the flowers.

The annuals cannot compete, with the possible exception of **C. propinqua grandiflora,** a branching plant with violet and mauve flowers.

CAMPION. See *Lychnis*

CANDYTUFT. See *Iberis*

CANNA
A genus of half-hardy perennials native to tropical Asia and America, generally grown under glass but also used for planting-out in sunny beds of loam richly dressed with manure. Propagation is by division or seed sown in Feb.–Mar. in pans or pots in a temperature of 60 deg. F. Before sowing, soak the seed for a day in warm water. Prick out, pot-up singly, and pot-on as required, finishing in 10–12-in. pots for greenhouse use. For outdoor planting set out in June about 24 in. apart, and about the end of Sept. lift and winter under glass or in a frost-proof building in boxes of moist soil and peat. In regions where the winter is mild they can be left in the ground protected with a layer of straw, leaves or ashes. All varieties flower Aug.–Oct. and reach a height of 6 ft. or more. There are several species with many beautiful, named varieties.

CAPE COWSLIP. See *Lachenalia*

CAPE DAISY. See *Dimorphotheca*

CAPE GOOSEBERRY. See *Physalis*

CAPE HYACINTH. See *Galtonia*

CAPE LILY. See *Crinum*

CAPE POND-WEED. See *Aponogeton*

CARDAMINE (*Bitter Cress, Cuckoo Flower*)
Native to the cooler parts of Europe, the species are mostly dwarf or annual plants of little merit, but a few of the perennials are excellent for borders, particularly on the heavier soils and in moist shaded places. The stems are generally leafy and the flowers borne in spikes or clusters. Propagation is by division.

C. macrophylla. Leaves hairy and toothed. Flowers pale purple, ½ in. across, June. 1–1½ ft. Specially suitable for cool moist places.
C. pratensis. Leaves roundish. Flowers white to pale purple, ½ in. across, in flat clusters, Apr.–May. 1–1½ ft. Prefers moist soils and partial shade.
C. trifolia is a dwarf species (6 in.) with white flowers, Mar.–May.

CARDUNCELLUS

A small genus of thistle-like perennials sometimes grown in borders, the species varying in height from 9–24 in. Propagation by division. Flowers blue, June–July. Apt to become weed-like on rich soils.

CARLINA (*Carline Thistle*)

A genus of annual, biennial and perennial thistle-like plants with one species suitable for growing in a border, preferably in full sun. Most kinds of soil are suitable. Propagate from seed.
C. acanthifolia. Leaves spiny and angular, downy beneath. Flowers white, typically thistle-like, June. 2 ft.

CARNATION (*Dianthus caryophyllus*)

Carnations are members of the genus *Dianthus* and are propagated by seeds, layers and cuttings. For cultural purposes they can be dealt with under two main headings: Borders and Perpetuals.

Border carnations are classified as 'Selfs', 'Flakes', 'Bizarres' and 'Fancies'. Selfs are those with flowers of one colour only. Flakes are those which have the ground colour striped with one of another shade. Bizarres are those which have the ground colour marked and flaked with two or three other tints. Fancies are those varieties which do not come within the other classes. There is also another class termed 'Picotee' which embraces those having a ground colour distinctly edged with another colour. They may be grown both in the outside border or in the greenhouse. Modern varieties produce perfect rounded flowers with a good calyx and stiff stem and the highest perfection is obtained by pot culture under glass. Commencing from scratch, young layers are potted singly into 3-in. pots in Sept. in a compost of two-thirds loam and one-third well-decayed leaf-mould or peat with the addition of some coarse sand, the loam if possible having been sterilized. The plants may be overwintered in a frame or a cold greenhouse, the chief point being that ample air circulation is permitted. In Mar. they should be potted-on, two plants in an 8-in. pot using a similar compost but with the addition of a little well-decayed manure and a sprinkling of chalk. Stand the pots on an ash base in the greenhouse and keep close for a few days, after which allow a good air circulation. Watering must be done with care but increasing quantities given as growth proceeds and as the flower spikes develop stakes must be provided and gentle feeding at alternate waterings be given. Disbud the flowers to one central bud at an early stage for the finest blooms. After flowering the plants may be layered in their pots. This is an acquired art and requires practice for the novice. First remove some of the lower leaves from the best growths, loosen and remove some of the top soil from the pot, replacing it with a fine sandy mixture; using a sharp knife slit the stems longitudinally and giving them a slight twist bring them down and peg the open tongue firmly into the compost. Keep the house close and syringe overhead daily during rooting, watering as required. When well rooted, again give plenty of air, pot-up and grow-on as before. Under this system the young layers will be ready for their final pots in the late summer and subsequent flowering will be correspondingly earlier.

Open border culture: Prepare the border three weeks or so before planting time which should be in Sept. or early Oct. Well-cultivated fertile soil with the addition of no recent manure is desirable. On very heavy soils raised beds will give the best results and planting should be deferred until Apr., potting the layers and keeping them in a cold frame for the winter. Well-tended beds may be allowed to stand for 2 or 3 years but a proportion of the required number should be layered and planted annually to maintain a healthy young stock. Staking and disbudding will require attention but the disbudding need not be so severe unless extra fine flowers are desired. These also are propagated by layering selected growths after flowering is finished. Prepare the shoots in the same manner as for pot layering, well water the plants if at all dry, break up with a fork the soil around the base, provide a layer of fine soil and proceed as described above.

Perpetual carnations under glass: These are of value for providing flowers throughout the year. They require cool treatment at all times with, in winter, an average temperature of 50 deg. F. Propagation is by means of cuttings of young shoots taken from about mid-way of the flowering stem and may be rooted in beds or pans of silver sand in a propagating case with a temperature of about 50 deg. F. Nov. to Mar. are good months for propagating, at which time suitable material is usually available. When rooted, pot singly into 3-in. pots, from thence, when ready, move on into 5-in. pots and finally to 7 or 8 in. size for flowering. When the young plants are about 6 in. high pull out cleanly the growing point and thereafter as the side-shoots develop to 6 or 8 in. they should in turn be stopped, the final stopping taking place not later than mid-July, as a stopped shoot will take about 3 months to produce a flower. If it is desired, after the final potting, the plants may be stood outside on a firm ash bed for the summer months returning them to the greenhouse in late Aug. or early Sept. Carnations should always be potted firmly and the soil for the final potting should consist mainly of good fibrous loam with a little granulated peat and coarse sand.

Malmaison carnations which were at one time considered the aristocrats of the carnation world are now seldom seen.

The following lists give some of the best border and perpetual-flowering varieties but readers are advised to consult trade lists as new varieties are constantly being introduced.

Border, Selfs:
- 'Bookham Grand' (crimson)
- 'Clarinda' (salmon)
- 'Eudoxia' (white)
- 'Fusilier' (scarlet)
- 'Lavender Clove' (heliotrope and grey)
- 'Pink Pearl' (soft pink)

Flakes:
- 'Katherine Brookes' (yellow and scarlet)
- 'Catherine Glover' (bright yellow and scarlet)
- 'Dorothy Robinson' (white, splashed rose-pink)
- 'Harmony' (soft grey, striped cerise)
- 'Mendip Hills' (pink, flaked scarlet)

Fancies:
- 'A. A. Sanders' (apricot-orange, edged and splashed heliotrope)
- 'Bennie Clove' (dusty pink, speckled lavender)
- 'Bookham Glory' (yellow, edged and striped crimson)
- 'Bookham Lad' (white, striped scarlet)
- 'Desert Song' (apricot-salmon, overlaid lavender)
- 'Leslie Rennison' (purple, overlaid rose)

Picotees:
- 'Ganymede' (white, edged crimson)
- 'Eva Humphries' (white, edged purple)
- 'Helen' (yellow, edged crimson)
- 'Ripston Piquette' (golden-buff, edged garnet-lake)
- 'Santa Claus' (yellow, edged purple)
- 'Starlight' (yellow, edged crimson)

Perpetual flowering:
- 'Cardinal Sim' (scarlet)
- 'Golden Gleam' (yellow)
- 'Heather Beauty' (mauve-pink)
- 'Lavender Lady' (orchid-mauve)
- 'Pink Gem' (pale pink)
- 'Paris' (salmon-pink)
- 'Snow Maiden' (white)
- 'Quaker Maid' (rose-pink, overlaid French grey and purple)
- 'Brocade' (white, overlaid crimson)
- 'Pigalle' (white ground, edged and flecked violet)

CARPENTER'S LEAF. See *Galax*

CARTWHEEL FLOWER. See *Heracleum*

CASTOR-OIL PLANT. See *Ricinus*

CAT THYME. See *Teucrium*

CATANANCHE (*Cupid's Dart*)
A small genus of which one perennial species,

makes a good border plant, particularly on the lighter soils in full sun. The flowers resemble cornflowers. Propagation is by seed or division.
C. caerulea. Leaves narrow, hairy. Flowers blue, white or blue and white, June–Aug. 2½ ft. The flowers can be cut and dried for winter use.

CATMINT. See *Nepeta*

CELOSIA (*Prince of Wales' Feathers, Cockscomb*) PLATE 7
A genus of half-hardy annuals native to many warm regions and including the popular species **C. cristata** which requires a warm, sheltered position, and may, with a little care, flower throughout the winter in a greenhouse. Sow the seeds thinly in pans in Mar. in rich, sandy loam and peat with a bottom heat of 70 deg. F. and cover with fine soil. Transplant into boxes, and when big enough pot singly into 3-in. pots and place on shelves near the glass. Syringe regularly, allow good ventilation and ensure that the roots are not too moist. Harden off and plant out about 6–10 in. apart in June. If for the greenhouse pot-up in 6-in. pots and keep the seedlings in a warm, moist atmosphere until the flowers appear. As soon as the buds form apply weak liquid manure until the colour shows. The flowers range from yellow to red or scarlet depending on variety and the height ranges from 12–18 in.

CELSIA (*Cretan Mullein*)
A genus of hardy and half-hardy annuals, biennials and perennials native to the Mediterranean and Near East, growing in ordinary soil in sunny, sheltered positions or in a cool greenhouse. Propagate from seed sown in pans or for the shrubby species **(C. arcturus)** from cuttings of young wood, struck in a cool greenhouse or frame.
C. arcturus (perennial). Large yellow flowers, often spotted purple, June–Nov. Up to 4 ft.
C. bugulifolia (perennial). Yellow flowers with purplish veins and blue-green markings, June–Sept. 1 ft.
C. cretica (biennial). Golden-yellow flowers spotted brown, June–July. 4–5 ft.

CENTAUREA (*Knapweed*)
This large genus contains annuals, biennials and perennials but is probably best known for its annual Cornflower and Sweet Sultan. Mostly natives of Europe and W. Asia, the plants grow well in most soils, either in sun or partial shade, but under rich conditions tend to make foliage at the expense of flowers. Propagation of annuals is by seed, perennials by division.

C. babylonica. Leaves silvery. Flowers numerous, small, yellow, July. Grows at least 6 ft. high and sometimes up to 10 or 12 ft., and is therefore suitable only for the back of large wide borders.
C. cyanus (*Annual Cornflower*). Flowers white, blue, rose, July. 2–3 ft.
C. depressa. Leaves silvery forming a flat growth. Flowers blue, June–Aug. 1 ft.
C. gymnocarpa. A shrubby type with branching woody stems and attractive silvery leaves. Flowers rosy-purple, partly hidden by the leaves, Aug. 1½ ft.
C. moschata (*Sweet Sultan*) (annual). Flowers white, yellow or purple, July–Aug. 2–3 ft.
C. pulchra. Long toothed leaves, green above and almost white below. Handsome pink flowers, July–Aug. 2 ft.
C. rutifolia. Leaves hairy and silvery. Flowers pale purple, July–Aug. 2½ ft.

CENTAURIUM (syn. *Erithraea*)
A genus of annuals, biennials and perennials mainly from the northern hemisphere with one of the hardy species making a good rock-garden plant. They require a sandy loam with plenty of peat and good drainage. Propagation is by seed or division.
C. scilloides. Flowers deep rose, June–Aug. 3 in.

CEPHALARIA
One species only is suitable for growing at the back of large wide borders. They will do well in most soils and will tolerate partial shade. Propagation is by division or seed.
C. tatarica. Leaves deeply cut, toothed. Flowers yellow, resembling those of scabious, June–Aug. 5 ft.

CERASTIUM (*Mouse Ear Chick-weed, Snow-in-Summer*)
A genus of hardy dwarf-growing annuals and perennials native to northern regions of the Old World and including several weeds. They grow well in ordinary soil and the better species make useful carpeting for the rock or paved garden. Propagate from seed, division or cuttings.
C. biebersteinii. Silvery foliage. White flowers, May–June. 6 in.
C. tomentosum. Silvery foliage. White flowers, June–Aug. 6 in. An attractive variety is **columnae.** Apt to spread unduly in rich soil.

CERATOPHYLLUM (*Water Hornwort*)
A small genus of water plants useful as oxygenators. The stems are forked with the leaves in whorls. May be planted in the soil at the bottom of the pond or allowed to float. Propagation by pressing pieces into the pond soil. The growth generally sink in winter and rise again in spring.

CERATOSTIGMA (*Leadwort*)
A small genus of shrubs and perennials native to Far East and including the herbaceous **C. plumbaginoides** which likes a sunny position in a sandy loam and makes a good border plant. Propagation from cuttings or by division. Striking cobalt-blue flowers, July–Sept. 10–15 in. For **C. willmottianum** see page 322.

CHAMOMILE. See *Anthemis*

CHEIRANTHUS (*Wallflower*)
A small genus of biennial and perennial plants including the well-known Wallflower and Siberian Wallflower. They are normally treated as biennials, the seed being sown outside in May or June, for transplanting to permanent positions in the autumn.
C. × allionii (*Siberian Wallflower*). Flowers yellow to orange. May–July. 1 ft.
C. cheiri (*Wallflower*). Flowers in striking colours and mixtures, white, yellow, orange to brown, pink to scarlet, some double, all fragrant, spring to early summer. Height generally about 1½ ft. with dwarf varieties 6–9 in. A large number of named varieties are available.

CHICK-WEED. See *Cerastium*

CHILEAN BELLFLOWER. See *Lapageria*

CHINA ASTER. See *Callistephus*

CHINCHERINCHEE. See *Ornithogalum*

CHINESE BELLFLOWER. See *Platycodon*

CHINESE LANTERN. See *Physalis*

CHIONODOXA (*Glory of the Snow*)
Bulbous plants native to Mediterranean and Near East. Thrive in ordinary, well-drained soil. Plant in Oct. 2½ in. deep and about 4 in. apart. Lift from the soil only when overcrowded and then only after the leaves have died down. They may also be planted in pots for growing under glass in the same way as many other bulbs. Propagate from offsets in Oct. or raise from seed.
There is little difference between the species. All have blue or violet-blue flowers with white centres in Mar. and grow 6–9 in. high. Varieties with white and pink flowers are obtainable.

CHRISTMAS ROSE. See *Helleborus*

CHRYSANTHEMUM PLATES 9–10
The genus comprises more than a hundred species of annual and perennial plants and contains some of the most popular flowers of today, the most important being the border and greenhouse chrysanthemums, the Shasta daisies, Marguerites and pyrethrums. The true origin of some of these is not known or is obscured by the selection and crossing that has gone on for many years in China and Japan, and for short periods in Europe, America and Africa. **C. indicum** and **C. morifolium** (syn. *C. sinense*) are the probable parents of the border and greenhouse or 'florists' chrysanthemums' which may now be made to flower all the year round. This, however, is an intricate process to be left to the specialist grower only, the average person still regarding the chrysanthemum as a late summer and autumn flower in the open garden, the season being

extended by late varieties which flower under glass.

Culture of Outdoor Varieties. Commencing in the late autumn when flowering has finished, cut down the plants and lift sufficient stools to provide stock for the next season. These may be placed close together in shallow boxes of fairly dry soil and stood in a cold frame or greenhouse, making sure that all are clearly labelled. From Mar. onwards cuttings of basal shoots will root readily in small pots of sandy soil in a case or on the open stage if shaded from bright sun. Pot singly into 3-in. pots when well-rooted and grow-on cool, hardening them off for planting-out in late Apr. or early May. About mid-June if the plants have not sent out side-shoots naturally the points should be taken out and if the breaks resulting from this stopping form a flower bud too quickly they may again be stopped but no stopping should be done after mid-July. Staking and tying will of course require attention as the plants grow and for the best flowers the stems may be disbudded to one central bud. Keep the plants well watered in dry periods, feed gently when in full growth and if earwigs are troublesome place a small inverted pot on each stake with a little dry moss in the bottom and inspect daily. Black-fly or green-fly may appear from time to time but this is easily kept in check by spraying with any mild contact insecticide such as Abol or D.D.T. emulsion.

Culture of Indoor Chrysanthemums. These also are best propagated from cuttings. After flowering the stems together with any weak shoots springing from the base should be cut down to about 6 in. from the base, the pots being kept in a cool greenhouse will require but little water for a time. As basal cuttings become available of the Japanese types during Dec. and Jan., a start may be made with propagating. Propagation of the smaller flowered 'Decorative' varieties may be deferred until Feb. when better growing conditions will prevail. At this season cuttings of chrysanthemums will root well in a frame placed in a cool house. The cuttings should always be of a short, sturdy type and the rooting compost of an open texture. Rooting will take from 3 to 5 weeks and when ready they should be potted singly into 3-in. pots and grown-on in the best light conditions available. The next shift will be into 5- or 6-in. pots commencing about the first week in Apr. At this stage a little well-decayed manure and a sprinkling of bone meal may be added to the compost which may be of a slightly coarser texture. The roots should be disturbed as little as possible and when completed the plants may be stood out in a cold frame. For a few days maintain a close atmosphere and shade from bright sunshine but thereafter air must be admitted freely. By the middle of May it will be safe to stand them outside and soon after preparations must be made for final potting which can be commenced in mid-June. Large pots, 8 to 10 in. diameter, will be necessary for finals and the compost should consist of two-thirds broken fibrous loam, one-sixth well-decayed manure, one-sixth granulated peat together with a good sprinkling of sharp sand and a 5-in. pot of bone meal to each barrow-load of loam. It is a good plan to see that the plants are staked before standing them out in a sheltered but open position on a bed of ashes or slates for the summer. Stopping and disbudding will require attention particularly for exhibition blooms. The stopping may vary slightly according to the variety but usually the first 'break' is a natural one, all that is required is to pinch out the flower bud and remove all the shoots below except for three of the best placed shoots into which the whole energy of the plant is concentrated. With some varieties a second stopping may be necessary but in any case no stopping should be done after mid-July. With 'decorative' varieties for which bushy plants are required the tip should be pinched out when the plants are about 6 in. high. All exhibition types should have the side flower buds removed leaving but one central bud on each of the three stems. Other types are dealt with as necessary according to whether single blooms or sprays are desired. Feeding may be commenced in Aug. and continued until the flowers commence to open. A general fertilizer or liquid manure will be suitable for growth and after the buds are formed sulphate of potash applied at about 10-day intervals on three occasions will improve the colour of the flowers. By the beginning of Oct. the plants should be removed to the greenhouse where, if the weather is fine and open, they should be syringed overhead twice daily to preserve the foliage. Keep the house cool and airy, but as the flowers commence to open a little fireheat at night may be necessary to prevent damping, but even then the top ventilators should never be entirely closed. A good temperature to aim at is 50 to 55 deg. F. The latest flowering varieties should be allowed to remain in the open as long as possible always providing that severe frosts do not occur.

Varieties, Japanese Exhibition:
'Cossack' (crimson)
'Dennis Wroe' (white)
'Jaffa' (orange-terra cotta)
'Margaret Shoesmith' (pink)
'Mrs. John Woolman' (rose)
'Lilac Prince' (lilac-pink)
'Shirley Perfection' (bright pink)
'Shirley Primrose' (primrose-yellow)
'Woolman's Victor' (rose-pink, silver reverse)

Japanese Incurved:
'Curlew' (gold)
'Maxine' (white)
'Ondine' (white)
'Ron Shoesmith' (white)
'Susan Alesworth' (soft pink)
'Vera Woolman' (yellow)
'Maylen Improved' (ivory-white)

Decorative, mid-season:
'Balcombe Perfection' (bronze)
'Cream Princess Anne' (pale cream)
'Marie Brunton' (deep yellow)
'Princess Anne' (pink)
'Rose Wells' (rose pink)
'Worthing Success' (deep pink)

Decorative, late:
'Christmas Flame' (bright scarlet)
'Florence Shoesmith' (crimson)
'Fred Shoesmith' (white)
'Loula' (crimson and gold)
'Red Crensa'
'Shirley Late Red'
'Sussex Crimson'
'Yellow Mefo'

Border varieties:
'Alex Cumming' (cerise-rose)
'Brenda Talbot' (pink)
'Evelyn Bush' (white)
'Golden Rule'
'Harold Park' (yellow)
'Imperator' (coppery-red)
'Kathleen Doward' (soft pink)
'Pink Pride'
'Regalia' (rosy-purple)
'Westfield Bronze'

Single varieties (greenhouse):
'Caroline' (pink)
'Eclipse' (yellow)
'Flarepath' (crimson)
'Firebird' (orange)
'Peggy Stevens' (yellow)
'Uranus' (bronze-red)

Anemone-Centred:
'Aphrodite' (mauve-pink)
'Bronze Enchantress'
'Long Island Beauty' (white)
'Thora' (rose-pink)
'Yellow Grace Land'

Pompons:
'Anastasia' (purple)
'Andy Pandy' (yellow)
'Imp' (crimson)
'Jante Wells' (yellow)
'Snow Elf' (white)

Rayonnante:
Varieties with rolled petals in bronze, pink, white, yellow and green.

Korean:
Introduced in 1930s and are crosses between early outdoor florists' varieties, and **C. coreanum.** There are two main types, the tall with wiry but strong stems and the dwarfer more branching type that form bushes suitable for the front border. All are hardy. Large number of varieties, double and semi-double, in vast range of colours. Flower late Aug. to Nov., 18–36 in. Single varieties can be grown from seed, and named varieties must be propagated from cuttings. Catalogues should be consulted.

Cascade chrysanthemums:
Developed from **C. indicum** and produces masses of white, pink or yellowish-bronze flowers and excellent for the cool greenhouse.

Propagated from cuttings or seed sown in Feb. and potted on into 9- or 10-in. pots as for late-flowering chrysanthemums, they should be grown outside during summer on a bench 6 ft. from the ground with training canes running at about 75 deg. The plants should be fed liberally, the laterals stopped repeatedly and tied in until mid-Aug. and the pots brought inside in Sept. when the ties should be released.

Charm chrysanthemums:

They produce masses of single scented flowers in autumn, in white or shades of pink, bronze, yellow and red. They are raised from seed sown in Feb., potted on, stopped once at 6 in. and grown on into 7–9 in. pots.

Summer flowering annuals:

C. carinatum and **C. coronarium** have given rise to most of the annual or summer flowering varieties which produce single or semi-double flowers in striking colours from July to Sept. and grow 1½–2½ ft. high. They are easy to grow, may be sown in boxes in Mar. and later planted out in beds or borders or may be sown direct where they are to flower in Apr.

Varieties:

- 'Northern Star' (white)
- 'Eastern Star' (yellow with dark centre)
- 'Evening Star' (yellow)
- 'Morning Star' (soft yellow)
- 'Attrococcineum' (deep scarlet)
- 'Eclipse' (zoned flowers of various colours)

Chrysanthemum frutescens (*Marguerite*). Popular border plants thriving in any average garden soil. Sow under glass in Apr. or strike cuttings taken from flowering plants in Sept., rooting in a cold frame. Grow-on in 4-in. pots and harden off for planting-out in late May. They also make good greenhouse plants for which purpose they should be potted into 6-in. pots, grown outside on an ash base until Sept., when they may be potted into larger pots and grown in a cool house for flowering the following spring. To induce a bushy habit stop the young growths during the spring and summer. Both white and yellow varieties are obtainable.

C. coccineum (*Pyrethrum*). Leaves delicately lobed and fern-like, vivid green. Flowers white, pink, red or crimson, May–June, 30 in. Large number of varieties available so consult catalogues.

C. leucanthemum (*Ox-eye Daisy*). Leaves oblong, lobed. Flowers white with yellow eye, July–Sept., 30 in.

C. maximum (*Shasta Daisy*). Leaves smooth, lance-shaped, toothed. Flowers large, single or double, white with gold or yellow eye, July–Sept., 18–36 in. Excellent varieties available.

C. rubellum. Long, lobed or broadly-toothed leaves, hairy beneath. Flowers white, pink, red, purple or yellow, fragrant, Aug.–Oct., 24–36 in. Consult catalogues.

C. uliginosum (*Moon Daisy*). Leaves long, sharply but coarsely toothed. Flowers white with greenish centres, Aug.–Oct., 4–5 ft. Suitable for rear of border.

CICHORIUM

The genus includes endive and chicory, the latter **C. intybus** making a good border plant with blue, white or pink flowers and growing up to 5 ft. high. Unfortunately the flowers close early in the day and sometimes the shed seed gives rise to quantities of unwanted seedlings. Propagation is by seed or division.

CIGAR FLOWER. See *Cuphea*

CINERARIA

Beautiful greenhouse perennials now included in the genus *Senecio*. Treated as biennials but which by early sowing may be had in flower later the same year. The best results are obtained from a May or June sowing giving plants which flower from Feb. to Apr. There is a wide range of colours available including shades of blue, pink and red, also white; these may be had in self colours or mixed and, in addition, in some varieties the flowers are edged with a second colour. The type of plant and size of flower also varies thus the hybrida grandiflora section gives a plant with large flowers and growing to a height of some 18 in. The multifloras make small, compact plants 9 to 12 in. The stellata types, with smaller flowers, will grow up to 3 ft., whilst intermediate strains may be had in a height range of 1 to 2½ ft.

Seed should be sown in well-drained pans of light, open compost, the seeds covered very lightly and the pans placed in very gentle warmth, covering them with glass and paper until germination takes place. As soon as ready, prick out or pot singly into 3-in. pots, gradually harden off and grow-on in a cold frame well spaced out. Pot-on as required until by the end of Sept. or early Oct. the plants should be in their final pots of 6 or 8 in. diameter. After each potting maintain a close, slightly moist atmosphere until established when air should be given freely. Shade the plants from too bright sunshine and transfer to a cool greenhouse before there is any danger from frost. Established plants will benefit from alternate waterings with weak liquid manure or soot water. Seed may be sown from Apr. to late June but as mentioned a mid-May or early June sowing is likely to be the most valuable. The silver-foliaged variety used for bedding purposes or the cold greenhouse is *C. maritima.* This should be sown under glass in Mar. and grown-on and hardened off for outdoor planting in the usual way.

CINQUEFOIL. See *Potentilla*

CLARKIA

This small genus of hardy annuals from N. America includes two species **C. elegans** and **C. pulchella** from which the modern garden clarkias have been derived. They are easily grown in most soils from seed sown in spring and thinned or transplanted 6–9 in. apart. They may also be grown in pots in the greenhouse. Flowers may be single or double in a wide range of colours, June–Sept. 1–2 ft.

CLAYTONIA (*Spring Beauty*)

A genus of dwarf-growing hardy annuals and perennials native to N. America, with only two of the perennial species worth growing. They do best in moist but well-drained soils and are suitable for rock gardens or wild gardens. Propagate from seed or from offsets.

C. sibirica. White or rose-coloured flowers, spring. 6 in.

CLEMATIS. See page 323.

CLIVIA

Evergreen bulbous plants for the greenhouse and natives of S. Africa, requiring cool, dry conditions when resting and a temperature of 50–60 deg. F. when growing in spring and summer. They should be grown in 5 to 10-in. pots but rarely need re-potting as they seem to thrive when pot-bound. Water well in summer and, when the buds are forming, give weak liquid manure. Propagate from seeds sown when ripe or division of suckers in Feb.

C. miniata. Leaves long, deep green. Orange-scarlet flowers with a yellow throat borne in open heads, Mar.–May. 2 ft.

C. nobilis. Numerous reddish-yellow flowers, May. 20 in.

COBAEA SCANDENS (*Cup and Saucer Plant*)

A genus of evergreen climbers native to C. America. Sow thinly under glass in light, rich soil in Feb. at temperature of 45 deg. F. Can also be propagated from cuttings of young shoots in Jan.–Feb. and raised in a propagating frame. Pot-up in 4-in. pots, harden off and, if for growing in open, plant out 24 in. apart in June. If for greenhouse allow to grow on in cool greenhouse. Prune back laterals to two buds in Feb. and remove all weak growth. The purple and greenish-white flowers bloom July–Sept. and reach a height of 20–24 ft.

CODONOPSIS

The species are mainly twining plants, natives of Asia and Japan, having flowers with attractive centres. Unfortunately, the flowers hang down and must therefore have some support or be grown high up, on the top of a bank, if they are to be seen. They will grow well in the lighter soils, in a sunny position.

C. convolvulacea. An uncommon slender plant requiring light but ample support. Flowers blue, bell-shaped, up to 2 in. across, Aug. 2–3 ft.

C. tangshen. Flowers greenish outside, with purple spots and stripes within, July–Aug. Given suitable supports such as pea sticks, will grow up to 10 ft. high.

COLCHICUM (*Autumn Crocus, Meadow Saffron*)
A genus of bulbous plants widely distributed in Europe, the Mediterranean and Near East, generally preferring a sunny, well-drained loam. The corms should be planted in July–Aug. 4 in. deep and 6 in. apart and left undisturbed unless increase is desired, when they should be lifted in July and divided, every 3 years. They may also be propagated from seed. Some species produce the flowers before the leaves and many of the hybrids have large, occasionally double, flowers.
C. autumnale. White or lilac flowers, single or double, Sept.–Oct. 6–10 in.
C. speciosum. Rose, purple or white flowers, Aug.–Sept. 10 in.

COLEUS
Half-hardy annual and perennial plants with decorative leaves, native to tropical regions of Old World, used mostly as greenhouse plants with some suitable for bedding out. Propagation is by cuttings or seed, both requiring a temperature of 50–60 deg. F., the rooted cuttings and seedlings being potted on as necessary. Plants for bedding out should be finished in 4–6-in. pots and those for the greenhouse grown into 10-in. pots, being pinched back as required. The perennial species get straggly at the end of the season and should be replaced by newly-raised stocks.
C. blumei (perennial). Leaves deeply toothed, yellowish, red or purple. Small white and purple flowers, 12–18 in. Several named varieties are available.
C. frederici (annual). Large deep blue flowers in open sprays, winter. Up to 4 ft.
C. thyrsoideus (perennial). Bright blue flowers, winter. Up to 3 ft.

COLLINSIA
Hardy annuals native to N. and C. America. They thrive in most garden soils preferably in a sunny position. Propagate from seeds sown in autumn or spring and thin to about 4 in. apart.
C. bicolor. White or reddish-purple and white flowers, July–Sept. 12–20 in.
C. grandiflora. Reddish-purple and white flowers, May–June. 6–12 in.

COLLOMIA
A small genus of hardy American annuals easily grown in most soils and sometimes used as a filler in borders. The flowers are borne in dense heads, yellow to red, July–Aug. 1–1½ ft.

COLUMBINE. See *Aquilegia*

COMFREY. See *Symphytum*

COMMELINA (*Day Flower*)
A large genus of half-hardy tuberous perennials native to C. America, with a few species suitable for greenhouse use or for bedding out when they should be lifted and stored for the winter as with dahlias. The species generally grown is **C. coelestis** which requires a good light soil in a sunny position, has white, blue or blue and white flowers in June. 1½ ft. Propagation is by seed or division. (**C. erecta** is similar but with smaller flowers and being more hardy will survive normal winters out of doors.)

COMMON COTTON THISTLE. See *Onopordon*

COMPASS PLANT. See *Silphium*

CONANDRON
A single species of a semi-hardy tuberous perennial native to Japan, and excellent for sheltered spots in the rock garden, or in the alpine house. Thrives in well-drained leafy soil. Propagate from seeds sown under glass, or from division. Bright green foliage. Violet-blue or white flowers, summer. 4–6 in.

CONEFLOWER. See *Rudbeckia*

CONVALLARIA MAJALIS
This single species, the popular Lily of the Valley, is widely distributed in the northern hemisphere. It grows well in most garden soils but prefers a moist position in shade, and flowers in Apr. and May. It may also be forced in a heated greenhouse when flowers may be had from Dec. to Mar. For forcing strong 2- to 3-year-old crowns should be selected in Nov., packed into pots or boxes

with a little soil, well watered and given a temperature of at least 60 deg. F. Growth is hastened by excluding light until the shoots are 3–4 in. high. 'Retarded' crowns can be purchased and will succeed in a lower temperature 50–55 deg. F. There are varieties with white or rosy-mauve flowers and one with double flowers.

CONVOLVULUS (*Bindweed*)
Hardy annual and perennial climbing and trailing plants widely distributed, especially in Mediterranean region. A sunny position in ordinary soil is suitable for the hardy species, but for the less hardy a mixture of fine loam, peat and leaf-mould is necessary. For the annuals sow seed thinly in the open from May–June near a trellis or other supporting structure and thin out to about 10 in. apart. For dwarf species sow seeds from Mar.–June and thin out to about 5–10 in. apart. For perennials propagate from seed, cuttings or division.
C. althaeoides (perennial). A trailing species suitable for rock garden. Flowers pale red or lilac, summer.
C. arvensis is the well-known troublesome weed.
C. cneorum (shrubby perennial, not fully hardy). Leaves covered with silvery hairs. Soft pink flowers, June–Sept. 1–3 ft. Also suitable for cool greenhouse.
C. mauritanicus (perennial). Blue flowers with white throat, June–Sept. Trailing, suitable for baskets.
C. tricolor (annual). Flowers blue and white, July–Sept. 1 ft.

CORAL BELLS. See *Heuchera*

CORAL-BERRIED DUCKWEED. See *Nertera*

COREOPSIS (*Tickseed*) PLATE 11
A genus of annuals and perennials mostly natives of N. America and valuable for their long flowering periods, the flowers being borne on long, slender stems having few leaves. The annuals are often known as Calliopsis. All are suitable for cutting, and will grow in most soils, preferably in sunny positions. Propagation of annuals is by seed and perennials by seed or division.
C. auriculata (perennial). Stems slender but wiry. Flowers single, golden-yellow with a crimson-maroon blotch at the base of the petals, June–Sept. 2 ft.
C. grandiflora (perennial). Stems long and strong. Flowers yellow, up to 3 in. across, July–Sept. 3 ft.
C. lanceolata (perennial). Stems more branching. Flowers bright yellow, up to 2½ in. across, June–Sept. 2 ft.
C. tinctoria is the annual species and comprises two groups, **nana** growing about 12–18 in. high and **nana compacta** 6–9 in. Flowers yellow or crimson often with brown, maroon or scarlet centres according to variety. Other useful annual species are **C. douglasii** and **C. drummondii.**
C. verticillata (perennial). Leaves narrow, divided. Flowers small but numerous, golden-yellow, July–Sept. 2 ft.

CORN FLAG. See *Gladiolus*

CORNFLOWER. See *Centaurea*

CORNISH MONEYWORT. See *Sibthorpia*

CORTADERIA
A small genus of perennial grasses native to S. America, and including the well-known Pampas grass **(C. argentea).** It thrives in a sunny position in well-drained soil, and is better propagated by division of roots in Apr.–May than by seeds which do not come true. The plant throws up magnificent, long, silky plumes 6–8 ft. high in summer. There are several varieties, differing in the leaves and colour of plumes from white to pink or purplish.

CORTUSA MATTHIOLII (*Bear's Ear*)
A dwarf-growing perennial widely distributed in Europe and Asia, closely resembling the Primula. The plant likes partial shade in rich sandy loam and leaf-mould. Propagate from seeds or division. Rosy-purple flowers, July.

CORYDALIS (*Fumitory*)
A small genus of annuals and perennials, mostly rock-garden plants, but with two species suitable for the front of a border. They will grow in most kinds of soil but prefer the lighter types and partial shade. Propagation is by division or seed.
C. cheilanthifolia (perennial). Leaves up to 8 in. long, erect, divided and fern-like. Flowers yellow, tubular, borne in loose sprays, May. 1 ft.
C. glauca (annual). Flowers red and yellow, July. 12–18 in.
C. lutea (perennial). Leaves divided and fern-like. Flowers yellow, in clusters, May–July. 1 ft. Will grow almost too well on good soil.

COSMOS (*Mexican Aster*) PLATE 12
Half-hardy annuals and perennials native to C. America, doing well in sunny positions in ordinary soil. The annuals are propagated from seed preferably sown under glass for planting out in May, the perennials by seed or division. Most garden varieties of annuals have been derived from **C. bipinnatus,** having white, rose or purple flowers with yellow centres, and **C. sulphureus** having sulphur-yellow flowers. All bloom from July to Sept. and grow 2 to 3 ft.
C. diversifolius is perennial and has rose to white flowers with yellow centres, summer. Up to 2 ft.

COTULA
Hardy perennials native to the Southern Hemisphere, especially New Zealand. They grow well in gritty loam in a sunny position and make excellent plants for the rock or paved garden, but in rich soil may need checking. Propagate by division in Mar. or Oct.
C. dioica. Small yellow flowers, summer. 2–4 in.
C. squalida. Mat-forming. Small purple flowers, summer. 2–4 in.

COTYLEDON. See *Echeveria*

CRANE'S BILL. See *Geranium*

CRASSULA
A genus of shrub-like plants native to Africa, with only one species sufficiently hardy for growing out of doors. Propagate from cuttings grown in sand under glass or by seed. Greenhouse plants should be kept fairly dry in a winter temperature of 45 deg. F., and 65 deg. F. in summer.
C. lactea. White starry flowers, summer. 10–14 in. Greenhouse.
C. sarcocaulis. Small pink or reddish flowers, summer. 12 in. Hardy. Rock garden.

CREAM-CUPS. See *Platystemon*

CREEPING JENNY. See *Lysimachia*

CRETAN MULLEIN. See *Celsia*

CRIMSON FLAG. See *Schizostylis*

CRINUM (*Cape Lily*)
Half-hardy bulbous plants native to the more tropical regions of the world, most of the species require a heated greenhouse, although a few will succeed out of doors in sunny, sheltered positions in well-drained sandy loams with some winter protection. Alternatively the bulbs may be lifted, stored and replanted. For outdoor cultivation plant 6 in. deep in Apr. or May. For the greenhouse pot-up in the spring (every third year or so), one bulb to each 9–10-in. pot in a compost of 2 parts fibrous loam and 1 part peat. Propagate by seed sown in a temperature of 70 deg. F. or from offsets in Mar.
C. asiaticum. Rosette of long leaves, up to 48 in. White flowers tinged green or red, long-lasting, summer. For the greenhouse.
C. bulbispermum. Leaves up to 24 in. White or pink flowers, summer. For the greenhouse.
C. moorei. Leaves up to 36 in. White or pink flowers, summer. For the greenhouse.
C. × powellii. Leaves up to 48 in. Rose-red or white flowers. Can be grown outdoors in sunny, sheltered position.

CROCOSMIA
This genus of two species of S. African plants has provided the 'montbretias' of gardens. They grow from corms which may be left

down, and in suitable conditions will increase steadily, although they are better lifted after a few years, separated and replanted. They prefer a rich, light soil and a sunny position. Propagation is by offsets or seed. The garden varieties have been produced by crossing the two species **C. aurea** and **C. pottsii.** The leaves are narrow, up to 20 in. long and the flowers funnel-shaped, borne in graceful spikes of brilliant colour, yellow, orange, red or scarlet, often with striking combinations. Aug.–Sept. A number of named varieties are available.

CROCUS PLATE 13
Hardy, bulbous plants widely distributed in Europe, Asia and Africa. Most of the species flower in the spring, but a few in autumn or winter, and all grow well in most garden soils in sun or shade and are also suitable for rock gardens. See Chapter 9. They may also be grown in pots, six to seven in a 6-in. pot planted in the autumn in a compost of light sandy loam and peat, plunged in ashes until root growth is well advanced and then put in a frame or cool greenhouse. Any attempt at quick forcing or the use of a high temperature will prevent flowering.

CRYPTOGRAMMA (*Mountain Parsley*). See *Ferns*

CUCKOO FLOWER. See *Cardamine*

CUP AND SAUCER PLANT. See *Cobaea*

CUPHEA (*Cigar Flower*)
Several species of these half-hardy shrubby plants, native to the tropical regions of America, make good greenhouse plants and may also be used for summer bedding, since they are suitable for most ordinary soils. Propagation is from seed, preferably sown in Jan. or Feb. in heat or by cuttings.
C. ignea. Evergreen, with white or scarlet, black and white flowers, summer. 12 in.
C. lanceolata (annual). Bluish flowers, summer. 18 in.
C. micropetala. White and red flowers, July. 12 in.
C. miniata. Evergreen with pale vermilion flowers, June–Sept. 2 ft.

CUPID'S DART. See *Catananche*

CUSHION PINK. See *Armeria*

CYANANTHUS
A genus of trailing plants native to E. and C. Asia, suitable for moist positions in the rock garden. Propagate from seed, or preferably from cuttings in spring or early summer struck in moist sandy loam and peat.
C. delavayi. Bell-like flowers of deep blue, Aug.–Sept. 3–4 in.
C. incanus. Azure-blue flowers, July–Aug. 4–6 in.
C. lobatus. Striking purple-blue flowers, Aug.–Sept. 4 in.
C. microphyllus. Violet-blue flowers, Aug.–Sept. 2–4 in.

CYCLAMEN (*Sowbread*)
For garden purposes these well-known and highly popular plants may be divided into two groups, the hardy outdoor cyclamens and the greenhouse cyclamens. All have tuberous rootstocks and are propagated by seed but it is often more convenient to buy the corms. Seed of the hardy species may be sown in Apr. in a bed out of doors or preferably in pans in a frame or cold house in Mar., and planted out in June or July when the corms are as big as peas. Seed of the greenhouse species should be sown under glass in Aug. or Sept. being merely pressed into the seed compost. The seedlings should be grown on at 55–60 deg. F., pricked out, potted-up and at the end of May put into a cold house or frame. By June or July they should be moved into 5- or 6-in. pots and brought back to the warm house 45–50 deg. F. at the end of Sept. for flowering from Nov. onwards. A good potting compost and good light are essential throughout and the corms should never be more than half-covered. After flowering the corms should be kept watered until the leaves die down, when they should be dried off and rested, prior to re-potting for the following year. Purchased corms should be potted in Aug. to

allow good root growth to be made before moving into the greenhouse.

C. europaeum, flowering in autumn with white, rose or carmine flowers, and **C. repandum,** flowering in Apr. with carmine flowers, are particularly suitable for the rock garden.

C. neapolitanum is the best species for outdoor use, having white or rose flowers with carmine blotch, from July to Nov., and is particularly suitable for growing under the shade of trees.

C. persicum is half-hardy and has provided the greenhouse varieties with large flowers in white or beautiful shades of pink, red or carmine and sturdy, self-supporting growth.

CYNOGLOSSUM (*Hound's Tongue*)

PLATE 14

A genus of biennial and perennial plants with only a few species sufficiently hardy for general use, and even then the perennials do not usually last for many years. But they are attractive plants with funnel-shaped flowers borne in forked sprays, and grow well in most kinds of soil. Propagation is by seed which should be sown where the plants are to flower since transplanting is often unsuccessful.

C. amabile (biennial). Flowers blue, pink or white, July–Aug. 2 ft.

C. grande (perennial). Leaves up to 12 in. long, oval, hairy beneath. Flowers blue, numerous, in branching sprays, July. 2½ ft.

C. virginianum (perennial). Leaves up to 10 in. long, oval, rough. Flowers pale blue, July. 1–2½ ft.

CYPERUS

A genus of perennial grasses which is widely distributed throughout the world. Some thrive in a bog or marsh garden and others in a greenhouse. Propagate from seed preferably sown in gentle heat or by division.

C. diffusus. Greenish-yellow or brownish-yellow spikes. Leaves green or variegated. Up to 3 ft. Greenhouse. Needs plenty of moisture.

C. longus. Leaves light green. Spikes reddish. Up to 4 ft. For margins, pools and the like.

CYPRESS VINE. See *Quamoclit*

CYPRIPEDIUM (*Lady's Slipper*)

A large and important genus of orchids with a few species sufficiently hardy for growing in a sheltered spot in a rock garden, preferably in semi-shade in a compost of sandy peat with good drainage. Propagated by division in Apr. or Sept.

C. calceolus. The Lady's Slipper is the native species now rarely found in woods on limestone soil. It grows about 1 ft. high with reddish-brown flowers having a yellow lip, June–July. Other hardy species include:

C. arietinum. Greenish-brown flowers, May. 6–10 in.

C. candidum. Greenish-brown flowers with white lip, June. 12 in.

C. macranthon. Rose-purple flowers, May–July. 9–12 in.

C. montanum. Brownish flower with white lip and striped red, May–July. 10–12 in.

C. reginae. Rose and white flowers, June–July. 20 in.

See also *Orchids.*

CYSTOPTERIS (*Bladder Fern*). See *Ferns*

DAFFODILS. See Chapter 9

DAHLIA PLATE 15

The cultivation of dahlias presents no difficulty in the average garden. All they ask is that the soil should be well supplied with humus so that it does not dry out too readily and that the young plants should not be subjected to frost in the spring. When the autumn frosts have blackened the tops the tubers must be lifted and stored in a frost-proof place for the winter. There are three methods of propagating the dahlia. The tuberous rootstock may be divided in Apr. by cutting off tubers at the crown with an eye or two attached. These may be planted direct into the border, or placed in shallow boxes with a little soil in a cool house to start into growth. Seeds may be sown in pots or pans in Mar. in a light compost. A warm greenhouse is necessary to raise the seedlings which, when germinated, should be either boxed or potted singly in small pots to grow. In Apr. they may be placed in a cold frame in readiness for hardening off for early June planting-out.

This method of propagating is frequently used for dwarf bedding types but it should be noted that seedlings do not produce tubers freely and therefore do not keep well during the winter. The most widely used method of propagation is by cuttings. In Feb. or Mar. old overwintered tubers are placed in shallow boxes with a little fine light soil and brought into a warm greenhouse—temperature 60 to 65 deg. F.—to start into growth. Strong shoots will soon appear from the base and when these are about 3 in. long they may be taken off and placed around the edges of 4-in. pots filled with sandy loam and peat. In a warm house they will root on the open stage if well watered in, shaded from bright sun and sprayed overhead on bright days. When rooted pot-up singly and gradually harden off for early June planting out.

Dahlias like a deep fairly rich soil and initial preparations are best carried out in the autumn or early winter. The site should be open but sheltered as strong winds can do much damage to the plants. Dig the ground two spits deep at the same time incorporating a good dressing of well-decayed manure and bone meal at the rate of 3 to 4 oz. per sq. yard. Toward the end of May break down the surface and if any old soot is available this may be worked in. Before planting place the stakes in position allowing a distance of from 2 to 5 ft. according to the height of the plants. Where a quantity of plants are grown it is a good plan to plant them in beds of two rows each allowing an alley-way between them. In this way the plants are well seen and the necessary attentions are performed with greater ease. Plant firmly and just cover the ball of soil around the roots.

Aftercare consists of tying as required to keep the plants neat and trim, conserving soil moisture by periodic hoeings and watering well during dry weather. A surface mulch of well-decayed compost or manure will serve two purposes—assist the moisture holding capacity of the soil and afford nourishment to the plants. Should this not be possible, liquid manure or a readily soluble general fertilizer lightly applied and well watered in will be helpful during Aug. and Sept. If earwigs are troublesome insert a small pot with a little moss in the bottom on the top of each stake and examine daily. If extra fine flowers are desired or showing anticipated, then a system of limiting the number of growths per plant and disbudding must be adopted. When the plants are some 15 to 18 in. high and showing no side-shoots the growing tip should be pinched out and the resulting growths limited to five or six and on these as the flower buds form they should be reduced to one on each shoot. For general purposes and a good show of flowers in the garden all that is necessary is that a periodic thinning out of straggling or unwanted stems is carried out. After the first autumn frost, cut down the stems to about six inches, take up the tubers removing all surplus soil and stand or hang them, tubers uppermost, in a suitable place for drying. When quite dry clean off and store in a frost-proof place for the winter. A few dry, old ashes scattered among the tubers will help to preserve them from damp and if desirable a dusting over with powdered lime and flowers of sulphur may be given once or twice during the winter. The following list gives some of the best varieties in each section:

Large and Medium Decorative:
- 'Alvas Supreme' (yellow)
- 'Barbara Rooke' (orange)
- 'Croydon Snotop' (white)
- 'Evelyn Rumbold' (purple)
- 'Kelvin' (salmon-pink)
- 'Skyride' (lavender-pink)
- 'Uchuu' (deep red)
- 'World News' (white, tipped lavender)

Small Decorative:
- 'Angora' (white)
- 'Front Row' (apricot)
- 'Lady Tweedsmuir' (mauve)
- 'Major Graham' (crimson)
- 'Meiro' (lavender)
- 'Thelma Mitchell' (orange)
- 'Worton Jane' (pale pink)
- 'Tipperne' (yellow, tinged bronze)
- 'Worton Melody' (deep pink)

Large and Medium Cactus:
- 'Belle of the Ball' (soft pink)
- 'Brandane' (yellow)
- 'Bravissimo' (vermilion)
- 'Cocktail' (yellow)

PLATE 23

HIBISCUS (Hemp Mallow, Rose Mallow). This late-flowering shrub produces a veritable mass of flowers as the photograph above demonstrates.

PLATE 24

HOSTA (Plantain Lily). These are best grown as specimen or key plants in beds, or as woodland or shrubbery plants.

PLATE 25
Flower spike of the hyacinth, 'Queen of the Pinks'.

PLATE 26
Above, HYDRANGEA X MACROPHYLLA (Hortensia). A summer-flowering shrub, there are a number of named varieties available.
Below, HYPERICUM (Rose of Sharon, St. John's Wort). An evergreen shrub which flowers during June to Aug.

PLATE 27
ILEX (Holly). The species shown here is the common holly, I. aquifolium.

PLATE 28

IRIS. A large number of named garden varieties are available, in a wide range of outstanding colours and shades.

PLATE 29
KALMIA LATIFOLIA (American Laurel).
Several species are suitable for the border.

PLATE 30

LATHYRUS (Sweet Pea). The variety illustrated here is 'Frolic'. A large number of named varieties in a wide range of delicate colours are available.

'Dolce Vita' (salmon-pink)
'Eclipse' (red with wine reverse)
'Glen Riches' (amber-bronze)
'Golden Autumn' (golden-apricot)
'Paul Critchley' (pink)
'Respectable' (golden-amber)
'Sapper Loot' (orange-red with yellow tips)
'Silent Beauty' (lavender-pink and white)
'Top Affair' (yellow)
'Veritable' (white and purplish-pink)

Small Cactus:
'Betty' (apricot-pink)
'Brig O'Doon' (scarlet)
'Cheerio' (carmine-red)
'Delicate Beauty' (lavender)
'Deerplay' (yellow)
'Elmer' (yellow)
'Grace' (pink)
'Jill Edwards' (cream, flushed rose)
'Preference' (salmon)
'Resplendent' (orange)
'White Rays'
'Worton Sally-Ann' (mauve)

Charm and Paeony-flowered:
'Bishop of Llandaff' (scarlet, dark foliage)
'Dorothy Russell' (scarlet)
'Lemon Beauty' (yellow)
'Norah Bell' (pink and yellow)

Large Pompons:
'Florence Vernon' (lilac)
'Rothesay Superb' (scarlet)
'Good Show' (white)

Medium Pompons:
'Bachus' (scarlet)
'Baseball' (white)
'Cassam's Red'
'Clarissa' (yellow)
'Globular' (purplish-pink)

Small Pompons:
'Avilla' (lavender, tipped silver)
'Cheeky' (lilac, purple edge)
'Crossfield Ebony' (deep crimson)
'Jessie Buchanan' (pink)
'Little Conn' (crimson-scarlet)

Collerette:
'Brides Bouquet' (white)
'Claire de Lune' (yellow)
'Easter Sunday' (cream)
'Fashionmonger' (red, white tips)
'Kaiserwaltzer' (scarlet, yellow collar)
'Libretto' (red, white collar)
'Vera Lynn' (rose-pink, cream centre)

Bedding Types:
'Border Triumph' (orange-scarlet)
'Corona' (vermilion-scarlet)
'Jean Thompson' (cherry-salmon)
'Lilianne Ballego' (orange and apricot)
'Maureen Creighton' (red)
'Park Princess' (pink)
'Park Wonder' (yellow)
'Shirley Yellow'

Ball Dahlias:
'Asgog' (lavender-pink)
'Blossom' (pink)
'Nellie Birch' (dark red)
'Good Show' (white)
'Linda' (apricot-orange)
'Mary Griggs' (white)

DAISY. See *Bellis*

DAVALLIA. See *Ferns*

DAY FLOWER. See *Commelina*

DAY LILY. See *Hemerocallis*

DELPHINIUM PLATE 16

The genus comprises a large number of species found over most of the temperate parts of the world. The great majority are fully hardy and include a number of annuals, biennials and perennials that are suitable for all parts of the garden, the best known being the annual larkspurs and the perennial delphiniums. The perennials are beautiful stately plants without which no border can be complete, but which can also make a wonderful display when grown in a bed by themselves. Delphiniums will grow in most soils but give the finest results in a sunny position on well-drained fertile loams and respond magnificently to liberal feeding. On wet or poorly-drained soils they usually suffer in winter and may even die out. They are a favourite food of slugs. Propagation of annuals is by seed and of perennials by seed, division or by cuttings of basal shoots taken in early spring.

Perennials

The parentage of the perennial garden delphiniums is not known and much of the plants' past history has been lost in the crossing and selection that has gone on for many years to produce the beautiful varieties that are grown today. But three main groups are generally recognized:

1. Typical delphiniums, large-flowered hybrids originating from **D. elatum,** and producing a long central spike, often branched at the base. They flower from June to July with single, double or semi-double flowers and grow 4–5 ft. high. Selected varieties (semi-double, unless otherwise stated):

'Alice Artindale': lilac and blue, double. 5 ft.
'Anne Page': cornflower blue. 6 ft.
'Anona': sky blue flushed pink, with white eye. 5 ft.
'Beau Nash': deep purple-dark mauve, with black and gold eye. 5 ft.
'Blackmore's Blue': sky blue, with white eye. 5 ft.
'Blackmore's Glorious': mauve and pale blue with white eye. 5½ ft.
'Blue Gown': deep blue, semi-double. 5 ft.
'Blue Lagoon': gentian-blue with rose flush at base of florets. 5 ft.
'Cambria': blue-mauve, with black eye. 5½ ft.
'C. H. Middleton': medium blue, with sulphury-white eye. 5 ft.
'Charles F. Langdon': medium blue, with black eye. 6 ft.
'Crystal': sky blue, with white eye. 5½ ft.
'Guy Langdon': violet, with white eye. 5½ ft.
'Jennifer Langdon': pale blue and mauve, with black eye. 5 ft.
'Julia Langdon': mauve and pale blue, with white eye. 5 ft.
'Lady Eleanor': double, sky blue, shaded mauve. 6 ft.
'Lorna': deep blue, with brown eye. 5 ft.
'Nell Gwynne': mauve, with white eye, 5 ft.
'Purple Prince': violet-purple, with white eye. 6 ft.
'Royalist': deep blue, with white eye. 6 ft.
'Silver Moon': silver-mauve, with white eye. 5 ft.
'Startling': violet, with white eye. 5½ ft.
'Swanlake': white with black eye. 4 ft.
'Wm. Richards': bright blue, with brown eye. 5 ft.
'Welsh Boy': sky blue and mauve. 5 ft.

2. Belladonna delphiniums of branching habit with several short, rather than one main or central spike, flowers single, plants shorter, 2½ to 4 ft. high, flowering June to August. Selected varieties:

'Blue Bees': single pale blue, with white eye. 3 ft.
'Capri': sky blue, with white eye. 3 ft.
'Cliveden Beauty': sky blue. 3 ft.
'Lamartine': single, dark blue. 3 ft.
'Naples': single, gentian-blue. 3 ft.
'Semi plena': sky blue tinted pink, semi-double. 2½ ft.
'Wendy': deep blue flecked mauve. 4 ft.

3. The Ruysii delphiniums which are hybrids of **D. nudicaule** (and are often included in group 2) have given pink colours as seen in:

'Pink Sensation': single, rose-pink. 3 ft.
'Rose Beauty': single, pink. 3 ft.

A fourth and fairly well recognized group consists of a number of hybrids raised in America and rather loosely known as 'Giant Pacific Hybrids' or 'Pacific Strain Hybrids'. The flowers range from white to deep purple, but the plants do not usually last for more than a few years.

Other species suitable for garden cultivation and including a number of dwarf-growing varieties which look well in rock gardens are:

D. grandiflorum. A branching type, best treated as an annual or biennial bedding plant. Varieties:

'Azure Fairy': pale blue. 1½ ft.
'Blue Butterfly': deep blue with a brown spot on the petals. 1½ ft.
'Blue Gem': deep blue. 1 ft.
'White Butterfly': white. 2 ft.

D. nudicaule. Leaves more fleshy and deeply cut. Flowers yellow, orange, red or purple, July–Aug. 1–1½ ft.

Delphiniums are so popular and attractive that new varieties and even new types are continually being produced. Those who wish to specialize should keep in touch with nurserymen who make a feature of the plant and those who are not so particular about growing named varieties only may find absorbing interest in raising their own plants from seed bought from one of the well-known sources.

Annuals (*Larkspur*)
The garden varieties have originated from **D. ajacio** and **D. consolida** and comprise plants growing from 18 in. to 4 ft. high with flowers in a wide range of colours, white, pink to scarlet, blue to mauve, many varieties being double and excellent for cutting. Seed should be sown in spring in the open, the seedlings being thinned to 6–9 in. apart.

DENDROBIUM. See *Orchids*

DENTARIA (*Toothwort*)

These are mainly dwarf-growing plants, natives of temperate regions and suitable for shaded positions or a woodland garden. But three species are suitable for the front of a border, provided the soil is rich and moist and the position not exposed to full sun. They flower early, Apr.–June. Propagation is by division.

D. bulbifera. The leaf-axils usually produce bulbils which may be used for propagation. Flowers few but large, purple, Apr. 1½–2 ft.

D. diphylla. Flowers white with purplish tinge, June. 6–12 in.

D. laciniata. Leaves on short stalks, deeply toothed. Flowers rose to white, Apr. 1 ft.

DIANELLA

Half-hardy perennials native to Australasia and E. Asia, mainly suitable for a cool greenhouse, although in warm districts they may be grown outdoors in a mixture of 2 parts peat to 1 part sandy loam. Propagate from seeds sown under glass, or root division in Mar.

D. laevis. Flowers bluish, in a loose spray, May. 2 ft.

D. tasmanica. Light blue drooping flowers, May. Up to 4 ft.

DIANTHUS (*Pink*) PLATES 18 and 19

This is a large genus of annual and perennial plants mostly natives of Europe and the Mediterranean, and includes Sweet Williams as well as pinks and carnations, in addition to a number of rock-garden plants. They grow best in well-drained soils containing plenty of lime and prefer full sun. Being evergreen, with silver-green foliage, and dwarf-growing free-flowering plants, the perennials are particularly useful for the front of a border. Propagation is by layering, cuttings or seed.

D. caryophyllus. This species is a native of Europe and has for long been known as the clove-pink, carnation or gillyflower (more correctly July-flower) and from it the modern varieties of carnation have been derived. The border type has the characteristic narrow, smooth, silvery leaves and solitary flowers of the species, but is not so satisfactory as the various types of pinks for inclusion in a border. Some form of light support for the flowers is necessary and the temptation to spend time in disbudding in order to produce larger and finer flowers is too often wasted. Nevertheless, the flowers are attractive and usually fragrant, the named varieties giving a wide range of colours in shades of white, yellow, pink, red and mauve, flowering from July to August, and growing 1–2 ft. high. See *Carnation*.

D. plumarius is the original cottage pink from which the modern garden pinks have been derived. They are invaluable as edging plants, flowering profusely throughout June in a wide range and combination of colours and, after the flowering stems have been cut off, making a border of silvery-green foliage the whole year round. A wide range of colours may be obtained particularly by raising plants from seed, and many of them are fragrant, single or double. There are also a number of named varieties, including the old favourite 'Mrs. Sinkins', with its large white, double flowers.

Among other types that have been evolved from crosses between original species, the most outstanding are: **D. allwoodii**, a race of perpetual-flowering pinks resulting from the crossing of **D. plumarius** with the perpetual-flowering carnation. They are generally double, bloom from June to Oct., have a wide range of colour and many are scented. There are a number of named varieties. 'Sweet Wivelsfield' comprises hybrids of **D. allwoodii** and **D. barbatus** (Sweet William) and can also be grown as a greenhouse plant. Though perennial it is better raised annually from seed. There are a number of named varieties, single and double, which are generally sweet-scented. Among the species suitable for border edging or rock garden are:

D. alpinus. Flowers white, pink to purplish red, June. 4 in.

D. deltoides. The Maiden Pink. Flowers white, pink, red or crimson, June–Sept. 9 in.

D. gratianopolitanus. The Cheddar Pink. Flowers pink or red, very fragrant. May–July. 1 ft.

D. knappii. Flowers yellow, June. 1–1½ ft.

Annuals and Biennials

D. armerica is the native Deptford Pink, an annual growing 12–18 in. high, with small purplish flowers in dense heads.

D. barbatus (*Sweet William*). Although perennial is better treated as a biennial. Seed should be sown in May, the seedlings pricked out for planting out in the autumn. The densely packed flowers are brilliant in a wide range of colours, some striped, some parti-coloured and others descriptively named 'auricula-eyed'. All flower early in summer and grow about 1½ ft. high. A true annual strain has recently been developed.

D. chinensis (*Chinese* or *Indian Pink*) is an annual sometimes treated as a biennial, with flowers in white or deep rich reddish colours, June–Sept. 12–18 in.

DICENTRA (*Bleeding Heart*)

These are dainty herbaceous perennials, natives of America, Siberia and Japan, having fernlike leaves and pendant flowers borne in arching sprays. They grow best in moist but well-drained soils and tolerate partial or light shade. Most of the species are dwarf-growing and are suitable for rock gardens or the front of borders. Propagation is by division.

D. eximia. Leaves deeply lobed. Flowers reddish-purple, drooping, in long sprays, May–June. 1½ ft.

D. formosa. Leaves coarsely divided. Flowers pink or dull red, May–June. 1½ ft.

D. oregana. Leaves coarsely divided. Flowers cream, tipped purple, June–July. 6 in.

D. spectabilis. Leaves much divided. Flowers white or rosy-crimson, up to 1 in. long, heart-shaped, drooping in graceful arching sprays, May–June. 1–2½ ft.

DICTAMNUS (*Burning Bush, Dittany*)

There is one species which is not only attractive in itself, but has also the curious capacity of exuding a volatile and inflammable oil. On a hot, still day it is sometimes possible to ignite this oil by putting a lighted match close to the flowers and doing no harm to the tissues. It will grow in most soils, preferably in a dry place, and should not be unnecessarily disturbed. Propagation is by division or seed.

D. albus. Leaves in pairs, finely toothed. Flowers fragrant, white or pale purple, borne in long spikes, June–July. 1½ ft.

DIEFFENBACHIA

Evergreen greenhouse plants native to tropical America. No part of this plant should be put in the mouth as it is acrid and poisonous. For luxuriant growth the plants need a high moist temperature. Propagate from suckers or cut up portions (2–3 in.) of stem. These root quickly in a sand-bed.

D. picta, dark green leaves with white or yellow patches or spots between the veins.

DIERAMA

A small genus of South African corm-rooted plants suitable for the cool greenhouse and sheltered sites outdoors in a well-drained moist soil. Propagated from seed sown in a frame in Sept. or offsets in Oct.

D. pulcherrimum. Bell-shaped flowers varying in colour from dark blood-red, purple, rose to white, early autumn. 3–6 ft.

DIGITALIS (*Foxglove*)

In addition to the well-known common foxglove which is a biennial, there are several perennial species suitable for growing in a border where their strong straight stems, bearing many closely-packed flowers, can be used to break levels of height or to grow up between the green foliage of other plants that flower earlier or later in the season. They are natives of,

Europe, N. Africa or W. Asia and grow well in most soils, preferring a cool or partially-shaded position. Propagation of biennials is by seed and of perennials by division or seed.

D. ambigua (perennial). Flowers yellowish, netted with brown, up to 2 in. long, July–Aug. 2–3 ft. Does not usually persist for more than a few years.

D. lanata (perennial). Flowers small but numerous and closely packed, greyish-white with white or purple lip, July–Aug. 2–3 ft.

D. lutea (perennial). Flowers small but numerous and closely packed, yellow, July. 2 ft.

D. purpurea (biennial). Excellent for shaded positions. Seed should be sown in May and the seedlings planted out 6–9 in. apart as soon as large enough to handle. Flowers in various colours from white, cream, pink to purple with contrasting marks or blotches in the tube, June–July. Up to 5 ft.

DIMORPHOTHECA (*Cape Daisy, Star of the Veldt*)

A genus of half-hardy annuals and perennials native to S. Africa, useful for summer flowering or growing in a cool greenhouse. Sow seed thinly in Apr. in a sunny position and in a light soil, or sow under glass in Mar. for planting out in May or for growing on in the greenhouse. Perennials may also be propagated from seed or cuttings.

D. aurantiaca (perennial but usually treated as annual). Marigold-like orange to yellow flowers with black disk in centre, May–Sept. 12 in.

D. ecklonis. Flowers white above and purplish beneath, summer. 24 in.

D. pluvialis (annual). Similar to above, June–Aug. 12 in. Hardy.

DISPORUM (*Fairy Bells*)

A genus of perennials with pleated leaves and nodding flowers doing well in rich, moist, shaded positions. Propagation is by seed or division.

D. lanuginosun. Flowers yellow and green, May. 1 ft.

D. pullum. Flowers white, purple or brownish-pink, May. 1½ ft.

DITTANY. See *Dictamnus, Origanum*

DODECATHEON (*American Cowslip, Shooting Stars*)

Hardy perennial herbs native to N. America. Suitable for cool, shady places in the rock garden or for growing in a cool greenhouse. Propagate from seed sown as soon as ripe or by division preferably in the autumn. Pot-up for the greenhouse in the autumn, using 6-in. pots.

D. clevelandii. Deep red-purple flowers with yellow bases and a few purple spots, Apr.–May. 15–18 in.

D. jeffreyi. Deep red-purple flowers, May. 18–24 in.

D. meadia. White or rose-coloured flowers with a white base, May. 18–24 in.

DOG'S TOOTH VIOLET. See *Erythronium*

DORONICUM (*Leopard's Bane*) PLATE 20

Doronicums are among the earliest-flowering perennials and are indispensable in a border if it is desired to have bloom in Apr. or May. Natives of Europe and temperate Asia, they grow well in most soils in sun or partial shade, producing daisy-like flowers that are excellent for cutting and will usually give a small second crop in the autumn. Propagation is by division.

D. austriacum. Leaves toothed, heart-shaped to ovate. Flowers large, yellow, up to five on a stem. Apr.–May. 1½ ft.

D. carpetanum. Roots stoloniferous. Flowers yellow, up to 2 in. across, Apr.–June. 1 ft.

D. caucasicum. Leaves deeply toothed. Flowers yellow, 2 in. across, solitary, Apr.–May. 1 ft.

D. plantagineum. Leaves heart-shaped, hairy. Flowers usually solitary, golden-yellow, Apr.–May. 'Harpur Crewe' (golden-yellow) up to 5 ft., 'Miss Mason' (pale yellow) 2 ft.

DOUGLASIA

A small genus of dwarf evergreen rock plants native to the Alps and Pyrenees, requiring perfectly drained positions. Propagate from seed.

D. vitaliana is the only accommodating species and is occasionally seen in rock gardens. The flowers are yellow, primrose-like, spring.

DRABA
A genus of dwarf-growing annuals, biennials and perennials widely distributed in alpine regions and suitable for the rock garden. The flowers are small but often showy and the plants require sunny positions in well-drained gritty loam. Propagate annuals from seed sown under glass as soon as ripe, or in Mar.–Apr. and perennials by division of roots in Mar.

D. aizoon. Bright yellow flowers, spring. 6 in.

D. dedeana. White flowers with a slight touch of violet, spring. 4 in.

D. incana (biennial). White flowers, spring. 4 in.

D. rigida. Golden-yellow flowers, spring. 3 in.

DRACOCEPHALUM (*Dragon's Head*)
The genus consists mainly of rock-garden plants both annual and perennial, with a few species suitable for a border. Natives of Europe and temperate Asia they grow well in most soils, preferring the lighter kinds and a cool or partially shaded position. The flowers resemble those of catmint. Propagation of annuals is by seed sown in Apr., of perennials by division or cuttings of young shoots taken in Apr. or May. The following are the best perennials.

D. grandiflorum. Flowers blue, in spikes about 3 in. long, July. 6–9 in. Rock garden.

D. isabellae. Leaves deeply cut. Flowers deep purple-blue, in long spikes, July–Aug. 18 in. Rock garden.

D. sibiricum. Leaves up to 3½ in. long, toothed, dark green. Flowers bluish or lavender-violet, tubular, 1 in. long, borne in whorls, July. 2–3 ft.

D. veitchii. Leaves toothed. Flowers up to 1¼ in. long, bluish-violet, tube straight, July. 2 ft.

D. wilsonii. Leaves blunt. Flowers 1 in. long, blue, tube curved, July. 1½–2ft.

DRAGON'S HEAD. See *Dracocephalum*

DROPWORT. See *Filipendula*

DROSERA (*Sundew, Youthwort*)
A genus of annual and perennial insectivorous plants, found in Europe, Africa, America and Australia, requiring warm sheltered positions in a bog or wild garden, and best treated as greenhouse plants. Propagation is generally by seed.

D. binata. Easily grown and increased by division, or by root-cuttings placed on the surface of a sandy, peat compost in a warm house in spring. Bears white flowers, June–Sept. 6 in.

D. capensis. Vivid purple flowers, June–July. 6 in.

D. rotundifolia (annual). Can be grown out-doors or in the alpine house. White flowers, June–July. 6 in.

DRYAS (*Mountain Avens*)
A small genus of hardy, evergreen, trailing, shrubby perennials found in northern hemisphere. They like sun or partial shade in gritty loam with lime and leaf mould. Propagate by cuttings taken in Aug. or by seed. Seedlings take 2–3 years to reach flowering size.

D. octopetala. White strawberry-like flowers, June–July. 3 in.

DRYOPTERIS (WOOD FERN). See *Ferns*

DYER'S GREEN WEED. See *Isatis*

ECCREMOCARPUS
A small genus of evergreen climbing plants native to S. America, with one species, **E. scaber,** sufficiently hardy for growing in sheltered positions in well-drained light loam against walls, trellises and pillars. Although perennial, it may more safely be treated as a half-hardy annual, sowing seeds in gentle heat in Feb. and planting out in Apr. or May. As a perennial it may be propagated from cuttings and after flowering cut away old wood and protect the roots in winter. Orange-red or yellow flowers, Aug.–Sept. 10–15 ft.

E. longiflorus with yellow flowers is suitable for the greenhouse.

ECHEVERIA
Half-hardy dwarf-growing succulent plants native to America (formerly included in the genus *Cotyledon*) with pretty coloured leaves in rosettes. They like a warm, sheltered position

in well-drained sandy loam mixed with a little grit. It is essential to bring them inside in Oct. for the winter. Propagate by seed, offsets or leaf cuttings in the summer. For growing in a cool greenhouse pot-up in Mar. in 4–5 in. pots.
E. atropurpurea. Rosettes of purple leaves with glaucous bloom. Bright red flowers, summer. 12 in.
E. fulgens. Bluish-green leaves. Bright red flowers, summer. 6–9 in. Winter-flowering hybrids are obtainable and are excellent for the greenhouse.
E. gibbiflora. Greenish-grey leaves with a touch of purple-red. Scarlet flowers, summer. 12 in.
E. grandiflora. White-grey leaves in rosettes. Yellow-green flowers, summer. 12 in.

ECHINACEA (*Purple Coneflower*)

There are only two species in the genus, both closely resembling *Rudbeckia* and sometimes included there. They prefer a good soil and a sunny position. Propagation is by division.
E. angustifolia. Leaves narrow, up to 6 in. long. Flowers 4–6 in. across, rays drooping, purple or rose, July–Aug. 2–4 ft.
E. purpurea. Leaves large, ovate, slightly toothed, rough. Flowers reddish-purple with orange centre up to 4 in. across, solitary, July–Sept. 3–4 ft. The best recognized variety is 'The King'.

ECHINOPS (*Globe Thistle*)

These are stately plants useful for the back of a border, resembling tall thistles in their foliage and flowers. A few species grow too high (up to 16 ft.) for garden use and care is needed in selection. They are natives of Europe and Asia and will grow well in most soils, preferably in a sunny position. Propagation is by division or root cuttings.
E. bannaticus. Leaves rough, hairy and spiny. Flowers blue, July–Aug. 2–3 ft.
E. humilis. Leaves almost spineless, cobwebby above, hairy beneath. Flowers blue, in large heads, Sept. 3–4 ft.
E. ritro. Leaves divided, spineless, cobwebby above, downy beneath. Flowers blue or steely-blue, July–Aug. 3–4 ft.
E. sphaerocephalus. Leaves spineless, green above, whitish-grey beneath. Flowers silver-grey, July–Aug. 5–6 ft.

ECHIUM

A genus of annual, biennial and perennial shrubby and herbaceous plants native to the Mediterranean, thriving in all but rich soils and particularly suitable for the wild garden. Propagate from seed or cuttings. Hardiness varies.
E. albicans (perennial). Flowers rose-coloured turning to violet, summer. 8–18 in. Hardy.
E. candicans (biennial). Bluish-white flowers, May. 24–48 in. Greenhouse.
E. creticum (annual). Reddish-violet colours, July. 24 in. Hardy.
E. plantagineum (annual or biennial). Purplish-blue flowers, July. 24–48 in.
E. rubrum (biennial). Reddish-violet flowers, May. 24–48 in.
E. wildprettii (biennial). Pale red flowers, summer. 2–3 ft. Greenhouse.

EDELWEISS. See *Leontopodium*

EDRAIANTHUS. See *Wahlenbergia*

ELISENA

A small genus of striking bulbous plants, native to S. America with one species, **E. longipetala,** making a good greenhouse plant. Needs a light, loamy soil with sand generously added and well drained. Propagate from offsets. Handsome white flowers in May. Grows up to 30 in.

ELODEA

A small genus of oxygenating plants useful in outdoor fishpools or aquaria. **E. canadensis** often needs checking. **E. crispa** is more close-growing with ascending stems.

EMILIA (*Tassel Flower*)

A small genus of hardy annuals and perennials native to Tropical America, with one species, **E. flammea,** making a good garden annual. It likes a light soil with plenty of leaf mould. Sow seed in gentle heat in early spring or outside in Apr. Orange-red or golden-yellow daisy-like flowers, July–Oct. 12–24 in.

EPIMEDIUM

All the species have handsome foliage usually forming a dense ground cover, and creeping roots, and are best grown in peaty soils in partial shade. Many are dwarf-growing and suitable for the rock garden or wild garden. Propagation is by division.

E. alpinum. Numerous red and yellow flowers in a loose spray, June. 6–9 in.

E. grandiflorum. Leaves up to 1 ft. long with heart-shaped leaflets. Flowers white, pale yellow, rose or violet, in close spikes, May–July. 1–1¼ ft.

E. pinnatum. Leaves up to 18 in. long, leaflets ovate, hairy, toothed. Flowers yellow, June–July. 1 ft. This species is generally evergreen.

E. × versicolor. Leaves reddish when young. Flowers yellow tinged red, pendulous, May–June. 1 ft.

EPISCIA

Half-hardy herbaceous perennial plants native to Tropical America, having attractive foliage and making good basket-plants for the greenhouse. They grow successfully in a compost of fibrous loam, peat and sand with good drainage and plenty of water. Cuttings set in sandy soil and kept in a close case will root at any time of the year.

E. chontalensis. Foliage green with purple underside. White flowers with yellow centre, sometimes pale lilac, July. 6–8 in.

E. cupreata. Copper-coloured foliage. Scarlet flowers, June–July. 6–8 in. Makes an excellent basket-plant.

E. fulgida. Dark green–coppery foliage. Bright red flowers, July. 6–8 in. Makes an excellent basket-plant.

E. melittifolia. Dark green foliage. Crimson flowers, Apr.–May. 12 in.

EQUESTRIAN LILY. See *Hippeastrum*

ERANTHIS (*Winter Aconite*)

Dwarf tuberous perennials native to Europe, Asia and F. East. They grow in woodland soil or under shrubs. Plant in Oct. 2 in. apart and 2 in. deep, and do not lift from the ground. Propagate by division of the tubers in Oct. or from seed as soon as ripe.

E. hyemalis. Yellow flowers with a slight green tinge, Feb.–Mar. 3–4 in.

E. × tubergeniana. Large bright yellow flowers, Feb.–Mar. 6 in.

EREMURUS (*Foxtail Lily*)

Natives of Asia, few of the species are fully hardy, but the flowers are so attractive that the risk is worth taking, except in cold or exposed positions. The danger period seems to be in spring when the new growth is beginning and some covering should then be given as a routine job. The thick claw-like rootstocks should be planted in early autumn at least 6 in. deep, preferably more, in a good light to medium loam, in a sunny position, and should not be disturbed for at least three years. Propagation is by division or by seed, but seedlings take up to six years to reach flowering size.

The most hardy species are:

E. bungei. Leaves narrow, up to 1 ft. long. Flowers bright yellow or gold, borne in densely packed spikes up to 5 in. long, June. 2–3 ft.

E. elwesii. Leaves long and fleshy. Flowers pink or white, tightly packed, May. 6–9 ft. Stems are strong and rarely need support.

E. robustus. Leaves up to 4 ft. long, bright green. Flowers peach-coloured in spikes up to 3 ft. long, June. 6–9 ft.

E. × shelford. Variable hybrids of garden origin. Flowers yellow, white, pink or shades of orange, June. 4–6 ft.

ERIGERON (*Flea Bane*)

A large genus of annuals, biennials and perennials, the latter making good rock garden and border plants with narrow oblong leaves and aster-like flowers that bloom over a long period. Mostly natives of America and Asia, they grow well in most garden soils that do not dry out easily, prefer full sun, but will also tolerate partial shade, and are suitable for cutting. Propagation is by division or seed.

E. aurantiacus. The Orange Daisy. Flowers semi-double, bright orange, up to 2 in. across, June–July. 1 ft.

E. compositus. Flowers white or pale blue, June. 6 in. Rock garden.
E. foliosus-confinis. Flowers mauve with orange centres, July–Aug. 1 ft. Rock garden.
E. macranthus. More leafy. Flowers blue or purple with yellow eye, July–Aug. 2 ft.
E. philadelphicus. Flowers small but numerous, pale reddish-purple or flesh-coloured, June–Aug. 2 ft.
Most of the named garden varieties have been derived from **E. × hybridus** amd **E. speciosus.** Among the best are:

- 'Amos Perry': rich lavender-blue, June–July. 15 in.
- 'B. Ladhams': rose-pink, May–July. 1½–2 ft.
- 'Dignity': violet-mauve, June–Aug. 2 ft.
- 'Elstead Pink': rose-pink, June–July. 1 ft.
- 'Felicity': pink, June–July. 1 ft.
- 'Merstham Glory': violet-blue, May–Aug. 2 ft.
- 'Mrs. H. Beale': violet-blue, June–Aug. 1 ft.
- 'Quakeress': silver-lilac, June–Sept. 2 ft.
- 'White Quakeress': white, June–Sept. 2 ft.

ERINUS ALPINUS (*Summer Starwort*)

A species of alpine plant from mountains of W. Europe. Thrives in sun or shade in sandy loam and rubble. Propagate from seed sown as soon as ripe, cuttings set in sandy soil and kept in a close frame, or by division. The plant carries purple, carmine or white flowers, Apr.–June. Grows 2–3 in. high.

ERIOPHYLLUM

Two species of this small genus of American plants are suitable for garden use. They require fairly good, well-drained soil and full sun. Propagation is by division or seed.
E. confertifolium. Leaves small, wedge-shaped, whitish, woolly. Flowers yellow, borne in compact clusters, July–Aug. 2 ft. Borders.
E. lanatum. Leaves deeply cut. Flowers yellow, numerous, July–Aug. 6–12 in.

ERITRICHIUM (*Fairy Borage*)

Dwarf alpine perennial plants of the northern hemisphere, suitable for the alpine house. If grown outside they require sheltered semi-shaded positions in gritty loam, leaf-mould, peat and sand. Propagation is by division or seed.
E. nanum. Blue flowers, June–Aug. 6 in. Care must be taken not to water the leaves. Alpine house. Most difficult to cultivate.
E. rupestre. Blue flowers, June–Aug. 10–14 in. This plant is a little easier to grow than **E. nanum.**

ERODIUM (*Heron's Bill*)

Dwarf-growing rock plants, natives of Europe, Asia, N. Africa and Australia, resembling *Geranium* (*Cranesbill*) and requiring well-drained soil in a sunny position. Most of the species are perennial. Propagate from seed sown as soon as ripe. Cuttings can also be taken in July. The roots can be divided in the early spring or autumn.
E. absinthoides. Pink, white or violet flowers and hairy foliage, July. 6 in.
E. chrysanthemum. Sulphur yellow flowers, June–July. 4–6 in. Alpine house.
E. corsicum. Rosy-pink flowers with veins of deeper colour, May–June. 3–5 in.
E. macradenum. Violet-pink flowers with deep purple markings, June–July. 4 in.
E. manescavi. Flowers large, up to 2 in. across, purplish-red, May–July. Up to 2 ft. Borders.
E. petraeum. Purple, violet or rose flowers, June. 4–6 in.

ERYNGIUM (*Sea Holly*)

This genus, mainly of S. American origin, includes several hardy species that make handsome border plants with striking foliage and bright, bluish teazle-like flowers, the colour often extending to the stems and leaves around the flowers. They do best in well-drained, light sandy soils in full sun. Propagation is by division, root cuttings or seed.
E. alpinum. Leaves heart-shaped, toothed. Flowers blue, in oblong heads with the colour extending into the stems and upper leaves, July–Aug. 1½–2 ft.
E. amethystinum. Leaves lobed, cut, spiny. Flowers in globose heads, amethyst blue, July–Aug. 1–2 ft.
E. caeruleum. Leaves lobed and heart-shaped. Flowers blue, July. 2–3 ft.
E. × oliverianum. Leaves deeply cut,

rounded. Flowers various shades of blue, generally spiny, July–Aug. 3–4 ft. Some varieties are too tall, growing up to 10 or 12 ft.

E. planum. Leaves oval to heart-shaped, the upper leaves usually extending beyond the flower-heads. Flowers blue, in roundish heads, July–Aug. 2 ft.

ERYSIMUM (*Fairy Wallflower, Hedge Mustard*)

Annuals, biennials and perennials native to northern hemisphere resembling wallflowers and growing well in moist soils. Propagate from seed, cuttings or division (perennials).

E. alpinum (perennial). Sulphur flowers, May. 6 in. There are two named varieties: 'Moonlight' (yellow) and 'Pamela Pershouse' (rich golden-yellow).

E. linifolium (evergreen). Purple-lavender flowers, May–July. 6–12 in.

E. perofskianum (annual). Reddish-orange, July–Oct. 12 in.

E. rupestre (perennial). Sulphur yellow flowers, June. 9 in.

ERYTHRAEA. See *Centaurium*

ERYTHRONIUM (*Dog's Tooth Violet, Adder's Tongue*)

Bulbous plants found in Europe, Asia, Far East and America, having flowers like cyclamen and making good edging or rock-garden plants. They thrive in light soils. Propagate from offsets planted 3 in. deep in groups in early autumn. For plants grown in pots plant in Aug. in 6-in. pots in a compost of loam and peat, put in a cold frame for the winter, kept fairly dry and brought into the greenhouse in Feb.

E. dens-canis. White or purplish flowers, Mar.–Apr. 6 in.

E. multiscapoideum. Creamy yellow flowers with orange-pink base, Mar.–May. 6–8 in.

E. revolutum. White, pink or cream with a tinge of pink, Mar.–May. 8–12 in.

E. tuolumnense. Yellow flowers, Mar.–Apr. 9–12 in. Most of these species have a number of named varieties.

ESCHSCHOLZIA (*Californian Poppy*)

Well-known hardy annuals, natives of N.W. America. They thrive in sunny beds in ordinary, even poor, soil. Sow seeds thinly from Mar.–June or in the autumn. Thin out to 9–12 in. apart. Autumn sown plants bloom in the early summer.

E. caespitosa. Yellow flowers, May–Oct. 6–9 in.

E. californica. Striking yellow flowers, summer. 12–18 in. A large number of garden varieties have been developed from this plant. Among the established ones are : 'Autumn Glory' (orange-copper), 'Carmine Queen' (carmine crimson), 'Enchantress' (carmine-rose), 'Fireflame' (scarlet-orange), 'Moonlight' (pale yellow), 'Orange King' (rich orange), 'Scarlet Glow' (scarlet).

EUCOMIS

Bulbous plants native to S. Africa. Although greenhouse pot plants they can be grown out of doors in a sheltered, warm position in a well-drained soil. Propagate from offsets in Mar. For the greenhouse pot-up in Mar. in 5-in. pots in a compost of 2 parts fibrous loam to 1 part sand and manure. Water well in the spring and summer but ease off in autumn. In winter keep dry and lay on their sides.

E. autumnalis. Green flowers, spring. 18–24 in.

E. comosa. Green flowers, summer. 18–24 in.

EULALIA. See *Miscanthus*

EUPATORIUM

This is a large genus which contains few species suitable for garden use and only one for outdoors in a border. It grows in most soils, in a sunny position. Propagation is by division.

E. atrorubens with reddish-like flowers and **E. riparium** with white flowers make good greenhouse plants.

E. cannabinum (*Hemp agrimony*). Leaves deeply cut, downy. Flowers reddish-purple in close heads, single or double, July–Aug. 2–4 ft.

EUPHORBIA (*Spurge*)

This is a large genus of spiny or spineless succulent plants and shrubs and a few hardy herbaceous plants suitable for border use. All

contain a milk latex, which is sometimes poisonous, and while the flowers are usually insignificant, their surrounding bracts are colourful and provide a show when massed together. The herbaceous species will grow in most kinds of soil, in sun, or partial shade. Propagation is by division or root cuttings.
E. cyparissias. Leaves slender. Flowers small, greenish-yellow, May–June. 1 ft. May spread too strongly if grown in rich soil.
E. wulfenii. Leaves bluish-green, hairy. Flowers yellow, May–June. 4 ft.

EUSTOMA
Handsome greenhouse plants from South U.S.A. Sow the seed in May and when the seedlings are large enough prick out singly into small pots and put in a light, airy position in a temperature of not less than 45 deg. F. Tend to keep the seedlings on the dry side. (It is important that the seedlings should be in a rosette stage during the winter.) In the early spring pot-up singly into 5-in. pots or 2 to a 6-in. pot, or 3 to an 8-in. pot. Use a compost of 3 parts loam, 1 part peat and 1 part sand. It is essential not to plant the seeds too soon.
E. russellianum (annual or biennial). Lavender-purple flowers, July–Aug. 12–24 in.
E. silenifolium (perennial). Purple flowers, July–Aug. 18–24 in.

EVENING PRIMROSE. See *Oenothera*

EVERLASTING FLOWER. See *Ammobium, Helichrysum, Xeranthemum*

EXACUM
Greenhouse biennials native to F. East. Seedlings should be grown in heat in a compost of fibrous loam and peat in equal proportions, with a good sprinkling of sand. If plants in 5-in. pots are needed, sow in Mar., but if larger specimens are desired sow in Aug. of the preceding year. The plants should be kept in a cool greenhouse, shaded from fierce sunlight and free from draughts. They can also be increased from cuttings set in sandy soil with bottom heat.
E. affine. Purple and violet flowers, fragrant, summer and autumn. 12–15 in.

FAIRIES' WAND. See *Galax*

FAIRY BELLS. See *Disporum*

FAIRY BORAGE. See *Eritrichium*

FAIRY WALLFLOWER. See *Erysimum*

FALKIA REPENS
A small creeping plant from S. Africa. Suitable for the cool greenhouse in pans or baskets. Propagate from seed or division in the spring. Convolvulus-like flowers in rosy-pink and white, May–June.

FALSE CHAMOMILE. See *Boltonia*

FALSE INDIGO. See *Baptisia*

FALSE SPIKENARD. See *Smilacina*

FEATHERFOIL. See *Hottonia*

FELICIA (*Blue Daisy, Blue Marguerite*)
A genus of perennial shrubby plants and a few annuals native to S. Africa, mainly suited to a cool greenhouse but sometimes used for bedding out. Easily raised from cuttings set in a compost of loam, peat and sand, and grown on in 5-in. pots. If the raising of the cuttings is spread out flowers can be obtained for a large part of the year.
F. amelloides (perennial). Blue daisy-like flowers, summer. 1–2 ft.
F. fragilis (annual). Violet-blue flowers. July–Sept. 6 in.

FENNEL. See *Foeniculum*

FERNS
Although not so popular as formerly, ferns still have a place in many gardens. They are useful as greenhouse plants, for floral decoration or for growing in particular positions where other plants will not flourish. Unfortunately they are too often regarded as being suitable for 'any old corner' when, as with other plants, results are disappointing. They are a part of one of the great divisions of the vegetable kingdom, are found in most parts of the world ranging from dwarf-growing plants to the Tree Ferns that reach 50 ft. or more and differ from flowering plants in their structure and the production of

spores instead of true seeds. Propagation is by division (or with some species by bulbils formed on the fronds) or by sowing spores, which however is not easy under ordinary garden conditions.

For general garden purposes ferns may be divided into two, those that are hardy and suitable for outdoor cultivation and those that are suitable for greenhouses.

Hardy ferns do best in cool, moist but well-drained positions, preferably under deciduous trees which shade them from strong light and summer heat, and give protection from high winds. They may be planted in autumn or spring. The following are generally suitable; providing hardy species ranging from 6 in. to 3 ft.

Adiantum (Maidenhair)
Asplenium (Spleenwort)
Blechnum (Hard Fern)
Cryptogramma (Mountain Parsley)
Cystopteris (Bladder Fern)
Dryopteris (Male Fern)
Osmunda (Royal Fern)
Polypodium (Polypody)
Polystichum (Shield Fern)

Greenhouse ferns require a moist atmosphere, shading from bright light and a winter temperature of around 45 deg. F. (Those requiring stove conditions are excluded here.) They should be grown in pots in a peaty fibrous compost, watered regularly and syringed when in growth. Suitable species are contained in the genera listed above and may also be found in:

Davallia (Hare's Foot)
Nephrolepis (Ladder Fern)
Pteris (Ribbon Fern)
Adiantum, Davallia and Nephrolepis provide good basket plants.

FERULA (*Giant Fennel*)

Most of the species of this genus are natives of Asia or the Mediterranean and provide stately plants with graceful deeply-cut foliage, but since they grow from 6 to 12 ft. high, few are suitable even for large wide borders. They excel as single specimens in a particular part of the garden, but since they may take several years before coming into flower they should not be disturbed after being planted in their permanent positions. They come into growth early in the spring, will thrive in most kinds of soil and tolerate partial shade. Propagation is by seed. Self-sown seedlings may need checking.

F. communis. Leaves finely cut, with large yellowish sheaths at the base. Flowers yellow, June. 8–12 ft.

F. tingitana. A more branching plant. Leaves shining, deeply cut and toothed. Flowers yellow, borne close together, June. 6–8 ft.

FIG MARIGOLD. See *Mesembryanthemum*

FILIPENDULA (*Dropwort*)

This small genus was formerly included in *Spiraea* and resembles the astilbes in foliage and flower. The species are natives of N. Asia, Europe and N. America and prefer a moist soil in sun or partial shade. Propagation is by division or seed.

F. camtschatica. Leaves large, lobed. Flowers white, pink or rose, borne in tall plumes, July. 4–10 ft.

F. hexapetala. Leaves fern-like. Flowers white tinged red, single or double, borne in loose sprays, June–July. 2–3 ft.

F. palmata. Leaves large, lobed, white, hairy beneath. Flowers pink, July. 2–3 ft.

F. purpurea. Leaves large, lobed. Flowers carmine, deep pink or white, borne in large plumes, June–Aug. 1–4 ft. Some varieties have tinted stems and leaves.

F. rubra. Leaves large, lobed, deeply cut and toothed. Flowers white, pink or carmine in large branching clusters, June. 2–8 ft.

F. ulmaria (*Meadow sweet*). Leaves deeply lobed, white, downy underneath. Flowers white in large compact plumes, single or double, June–Aug. 2–4 ft.

FLAX. See *Linum*

FLEA BANE. See *Erigeron*

FLOSS FLOWER. See *Ageratum*

FLOWERING GRASS. See *Lapeyrousia*

FLOWERING RUSH. See *Butomus*

FOENICULUM (*Fennel*)
This is a small genus containing only one species, the true fennel, that may sometimes be included in a border because of its attractive foliage. But its proper place is in the herb bed. Propagation is by seed, which germinates readily and may give rise in a border to unwanted seedlings.
F. vulgare. Leaves finely cut. Flowers yellow, Aug.–Oct. 4–5 ft.

FORGET-ME-NOT. See *Myosotis*

FOXGLOVE. See *Digitalis*

FOXTAIL LILY. See *Eremurus*

FRANCOA (*Bridal Wreath*)
Small genus of perennial plants native to Chile, suitable for the cool greenhouse and best treated as annuals. Propagate from seed sown in Mar. with slight bottom heat (55 deg. F.), or by division. Pot-up in 6–8-in. pots in a compost of equal parts sandy loam and peat. Keep the seedlings in a cool, airy frame during the summer and transfer to a cool greenhouse in autumn. Water well in spring and summer, but very sparingly in winter.
F. appendiculata. Pink flower spotted with red, summer. 20–24 in.
F. sonchifolia. Pink flower spotted with red, summer. 20–24 in.

FRANKENIA
Dwarf evergreen plants of sea margins in temperate and sub-tropical regions, suitable as carpet plants in a rock garden. They like plenty of sun and a light sandy loam. Propagate from seed sown as soon as ripe or in Mar., or from division of roots in the spring.
F. laevis. Pinkish flowers, July. 4–6 in.
F. pulverulenta. Rose-coloured flowers, June–Aug. 4–6 in.

FREESIA
Recent developments have made freesias one of the most popular flowers, particularly for growing in a cool greenhouse. They are suitable also for a sunny border but the flowers suffer in bad weather. Propagate from seed or offsets. Since the seedlings do not transplant well, the seed should be sown in Mar. in 5-in. pots containing well-sieved sandy loam and peat, in a cool greenhouse or frame. Thin out to five or six plants to each pot, put in a frame for the summer and bring into the house at the end of Sept. or early Oct. If corms are used, they should be potted-up in Aug. or Sept., 1 in. deep and 2 in. apart in a compost of medium loam and peat, six equal-size corms to a 6-in. pot. Put in a frame or under a south wall until the corms begin to grow then transfer to the cool greenhouse, close to the glass. Little water is needed until growth starts. In all cases, when the new growth has reached 3 in. support with thin stakes. As soon as the flower buds are formed water about twice weekly with liquid manure. After flowering ease off watering and keep dry in a frame from May to June to ripen the corms. Clean soil from corms and pot-up each year.
The garden Freesias have been derived from **F. refracta** and **F. armstrongii** and many brilliantly-coloured hybrids and named varieties are available in shades of white, yellow, pink, mauve, orange, often with blotches or markings of contrasting colours.

FRENCH MARIGOLD. See *Tagetes*

FRINGED LILY or **VIOLET.** See *Thysanotus*

FRITILLARIA (*Fritillary*)
A large genus of bulbous plants from northern hemisphere, doing well in most soils, but with some species particularly suited to sheltered positions or preferring heavy or gritty soil. Propagate from offsets in Oct. or seeds sown as soon as ripe in a cold frame. (Some species take 4 or 5 years to reach flowering.) For pot culture plant in the autumn in a 5-in. pot in a compost of loam, peat and manure with a little sand. Occasionally dose with liquid manure when flower buds form.
F. acmopetala. Olive-green and purplish-brown, spring, 12–18 in. Rock garden.
F. caucasica. Purplish-brown and greenish-blue, spring. 8–12 in. Rock garden.
F. citrina. Yellowish-green, spring. 12 in.
F. imperialis (*Crown Imperial*). Large flowers,

yellow, bronze or red, spring. 30–50 in. There are several varieties available. Prefers heavier soils.

F. lanceolata. Purple with yellow-green chequered spots, spring. 18–24 in. Woodland.

F. meleagris (*Snake's Head Fritillary*). Purple with whitish chequering, grey-purple or white with green, spring. 9–12 in. Prefers a peaty soil.

F. nigra. Purple or yellow-green with purplish flush, spring. 8–12 in.

F. pudica. Yellow to orange with purple tinge, spring. 4–8 in.

F. recurva. Red outside, bright yellow inside spotted red, spring. 18–30 in.

F. tubiformis. Purple chequered yellow, spring. 8–12 in.

FUCHSIA

In addition to their value out of doors (see page 331, 'Trees and Shrubs') fuchsias make excellent plants for a cool greenhouse and the new improved varieties have greatly increased their popularity. They root readily from cuttings of young growth taken in spring for potting into a standard compost in 3-in., then 5-in. pots. They may be trained as bushes, when they should be stopped twice, or as standards when they should be grown-on without stopping but with all side growths being removed, until the desired height is reached. Standards will need potting-on into 10-in. pots and well-grown specimens will eventually require tubs. During growth ample moisture and some shade should be given. After flowering the plants should be gradually dried off for storing over the winter in a cool but frost-proof place. There are large numbers of varieties with single or double flowers in a wide range of colours.

FUMITORY. See *Corydalis*

FUNKIA. See *Hosta*

GAILLARDIA (*Blanket Flower*)

Although one annual **(G. pulchella)** of this small genus of American plants is often grown in gardens it is the perennial **G. aristata** which has given rise to the varieties that add such brilliant colours to a border throughout the summer. Unfortunately even they do not usually last for more than a few years, and they are untidy plants requiring support which is not easily and inconspicuously given, short strongish pea-sticks being the best. The plants prefer a light to medium well-drained soil and a sunny position. They have oblong, toothed, rough leaves and striking flowers 3–4 in. across. Propagation is by seed, division or cuttings. Named varieties do not come true from seed and must be propagated vegetatively. Selected varieties flowering June to Oct.:

'Burgundy': rich wine-red, 2 ft.
'Firebrand': bright coppery-red. 2–2½ ft.
'Mrs. H. Longsten': deep yellow, red centre, 2 ft.
'The King': red, tipped yellow, 2 ft.
'Wirral Flame': cardinal red, wiry stems, 2 ft.
There are also dwarf types, growing about 1 ft. high.

GALANTHUS (*Snowdrop*)

Bulbous plant native to Asia Minor or E. Mediterranean, excellent for the rock garden, beds or for indoors in pots, preferring a well-drained sandy loam. Plant bulbs in Aug.–Sept. 3 in. deep and 3 in. apart. Lift every 4th year if required for further planting. Propagate from offsets or seed when ripe. For pot-planting set 6–8 bulbs 1 in. deep in Sept.–Oct. in 5-in. pots and plunged in ashes until well rooted when they may be brought into a cool house. They will not stand forcing temperatures.

G. byzantinus. Greenish-white flowers, Nov.–Jan. 6–8 in.

G. elwesii. White flowers marked with green, Jan.–Feb. 8 in. Prefers shelter and sun.

G. latifolius. White flowers with small green patch, Feb.–Mar. 6–9 in.

G. nivalis (*Common Snowdrop*). White flowers, Jan.–Feb. 6 in. There are many good forms available for the garden.

GALAX (*Fairies' Wand, Carpenter's Leaf*)

There is only one species, **G. aphylla,** a creeping evergreen native to N.E. America. Thrives in partial shade in a peaty soil. Propagate by division of roots in spring or early autumn. Bronze-coloured foliage in autumn. White flowers, summer. 12–24 in.

GALEGA (*Goat's Rue*)
Of the three species comprising the genus, only one is suitable for a border where it makes a good back-plant, and although somewhat untidy, requires little support. Native to S. Europe and W. Asia it grows well in most soils but does best in a fertile light loam and a sunny position. Propagation is by seed or division.
G. officinalis. Leaves dainty, feathery, smooth. Flowers resembling small sweet pea flowers, white, mauve or pink, June–July. 3–4½ ft. 'Duchess of Bedford' (lilac and white), 'Her Majesty' (clear lilac), 'Lady Wilson' (blue and white).

GALTONIA (*Cape Hyacinth*)
One species **(G. candicans)** of these tall bulbous plants from S. Africa thrives in sunny positions in good well-drained soils and is also useful in the greenhouse. Propagate from seed sown in the open as soon as ripe, or offsets in the autumn. Plant bulbs in Mar. or Oct. about 6 in. deep and 15 in. apart, and leave undisturbed for several years. For growing in pots set 1 bulb ½ in. deep in a 6-in. pot in a cool house. Only grow in a pot for 1 year and then return to the border. White flowers in summer, 3–4 ft.

GAURA
Two of the perennial species, originating in America, are sometimes grown in borders. They bloom over a long period but few flowers open at any one time. They grow best in a light soil, in full sun. Propagation is by seed.
G. coccinea. Leaves lance-shaped, toothed. Flowers rose-white in loose spikes, June–Aug. 1 ft.
G. lindheimeri is similar but grows to 3 ft.

GAZANIA (*Treasure Flower*)
A genus of showy plants native to S. Africa mainly perennial but not fully hardy, good for bedding out in a sunny position or growing on walls or in a cool greenhouse. Propagate from basal cuttings in summer in a cold frame and plant out in June in a sunny position. For the greenhouse pot-up in Mar. in loam and peat. Water moderately while growing and winter in a frame or cold house.
The garden varieties are hybrids derived from several species. Flowers in a wide range of colours, white, yellow, orange, shades of red with black or green, June–Oct. 6–12 in.

GENTIANA
A large genus of annual or perennial plants native to the alpine regions of the world, generally requiring great care and attention. They need a well-drained mixture of gritty, peaty loam and a continuous supply of moisture particularly during the summer. Propagate from ripe seed sown in pots or pans containing a well-drained compost of equal parts loam, sand and peat. Sink into ashes or sand up to the rim and cover with a light until the winter when they can be exposed to frost and snow. In early spring when seedlings appear place in cold greenhouse or frame. Water well and protect seedlings from sun. Prick-off singly into pots. Some gentians which have shoots sprouting from the base can be propagated from cuttings. Take off young shoots (1–2 in.) just above crown and set in sand in a frame or greenhouse. Keep moist and shaded. Pot-off singly when cuttings have rooted. Gentians with fibrous roots can be propagated by root division in spring.
Among the less difficult species are:
G. acaulis. Deep blue flowers, May–June, 2–4 in.
G. asclepiadea. Violet-blue flowers, spotted purple within, July–Aug. 12–18 in. Prefers partial shade.
G. farreri. Rich blue flowers tinged red at base and with some spots, July–Aug. 8–10 in.
G. gracilipes. Deep purple-blue flowers with greenish outer tube, July–Aug. 9–12 in.
G. lagodechiana. Deep blue flowers with green spots, Sept.–Oct. 8–18 in.
G. lutea. Yellow flowers with spots or veins, May–July. 36 in. Suitable for borders.
G × macaulayi. Deep blue flowers, 2 in. long, Sept.–Oct. 9–12 in.
G. pneumonanthe. Deep blue flowers. May–June. 6–12 in.
G. septemfida. Clusters of deep purple-blue flowers, July–Aug. 6–12 in.

G. sino-ornata. Dark blue flowers, Sept.–Oct. 4–6 in. Requires lime-free soil.

GERANIUM (*Crane's Bill*)

This genus includes a number of perennial species that make good rock-garden plants and a few that are suitable for borders. It does not include the pelargoniums which are commonly but wrongly called 'Geraniums'. Most of the species produce seed freely, the seed often being scattered explosively when ripe. They will grow in most soils, but prefer one that is well drained and a sunny position. Propagation is by seed or division.

G. aconitifolium. Flowers white with black veins, May–June. 9–18 in. Rock garden.

G. cinereum. Flowers purplish-pink, June. 6 in. Rock garden.

G. endressii. Virtually evergreen with lobed and toothed leaves resembling those of a buttercup. Flowers pink or rose, summer–autumn. 1 ft. Border or rock garden.

G. grandiflorum. Leaves lobed and roughly toothed. Flowers borne in clusters, blue with reddish veins and red-purple eye, July. 1–1½ ft. Border.

G. ibericum. Flowers white or bluish-violet, July–Aug. 9–12 in. Rock garden.

G. pratense. Leaves large, rounded and lobed. Flowers blue, white or purplish, single or double, about 1 in. across, June–Sept. Up to 4 ft. Border.

G. psilostemon. Leaves heart-shaped, silvery. Flowers magenta-red with black spot at the base, up to 1½ in. across, June–July. 3 ft. Border.

GERBERA (*Barberton Daisy*)

Although difficult to grow, these half-hardy African plants are worth trying for their showy flowers. The easiest species is **G. jamesonii** and should be grown in a cool greenhouse. Propagation is by seed sown in gentle heat in Mar. for potting-up in a sandy compost in May. Flowering takes 2–3 years, the flowers being white, yellow, orange, pink or flame, May–July. 15 in.

GERMANDER. See *Teucrium*

GEUM (*Avens*)

The genus is widely distributed in temperate regions and its well-known garden species are valuable in the rock garden and the border because they bloom over long periods. They grow well on most kinds of soil, in sun or shade. Propagation is by seed or division. Seed often does not come true to type and named varieties must therefore be increased vegetatively.

G. chiloense. Most of the border varieties have originated from this species. 'Mrs. Bradshaw' with semi-double scarlet flowers is still among the most popular, but there are others such as: 'Dolly North', orange, June–July, 2½ ft.; 'Fire Opal', scarlet, May–July, 2 ft.; 'Lady Stratheden', buttercup-yellow, semi-double, May–Aug., 2 ft.; 'Princess Juliana', bronzy-orange, semi-double, 2 ft.

G. heldreichii. Flowers orange-red, June–Oct. 9–12 in.

G. montanum. Flowers yellow or orange, June–July. 6–12 in.

G. reptans. Flowers yellow, July–Aug. 6–9 in.

G. rivale. Flowers pink or reddish, May–June. 9–12 in. Needs a moist soil.

GIANT FENNEL. See *Ferula*

GILIA

A genus of annual, biennial and perennial plants native to America, especially N. America, growing in ordinary soil in a sunny open position. Propagate annuals from seed sown in Mar. and thinned to 3 in. apart, biennials from seed sown in June, winter in a frame and plant out the following May.

G. androsacea (annual). Lilac-pink flowers with dark throat, Aug. 12–18 in.

G. densiflora (annual). Lilac-white flowers, June–Sept. 10–20 in.

G. lutea (annual). Yellow or orange flowers, June–Sept. 4–12 in.

G. rubra (biennial). Scarlet or pink with yellowish spots, June–Sept. Up to 60 in.

G. tricolor (biennial). White, yellow or reddish flowers with spotted throat, June–Sept. 18–30 in.

GILLENIA

One species, **G. trifoliata,** native to N.

America, makes a good perennial plant. Thrives in moist woodland soil in a shady position. Propagate by division in the spring. Dainty white or red flowers, June–July. Grows up to 48 in.

GLADIOLUS (*Sword Lily, Corn Flag*)
PLATE 20
Although several of the distinct species of these S. African plants are beautiful in themselves, they have been surpassed by the hybrids that have been raised by many years of selection and crossing. New and improved varieties continue to become available and it is now impossible to classify them according to species. Instead the accepted practice is to separate the garden varieties into three main groups, the Early-flowering (May–June), the Large-flowered and the Primulinus hybrids (both flowering Aug. and Sept.). All provide flowers in a vast range of colours and innumerable named varieties are available. Propagation is by seed or 'spawn', the small bulbils produced at the base of the corm. Seed should be sown in Mar. preferably in gentle heat, the seedlings thinned and hardened off, lifted in autumn and replanted the following spring to produce their first (small) flowers in the summer. Spawn must be used to reproduce varieties true to type. It should be planted in Mar., 4–6 in. apart, and will flower the following year.
The usual practice, however, is to buy corms of flowering size, for planting in Mar. in well-prepared, rich, lightish soil, 4–5 in. deep, 8–12 in. apart with 15 to 18 in. between rows. Successional plantings may be made up to the end of May. Staking and watering must be given as required, and the corms lifted in Oct. for storing in trays in a frost-proof and dry place. Varieties should be labelled and the spawn, if required, should be carefully preserved and stored separately.
Both early-flowering and large-flowered varieties may be grown in greenhouses. The former should be potted up in early autumn in a sandy compost, 4 or 5 corms to a 5- or 6-in. pot, stood in ashes outside and brought into a temperature of 50–55 deg. F. for flowering in Apr. and May. The large-flowered types will not stand forcing, but with the protection of a house make beautiful flowers grown one corm to a 6- or 7-in. pot.

GLAUCIDIUM PALMATUM
A single species of herbaceous perennial native to Japan, requiring half shade in woodland conditions. Propagate from seed sown in Apr. or division in Mar. or Sept. Beautiful pale mauve flowers in summer. Grows up to 18 in.

GLOBE AMARANTH. See *Gomphrena*

GLOBE DAISY. See *Globularia*

GLOBE FLOWER. See *Trollius*

GLOBE THISTLE. See *Echinops*

GLOBULARIA (*Globe Daisy*)
A small genus of perennial and often shrubby rock plants native to the Mediterranean area. They like light limy soil in a dry sunny position. Propagate from seed or division in the spring.
G. cordifolia. Small white, rose or blue flowers, summer. 3–4 in.
G. incanescens (shrubby). Violet-blue flowers, summer. 3 in.
G. nudicaulis. Blue flowers, summer. 6 in. Will tolerate partial shade.
G. vulgaris (*Blue Daisy*). Bright blue flowers, summer. 6–8 in.

GLORY OF THE SNOW. See *Chionodoxa*

GLOXINIA
Tuberous-rooted perennials developed from **Sinningia speciosa,** a native of Brazil. They thrive in a fibrous peaty loam with some sharp sand. Start the tubers in a shallow box or pan in succession from Jan.–Apr. in a compost of the above kind at a temperature of 60 deg. F. Keep slightly moist until 2–3 in. of growth has been made, then plant one tuber to a 3–4 in. pot with the tops of the tubers just above soil level. When well rooted water liberally and shade from direct sun. Pot-on into 5-in. pots and when buds form to a 6- or 8-in. pot, according to vigour. As soon as the buds are open lower temperature and decrease watering. After flowering dry off the tubers and store in peat or fibre. Propagate from seed at the end of Jan. in a compost of peat, sand and fine loam, thinly

covered with coarse sand and a bottom heat of about 65 deg. F. Prick-off to about 1 in. apart and reduce heat to 60 deg. F. When strong enough pot-up singly into 3-in. pots and place near glass. Maintain temperature and keep moist, but do not water leaves. Pot-on as required. Another method of propagation is by cuttings of shoots from old tubers. Place in a close frame and maintain a gentle heat, and keep moist. Gloxinias can also be propagated from leaf cuttings taken with a piece of leaf-stalk at any time of the year, or by pegging down a mature leaf after the midrib has been cut. All should be raised in a fine sandy compost.

There are a number of named garden varieties, the majority having large tubular flowers in striking rich colours, white, scarlet, violet and pink, often with vari-coloured edges. Consult catalogues.

GOAT'S BEARD. See *Aruncus, Astilbe*

GOAT'S RUE. See *Galega*

GODETIA

Hardy annuals native to N. America. Grow well in ordinary soils preferably fairly moist. Propagate from seed sown thinly in open in Mar.–May for summer flowering, or in Sept. for spring flowering, thinning the seedlings to 4–6 in. apart.

The garden varieties have been derived from two species **G. amoena** (2 ft.) and **G. grandiflora** (9–12 in.). Flowers June–Oct. in white and various shades of pink, red, mauve and blue. Named varieties are available. Consult growers' catalogues.

GOLDEN ROD. See *Solidago*

GOMPHRENA GLOBOSA (*Globe Amaranth*)

A half-hardy annual native to India, and a good plant for the cool greenhouse. Raise from seed sown in gentle heat in Mar. or Apr., prick out for planting in May–June. For greenhouse use pot-on singly to 5-in. pots by June and put near glass to flower. There are several varieties of this species with small red, purple, orange or white 'everlasting' flowers on stems about 12 in. high, and a dwarf form with red flowers. 6 in.

GRAPE HYACINTH. See *Muscari*

GRASS OF PARNASSUS. See *Parnassia*

GREAT REED. See *Arundo*

GROMWELL. See *Lithospermum*

GUNNERA

Perennial foliage plants native to Australasia requiring rich damp soil in a sunny but sheltered position, with two species suitable for margins of ponds or shrubberies. Propagate from seed or division in spring. The crowns need some protection in winter.

G. chilensis. Large leaves (up to 5 ft. across). Numerous small red flowers in sprays. 6 ft.

G. manicata. Leaves 4–6 ft. across, stems up to 8 ft. Reddish flowers.

GYPSOPHILA

The genus comprises a number of dainty annual and perennial plants, suitable for rock gardens or borders, and valuable for their feathery foliage and masses of small delicate flowers. They grow best in good fertile soil and prefer full sun. Propagation of annuals is by seed and of perennials by seed or by root cuttings. Varieties of **G. paniculata** have to be grafted and are therefore generally purchased from nurseries.

G. elegans (annual). Flowers white, pink or crimson, in graceful sprays, May–Aug. 12–18 in.

G. paniculata (perennial). Smaller flowers, June–Aug. single or double. The best varieties are 'Bristol Fairy', double, white, July–Aug., 3 ft.; 'Flamingo', double, pale rose-pink, July–Aug., 3 ft.; 'Royal Veil', double, white becoming pink, July–Sept., 1½ ft. Foliage silvery-grey.

G. repens (perennial). Flowers white or rose, June–Aug. 4–6 in. Trailing growth suitable for rock gardens.

HABERLEA

A hardy perennial native to the Balkan region, and suitable for rich soil in a shady position in a

rock garden. Propagate from seed or division.
H. rhodopensis. White or pale lilac flowers, May. 6 in.

HACQUETIA EPIPACTIS

Pretty small European plant which grows well in a rock garden where the soil is on the stiffish side. Propagate by division of the roots before growth starts in the spring, and only divide strong plants. The little yellow flowers bloom Apr.–May, and the plant grows 3–6 in. high.

HAEMANTHUS

A genus of half-hardy bulbous rooted plants native to S. and tropical Africa, suitable for a cool greenhouse and flowering better if kept under-potted. Water regularly and feed with weak liquid manure while growing. Dry off and rest when dormant. Propagate from offsets potted-up as soon as new growth begins.
There are many hybrids and a number of variable species, with white, pink, red or crimson flowers blooming between Apr. and Sept. and growing from 1–3 ft. high.

HAWORTHIA

A genus of variable dwarf-growing succulents from S. Africa, suitable for the cool greenhouse and grown for their attractive leaves. Pot-up in a compost of sandy loam and peat in Mar. or Apr. and re-pot every second year. Water regularly when growing but keep just moist in the winter. Propagate from offsets or seeds, which, however, do not come true. There are a number of species, all having inconspicuous flowers and growing 3–9 in. high.

HEBENSTREITIA

A S. African genus of half-hardy shrubs and plants of which one perennial **H. comosa** is suitable for a cool greenhouse. Pot-up singly in 5-in. pots in a compost of loam, peat and sand. Propagate from soft-wood cuttings. Orange-red and white flowers from July–Sept. Grows to a height of about 2 ft.

HEDGE MUSTARD. See *Erysimum*

HEDYCHIUM (*Butterfly Lily*)

Half-hardy perennial plants native to S. and E. Asia, suitable for a cool greenhouse or for summer bedding and having attractive flowers in long or dense spikes. Propagate by division of rhizomatous roots and pot-up in Mar. in a compost of loam and sand. They need ample and regular water while growing.
H. coccineum. Orange-scarlet flowers, summer. 4–6 ft.
H. coronarium. Pure white flowers, summer. 3–4 ft.
H. flavum. Orange or yellow flowers, summer. 4 ft.
H. gardnerianum. Lemon-yellow flowers, summer. 5–7 ft. For bedding out.
H. greenei. Scarlet flowers, summer. 2–6 ft.
H. spicatum. Yellow flowers, summer. 2–3 ft.

HEDYSARUM

Biennial and perennial plants for the rock garden and native to the northern hemisphere. They thrive in sunny positions in ordinary soil. For the biennials sow seed in the open in May, and plant out in the following autumn or spring. With perennials sow seed in the open in Apr. Some species can be increased by division in Mar. or by layering in autumn.
H. capitatum (perennial). Rose-purple flowers, summer. 12–24 in.
H. coronarium (*French Honeysuckle*) (biennial). Scarlet flowers, summer. 36–48 in.
H. obscurum (perennial). Violet-red flowers, June–Aug. 6–12 in.

HELENIUM (*Sneezeweed*)

Natives of N. America, these well-known plants are particularly valuable because they produce large daisy-like flowers freely over a long period, and are good for cutting. The stems are generally strong and need only light support. They will grow well in most kinds of soil preferably in full sun. Propagation is generally by division but seed may also be used. The genus contains a few annuals but the three main garden species are the perennials **H. autumnale, H. bigelovii** and **H. bolanderi.** The first has given rise to most of the varieties grown today, particularly the late-flowering and taller ones, the other two producing generally shorter and earlier plants.

Selected varieties:
'Baron Linden': orange-yellow shaded bronze, July–Sept. 3 ft.
'Chipperfield Orange': orange-yellow striped red, July–Aug. 4½ ft.
'Crimson Beauty': bronzy-red, Aug. 2 ft.
'Moreheim Beauty': brownish-red with black centre, July–Sept. 3 ft.
'Riverton Gem': crimson shot gold, Sept. 4½ ft.
'The Bishop': deep yellow with brown eye, July. 3 ft.
'Wyndley': orange-yellow, July. 3½ ft.

HELIANTHUS (*Sunflower*)

Native to N. and S. America the genus provides both the annual and the perennial sunflowers. The perennials are particularly useful for the back of a border but they need to be well manured and divided every three years or so to prevent deterioration which often results in the double varieties reverting to singles. On the other hand, good feeding may encourage excessive spread and some checking may then have to be done. They should be grown in full sun. Propagation of perennials is by division and of annuals by seed sown in Apr. and thinned to 1 ft. apart.

H. annuus (*Common Sunflower*) (annual). Flowers up to 1 ft. across, single or double, yellow or reddish, July–Sept. Up to 10 ft.

H. debilis (*Miniature Sunflower*) (annual). Flowers 2–3 in. across, yellow, orange or pinkish-purple, July–Aug. 1–3 ft.

H. decapetalus (perennial). Leaves long, oval, rough and toothed. Flowers large, up to 3 in. across, yellow, July–Sept. 4–6 ft. 'Capenock Star' (single, Sept., 4 ft.), 'Loddon Gold' (double, Sept., 5 ft.), 'Soleil d'Or' (double, Aug.–Oct., 5 ft.).

H. salicifolius (perennial). Grows less coarsely and has attractive leafy stems. Flowers small but numerous, borne in loose sprays, Sept.–Oct. 6–8 ft.

HELICHRYSUM (*Everlasting Flowers*)

A genus of hardy and half-hardy annuals, perennials and shrubs mostly native to S. Africa and Australasia. Several species make excellent plants for the border or pot plants indoors, while the dwarf species make good plants for the rock garden. To raise annuals sow seed thinly (Feb.–Mar.) preferably in gentle heat, prick out, harden off and transplant in mid-May to 9–12 in. apart. Hardy species can be sown in the open in Apr., being thinned to 12 in. apart. Propagate perennials by division in the spring.

H. bracteatum (half-hardy annual). White, pink, red or yellow flowers, single or double, June–Aug. 24–48 in.

H. graveolens (half-hardy perennial). Yellow flowers, summer. 12–18 in.

H. orientale (hardy shrubby, perennial). Yellow flowers, summer. 6–18 in.

H. stoechas (*Goldy-Locks*) (hardy shrubby, perennial). Yellow flowers, summer. 12–24 in.

HELIOPHILA

A genus of S. African plants which includes a half-hardy annual **H. longifolia** suitable for bedding out. Seed should be sown in Mar. under glass or in Apr. in the open. Flowers blue with a white eye, freely produced, July–Aug. 18 in.

HELIOPSIS (*Orange Sunflower*)

This small genus of American origin resembles *Helianthus* but the plants flower earlier and do not grow so tall or so strongly. They will grow well on dryish soils and are good for cutting. Propagation is by division.

H. helianthoides. Leaves coarsely toothed, roughish above. Flowers yellow, numerous, up to 3 in. across, July–Aug. 3–6 ft.

H. scabra. Leaves rough, coarse. Flowers pale yellow to orange, July–Sept. 2–4 ft. 'Golden Sun', deep yellow, July–Aug., 3½ ft.; 'Orange King', orange, Aug.–Sept., 4 ft.

HELIOTROPIUM

A large genus of half-hardy, shrubby plants of which one species **H. peruvianum** has provided the well-known 'Cherry Pie' popular for bedding out. Although perennial and often grown and over-wintered in a greenhouse and propagated by cuttings taken in Aug., the usual practice is to raise bedding plants from seed sown in gentle heat in Mar., pricked out, pinched back when 3–4 in. high and planted in the open in mid-June. Flowers lilac, fragrant, July–Sept. 12–18 in.

HELIPTERUM

A genus of annuals, perennials and shrubs from Australasia and S. Africa, of which only two of the annuals are suitable for summer bedding in a dry, sunny position in well-drained loamy soil or for the greenhouse. Sow seed in gentle heat in Mar. in a compost of 2 parts loam to 1 part peat and only just cover with soil. Grow on in pots near glass.

H. manglesii. Rose, red or purple flowers, July–Sept. 12–24 in. Greenhouse or bedding out.

H. roseum. White or pink flowers, Sept. 12–24 in. Greenhouse.

HELLEBORUS (*Hellebore, Christmas Rose*)

The genus contains the popular Christmas and Lenten roses, and while the plants are hardy enough to be grown out of doors, they are often spoiled by the weather unless some protection is given. They are not therefore suitable for open beds or borders but in a sheltered position or among shrubs give great attraction with their winter-green foliage and long-lasting unusual flowers in which the sepals provide the colour and the petals are reduced to tubular nectaries. They grow best in moist, well-drained rich soil, preferably in partial shade, and should be left undisturbed after planting. Propagation is by seed or by division which should be done after flowering. The seedlings grow slowly, taking about three years to reach flowering.

H. niger (*Christmas rose*). Evergreen, with divided dark green leaves. Flower saucer-shaped, white or tinged rose, up to 4 in. across, nectaries yellow, Jan.–Feb. 1 ft. Also suitable for a cool greenhouse.

H. orientalis (*Lenten rose*). Usually evergreen. Flowers cream, turning to brownish or yellow-green, pink or purple, Feb.–Apr. 1–2 ft.

H. viridis. Flowers cup-shaped, nodding, green, Feb. 1 ft.

HELONIAS BULLATA (*Swamp Pink*)

A single perennial species from N. America, suitable for the bog garden and requiring a moist peaty soil and some shade. Propagate by division of the roots in the spring. The plant bears purplish-rose flowers in the summer and reaches a height of 12 in.

HEMEROCALLIS (*Day Lily*)

PLATE 22

As the common name implies, the flowers open only during the day and generally each one lasts only for a day or two. But since the flowers are numerous and open successively, the period of blooming is long. The leaves are narrow, long and arching and in many species are attractive with their yellowish-green colour. Some species prefer moist, cool or even marshy conditions, but the majority will do well in most soils, in sun or shade. Propagation is by division.

Many of the species are variable and since they cross readily, a large number of hybrids have been obtained from which most of the garden varieties have been developed without the exact parentage being known. Among those generally popular are:

'Citrina': pale citron-yellow, scented, June. 2½ ft.

'C. P. Raffill': maroon-pink, shaded apricot, July–Aug. 2½ ft.

'George Yeld': orange-scarlet, July–Aug. 2½ ft.

'Hesperus', citron-yellow, July–Aug. 4 ft.

'Hyperion': canary-yellow, July. 3 ft.

'Marcus': orange-yellow tinged bronze, July. 2½ ft.

'Pink Damask': salmon-pink, July–Aug. 2½ ft.

'Potentate': pansy-purple, July–Aug. 3½ ft.

'Royal Ruby': crimson, July–Aug. 3 ft.

'Sirius': orange-buff, July–Aug. 2½ ft.

'The Doctor': deep velvety red, July–Aug. 2½ ft.

HEMP AGRIMONY. See *Eupatorium*

HEPATICA. See *Anemone*

HERACLEUM

A genus of large coarse plants suitable only for a large wild garden, moist woodland or the banks of streams, containing the common weed

Cow Parsnip. One species **H. mantegazzianum** (*Cartwheel Flower*) is attractive for its large leaves, up to 36 in. across on stout coppery stalks. It bears numerous white flowers and in good conditions will reach a height of 12 ft.

HERB LILY. See *Alstroemeria*

HERBERTIA
Half-hardy, cormous plants native to C. and S. America, requiring a sunny position in sandy loam. Propagate by seed or offsets.
H. amatorum. Violet flowers with brown spots, July. 12–20 in.
H. drummondiana. White and blue flowers, July. 9 in.

HERMODACTYLUS TUBEROSUS
A single species resembling an iris, growing in most soils provided they are well drained. Propagate by seed or offsets. Flowers purple, Apr.–May. Up to 1 ft.

HERON'S BILL. See *Erodium*

HESPERIS (*Sweet Rocket*)
A genus of biennials and perennials, native to S. and E. Europe, with one perennial species that is suitable for a border. It does not, however, usually last for more than 3 years unless divided and the youngest roots replanted. A moist but well-drained and fairly rich soil is needed and preferably some shade. Propagation is by seed for the single varieties and division for the doubles.
H. matronalis. Leaves oblong, smooth, 3–4 in. long. Flowers single or double, white or purple, borne in long spikes, fragrant, June. 2–3 ft. Good for cutting.

HEUCHERA (*Coral Bells*)
Natives of N. America, two of the species **H. × brizoides** and **H. sanguinea** have provided most of the garden varieties grown today. They are low-growing evergreen plants with heart-shaped, lobed leaves and slender stems carrying small, pendulous bell-shaped flowers. They grow well in most soils provided they do not dry out, and prefer full sun, although they will tolerate some shade. Propagation is by seed or division. The seed rarely comes true and division should be carried out fairly regularly as parts of the plants frequently die out.
There are a number of varieties, many showing only slight variations from others. The flowers are white, or in shades of pink and red, June–Sept. 1–1½ ft.
Heucherella is the name given to hybrids obtained by crossing with **Tiarella cordifolia** resulting in a tufted perennial, 4 in. high, suitable for rock gardens or edging and having white, pink or carmine flowers, June–Sept. These hybrids do not set seeds and must be increased by division.

HIBISCUS
In addition to the well-known shrubs the genus contains a few species of annuals and herbaceous perennials of which two that are hardy are sometimes grown out of doors. Propagate by seed.
H. militaris (perennial). Flowers up to 5 in. across, white or rose, July–Aug. 3 ft.
H. trionum (annual). Flowers yellow or white with purplish-brown centres, July–Sept. 18 in.

HIDALGOA WERCKLEI
A climbing, half-hardy perennial native to Costa Rica and suitable for the cool greenhouse. Increase by cuttings in the autumn and provide support. Striking orange-scarlet flowers very like a dahlia, all the summer.

HIERACIUM (*Hawkweed*)
Two or three species of this vast genus are sometimes recommended, but, with the exception of **H. villosum** which has downy foliage and golden yellow flowers and is suitable for a rock garden, they are the least objectionable of what are really weeds, and should have no place in a garden.

HIPPEASTRUM (*Equestrian Lily*)
A large genus of bulbous plants native to tropical regions of S. America and popularly called **Amaryllis**. The growing season is from early spring, after they have flowered, until about Sept., in a minimum temperature of

60 deg. F., with sufficient water and air to assist with ripening. After Sept. they should be rested and kept in a moderately dry house in a temperature of 45–50 deg. F. until Feb. when the flower-scapes appear. For early flowering, batches of bulbs can be brought into heat from the end of Dec. Young bulbs should be re-potted if they require it. Just as growth is about to start shake out the old soil and fill in firmly with fresh compost. Established bulbs need not be re-potted for 4 or 5 years but should be top dressed annually when growth commences; this is generally sufficient with the aid of manure-water during the growing season. Good heavy loam with charcoal and bone meal should be used, and it is very important to have good drainage. They require plenty of light and, except when in flower, all the sun-shine possible.

Propagation by offsets is adopted to increase named species or varieties, and should be carried out when the bulb is at rest, but only if the offset comes away easily without damaging the roots. Offsets should be placed singly in pots in a compost of 2 parts loam, 1 part decayed manure and ½ part of sand, taking care not to over-pot. Keep the bulb ⅓ above the level of the soil, and plunge the pot in peat or fibre with bottom heat. It should be placed in a light position and syringed freely, but watered sparingly until growth has started. They should be kept growing the first year or two, to build up good flowering bulbs. Later give the same treatment as for established plants.

Propagation by seed is for raising new varieties, and is the usual one for producing bulbs for ordinary decoration. Seed should be sown as soon as ripe in pans of loam and peat, with sufficient sand to keep it open. Place the pan in a temperature of 60–70 deg. F., shading it from the hot sun. When the seedlings appear give them plenty of light and a moist atmosphere. Keep the seedlings in the pan until a few leaves appear, then pot them up singly in small, well-drained pots in a similar compost, but slightly rougher than that used for the seed. Seedlings should not be rested in their early stages, but kept growing to build up good bulbs, as in the case of young offsets. Seedlings may be had in flower 2 to 3 years from the sowing of the seed.

There has been much inter-crossing of species and most garden varieties are hybrids, with flowers in white, orange, shades of red, scarlet, yellow or green, often with reddish spotting, and grow 1½–3 ft.

HOLLYHOCK. See *Althaea*

HONESTY. See *Lunaria*

HOP. See *Humulus*

HORMINUM PYRENAICUM
(*Pyrenean Dead-nettle*)

A single species of a hardy perennial native to European alpine regions. It likes a sunny position in ordinary soil in rock garden or border. Propagate from seed or division. Flowers nodding, bluish-purple or rose-purple, July–Aug. 6–12 in.

HORNED RAMPION. See *Phyteuma*

HOSTA syn. **FUNKIA** (*Plantain Lily*)
PLATE 24

Several species of these Asiatic perennials make attractive garden plants but many are best grown as specimen or key plants in beds, or as woodland or shrubbery plants. The leaves are often variegated in attractive arrangements of green and white or occasionally yellow. They prefer a moist rich soil and partial shade, and should not be disturbed unnecessarily. Propagation is by division.

The following are among those most suitable for borders:

H. fortunei. Leaves heart-shaped, bluish-green, variegated. Flowers pale lilac, borne in sprays, May. 2 ft. A good bog or waterside plant.

H. lancifolia. Leaves green, or with white margin. Flowers pale lilac, July–Sept. 1½–3 ft.

H. plantaginea. Leaves oval, green. Flowers white, fragrant, borne in short sprays, Aug.–Sept. 2 ft.

H. undulata. Leaves large, green or splashed white. Flowers pale lilac, Aug. 2½ ft. A good bog or waterside plant.

HOTTONIA (*Water Violet, Featherfoil*)
There are two species of this genus of perennial aquatic plants, **H. palustris** being the better and more attractive. Propagate from seeds sown in ordinary soil in shallow water in Mar., or division of roots in Apr. Plant at water's edge with from 6 to 18 in. of water above the crowns. Flowers lilac with yellow eye, June. 12–24 in.

HOUND'S TONGUE. See *Cynoglossum*

HOUSELEEK. See *Sempervivum*

HOUSTONIA
Attractive tufted plants native to N. and C. America and suitable for the rock garden, flowering most of the year round. When grown in pans under cold-frame treatment they are very useful for the alpine house, with a carpet of foliage beneath the flowers of blue, white or purple. They require a good loam, with peat and sand, and need to be kept moist. When not required for the alpine house, the pans should be kept plunged in ashes in a partially shaded position. Increased by seed sown as soon as ripe, or by division in the early autumn.
H. caerulea (*Bluets, Quaker Lady*). Flowers vary from blue to white with a yellow eye, summer. 3–6 in.
H. purpurea. Purple flowers, summer. 6–18 in.
H. serpyllifolia. Creeping plant. Violet-blue flowers, sometimes white, spring–early summer. 3–4 in.

HOYA (*Wax Flower*)
A genus of greenhouse, climbing, evergreen plants, natives of F. East and Australia and remarkable for their wax-like flowers. Pot in a compost of lumpy peat and loam containing a little coarse sand and charcoal, and keep under-potted. Re-pot every 5 or 6 years. Hoyas may also be grown up a pillar or along wires on the roof if planted in a well-drained greenhouse border or in 8-in. pots. Water well while growing and keep dry in winter (average temperature 45 deg. F. winter, 65 deg. F. summer). Propagation is easier by means of layering in spring or summer, though cuttings of the previous year's shoots, 4 in. long, may be taken and struck in sandy soil in a temperature of about 65 deg. F. in spring or early summer. Do not cut off the spurs that remain after the flowers have passed, as these spurs will flower again.
H. bella. Pure white flowers with violet centre, July–Oct. 15–20 in. Good basket plant.
H. carnosa. Pinkish-white flowers, July–Oct. 12–15 in. There is a variegated form.
H. imperialis. Reddish-brown or dull purple flowers, July–Oct. 15–20 in.

HUMEA ELEGANS (*Incense Plant*)
A biennial foliage plant from Australia, rather difficult to grow and demanding a rich sandy loam and sunny beds and borders. Better treated as a greenhouse plant. Propagate from seed sown in July and rear in greenhouse until ready to go out the following June. Brownish-red, crimson or pink small but numerous flowers bloom July–Oct. The growth is from 4–8 ft.

HUMULUS (*Hop*)
The hop plant **H. lupulus** is often used as a screen. Grows well in deep rich loam. Propagate from seed or division.

HUNTSMAN'S HORN. See *Sarracenia*

HUTCHINSIA
Dwarf-growing annual and perennial plants native to Europe, and suitable for open positions in the rock garden. Propagate from seed or division.
H. alpina. Fern-like foliage. Small white flowers, May–June. 2–4 in.
H. auerswaldii. Leaves purplish beneath. Small whitish flowers, May–June. 2–6 in.

HYACINTHUS PLATE 25
There are two main groups of these well-known plants which are natives of Mediterranean regions and parts of Africa, Roman hyacinths (early flowering) and Dutch hyacinths (large flowered). For growing in the open hyacinths like a deep-dug, well-manured, sandy loam in a sunny position. Plant Sept. to Nov. about 3–4 in. deep and from 6–10 in. apart,

according to variety. For pot culture plant in succession from Aug. to Nov. for flowering from Dec. to Apr. using a compost of 2 parts turfy loam to 1 part of rotted manure, peat and sand. Plunge in ashes until shoots are 2 in. high, then bring into gentle heat and full light. For indoor display use bulb fibre and place the bowls in a cool, airy place until shoots are 1–2 in. high. Then treat as for greenhouse culture. Size of pots and/or bowls are a matter of personal choice, but whereas a 6-in. pot will take 3 or 4 Roman hyacinths, it may only give enough room for one of the large-flowered varieties. Bulbs in pots and bowls should be planted with the tips just showing.
There is a large number of named varieties and new introductions occur in most years. Catalogues should be consulted. See Chapter 9 .

HYDROCHARIS MORSUS-RANAE (*Frog Bit*)
A floating aquatic plant from Europe and N. Asia, having yellow-green leaves in rosettes and white flowers in summer. Propagation is by runners or seed. Makes a good pond plant and is to be preferred to the floating duckweeds (*Lemna*, spp.) which easily get out of hand.

HYMENOCALLIS (*Spider Lily*)
A genus of bulbous plants native to S. America and Africa with large, fragrant flowers. Some species are sufficiently hardy for planting out in sheltered positions but will not survive a severe winter, and it is better therefore to treat as greenhouse plants. 45–50 deg. F. They should have good turfy soil and drainage and be rested after flowering. Propagation is by offsets.
H. amancaes. Bright yellow flowers, Feb.–Mar. 18–24 in. For the greenhouse.
H. calathina. White flowers, Mar.–Apr. 20–24 in. For the greenhouse.
H. macrostephana. White flowers, Feb.–Mar. 24–30 in. For the greenhouse. Requires a higher temperature (60 deg. F.).

HYPERICUM (*St John's Wort*)
This large genus consists mainly of shrubs and sub-shrubs (see page 334), but has also a few herbaceous species of which **H. polyphyllum** is the best. It is low-growing with golden-yellow flowers, often spotted red, July–Sept. 9–12 in.

IBERIS (*Candytuft*)
Annual, biennial and perennial plants native to Europe and Asia, the perennials being mostly of a shrubby character. They will grow in almost any soil but prefer dry sandy loam and a sunny position. Propagate from seed, division or cuttings which root very easily.
The garden annuals have been derived from two species, **I. amara** and **I. umbellata,** the former giving the white 'spiral' type, the latter those with purplish, lilac or rosy-crimson flowers. All grow 6–12 in. high and flower in summer.
I. sempervirens (evergreen, shrubby perennial). White flowers, May–June. 6–12 in. There are several named forms.

IMPATIENS (*Balsam*)
A genus of hardy and tender annuals and perennials found in mountainous areas of Asia and Africa. The hardy annuals make good border plants and are easily raised from seed and grown in ordinary moist loam. The perennial greenhouse species may be propagated from seed sown in gentle heat, or from cuttings struck at any time in a close frame.
I. amphorata (annual). Pale purple flowers speckled red, Aug.–Sept. 3–5 ft.
I. balsamina (*Garden Balsam*) (half-hardy annual). Rose and yellow flowers, summer. 18 in.
I. holstii (perennial). Scarlet flowers, summer. 24–36 in. Greenhouse.
I. noli-tangere (*Touch-me-not*) (annual). Yellow flowers spotted red, July–Aug. 12–18 in. Requires moist soil.
I. roylei (annual). Deep purple flowers, July–Aug. 60–90 in. There are several varieties of this species.
I. sultani (perennial). Large purple or scarlet flowers, summer. 12–24 in. Greenhouse. This and **I. holstii** are often called 'Busy Lizzie'.

INCARVILLEA
This small genus of Chinese origin contains two species that are sufficiently hardy and

suitable for border plants. Both foliage and flowers are attractive and since they seem to resemble certain greenhouse plants are often regarded as unusual when growing in the open. They grow best in a well-drained, light but rich loam, in full sun. Propagation is by seed or division.

I. delavayi. Leaves dainty and feathery, dark green. Flowers rose-red, tubular, up to 6 on each stem. May–June. 1½ ft.

I. grandiflora. Leaves more rounded. Flowers rose-red, with yellow tube and white blotch, only 1–2 on each stem, but up to 4 in. across, May–June. 1 ft.

INCENSE PLANT. See *Humea*

INDIAN CRESS. See *Tropaeolum*

INDIAN PINK. See *Dianthus, Spigelia*

INULA

Natives of Europe, Asia and Africa, having brightly-coloured daisy-like flowers, only three species are suitable for borders, many of the others being too vigorous although excellent in a wild garden. All grow well in most soils and prefer full sun. Propagation is by seed or division.

I. hirta. Leaves narrow, hairy. Flowers bright orange-yellow, June–Aug. 1 ft.

I. oculis-christi. Leaves slightly toothed and downy. Flowers bright golden-yellow, up to 3½ in. across, the centre having a whitish waxy covering, June–Aug. 1 ft.

I. orientalis. Leaves oblong, hairy. Flowers orange-yellow, up to 5 in. across, June–Aug. 2 ft.

IONOPSIDIUM ACAULE (*Violet Cress*)

Annual plant native to C. and S. America and W. Indies suitable for the rock garden, preferably in a shady position. They increase by self-sowing in their growing position or can be raised from seed sown in pots in spring or summer. Violet or white flowers tinged with purple, summer. 3 in.

IPOMOEA

A large genus of evergreen and deciduous creeping or climbing plants from tropical regions. The hardier species may be grown in a warm, sheltered position but the majority are greenhouse plants. Sow seed in Apr. 2–3 in a small pot under glass (55–60 deg. F.). Harden off and plant out 24 in. apart in May–June against some support. For greenhouse pot-on. The evergreen species can also be increased from stem cuttings in a peaty soil with bottom heat. The Sweet Potato **(I. batatas)** belongs to this genus.

I. angustifolia (annual). Whitish flower with purple throat, summer. 72 in. Greenhouse.

I. digitata (perennial). Pink-purple flowers, summer. 15–30 ft. Greenhouse.

I. leptophylla (*Bush Moon-flower*) (perennial). Rose flowers with purple throat, summer. 24–48 in. For the greenhouse.

I. pandurata (*Man of the Earth*) (perennial). White flowers with purple throat, summer. Hardy.

IRESINE

Ornamental foliage plants from tropical regions of America, suitable for planting out in sunny beds of sandy soil or for pot-culture in a greenhouse. Plant out 8 in. apart in June (not earlier) or pot-up in 5- to 8-in. pots in Mar. in a compost of peat, loam and sand. Propagate from cuttings of young shoots taken in late summer, put in a frame and transfer to greenhouse by early Oct. 50 deg. F. Further cuttings for bedding may be taken in Mar.

I. herbstii. Purplish-red foliage often with green blotches. 12–18 in.

I. lindenii. Blood-red foliage. 12 in.

IRIS PLATE 27

This large genus contains many of the most popular and useful of the garden plants that are commonly grown today. There are two forms of growth, those with fleshy rhizomes or 'roots' and those with bulbs, and they are further subdivided into 10 or 11 groups. Many of the rhizomatous irises of today have come from a number of original species and a large number of varieties have been produced by crossing within or between the species. Precise classification is therefore not easy, but the largest and most popular garden group is known as the bearded irises and is divided into tall bearded irises covered by the name **Iris barbata** (or more commonly but less correctly **I. germanica**) and the dwarf bearded irises which have been derived from three species **I. flavescens, I. pumila and I. chamaeiris,** and are primarily rock-garden plants.

The tall bearded irises grow best in a well-drained soil not deficient in lime and enjoy full sun. The leaves are silvery-grey and erect, and the flowers have the characteristic 'beards' on their petals. These irises are often grown in beds by themselves but they make attractive groups in a border and while the individual flowers do not usually last long, they come out successively and so give colour for a lengthy period.

Propagation is by seed or division, which should be done every third year, as soon as flowering is finished, the rhizomes being planted firmly with the top left exposed. Plants raised from seed normally flower in their second year, but do not come true.

Hundreds of named varieties have been raised and the number is constantly being increased with the result that it is impossible to give a short list of the best. The soundest advice to any purchaser is to obtain a catalogue from a nursery that specializes in irises. The range of colours also continues to widen, from white to shades of yellow, blue, purple, mauve, brown, pink and red and with different colours appearing in the standards or falls the most fascinating mixtures and combinations are obtained. The height varies from 2½ to nearly 4 ft., but the tallest should usually be avoided because they need support which cannot be given unobtrusively.

The dwarf bearded irises grow from about 6 in. to 10 in. high and make excellent rock-garden plants. There are a number of named varieties blooming in Apr. and May with flowers in shades of white, yellow, rose, lilac and purple. Hybrids with the tall bearded irises have given rise to what are often called 'intermediate' irises.

The bulbous irises include the well-known English irises **(I. xiphioides)** flowering June–July, the Spanish irises **(I. xiphium)** flowering in May and June and the Dutch irises (raised by crossing **I. tingitana** with an early-flowering type of **I. xiphium**) flowering in May, all in shades of white, blue or yellow. They are treated in the same way as other bulbs and may also be brought on early under glass, but will not stand more than a low gentle heat. They are propagated by seed or by offsets, both methods taking about 3 years to produce flowering plants. Named varieties do not come true from seed and must be propagated by offsets. Other bulbous irises are the well-known **I. reticulata** which does well in bowls, grows about 9 in. high and has white, blue or reddish-purple flowers in Feb., **I. danfordiae** growing up to 1 ft., with bright yellow flowers in Jan–Feb., and **I. histrio** growing 6–10 in. with lilac flowers, often spotted yellow, in Jan. Although hardy, these early-flowering irises need protection to prevent the blooms being spoiled by weather and are therefore best grown in a frame or cold house.

In addition there are a number of other species that provide excellent garden plants. Some require the same conditions of soil and position, others need moist or marshy conditions, while a few are aquatic. Others (not included here) require special treatment to ensure they are kept dry during their resting stages.

I. kaempferi. The flowers are large and flattish, up to 8 in. across in white, pink, red, purple or blue with combinations of these shades in fascinating markings, July. The stems are often branched. There are a number of named varieties as well as a whole range of unnamed hybrids. They grow 2–2½ ft. high and require a good but acid soil that does not dry out in summer. Borders.

I. laevigata is similar but has blue or white flowers in June and needs to be grown in water, with the roots just below the surface.

I. pseudacorus is the Yellow Flag of ponds and streams and needs water to cover its roots. There is also a white-flowered variety. May–June. 2–3 ft.

I. sibirica. Leaves narrow, about ¼ in. wide but up to 1 ft. long. Flowers 2–5, white, blue, purple and intermediate shades. Several named varieties are available, many of them showing the

characteristics of **I. orientalis** which has been much used by plant breeders in inter-crossing. All require a moist soil or water-side.
I. unquicularis is probably better known by its former name **I. stylosa.** It differs from most species by requiring poor but well-drained soil in a warm place, preferably under a south wall. Flowers lilac with white, fragrant, Nov.–Mar. There are also white and purple varieties.

ISATIS (*Dyer's Green Weed, Woad*)
A small genus of plants native to Europe and Asia, including the biennial **I. tinctoria** from which the Ancient Britons obtained the dye 'woad' with which they stained their bodies. It thrives in any well-drained soil in a sunny position. Propagate from seed. The plant bears tiny yellow flowers in open sprays in May. Grows 24–48 in. The perennial species **I. glauca** is more showy and less rampant, but neither deserves a prominent position.

IXIA (*African Corn Lily*)
These half-hardy South African plants will succeed in warm, dry, sunny borders or rock gardens in rich, sandy loam, but are more suitable for a greenhouse. Pot-up in Sept.–Oct. placing 6 corms 1 in. deep in a 6-in. pot. Keep cool but frost-proof during the winter, and when the flower spikes appear give plenty of light and air. Water well after blooming until the foliage dies, then dry off when the leaves have died down. Propagate by means of seed sown in a frame in Sept. or by offsets in Oct. Offsets generally flower in their second year but seed takes 3 or 4 years.
There are a number of named varieties derived from several species, all having flowers in loose spikes and striking colours from white to shades of pink, red, violet and yellow. Those derived from **I. viridiflora** have attractive green flowers with black centres. All flower Apr.–May under glass or June–July in the open, and grow between 1 and 2 ft.

JACOB'S LADDER. See *Polemonium*

JAPANESE HYACINTH. See *Ophiopogon*

JASIONE (*Sheep's Scabious*)
A genus of dwarf-growing hardy annuals and perennials with tufts of narrow leaves and rounded heads of blue flowers, suitable for sunny positions in the rock garden. Propagate annuals by seed sown in Mar., perennials by seed sown in autumn.
J. jankae (perennial). Blue flowers, summer. 6 in.
J. perennis (perennial). Blue flowers, summer. 9 in.
J. montana (annual). Flowers pale blue or white, summer. 9 in.

JASMINE PLANT. See *Bouvardia*

JEFFERSONIA DIPHYLLA
(*Twin Leaf, Rheumatism Root*)
Perennial herbaceous plant from N. America. It thrives in a shady position in sandy peat or woodland soil. Suitable for the rock garden or alpine house. Propagate by division which should be done just as growth is about to commence, or from seed sown as soon as ripe. Solitary white flowers in spring, 4–6 in.

KALANCHOE
One species of this genus of tender plants from Africa and F. East is suitable for a cool greenhouse. Pot-up the young seedlings or cuttings in spring when new growth starts. Water sparingly until the plants are well rooted and then pot-on to 6-in. pots. Water regularly and generously while making growth. Keep only just moist in winter. Seed may be sown in pots or pans in slight heat in Mar., or cuttings of new shoots taken in late summer.
K. blossfeldiana. Bright red flowers, borne in spikes in early spring. 12–18 in.

KENNEDYA (*Australian Bean Flower*)
A climbing plant native to Australia and suitable for a cool greenhouse. Pot-up in Mar., water well in summer, and keep fairly dry in winter. Trim back straggly shoots and cut off dead flower-heads in the autumn. Propagate from seed sown in Mar.–Apr.
K. rubicunda. Red flowers, Apr.–June. 4–6 ft.

KENTRANTHUS (*Valerian*)
This is a small genus of Mediterranean annuals and perennials particularly suitable for dry conditions such as are found in rock gardens and walls but also perfectly happy in the more moist soils of beds and borders. It does best in full sun. Propagation is by seed.
K. macrosiphon (annual). Flowers white or rose, July. 2 ft.
K. ruber (perennial). Leaves ovate, slightly toothed. Flowers white, pink or red, borne in clusters, June–July. 2–3 ft.

KIRENGESHOMA
There is one species of Japanese origin, a beautiful vigorous plant which unfortunately only does well in moist peaty soil and light shade. Propagation is by seed or division.
K. palmata. Leaves large, lobed, toothed and hairy. Flowers cup-shaped, yellow, wax-like, nodding, up to 1½ in. across, Sept. 2–4 ft.

KNAPWEED. See *Centaurea*

KNIPHOFIA (*Red-hot Poker* or *Torch Lily*)
Some species of this African genus make good greenhouse plants but a few are sufficiently hardy for growing in the open, although they may need some winter protection in cold or exposed positions. They are aptly named, striking plants that grow best in fertile light soils in full sun or partial shade. Many named varieties have been raised. They should not be disturbed unnecessarily. Propagation is by seed or division which should be done quickly so that the portions do not dry out before replanting.
K. caulescens. Produces handsome plants suitable for growing as specimens. Leaves blue-grey arising from a main woody stem. Flowers reddish-salmon becoming white with greenish-yellow tinge, in a dense head, 6 in. long, Sept.–Oct. 4–5 ft.
K. praecox. Leaves up to 2 ft. long, toothed. Flowers bright red or yellow, in spikes, May–June. 2 ft.
K. tysonii. Similar to **K. caulescens** and again useful as an individual specimen. Leaves bright green. Flowers rose-scarlet, becoming yellow, Aug. 3–4 ft.
K. uvaria. The common red-hot poker which has given rise to many hybrids and named varieties. Leaves up to 3 ft. long, grey-green. Flowers cream, yellow, orange or red, generally becoming greenish-yellow, borne in a dense spike, July–Sept. 2½–5 ft. Selected varieties:
'Autumn Queen': citron-yellow, flushed bronze, Aug. 3–4 ft.
'Corallina': tangerine-red, July–Aug. 2½ ft.
'Lord Roberts': brilliant red, July–Aug. 3 ft.
'Mount Etna': scarlet, Aug.–Sept. 5 ft.
'Royal Standard': scarlet and yellow, July. 3½ ft.
'Sir C. K. Butler': coral-red and yellow, June–July. 3 ft.
'Star of Baden': yellow, Aug. 5 ft.
'Watkin Samuel': orange-scarlet, Aug.–Sept. 4–5 ft.

KNOTWEED. See *Polygonum*

KOCHIA (*Burning Bush*)
A genus of annuals and perennials with one half-hardy annual that grows well in moist soils. Sow seed in the open in Apr., or in Mar. under glass in gentle heat. Prick out, harden off and plant out about 12 in. apart at the end of May.
K. scoparia (*Belvedere*). Small green flowers, July–Oct. 24–28 in. Fine autumn foliage.

LACHENALIA (*Cape Cowslip, Leopard Lily*)
Bulbous greenhouse plants native to S. Africa, with nodding cowslip-like flowers in graceful spikes. Pot-up in Aug. ½ in. deep in a compost of peat, loam and sand, 4–5 bulbs to a 6-in. pot. Keep in a cold frame until Oct. or Nov., water only when required then transfer to the greenhouse, temperature not exceeding 50 deg. F., and start to water as growth commences. After flowering dry off in a sunny frame from May–Aug. Propagate from offsets in Aug., or from seed.
Most garden varieties have been derived from **L. aloides** and **L. bulbifera** with flowers in a wide range of colours, white, green, yellow, red or purple, Apr.–May. 6–12 in. **L. bulbifera** makes an excellent basket plant.

LADIES' FINGERS. See *Anthyllis*

LAD'S LOVE. See *Artemisia*

LADY OF THE NILE. See *Zantedeschia*

LADYBELL. See *Adenophora*

LADY'S MANTLE. See *Alchemilla*

LADY'S SLIPPER. See *Cypripedium*

LAPAGERIA ROSEA (*Chilean Bell Flower*)
A single species of evergreen climber native to Chile, suitable for a cool greenhouse. Propagate from seed sown as soon as ripe in gentle heat (50 deg. F.), or by layering after flowering. Grow in a compost of turfy loam with equal parts of sand and peat. They may be grown in pots but are better in the greenhouse border and trained on a trellis. Plant in Mar., shade and water well in summer. Cut out weak shoots after flowering, but do not prune. Keep fairly dry in winter. The plant produces waxy, pendent, white or rosy-crimson flowers, Sept.–Nov. Grows up to 10 ft.

LAPEYROUSIA (*Flowering Grass*)
Bulbous greenhouse plants native to Africa, with one species **L. cruenta** hardy enough for sheltered, sunny positions out of doors. Pot-up in a light, sandy loam and peat in Mar., 4–5 bulbs to a 6-in. pot. Propagate from offsets, or seeds sown in spring.
L. cruenta. White or crimson flowers, June–Oct. 6–12 in.
L. grandiflora. Similar to above with large flowers, Sept.–Nov. 12 in.

LARKSPUR. See *Delphinium*

LATHYRUS PLATE 30
A large genus of annual and perennial climbers widely distributed throughout the world. The best-known species is **L. odoratus,** the Sweet Pea (see page 280). Other species also make good garden plants for beds or borders, or as climbers in the open or in the greenhouse. They thrive in good average garden soil. Propagate the annuals from seed and the perennials by division or seed. As the roots of the perennials are long and somewhat fleshy they should not be disturbed more than is necessary.
L. latifolius (*Everlasting Pea*) (perennial). Large white or rose flowers, summer. 4–6 ft.
L. odoratus (*Sweet Pea*) (annual). See page 280.
L. pubescens (perennial). Lilac-blue flowers, early summer. 3–5 ft. Greenhouse.

LAVATERA (*Tree Mallow*)
A small genus of annuals, biennials, perennials and shrubs, mostly natives of S. Europe, and growing well in sunny positions in ordinary soil. Propagate annuals and biennials from seed, perennials from seed or cuttings.
L. olbia. Although a shrubby type, is often used in herbaceous borders. Flowers reddish-purple or rose, resembling hollyhocks. June–Oct. 5–6 ft.
L. trimestris (annual). Flowers white or rose, July–Oct. 3–6 ft.

LAVENDER. See 'Trees and Shrubs', page 336

LAYIA (*Tidy Tips*)
Hardy annuals from N.W. America. They like a sunny position in ordinary soil. Propagate from seed sown thinly in Apr. under glass or in the open.
L. elegans. Yellow flowers with white tips, July–Sept. 10–12 in.
L. glandulosa. White flowers, July–Sept. 10–12 in.

LEADWORT. See *Ceratostigma, Plumbago*

LEONTOPODIUM ALPINUM (*Edelweiss*)
Perennial herb from the Alps. It is hardy and can be grown in a rock garden, but is better suited to the alpine house. Propagate from seed, prick out seedlings into gritty or sandy loam and plant out. The plants should be tightly wedged between pieces of stone or old lumps of mortar. Division is not always satisfactory. Has a silvery-grey foliage and creamy flowers from June–July. Grows to 4–6 in.

LEOPARD LILY. See *Lachenalia*

LEOPARD'S BANE. See *Doronicum*

LEUCOJUM (*Snowflake*)
Hardy bulbous plants native to C. Europe and

Mediterranean. They will grow in most ordinary garden soils in the open or semi-shaded. They can also be grown in a cold greenhouse or alpine house. Plant in Sept., 3–4 in. deep and 5–6 in. apart. Propagate from offsets or seed.

L. aestivum (*Summer Snowflake*). Drooping white flowers with green spots, May. 15 in.

L. autumnale (*Autumn Snowflake*). Drooping white flowers with pink base, Oct. 6 in.

L. vernum (*Spring Snowflake*). Drooping white flowers, tinged green or yellow, Mar. 9 in.

LEWISIA

Perennial rock-garden plants, natives of W. N. America. They need a well-drained, rich soil in a sunny, sheltered position and are also suitable for an alpine house. Propagate by division or seed, which, however, does not come true.

L. colombiana. Pink or white flowers, May–June. 4–6 in.

L. cotyledon. White flowers with pink veins, Apr.–May. 8–10 in.

L. tweedyi. Pink flowers, May–June. 8–12 in.

LIATRIS (*Blazing Star, Kansas Feather*)

This is a small genus of N. American plants, showy and somewhat unusual with their long, narrow leaves rising from ground level and handsome, closely-packed spikes of flowers. They grow best in good light soil in full sun or partial shade. Propagation is by seed or division.

L. callilepis. Flowers bright carmine, July–Sept. 2 ft.

L. elegans. Leaves spotted, often spiny at the tips. Flowers purplish in spikes up to 20 in. long, summer and autumn. 2–4 ft.

L. scariosa. Flowers white or purple, in loose spikes up to 2 in. across, Sept. 2–4 ft.

L. spicata. Prefers moist conditions. Flowers white or purple, Sept. 2 ft.

LIBERTIA

Perennial herbs with iris-like leaves from Chile and New Zealand. They require well-drained, peaty soils or a cool greenhouse. Propagate from seed sown in a cool frame or greenhouse, or division.

L. formosa. White flowers, May. 16 in.

L. grandiflora. Pure white flowers, summer. 30–36 in.

L. ixioides. White flowers summer. 18–24 in.

LIGULARIA

This genus contains both hardy species suitable for a border and half-hardy species for the greenhouse. The plants have handsome foliage resembling *Senecio* and in the open do best in a good, moist, peaty soil in full sun. Propagation is by seed or preferably division.

L. clivorum. Flowers 3–4 in. across, orange-yellow, July–Aug. 3–4 ft. Good for water-side.

L. japonica. Leaves up to 1 ft. wide, deeply cut into lobes. Flowers up to 3 in. across, orange-yellow. Aug.–Sept. 5–6 ft.

L. tussilaginea. Flowers yellow, on a woolly stem, July–Aug. Leaves variegated. 2 ft. Greenhouse.

L. veitchiana. Leaves up to 2 ft. wide. Flowers golden-yellow in dense spikes. July–Sept. 4–6 ft.

LILIUM (*Lily*) PLATE 31

This genus comprises the true lilies. There are a number of species, hybrids and varieties, many of them suitable for growing both in the open and under glass. They thrive in deep, rich, well-dug soil, preferably a moist, well-drained, fibrous loam. A few, such as **L. auratum, L. giganteum, L. speciosum,** and most of the American lilies like a peaty soil, but with some the presence of peat in their soil will cause failure. Although very few are really successful on a calcareous soil, **L. candidum, L. henryi, L. martagon, L. pyrenaicum, L. regale** and **L. testaceum** are exceptions. Lilies which form roots from the base of the stem as well as from the bulb should be planted among low-growing shrubs, which will afford shade to the base of their stems, or in the greenhouse potted deeply. As lily bulbs dry up quickly, it is a good plan to keep them covered in a cool place previous to planting. When in bloom all lilies must be carefully staked, and all dead flowers must be removed, but the stems must not be cut down until they have died off.

Plant in late summer to early autumn. For pot culture select suitable sizes of pots from 6 in. to 10 in. and cover the bulbs with about 1 in. of soil, which should be made firm, leaving room to add more soil as necessary, particularly for stem-rooting kinds. Treat as for other pot-bulbs, plunging the pots in ashes or fibre or in a frame until the plants begin to grow. As the stems grow, the pots are gradually filled up to within about 1 in. of the rim, and brought on in a temperature of 45–50 deg. F. Plenty of ventilation should be given and watering done very carefully, and not commenced until the plants have started growth. When the colours of the flower begin to show, stop giving any liquid manure. Late bloomers should remain outdoors in a sheltered situation.

The Madonna Lily **(L. candidum)** and Nankeen Lily **(L. testaceum)** require planting early in Aug. They resent disturbance, and should be lifted only when necessary. Top dress with well-rooted manure each spring.

Propagation is carried out by means of offsets in Oct., by planting scales from bulbs in sandy soil in a cold frame, or by seed in pans in a cold frame in Aug. Seedlings generally flower when they are from 2–5 years old, according to species.

Some selected species:

L. amabile. Red flowers spotted black, July–Aug. 18–48 in.

L. auratum (*Golden-rayed Lily of Japan*). White or yellow flowers with crimson, purple or brownish bands or spots, Aug.–Sept. 40–60 in.

L. brownii. White flowers tinged purple or green, July–Aug. 36–48 in.

L. candidum (*Madonna Lily, White Lily*). White flowers, June–July. 18–50 in.

L. concolor. Yellow, orange or scarlet flowers, spotted, June–July. 2 ft.

L. dauricum. Scarlet flowers with brown spots, June–July. 12–24 in.

L. davidii. Scarlet or orange-red flowers with black spots, July–Aug. 36–48 in.

L. henryi. Orange-yellow flowers, dotted reddish-brown, Aug. 5–6 ft.

L. longiflorum. Pure white flowers, July. 24–36 in.

L. × maculatum. There are a large number of named varieties and it is best to consult a trade catalogue.

L. martagon (*Turk's Cap Lily*). White or purple-red flowers with purple spots, June–July. 24–48 in.

L. pyrenaicum (*Pyrenean Lily*). Greenish-yellow flowers with dark spots, May–June. 24–36 in.

L. regale. White and yellow flowers, July. 24–60 in.

L. speciosum. Pure white flowers with red spots. Aug.–Sept. 12–48 in.

L. superbum (*Swamp Lily*). Scarlet-orange flowers with purple spots, July–Aug. 24–84 in.

L. × testaceum (*Nankeen Lily*). Yellow flowers, June–July. 48–72 in.

L. tigrinum (*Tiger Lily*). Scarlet-orange flowers with purple spots, Aug.–Sept. 24–48 in. Catalogues should be consulted for named varieties.

LILY OF THE VALLEY. See *Convallaria*

LIMNANTHES DOUGLASII

A dwarf annual native to California. It can be grown in any reasonable garden soil and easily propagated from seed sown in Mar.–Apr. White flowers often tinged yellow, summer. 6–12 in.

LIMONIUM (*Sea Lavender*)

Still commonly known as *Statice* this genus provides some of the popular everlasting flowers. The species include annuals, biennials and perennials some of which are suitable for the greenhouse, others for growing in the open. The flowers look as if made of paper and are suitable for drying. In the open, a light, well-drained soil and sunny position are required. Propagation of annuals is by seed and of perennials by seed or division in spring.

L. bonduelii (perennial). Leaves deeply cut and lobed. Flowers yellow, July–Aug. 2 ft. Greenhouse.

L. gmellinii (perennial). Leaves up to 5 in. long and 2 in. wide in rosettes. Flowers pink, in branched heads, July–Aug. 1½–2 ft.

L. imbricatum (perennial). Leaves downy,

PLATE 31
LILIUM (Lily). There is a large number of named varieties suitable for growing both in the open and under glass. A fine group of vigorous hybrids are the 'Bellingham Hybrids', a specimen of which is illustrated on the left.

PLATE 32

LONICERA (Honeysuckle). Some species make excellent climbers for walls, screens or the like. The species shown here is L. caprifolium.

PLATE 33

Left, LABURNUM (Golden Chain). This tree produces masses of pendulous yellow flowers in May and June. Below, LONICERA (Honeysuckle). There are many attractive species, the one shown here is L. tatarica which flowers in May.

PLATE 34

LYTHRUM (Loosestrife). An excellent perennial for the back of the border. Blooms continuously from June to September.

PLATE 35
MAGNOLIA. These are among the most beautiful of the garden shrubs. A number of hardy species are available.

PLATE 36

Above, MALUS (Flowering Crab). A number of varieties are available, all flower April and May. Right, PHILADELPHUS (Mock Orange). These shrubs flower during June and July and are sweetly scented.

PLATE 37

NICOTIANA (Tobacco Plant). These fragrant plants are suitable for sunny beds and borders. Many colour forms are available.

PLATE 38

NARCISSUS. The variety shown here is 'Actaea', a tall-stemmed, free-flowering variety.

lobed. Flowers blue, July–Aug. 1½ ft. Greenhouse.

L. latifolium (perennial). Leaves downy. Flowers July–Sept. 2 ft. 'Violetta' (deep violet), 'Chilwell Beauty' (deep blue), 'Grittleton' (mauve-lavender, in large sprays).

L. roseum (shrubby perennial). Flowers deep rose, May. 1½ ft. Greenhouse.

L. sinuatum (perennial but generally grown as an annual). Flowers lilac and white, July–Aug. 1 ft.

L. suworowii (annual). Flowers lilac, Aug. Up to 4 ft.

LINARIA (*Toadflax*)

Native to the northern hemisphere, most of the species make good annuals or rock-garden plants, but a few are suitable for beds or borders. They grow well in most soils, in full sun but will tolerate partial shade, and flower over a long period. Propagation of annuals by seed and perennials by division.

L. alpina (perennial). Flowers white, pink or bluish-violet, July–Sept. 4 in.

L. cymbalaria (creeping perennial). Flowers white, blue, pink or lilac. Makes a good basket plant.

L. macedonica (perennial). Leaves narrow, on erect stems. Flowers cream or yellow borne in slender spikes, June–Sept. 3–4 ft.

L. maroccana (annual). Flowers white, yellow or purplish, June. 9–12 in.

L. purpurea (perennial). An erect, branching plant. Flowers bluish-purple, touched with white, July–Sept. 1–3 ft. 'Canon Went' (pink, touched orange).

L. reticulata (annual). Flowers purple, May–July. 2–3 ft.

LINNAEA BOREALIS (*Twin-flower*)

Trailing evergreen of the northern hemisphere suitable for shady positions in a rock garden, preferably in moist, peaty soil. Propagate by division or by layers or cuttings in spring. White flowers flushed with pink, June–July.

LINUM (*Flax*)

A genus of annuals, biennials and perennials, suitable for rock gardens or borders. Unfortunately the flowers are only at their best in brilliant sunshine. They require a light, well-drained soil in a warm, sunny position. Propagation of annuals is by seed and of perennials by seed or by cuttings taken in July.

L. alpinum (perennial). Flowers pale blue, July–Aug. 6 in.

L. austriacum (perennial). Leaves narrow, erect, dotted. Flowers blue or white, June–July. 1–2 ft.

L. grandiflorum (annual). Flowers rose or crimson, June–July. 12 in.

L. narbonense (perennial). Leaves small, stiff, erect and pointed. Flowers various shades of blue, May–July. 1–2 ft.

L. perenne (perennial). Flowers blue, white or pink, June–July. 1–1½ ft.

L. viscosum (perennial). Leaves broader, on hairy stems. Flowers white, blue or lilac-rose, June–Aug. 1½ ft. Will tolerate some shade.

LIPPIA CITRIODORA (*Sweet Verbena*)

Sweet-smelling shrub native to Chile. It can be grown outside in warm regions, but is best cultivated in a cold greenhouse. Propagate from cuttings of young wood in gentle heat (60 deg. F.) in spring. Cut young shoots hard back in Feb. Pale purple flowers in Aug. Grows up to 20 ft.

LIRIOPE GRAMINIFOLIA

A perennial herb native to China and Japan suitable for the cool greenhouse, with arching green leaves and violet-blue flowers in autumn. Propagate by division in spring. 9–12 in.

LITHOSPERMUM (*Gromwell*)

A genus of biennial and perennial herbs and shrubs and natives of Europe, N. Asia and N. America. They thrive best in well-drained, sandy loam. Propagate from seed, by cuttings of half-ripened wood set in sand in a cold frame, or division in spring.

L. diffusum (shrubby evergreen). Deep gentian blue flowers, summer. 12 in. A well-known variety is 'Heavenly Blue'. Dislikes lime.

L. fruticosum (shrubby). Hairy leaves. Purple-azure flowers, summer. 8–12 in.

L. gastoni (herbaceous perennial). Sky blue flowers with a white eye, summer. 6–12 in.

LOBELIA

A genus of pretty, profusely blooming plants, half-hardy annuals and herbaceous perennials, widely distributed, especially in America. The low-growing kinds are suitable for edgings and baskets. The various species grow from 5–36 in. in height, and bloom from July–Oct. and thrive in sunny positions with deep, well-manured, and moist soil.

L. gracilis, a half-hardy annual, with its bush-like habit and profusion of celestial blue flowers in July is extremely beautiful in pots, beds or when used as an edging. All the varieties of the greenhouse perennial **L. erinus** as well as others with yellowish or bronzy foliage, the double-flowered variety known in gardens as 'Kathleen Mallard', and **L. tenuior** with blue and white eye, flowering from July to Oct. and growing 15–18 in. high, are valuable for edging, for intermixing with other plants in the greenhouse, for hanging baskets, or for rustic-work vases, over whose edges they droop in graceful manner. Treat all these as half-hardy annuals. The tall perennial species, **L. cardinalis, L. fulgens** and **L. syphilitica,** with their handsome spikes of flowers, are very ornamental and valuable for pot culture. There are also a number of beautiful varieties and hybrids of these species.

To propagate annuals sow seed thinly in gentle heat under glass in Mar., on the surface of pans of very fine, moist sandy soil, that have been soaked well before sowing. Prick off 1 in. apart in boxes, harden off in a cold frame in Apr., and plant out early in May. If required for greenhouse use pot-up singly into 3–4-in. pots, using a compost of rich loam and peat.

To propagate perennials sow seed in a frame, take cuttings of young growth in Mar., or propagate by means of division in late Apr., and plant out in rich, moist soil or pot-up for greenhouse use. Water liberally while the plants are making growth. As soon as the foliage is dead in autumn the stems should be cut down and the roots lifted and stored in boxes of dry soil in a frost-proof frame. Water should be given in Mar. to restart growth, and late in Apr. the roots should be divided and the most vigorous planted out.

For growing in pots pot-up in Mar., using 6–8-in. pots. Keep in a well-ventilated frame on ashes until about to bloom, then transfer to the cool greenhouse.

L. cardinalis (*Cardinal Flower*) (perennial). Crimson-scarlet flowers, July–Aug. 24–36 in. There are many named garden varieties.

L. erinus (*Blue Lobelia*) (perennial). Blue flowers with white-yellow throat, summer. 6 in. There are many named garden forms.

L. fulgens (perennial). Scarlet flowers, June–Sept. 18–36 in.

L. gracilis (annual). Deep blue flowers, summer. 12–24 in.

L. laxiflora (perennial). Red-yellow flowers, June–Aug. Up to 60 in. This species needs greenhouse treatment.

L. syphilitica (perennial). Light blue flowers, Aug.–Oct. 12–36 in.

L. tenuior (annual). Blue flowers with a white eye. Sept.–Oct. 12 in.

LOBULARIA. See *Alyssum*

LOTUS

Only two of the hardy perennial species of this genus are worth growing, either in the alpine house or the cool greenhouse. Pot-up in Mar. using a compost of loam, peat and sand. Water very sparingly in autumn and winter and give only a moderate amount even in summer. Propagate by means of cuttings struck in a frame in July, or sow seed in gentle heat in Mar.

L. bertholetii (*Coral Gem*). Scarlet flowers, May–June. 10 in. A good basket plant.

L. jacobaeus. Dark purple flowers, summer. May–June. 10 in.

LOVE-LIES-BLEEDING. See *Amaranthus*

LUNARIA (*Honesty*)

A genus of two species, one annual **(L. annua),** which is often biennial, one perennial **(L. rediviva),** the former being the better known. Native to Europe and Asia, they thrive in partly shaded positions in sandy soil. Propagate from seed sown in May in the open. Violet-mauve or white flowers, May–July. 18–24 in.

LUNGWORT. See *Pulmonaria*

LUPINUS (*Lupin*)

Apart from the odd exception, the lupins grown in gardens today are the famous Russell hybrids. The first step was taken when James Kelway crossed the tree lupin **(L. arboreus)** with the herbaceous American lupin **(L. polyphyllus)** of which a pink seedling occurred later and introduced the colour which George Russell used with such skill, combining it with the colours of other species including some annuals, to give the large and enchanting range that is now available.

Lupins need no description. They will grow in most soils, but do best in those that are light and slightly acid, and while they prefer sun will also flourish in partial shade. They flower in June and July, reaching heights of 2½ to 3 ft. or more, and for these reasons should be planted towards the back of the border so that other later-flowering plants can screen their foliage. They generally look better in groups of roughly the same colour than in a mixture and are perhaps at their best when grown in a bed by themselves, provided there is enough garden space for such a luxury.

Unfortunately many of the modern varieties do not last for more than a few years, particularly if the flower-heads are allowed to run to seed instead of being cut off. The best plan therefore is to prepare to renew the stock every third or fourth year, or to raise a few plants every year as an insurance against the inevitable casualties. Propagation is easy, either by seed or by cuttings taken in Mar. or early Apr.

Hundreds of named varieties have been raised and vast quantities of hybrid seed have been sown since the modern types first appeared, and it is impossible to make a short list of the best. Many nurserymen keep large stocks which may be seen and selected when in flower or alternatively plants may be raised from seed and a good deal of interest obtained from seeing what develops. If it is desired to multiply named varieties or particular colours propagation must be by cuttings; seed may produce only a further but interesting variation. Practically every flower colour and shade, with a large number of combinations, can be obtained. Of the original species the only one that is still seen occasionally and is still worth growing is the tree lupin, **L. arboreus.** It is a branched shrub suitable for a border or as an individual specimen, growing up to 5 ft. high with fragrant yellow, or less commonly blue, lilac or violet flowers. It is hardy in all except severe winters but can be raised easily from seed. It may be trained and grown as a standard.

LYCHNIS (*Campion*)

Many of the species now included in this genus are synonymous with those formerly found in other genera and some of the few that are of garden value may be listed in catalogues under *Agrostemma, Coronaria, Melandrium, Silene*, etc. They grow well in most good soils, some preferring drier conditions than others, while a few will tolerate shade. The best have vivid colours and for this reason need careful placing in a mixed border. Propagation is by seed or division.

L. chalcedonica. Stiff and erect. Flowers borne in flat heads, brilliant scarlet, white or pink, June–Aug. 2–3 ft. There is a double scarlet variety which is rare.

L. coronaria. A dense covering of silvery hairs makes the plants look white and woolly. Flowers single, white to rose-crimson borne on branching stems, June–Aug. 2½ ft.

L. flos-cuculi is the wild Ragged Robin, but a garden variety with double flowers is worth growing.

L. flos-jovis. White and woolly. Flowers white, pink, purple or scarlet, June–July. 1–2 ft.

L. × haageana. Hybrids with flowers up to 2 in. across, white, orange, scarlet or crimson, June–July. 1 ft.

L. viscaria. The stem is sticky and often traps insects. Flowers rosy-crimson, on rigid branching stems, single or double, May–July. 1 ft.

LYCORIS

A small genus of bulbous plants from China and Japan, suitable for the cool greenhouse. They need the same treatment as the Hippeastrum (q.v.).

L. aurea (*Golden Spider Lily*). Bright yellow flowers, Aug.–Sept. 12 in.

L. radiata. Deep pink or white flowers, Aug. 15–18 in.
L. squamigena. Rosy-lilac flowers, July–Aug. 18–24 in. Can be grown outside in a warm, sheltered position.

LYSIMACHIA (*Yellow Loosestrife*)
Widely distributed, most of the species are vigorous perennial plants and some may grow even too strongly. They have dainty flowers borne in erect or arching spikes and prefer a moist soil, or the banks of ponds, and do equally well in sun or shade. Propagation is by division.
L. clethroides. Leaves ovate, up to 6 in. long, attractively tinted in autumn. Flowers white in arching spikes, July–Sept. 1½–3 ft. Good for cutting.
L. nummularia (*Creeping Jenny*). Prostrate. Flowers yellow, July–Aug. Useful for baskets or moist banks.
L. punctata. Erect stems. Flowers yellow, borne in whorls, June–July. 2–3 ft.
L. thyrsiflora. Flowers yellow, July–Aug. 1–2 ft. Suitable for water-side.
L. vulgaris. Erect and downy. Flowers yellow dotted orange, in sprays, June–Aug. 2½ ft. Does best in moist positions.

LYTHRUM (*Purple Loosestrife*) PLATE 34
Two species of this small but widely-distributed genus make showy border plants, and one makes a useful trailing plant in a greenhouse. They do best on a moist, fairly heavy soil, in partial shade. Propagation is by division.
L. flexuosum. Trailing stems up to 3 ft. Flowers pink, July–Sept.
L. salicaria. Leaves heart-shaped, in whorls. Flowers pink, red or purple, in long spikes, June–Sept. 2–4 ft. 'Robert' (deep pink, 2 ft.), 'The Beacon' (rose-red, 3 ft.).
L. virgatum. Flowers purple, borne in threes on graceful spikes, June–Sept. 2–3 ft. 'Rose Queen' (bright rose).

MACLEAYA (*Plume Poppy*)
Of Chinese origin, the genus contains two species only, the plants being tall and stately, suitable for the back of a wide border or as individual specimens. They do best in a moist fertile soil, in sun or partial shade. Not suitable for cutting because the yellowish, staining sap runs freely. Propagation is by seed or by suckers.
M. cordata. Leaves large, deeply veined and lobed. Flowers buff or pink, numerous in large branching sprays, July–Sept. 5–8 ft.
M. microcarpa. Similar to above. Flowers bronzy, in spreading plumes, July–Sept. 6–7 ft.

MADAGASCAR JASMINE. See *Stephanotis*

MADONNA LILY. See *Lilium*

MADWORT. See *Alyssum*

MAIANTHEMUM BIFOLIUM
A small perennial from northern temperate regions, useful for carpeting the rock garden. Likes a shady moist situation. Propagate by division. Small white flowers, May–June. 4–6 in.

MALCOMIA
A genus mainly of hardy annuals native to the Mediterranean area and including **M. maritima,** Virginian Stock, which grows in most soils preferably in the sun. Propagate by seed sown in early spring or autumn. Lilac, red, yellow or white flowers, June–Oct. 6–8 in.

MALLOW-WORT. See *Malope*

MALOPE TRIFIDA (*Mallow-wort*)
Hardy annual from the Mediterranean regions, growing best in a sandy soil in a sunny site. Propagate from seed sown under glass in Mar. or in the open in Apr. or May. Crimson, red, pink or white flowers, June–July. 12–18 in.

MALVA (*Musk Mallow*)
A genus of annuals and perennials, the former often classed as weeds, the latter including two species suitable for borders. They resemble hollyhocks with large, open, showy flowers and are also often spoiled by rust. They will grow in almost any kind of soil, in sun or shade. Propagation is by seed or cuttings.
M. alcea. Leaves lobed, toothed, downy. Flowers red or rose-purple, about 2 in. across, borne in clusters, July–Oct. 2–4 ft.
M. moschata. Leaves deeply and finely cut. Flowers white, pink or rose, June–Oct. 2–2½ ft.

MALVASTRUM

A genus of perennial plants resembling **Malva** and containing a few species grown for their prettily-cut foliage as much as their flowers. Propagation is by seed or cuttings.

M. coccineum. Flowers scarlet, July–Oct. 18 in.

M. × hypomadarum. Shrubby. Flowers white flushed pink. Doubtfully hardy. Greenhouse.

MARSH MARIGOLD. See *Caltha*

MARSH TREFOIL. See *Menyanthes*

MARTYNIA (*Unicorn Plant*)

Half-hardy annuals native to N. America and suitable for warm, sunny borders or the greenhouse. Propagate from seeds sown in spring in the greenhouse, transplant or pot-up in June.

M. fragrans. Violet-orange flowers, Aug.–Sept. 18–24 in.

M. louisiana. Yellowish flowers with green, yellow and violet spots and bars, June–July. 24–36 in.

MARVEL OF PERU. See *Mirabilis*

MASK FLOWER. See *Alonsoa*

MASTERWORT. See *Astrantia*

MATTHIOLA (*Stock*)

Although the genus contains a few perennials it is the annuals and biennials that provide the popular garden plants. They grow well in most soils, but prefer a sunny position. The annuals should be sown outdoors in spring, the biennials in June or July in pans in a frame, pricked out and grown on over the winter. For the greenhouse the seedlings should be potted-up in early autumn and brought into the house from Oct. onwards, to a cool temperature and plenty of ventilation.

M. bicornis (*Night-scented Stock*) (hardy annual). Lilac to pale purple flowers which open at night, very fragrant summer. 12–15 in.

M. incana and **M. sinuata** have given rise to the garden stocks of today, which are generally grouped as follows:

Ten-week Stocks. The different types of this half-hardy annual 'Dwarf', 'Giant' or 'Mammoth' grow 6–24 in. high and usually bloom 10–12 weeks after being sown. Sow seed thinly, in Mar., under glass, or in Apr. in the open. Under glass the seedlings must not be overwatered or given too much heat. Prick off as soon as possible, 3 in. apart, into boxes, harden off in Apr., and plant out firmly late in May, 12 in. apart, in well-manured soil. The over-vigorous seedlings should be thrown away, as they are usually single-flowered. 'All Double' strains are now available.

Intermediate or East Lothian Stocks. These flower in the borders from June to Oct., and are also excellent for growing in a cold greenhouse for flowering in late winter and early spring. Sow thinly in light soil in boxes or pots in a cold frame in July. Prick out or for the greenhouse pot-up when fit to handle. Stand in the open until early autumn, then transfer to a frame. Pot-on into 6- to 7-in. pots, transfer to the cold greenhouse from Oct. to Feb. for successional flowering, or if for summer-flowering in the open, keep in the frame until Apr., and plant out in May.

Brompton Stocks. Sown in July, these stocks will flower in the open in May, June and July. They may also be used for greenhouse culture.

Nice or Winter-flowering Stocks. These are useful in the cool greenhouse. For winter-flowering, sow July, grow on in a frame three to a 5-in pot, and transfer to the house early in Dec. For spring-flowering, sow in a frame in Aug., grow on as above, and take into the house when the winter-flowering plants are over. There are a number of named varieties in each group. Catalogues should be consulted.

MAURANDIA

A genus of half-hardy perennial climbing plants from C. America, suitable for a greenhouse or for planting out in June on a trellis in a rich soil in a sunny position. Although they may be propagated from cuttings the usual practice is to treat them as annuals and sow seed in heat in Mar. each year.

M. barclaiana. Violet-purple, rose or white flowers, summer. Grows up to about 10 ft.

M. lophospermum. Flowers rose-purple, dotted white, summer. 8–10 ft.

MAY APPLE. See *Podophyllum*

MAZUS
Creeping perennial plants native to S.E. Asia and New Zealand and suitable for the rock garden. Need good, well-drained soil in a sunny position. Propagate by seed or division.
M. pumilio. Bluish-white flowers with yellow centre, summer.
M. reptans. Mauve-blue flowers with red, purple and white blotches, summer.

MEADOW RUE. See *Thalictrum*

MEADOW SAFFRON. See *Colchicum*

MECONOPSIS
Large genus of hardy herbaceous plants native to Europe and Asia containing a number of perennial species that are monocarpic, that is, they exhaust themselves by producing seed, and for garden purposes must therefore be regarded as biennials. They thrive in well-drained, peaty soils in partial shade and are particularly suitable for woodlands, and a number are excellent for the rock garden. Propagate from seed sown in pans in the autumn as soon as ripe. Prick off when strong enough into a seed box, place in a cool greenhouse and plant out in spring.
M. betonicifolia (syn. **M. baileyi,** monocarpic). Blue to lavender flowers, May–Aug. 36–60 in.
M. cambrica (perennial). Yellow or orange, single or double flowers, May–Aug. 12–24 in.
M. grandis (perennial). Blue-purple or deep blue flowers, May–Aug. 18–36 in.
M. integrifolia (monocarpic). Yellow flowers, May–Aug. 18–24 in.
M. napaulensis (monocarpic). Pale blue, red or purplish flowers, May–Aug. Up to 72 in.
M. paniculata (monocarpic). Yellow flowers, May–Aug. 48–72 in. Large, deeply cut leaves, up to 2 ft. long.
M. quintuplinervia (perennial). Lilac-blue flowers, May–Aug. 12 in. Rock garden.
M. regia (monocarpic). Yellow flowers with attractive silvery foliage, May–Aug. 48–60 in.
M. villosa (perennial). Yellow flowers, May–Aug. 18 in. Rock garden.

MEDITERRANEAN CRESS. See *Morisia*

MEDITERRANEAN LILY. See *Pancratium*

MEGASEA. See *Bergenia*

MELITTIS MELISSOPHYLLUM
A single species of hardy herbaceous perennial having nettle-like flowers resembling Salvia, and particularly suited to semi-shaded places on good loam. Propagation by seed or division. Flowers white or white spotted purple or pink, May. 1 ft.

MENTZELIA (BARTONIA) LINDLEYI
A hardy annual from California and a suitable plant for the rock garden. They thrive in ordinary soil. Propagate from seed sown where the plants are to grow in Mar.–May. Fragrant golden-yellow flowers, opening in the evening, June–Oct. 12–15 in.

MENYANTHES TRIFOLIATA (*Buckbean, Marsh Trefoil*)
Hardy aquatic perennial which thrives in ordinary soil in a boggy situation or as a pocket plant in a pool. Propagate from cuttings 12 in. long struck in mud in the summer. Pinkish-white, fragrant flowers, Mar.–June. 1 ft.

MERTENSIA
A genus of hardy perennials native to Europe, Asia and America, thriving in moist, cool, woodland, or shaded position in the rock garden. Propagate from seed sown as soon as ripe or by division.
M. alpina. Light blue flowers, May–Aug. 8–12 in.
M. ciliata. Blue flowers, May–July. 2 ft.
M. primuloides. Deep blue flowers turning to yellow, May–Aug. 4–6 in.
M. sibirica. Purple-blue flowers, May–Aug. 12–18 in.
M. virginica (*Virginian Cowslip*). Purple-blue flowers, May–Aug. 12–24 in.

MESEMBRYANTHEMUM (*Fig Marigold*)
This name covers a large group of succulent

plants of several genera, largely natives of S. Africa with a few found in New Zealand, Australia, the Canary Islands and in the Mediterranean region. Generally, they may be regarded as greenhouse plants, although some of them are hardy and grow well outdoors. While most of them are perennials, there are a few annual species which have for many years been fairly common in gardens, the best known being **M. criniflorum** (*Dorotheanthus criniflorus*), which resembles **M. gramineum,** but the leaves have red tips; **M. crystallinum** (*Cryophytum crystallinum*) (*Ice Plant*); **M. gramineum** (*Dorotheanthus gramineus*) with rose, red and white flowers; and **C. pomeridianum** (*Carpanthea pomeridiana*) with yellow flowers. Some of them are excellent for window-gardening, while many of the strong growing and sub-shrubby species are very suitable flowering plants for the cool greenhouse, or for hot, sunny positions outdoors during the summer months. The greenhouse specimens will flower during the spring and summer.

Most of them are readily propagated by means of seed, cuttings or division. They thrive in a compost of good medium loam with a little leaf-mould, and enough coarse sand to keep the whole open and porous. Perfect drainage is essential, and watering must be done carefully during the winter months.

The following are a few of the most showy sub-shrubby species which may be used for planting out in summer: **M. aurantiacum** (deep orange); **M. aureum** (orange); **M. blandum** (white, changing to rose and red); **M. brownii** (purple, changing to reddish-yellow); **M. coccineum** (scarlet); **M. falciforme** (purplish-pink); **M. roseum** (rose); **M. spectabile** (red); **M. violaceum** (violet). All reach from 12 to 18 in. in height.

The other section, with compressed stems and very thick, fleshy leaves, are interesting on account of their strange forms and coloration, which in many cases has a striking resemblance to the ground and stones or pebbles among which they grow. The plants may be grown in pans of well-drained soil, and seed may be thinly sown in the pans. During the summer they appreciate a rather moister atmosphere, and during the late afternoon a slight syringing with a fine spray is beneficial (temp. 50 deg. F. winter, higher in summer). On account of their small size, a large collection may be accommodated in quite a small greenhouse, while many may be successfully grown in sunny windows. They are generally only a few inches high, and flowering is very uncertain. In this section the growing period is, in most cases, during our winter. This necessitates great care in giving them water, especially during spells of dull weather.

The following are some of the fairly common and distinct species (with the new generic names in brackets): **M. bolusii** (*Pleiospilos bolusii*), **M. calcarium** (*Titanopsis calcarea*), **M. ficiforme** (*Conophytum ficiforme*), **M. fissum** (*Rismaria dubia*), **M. fulviceps** (*Lithops fulviceps*), **M. lesliei** (*Lithops lesliei*), **M. pseudotruncatellum** (*Lithops pseudotruncatella*), **M. simulans** (*Pleiospilos simulans*), **M. testiculare** (*Argyroderma testiculare*), **M. thecatum** (*Conophytum minutum*), **M. tigrinum** (*Faucaria tigrina*), **M. truncatellum** (*Conophytum truncatellum*).

MEXICAN ASTER. See *Cosmos*

MEXICAN BERGAMOT. See *Agastache*

MEXICAN MARIGOLD. See *Tagetes*

MICHAUXIA TCHIHATCHEFFI

A tall biennial native to E. Mediterranean, suitable for the border but requiring a warm, sunny position. Propagate from seed sown in Apr. White flowers, July–Aug. Up to 6 ft.

MIGNONETTE. See *Reseda*

MILFOIL. See *Achillea*

MILK VETCH. See *Astragalus*

MILKWEED. See *Asclepias*

MIMULUS (*Musk, Monkey Flower*)

A genus of hardy and half-hardy annuals and perennials natives of W. America. They have brightly-coloured flowers resembling a monkey's face. All require moist conditions, and do well on the banks of ponds. None of the species or varieties is fragrant, the scent of the original common musk **(M. moschatus)** having been lost about 50 years ago. Propagation is by seed, cuttings or division. The following are hardy and suitable for borders but should not be allowed to get dry during the summer.

M. cardinalis (perennial). Flowers white, pink or crimson, June–July. 2–3 ft.

M. cupreus and **M. luteus** have together given rise to most of the present-day garden varieties with flowers ranging from pink to crimson, yellow to orange or vermilion and generally with two dark marks at the mouth, up to 2 in. across, June–Sept. 12 in. Four good vars. are 'Bee's Dazzler' (crimson), 'Bonfire' (crimson-scarlet), 'Canary Bird' (yellow) and 'Whitecroft Scarlet' (Vermilion).

M. glutinosus (shrubby). Flowers orange, buff or scarlet, June. Up to 5 ft. Cold greenhouse.

MIRABILIS (*Marvel of Peru*)

A genus of annuals and perennials native to S. America, including one species **M. jalapa** which may be grown as a half-hardy perennial. Propagate from seed sown in gentle heat in Mar.–Apr. and plant out the hardened seedlings towards the end of May. They should be lifted similar to dahlias in Oct., stored in sand or fibre for the winter and planted out in Apr.–May. The flowers are variable, ranging from white, red or pink, July–Sept. 2 ft.

MISCANTHUS (*Eulalia*)

A small genus of ornamental perennial grasses native to F. East, suitable as specimen plants in lawns or borders. Easily propagated by division in Mar.–Apr.

M. sinensis. Panicle up to 12 in., white tinged red, Aug.–Sept. Leaves striped or barred according to variety. 3 ft.

MISSOURI HYACINTH. See *Brodiaea*

MOLTKIA

A small genus of dwarf shrubby perennials native to Greece, resembling Lithospermums and suitable for the alpine house or sunny positions in the rock garden, in a well-drained loam containing lime. Propagate from seed, cuttings or layers.

M. petraea. Flowers pinkish-blue, June–July. 9–12 in.

M. suffruticosa. Flowers pale blue, June-Aug. 6–9 in.

MOLUCELLA (*Shell Flower*)

Of the two species in this genus one, **M. laevis,** is a hardy annual sometimes grown for its shell-like flowers which last for a long time. The flowers are greenish turning white as they mature with pink tips, Aug.–Oct. 1–1½ ft.

MONARDA (*Bergamot, Bee Balm*)

A genus of hardy annual and perennial herbs native to N. America, and having a pleasant fragrance. Two of the perennials make good garden plants. They are somewhat unusual, having square stems and fragrant leaves with more brightly coloured leaves or bracts forming part of the flower-head. They grow well in most soils, provided they do not dry out, and while they prefer full sun, will tolerate partial shade. Propagation is by seed or division, preferably in spring.

M. didyma. Leaves ovate, hairy. Flowers pink, red or scarlet, bracts tinged red, July–Sept. 24–36 in.

M. fistulosa. Leaves heart-shaped. Flowers white, pink or purple, bracts tinged purple, June–Aug. 24–48 in.

MONKEY FLOWER. See *Mimulus*

MONK'S HOOD. See *Aconitum*

MONSONIA

Shrubby greenhouse plants native to Tropical Asia and Africa. They need a well-drained compost of 2 parts sandy loam, 1 part peat and 1 part sand. Propagate from cuttings set in sandy soil in the early autumn or by seed sown in gentle heat in the spring. Pot-on as required.

M. lobata. The flowers are greenish, variegated, with purple, red or white on the outside, pale blue inside with a darker centre, spring. 12 in.

M. speciosa. Similar but the flowers are rose-coloured inside wth a dark eye, spring. 6–12 in.

MONTBRETIA
The true montbretia is a small genus native to S. Africa growing from corms, resembling and sometimes included in *Tritonia* (q.v.). The 'Montbretias' as commonly accepted by gardeners belong to the genus *Crocosmia*.
M. flava. Flowers yellow, Feb. 12 in. Greenhouse.
M. laxifolia. Leaves narrow, straight and rigid, up to 12 in. long. Flowers cream and pinkish-orange, borne in a loose spike, Sept.–Oct. 6–18 in.

MORAEA
Bulbous plants rather like irises and native to S. Africa. They may be grown in rich, sandy loam in sunny, sheltered positions but are best suited to a cool greenhouse, treated as for bulbous irises. Propagate from offsets or seed. Pot-up in Oct. Plant in the open in Mar. and lift when the foliage has died down.
M. robinsoniana (*Wedding Iris*). Large, pure white flowers often with red and yellow spots, June. 36–48 in.
M. spathacea. Flowers yellow with purple lines, May–June. 1 ft.

MORINA
A small genus of thistle-like plants, the taller species being suitable for borders. They grow best on light soils in partial shade. Propagation is by division or seed.
M. longifolia. Leaves large, spiny, up to 12 in. long. Flowers crowded in whorls on long spikes, white turning to pink, then crimson, June–July. 24 in.
M. persica. Leaves shorter but broader, hairy. Flowers pink, in long spikes, June–July. 36–48 in.

MORISIA MONANTHA (*Mediterranean Cress*)
A single species of perennial native to Corsica. Grows well in average soil and is suitable for the rock garden or alpine house. Propagate from seed or root-cuttings set in sand. Golden-yellow flowers, Mar.–May. 2–3 in.

MOSCHOSMA RIPARIUM
Half-hardy perennial from S. Africa, suitable for the cool greenhouse. Propagate from cuttings 2–3 in. long in spring and with slight bottom heat. They should be stopped back and potted-on as needed, reaching their final potting stage (6-in. pot) at the end of June. Stand in open during summer. After flowering prune well back, and re-pot in Mar. Small but numerous creamy-white flowers, Dec.–Feb. 24–48 in.

MOSS CAMPION. See *Silene*

MOUNTAIN AVENS. See *Dryas*

MOUNTAIN PARSLEY. See *Ferns*

MOUSE EAR. See *Cerastium*

MULLEIN. See *Verbascum*

MUSCARI
Hardy bulbous plants, natives of Europe and the Mediterranean. They thrive in a good loam and are most suitable for borders, rock gardens or for growing in pots. They have the advantage of thriving for many years without attention. Propagate from offsets in Oct. For growing in a greenhouse pot into a 5- to 6-in. pot in Oct., water moderately while growing and dry off in a cold frame after flowering.
M. armeniacum. Azure-blue flowers, Apr.–May. 6–8 in. A popular var. is 'Heavenly Blue'.
M. botryoides (*Grape Hyacinth*). Deep or pale blue or white flowers, spring. 8–12 in.
M. comosum (*Feather Hyacinth*). Pale violet-blue flowers, Apr.–May. 8–10 in.
M. moschatum (*Musk Hyacinth*). Yellow or purple flowers later turning greenish-yellow, spring. 8–10 in.

MUSK. See *Mimulus*

MUSK MALLOW. See *Malva*

MUTISIA
A genus of climbing plants native to S. America, most of them doubtfully hardy and best grown in a cold greenhouse. The one species listed below often grows well in ordinary soil in a sunny position. Propagate from seed sown as soon as ripe, or from cuttings of young shoots set in gentle heat in Mar. For a greenhouse pot-up in spring when growth is about to start or

plant in the greenhouse border. Water well and syringe overhead from May to June, but keep fairly dry during the autumn and winter.

M. clematis. Scarlet-orange flowers, July–Aug. Reaching up to 20 ft.

MYOSOTIDIUM HORTENSIA

A single species of herbaceous perennial from the Chatham Islands, requiring a moist soil in a damp, sheltered position. It is generally short-lived and difficult to grow. Propagate from seed sown May–June. It has large fleshy leaves up to 12 in. long, and flowers with a dark blue centre and lighter margins, spring. Grows 12–18 in.

MYOSOTIS (*Forget-me-not*)

Annual and perennial plants native to temperate regions, mainly Europe and Australia, usually treated as biennials. They thrive in ordinary but preferably moist soil in sunny positions. Propagate annuals from seed sown in June–July, and perennials from seed sown Apr.–July, or by division in Oct.

M. alpestris (perennial). Azure-blue flower with yellow eye, summer. 4–8 in. There are several named varieties.

M. azorica (perennial). White or purple flowers fading to blue, summer. 6–10 in. Not fully hardy, but good for potting.

M. caespitosa (perennial). Blue flowers, summer. 2–3 in.

M. dissitiflora (perennial but better treated as biennial). Sky-blue flowers, Mar.–May. 6–10 in.

M. scorpioides (perennial). White or sky-blue flowers with yellow eye, May–Sept. Creeping, 6–12 in. A good water-side plant.

MYRTLE GRASS. See *Acorus*

NARCISSUS

The first point to get clear is that of nomenclature. It is often asked 'What is the difference between a narcissus and a daffodil?' The answer is that all narcissi are daffodils and *vice versa*, daffodil being the common name and narcissus the Latin name of the family. The narcissus has been grown in gardens for hundreds of years but the present century has seen their greatest development and the modern improvement of the flower is almost unbelievable as anyone who has visited spring shows will readily agree. For convenience of reference the family has been classified into sections each of which bears reference to the colour or to the size and general shape of the flower; the latter having special regard to the proportion of the central part of the flower, that is, the trumpet or 'corona', and the outer surrounding part consisting of the petals or 'perianth' segments. The following gives a brief guide to the main sections. Readers requiring more detailed information should consult a classified list of daffodils. Division 1 embraces the 'trumpet' narcissi, followed by the 'large-cupped', 'small-cupped', 'double', 'triandrus', 'cyclamineus', 'jonquilla', 'tazetta' and 'poeticus'.

All narcissi like a warm, well-drained soil, but one which retains its moisture into the early summer while the new bulbs are developing, which is why they do so well in the higher rainfall districts. Planting should be done in the early autumn, aiming at completion by mid-Oct. Plant the bulbs 3–4 in. deep and at a distance apart to suit the purpose for which they are used. When planting in clumps 6–8 in. is a good distance or, when used with other plants, place alternate to them. The soil of beds and borders should be well cultivated but the addition of fresh manure is not recommended. After flowering the bulbs should be allowed to remain to complete their growth or until the foliage dies down naturally. It is not necessary to lift the bulbs every year but they should not be allowed more than 3 or 4 years without lifting and dividing. Should it be necessary to lift them to make way for other plants, then lay them in on a reserve border keeping the foliage intact. Under no circumstances should the foliage be cut off while it is green. When growth is completed the bulbs may be lifted, cleaned and laid out to dry in shallow trays but should not be exposed to strong sunshine. Before storing, examine the bulbs, destroying any showing signs of decay, store under cool, airy conditions and check through occasionally removing any which are deteriorating. Replant sound bulbs as early in September as possible.

Many varieties of narcissus do well naturalized in grass; in fact, some sorts are better under such conditions than when planted in cultivated soil. It is necessary for this type of planting to wait until the autumn rains have moistened the soil, and for planting it will be found more convenient to use a bulb planter than attempt the work with a spade. Bulb planters are available in small or larger sizes and by their use the minimum labour and disturbance of grass is required. Naturalized bulbs may be either mixed or the varieties kept distinct. Whichever method is preferred the plantings should be as informal as possible with no straight lines or defined circles. The pot culture of bulbs has been dealt with elsewhere in this volume, suffice it here to say that good bulbs should be obtained for this purpose, that they should be potted in Sept. for forcing and not introduced to heat until the pots are well filled with roots. Bulbs which have perforce to be grown in the dwelling house all the time may be potted in Oct. and should be kept in the dark for some weeks to induce rooting before top growth.

In addition to the large flowered varieties of narcissus there are also a number of small or miniature-flowered types. These species do well either on the rock garden or naturalized. It should be noted that the miniature 'trumpets' and 'triandrus' species do well in light shade, the 'jonquils' like full sun and the 'cyclamineus' and 'bulbocodium' sections have a liking for moist situations. Wherever planted it should be on informal lines and in sizeable clumps and as with all naturalized bulbs it follows that the grass must not be cut until the foliage has died down. A selection of these miniature types might include the following:

- *N. biflorus*, white perianth, pale yellow corona
- *N. bulbocodium 'Obesus'*, bright yellow
- *N. b. vulgaris conspicuus*, deep yellow
- *N. cyclamineus 'Beryl'*, perianth yellow, corona brick-red
- *N. c.'Larkelly'*, yellow perianth, orange-red cup
- *N. c. 'Charity May'*, canary yellow
- *N. c. 'Snipe'*, white
- *N. juncifolius*, small yellow, sweetly scented
- *N. jonquilla*, single and double forms; yellow, with several flowers per stem
- *N. j. 'Lintie'*, yellow with orange cups
- *N. j. 'Orange Queen'*, perianth and cup orange-yellow; all the jonquils are sweetly scented
- *N. minimus*, sulphur-yellow, the smallest trumpet daffodil
- *N. tazetta lacticolor*, a real miniature, white perianth, pale yellow cup, sweetly scented
- *N. triandrus* (Angels' Tears), creamy-white

Those wishing to make a good choice of the large flowered narcissus should consult a trade list but the following may serve as a guide.

Trumpet varieties:

- 'King Alfred' (deep yellow trumpet)
- 'Golden Harvest' (golden yellow trumpet)
- 'Beersheba' (pure white)
- 'Music Hall' (creamy-white and yellow)
- 'World's Favourite' (pure white and soft yellow)
- 'Robin Hood (deep yellow)

Large Cupped varieties:

- 'Carlton' (clear yellow cup with frilled edge)
- 'Carbineer' (rich yellow perianth, rich red cup)
- 'Dunkeld' (yellow perianth, orange-scarlet cup)
- 'Rustom Pasha' (deep yellow perianth, red cup)
- 'Yellow Sun' (yellow perianth, golden yellow frilled cup)

Small Cupped varieties:

- 'Edward Buxton' (pale perianth, orange cup)
- 'Lady Kesteven' (white perianth, deep red cup)
- 'Snow Princess' (white perianth, yellow, edged orange-scarlet cup)

Double varieties:

- 'Yellow Cheerfulness'
- 'Irene Copeland' (creamy-white and sulphur yellow)
- 'Primrose Phoenix'

Jonquil varieties:

- 'Golden Sceptre'
- 'Golden Perfection'

Poeticus varieties:

- 'Actaea' (white perianth, bright yellow, edged scarlet eye)
- 'Daphne' (Double Poeticus, pure white)
- 'Pheasant Eye' (white perianth, eye edged orange-scarlet)

NASTURTIUM. See *Tropaeolum*

NEMESIA
A genus of annuals and perennials native to S. Africa, containing the well-known **N. strumosa,** the Nemesia of the garden, suitable for bedding, rock gardens or pot plants. They thrive in ordinary soil in a sunny position. Propagate from seed sown in Mar. under glass, thin out and harden off. Plant out in May, or pot-up, stand the pots in the open during the summer, and bring into the cool greenhouse in Oct.

N. strumosa var. **suttonii.** Flowers variable, white, pink, orange, yellow, red, blue, summer. 12–24 in. There are a number of named varieties and a dwarf type, growing 9 in.

NEMOPHILA (*Californian Bluebell*)
Hardy annuals native to N. America. Grow in average soil in full sun. Propagate from seed sown in Aug. for flowering in spring, and Apr. for flowering in summer.

N. menziesii. White, blue or purplish flowers usually with vari-coloured lines or blotches, spring or summer. 4–8 in.

NEPETA (*Catmint*)
Of this large and widely-distributed genus of annuals and perennials only a few of the perennials are suitable for garden use. They prefer light sandy soils and a sunny position. Propagation is by seed, cuttings or division.

N. × faassenii. This is the perennial catmint grown in gardens and usually but wrongly named **N. mussinii** which is an inferior species. It is a branching plant with small, silvery-grey leaves and pale lavender flowers borne in whorls and forming a long spike, May–Sept. 12–18 in. It is a useful edging plant but as it sets no seed must be propagated by cuttings of young growth taken in June or July. 'Six Hills Giant' grows up to 36 in.

N. nervosa. Leaves narrow, strongly veined. Flowers blue, in spikes, July–Sept. 12–24 in.

N. spicata. Spreading, branching. Leaves ovate, toothed, up to 4 in. long. Flowers pale blue in cylindrical spikes, Sept. 12–36 in.

NEPHROLEPIS (*Ladder Fern*). See *Ferns*

NERINE
Bulbous plants native to S. Africa, several of the species providing beautiful flowers for a cool greenhouse. Plant singly in Aug. in 4- to 5-in. pots, so that the top of the bulb just shows above the soil. Water when the first growth appears, gradually increasing the quantity, and feed with liquid manure. After flowering and when the leaves turn yellow, gradually decrease the water supply, and keep the bulbs quite dry until Aug. comes round again when the pots should be well soaked and a top dressing of fibrous, loamy soil should be given. There is no need to re-pot annually if this dressing is provided; re-potting every fourth year will be sufficient. Propagate by means of offsets removed in Aug., or sow seed when ripe. To produce seed, however, the flowers must be hand fertilized.

N. bowdenii. Pink flowers, Sept.–Dec. 15–18 in. Hardy enough for outdoors in a warm position.

N. curvifolia. Bright scarlet flowers, Sept.–Dec. 15–18 in.

N. pulchella. Pale pink flowers, Sept.–Dec. 6–10 in.

N. sarniensis (*Guernsey Lily*). Pale salmon, rose-red or scarlet flowers, Sept.–Dec. 20–30 in.

N. undulata. Flesh-pink flowers, Sept.–Dec. 12–15 in.

There are a number of varieties and hybrids of most of these species.

NERTERA GRANADENSIS (*Coral-berried Duckweed, Bead Plant*)
The hardiest and best of a small genus of dwarf-growing plants native to Australasia and S. America. It is well suited to the alpine house, but will also grow in the rock garden in semi-shade in warm, moist, sandy loam provided it is protected from frost. Propagate from seed sown Mar.–Apr. in a little heat or by division in spring. The plant creeps along the ground, rarely reaching more than 3 in. high. Small greenish flowers followed by orange-scarlet berries.

NEW ZEALAND BURR. See *Acaena*

NEW ZEALAND FLAX. See *Phormium*

NICOTIANA (*Tobacco Plant*) PLATE 37
A genus of annual and perennial plants native to America and Australia. They thrive in rich soil in sunny beds and borders, and also make attractive greenhouse plants. Propagate from seed sown in Mar. under glass, harden off and plant out in June, or pot-on if for the greenhouse.
N. alata (perennial but better treated as an annual). Flowers yellowish-green outside and white inside, strongly fragrant, summer. 18–24 in.
N. × sanderae (annual). Rosy-red and greenish-white flowers, but not fragrant, summer. 24–36 in.
N. suaveolens (annual). White and purply-green flowers, fragrant at night, summer. 12–24 in. Greenhouse.
N. sylvestris (annual). Long white flowers, fragrant, summer. 48–60 in.

NIEREMBERGIA (*Bell Flower*)
Hardy and half-hardy perennial plants, natives of S. America. They need a light, moist soil and are suitable for the rock garden or alpine house. Propagate from seed sown in Mar. under glass, or cuttings taken in Aug. and set in sandy loam and peat in late spring or autumn.
N. caerulea. Numerous deep bluish-violet flowers, June–Sept. 6–12 in. Hardy.
N. gracilis. Flowers white, streaked purple, June–Aug. 12 in. Greenhouse.
N. frutescens. White, violet or light blue flowers, June–July. 12–18 in. Half-hardy.
N. repens. Creamy-white flowers streaked with yellow or pink, June–July. 3–6 in. Hardy.

NIGELLA
Hardy annuals, natives of S. Europe and N. Africa. They grow well in average soil in sunny positions in beds and borders. Propagate from seed sown where the plants are to flower in Mar. or autumn.
N. damascena (*Love-in-a-mist, Devil-in-a-bush*). Blue or white flowers, single or double, June–Sept. 12–24 in.
N. hispanica (*Fennel Flower*). Deep blue or white flowers with red stamens, June–Sept. 12–24 in.

NOLANA HUMIFUSA
Small hardy annual, native to Peru, suitable for a sunny position in the rock garden. Propagate from seed sown in Mar.–Apr. Bell-shaped, light blue flowers, summer. 3–12 in.

NUPHAR (*Yellow Water Lily*)
A small genus of aquatic plants native to northern hemisphere, suitable for still or slow-moving water, and succeeding in partly-shaded positions that are not sufficiently light or sunny for Nymphaeas, the true water lilies. Require 1–2 ft. of water.
N. advena. Large erect leaves. Yellow flowers, June–Sept.
N. lutea. Floating leaves. Yellow flowers, June–Sept.

NYMPHAEA (*Water Lilies*)
These well-known aquatic plants are natives of Europe, Asia, Australia and S. Africa. Several species require a tropical house, but those that are hardy do best in a sunny pool or very slow-moving water from 6–24 in. deep. The hardy species should be planted firmly in a basket or in the bottom of the pool in fibrous loam. A basket is preferable because young plants do best when the depth of water above them is not more than 1 ft. to begin with and is increased gradually as growth progresses. The basket can be supported on bricks or flat stones and lowered later on. Propagation is generally by seed which must be collected as soon as the pods burst since it floats for only a short time. The seed should be sown in pans barely covered with water, in gentle heat. Large plants can, with care, be divided.
There are a large number of named varieties derived mainly from **N. alba** and **N. marliaca** with flowers in various shades of white, yellow, pink, rose, red and purple.
N. odorata, white, pink or yellow, is fragrant and being less vigorous is suited for small pools. Most varieties require about 2 ft. of water, a few prefer 1 ft. and others up to 3 ft. (These particulars are always given when purchasing.) The dwarf varieties of **N. pygmaea** need only 4–9 in. and are often grown in bowls.

OBEDIENT PLANT. See *Physostegia*

OENOTHERA (*Evening Primrose*)
This is a large genus, mostly native to N. America, and includes the well-known biennial species with fragrant flowers opening only at night. Some of the perennials are also fragrant and fortunately are open during the day and flower over a long period, but often die after flowering. They grow in most soils but do best on the lighter well-drained kinds and in full sun. Propagation is by division.
O. biennis (biennial). The common Evening Primrose sometimes grown in borders, but best suited to the wild garden. Flowers yellow, evening, June–Sept. Up to 4 ft.
O. caespitosa (perennial). Tufted or prostrate. Flowers white to pink, fragrant, May–Aug. 9–12 in.
O. fruiticosa (perennial or biennial). Stems erect, reddish and branched. Leaves ovate, up to 2 in. long. Flowers deep yellow, up to 2 in. across, June–Sept. 24 in.
O. odorata (perennial). Leaves slightly toothed, up to 4 in. long. Flowers yellow turning red, up to 2½ in. across, opening in the evening, fragrant, Apr.–June. 12–18 in.
O. perennis (perennial). Leaves 2 in. long. Flowers small, yellow, in loose leafy spikes, July. 12–24 in.
O. speciosa (perennial). Leaves partly toothed. Flowers white turning to rose, fragrant, July–Aug. 12–24 in.
O. tetragona (perennial or biennial). A variable species, generally branching. Leaves up to 8 in. long. Flowers 1–2 in. across, numerous, yellow, June–July. 12–30 in.

OLD MAN. See *Artemisia*

OMPHALODES
Annual and perennial creeping plants, natives of E. Asia and Mediterranean, suitable for rock gardens in semi-shade in moist, sandy soil. Propagate from seed or by division.
O. cappadocica (perennial). Clear, rich blue flower, June–Aug. 6–8 in.
O. linifolia (*Venus' Navel-wort*) (annual). White flowers, sometimes tinged blue, June–Aug. 6–12 in.
O. luciliae (perennial). Flowers vary from light blue to pinkish-purple, June–Aug. 6–8 in. Difficult.
O. verna (*Creeping Forget-me-not, Blue-eyed Mary*) (perennial). Light blue flowers, with white throat, Apr.–May. 2–6 in.

ONONIS
A genus of hardy sub-shrubs and annual, biennial and perennial herbs, native to S. Europe and N. Africa. They thrive in almost any soil in sunny positions such as a rock garden. Propagate from seed, perennials also by cuttings.
O. cenisia (perennial). Flowers purplish-pink, June–Aug. 3–9 in.
O. speciosa (shrub). Rose-purple flowers, May–June. 3–4 ft.
O. viscosa (annual). Yellow flowers, streaked purple-red, May–June. 6–18 in.

ONOPORDON
A genus of annual, biennial and perennial herbs, natives of Europe, Asia and N. Africa, that grow in most garden soils. Propagate from seed sown in spring.
O. acanthium (*Common Cotton Thistle*) (perennial). Large purple flowers, July. 36–60 in.
O. tauricum (biennial). Large violet-purple flowers, summer. 24–36 in.

ONOSMA (*Alpine Comfrey*)
A genus of hardy annuals, biennials and perennials, natives of Asia and the Mediterranean, and suitable for the herbaceous border, rock garden or the alpine house. They thrive in sunny positions in well-drained sandy loam. All species can be propagated from seed and perennials also by cuttings set in sandy soil in a close frame in summer.
O. albo-pilosum (shrubby). White flowers later changing to rose, summer. 6–8 in.
O. echioides. Pale yellow to white flowers, summer. 6–8 in.
O. hookeri. Reddish-violet or purple flowers, early summer. 4–8 in.
O. stellulatum. Yellow flowers, early summer. 2–4 in.
O. tauricum. Citron-yellow flowers, summer. 4–8 in.

OPHIOPOGON (*Snake's Beard, Japanese Hyacinth*)
A small genus of doubtfully hardy perennial plants, natives of Far East, suitable for a cold greenhouse or outside in sandy soil, but need winter protection. Propagate by division.
O. jaburan. Long, white grass-like leaves. White to lilac flowers, July. 18–36 in.
O. japonicus. Long, grass-like leaves, often variegated. White flowers, June. 10–15 in.

ORANGE SUNFLOWER. See *Heliopsis*

ORCHIDS
Although orchid growing is a highly specialized job, it is by no means essential for an amateur grower to be a millionaire. What is essential is to have the necessary facilities, equipment and knowledge in order to provide the plants with conditions that as far as possible resemble their natural environment. The majority are natives of warm humid forests where they grow on the bark of the trees or in the fibrous forest soil. The different groups therefore require their own special conditions of warmth, humidity, shade and air and since they take up their food in ways that are different from those employed by the plants usually grown in greenhouses they need special composts and in some cases special containers and special positions. Generally they need more humidity, less air and less light than other plants and this means that they must have a house to themselves where the temperature, humidity, ventilation and light can be controlled within fairly close limits, and the amateur who wishes to specialize must usually confine himself to a particular group of species, selecting from those that require a high temperature (70 deg. F. in winter), an intermediate temperature (60 deg. F.) or a cool temperature (50 deg. F.). And although there are some 600 genera and 15,000 species, most amateurs choose only from the few that are the most easily managed. Even then, before making any decision it is essential to understand what will be involved. The first step is to study a specialist book such as F. G. Preston's, *The Greenhouse*, and to consult a commercial orchid nurseryman. This will give a picture of the type of house required, the form of heating, shading and ventilation, the types of compost, pot drainage, methods of potting and all the other miscellaneous requirements of the job. The first purchases should be confined to the less expensive kinds of those that succeed in a cool house, or to the few that will tolerate sharing a general purpose house, provided they can be kept together in one end where they can be specially tended. The nurseryman supplying the plants will advise on particular species or varieties and on their general growth requirements. He will probably also be ready to sell the particular fibrous composts that are needed and to show how potting should be done, both being very different from the usual.
The first choices may be made from:
Anguloa (*Bull's Head* or *Cradle Orchid*). Pot-up in spring when new growth begins, using a compost of 2 parts of fibrous peat to 1 part of osmunda fibre and sphagnum moss. Water well while growing, but sparingly when mature, and give rest in the winter at 50 deg. F. Propagate by division at potting time.
There are several species with large flowers generally 6–9 in. round, golden-yellow and white with coloured spots, June–July. About 20 in.
Brassia. Most species require a winter temperature of 60 deg. F. Pot-up in Feb. triennially in shallow pans or on blocks of wood in a compost of 1 part of sphagnum moss to 3 parts of chopped osmunda fibre. **B. brachiata** will succeed in a cool house, in small pots in partial shade. It is vigorous and spreading, has large yellowish-green flowers with purplish spotting, 6 in. long.
Coelogyne. The Indian species will succeed in a winter temperature of 50 deg. F. in a compost of ½ osmunda fibre and ½ sphagnum moss, in pots or on rafts. Water liberally during spring and summer. The most suitable is **C. cristata** and its varieties. Flowers fragrant, white, with golden-yellow lip, Jan.–Mar. 6–9 in.
Cymbidium. Several species are suitable for a cool house, the long sprays of flowers being most attractive. They require plenty of room, and a compost of fibrous loam with some peat or sphagnum moss. Give reasonable air, and

ample light, but shade from strong sun. Water well while growing. Keep moist and cool in summer. Reduce water supply for a few weeks after flowering. Propagate by division in Mar.
C. eburneum. Ivory-white, Mar. 30 in.
C. erythrostylum. White or yellowish, with red or crimson lines.
C. grandiflorum. Flowers yellow with blotches of purple or red, 4 to 5 in. wide, up to 30 in.
C. insigne. White or rose and white, Mar.–May. 30 in.
C. lowianum. Flowers numerous, yellow and green, with brown or purplish blotches, Mar.–Apr. 30 in.
C. parishii. Flowers white and yellow, with orange and purplish tipping and spotting, summer. 30 in.
Cypripedium (*Lady's Slipper*). A large genus of attractive, terrestrial orchids, containing some hardy species suitable for growing outside and others that require either a warm or cool greenhouse.
The greenhouse species are sometimes treated as belonging to other genera, **Paphiopedilum, Phragmipedilum** and **Selenipedium,** but for practical purposes all are accepted as Cypripediums. They require a compost of 2–3 parts fibrous loam, 1 part osmunda fibre and 1 part sphagnum moss, a winter temperature of 45 deg. F. to 55 deg. F. according to species, reasonable watering and shading in bright weather. Propagation is by division of large plants. Many of the species contain a large number of hybrids and named varieties. Among the more hardy are: **C. acaule,** pinkish-purple solitary flowers, May–June, 6–8 in.; **C. candidum,** greenish-brown and white, June, 12 in.; **C. japonicum,** pink and white, tinged with crimson, June, 8–10 in.; **C. macranthum,** purple, May and June, 9–12 in.; **C. montanum,** white, veined with purple, June, 18–24 in. For a cool house any of the above will do well, but the best is **C. insigne** which has a number of hybrids and varieties and a wide range of colours in shades of green, yellow and white with brown, purple or reddish markings. Flowers up to 5 in. on stems up to 20 in. high, winter.
Dendrobium (*Rock Lily*). A large genus with many hybrids in the popular species, all having distinctive noded stems. Those suitable for a cool house require a compost of 3 parts of osmunda fibre to 1 of sphagnum moss, a temperature of 50 deg. F., fairly regular watering except when dormant, and ample light with shading in summer. Propagate by means of offsets. The best cool house species is **D. nobile** with white fragrant flowers, tipped or marked with purple or crimson, Jan.–Apr. Up to 2 ft. Many named varieties. Other species are **D. falcorostrum,** white, marked crimson, spring. **D. longicornu,** white, May–June, and **D. speciosum,** yellowish-white with red spots, autumn.
Disa (*Table Mountain Orchid*). Requires a compost of equal parts osmunda fibre and sphagnum moss with some coarse sand. Ventilate freely while growing. Keep moist, and shade from direct sun. Temperature 45–50 deg. F. Syringe overhead in spring and summer. Propagate by division of the roots in Nov. The most suitable species is **D. uniflora,** scarlet and crimson, June–July. 2–3 ft.
Odontoglossum. The difficulty is to keep a temperature of 55 deg. F. summer and winter, with a moist well-aired atmosphere. But some of the hybrids are so beautiful that many amateurs specialize in this genus alone. They require a compost of 1 part sphagnum moss and 1 part of osmunda and full drainage. Ventilate freely, shade and keep cool in hot weather. Give plenty of light while flowers are forming, and keep the atmosphere moist when warm and fine. Water liberally during summer, but give only sufficient water to keep bulbs plump in winter. Propagate by means of division of large plants in Sept. Most of the best and most suitable varieties have been derived from **O. crispum** with flowers generally white or yellow and marked or spotted with shades of brown, red or purple.
There are also many beautiful hybrids the results of crossing Odontoglossum with species of Cochlioda, the latter bringing in shades of brown, rose, red and mauve, and all known as Odontiodas.
Oncidium. A large genus with groups of

species requiring widely differing treatments. The most suitable is **O. macranthum** which can be grown in the same way as Odontoglossums, and has golden-yellow and purplish flowers. Other species that may be tried are: **O. concolor,** bright yellow, Apr.–May, 30 in.; **O. incurvum,** purple, edged white, Oct., 30 in.; **O. ornithorhynchum,** rose-purple, Sept.–Nov., 15–20 in.; **O. tigrinum,** yellow and brown, Nov.–Dec., 30 in.; **O. varicosum,** green, reddish-brown and yellow, Nov.–Dec. 30 in.

Pleione. A small genus resembling Coelogyne with large flowers which do not however last more than 10–14 days. They require a compost of 2 parts loam fibre, 2 parts osmunda and 1 of sphagnum moss and re-potting every year. Water well only in growth. **P. hookeriana.** Flowers with rose, blotched purple, May. **P. praecox.** Flowers white or purplish with yellow blotches, May–June.

ORIGANUM

A genus of herbaceous perennials, natives of the Mediterranean, with two species suitable for the rock garden. Thrive in ordinary well-drained soil. Easily raised from seed, cuttings from young growth or division in the spring.

O. dictamus (*Dittany*). Leaves covered with dense wool on both sides. Pink flowers, summer. 8–12 in.

O. hybridum. Woolly leaves. Pink flowers, summer. 8–12 in.

O. marjorana is the herb Sweet Marjoram. (See 'Herbs'.)

O. onites (Pot Marjoram). Toothed, hairy leaves. White flowers in dense spikelets, summer. 12 in.

ORNITHOGALUM

Bulbous-rooted plants, natives of Europe, Africa and Asia, the hardy species are suitable for borders or the wild garden, the more tender ones for growing in pots in a cool greenhouse. Propagate from seed.

O. arabicum. White flowers with dark centres, summer. 24–30 in. Although hardy the plant seems to flower best in a cool greenhouse.

O. nutans. White flowers, greenish outside, Apr.–May. 12–18 in.

O. thyrsoides (*Chincherinchee*). White to yellow flowers, early summer. 6–12 in. Cool greenhouse.

O. umbellatum (*Star of Bethlehem*). White with a green stripe, summer. 6–12 in.

OSMUNDA (*Royal Fern*). See *Ferns*

OSTROWSKIA MAGNIFICA (*Giant Bellflower*)

A single perennial species making a grand border plant, growing 5–6 ft. high with attractive foliage and light purple cup-shaped flowers in July. Requires a good sandy loam sufficiently well drained to prevent excessive moisture in winter when a protective covering of ashes should be given. Resents disturbance and should therefore be raised from seed sown as soon as ripe. After transplanting, the seedlings will take 3–4 years to come into flower.

OURISIA

Perennial alpine plants, natives of New Zealand and S. America. Suitable for the rock garden. They thrive in a moist but well-drained soil in a sheltered position shaded from the mid-day sun. Propagate from seed or division in Mar.–Apr.

O. alpina. Red to pink flowers, summer. 4–10 in.

O. coccinea. Scarlet flowers, summer. 6–12 in.

O. macrophylla. White flowers, sometimes with purple streaks, July. 12–18 in.

OXALIS

A large genus of hardy and half-hardy annuals, perennials, and bulbous plants, natives of S. Africa and Tropical America. Many species are weedy but others make suitable garden plants with their beautiful green, clover-like foliage, which forms a fine contrast to their richly coloured blossoms, or are admirably adapted for pot culture. **O. adenophylla, O. enneaphylla, O. lobata** and **O. magellanica** grown in a 5- to 6-in. pan make useful little plants for culture in the alpine house. In the cool greenhouse autumn-flowering species may be had in bloom in summer. **O. corymbosa** is an ideal hanging-basket plant, and

O. ortgiesii, a free, yellow-flowering species, is a most useful subject for pot culture in the warm greenhouse. They succeed in any well-drained, light, sandy soil mixed with leaf-mould; the rock garden species need a gritty loam and a semi-shaded position.

Sow seed of annuals thinly in Mar. or Apr. Prick off in pots for the greenhouse, or plant out in June. Propagation of bulbous species is by means of offsets planted in Sept. 3 in. deep, or for the greenhouse potted in Mar., putting 5 bulbs $\frac{3}{4}$ in. deep, in a 5-in pot. Keep cool, and water sparingly until growth commences, then water liberally. Dry off after flowering, and keep dry through the winter.

O. acetosella (*Wood Sorrel*). White flowers with purplish veins, spring. 4–6 in. Hardy, for shaded places.

O. adenophylla. Lilac-pink flowers with a dark eye, May–July. 4–6 in. Rock garden.

O. corymbosa. Bluish violet or mauve or white flowers, spring. 6–8 in.

O. enneaphylla. White or pink flowers, May–Sept. 6–8 in. Rock garden.

O. hirta. Deep rose to lavender flowers, autumn. 8–12 in.

O. lasiandra (*O. floribunda*). Rosy-crimson flowers, spring. 12–15 in.

O. lobata. Pale yellow flowers, Sept.–Oct. 4–6 in.

O. magellanica. Pale pink or whitish flowers, summer. 2–4 in. Rock garden.

O. rosea (annual). Rose and white flowers, spring. 6–18 in.

O. stricta (annual). Yellow flowers, spring. 12–18 in.

O. tuberosa. Yellow flowers, late summer. 6–12 in.

OYSTER PLANT. See *Mertensia*

PAEONIA (*Paeony*) PLATE 41

This is a small genus although its species have come from parts of Europe, Asia, America and China, to provide some of the finest garden plants of today. The shrubby species (principally **P. delavayi, P. lutea** and **P. suffruticosa** and their hybrids) provide the 'tree peonies', striking plants which need a rich soil and sheltered positions, with some protection for the early shoots which may suffer in late frosts. Propagation is by grafting on to **P. officinalis** or **P. lactiflora** or by layering. Plant in Mar. or Apr., with graft union below soil level.

The herbaceous paeonies also require a deep rich soil and prefer partial shade. They resent being disturbed and for this reason are often grown in beds by themselves or among or in front of shrubs. Propagation is by division in autumn.

P. lutea. Shrub up to 4 ft. Flowers yellow, some varieties with red blotches, single or double, May–June.

P. suffruticosa (*Moutan Paeony*). Shrub up to 6 ft. Flowers mostly double, white, pink, red or scarlet, May–June.

In both species there are several named varieties.

The two principal herbaceous species are:

P. lactiflora. The Chinese paeony has provided most of the modern herbaceous varieties, imparting a lighter foliage and more upright but more slender growth than **P. officinalis.** A large number of named varieties have been raised, both single and double, and lengthy lists can be obtained from most nurseries. The colours range from white to pink, red, crimson, mauve, yellow and gold, often with delicate shading or blotching.

P. officinalis. The common paeony, which gave rise to the old-fashioned varieties still seen in gardens today and still worth some space. The leaves are large and deeply cut into segments and the flowers single or double, white, pink, red or crimson, blooming in May. The plants grow about 30 in. high but the heavy double flowers must have good support if they are to survive wind and rain.

Many retain the fragrance of the species and all flower in June, growing between 24–40 in. high.

Selected varieties (all double unless stated otherwise):

Whites: Alice Harding, Baroness Schroeder, Clairette (single), Duchesse du Nemours (scented), Frances Willard, Marie Lemoine, Mrs. A. M. Brand, Solange, The Bride (single).

Pinks: Albert Crousse, Blanche King, Claire Dubois, Emma (single), Georgiane Shaylor, Jeannot, La France (scented), Loren Franklin, President F. D. Foosevelt, Sarah Bernhardt.
Reds: Adolphe Rousseau, Balliol, Border Gem, Defender, Felix Crousse, Gen. MacMahon, Karl Rosenfeld, Longfellow, Mark Twain, Mary Brand, Philippe Rivoire, Sir John Franklin, The Moor (single).
Purple: M. Martin Cahuzac.
Other species are:
P. mlokosewitschi. Leaves dark bluish-green, tinted red. Flowers yellow, up to 5 in. across, Apr. 18–24 in.
P. peregrina. Leaves much divided, coarsely toothed. Flowers red, up to 4 in. across, May. 36 in.
P. tenuifolia. Leaves many, dark green, finely cut. Flowers deep crimson, cup-shaped, 3 in. across, single or double, May. 18–24 in.
P. wittmanniana. Leaves up to 7 in. long, shining green above, hairy and white beneath. Flowers yellow, bowl-shaped, up to 5 in. across, Apr.–May. 36 in.

PANCRATIUM (*Mediterranean Lily, Sea Daffodil*)

A genus of bulbous plants native to S. Europe, mostly requiring high temperatures but two species succeed in the open in light, rich loam and peat that is well drained and in sunny, sheltered positions. Propagate from seeds sown in spring in heat or offsets at potting time (Mar. or Oct.). Those grown in the open should be protected with fibre or the like in winter.
P. illyricum. Broad strongly veined leaves. Small white flowers, May–June. 18 in.
P. maritimum. Small white flowers, May–June. 18–24.

PANDOREA

A genus of striking climbing plants, natives of Australia, and suitable for a cool greenhouse. Propagate by means of matured side-shoots struck in sand in heat in late summer. When fairly advanced in growth these plants may be trained over the roof of the greenhouse. They need rich, well-drained compost in full sun, ample ventilation and plenty of water in spring and summer. In Jan. prune back all weak growths by at least half their length and reduce the more vigorous stems by one-third.
P. jasminoides (*Bower Plant*). White flowers sometimes suffused with pink, summer.
P. pandorana (*Wonga-wonga Vine*). Pinkish-white to yellow flowers, summer. Finely cut fern-like foliage.

PANSY. See *Viola*

PAPAVER (*Poppy*) PLATE 43

Native to the temperate regions of Asia, N. Africa and Europe, the genus includes many annuals, biennials and perennials. All grow well in most kinds of soil but prefer a rich, deep, sandy loam and a sunny position. Propagation is by seed or for named varieties of perennials by division or root cuttings. The best garden perennials are the Iceland poppies derived from **P. nudicaule** and the Oriental poppies from **P. orientale.**
The Iceland poppies are dainty plants suitable for the front of a border, with oblong, basal leaves, 4–6 in. long, and solitary flowers up to 2 in. across, often fragrant. A number of named varieties or strains are available in white, shades of yellow, orange or red, flowering June to Aug. and growing 12–18 in. high. This species is often best treated as a biennial.
The Oriental poppies are bigger, taller and more vigorous, growing from 24 to 36 in. high and having large divided leaves up to 10 in. long and flowers up to 6 in. across. Unfortunately they usually become untidy as the foliage begins to die off after flowering, and for this reason should be planted in the middle of a border so that other plants in front will act as a screen, and the foliage should be trimmed as soon as it loses colour. Many named varieties are available, from the original scarlet to more delicate shades of red, pink or mauve, and white usually with deeper-coloured blotches. Some are double. Most of them flower in May and June, but a few late varieties flowering in July and early Aug. have been developed. The best are 'Marcus Perry' (orange-scarlet, which does not need staking), 'Ethel Swete' (crimson-pink), 'Perry's White', 'Salmon Flow', 'King George' (red).

The Shirley Poppies and Opium Poppies are annuals and have been derived from **P. rhoeas** and **P. somniferum.** They should be sown in Apr. and May in their permanent positions and thinned to 9–12 in. apart, flowering in July–Sept. The Shirley poppies flower in a large variety of colours, often shaded with a second tint, and grow up to 2 ft. high. The Opium poppies are usually white, red or purple, often blotched and fully double and grow up to 3 ft.

PARADISEA (*St. Bruno's Lily*)

There is one species only, native to S. Europe, having a thick rhizomatous root and growing well in rich, light soils in full sun. Propagation is by division in Sept. or Oct.

P. liliastrum. Leaves narrow, up to 24 in. long. Flowers lily-like, transparent white, 2 in. long, petals tipped green, borne in loose spikes, June. 12–24 in.

PARNASSIA

A small genus of hardy perennials, natives of the northern temperate regions. One species is suitable for the bog or water garden. Propagate from seed or division.

P. palustris (*Grass of Parnassus*). Heart-shaped leaves. White flowers, June–July. 4–6 in.

PARONYCHIA

Mat-forming creeping plants natives of S. Europe and Mediterranean, suitable for a rock garden in light, gritty soil in full sun. Propagate by division in Mar., or from seed.

P. kapela and **P. serpyllifolia** form dense carpets of attractive leaves but have insignificant flowers.

PASQUE FLOWER. See *Pulsatilla*

PASSIFLORA (*Passion Flower*)

A genus of climbing plants, mostly perennial and natives of S. and E. America. The majority require a high temperature, but several do well in a cool greenhouse and a few succeed out of doors. They will grow well in almost any well-drained soil, though sandy loam is the best. Propagate from cuttings of young shoots taken in spring, pot-on, finally into large pots, or plant in the border and train to the roof or rafters. If planted in the border the roots should be restricted to encourage flowering. After flowering prune back the old wood and cut out weak shoots.

P. banksii. Brick-red flowers, June–Sept. Cool greenhouse.

P. caerulea. Whitish-pink flowers with bluish filaments, June–Sept. A recommended variety is 'Constance Elliott'. Hardy in protected positions outside.

P. gracilis (annual). Flowers pale green, Aug. Hardy.

PASSION FLOWER. See *Passiflora*

PATRINIA

A small genus of perennial herbs, native to Asia, one species, **P. triloba,** being suitable for the rock garden or front of a border. It has a reddish stem and golden-yellow fragrant flowers in July. It grows in most soils and is propagated by seed or division. 9–12 in.

PEARLWORT.

PELARGONIUM

Although commonly called Geraniums, the Pelargoniums are a distinct genus. The true geraniums (see p. 224) are hardy whereas the pelargoniums are not, and for this reason are grown in cool greenhouses or used for bedding out, making wonderful displays in either case. They grow well in most soils and are easily raised from seed or from cuttings taken in spring or late summer in gentle heat. The cuttings should be 3–4 in. long, cut below a joint, and will take about 6 months to come into flower.

When growing a moderate and regular amount of water is required, but in winter only sufficient moisture to keep roots from becoming dust-dry is needed. Weekly doses of weak liquid manure or soot-water are beneficial to pot-plants when the flower buds are forming.

Most of the plants grown in gardens are hybrids and modern plant breeding has produced a number of striking varieties many of which are named. They are divided into 4 main groups:

Zonal Pelargoniums are the best-known 'Geraniums' and probably originated from **P. inquinans** and **P. zonale.** They are used extensively as bedding plants and also make excellent pot-plants for decoration in the greenhouse, where they may be had in flower almost the whole year through. The flowers, some of which are double, vary in size almost as much as they do in colour, which ranges from brilliant crimson-red or purple to pink, and from salmon to white. The leaves usually show a 'horseshoe' but they may also be variegated which are most effective for summer bedding. Dwarf varieties are available.

Ivy-leaved Pelargoniums. These are forms of **P. peltatum** and are attractive plants of trailing habit, with brilliant flowers of various colours, mostly shades of red, rose, pink or white, some varieties being double. They make excellent plants for hanging baskets and for window-boxes or balconies or may be trained up the greenhouse wall or pillars. Those of less trailing habit may be used for summer bedding.

Regal or Show Pelargoniums are forms of **P. domesticum** particularly suitable for greenhouse decoration, often making large plants with fine brilliant blooms, which vary from deep maroon to shades of red, pink, to pure white. They bloom in early summer, from May to July. After flowering, they should be cut back and rested. When they commence to break they should be re-potted with new soil in the same sized pot and early in the new year transferred to their flowering-pots and stopped as required. In this way established plants may be grown for a number of years in pots of a similar size, the soil being renewed annually.

Scented-leaved Pelargoniums have, as their name implies, fragrant foliage. They make good pot-plants often of large size, and can also be used with effect in bedding schemes and for indoor decoration, although their flowers are insignificant.

Varieties:

Large numbers of varieties have been raised and specialist nurseries offer a wide choice from comprehensive catalogues. The following is a small selection of the best and most popular:

ZONAL: 'Elizabeth Cartwright (carmine), 'Paul Crampel' (scarlet), 'Decorator' (scarlet), 'Gustav Emich' (orange-scarlet), 'Hermione' (white), 'King of Denmark ' (salmon-pink), 'A. M. Mayne' (purple), 'Maxim Kovalesky' (orange-vermilion), 'Prince of Wales' (purple), 'Queen of Denmark' (pink).

IVY-LEAVED: 'Abel Carriere' (purple), 'Chas. Turner' (rose madder), 'L'Élegant' (white with purple), 'Galilee' (rose-pink), 'Mme Crousse' (pink).

REGAL: 'Bridesmaid' (white with pink markings), 'Carisbrooke' (rose-pink), 'Grand Slam' (red with maroon), 'Lady Torsden' (cherry madder), 'Lord Bute' (purple).

SCENTED-LEAVED: 'Clorinda', **P. tomentosum.** (white, veined purple).

Although practically the whole of the genus needs protection, **P. endlicherianum** (Asia Minor and Syria) can be grown in a sheltered part of the rock garden. It should be planted in well-drained soil and the pans plunged in ashes in a frame during the winter. Flowers rose.

PELTANDRA VIRGINICA

A handsome aquatic plant native to N. America, suitable for shallow water and the margins of ponds. Propagate by division of roots in spring. White flowers, June–July. 24–36 in.

PELTIPHYLLUM PELTATUM
(*Umbrella Plant*)

A single species of hardy perennial native to California, suitable for margins of streams and ponds. Propagate by division of the rhizomes. Leaves about 6 in. across. White or pink flowers, spring. 3–4 ft.

PENSTEMON (*Beard Tongue*)

A genus of perennial plants native to N. and C. America, not sufficiently hardy to stay outside in winter. The taller species are excellent for beds and borders, and the dwarfs for the rock garden. All need rich, lightish and well-drained soil. They are susceptible to wet, but will stand dry conditions well. In cold, wet areas they need a sheltered position and protection from frost. Propagate from cuttings taken in Sept., and kept free from frost during winter, or from seed sown under glass in early Mar., pricked out and hardened off for planting out in May.

There are a number of named varieties, most of them derived from the following species:
P. barbatus. Red, salmon or pink tubular flowers, June–Aug. 24 in.
P. cobaea. Flowers purple or white, Aug. 12 in.
P. eatonii. Scarlet flowers, Aug. 12–24 in.
P. glaber. Flowers blue, purple, pink or rose, Aug. 12–24 in.
P. hartwegii. White, rose, red, crimson or purple flowers, July–Sept. 18–30 in.
P. heterophyllus. Flowers blue with pink flush, July. 12 in.
P. newberryi. Pink or cerise flowers, summer 12 in. Dwarf forms 6 in.

PEROVSKIA ATRIPLICIFOLIA
One species of a small genus of shrubby perennials native to N. Asia. It has a sage-like scent and thrives in full sun in a well-drained, ordinary soil. Propagate from cuttings. Bright lavender-blue flowers, Aug.–Sept. 3–4 ft.

PERUVIAN LILY. See *Alstroemeria*

PETUNIA PLATE 42
The garden petunias have been derived from two species, **P. integrifolia** and **P. nyctaginiflora,** both native to S. America, and although perennial are treated as half-hardy annuals. There are single and double varieties, and the prevailing colours are white, rose, carmine, magenta, blue and purple. They like a sunny position in moderately rich, light soil, and flower in the summer and autumn. Single varieties grow about 12 in. in height, and double varieties about 24 in. Both are suitable for cultivation in the greenhouse, in sunny borders, in hanging baskets and for pot culture, particularly the double varieties. Propagate from seed sown thinly in Mar. in gentle heat, and only just cover with soil. Prick out, harden off and plant out in May and June, 12 in. apart. For the greenhouse pot into 5- or 6-in. pots in May, pinch back, train and stake as required. Named or special varieties may also be propagated by means of cuttings taken in Mar. from plants over-wintered in a cool house. A large number of garden varieties are available; consult seedsmen's catalogues.

PHACELIA
Most of the species are dwarf-growing hardy annuals, and natives of America. Grow well in ordinary soil. Propagate from seed sown thinly in spring or summer, in permanent positions.
P. campanularia. Deep blue, bell-like flowers, June–Aug. 6–8 in.
P. tanacetifolia. Blue to pale mauve, bell-like flowers, June–Aug. 4–30 in.
P. whitlavia (*California Bluebell*). Deep blue, bell-like flowers, June–Aug. 6–12 in.

PHAEDRANASSA CARMIOLI (*Queen Lily*)
A species of a small genus of half-hardy, bulbous plants from S. America. It will grow in a well-drained, deep, sandy loam in a sunny, sheltered position in summer but must be brought into a cool greenhouse for winter. Propagate by offsets in Mar. or Oct. Crimson flowers with greenish tips, spring. 2 ft.

PHALARIS (*Ribbon Grass, Gardener's Garters*)
A genus of annual and perennial ornamental grasses suitable as specimen plants or for mixing in borders. They grow well in most soils and are propagated by seed, perennials also by division.
P. arundinacea (perennial). Leaves variegated or striped. Inflorescence a spray, 4 in. long, June–July. 2–5 ft.
P. canariensis (annual). Leaves long, narrow. Inflorescence rounded, greenish-white, July–Aug. 2 ft.

PHEASANT'S EYE. See *Adonis*

PHLOMIS (*Jerusalem Sage*)
The genus consists mainly of shrubs and subshrubs natives of Asia and the Mediterranean, but includes two species suitable for borders. Resembling the true sages they grow best in the lighter, well-drained soils in full sun. Propagation is by division or seed.
P. cashmeriana. Leaves downy or hairy above, white beneath. Flowers pale lilac, in whorls, July. 24 in.
P. samia. Leaves green above, grey beneath, hairy. Flowers creamy-white tinged green, pinkish within, in whorls, June. 24–36 in.

PHLOX

Many of the species of this N. American genus provide plants specially suited to the rock garden or border. Most of them are perennial, hardy and easy to grow, require little or no support, and their brightly-coloured flowers cover a long period during the summer. They will flourish in a wide range of soil but do best on fertile loams with a good supply of moisture, in full sun or partial shade. Propagation of annuals is by seed and of perennials by division or cuttings or, less commonly, bv seed.

Most border varieties have been derived from **P. paniculata** (Syn. **P. decussata**) They range from 2–4 ft. and flower between July and Sept. in a wide range of colours, pinks, reds, purples and white, with various shades and combinations, the flowers being borne in loose heads easy to look at. A vast number of named varieties are available, the following being a small selection:

'A. E. Amos': brilliant scarlet. 36 in.
'Amethyst': lavender blue. 36 in.
'Balmoral': rosy-mauve. 36 in.
'Cecil Hanbury': orange-salmon, with carmine eye. 24 in.
'Dresden China': shell-pink. 36 in.
'Frau Ant. Buchner': white. 36 in.
'Graf Zeppelin': white, with carmine eye. 36 in.
'Jules Sandeau': pure pink. 30 in.
'Le Mahdi': dark violet. 30 in.
'Leo Schlageter': scarlet-crimson, with dark eye. 36 in.
'Lord Lambourne': carmine-pink, with white eye. 36 in.
'Sandringham': pink. 36 in.
'Spitfire': geranium-lake, with crimson eye, Sept. 30 in.
'Windsor': rose-carmine. 36 in.

Other species suitable as border plants are:

P. × arendsii. These are hybrids, generally more dwarf than the paniculata varieties, flowering earlier and having large somewhat loose trusses of flowers, in white, pink and lilac, June–July. 14–24 in.

P. maculata. Stems hairy with red spots. Flowers violet-blue or purple, July–Aug. 36 in.

The dwarf or alpine phloxes were derived mainly from **P. subulata** although one or two other dwarf species such as **P. adsurgens, P. nana** and **P. stolonifera** are sometimes grown. They require a well-drained, sunny position and often fail if the winter is over-wet. Few of them produce seed and propagation must therefore be effected by division, preferably in autumn or by cuttings taken in July. All flower profusely in a wide range of colours, May–July. 3–9 in. There are several named varieties.

The annual phloxes are derived from **P. drummondii** and are divided into two sections, **grandiflora** growing 12–18 in. and **nana compacta** growing 6–9 in., both providing a wonderful range of colours and mixtures. They should be treated as half-hardy annuals, the seed being sown in Mar. under glass or Apr. in the open, the seedlings pricked out, hardened off and planted 1 ft. apart in June, for flowering from July to early Oct.

PHORMIUM (*New Zealand Flax*)

A genus of two species of tall perennials native to New Zealand. Being not quite hardy they require a fairly sheltered position in a moist but well-drained loam, preferably in a sunny position, although they will tolerate partial shade. Excellent foliage plants for the water-side. Propagate from seed or division of roots in Apr.

P. colensoi. Large, smooth, sword-like leaves, sometimes variegated, from 24 to 36 in. Yellowish flowers, summer. 4–6 ft. Fairly hardy.

P. tenax. Purplish or dark green, sword-like leaves with reddish margins, up to 7 ft. Dull red flowers, summer. 6–15 ft. Less hardy.

PHYGELIUS

Shrubby plants, natives of S. Africa. They thrive in well-drained ordinary soil in full sun, and being doubtfully hardy are specially suitable for a sunny wall. Propagate from seed sown in spring with slight heat or from cuttings.

P. aequalis. Coral-red or dull salmon flowers, Aug.–Sept. 24–36 in.

P. capensis. Bright red flowers with yellow throats, Aug.–Sept. Can grow up to 72 in.

PHYLLODOCE
Small heath-like shrubs of alpine-arctic regions. They like an open, peaty soil in partial shade. Best propagated from cuttings set in sandy peat in July.
P. breweri. Purplish-red flowers, May–June. 6–10 in.
P. × intermedia. Purple or pinkish-yellow flowers, Apr.–May. 6–10 in. Recommended var. is 'Fred Stoker'.
P. nipponica. White and pink flowers, May–June. 4–8 in.

PHYSALIS (*Chinese Lantern, Cape Gooseberry*)
A genus of annual and perennial herbs from Mexico and N. America. Many of the species are tender or of little value, but two are sufficiently hardy for growing out of doors and when the flowers are over will produce fruits or berries that are useful for winter decoration. They grow well in most well-drained soils, in full sun, but on rich soils may spread too much and require some checking. Propagation is by division.
P. alkekengi. Leaves pointed, 3–4 in. long. Flowers small, white, July. Fruit scarlet, edible. 12 in.
P. franchettii. Leaves large with long stalks. Flowers whitish-violet, July. Fruit red or tinged orange, borne in an inflated bladder-like calyx, up to 3 in. long and 7–8 in. in circumference. 18 in.

PHYSOSTEGIA (*Obedient Plant*)
One species of this small N. American genus is suitable as a tall, late-flowering perennial. Its common name has arisen from the fact that the flowers stay where they are put when moved from one position to another. It will grow in most soils, in sun or partial shade. Propagation is by division.
P. virginiana. Leaves narrow, irregularly and sharply toothed. Flowers flesh-coloured or purple, tubular, up to 1 in. long, borne in spikes, July–Sept. 18–48 in.

PHYTEUMA (*Horned Rampion*)
A genus of hardy dwarf-growing perennial herbs, native to Europe and suitable for the rock garden or front of the border. Grows easily in average well-drained soil. Propagate from seed or division in spring.
P. comosum. Tufted. Flowers purplish-blue, July. 3–6 in.
P. spicatum. Flowers white or blue, July. 1–3 ft.

PHYTOLACCA (*Poke Weed*)
Two species are often recommended but their claims are doubtful. They have large attractive often variegated leaves up to 6 in. long, that turn purple in the autumn, and flowers borne in close spikes, followed by purple or black berries. But the plants are poisonous, particularly the roots which are large and fleshy and may reach 3 in. in diameter. Propagate from seed sown in Mar. under glass or division of roots in spring or autumn.
P. americana. Flowers white or pale yellow, spotted green, June–Sept. Berries purple. 5–6 ft. or, on good soil, up to 10 ft. The plant has a disagreeable scent.
P. clavigera. Flowers pink and green, in compact spikes, June–Sept. Berries black. 3–5 ft.

PICK-A-BACK PLANT. See *Tolmiea*

PIMPERNEL. See *Anagallis*

PINCUSHION FLOWER. See *Scabiosa*

PINGUICULA (*Butterwort, Bog Violet*)
A genus of insectivorous bog plants, tender or hardy, perennial or annual and mostly natives of America and Europe. Thrive in moist, peaty loam in a shady position. Propagate from seed or by division.
P. bakeriana. Narrow, fleshy leaves in rosette. Deep carmine flowers, Aug.–Sept. 4–6 in. Greenhouse.
P. grandiflora. Fleshy oval leaves in rosette. Violet flowers, summer. 4–6 in. Bog garden.

PINK. See *Dianthus*

PINK ROOT. See *Spigelia*

PLANTAIN LILY. See *Hosta*

PLATYCODON (*Chinese Bellflower*)
PLATE 54
Native to China and Japan, the one species,

makes a fine border plant with its branching stems and numerous bell-shaped flowers. It grows in most soils, but prefers those that are fairly rich and well drained, in full sun. Propagation is by division or seed.

P. grandiflorus. Leaves ovate, toothed, lower ones in whorls. Flowers blue or white, up to 2 in. across, single or semi-double, July–Sept. 12–24 in.

PLATYSTEMON CALIFORNICUS (*Californian Poppy, Cream-cups*)

Hardy annual native to California. Thrives in a light ordinary soil in a sunny position. Propagate from seed. Yellow flowers, summer. 12 in.

PLUMBAGO (*Leadwort*)

A small genus of shrubs, annuals and perennials widely distributed in warmer regions of the world, and mostly suitable for the cool or warm greenhouse. The shrubs are propagated by means of cuttings struck in early summer with gentle bottom heat, by root cuttings or by basal shoots which have rooted in the surrounding soil. They should be grown in pots and pinched back as required. Climbers may be grown in the greenhouse border and should be trained in a single stem in much the same manner as a vine, cutting back the laterals to within 5 in. of their base after flowering. Perennials may be propagated by division and annuals by seed.

P. caerulea (annual). Flowers blue in loose sprays, summer. 18 in. Greenhouse.

P. capensis (climbing shrub). White or pale blue flowers, summer. 2–8 ft. Greenhouse.

P. europaea (hardy perennial). Violet-rose flowers, Sept. 2–3 ft.

PLUME POPPY. See *Macleaya*

PODOPHYLLUM (*May Apple*)

The species of this small genus of American and Chinese origin provide useful plants for growing in shaded positions, doing best on rich, moist soils. The foliage is particularly attractive, generally growing above the cup-shaped flowers. The leaves and roots are poisonous but the berries are edible. Propagation is by division or seed.

P. emodi. Leaves up to 10 in. across, in deep wedge-shaped lobes, sharply toothed. Flowers white or rose, up to 1½ in. across, Apr.–May. 12 in. Berries red, edible, 1–2 in. long.

P. peltatum. Leaves lobed, wrinkled, shiny. Flowers white, 2 in. across, Apr.–May. Fruit up to 2 in. long, yellowish-green, ripe and edible in July. 12–18 in.

P. versipelle. Leaves large and lobed, carried above the flowers. Flowers crimson, May–June. Berries rare, dark red. 18 in.

POKE WEED. See *Phytolacca*

POLEMONIUM (*Jacob's Ladder*)

Native to many temperate regions, the species provide a number of free-flowering plants mostly suitable for the rock garden with a few for the border. The common name reflects the characteristic straight leafy stems. They grow well in most soils provided there is sufficient but not too much moisture. Propagation is by division or seed.

P. carneum. Leaves divided, generally oblong. Flowers blue, pink or yellow, May–Aug. 12–24 in.

P. coeruleum. Leaves smooth, slender, pointed. Flowers blue or white, June–Aug. 12–30 in.

P. confertum. Flowers blue in dense clusters, June–Aug. 6 in.

P. lanatum. Flowers blue in short spikes, July–Aug. 1 ft.

P. reptans. Flowers blue or white, Apr.–May. 6–18 in.

POLIANTHES TUBEROSA (*Tuberose*)

A single species of half-hardy, bulbous plants native to Mexico, suitable for growing in a greenhouse or sometimes in sunny, sheltered positions out of doors, during summer. The bulbs generally fail after flowering and must therefore be purchased annually. Pot-up singly in 4- or 5-in. pots in succession from late autumn to early spring, preferably with bottom heat. Water sparingly until they begin to grow. White fragrant flowers in long clusters, single or double, Sept. 3–4 ft.

POLYGALA
A genus of hardy and tender shrubs and perennials, distributed widely. The hardy species thrive in a mixture of cool, moist, gritty loam and peat, in partial shade in sheltered positions, are excellent for the rock garden, border, wild garden or for the alpine house. The tender species are useful for decoration in the greenhouse. Propagate from cuttings of young shoots or by division.
P. calcarea. Purple, blue, rose or white flowers, May–Sept. 4–6 in. Rock garden.
P. chamaebuxus (*Bastard Box*). Creamy-yellow or purple flowers, May–June. 3–6 in. Rock garden.
P. myrtifolia (branching shrub). Bright purple flowers, summer. 3–6 ft. Greenhouse.
P. oppositifolia (shrub). Flowers purplish and yellowish-green, summer. 3–4 ft. Greenhouse.

POLYGONATUM (*Solomon's Seal*)
The species are mostly hardy and have gracefully-arching stems with hanging, bell-shaped flowers. They grow in most soils and do best in shaded positions. Propagation is by division.
P. latifolium. Leaves oblong, up to 6 in. long. Flowers greenish-white, July. 24–48 in.
P. multiflorum. Leaves oblong, up to 4 in. long, occasionally variegated. Flowers white, single or double, June. 24–48 in. Forces well if potted in Nov., plunged in ashes and brought into the greenhouse when growth begins.

POLYGONUM (*Knotweed*)
This genus contains a number of widely-differing species, both annual and perennial, some of them weeds, others climbers, and a few suitable for growing in a border with one or two that make fine specimen plants where space allows. They grow in most soils, in sun or partial shade, and do best with a good supply of moisture. Propagation of annuals is by seed and perennials by division.
P. affine. Leaves deep green, becoming bronzy. Flowers red, in dense spikes, Aug.–Oct. 9–12 in. Rock garden.
P. amplexicaule. Leaves heart-shaped. Flowers bright crimson, purplish-red or white (which are fragrant) in single or twin spikes, Aug.–Oct. 24–36 in. Good water-side plant.
P. baldschuanicum is the well-known climber, reaching to 30–40 ft. and excellent for growing up old trees. Flowers white or tinged rose, July–Oct.
P. cuspidatum. Leaves large and oval, on bamboo-like stems, which curve outwards. Flowers creamy-white, borne in feathery sprays, 4–5 in. long, July–Oct. 6–9 ft. A strong grower best used as a specimen on its own, when the stems which turn reddish-brown in winter may be left for cutting down in spring.
P. sachalinense. Leaves large, oblong, up to 12 in. long, and 4–5 in. wide. Flowers greenish-yellow, July–Oct. A rampant grower, reaching 12 ft.
P. vacciniifolium. Flowers rose, Sept.–Oct. 6–9 in. Rock garden.

POLYPODIUM, POLYSTICHUM. See *Ferns*

PONTEDERIA CORDATA (*Water Plantain*)
A species of a small genus of perennial aquatics, natives of N. America, making a good plant for still, shallow water, 6–12 in. deep. Specially suitable for small pools. Propagate by division. The leaves are long, bright green, the flowers blue or white, in close spikes, summer. 1½–2 ft.

POPPY. See *Papaver*

POPPY MALLOW. See *Callirhoe*

POOR MAN'S ORCHID. See *Schizanthus*

POOR MAN'S WEATHER GLASS. See *Anagallis*

PORTULACA (*Purslane*) PLATE 45
A genus of half-hardy annual and perennial herbs mostly from S. America, two species being grown in gardens. They need a sunny site and sandy soil, and are propagated from seed sown in the open in Apr. or under glass in Mar. Thin out or transplant in May–June.
P. grandiflora. Purple, red, yellow or white flowers, June–Sept. 6–12 in.

P. oleracea. Flowers yellow, June–July. 6 in. Also used as a salad plant.

POTENTILLA (*Cinquefoil*)
This large genus, mostly originating in the northern hemisphere, contains a few perennials suitable for a border or rock garden, some shrubs and several weeds difficult to get rid of. All grow well in most soils including the drier kinds, in sun or partial shade. Propagation is by division or seed.
P. argyrophylla. Leaves toothed, silky above, white and hairy beneath. Flowers yellow, 1 in. across, May–Sept. 24–36 in.
P. atrosanguinea. Most of the garden varieties have been derived from this species probably by crossing with one of the other species listed here. There are a number of named varieties all flowering between June and Sept. and growing 18–24 in. high, among which are: 'Gibson's Scarlet' (brilliant scarlet, July–Sept.), 'Wm. Rollisson' (semi-double, dark orange with yellow centre, July–Sept.), 'Yellow Queen' (bright yellow, July–Aug.).
P. nepalensis. Leaves coarsely toothed, basal leaves up to 3 in. long, upper leaves 1 in. long, lobed. Flowers crimson or purple, July–Aug. 24 in. 'Miss Willmott' (cherry red, 24 in.), 'Roxana' (orange-scarlet, June–July, 18 in.).
P. nitida. Tufted. Flowers pink or white, May–Aug. 6 in. Rock garden.
P. recta. Leaves lobed to oblong, toothed. Flowers yellow, up to 1 in. across, in compact heads, June–July. 12–24 in.

PRICKLY THRIFT. See *Acantholimon*

PRIMULA (*Primrose*)
This large genus of both tender and hardy plants provides some of the most attractive flowers for growing in greenhouses, rock gardens, borders, woodland or water side. The majority require a soil rich in humus, some a good supply of moisture particularly when in growth and many prefer partial shade. Propagation is by seed or division. Among the most valuable and popular species are:
P. auricula. This is the well-known auricula with velvety flowers and powdery leaves, excellent for the alpine house, rock garden or as an edging plant. While it does not require such moist conditions as other species, it will fail in a drought. Many named varieties are available in striking colours and combinations, flowering from Apr.–May and growing 6 to 9 in. high. (See *Auricula.*)
P. denticulata. This species will grow well in moist, rich soils in the open but thrives in abundant moisture and plenty of shade. The flowers are borne in large rounded heads, mauve, purple, red, rose or white, Mar.–May. 12 in.
P. vulgaris. This is the common primrose and while it is essentially a woodland plant, may find a place in a shady spot in a border, if only to show when spring has come. It will put up with drier conditions than most, provided the soil is well supplied with humus. In addition to the typical colour, pink, red and purple can be obtained, flowering from Mar. to Apr. and growing 6 in. high.
The Polyanthus primroses have been derived from this species crossed with **P. veris** (*Cowslip*) and **P. elatior** (*Oxlip*). These showy plants are ideal for bedding. They may be raised from seed sown in May or June, the seedlings pricked out and planted in the beds in Oct. They make most attractive displays with masses of flowers ranging from white to cream, yellow, pink, rose, red or crimson and shades of blue-mauve and purple, flowering Mar. to Apr. and growing about 12 in. high. Unfortunately the bright colours seem to fascinate birds and if one starts on the petals others will copy and soon the flowers will be stripped to pieces. Generally a few strands of black cotton will be effective, provided they are put on just above blossom height, immediately the first damage is seen. On no account must the plants be allowed to dry out during the summer. After flowering they should be moved to a moist, partially-shaded part of the garden, divided and grown on for replanting for the next season.
For the rock garden many species are suitable provided they have a good supply of moisture during their growing season. Among the dwarfs are **P. juliae** which grows about 4 in. and flowers in Mar.–Apr., in white, yellow and shades of pink, red and purple, and **P. rosea**

growing 3–5 in., with rose or magenta flowers in Apr. Both are at their best at the side of rock-garden pools.

For the greenhouse three species are outstanding. They are easily grown from seed, potted in a loam-peat compost, grown outside during summer and brought into a night temperature of 45 deg. F. in Sept. for flowering during winter. **P. obconica** with large, white, pink, crimson, purplish or blue flowers and **P. sinensis** with larger flowers in the same colour range, single or double, are both raised from seed sown in gentle heat in Apr. or May, while **P. malacoides** has smaller but more graceful flowers and is raised from seed sown in a frame in June. (**P. obconica** unfortunately produces a skin rash on some people.) There are a number of named varieties, the following being a small selection for the greenhouse:

P. obconica
'Crimson King Improved'
'Red Chief'
'Wyaston Wonder' (crimson)
P. malacoides
'Delight' (rose-pink)
'Enchantment' (purple-mauve)
'Lilac Queen'
'Princess Mary' (rose-pink)
'Rosita' (rosy mauve)
P. sinensis
'Dazzler' (mandarin-red)
'Giant Royal White'
'Pink Enchantress' (rose-salmon)
'Double Dazzler'
P. sinensis stellata
'Crimson Star'
'Fire King' (crimson)
'Guardsman' (orange-red)
'King of the Stars' (crimson)
'Rose Marie' (rich rose)

PRINCE OF WALES' FEATHERS. See *Celosia*

PROPHET FLOWER. See *Arnebia*

PTERIDOPHYLLUM RACEMOSUM

A single species of dwarf plant, native of Japan. Needs a shaded position in moist, well-drained peaty soil or woodland. Suitable also for the alpine house. Propagate from seed. Ivory-white flowers, summer. 4–8 in.

PTERIS (*Spider Fern*). See *Ferns*

PULMONARIA

A genus of dwarf-growing perennial plants native to Europe. They grow well in any good moist soil and like a partially shaded situation. Propagate by division in early spring.

The garden species cross readily and are not easily distinguished. The leaves may be green, marbled or spotted with white, the flowers pink, turning to red, purplish-blue or blue, spring. 6–9 in.

PULSATILLA (*Pasque Flower*). See *Anemone*

PURPLE CORNFLOWER. See *Echinacea*

PURPLE LOOSESTRIFE. See *Lythrum*

PURSLANE. See *Portulaca*

PUSCHKINIA SCILLOIDES (*Striped Squill*)

Hardy bulbous plants natives of Far East. Thrive in rich, sandy loam and are suitable for the rock garden. Propagate by division of bulbs every 2–3 years. Blue to whitish flowers, Apr.–May. 4–6 in.

PYRENEAN DEAD-NETTLE. See *Horminum*

PYRETHRUM. See *Chrysanthemum*

PYROLA (*Wintergreen*)

Dwarf-growing perennials, natives of Europe, Asia and America, often failing after a few years. They need semi-shade in gritty, peaty loam, and are suitable for rock garden or wild garden. Propagate by division in spring or seed, and do not move unnecessarily.

P. minor. Pinky-white flowers, June–July. 1–3 in.

P. rotundifolia. White flowers, June–Aug. 6–8 in.

P. virens. Greenish-white flowers, June–July. 6–10 in.

QUAMASH. See *Camassia*

QUAMOCLIT

Half-hardy climbers, natives of America, requiring a warm, sheltered position in well-drained, rich soil or cool greenhouse. Propagate from seed sown in Apr.–May under glass.

Q. coccinea (*Star Glory*). Scarlet flowers with yellow throat, summer. 8 ft.
Q. lobata. Crimson and yellow flowers, summer. 10–20 ft.
Q. pennata (*Cypress Vine*)
Scarlet flowers, summer. 6–8 ft.

QUEEN LILY. See *Phaedranassa*

RAMONDA
Small hardy perennials, natives of S. Europe, suitable for the alpine house or rock garden in well-drained peaty soil. Propagate from seed or by division.
R. myconi. Leaves covered with reddish hairs, in a rosette. White, rose or purple flowers with orange centre. May–Aug. 6 in.
R. nathaliae. Similar to above, but flowers more numerous, white or lavender-blue, May–Aug. 6 in.

RANUNCULUS (*Buttercup*)
This is a large genus containing both annuals and perennials including the common buttercup and the well-known garden ranunculus. All will grow in most soils but prefer those that are moist and well drained. Propagation is by seed or division.
R. aconitifolius (*Bachelor's Buttons*). Leaves lobed and toothed. Flowers white, single or double, May–June. Up to 24 in.
R. amplexicaulis. Flowers white, single or double, Apr.–May. 3–9 in.
R. asiaticus (*Garden Ranunculus*). Flowers of various shades of white, yellow, orange to red, May–June. 6–9 in. The roots must be planted 'claw' downwards.
R. gramineus. Leaves narrow, shiny. Flowers citron-yellow, single or double, Apr.–June. 12 in.
R. lingua (*Spearwort*). Flowers yellow, 2 in. across, July–Sept. 2–3 ft. Good in shallow water or sides of a pond.
R. monspeliacus. Leaves woolly with wedge-shaped lobes. Flowers golden-yellow, Apr.–May. 12–18 in.

RED-HOT POKER. See *Kniphofia*

REED MACE. See *Typha*

REHMANNIA
A small genus of tender perennials, natives of Japan and China, sometimes grown in a cool greenhouse. Propagate from seed or cuttings.
R. angulata. Pink, purplish or red flowers, summer. 24–36 in.
R. glutinosa. Yellowish-buff and purple flowers, early summer. 12–18 in.

RESEDA
The genus contains the well-known Mignonette (**R. odorata**) grown for its sweet scent. The seed should be sown in Mar. in a sunny position in fairly rich soil and thinned to 6 in. apart. It may also be grown in pots in a cold or cool house. Yellowish-white flowers, May–Sept. 8–18 in. There are a number of named varieties.

RHABDOTHAMNUS SOLANDRI (*Wainatua*)
A single species of half-hardy shrub, native of New Zealand, slow growing but otherwise suitable for the cool greenhouse, Propagate from seed or cuttings. Rich orange flowers striped red or purple, several months. Up to 4 ft.

RHEUM (*Rhubarb*)
In addition to the common rhubarb, the genus also includes other species which can be grown in large wide borders or as specimen plants, although their best place is, perhaps, in the wild garden. They have the usual large leaves but often with tinges of colour and deep lobing, and produce tall plumes of white, greenish-white, red or purple flowers, some reaching up to 10 ft. high. They do best in deep rich, moist soils, in sun or partial shade. Propagation is by division or seed.
R. emodi, white, 6–10 ft. **R. palmatum,** white or red, 5 ft.

RHEUMATISM ROOT. See *Jeffersonia*

RHODOCHITON ATROSANGUINEUM
A single species of Mexican climber suitable for a cool greenhouse. Seed should be sown in Mar. in gentle heat, for potting-on and flowering later in summer. Flowers red-purple, July–Sept. Up to 10 ft.

RHODOHYPOXIS BAURII
Perennial plant, native to S. Africa, suitable for a sunny position in ordinary soil, or for the alpine house. Propagate by division. Hairy leaves. Rose-red or white flowers, summer. 8–10 in.

RICINUS COMMUNIS (*Castor-oil Plant*)
This single species of half-hardy plants native to Africa, make good foliage plants in rich loam in warm beds or in a cool greenhouse. Propagate from seeds sown in heat in Mar. and plant out in June. If for the greenhouse pot-on to 6 to 8-in. pots. There are several varieties with bronzy-green, dark-red or bronzy-purple foliage and greenish flowers, July–Aug. 3–5 ft.

ROCK CRESS. See *Arabis, Aubrieta*

ROCK JASMINE. See *Androsace*

ROCK PURSLANE. See *Calandrinia*

RODGERSIA (*Saxifragaceae*)
This genus of five species native to China and Japan contains three that provide plants with fine ornamental foliage suitable for large borders or individual positions. They will grow in most good soils but do best in moist peaty conditions in full sun. Propagation is by division or seed.
R. aesculifolia. Leaves up to 18 in. across, glossy bronze. Flowers white, in large plumes up to 2 ft. long, July. 3 ft.
R. pinnata. Leaves oval, up to 8 in. long. Flowers white or reddish, borne in branching sprays, July. 3–4 ft.
R. podophylla. Leaves up to 10 in. long. Flowers yellowish-white, in nodding sprays, June–July. 3–4 ft.

ROELLA CILIATA (*African Harebell*)
Half-hardy perennial, native of S. Africa, suitable for a cool greenhouse. Propagate from seed or cuttings. Blue or rose-purple flowers, Aug.–Sept. 6–12 in.

ROMNEYA (*Bush Poppy*)
A genus of two species of near hardy perennials, native to California. They thrive in a sunny, sheltered position in rich, sandy loam or may be grown in pots in a greenhouse. Propagate from seed or division of roots in Mar. Protect in severe winter.
R. coulteri. Silvery-grey leaves. Large snowy-white, poppy-like flowers, June–Sept. 5–8 ft.
R. trichocalyx. Similar to above but less branched. 3–4 ft.

ROMULEA
Hardy and half-hardy plants, natives of Europe, Mediterranean and Africa. Thrive in a sunny position in mixture of sandy loam and peat. Propagate from seed or offsets.
R. bulbocodium. Violet and yellow flowers, Mar.–Apr. 4–6 in. Hardy.
R. columnae. Blue, pale mauve or whitish flowers, yellow at base, spring. 4–6 in. Hardy.
R. rosea. Rose and yellow flowers, early summer. 4–6 in. Greenhouse.

ROSCOEA
This small genus of Himalayan and Chinese plants is just hardy enough for European conditions provided the thick fleshy roots are planted 6 in. deep. They grow best in well-drained rich soil in partial shade, and have attractive funnel-shaped flowers. Propagation is by division.
R. cautleoides. Leaves grey or glossy green, sheathed round the stem. Flowers yellow, hood-like, in a close spike, June–Aug. 12 in.
R. humeana. Leaves up to 8 in. long. Flowers violet-purple, $1\frac{1}{2}$ in. across, June–July. 12 in.

ROSES. See Chapter 10

RUDBECKIA (*Coneflower*)
This N. American genus provides some excellent annuals and autumn perennials having the well-known prominent cone in the centre of the flowers. They are almost indistinguishable from the echinaceas except that the latter is now accepted as having rosy or purple flowers, whereas the true rudbeckias are yellow. They grow well in most garden soils in full sun, but should not be allowed to get dry in the summer. Good for cutting. Propagation of annuals is by seed and perennials by division or seed.
R. bicolor (annual). Flowers yellow, with purple centre, July. 1–2 ft.

R. hirta hybrida (perennial). These hybrids include a number of named varieties generally yellow with dark centres, flowering between Aug. and Oct. and growing 2–5 ft. high. 'Black-eyed Susan' (2 ft.), 'Goldquelle' (semi-double, 3 ft.).

R. laciniata (perennial). Leaves divided, deeply cut. Flowers yellow, single or double, up to 3 in. across, with green centre, Aug.–Sept. 2–7 ft.

R. nitida (perennial). Leaves bright green, rounded. Flowers yellow with green centre made more prominent by the reflexed petals, Aug.–Oct. Up to 6 ft.

R. speciosa (perennial). Leaves ovate, toothed, slender. Flowers large, yellow, up to 4 in. across, cone black-purple, July–Oct. 2 ft.

SAGE. See *Salvia*

SAGINA (*Pearlwort*)

A genus of small tufted plants natives of alpine regions of Europe containing some well-known weeds, but with one species, **S. glabra,** suitable for the rock and paved garden. Thrives in a sunny position in gritty loam. Propagate by division of roots in spring. Creeping habit. White flowers, summer. 1–4 in.

SAGITTARIA

A genus of tender and hardy aquatic plants, natives of America and Europe, the hardy species suitable for shallow water margins of ponds or the marsh garden. Propagate from seed or division in Apr.

S. latifolia. Arrow-shaped leaves. Flowers white, single or double, summer. 1–3 ft. In still water 6 in. deep.

S. sagittifolia. (*Common Arrowhead*). White flowers with purple claws, summer. 1–1½ ft. In still water 12–18 in. deep.

ST. BERNARD'S LILY. See *Anthericum*

ST. BRUNO'S LILY. See *Papaver*

ST. GEORGE'S HERB. See *Valeriana*

SAINTPAULIA IONANTHA (*African Violet*)

This species of a small genus of perennial plants native to Trop. Africa has provided the highly-popular African Violets. They make decorative house plants and are widely grown in U.S.A. where numerous varieties have been developed. Propagate from seed sown in Mar. in heat, preferably in a propagating frame (60 deg. F.) or in June. Prick off as soon as possible and pot-on singly until they reach their flowering pots which should be 3 to 5 in. They may also be propagated from leaf-cuttings or division in spring, and this method must be used to get named varieties true to type. The cuttings should be from mature leaves taken with 1–1½ in. of leaf stalk and inserted round the edge of a pot of sandy compost in a temperature of 60 deg. F. There are a large number of named varieties with flowers in various shades of blue, violet, pink or white; all growing about 4 in. high. Flowering is almost continuous.

SALPIGLOSSIS

A genus of half-hardy annuals and perennials, native of Chile, providing **S. sinnata** the well-known annual grown either in borders or cool greenhouse. It needs a rich, light soil in a sunny position. Propagate from seed sown in Mar. under glass in gentle heat. Harden off and plant out in May–June, or pot-on for greenhouse culture. Large-veined, funnel-shaped flowers of rich shades of deep purple, violet, crimson, gold, yellow or white, July–Sept. 18–24 in. Sow also in Aug. for winter flowering in the greenhouse.

SALVIA (*Sage*)

This is a large genus containing annuals, biennials, perennials and shrubs, most of them hardy or half-hardy, with others requiring greenhouse treatment. All have characteristic and generally showy spikes of nettle-like flowers. In the open they prefer a good well-drained soil in full sun and will grow in dryish conditions; under glass they require a well-manured loam. Propagation is by seed, which is convenient also for perennials since they generally come true, but division or cuttings may be used.

S. azurea. Leaves oblong, toothed. Flowers deep blue in dense spikes, Aug. Up to 5 ft. Hardy perennial for borders or for cool greenhouse.

S. greggii (greenhouse shrub). Flowers white or carmine-cerise, 3 ft. Oct.–Nov.
S. haematodes (biennial). A good specimen plant. Flowers bluish-violet, June–Sept. 3 ft.
S. leucantha (greenhouse shrub). Flowers white and violet, woolly. 2 ft.
S. nutans (hardy perennial). Leaves oblong, toothed and wrinkled, up to 5 in. long. Flowers violet, drooping, July. 2–3 ft. Nov.–Dec.
S. officinalis is the common sage and in addition to its culinary value makes an attractive shrub with purple, blue or white flowers.
S. patens (half-hardy perennial). Flowers white, light blue or deep blue, Aug.–Sept. 1½–2 ft. The tuberous roots may be stored over winter as with dahlias.
S. pratensis. Leaves oblong, wrinkled up to 6 in. long, Flowers white, bright blue, purple or rosy-red in spikes up to 18 in. long, June–Aug. 2 ft.
S. splendens. The well-known bedding salvia. Perennial but best treated as half-hardy annual. There are several named varieties, generally with red or scarlet flowers, but white, blue and shades of purple are also obtainable. 1–2 ft.
S. × superba (hardy perennial). Leaves oblong up to 3 in. long, toothed, aromatic. Flowers blue-purple, in erect spikes up to 8 in. long, July–Aug. 2–3 ft.
S. virgata (hardy perennial). Leaves oblong to heart-shaped, irregularly toothed, hairy, aromatic. Flowers light blue or white, in long branching sprays, July–Aug. 2 ft.

SANDWORT. See *Arenaria*

SANGUINARIA CANADENSIS (*Bloodroot*)

Dwarf perennial herb, native to N. America, suitable for the rock garden or alpine house. Thrives in sandy loam in sun or shade. Propagate by division in Aug. when leaves have died down. Bluey-grey, scalloped, kidney-shaped leaves. Large white flowers, Apr.–May. 4–6 in.

SANGUISORBA

A small genus of perennials from temperate zones, two of the species making handsome border plants flowering over a long period. They grow well in most soils and are propagated by seed or division.
S. canadensis. Leaves deeply cut, grey-green. Flowers white, borne in cylindrical heads, summer. 3–5 ft.
S. obtusa. Leaves up to 20 in. long, pale green. Flowers white or rose-purple, summer. 4 ft.

SANVITALIA PROCUMBENS

Hardy trailing perennial, native of Mexico, suitable for edgings or the rock garden. Likes a sunny position in sandy, peaty loam. Propagate from seed sown in Apr. Bright yellow flowers with dark centre, single or double, June–Sept.

SAPONARIA (*Soapwort*)

A small genus of hardy and half-hardy annuals, biennials and perennials from Europe and Asia. The garden species make good rock plants, and one is suitable for borders particularly on poorish soil. In rich soil it is inclined to do too well. Propagate annuals by seed, perennials by seed or division.
S. calabrica (hardy annual). Flowers white, pink or red, June–Oct. 6 in.
S. ocymoides (trailing perennial). Flowers white, pink or deep rose, May–June. 6 in. Rock garden.
S. officinalis (perennial). Leaves elliptical up to 5 in. long and 2 in. wide. Flowers white, pink or red, single or double, up to 1½ in. across, Aug.–Sept. 12–36 in.

SARRACENIA PURPUREA (*Huntsman's Horn*)

One species of a genus of half-hardy insectivorous perennials, natives of N.E. America, sometimes grown out of doors in a sunny position in a bog or marsh garden but is more reliable in a cool greenhouse in a compost of peat and sphagnum moss with plenty of water. Propagate from seed sown on chopped sphagnum moss or division of roots in Apr. Leaves in the form of a huntsman's horn, 6–12 in. Purplish flowers, Apr.–May. 10–20 in.

SAXIFRAGA

This is a large genus composed mainly of perennial rock-garden plants but containing also the well-known London Pride that is suitable for growing in many parts of the garden, including the front of a border. All grow well in most soils, some in sun, some in shade with others excellent for the alpine house. Propagation is by division or offsets and with some species by cuttings.

The genus is divided into 16 separate sections but since there has been much hybridization and natural crossing both within and between several of the sections, many of the original species have been replaced by hybrids and named varieties. The more important sections are:

Cushion or *Tufted Saxifrages* (Kabschia). Leaves generally spiny. Flowers solitary or many, borne on a stem, in shades of white, yellow, pink or red, spring. 3–6 in. Propagation by cuttings. Excellent for the alpine house.

Encrusted Saxifrages (Euaizoonia). Leaves in rosettes. Flowers in sprays, white, yellow, rose, red or spotted, May–July. 9–18 in. Propagation by division, cuttings or seed, the seed giving rise to considerable variation. Excellent for the rock garden or terrace, preferably in full sun.

Mossy Saxifrages (Dactyloides). Leaves in rosettes forming dense carpets. Flowers in shades of white, pink, rose or red, May–June. 3–9 in. Propagation by division or seed. Excellent for the rock garden, particularly in partial shade with a good supply of moisture.

Creeping Saxifrages (Porphyrion). Mat-forming with creeping stems. Flowers purplish or white, Mar.–July. 3–6 in. Propagation by division or cuttings of unflowered shoots. Require porous soil in partial shade.

In the Robertsonia section is **S. umbrosa** (*London Pride*). Leaves rounded, often blotched or variegated. Flowers small, star-like, pink, borne in loose sprays on slender stems, May–July. 1–1½ ft.

In the Ligularia section is **S. stolonifera** (*Aaron's Beard* or *Mother of Thousands*), a tender species making a good basket or window plant and having white flowers and reddish stolons.

SCABIOSA (*Scabious, Pincushion Flower*)

This genus native to Europe, Asia and N. Africa contains the well-known annual Sweet Scabious, and a few perennials suitable for the rock garden or border. They grow well in most kinds of soil, particularly those with a high lime content, and prefer full sun. Propagation is by division or seed.

S. atropurpurea (*Sweet Scabious*) (annual). Flowers white, yellow, red, rose, blue or mauve, July–Sept. 2–3 ft.

S. caucasica (perennial). Leaves narrow, feathery. Flowers in pincushions of white or shades of blue and mauve, up to 3 in. across, June–Oct. 18–30 in. 'Clive Greaves' (lavender-mauve), 'Constancy' (violet-blue), 'Wensleydale' (light blue).

S. graminifolia (perennial). Leaves silvery-white. Flowers rose or mauve, July. 9 in. Rock garden or front of border.

SCARBOROUGH LILY. See *Vallota*

SCHIZANTHUS (*Butterfly Flower, Poor Man's Orchid*)

Half-hardy and hardy annuals, natives of Chile, with beautiful flowers in tall sprays. The half-hardy species are excellent for flowering in a cool greenhouse in spring and should be raised by sowing seeds in Sept., wintering in pots in the greenhouse or frost-proof frame and potting on into 7-in. pots in Feb. They may also be sown in Mar. in gentle heat for planting out in a border, to flower in the summer. The hardy species should be sown in Mar.–Apr. in the open.

S. pinnatus (hardy). Various colours, usually mixed violet, pink, white and yellow, June–Oct. 18–24 in.

S. × wisetonensis. The crossing of **S. pinnatus** with **S. grahamii** has provided the attractive strains and varieties used for greenhouse cultivation. There are a large number of hybrids and named varieties with flowers in shades of apricot, yellow, pink, carmine, mauve and purple, veined or pencilled sometimes in black. Up to 4 ft. Support must be given by thin sticks inserted in the pots.

SCHIZOSTYLIS COCCINEA (*Kaffir Lily, Crimson Flag, Winter Gladiolus*)

Half-hardy rhizomatus species, native to S. Africa, suitable for a sheltered, sunny border in moist, well-drained, light soil, and excellent in pots in a cool greenhouse. Propagate from division of the rhizomes in Mar. Red or pink flowers in tall spikes, Oct.–Nov. 20–30 in. Recommended varieties: 'Mrs. Hegarty' (rose) and 'Viscountess Byng' (pink).

SCILLA (*Wild Hyancith, Squill*)
A genus of hardy and half-hardy bulbous plants, natives of Europe, Africa, and Asia, the hardy species thrive in warm, sunny borders, in a rock garden or naturalized in grass or woodland. The greenhouse species should be potted into 5-in. pots from Aug.–Oct., stood in ashes and brought into the house when growth begins. Propagate from offsets in Sept. or from seed which, however, takes 4–5 years to reach flowering.
S. hispanica (*Spanish Squill*). White, pink or bluish flowers, Apr.–May. 6–9 in.
S. non-scripta (*Bluebell, Harebell, Wild Hyacinth*). Purple, red, pink, blue or white flowers, Apr.–May. 12–18 in.
S. peruviana (*Cuban Lily* or *Hyacinth*). Purple, reddish or white flowers, May–June. 6–12 in.
S. sibirica (*Siberian Squill*). Blue or white flowers, Mar. 4–6 in.

SCIRPUS
This large genus contains the well-known Bulrush, **S. lacustris**, a hardy perennial, widely distributed over the world. Thrives in moist loamy soil in a bog garden or on the margin of a pond. Stems grow from 1–8 ft. Red-brown spike on head of stem, July–Aug.

SCUTELLARIA
A genus of hardy and tender annuals and perennials, with some shrubs, natives of Europe, Asia and America, most of the tender species require stove conditions. The hardy species thrive in ordinary soil in a border or rock garden. Propagate the hardy herbaceous species from seed or division.
S. alpina. White, rose or purple and yellow flowers, Aug. 9–12 in.
S. indica. Bluish flowers, June–Aug. 6–12 in.
S. orientalis. Yellow or yellow and purple flowers, Aug. 8–12 in.

SEA CAMPION. See *Silene*

SEA DAFFODIL. See *Pancratium*

SEA HOLLY. See *Eryngium*

SEA LAVENDER. See *Limonium*

SEA PINK. See *Armeria*

SEDUM (*Stonecrop*)
This is a large genus consisting mainly of hardy perennials suitable for the alpine house or rock garden with three species that make good border plants. They grow in most kinds of soil, in full sun. Propagation is by division or seed.
S. acre (creeping perennial). Flowers yellow, May–June. 2–3 in.
S. maximum (border perennial). Leaves ovate, up to 3 in. long, slightly toothed, purple, dark green or variegated. Stems generally pinkish or reddish. Flowers greenish-white, white or pink, borne in dense heads, Aug.–Sept. 12–36 in.
S. spathulifolium (running perennial). Leaves green or purplish. Flowers yellow, June–July. 3 in.
S. spectabile (border perennial). Leaves large, up to 3 in. long and 2 in. wide, generally in threes. Flowers numerous, white, pink or red, borne in large flat heads up to 6 in. across, Sept–Oct. 12–18 in.
S. stahlii (doubtfully hardy). Leaves reddish-brown. Flowers yellow, Aug.–Sept. 4–6 in. Alpine house.
S. telephium (border perennial). Leaves scattered, up to 3 in. long, toothed, rounded, green or red. Flowers pink to purple, Aug.–Sept. 12–18 in.

SELAGINELLA
A large genus of evergreen plants, mostly perennials, natives of many parts of the world, resembling mosses and, like ferns, grown for their striking foliage. The majority are greenhouse plants, many requiring high temperatures (70 deg. F.), humidity and some shade. Only a few species are suitable for a cool greenhouse or outdoor cultivation. They require a compost of ordinary loam with plenty of coarse grit, a good supply of moisture, and preferably some shade.

The best hardy plant is **S. helvetica.** Species suitable for a cool greenhouse are **S. apus, S. braunii, S. kraussiana, S. lepidophylla,** the *Resurrection Clubmoss,* **S. martensii** and **S. willdenovii,** a climbing form. **S. caulescens** and **S. uncinata** which makes a good basket plant do best in slightly higher temperatures (60 deg. F.).

SELF-HEAL. See *Prunella*

SEMPERVIVUM (*Houseleek*)
A genus of succulent plants, natives of C. and S. Europe, mostly hardy perennials. They are well suited to small openings in walls, bare ledges in a rock garden or old roofs and prefer a sunny position. Propagate by division in Apr., cuttings in summer, or by seed, which, however, rarely comes true.

S. arachnoideum. Leaves in rosettes, covered with cobweb-like hairs. Reddish-pink flowers, June–July. 4–6 in. Generally needs some winter protection.

S. × calcaratum. Leaves in rosettes, purple and reddish at base. Pink or reddish-purple flowers, June–July. 9–15 in.

S. montanum. Leaves in rosettes, hairy. White or purplish-violet flowers, June–Aug. 4–6 in.

S. schlehanii. Leaves green, brown or reddish. Flowers purple with white margin, Aug. 4–6 in.

S. soboliferum (*Hen and Chicken Houseleek*). Leaves in rosettes. Yellow flowers, July, 4–8 in.

S. tectorum (*Common Houseleek, St. Patrick's Cabbage*). Purple-tipped leaves in rosettes. Pale red or purple flowers, July. 8–12 in.

SENECIO
Although this large genus provides some excellent shrubs (see Chapter 15) and one of its species (**S. cruentus**) by crossing with others has given the garden Cinerarias, it also includes native or introduced species of weeds or weed-like plants such as groundsel and ragwort. Some of the herbaceous species are occasionally recommended for garden use but on good soils they often get out of hand within a few years and in any event are of no special merit. Those given below may however be tried. They thrive in a loamy soil, the annuals being easily propagated from seed and the perennials by division or cuttings.

S. doria (perennial). Flowers yellow, July–Sept. 4 ft.

S. elegans (annual). Flowers white or purple with yellow centre, June–Sept. 1–2 ft.

S. pulcher (perennial). Flowers rosy-purple, 2 in. across, Aug.–Oct. 1–2 ft. Needs a sheltered position.

SHAMROCK. See *Trifolium*

SHEEP'S SCABIOUS. See *Jasione*

SHELL FLOWER. See *Tigridia*

SHORTIA
A small genus of hardy, dwarf-growing perennials, natives of N. America and Japan, best suited to a sheltered position in the rock garden or woodland in well-drained sandy loam with peat. Propagate by division of roots in Apr.

S. galacifolia. Leathery green leaves turning to rich bronze or red in autumn. White flowers, tinged with pink, spring. 6 in.

S. uniflora. Flowers pink, veined white, spring. 4–6 in. Best in an alpine house.

SIBTHORPIA (*Cornish Moneywort*)
A small genus of creeping perennials, natives of Europe. Thrive in moist sandy loam and peat in a shady position in a rock garden, alpine house or cool greenhouse. Propagate by division of roots in Apr. or cuttings taken in Aug. and struck in sandy soil in a frame.

S. europaea. Creeping stems up to 12 in. long. Flowers minute, pink and yellow, July. 2 in.

S. peregrina. Pendent stems. Flowers yellow, July. 2 in. Greenhouse.

SIDALCEA
This small genus of N. American plants contains two species from which most of the garden varieties have been derived. These make graceful and attractive border plants which will grow well in most soils, preferably the lighter, well-drained loams and in full sun. Propagation is by seed or, for named varieties, by division.

S. candida. Leaves roundish, lobed. Flowers white or pink, up to 1 in. across, in loose slender sprays, June–Aug. 2–3 ft.

S. malvaeflora. Basal leaves roundish and lobed. Stem leaves divided into segments, generally toothed at the tips. Flowers borne in erect graceful sprays, pink, rose, rosy-crimson or purple, July–Aug. 2½–4 ft.

The following varieties have probably come from crossing the two species:

Pink: 'Elsie Heugh', 3 ft. with fringed flowers; 'Rev. Page Roberts', 3½ ft.; 'Rose Queen', 3½ ft.; 'Sussex Beauty', 4 ft.

Carmine red: 'Brilliant', 3½ ft.

Silver pink: 'Interlaken', 4 ft.

Rose-crimson: 'Crimson King', 3 ft.; 'Monarch', 3½ ft. with crinkled flowers.

SILENE

A large genus of annuals and perennials native to northern temperate regions. Many of the species are weed-like but a few are suitable for the rock garden or border. They thrive best in a sunny position in well-drained sandy loam. Propagate by seed, cuttings or division.

S. acaulis (*Moss Campion*) (perennial). Close-set leaves forming a bright green cushion. Flowers pink, rose or white, May–June. 2 in.

S. armeria (annual). Oval lance-like leaves. Flowers pink or white, May–Sept. 12–24 in.

S. maritima (*Sea Campion*) (perennial). Oval lance-like leaves. Large white or white tinged pink, sometimes double, flowers, July–Sept. 6–8 in.

S. pendula (annual). Rose, white or purplish flowers, May–Sept. 4–6 in.

S. rupestris. Short fine leaves forming blue-green tuft. Flowers pink or white, June–Aug. 4–8 in.

S. schafta. Flowers rose-magenta, June–Oct. 6 in.

SILPHIUM (*Compass Plant*)

This N. American genus of perennial herbs contains a few species suitable for the back of the border and having striking foliage and sunflower-like flowers. They will grow in most kinds of soil, in full sun. Propagation is by division or seed.

S. albiflorum. A prickly plant with ovate, lobed leaves up to 5 in. long. Flowers creamy-white, 3 in. across, July–Aug. 2–4 ft.

S. laciniatum. This is the true compass plant, so called because in the young growth the leaves, which reach up to 2 ft. long, face north and south. The flowers which are yellow, up to 2 in. across and borne in graceful heads, face east, July–Aug. 3–6 ft.

S. terebinthinaceum. Leaves ovate to heart-shaped, rough, toothed, up to 2 ft. long. Flowers numerous, yellow, up to 3 in. across in fairly loose heads, July–Sept. Up to 8 ft.

SISYRINCHIUM

A genus of annual and perennial herbs native to N. and S. America, most of the species being hardy and mainly suitable for the rock garden. One species, however, makes a good border plant, somewhat resembling an iris. All do best on well-drained, lightish soil, in full sun. Propagation is by seed or division.

S. bermudiana. Flowers violet-blue with yellow base, May–June. 9–12 in.

S. californicum (yellow, 2 ft.) and **S. iridifolium** (yellow and white, 1 ft.) are half-hardy and may be grown in pots in a cool greenhouse, standing in the open in summer.

S. douglasii. Flowers white or purple, June. 9 in.

S. filifolium. Flowers white, veined purple, May. 9 in.

S. striatum. Leaves long, narrow, sheathing. Flowers yellowish, borne in long fairly open spikes, June. 1–2 ft.

SLIPPER FLOWER. See *Calceolaria*

SMILACINA (*False Spikenard*)

Native to N. America and Asia this genus of mostly hardy perennial herbs contains one species that is suitable for borders. It needs good soil that is fairly moist and will not dry out in summer, and prefers partial shade. Propagation is by division.

S. racemosa. Leaves oblong, slender-pointed up to 9 in. long, downy beneath. Flowers small, whitish, borne in sprays up to 6 in. long, May. 2–3 ft.

SMILAX

A genus of climbing plants natives of America and the Far East, most of them needing green-

house treatment, a few being hardy and requiring good loamy soil in a sunny site. Propagate from seed sown in gentle heat or division in spring.
S. aspera (evergreen). Narrow oval leaves. Flowers pale green, Aug.–Sept. Greenhouse.
S. excelsa (deciduous). Ovate, pointed leaves. Flowers greenish, June. Hardy.
S. rotundifolia (deciduous). Lustrous ovate-rounded leaves. Flowers yellow-green, June. Up to 30 ft. Hardy.

SNAKE'S BEARD. See *Ophiopogon*

SNAPDRAGON. See *Antirrhinum*

SNEEZEWEED. See *Helenium*

SNEEZEWORT. See *Achillea*

SNOWDROP. See *Galanthus*

SNOWFLAKE. See *Leucojum*

SOAPWORT. See *Saponaria*

SOLANUM

In addition to the shrubby climbers described on p. 300 and of course the potato **(S. tuberosum)** the genus also contains the well-known Winter Cherry **(S. capsicastrum)** so popular as a cool greenhouse plant. Although perennial and capable of being propagated by cuttings, it is usually raised from seed sown in Mar. in gentle heat, pricked off into 3-in. pots, potted-on to 5 in., stood outside during summer and brought into the house in early Oct., 50 deg. F. or slightly lower rather than higher. The flowers are white and small, the berries orange-red to scarlet, making attractive winter decoration.

SOLDANELLA

Hardy, perennial rock plants native to alpine regions of Europe. Like a shaded position in a moist gritty soil, and should be protected from excessive wet in winter. Propagate from seed or by division. There are many garden hybrids, the main species being:
S. alpina. Small roundish leaves. Flowers violet-blue, Apr.–May. 4–6 in.
S. montana. Roundish leaves on hairy stalk. Flowers violet-blue to blue, Apr.–May. 6–8 in.
S. pusilla. Roundish glossy leaves. Flowers pale violet or blue, May–June. 3–4 in.

SOLIDAGO (*Golden Rod*)

The several species of this genus are generally so variable in character and hybridize so easily and naturally that botanists have found classification difficult. It is, however, generally recognized that the garden varieties grown today have been derived from **S. canadensis** which grows up to 6 ft. and flowers between Aug. and Oct. and **S. virgaurea** which grows up to 2 ft. and begins to flower in July continuing to Oct. These characteristics have given the modern varieties their wide range in height and time of flowering and made them far superior to the old-fashioned, rather coarse plants that were common 20 or 30 years ago. Golden Rod grows well in most kinds of soil preferably in a sunny position. Propagation is by division.
Selected varieties:
'Ballardii': golden-yellow in branching sprays, Aug.–Sept. 5–6 ft.
'Golden Gate': lemon-yellow, compact, Sept. 2 ft.
'Goldenmosa': mimosa-yellow, compact, Aug. 2½ ft.
'Golden Plume': lemon-yellow, compact, Aug. 2½ ft.
'Golden Wings': deep yellow, branching, Aug.–Sept. 5 ft.
'Goldstrahl': canary-yellow, neat sprays, Sept. 3 ft.
'Leda': sunshine yellow, erect spikes, July–Aug. 3½ ft.
'Leraft': golden-yellow, sprays. Aug.–Sept. 2½ ft.
× **Solidaster.** This is an inter-generic hybrid derived from crossing **Aster ptarmicoides** with a species of **Solidago.** It was introduced from France about 1909 and is now often grown in gardens. Its treatment should be the same as for asters or golden rod.
× **S. luteus.** Leaves narrow, aster-like. Flowers numerous, borne in flattish heads, bright yellow fading to creamy-yellow, Sept.–Oct. 2½ ft.

SOLLYA FUSIFORMIS (*Australian Bluebell Creeper*)
Evergreen creeper, native of Australia. Needs a cool greenhouse, and planting in 5–6-in. pots in a compost of sandy loam and peat. Water regularly and keep moist in winter. Propagate from cuttings of new shoots in spring or summer set in pots of sandy soil kept close in gentle heat. Slender, pointed, lance-like leaves. Flowers are rich blue, May–July. 6–7 ft.

SOLOMON'S SEAL. See *Polygonatum*

SOUTHERNWOOD. See *Artemisia*

SOWBREAD. See *Cyclamen*

SPARAXIS
Genus of half-hardy, bulbous plants, native to S. Africa. Thrive in sunny positions in well-drained sandy soil, or in pots in a cool greenhouse. Plant in Sept.–Oct. about 2½ in. deep and 3 in. apart or pot-up, 6 bulbs to a 5-in. pot, and treat as for Ixia. Propagate from offsets or seed.
S. grandiflora. Long, lance-shaped leaves. Flowers purple, white, yellow, pink or crimson, Apr.–May. 18 in.
S. tricolor. Flowers white, orange-red or purple and generally flushed yellow, May. 20–24 in.

SPEEDWELL. See *Veronica*

SPIDER LILY. See *Hymenocallis*

SPIDERWORT. See *Tradescantia*

SPIGELIA MARILANDICA (*Pink Root, Indian Pink*)
A hardy species of a small genus of perennial herb native to N. America, many requiring warm temperatures. Thrives in a sunny position in compost of loam and peat. Propagate from seed or cuttings of young growth in gentle heat. Oval, lance-shaped leaves. Long tubular red flowers with yellow throat, July. 12–18 in.

SPLEENWORT. See *Ferns*

SPRING BEAUTY. See *Claytonia*

SPRING MEADOW SAFFRON. See *Bulbocodium*

SPURGE. See *Euphorbia*

SQUILL. See *Scilla*

STACHYS (*Woundwort, Betony*)
This genus of annuals and perennials, mainly of Asian origin, many of them weed-like, contains few species of garden value. Some of the perennials are however useful for their attractive foliage as well as their flowers. They will grow in most kinds of soil, including those that are poor or dry, in sun or partial shade. Propagation is by division or seed.
S. corsica. Mat-forming. Flowers pinkish-white, summer. 1 ft. Rock garden.
S. lanata. Leaves thick, soft, densely white-woolly. Flowers purplish, borne in whorls on an erect spike, July–Aug. 1–1½ ft.
S. macrantha. Leaves ovate or roundish, rough, hairy. Flowers rose or violet, up to 1 in. long, May–June. 1–2 ft.

STAPELIA
A genus of leafless succulents native to S. Africa, suitable for a cool greenhouse in a porous compost of loam and coarse sand. Water carefully and regularly, give some shade and keep moist when dormant. Re-pot every 2 years. Propagate from seed or division of roots. Some species have unpleasant aromas.
S. gigantea. Flowers purple, light yellow and crimson, up to 12 in. across. 5–7 in.
S. grandiflora. Flowers purplish-brown, white base with purple hairs, 6 in. across. 8–10 in.
S. nobilis. Flowers pale buff to yellow with purple or crimson markings, 9 in. across. 6–8 in.

STAR FLOWER. See *Trientalis*

STAR GLORY. See *Quamoclit*

STAR OF BETHLEHEM. See *Ornithogalum*

STAR OF THE VELDT. See *Dimorphotheca*

STARWORT. See *Boltonia*

STATICE. See *Limonium*

STEPHANOTIS (*Madagascar Jasmine*)
A genus of evergreen climbers, natives of

Madagascar, mostly requiring winter temperatures of 55–60 deg. F. **S. floribunda** will, however, succeed at slightly lower levels. It can be grown either in pots or the greenhouse border in a compost of fibrous loam and leafmould. Should be occasionally syringed during the growing season. Propagate from cuttings of the previous year's wood struck in a close frame at 60 deg. F. in spring. Large, thick, oval leaves. Flowers in clusters, waxy white, May–June. 10–30 ft.

STERNBERGIA

Genus of bulbous plants native to S. Europe, M. East and F. East requiring a sheltered, sunny position in well-drained borders or in an alpine house. They need a sandy soil with a little peat. Propagate from offsets in Apr.

S. fischeriana. Flowers bright yellow, Mar. 10 in.

S. lutea (*Winter Daffodil*). Flowers yellow, Sept. 10–12 in.

STOCKS. See *Matthiola*

STOKESIA (*Stokes's Aster*)

The genus contains only one species, providing handsome flowers, good for cutting. The plants grow well in most kinds of soil, in sun or partial shade. Propagation is by division.

S. laevis. Leaves smooth, narrow. Flowers generally blue, but also white, yellow or purple, fringed somewhat like a China aster, up to 3 in. across, Aug.–Sept. 12–18 in.

STONECROP. See *Sedum*

STRATIOTES ALOIDES (*Water Soldier*)

A single species of an aquatic herb native to Europe. Although an interesting plant with its leaves rising in spring to produce white flowers in summer, then sinking again in autumn, it should be grown with discretion as it sometimes makes rapid growth and may choke up the water garden.

STRELITZIA REGINAE (*Bird of Paradise Flower*)

Perennial herb native to S. Africa, requiring a winter temperature of 50 deg. F. It should be grown in 9-in. pots or in the greenhouse border in a compost of 2 parts good loam and 1 of peat with a little sand. Needs good ventilation, full sun and regular watering. Propagate by division or suckers or from seed which must be hand-pollinated, sown in spring with bottom heat. Sword-like leaves (18–20 in.) Flowers orange and blue-purple on long stems (up to 36 in.), Mar.–Apr. There are several varieties.

STREPTOCARPUS

Genus of dwarf perennials natives of Africa and Near East, requiring a cool greenhouse and a rich compost of good loam and peat in 6-in. pots. Water well when growing but keep almost dry in winter. Propagate from seed sown in gentle heat in Feb. or by leaf-cuttings or division in Mar. Most of the garden varieties have been derived from **S. rexii** and its crosses with other species, giving flowers in a wide range of colours, blue, mauve, pink, salmon, red or white, May–Oct. on stems growing up to 3 ft.

STREPTOSOLEN JAMESONII

A single species of evergreen climber suitable for a cool greenhouse, requiring a rich, light compost in pots or the greenhouse border. Water freely in summer, keep fairly dry in winter and cut fairly hard. Re-pot in spring. Propagate by cuttings of young shoots in a close frame. Orange-red flowers, June. 8 ft.

STRIPED SQUILL. See *Puschkinia*

STROBILANTHES

A genus of shrubby herbs, natives of S.E. Asia, most of the species requiring stove conditions to get the best of their magnificent foliage with a few suitable for a cool greenhouse. Grow easily in light soil. Need plenty of water and syringing. Propagate from cuttings, 60 deg. F.

S. attenuatus. Dark green, ovate leaves. Flowers purple and yellow, June. 3 ft.

S. pentastemonoides. Lance-like leaves. Flowers blue-violet. 2–3 ft.

STYLOPHORUM (*Celandine Poppy*)

A small genus of poppy-like perennials, one species, **S. diphyllum,** making a useful plant for woodland or shaded border. Propagate by seed or division. Flowers yellow, May. 1 ft.

SUMMER STARWORT. See *Erinus*

SUNDEW. See *Drosera*

SUNFLOWER. See *Helianthus*

SWAINSONA

One species **(S. galegifolia)** of this Australian genus is suitable for a cool greenhouse. Seed should be sown in Mar. in heat, the seedlings potted up, pinched out and grown on through the summer and winter. Pot-on the following spring and pinch again in Apr., to flower in July. Large white, orange, pink, red, blue or mauve flowers, 2–4 ft.

SWAMP LILY. See *Lilium*

SWAN RIVER DAISY. See *Brachycome*

SWEET FLAG. See *Acorus*

SWEET MARJORAM. See *Origanum*

SWEET PEAS

The Sweet Pea is an annual of great possibilities and therefore merits special attention. The first variety offered for sale in about 1730 bore little resemblance to the sweet pea varieties as we know them today. It was a small-flowered, more or less wild variety with purple flowers which had been grown from seed sent to this country by an Italian monk. Development of the sweet pea was at first slow and by the end of the eighteenth century a few varieties only began to appear. The larger seed firms then took up the work of improving and adding to the number of varieties and by 1860 were offering a number of varieties. But it was Henry Eckford about the turn of the century who laid the foundation of the popularity enjoyed by the sweet pea today with such varieties as 'Dorothy Eckford' (pink), 'Lady Grisel Hamilton' (lavender) and 'King Edward' (scarlet). These were unfrilled types. The first waved varieties were raised by Mr. Silas Cole, gardener to Countess Spencer, and were hence known as the Spencer varieties. 'Countess Spencer', a pink variety, was the first of this type to be exhibited in 1901. At the same time Mr. W. J. Unwin who was working on somewhat different lines produced 'Gladys Unwin' (pink), a variety of rather different form, and it is from these two types that our modern forms and varieties have come. A modern list may now run into over a hundred varieties with a wonderful range of colouring.

The most important point is to start with a good strain of well ripened and properly harvested seed; an inferior strain will always throw a certain percentage of off-type flowers. The seeds may be sown in pots, pans or boxes at the end of Sept. or early Oct. using John Innes compost No. 1 or any light mixture available. In boxes or pans the seeds should be spaced 2 in. apart and 1 in. deep, 5-in. pots will take four or five seeds, or a single seed may be sown in a 3-in. pot. For this sowing a cold frame with an ash bottom is necessary. See that the soil is well moist after sowing and keep the light closed and shaded against sunshine until germination takes place. The closed lights and shade prevent the evaporation of moisture and no more water should be given until after germination. Sweet peas are quite hardy—make no mistake about this—and air must be admitted freely as soon as growth is apparent, removing the lights altogether on all favourable occasions. Should birds be troublesome to the young seedlings spread a net over the frame but do not be tempted to cover with lights. Throughout the winter the only time the lights should be on is during rainy periods or very severe frost and even then they should be blocked up. To protect the pots from frost it is a good plan to plunge them up to the rim in old ashes. Should the plants become frozen, cover the lights to shade them from sunshine during the thaw. When each seedling has three pairs of leaves pinch out the growing tip and shortly afterwards pot each one separately into 3-in. pots, using John Innes compost No. 2. Prepare to plant out at the first favourable opportunity from the end of Feb. onwards, but do not be tempted to plant in wet weather or in unsuitable soil but wait until the right day arrives even though it may be a month or more. The soil for planting should have been deeply dug and well manured in the autumn and the surface having been left rough should be broken down to a good tilth. If it is intended to grow the plants on the cordon system—which will be described below—a stout pole must be erected at each end of the row to which a cross-piece 1 ft. long is firmly fixed at right angles. From the two ends of each cross-piece a wire is stretched tightly and to the wire bamboo canes 6 in. apart are tied, each cane being 6–7 ft. out of the ground. These should be in position before planting is done. When planting, the roots should be shaken free of all potting soil and extended downwards or laterally as much as possible, firming the soil well around them. And now to explain something of the cordon system of growing. There will not be much activity until mid-Apr. when it will be noted that several shoots begin to develop. Finally only one of these will be required and they should be reduced gradually, in case of slug or wind damage, tying the best shoot to the cane in good time. Each single stem must have the side shoots removed regularly together with the leaf tendrils and the main stem kept tied to the canes. Provided the hoe is used frequently, water should seldom be necessary but if required let it be copiously applied as driblets of water can do much harm. When the cordons reach the top of the canes they may be taken down and retrained. To do this, lower the first six plants carefully away from the row, the seventh, tie along the bottom of the freed canes and carefully turn the head upright and tie to the first cane. Repeat this process along the row using the first six plants from the opposite side to clothe the vacant end canes, the same method being used to finish the row. Throughout the season prevent the formation of seed pods by the regular removal of spent flowers.

The above method of growing has as its object the production of good quality, long-stemmed flowers, but good blooms for general purposes may be obtained either by sowing in pots or boxes in the spring and planting out or direct outdoor sowing may be made from mid-Feb. onwards according to the district and soil conditions. By this method ordinary pea sticks will give sufficient support. In all cases the preparation of the soil is of paramount importance and should farmyard manure or compost be in short supply it should be supplemented by using 2 oz. hoof and horn grist when digging, and 4 oz. superphosphate and 2 oz. sulphate of potash per sq. yd. a few weeks before planting-out.

Under good cultivation pests and diseases should give little trouble; "Streak" is undoubtedly the worst and this is a disease of the virus type. The symptoms are yellowing of the foliage, turning to browning and dropping together with withering of the stem. Examination will show the typical blackish-brown streaking on affected stems and all such must be pulled up and destroyed by burning. The trouble is most likely to occur as the result of unbalanced manuring with an excess of nitrogen, over-watering or excessive rainfall, or sudden fluctuations of temperature. A sufficiency of lime and potash in the soil tends to make the plants resistant. The other worry may be bud-dropping; this is not a disease but a physiological disorder caused by some interruption to the normal functional processes of the plant, such as a sudden cold spell or fluctuation of soil moisture.

Varieties:

Among others the following are recommended as reliable under average conditions.

Pink shades:

'Challenge', 'Carlotta', 'Elizabeth Arden', 'Fairy Princess', 'Mrs. R. Bolton', 'Margaret Rose', 'Piccadilly', 'Pinkie', 'Shillingford'.

Lavender or mauve:

'Ambition', 'Blue Pearl', 'Basildon', 'Chieftain', 'Lavender Lass', 'Prince Charles', 'Powerscourt'.

Blue and purple shades:

'Blue Bonnet', 'Blue Heaven', 'Blue Ice', 'Calcot', 'Marlow', 'Mabel Gower', 'Purple Cloak', 'Purple Monarch', 'Zeta'.

Crimson and maroon:

'Black Diamond', 'Loch Lomond', 'Mahogany', 'Warrior.'

Cerise and scarlet:

'Air Warden', 'Cheerfulness', 'Mollie', 'Runnymede', 'Red Admiral', 'Streatley.'

White and cream:

'Blushing Beauty', 'Gigantic', 'Swan Lake', 'Cream Frills', 'Puritan', 'Valerie'.

SWEET ROCK. See *Hesperis*

SWEET SEDGE. See *Acorus*

SWEET SULTAN. See *Centaurea*

SWEET VERBENA. See *Lippia*

SWEET WILLIAM. See *Dianthus*

SWORD LILY. See *Gladiolus*

SYMPHYANDRA

A genus of hardy perennial herbs natives of F. East and E. Europe, suitable for borders or rock gardens, preferably on lightish loam. Propagate from seed sown under glass in Mar., or division of roots in spring or autumn.

S. asiatica. Toothed leaves, coarse white hairs. Flowers violet, nodding, summer. 18–30 in.

S. hofmannii. Toothed, lance-like leaves. Flowers white, summer. 12–24 in.

S. wanneri. Hairy, toothed leaves. Flowers blue, summer. 6 in.

SYMPHYTUM (*Comfrey*)

This genus, native to Europe and W. Asia, contains a few showy species that flower over a long period and will succeed in shaded positions. They grow well in most soils, often too well if fertility is high. Propagation is by division or seed.

S. officinale. Leaves oblong, pointed, up to 8 in. long. Flowers white, rose, purple or crimson, June–Sept. 2–4 ft.

S. peregrinum. Leaves ovate-oblong, up to 10 in. long. Flowers rose, becoming blue, bell-shaped, June–Sept. 3–5 ft.

SYNNOTIA

A small genus of bulbous plants native to S. Africa and suitable for a cool greenhouse for growing in pots in the same way as freesias. Propagate from offsets or seed.

S. bicolor. Flowers violet or yellow, Mar. 6–9 in.

TAGETES

A genus of annual and perennial herbs native to America. The garden varieties have originated from the species listed below and are annuals. They thrive in sunny beds in average soil. Propagate from seeds sown in Mar. or Apr. where required to bloom, thin to 1 ft. apart or transplant.

T. erecta (*African Marigold*). Toothed, lance-like leaves. Flowers in yellow, orange or buff shades, June–Sept. 18–24 in. There are a number of named varieties, generally divided into three types, giant-flowered and carnation-flowered, $2\frac{1}{2}$ ft. and dwarfs $1\frac{1}{2}$ ft.

T. lucida, the Mexican Marigold, is less commonly grown. It has sharply toothed, lance-like leaves. Flowers yellow, July–Aug. 8–12 in.

T. patula (*French Marigold*). Toothed, lance-like leaves. Flowers yellow or brownish-yellow, orange or maroon, June–Sept. Tall varieties $2\frac{1}{2}$–3 ft., dwarfs 9–15 in., single or double.

TANACETUM (*Tansy*)

A genus of annual and perennial herbs with a few species suitable for garden cultivation and even then their spread may need regular checking. They grow well in most kinds of soil, preferably in full sun. Propagation is by division.

T. herderi. Leaves in silvery rosettes. Flowers yellow, July. 6–9 in. Rock garden.

T. vulgare. Leaves oblong, up to 5 in. long. Flowers small, yellow, button-like, borne in flattish heads, Aug.–Sept. 3 ft.

TANAKAEA

A genus of a single species, **T. radicans,** native to Japan. This creeping perennial plant thrives in sandy loam or in an alpine house. Propagate by division in spring. Evergreen, heart-shaped leathery leaves. Flowers small, white, Apr.–June.

TANSY. See *Tanacetum*

TARRAGON. See *Artemisia*

TASSEL FLOWER. See *Emilia*

TECOMA (*Trumpet Flower*)

A small S. American genus of tender climbing plants, two species being suitable for a cool greenhouse. Propagate by seed or cuttings in gentle heat.

T. garrocha. Graceful slender leaves. Flowers scarlet and yellow, 1 in. across, in sprays, summer. 5 ft.
T. smithii. Flowers tubular, yellow-orange, winter. 3 ft.

TEUCRIUM

A genus of herbs, sub-shrubs and shrubs, widely distributed, but with few species which are suitable for the garden. They succeed in a well-drained, moderately good soil. Propagate the herbaceous species by division in spring and the shrubby species by cuttings.
T. chamaedrys (*Wild Germander*) (perennial). Ovate leaves. Flowers rose, lower lip spotted red and white, July–Sept. 6–18 in. Rock garden.
T. fruticans (*Tree Germander*). Evergreen, ovate, hairy leaves. Flowers pale lavender-blue, Mar.–Sept. 2–4 ft. Greenhouse. Shrubby.
T. marum is often known as Cat Thyme and should not be grown. Cats are so attracted that they bite it, tear it and trample on it, and in so doing, damage adjacent plants.

THALICTRUM (*Meadow Rue*)

A large genus of perennial herbs, mostly native to temperate regions, containing several species with attractive foliage and somewhat unusual flowers, some having ornamental sepals, others having conspicuous stamens. They do best in a fairly rich, moist loam and prefer partial shade. Propagation is by division or seed.
T. alpinum. Leaves basal. Flowers purplish, July–Aug. 4–6 in. Rock garden.
T. aquilegiifolium. Leaves feathery, divided, lobed. Flowers greenish-white to purple, the sepals green or white, stamens prominent, white to purple, borne in loose feathery or fluffy heads, May–July. $2\frac{1}{2}$–4 ft.
T. dipterocarpum. Leaves 3-lobed, fern-like. Flowers white or violet-amethyst, stamens yellow, drooping, borne in branching sprays, June–Aug. 2–5 ft.
T. flavum. Leaves grey-green, delicately cut and lobed. Flowers small numerous, yellow with bright yellow stamens, July–Aug. 2–3 ft.
T. speciosissimum. Leaves delicately cut and lobed, up to $1\frac{1}{2}$ in. wide. Flowers small, numerous, in fairly compact sprays, yellow, July–Aug. 2–5 ft.

THE PRINCE'S FEATHER. See *Amaranthus*

THERMOPSIS

This is a small genus of perennial herbs with a few N. American species suitable for garden use. The flowers resemble those of lupins and the plants will grow best in lightish but fairly rich soil, in full sun. Propagation is by seed. (Division is not usually successful.)
T. caroliniana. Leaves smooth, hairy beneath, up to 3 in. long. Flowers yellow, borne in compact spikes, up to 10 in. long, July. 2–3 ft.
T. montana. Leaves narrow, up to 3 in. long. Flowers yellow, in compact spikes, up to 8 in. long, June–July. 1–2 ft.

THLASPI

A genus of annual and perennial herbs, widely distributed, mostly weeds, but having a few dwarf perennial species such as **T. rotundifolium** suitable for the rock garden. Propagate from seed or division in spring. Flowers rosy-lilac, July–Aug. 2–4 in.

THOUSAND MOTHERS. See *Tolmiea*

THRIFT. See *Armeria*

THROATWORT. See *Trachelium*

THUNBERGIA

A genus of annual or perennial climbing plants native to Trop. Africa and Asia, mostly requiring stove conditions. Two species are however suitable for a cool greenhouse, particularly hanging baskets, and will stand out of doors during summer. Propagate from seed sown in Mar. in heat, or cuttings in a propagating frame. Pot singly in a loam peat compost and move into 5- or 6-in. pots.
T. alata (annual). Flowers white or yellow and purple, June–Sept.
T. gregorii (perennial). Triangular leaves. Flowers bright orange, waxy, June–Sept.

THYMUS

A large genus of hardy trailing and shrubby

plants native to the northern temperate regions of the Old World, containing the well-known culinary thyme **(T. vulgaris)** and several good species useful for the rock or paved garden. They thrive in well-drained sandy loam, and are propagated by seed or division in Mar. or by cuttings in June. Many of the species are closely related or even indistinct and possibly hybrids, but most alpine nurseries can offer a wide choice, giving various colours of foliage from green, grey-green to silvery and flowers from white to pink and crimson growing from 2–12 in.

THYSANOTUS (*Fringed Lily, Fringed Violet*)
A genus of greenhouse perennials native to Australia requiring a cool greenhouse and a sandy loam. Propagate from offsets.
T. dichotomus. Few short leaves. Flowers purple, July. 12–20 in.
T. tuberosus. Few narrow leaves. Flowers purple, June. 10–12 in.

TIARELLA
This is a small genus of N. American and Asian species, most of them suitable for woodland or rock gardens. They grow best in peaty soils, in partial shade. Propagation is by division.
T. cordifolia. Leaves green, turning bronze. Flowers white or pink, Apr.–June. 6–12 in. Rock garden. (On good soil its spreading roots may get out of hand and a dense plant mass then results.)
T. wherryi. Roots are compact not creeping. Leaves ovate, lobed, becoming reddish in autumn. Flowers star-like, white or rose, borne in feathery spikes, May–June. Up to 15 in. Border or rock garden.

TICKSEED. See *Coreopsis*

TIDY TIPS. See *Layia*

TIGER FLOWER. See *Tigridia*

TIGER IRIS. See *Tigridia*

TIGER LILY. See *Lilium*

TIGRIDIA (*Tiger Iris*)
A genus of half-hardy bulbous plants natives of S. and C. America, suitable for a cool greenhouse or for planting out in sheltered positions in a sunny border or rock garden but they must then be lifted in autumn and stored in a frost-proof place during winter. They thrive in light, sandy soil, 3 or 4 bulbs to a 5- or 6-in. pot. Propagate from seed or offsets in Apr.
T. pavonia (*Tiger Flower, Shell Flower*). Lance-like leaves up to 18 in. long. Flowers white, yellow, orange or reddish-purple, often marked or spotted, June. 12–24 in.
T. pringlei. Flowers crimson, orange and scarlet, July–Aug. 12–24 in.

TOADFLAX. See *Linaria*

TOBACCO PLANT. See *Nicotiana*

TOLMIEA (*Pick-a-Back Plant, Thousand Mothers*)
This is a genus of one N. American species which produces young plants from a bud on the leaf-stalk. If taken off and planted, young roots develop readily. The plant grows well in most soils, preferably in partial shade.
T. menziesii. Flowers greenish, nodding, in sprays up to 18 in. long, May. $1\frac{1}{2}$–2 ft.

TOOTHWORT. See *Dentaria*

TORCH LILY. See *Kniphofia*

TORENIA
A genus of half-hardy trailing plants native to Trop. Asia and Africa, mostly requiring warm temperatures, but two species are suitable for a cool greenhouse and are good plants for hanging baskets. They should be grown in a compost of loam and peat. Propagate from seed sown in heat in Apr.–May.
T. baillonii. Toothed, oval leaves. Flowers bright yellow and purplish-brown, May–Aug. 6–12 in.
T. fournieri. Toothed, oval leaves. Flowers pale violet-blue, with yellow and white throat, May–Aug. 8–12 in.

TOWNSENDIA
A genus of dwarf perennial herbs native to N. America. They are suitable for the rock garden

and alpine house, and thrive in a well-drained sandy soil with grit or chippings. Propagate from seed sown as soon as ripe.

T. exscapa. Almost stemless. Spatulate leaves. Flowers white, sometimes with purplish tint, Apr.–May. 2 in.

T. grandiflora. Narrow leaves. Flowers bright blue or violet, summer. 8–12 in.

TRACHELIUM

A genus mostly of hardy perennial herbs native to the Mediterranean region, suitable for rock gardens or sunny beds with one half-hardy species popularly grown in a cool greenhouse. Propagate from seed sown in slight heat in spring, or cuttings in Apr. and Aug.

T. caeruleum (*Throatwort*). Ovate leaves, deeply toothed. Flowers light blue or white in large dainty heads, June–Aug. 2–3 ft. Best treated as an annual from seed sown in Mar. in gentle heat or as a biennial from seed sown in July for flowering the following year. Use a loam peat compost, grow outside during the summer and bring into the house early Oct.

TRACHELOSPERMUM

A genus of doubtfully hardy evergreen climbing shrubs native to E. Asia. The best species, **T. jasminoides,** is suitable for warm districts, but is generally better in a cool greenhouse. Propagate from cuttings in spring and summer. Lance-like, shining green leaves. Flowers white and fragrant, July. Climbs up to 20 ft.

TRADESCANTIA (*Spiderwort*)

This is a large genus of widely differing species of American perennial plants, most of the best not hardy although excellent for a cool greenhouse or indoor decoration. One species however makes a good and somewhat unusual border plant. It grows on most soils but prefers fairly good moist conditions in full sun. Propagation is by division or seed.

T. fluminensis. A popular greenhouse and indoor species. There are forms with yellow and white striped leaves. Some of the variegated forms have a rose tint, making them very attractive.

T. virginiana. Leaves long, narrow, up to 14 in. long. Flowers white, blue, mauve, rose or red, some double, lasting only one day but quickly succeeded by others to give a long period of bloom, June–Sept. 1½ ft. 'Iris Pritchard' (white with violet shading), 'J. C. Weguelin' (azure), 'Leonora' (violet) and 'Osprey' (white) are probably the best varieties. Borders.

TREASURE FLOWER. See *Gazania*

TREFOIL. See *Trifolium*

TRIENTALIS

A genus of two species of perennials native to the N. Temperate regions. They are suitable for the rock garden or border edging and need a light peaty soil in a shady position. Propagate from seed in spring or by division.

T. borealis (*Star Flower*). Leaves lance-like and in rosette at top of stalk. Flowers white, Apr.–May. 6–9 in.

T. europaea. Leaves similar to above species. White flowers, June–July. 4–8 in.

TRIFOLIUM (*Clover, Shamrock, Trefoil*)

A genus of annual, biennial and perennial herbs, of little garden merit and often a nuisance on lawns, but interesting as containing shamrock (**T. repens**). **T. alpinum** and **T. uniflorum** are sometimes grown in rock gardens.

TRILLIUM (*Wood Lily*)

A genus of perennial rhizomatous plants native to N. America and Far East. They thrive in moist peaty soil in woodland or in a shaded position in a border. Propagate by division in Oct. or from seed sown in spring (plants from seed take 2–3 years to flower).

T. erectum (*Birth-root*). Broad, lozenge-shaped leaves. Flowers deep purple, May–June. 12 in.

T. grandiflorum (*Wake Robin*). Leaves similar to above. Flowers rose turning to white, Apr.–June. 12–18 in.

T. sessile. Leaves broadly oval. Flowers purple, Mar.–Apr. 6–12 in.

TRITONIA

Although this bulbous genus is botanically distinct, tritonias are often called, and included with, montbretias which in their turn properly belong to the genus Crocosmia (see page 205). The best way out of these difficulties is to assume that for general garden purposes the tritonias are plants for the cool greenhouse because the best species must be so treated whereas the crocosmias are fully hardy. But since the ordinary gardener will probably go on calling both 'montbretias', he may find it easier and simpler to remember that there are hardy montbretias and greenhouse montbretias, and that the two must be grown in different ways and not mixed up together.

T. crocata has the characteristic narrow leaves and bell-shaped flowers, yellow, orange, red, scarlet or purple in May and June, and grows about 2 ft. Pot-up in Oct., 5 bulbs to a 7-in. pot in a loam-peat compost and water well during the growing season. Temperature 45 deg. F.

TROLLIUS (*Globe Flower*)

This is a small genus of herbaceous perennials having showy flowers resembling buttercups. They grow best on moist and fairly heavy soils or the sides of pools but will also do well on most other kinds. They prefer full sun but will tolerate shade. Propagation is by division.

The garden varieties have been derived mainly from crosses of **T. europaeus** with **T. asiaticus** and **T. chinensis** and are now grouped under:

T. × cultorum. Leaves generally lobed and cut, toothed. Flowers yellow to orange, up to 2 in. across, May–July. 2–2½ ft. Among the best varieties are: 'Bee's Orange', 'Orange Globe', 'Orange Princess', 'Fire Globe' and 'Prichard's Giant' (3 ft.). All are good for cutting.

TROPAEOLUM

A genus of annuals and perennials, many of them climbers, native to S. America. They thrive in ordinary soil in sunny positions, the climbing species doing well against fences or trellis work, needing no training. Propagate from seed sown in spring or in pots under glass and planted out in May.

T. azureum (blue) and **T. tuberosum** (orange and red) are tender, tuberous, and make good climbers in a cool greenhouse.

T. majus (*Nasturtium, Indian Cress*) (annual). Leaves circular. Flowers gold, orange, red or salmon, single or double, summer. There are numerous named varieties, dwarf, tall or climbing.

T. peltophorum (tender annual). Leaves roundish. Flowers red, summer. Cool greenhouse.

T. pentaphylum (tender perennial). Leaves lobed, with long stalks. Flowers scarlet, summer.

T. peregrinum (annual or perennial) (*The Canary Creeper*). Large lobed leaves. Flowers yellow or orange, summer. Rock garden.

T. speciosum (*Flame Nasturtium*). Leaves lobed and notched. Flowers scarlet, summer. Good for a north wall.

TRUMPET FLOWER. See *Tecoma*

TUBEROSE. See *Polianthes*

TULIPS PLATE 59

The known history of the tulip dates back to the middle of the sixteenth century. About the middle of the next century an extraordinary boom in popularity took place which was known as 'Tulipomania' and many are the tales told of the fantastic prices paid for single bulbs in Dutch auction rooms by tulip fanciers of the period. It was not until about 1850 that the tulip became really popular and thereafter it seems to have been somewhat neglected until the introduction of the 'Darwin Tulip' in 1889 reinstated it. Today it is regarded as one of the most useful and brilliant flowers for the spring and early summer months.

Tulips will thrive in all good garden soils provided they are well drained and not too rich with freshly applied manure. On very heavy soils drainage will be assisted by planting in raised beds. The bulbs should be planted some 4 in. deep from Oct. to early Dec., regarding Nov. as the optimum planting date. A blunt dibber or trowel may be used for planting making sure that the base of the bulb is in contact with the soil. Tulips, especially the taller 'Cottage' varieties and the 'Darwins', are easily damaged by wind and should be given the most sheltered site available. After flowering, the bulbs may be carefully lifted and laid in on a reserve border to complete their growth or—

and this is preferable where possible—allowed to remain until the foliage dies down naturally in July. Lifted bulbs should be cleaned and dried in the shade outdoors, or in an airy shed, and stored in shallow boxes for replanting in the autumn. Bulbs left in the ground too long are prone to shed their skins when lifted and although little harm is caused by this, they should be handled as carefully as possible to preserve them intact.

With tulips the original bulb is expended in the production of the flower and foliage, an offset bulb being formed for the next season. Any small bulbs or offsets may be saved and if planted thickly and allowed to remain for two years will attain flowering size. The practice of leaving tulip bulbs in the ground for succeeding seasons is not to be recommended, much better results following lifting and replanting. In addition to the tulip varieties used for bedding and forcing there are also a number of interesting species. The following represents a selection from the different sections.

Species:
- *T. celsiana* (yellow, 6 in.)
- *T. clusiana* (The Lady Tulip, white interior, rosy-red outside, with dark blotch at base, 8 in.)
- *T. kaufmanniana* (Water-lily Tulip, a variable species, creamy-yellow within, outside carmine, 6–8 in.)
- *T. linifolia* (scarlet with black centre, 6–8 in.)
- *T. marjoletti* (lemon-yellow, 9 in.)
- *T. praestans* (scarlet, producing two or three flowers on a stem, 8 in.)

These are all suitable for growing on the rock garden.

Early-flowering, double:
- 'Aga Khan' (golden-yellow)
- 'Electra' (carmine-rose)
- 'Murillo' (white, flushed rose)
- 'Orange Nassau' (orange-scarlet)
- 'Scarlet Cardinal' (orange-scarlet)
- 'Schoonoord' (pure white)
- 'Peach Blossom' (rose-pink)

Average height of all the above 12 in.

Early-flowering, single:
- 'Cramoise Brilliant' (vivid scarlet)
- 'Diana' (pure white)
- 'Duchess de Parma' (scarlet-crimson, edged yellow)
- 'Fred Moore' (apricot)
- 'Ibis' (deep pink)
- 'Keizerskroon' (scarlet, edged yellow)
- 'Orange Wonder' (deep orange-red with paler edging)
- 'Prince of Austria' (orange-scarlet)
- 'Proserpine' (carmine-rose)

Average height of the above 12–14 in.

Triumph or Early-flowering Darwins:
- 'Bruno Walter' (orange-yellow, 15 in.)
- 'Crater' (crimson, 20 in.)
- 'Dreaming Maid' (violet, edged white, 17 in.)
- 'Kansas' (pure white, 22 in.)
- 'Nova' (salmon-pink, 18 in.)
- 'Rheinland' (crimson, edged yellow, 20 in.)
- 'Teheran' (apricot, 22 in.)

This section is excellent for bedding, flowering during late April.

Darwins:
- 'Baron de la Tocnaye' (deep rose-pink, paler margin, 28 in.)
- 'Clara Butt' (salmon-rose, 22 in.)
- 'Copland's Purple' (wine-red, 22 in.)
- 'Charles Needham' (scarlet, 24 in.)
- 'Dorrie Overall' (violet-mauve, 26 in.)
- 'Golden Age' (23 in.)
- 'Golden Harvest' (lemon-yellow, 28 in.)
- 'Mr. Van Zijl' (rose-pink, 26 in.)
- Farncombe Sanders' (rose-scarlet, 27 in.)
- 'Pandion' (purple, white margin)
- 'William Pitt' (scarlet, blue and white base, 24 in.)
- 'William Copland' (lavender, 22 in.)

All the Darwin tulips are May flowering.

Cottage Tulips (May flowering):
- 'Carrara' (pure white, 24 in.)
- 'Ellen Willmott' (yellow, 24 in.)
- 'Inglescombe Yellow' (18 in.)
- 'Marshall Haig' (scarlet, with yellow base, 28 in.)
- 'Princess Margaret Rose' (yellow, edged and flushed orange, 18 in.)
- 'Smiling Queen' (rose-pink, lighter flushed edge, 27 in.)

All the 'Cottage' varieties are excellent for bedding.

Parrot Tulips:
'Discovery' (rose-pink, 24 in.)
'Fantasy' (multi-coloured, shades of rose and white, 22 in.)
'Parrot Wonder' (carmine, 25 in.)
'Pierson Parrot' (crimson-maroon, 25 in.)
'Orange Favourite' (20 in.)
The 'Parrot' tulips flower in early May; while the flowers are attractive they frequently have weak stems. Those selected will generally be found satisfactory in this respect.

TUNICA
A genus of annual and perennial herbs native to S. Europe. The most suitable garden species is **T. saxifraga,** which can be grown in the rock garden or alpine house. It thrives in well-drained, light soil. Propagate from seed sown as soon as ripe or division in spring. Leaves narrow, small. Flowers white or lilac, June–Sept. 4–8 in.

TURTLE HEAD. See *Chelone*

TWIN FLOWER. See *Linnaea*

TWIN LEAF. See *Jeffersonia*

TWIN-LEAVED LILY-OF-THE-VALLEY. See *Maianthemum*

TYPHA (*Reed Mace, Narrow-leaved Bulrush*)
A genus of aquatics widely distributed in tropical and temperate regions of world. They thrive in moist banks of bog gardens or ponds in 6 in. of water. Propagate by seed or division.
T. angustifolia (*Small Reed Mace*). Dark green leaves. Flower spikes brown, July. 3–4 ft.
T. latifolia (*Reed Mace, Cat-tail*). Long nearly flat leaves. Flower spikes dark brown, July–Aug. 6–8 ft.
T. minima is a diminutive bulrush, only 1–2 ft. high, and is the most suitable for small ponds.

UMBRELLA PLANT. See *Peltiphyllum*

UNICORN PLANT. See *Martynia*

URSINIA
A genus of annual and perennial herbs and shrubs native to S. Africa and mostly half-hardy. The annuals are the more suitable for the garden and thrive in well-drained average soil. Propagation from seed sown in Apr. or May where they are to flower.
U. anthemoides. Flowers drooping, purplish, Aug. 6–12 in.
U. pygmaea is dwarf, with yellow or orange flowers. 4 in.
U. versicolor. Fern-like leaves. Flowers bright orange, summer. 8–12 in.

UVULARIA (*Bellwort*)
This is a small genus of rhizomatous perennials from N. America with bell-shaped flowers hanging gracefully in much the same way as Solomon's Seal. Only one species is suitable for garden use, and grows best in moist peaty soil, in partial shade. Propagation is by division.
U. grandiflora. Leaves oblong, membranous, clasping the stem, up to 4 in. long. Flowers yellow, usually in threes, drooping, May–June. 1–1½ ft.

VALERIANA
A genus of hardy perennial herbs and shrubs native to Europe, Asia and America. Only the species described below have any garden value. They thrive in ordinary soil and can be increased by division.
V. arizonica. Lobed, fleshy leaves. Flowers pink, Apr.–July. 3–4 in. Suitable for the rock garden.
V. officinalis (*All-heal, St. George's Herb*). Lance-like, toothed leaves. Flowers pink, June. 2–3 ft. Wild garden.
V. supina. Leaves shiny-green. Flowers white tinged pink, June–Aug. 4 in. Rock garden.
For the commonly called Valerian, see Kentranthus.

VALLOTA
A genus of half-hardy bulbous plants native to S. Africa resembling *Amaryllis* and comprising only one species, **V. speciosa** (*Scarborough Lily*), which requires a compost of sandy loam and peat and a cool greenhouse. Plant the bulbs 6–8 in. deep in sand with compost well firmed around them—do not re-pot for several years. Propagation is by offsets in Aug. Broad leaves up to 20 in. long. Flowers white, pink, red or scarlet, summer. 1–2 ft.

VENIDIO-ARCTOTIS
A hybrid recently introduced, excellent for a cool greenhouse. The plants combine all the merits of the original parents, producing attractive flowers in striking shades of yellow, orange, buff, pink, salmon, crimson and purple. 1½–2 ft. There are a number of named varieties. Being sterile, propagation can be effected only by cuttings.

VENIDIUM
A small genus of half-hardy annual and perennial herbs from S. Africa, providing showy plants with daisy-like flowers for a cool greenhouse, or sheltered, sunny positions outside. All are best treated as annuals, seed being sown in Mar. in gentle heat, pricked out for transplanting in the open in May or for potting on.
V. decurrens. Lyre-shaped leaves. Flowers white, yellow or orange, with black or brown centres, July–Sept. 2–18 in.
V. fastuosum. Leaves greyish, silky. Flowers yellow to orange, with purplish blotch and black centre, July–Sept. 2–3 ft.

VENUS' NAVEL-WORT. See *Omphalodes*

VERATRUM
This is a small genus, of hardy rhizomatous perennials, most of the species being native to Europe, Siberia or N. America and having attractive foliage and graceful spikes of flowers. They grow best in moist peaty soils, preferably in partial shade. The roots are poisonous. Propagation is by division.
V. album. Leaves large, dark green, downy. Flowers greenish-white, borne in dense spikes, July. 3–4 ft.
V. californicum. Leaves ovate. Flowers whitish-green, bell-shaped, drooping, June–Aug. 3–6 ft.
V. viride. Leaves oval, up to 12 in. long. Flowers yellowish-green, borne in branching spikes, July. 2–6 ft.

VERBASCUM (*Mullein*)
Most of the species are biennial, and all but a few of the perennials are better so treated. The best are stately but old-fashioned plants with attractive green or white-woolly foliage and tall spikes of flowers. They grow well on most soils, even in dry positions, in full sun or partial shade, and flourish on chalk. Propagation is by division, cuttings or seed.
V. chaixii. Leaves green or whitish-hairy. Flowers white or yellow, with purple stamens, borne in branching sprays, June–Aug. 3 ft.
V. nigrum. Leaves ovate or oblong at base, becoming heart-shaped higher up. Flowers white, yellow or purplish, June–Oct. 2–3 ft.
V. phoenicium. Basal leaves ovate, in a rosette, upper leaves few. Flowers up to 1 in. across, borne in branching sprays, violet, pink, rose or purple, May–Sept. 2–3 ft.
Most of the named varieties have been derived from this species, the best being:
'C. L. Adams': yellow, foliage silver, June–July. 5–6 ft.
'Cotswold Beauty': biscuit, June–July. 3–4 ft.
'Cotswold Gem': rosy-amber with purple centre, June–July. 3–4 ft.
'Cotswold Queen': buff terra-cotta, June–July. 3–4 ft.
'Gainsborough': sulphur-yellow, June–July. 4 ft.
'Miss Willmott': creamy-white, June–July. 5 ft.
'Pink Domino': rosy-pink, June–July. 3½ ft.
V. thapsus (*Aaron's Rod*). Woolly and hairy. Flowers yellow, June–Aug. 2½ ft.

VERBENA
This large genus of American plants provides a few shrubs, several attractive half-hardy annuals and a few perennials hardy enough for an open border in good loamy soil and a sunny position. Propagation is by seed or for perennials by division.
V. corymbosa (perennial). Leaves dark green, oblong or ovate, toothed. Flowers heliotrope to reddish-purple, borne in dense flat heads, fragrant July–Sept. 3 ft.
(**V. bonariensis** is similar but although perennial often seeds itself to death.)
The well-known annuals (**V. × hybrida**) are derived from several species. They are good for bedding or cutting, with flowers in white, pink, scarlet, lavender or blue, summer to autumn. There are many named varieties, growing about 1 ft., also dwarf strains about 6 in. Seed should be sown Feb.–Mar. in gentle heat, pricked off and planted out.

VERONICA (*Speedwell*)
This is a large genus containing many shrubs, weedy annuals and a number of perennials of which the majority are suitable for the rock garden. They do well in a fairly good soil, in full sun. Propagation is by division.

V. longifolia (herbaceous perennial). Leaves oblong, narrow, toothed. Flowers white, blue or purplish-pink, in dense spikes, July–Sept. 2 ft. Borders.

V. teucrium (herbaceous perennial). Leaves ovate to narrow, toothed. Flowers blue, in slender spikes, July. Up to 3 ft. Borders. In addition a number of named varieties are available, most of them derived from **V. spicata** and **V. longifolia.**

'Blue Peter': Oxford-blue, compact trusses, June–Aug. 1½–2 ft.

'Erica': orchid-purple, neat spikes, June–Aug. 1 ft.

'Romily Purple': blue-violet, upright spikes, June–Aug. 1½ ft.

'Royal Blue': true blue; 'Wendy': blue, June–July. 1½ ft.

For the rock garden a number of low-growing or creeping perennials are available, often in named varieties. Most of them have been derived from **V. fruticans** and **V. prostrata** and have blue or pink flowers, between May and Sept., and grow 4–12 in. **V. cineraria** has grey foliage and pink flowers, 6 in. **V. nummularia** has blue or pink flowers and makes a neat ground cover and **V. peduncularis** has bronzy leaves and white and rose flowers.

VIOLAS PLATE 60
This large genus includes the popular violas, pansies and violets but there is no clear-cut botanical distinction between the first two. What difference exists is to be found in the more tufted, perennial habit and wider range of clear, self-coloured flowers in the viola as compared with the pansy. There is no firm agreement as to the precise derivation of the pansy, suffice it here to say that our present-day large-flowered varieties are the result of selection and hybridization of such old species as *Viola lutea*, *V. tricolor*, *V. altaica*, *V. rothomogensis*, etc., and and its history can be traced back to the sixteenth century, the period of greatest development being the early nineteenth century. Developed largely from **V. tricolor,** pansies are divided into two main groups. Show pansies with flat rounded flowers having a circular blotch and Fancies with a wider range of colours and less formal shape and blotching. Propagation is by seed sown (in pans) in June for autumn planting or Sept. for spring planting, by cuttings or layers.

To return to the viola, it can be firmly stated that the early work in its development took place between 1860 and 1870 and that the two species used as the seed-bearing parents were *V. cornuta*, a very free-flowering mauve coloured species, and *V. lutea*, yellow, these being crossed with the larger flowered pansy varieties of the day. Thus it is seen that both the pansy and viola are essentially of garden origin.

The earlier varieties of viola were marked with 'rays' or lines running to the 'eye' or centre of the flower but gradually a type of flower was developed devoid of markings or rays and today in the best forms the flowers should be of a clear colour and stout substance and with a slight perfume; the habit of the plant should be compact and tufted and free-flowering. There is also a miniature, more dainty type known as 'violetta' in which the flowers are smaller—about 1 in. across—sweetly scented and carried on good stems well above the foliage. As an example of these mention may be made of 'Blue Tit', 'Delight' (creamy-yellow), 'Tom Tit' (deep blue) and 'Yellow Bird'.

As violas do not come true from seed it is necessary that particular varieties are propagated by vegetative means. Where only limited increase of stock is required and the plants are of a good tufted habit this may be accomplished by division of the rootstock either in the late summer or early spring. The best cuttings are obtained by selecting healthy young growths springing from the base of the parent plants in the late summer or autumn. To induce a plentiful supply of such shoots, the old plants should be cut back in early Aug. The preparation of the cuttings is done in the usual way by removing the lower leaves together with the stipules and cutting through the stem cleanly immediately below a joint. The prepared cutting should be about 2½ in. in length and in some cases even shorter. If taken sufficiently early, say before the end of Aug., an outdoor bed in a semi-shaded position may be quite satisfactory but from Sept. onwards a cold frame must be provided. To provide good rooting conditions a bed of compost some 3–4 in. in depth should be given. The compost should consist of good loam, peat and sharp sand in equal parts passed through a ½-in.-mesh sieve, this being spread over the levelled surface of the frame or bed and made firm by treading down on a flat board. After firming, a sprinkling of sharp sand over the surface to trickle into the holes as the cuttings are inserted will further assist in preventing damping off during rooting. Using a short, thin dibber insert the cuttings about 2 in. apart and make quite firm by applying pressure to the base of the cutting meanwhile taking care not to cause bruising at the 'collar'. The task completed, a gentle watering with a fine-rosed can should be given and with a cold frame, the light put on and left closed until the cuttings are rooted. After-care consists of giving ample air on all possible occasions—gradually at first—ensuring that the bed does not dry out and that any damaged material is regularly removed. By early spring the light can be completely taken off and the cuttings hardened for planting out in Apr. or as soon as weather and soil conditions will allow.

Violas will grow satisfactorily in most soil types found in the average garden but heavy soils are made more suitable by the addition of well-decayed compost and, at planting time, the use of a mixture similar to that of the cutting bed around the roots will assist the young plants to become established. On hot, dry soils a semi-shaded site is desirable otherwise they will thrive best in an open, sunny position. To keep the plants growing and flowering freely seed pods should not be allowed to form but the spent flowers regularly removed. When planted as a border and any tendency to a straggling habit is seen, it is a good plan to cut back alternate plants to encourage fresh young growths.

Varieties:
- 'Avalanche' (white)
- 'Arkwright Ruby' (ruby-crimson shaded terra-cotta)
- 'Campanula Blue'
- 'Derby Bronze'
- 'King Bronze'
- 'Kingcup' (yellow)
- 'Miss Brooks' (red)
- 'Mayday' (red)
- 'Moseley Perfection' (yellow)
- 'Purple Bedder'
- and the old favourite 'Maggie Mott' (lavender-mauve)

The *Sweet Violet* (**V. odorata**) is well known for its fragant flowers, the doubles being commonly called Parma violets. Propagated by layers, cuttings, division or seed sown in autumn, they flower from autumn to spring, but the choicest varieties should be grown in a cold frame to protect the flowers in bad weather.

VIOLET CRESS. See *Ionopsidium*

VIRGINIAN COWSLIP. See *Mertensia*

VIRGINIAN STOCK. See *Malcomia*

VISCARIA. See *Lychnis* with which the genus is generally included.

VITTADINIA

A small genus of attractive perennial herbs native to Australasia. One species, **V. australis,** is useful in the rock garden and thrives in sandy loam in a shady situation. Propagate from seed. Flowers white or pink, daisy-like, Apr.–Sept. 6–12 in.

WACHENDORFIA

A genus of half-hardy, tuberous-rooted perennials native to S. Africa, sometimes grown in warm, sheltered situations in well-drained, rich sandy loam to which should be added some peat, but they must be moved into a greenhouse or cold frame for winter—propagate from seed or offsets.

W. hirsuta. Long, hairy leaves. Flowers golden-yellow, Apr.–May. 18–20 in.

W. paniculata. Flowers golden-yellow, Apr. May. 18 in.
W. thyrsiflora. Flowers yellow, Apr.–May. 20–24 in.

WAHLENBERGIA
A genus of annual and perennial plants native to S. Europe, S. Africa and F. East, some of the annual species making attractive plants for the rock garden, the perennials needing a cool greenhouse or alpine house. They thrive in a well-drained loamy soil. Propagation from seed.
W. albomarginata (perennial). Leaves with reddish-brown edges. Flowers white or blue, June. 4–8 in. A dwarf form, 1 in. high, is suitable for the alpine house.
W. hederacea (annual). Small pale blue flowers, summer. 4–8 in.

WAKE ROBIN. See *Trillium*

WALLFLOWER. See *Cheiranthus*

WATER HAWTHORN. See *Aponogeton*

WATER HORNWORT. See *Ceratophyllum*

WATER PLANTAIN. See *Pontederia*

WATER VIOLET. See *Hottonia*

WATER-LILY. See *Nuphar, Nymphaea*

WATSONIA
A genus of half-hardy bulbous plants with large tubular flowers, native to S. Africa, suitable for sunny positions in warm, sheltered borders or in a greenhouse in sandy loam with some peat. Propagate from seed or offsets in Oct.
W. ardernei. Flowers white, Sept. 3–4 ft.
W. densiflora (evergreen). Flowers rose or pink, June–July. 2–3 ft.
W. fulgens. Flowers scarlet, June–July. 2–3 ft.

WAX FLOWERS. See *Hoya*

WILD HYACINTH. See *Scilla*

WILD MARJORAM. See *Origanum*

WINDFLOWER. See *Anemone*

WINTER ACONITE. See *Eranthis*

WINTER GLADIOLUS. See *Schizostylis*

WINTERGREEN. See *Pyrola*

WOAD. See *Isatis*

WOLF'S BANE. See *Aconitum*

WONGA-WONGA VINE. See *Pandorea*

WOOD LILY. See *Trillium*

WOODRUFF. See *Asperula*

WORMWOOD. See *Artemisia*

WOUNDWORT. See *Stachys*

WULFENIA
A genus of perennial herbs native to S. Europe and W. Asia. One species, **W. carinthiaca,** is suitable for the rock garden and thrives in a shady position in well-drained, light rich soil, but should be protected from excessive winter wet. Propagation is from seed or by division. Flowers purple-blue, June–Aug. 12–14 in.

XERANTHEMUM (*Everlasting Flowers*)
A small genus of hardy annuals native to the Mediterranean. They are attractive for their rather showy everlasting flowers. They grow well in a sunny position in rich, light soil. Propagate from seed.
X. annuum. Flowers white, pink or purple, single or double, July–Sept. 18–24 in.

XEROPHYLLUM
A small genus of hardy rhizomatous perennials native to N. America. One species, **X. asphodeloides,** making an attractive border or marsh garden plant. Thrives best in moist peaty soil in partial shade. Propagation is from seed or by division. Leaves in dense cluster at base. Flowers ivory-white, in tall spikes, summer. 2–4 ft.

YARROW. See *Achillea*

YELLOW LOOSESTRIFE. See *Lysimachia*

YELLOW OX-EYE. See *Buphthalmum*

YOUTHWORT. See *Drosera*

ZANTEDESCHIA

A genus of moisture-loving perennial plants native to S. Africa, often known as Richardias or Callas. These most attractive plants are quite easy to cultivate either in a cool greenhouse or a room. Pot-up in Sept. in good rich loam. A 6-in. pot may be used for each plant, or three may be placed in a 9- to 10-in. pot. They should have ample water and occasional doses of liquid manure, and the pots may be kept standing in a deep saucer full of water. After flowering they should be planted out in rich soil, or stood in the open in semi-shade, kept moist and given occasional doses of manure-water until Sept., when the offsets should be removed and the plant re-potted and brought in (45 deg. F. winter) when the same treatment should be repeated. Propagate from suckers.

Z. aethiopica (*Arum Lily, Calla, Lily of the Nile*). Dark green, arrow-shaped leaves. Flowers white, spring. 24–30 in. Will also grow in ponds provided there is sufficient water, at least 20 in. above roots, to protect them from frost.

Z. elliottiana. Wide, roundish leaves, blotched. Flowers golden-yellow, summer. 24–36 in. Prefers slightly higher temperatures.

Z. rehmannii. Lance-like, spotted leaves. Flowers rose, pink or white, summer. 18–24 in.

ZAUSCHNERIA

A small genus of dwarf perennials native to N. America. One species, **Z. californica,** being sufficiently hardy for the rock garden in warm, sheltered positions in sandy loam. Propagate from seed in spring, division or cuttings taken in Sept. and wintered in a cool house or frost-proof frame. Flowers scarlet in loose spikes, July–Sept. 12–18 in.

ZEBRA-STRIPED GRASS. See *Miscanthus*

ZEPHYRANTHES

A genus of bulbous plants native to America, one species being sufficiently hardy to thrive in sunny positions in well-drained peaty loam with some sand but needs some winter protection. Propagate from seed or offsets in Oct.

X. candida. Leaves long, evergreen. Flowers white, often flushed rose, Sept.–Oct. 6–10 in. In the cold or cool greenhouse **Z. grandiflora** (rose-pink, June–July) and **Z. rosa** (rose, July–Dec.) may be grown in pots, being stood out of doors while growing and brought into the house for the winter.

ZINNIA

A genus of half-hardy annuals native to Mexico, growing best in a deep loamy soil. Propagate from seed sown in gentle heat in Mar.–Apr., the seedlings being pricked out and hardened off for planting in late May or early June. The numerous garden varieties have been mainly derived from **Z. elegans,** and are variously described in catalogues as 'giant', 'chrysanthemum-flowered' or 'dahlia-flowered'. They are good for cutting or bedding and have flowers in various shades of white, yellow, orange, pink, red or mauve, single or double, long-lasting over the summer. Height 1–2½ ft.

CHAPTER THIRTEEN

Lawns and their Care

FROM the small surburban garden to the large country house or public park, the lawn is one of the most important features in the general layout, providing a perfect setting for flower beds or borders. The all-seasons' effect of mown and well-tended grass is as valuable an asset in mid-winter as it is in the height of summer and amply repays all the time and care taken in its establishment and maintenance.

Grass is like any other plant in the garden; if care is not taken to cultivate it, it will soon be displaced by weeds or moss. Yet there is a tendency to assume that a lawn requires little attention other than a weekly mowing in the summer and perhaps an occasional brush over in the winter.

There are two ways of forming a lawn, by seeding and by turfing down. Each has its own advantages and drawbacks, but whichever is adopted the selection and preparation of the site is all important.

The site

It is not always possible to be as selective as one would wish in choosing the site for a lawn, but there are certain points which should always be kept in mind. A slope to the south is unsuitable because it tends to dry out too readily and leads to scorching in the summer. Such sites, if chosen, should always be brought up to a level even if this means terracing for the purpose. While soil moisture capacity is important, so equally is drainage and for this reason it may prove to be impossible to maintain a good lawn on heavy clay without a considerable outlay of time and money during construction. The establishment of the better grasses under the shade and drip of large trees is also very difficult and such sites should be avoided if possible. This does not mean that a well-placed tree must be ruled out. On the contrary, such a tree can be valuable for its general effect and for the shade it affords for sitting out in the summer. If trees cannot be avoided, the grasses must be selected accordingly and leaves must not be allowed to lie and accumulate for lengthy periods in the autumn.

Preparation and levelling

Having selected the site, the first point on which to be assured is the drainage. Grasses are shallow rooting, and deep drainage is not called for, but within the area of the roots, there must be no stagnating water. This means that on heavy clay some provision must be made for getting rid of surplus water, and in certain cases the laying of pipe drains may be necessary to achieve this. Thorough trenching of the site will generally ensure sufficient drainage, particularly if a quantity of opening material such as breeze or old ashes can be incorporated. Alternatively, a layer of ashes about 4 in. thick may be placed a foot or so below the surface of the site.

Where drainage work is called for it can be carried out in conjunction with levelling. An absolute level is not necessary for a lawn constructed for general use, but pronounced variations in surface level must be corrected. In the case of shallow soils or where considerable soil moving is called for, the top soil should first be taken off, the necessary adjustment made to the sub-soil and then the top soil replaced.

An approximate level having been obtained by means of pegs and a straight edge (see page 90), the preparation of the surface soil may be undertaken. It is wise at this stage to be assured of the quality of the top foot or so of the soil. If the soil is unsuitable it is better to replace it rather than risk complete failure, but in most cases, except for fertile garden soils, some additional manurial treatment will be needed. Light soils may be given a good dressing of farmyard manure which should be well incorporated in the top spit so as to be about 4 in. below the surface. On medium soils decayed compost or leaf-mould may be worked into the top 9 in. or a good grass fertilizer at 3 oz. per sq. yd. may be applied a week or so before sowing the seed. Lime, too, is a necessary ingredient and if deficient must be made good.

Having completed these operations, time should be allowed for natural soil settlement before carrying on farther. This time lag will also have the advantage of allowing the germination of weed seeds which can then be destroyed before sowing down the grass.

The next step will be to break down and consolidate the soil evenly by treading. For this the soil must be in such a condition that no clogging takes place. Great care is needed when dealing with heavy soils which do not usually require any treading and may indeed be damaged by too much consolidation. Following this a fine tilth must be obtained by repeated rakings and removing all stones and coarse material. The final surface should be quite firm and even before the seed is sown.

Sowing the seed

The sowing of a lawn is a job which calls for much care and attention to detail. The condition of the soil is all important; it must be dry on the surface and work well without sticking to boots or tools.

Sowing can take place either in the autumn or spring, the autumn generally giving a quicker seed germination as the soil at that time still retains a good degree of warmth. The deciding factor must be the condition of the soil, and the weather must be still, because any wind will result in the uneven distribution of the seed. Further, following a dry summer sufficient rainfall to moisten the soil well is essential before sowing is begun, but the earlier it can be done after the end of Aug. the better. If sowing is not possible before the end of Sept., it is generally best to defer the work until the spring. Early Apr. is the most suitable time for spring sowing because severe frosts are then unlikely and there will be sufficient time for the young grasses to become established before the danger of early summer drought. The rate of sowing should be liberal since the important thing is to produce a good thick sward in the shortest possible time. For this reason it is false economy to attempt to cut down on the amount of seed used, and 2 oz. per sq. yd. should be taken as the minimum rate, to be increased if weather or soil conditions are considered to be not of the best or if birds are known to be exceptionally troublesome. In any case, birds will take a certain toll of the seed and it is advisable to afford some protection. Old netting, black cotton stretched on short sticks, or twiggy branches layed lightly over the seeded area will be suitable.

The actual sowing should be as accurate as possible and this is best obtained by marking out the ground into 1 yd. squares. Perhaps the easiest way to do this is to knot two lines at 1 yd. intervals and stretch these 1 yd. apart across the site. If desired, the knots may be at 2-yd. intervals, the sowing being then adjusted to 2 sq. yd. To avoid making depressions with the feet when sowing, pieces of wood may be tied to the boots or boards used for standing on. The seed must be weighed or measured for each given area and if there is any difficulty in sowing evenly it may be mixed with twice the amount of fine dry soil to give more bulk which is generally easier to handle. Alternatively a distributor may be used.

Selection of seed

The selection of the most suitable seed for the soil and situation is important and the amateur will be well advised to place himself in the hands of a reliable firm who will advise and supply a mixture of grasses to give the best results. As a general guide the following mixtures are recommended:

For general use

30% *Festuca rubra* var. *fallax* (Chewings Fescue)
20% *Festuca rubra* var. *genuina* (Creeping Red Fescue)
30% *Agrostis canina* (Brown Bent-grass)
20% *Poa trivialis* (Rough-stalked Meadow-grass)

For shaded areas

30% *Poa nemoralis* (Wood Meadow-grass)
30% *Festuca rubra* var. *fallax* (Chewings Fescue)
20% *Festuca rubra* var. *genuina* (Creeping Red Fescue)
10% *Anthoxanthum odoratum* (Sweet Vernal-grass)
10% *Cynosurus cristatus* (Crested Dogs-tail)

For light soils

30% *Festuca rubra* var. *genuina* (Creeping Red Fescue)
30% *Poa pratensis* (Smooth-stalked Meadow-grass)
20% *Cynosurus cristatus* (Crested Dogs-tail)
20% *Anthoxanthum odoratum* (Sweet Vernal-grass)

Following sowing a very light raking is required to cover the seed and a further light treading or rolling may be given provided the surface is quite dry. Under favourable conditions growth will be seen in about 10 to 14 days and when the young grass is 1 in. or so high a light rolling will be beneficial. The first cutting should be given when about 4 in. of growth is made and for this a sharp scythe is the best tool to use but the lawn mower may be used when the grasses are well established and there is no danger of pulling them out of the ground by their roots. During this time of initial growth the roller should be used periodically and any weeds that may appear removed. At the first mowing the blades should be set 1 in. or so higher than normal and allowed to remain so adjusted for the first three or four cuttings.

Lawns from turf

There is no doubt that turfing is the quickest way to form a usable lawn, but the cost of turfing is much more than that of seeding. The turves used must be of good quality, with the grasses fine and close and free from weeds. Frequently, purchased turves are of coarse meadow grasses and weeds, quite unsuited to form the close sward so desirable in a lawn, and unless one is prepared to pay high carriage costs on turves from a good district, such as Cumberland, then any advantage over seeding may be cancelled out. Sometimes too, the grasses of imported turf may not be suited to the soil in question, and sowing with a carefully selected mixture will give better results.

The preparation of the site for turfing consists of digging over to a good spade depth and incorporating a dressing of well-rotted manure. The digging finished, the surface should be broken down to fine tilth, large stones, clods, weed roots, etc., being removed. The ground should then be rolled to an even degree of firmness, any discrepancies in the level being corrected, and finally raked over. It will then be ready for laying the turves. To ensure the best results for the following season, turfing should be done in the autumn. If put off until the spring, there is a serious risk of loss in the event of an early dry spell, or if not completely destroyed, the valuable grasses will suffer damage, leaving the coarse grasses to take over.

Turves are usually cut 3 ft. long by 1 ft. wide and 1½–2 in. thick, each turf being rolled up with the grass on the inside. As an alternative, turves may be cut 1 ft. square to make them easier to manage, but in both cases careful handling is necessary to avoid tearing and permit good laying. An even thickness in the turves is essential for good laying and although slight unevenness can be adjusted by beating down, any great variation should be corrected beforehand. For this purpose a frame 1½ in. deep is required in which the turf is placed grass side down and trimmed by passing a knife—an old scythe blade will serve the purpose—across the frame to level off inequalities. Dry turves are almost impossible to handle and it is advisable to lay them as soon after cutting as possible. If they have to be held for a time they should be kept in a cool shaded place, but rolled turves will soon deteriorate and the grass lose its colour through lack of light, so stacking should be limited to the shortest possible time.

As laying proceeds any visible weeds should be removed from the turf, the edges fitted close together and the turves bonded so that no cross joint is opposite another but central with its neighbour in the same way as a builder bonds the bricks in a wall. Turves laid diagonally across the lawn will give a better finish than if laid straight up and down. The newly laid turf should then be moderately beaten down with a turf beater to bring it in close contact with the soil and to obtain a good level. Following this, finely sifted soil should be spread over the surface and worked into the joints between the turves with a new birch broom or bush harrow if the area is a large one. Any surplus soil should be removed and the lawn given a light rolling. Autumn-laid turf is not likely to require much in the way of immediate watering but in the spring no drying out must be permitted. As with seeded lawns, the first cutting should be given with a scythe in preference to the lawn mower and, during the first season, the periodic use of the roller when conditions are suitable will help to establish the grass.

Lawn maintenance

Having gone to considerable trouble and expense in the making of a lawn there next comes the question of maintenance. Without close attention weeds will multiply, the soil will become poverty-stricken, the grasses coarse and sparse and in the end the lawn may reach the stage when re-sowing or drastic renovation is required to bring it back to condition. With the application of a few principles and the expenditure of some time and care the lawn may be kept in good green condition throughout the year.

In dealing with this subject it is a good plan to regard the year as consisting of two periods, taking the spring and summer as the period of active growth and autumn and winter as the period of rest. The latter period is perhaps the most important so far as the work of general maintenance is concerned because many lawns at the end of the summer are in poor condition, periods of drought, weekly mowings and hard usage all having contributed to the worn out appearance. As soon as the autumn rains have softened the ground, work should begin. The grass should be well swept with a stiff broom and raked over to break any mat of old grasses or moss which may have accumulated, care being taken to remove all material so loosened by a further good sweeping. The result of this, if thoroughly done, will be to give the lawn a somewhat rough appearance but this need cause no concern. After raking, the turf should be thoroughly pierced either by using the garden fork or one especially made for use on lawns. To deal with a large lawn, a spiked roller is to be recommended and this implement can be obtained with sets of tines of varying lengths to give the penetration desired. This piercing, which materially improves aeration and drainage throughout the winter, is invaluable in the management of lawns. When the forking has been completed, a dressing of a suitable proprietary grass fertilizer should be given, the fertilizer being of a slow-acting type, or the following mixture may be made up and applied at the rate of 1½ oz. per sq. yd.: 1 part steamed bone flour, 1½ parts hoof and horn meal, ½ a part sulphate of potash. On light soils superphosphate may be used in place of bone flour provided the soil is not deficient in lime. To assist even distribution the fertilizer may be mixed with sharp sand which will further benefit the lawn by encouraging the finer grasses.

In the case of lawns showing considerable growth of mosses (indicating acidity) a dressing of powdered chalk or lime at the rate of 8 oz. per sq. yd., applied in late Nov. or early Dec., will be beneficial. Lime, if allowed to lie on the surface, has a tendency to cake and this excludes air. All such dressings should be worked in by raking and sweeping as soon as applied.

In addition to the above, top dressings of finely sifted soil or compost will do much towards maintaining the lawn in good condition. A good compost for the purpose may be made by building a heap in layers of about 1 ft. thickness of soil, sand and well rotted manure, the top and bottom layers always being of soil. The soil should be of a good medium loam and the sand of a sharp coarse nature; fine sand should never be used. The ingredients should be stacked some months prior to requirements and prepared for use by screening or sifting to remove coarse material which can be set aside to form a base for the next heap. When drawing from the stack it should be chopped down vertically so that each ingredient is taken in the same proportion and the material should be well chopped up with the spade to assist screening. As a guide to quantity required, 1 cu. yd. will dress an area of 150 sq. yd. to a depth of $\frac{1}{4}$ in., and this is the maximum amount recommended for a single application. This type of dressing can be used at any time from late Oct. to mid-Feb. and two or more applications may be given during that period, provided the previous dressing has been well worked in. In the case of heavy soils the proportion of sand may be increased.

Coming to the spring season, thoughts turn first to rolling and mowing. The correct use of the roller is still not perfectly understood and it still happens that what might otherwise have been a good lawn is often damaged by the indiscriminate use of a roller. The most usual causes of trouble are that the roller is too heavy and the ground is too wet with the result that the surface cakes down and air is excluded thus nullifying the good work done throughout the winter. Rolling should be done when the lawn is on the dry side rather than wet, and the roller of such a weight that it causes no undue compaction of the soil. It is better to use a roller of moderate weight twice than a heavier implement once. The most important time for rolling is in the spring just before mowing commences as this will bring the grass roots firmly in contact with the soil and stimulate growth.

For mowing, the first and most important thing is to have a good machine and to see that it is well and suitably adjusted to cut cleanly at the correct height. It is not always understood that the lowering or raising of the front roller controls the height of the cut and that the adjustment of the blade cylinder on to the bottom plate determines the cleanness of the cut. The method of adjusting may vary with the make of machine but it should always be carried out so that the blades cut evenly along the whole length of the bottom plate. The test is to hold a piece of paper between the blades and the plate as the cylinder is slowly turned by hand, working the paper from one side to the other. If the cut is not clean for the whole width, further adjustment is required. When properly set, the cylinder should revolve freely making light contact with the plate without a pronounced clicking noise (see Chapter 1).

The start of mowing is of course governed by the season, the first cut generally being needed in early Mar. and from then on continued as necessary until growth ceases in the autumn. It sometimes happens that in a mild season growth is continued into the winter and rather than allow the grass to become long and straggly, the mower may be lightly run over the lawn when conditions are suitable. In very hot weather the cutting height should be raised since to cut closely under such conditions will result in more severe drying out and possibly scorching.

Other things to consider during the growing season are watering, feeding and the control of weeds. There is no doubt that the only satisfactory way to water a lawn is by means of a sprinkler so that water falls in very small droplets or as a fine mist. A start should be made with watering before the grass shows signs of suffering and sufficient should be given to soften and penetrate the ground. If the winter operations detailed above have been carried out fully further feeding should not be necessary during the summer, but if growth is slow in the spring, a light dressing of nitro-chalk at the rate of 1 oz. per sq. yd. may be given about mid-Apr.

The control of weeds is always a problem. There are now a number of selective weed-killers on the market which, if used correctly, are extremely effective. If used carelessly, some of them can do a great deal of damage, extending to adjacent plants and even to neighbouring gardens. The maker's instructions should be strictly followed and the greatest care should be taken in applying, choosing a still day and keeping the nose of the watering can well down so as to avoid the spray drifting and causing damage to near-by plants in beds and borders. To ensure the even distribution of any weed-killer, whether in liquid or powder form, the lawn should be marked out by the use of two lines 1 yd. or 2 yd. apart so that any known quantity can be applied to a known area. When applied, the ground should be moderately moist, and 24 hours without rain is desirable after using. The larger weeds (plantains, dandelions and daisies) are often best removed by means of a weeding fork, spring or autumn being the best time for this task. Any depressions resulting from this weeding should be filled with finely sifted soil with which a little grass seed has been mixed.

Improvement and repair

Despite care in general maintenance it does sometimes happen that the stage is reached when some drastic measures for improvement and repair become necessary. Where the turf has become very poor and weed-infested it should be stripped off and discarded. The soil can then be well cultivated to a depth of some 4 in., new top soil of good quality being added to bring it up to the necessary level. This work is best undertaken in the autumn and the ground allowed to lie rough during the winter. In the spring the surface will break down readily and, by means of raking, a good tilth can be obtained for a seed bed. The seed should be sown as previously recommended and a good lawn should result in a shorter time than that required to nurse back neglected turf into good condition. Where such drastic measures are not called for, thorough raking in the autumn, followed in the spring by a top dressing of good soil to which some grass seed has been added, will considerably improve the lawn.

Apart from general poor condition, hard wear and tear may result in bare patches and these are best dealt with by laying new turves. In this case the selected turves should be of similar grasses to the rest of the lawn. The worn area should be stripped well back into good turf so that no obvious join will be apparent when finished. The ground should be broken up a few inches deep, the surface fined down and the new turves laid so that when finished they are slightly above the surrounding level to allow for settlement.

Edges sometimes become worn or sunken and to remedy this condition the turf should be taken off to good grass, any necessary adjustment to the soil level made and the turf relaid to extend about 2 in. beyond the required edge. No cutting back should be done until the newly-laid turves are established when the final edge can be cleanly cut. Any making good necessary should be done by inserting a strip of turf between the existing lawn and the back of those newly laid.

Should any hollows or humps appear in the lawn they can be smoothed out either by lifting and levelling or, if the area is small, by cutting through the turf at suitable intervals, turning it back and adding or taking out soil as required. It is strongly recommended that where grass gets into really bad condition or moss spreads over the area, a soil analysis should be made since acid conditions may well be the cause of the trouble. In such cases a dressing of carbonate of lime or ground chalk in Nov. or Dec. at 8 oz. per sq. yd., or at the recommended rate, will be the answer. Alternatively, to rid the lawn of moss, iron sulphate may be applied, 2 lb. in 4 gal. of water being sufficient for 25 sq. yd. of surface. The dead moss should be raked out and the treatment repeated if necessary.

CHAPTER FOURTEEN

Ornamental Trees and Shrubs

ORNAMENTAL trees and shrubs can play an important part in any garden, whether large or small. Correctly selected and sited, they can form the setting or the backbone for all other development. Of the many mistakes that can so easily be made some can arise from the very fact that there is so much good material from which to choose. The main factors always to be considered are: (1) soil type and texture; (2) size of the garden and the nature of its surrounds; and (3) the habit and ultimate size (both height and spread) the selected subject will grow to.

Other considerations such as the proportion of evergreen and deciduous types to be planted, seasonal effects of flower and/or foliage, light and shade effects upon other occupants of the garden should also be thought about. In putting these into practice discrimination even to the point of ruthlessness may at times have to be exercised. Perhaps the best advice one can give is that the reader should carefully consult the classified tables at the end of this volume as a reliable guide in the selection of suitable species.

The siting of a tree or shrub should always be considered in relation to its surroundings having full regard to the visual effects. Garden space is valuable and the best use should be made of it by ensuring that the trees or shrubs planted are of the right habit and shape for the space allotted to them, will not become over-crowded or, at a later stage in their development, have to be cut back severely to keep them within bounds. Specimen planting usually at some focal point requires careful consideration, and the effect of light and shade must always be borne in mind remembering that autumn colour is most effective when seen with the light behind the viewer.

Planting

Having decided to plant trees and shrubs in the garden on the lines indicated, preparations for planting may proceed. Much depends upon the nature and condition of the soil, and it must be emphasized that initial preparation is all important for satisfactory results; no amount of after-care will make up for unsuitable soil conditions at planting time.

Old garden soils are generally sufficiently well worked and in such a state of fertility that no special cultivations are called for, but in other cases the nature of the soil and its general condition must be taken fully into account. Virgin soils and new gardens will require to be deeply dug or trenched and generously manured to bring them into condition. The treatment must, however, be varied to suit the soil texture. Heavy or clay soils will require to have their drainage and aeration improved by being deeply worked with the addition of strawy manure or other opening material such as leaf-soil. Light soils, on the other hand, require to be made more retentive of moisture and also enriched with plant foods. This means increasing their humus content by using plenty of well-rotted manure or compost. Humus acts as a sponge to absorb and hold moisture in its passage through the soil. Humus deficiency on light soils will result in the too-free passage of water and the leeching of dissolved plant foods so that the soil is left dry and impoverished and incapable of supporting good growth.

Soil preparation having been completed a start may be made with planting. A great deal of conflicting advice is too often given on the best time for planting, but there should be no difficulty if the main principles are kept in mind. The planting season commences in late Sept. and extends to mid-May and, depending on the subject in question, during this period planting may take place in all open weather provided the soil is in suitable condition. On light soils most of the evergreens can be safely planted at any time during the period mentioned. With the more difficult evergreens such as holly, arbutus and *Garrya elliptica*, which have coarser and more spreading roots, the planting season is more restricted particularly on heavy soils, the two periods late Sept. to mid-Nov. and mid-Mar. to early May giving the best results. With deciduous types the general planting season extends from leaf-fall in late Oct. to early Apr. making full allowance for suspending planting on heavy soils during the mid-winter period should the weather be bad. Light frosts need not hold up planting, but frozen lumps of soil should not be buried around the roots.

Before planting the roots should first be examined and any damaged portions removed cleanly by an upward cut with a sharp knife. The hole should be prepared large enough to accommodate the roots without cramping, the depth being regulated by noting the soil mark on the stems which indicates the depth of planting in the nursery. On firm soils the bottom of the hole should be well broken up with a fork. The tree or shrub should then be placed in position and the soil filled in all round, making it fine enough to be worked in among the roots, the tree or

PLATE 39
NARCISSUS. The variety 'Mrs. R. O. Backhouse'.

PLATE 40

NARCISSUS. The variety 'Carbineer'.

PLATE 41

PAEONIA (Paeony). A single-flowered variety with a striking centre.

PLATE 42

PETUNIA. There are three basic garden groups: "bedding" varieties, "balcony" varieties and "large-flowered" varieties.

PLATE 43

Above PLATYCODON (Chinese Bellflower). P. grandiflora is suitable for beds and borders. Below PAPAVER (Poppy), of the 'Oriental' type.

PLATE 44

PHILADELPHUS (Mock Orange). The variety shown here is 'Virginal' and is one of the best and most reliable varieties available.

PLATE 45
PORTULACA (Purslane). Excellent plants for the rock and wall garden and available in a good range of colours.

PLATE 46

PYRACANTHA (Firethorn). Produces masses of brilliant red, orange and yellow berries in the autumn.

shrub being moved gently up and down as the filling in proceeds. The soil should be firmed well by treading in and finished off by lightly pricking over the surface avoiding a smoothly trodden finish. If the soil is in such a condition as to cause 'puddling' planting must be deferred, but, except in very wet weather, it can be carried out safely if some dry soil is available for working among and over the roots, the finishing off being left until soil conditions improve. Staking may be necessary and when this is so the stake should be placed in position and driven down into firm soil before filling in.

With all plants—particularly with trees and shrubs—the right kind is all important. The experienced eye can tell at a glance whether or not any given plant is of the right type to grow away well and give the desired results. With few exceptions any tree or shrub with strong, coarse roots and little fibre should be avoided as this generally denotes that transplanting in the nursery has been neglected and establishment will be difficult. The growth of branch and twig should also be of moderate vigour and short jointed in preference to long sappy shoots. These considerations alone emphasize the importance of dealing with a reputable nursery and avoiding inferior stock, which may result in losses after planting.

With young deciduous plants it is not necessary for the soil to be contained about the roots but all evergreens move best when lifted carefully with a good ball of soil. Nurserymen will frequently send out evergreens with such a ball of soil and roots wrapped in sacking. When planting, this sacking should be left in place until the plant is in the hole and then carefully removed.

Management

No matter how carefully a tree or shrub has been transplanted it must be accepted that the roots will have suffered some damage, and although the moving took place during the dormant season the young plant will not be fully established by the start of the next growing season. Some special care may therefore be required to avoid casualties. In the case of late autumn or early winter planting an inspection should be made after heavy rains or strong winds to see that no movement has taken place which might cause dragging at the roots or water flooding round the stems. The thawing out of the ground after frosts has also a loosening effect on the soil and in all such cases re-firming should be done as soon as the ground is in a suitable condition for treading. With newly planted evergreens, particularly those in open situations, some slight protection against wind is recommended. This may take the form of wattle hurdles, wide-meshed wire netting interwoven with bracken or straw or even rush mats or old sacking tied to stakes. These will ward off strong winds which, with evergreens, can result in a withering of the leaves and a general loss of vitality to the plant as a whole.

With the coming of spring the question of watering is certain to arise and it is safe to say that no other job is more open to abuse. Mistaken kindness in this respect can lead to more trouble and result in a greater number of losses than any other cultural practice. Water should only be given when the soil is becoming too dry to yield the necessary moisture to sustain growth, and should then be given in sufficient quantity thoroughly to soak the area around the roots. Repeated light waterings are of little use and may even be harmful.

Following watering, moisture is retained for a longer period if the surface soil is lightly pricked up and given a mulch of light material such as compost, well-decayed manure or leaf-mould which will check undue evaporation but will not impede the free passage of air. This surface mulch is of particular value on heavy soils to prevent the baking and cracking which often occurs in hot weather with consequent damage to roots. Further watering may be given when necessary by pulling aside the mulch, or if water is applied direct the mulch should again be lightened up when the water has had time to soak through.

Following transplanting evergreens frequently suffer more than deciduous plants since transpiration takes place continuously through the leaves and thus there is a bigger demand on the damaged root system. There are two methods—apart from watering—which will assist in making good this moisture loss. The first is to reduce the transpiration area by cutting back some of the branches or, if this appears impracticable, the leaf surface can be reduced by partial defoliation of some of the branches. The second method consists of a fine overhead spray two or three times daily in bright or windy weather. This is more beneficial than too frequent soil waterings.

Some deciduous plants which appear to be slow to start into growth in the spring will also be helped by overhead sprayings. In all cases, however, in addition to watering and mulching, a clean weed-free area should always be kept around the base of transplanted trees or shrubs in order to give good aeration to the soil and encourage quick, healthy root development and good top growth.

A number of trees and some shrubs, notably rhododendrons, are grafted or budded on a rootstock of an inferior species and when this is the case it is important that any growths which appear below the point of union between stock and scion should be removed. If this is neglected, the choicer grafted variety will be robbed of nourishment and its growth restricted—or it may even die out altogether. This is an easy matter where top-worked standard trees are concerned since all that is required is to remove any stem shoots or ground suckers, but the inexperienced gardener may find some difficulty with shrub varieties which are worked on species having similar growth characteristics. Rhododendrons and some viburnums may be used to illustrate this point and the best procedure where foliage characters are not readily recognized is to inspect the bushes annually when in flower, sucker growths being more easily spotted at this time. All such growths must be removed at their origin since to cut them off, leaving a portion intact, is to encourage several shoots in place of one.

The training of trees and shrubs has only limited application, and in practice is more or less confined to climbing or wall plants, the furnishing of screens, arches or pergolas, the clipping of hedges or the regulation of size and shape when some conventional form is required to produce a topiary specimen. This latter form of treatment, so popular in the Victorian era, has now ceased to interest the majority of gardeners and is only found in some old-world garden or where the strictly formal meets with approval. It is not proposed, therefore, to deal with this matter in any great detail here.

The species of trees or shrubs adapted to topiary work are few, the chief being yew, box and holly. The last has only limited use for training beyond clipping into rounded or pyramidal form and even then tends to become woody or scraggy after a few years. The English yew (*Taxus baccata*) and the common box (*Buxus sempervirens*) are the best types to use for topiary work since both will withstand the hard clipping necessary to keep the desired shape. When left to themselves these trees are generally dull and uninteresting, but they can be made attractive by training. Trees for training should be planted when quite small and allowed to grow and establish themselves for a few years before any treatment begins, and unless small specimens such as balls or pyramids are the aim they should be some 4 or 5 feet high before shaping commences. The yew in particular withstands clipping so well that it can be trained to almost any form desired whether bird, animal or other design, only requiring time and patience coupled with the use of some imagination. The design having been completed over the course of a few years, strict attention to annual clipping is necessary to maintain such specimens in good condition.

An example of training for wall furnishing is that of the cordon or espalier which may be upright or horizontal as conditions dictate. This form of training is suited to such subjects as pyracantha and wisteria. The latter with its long, drooping racemes of mauve flowers and the former of particular merit for its autumn crop of red, orange or yellow fruits are both great favourites. Where wall space is limited then growth can be restricted either to upright main stems with all side shoots close pruned each year or, to furnish narrow horizontal spaces at intervals, branches can be allowed to develop where required and trained outwards, the side shoots on these again being close pruned.

Pruning

The pruning of ornamental trees and shrubs requires some thought as there is no operation less understood or more easily messed up. The art of pruning can only be correctly performed when the gardener is familiar with the growth and flowering habits of the subject in question. Without such knowledge it is undoubtedly better that no pruning should be done and the plant left to develop on natural lines rather than that its true characteristics should be marred.

Pruning has as its aims: (*a*) the alteration and improvement of shape; (*b*) the inducement of well-regulated and better growth; and (*c*) an increased production of good quality flowers and fruits.

Some shrubs, notably the evergreens, including rhododendrons, kalmias and camellias, require little or no pruning, others, if left to themselves, will soon become congested with useless shoots and if too long neglected will begin dying out in the centre from lack of air and light. In this category come some of the early-flowering shrubs such as *Spiraea arguta*, *thunbergii* and *prunifolia* and the shrubby honeysuckles. Others object to hard pruning but at the same time must be kept from becoming weak and straggling by lightly cutting back each year, the best example of this type being lavender.

In order to clarify the matter it is best to group the shrubs under two main headings: (1) those which flower on growth made during the previous season; and (2) those which flower later, on growth of the current season. The governing principle with both groups is to prune at such a time as will give the maximum time for the new shoots to grow and ripen before the next flowering season.

Group 1 may perhaps be best dealt with by sub-dividing it into those which flower very early in the season such as *Jasminum nudiflorum*, *Prunus triloba*, *Forsythia*, etc., and the main group which includes a large proportion of our most familiar shrubs. The former are best treated as soon as flowering is finished by cutting out the flowered shoots thus allowing a whole season for new growths to develop. The main group may also be pruned after flowering but can, if circumstances require, be pruned at any time during the winter or early spring. The pruning in this case is really nothing more than a judicious thinning out of the flowered wood and also cutting back any weak growths which may not have produced flowers. This cutting out will let in light and air and so encourage good strong growth for flowering next season.

A few examples may serve to illustrate the methods of pruning to be employed.

The lilac (*Syringa*) is often seen overcrowded with weak shoots giving a poor display of inferior flowers. This is because a flowered shoot frequently produces two or more growths and, if left alone, the bush becomes filled with weak wood. To remedy this condition hard annual pruning is not required, but as soon as the flowers fade, they should be removed and at the same time the weakest growths should be completely cut out to a main branch. Should overall growth and flowering be unsatisfactory, then a proportion of the flowered shoots may be cut back by one-third of their growth. By following this method a shapely bush with strong, well-regulated flowering shoots will be maintained. The deutzias provide an illustration of a shrub having a natural tendency to become choked with a mass of twiggy shoots which spoil an otherwise graceful habit. A periodic, but not necessarily an annual, thinning out will improve the growth and appearance of the plant to an unbelievable extent.

Some shrubs, such as *Philadelphus*, often wrongly termed *Syringa*, have the very accommodating habit of annually throwing up strong shoots from the base. These, if given light and air by cutting out a proportion of the older growths after flowering, will nearly always flower the next season and the bush will be kept compact in habit instead of becoming tall and straggly. Any year-old wood left unpruned will produce short lateral flowering shoots. Finally in this group mention ought to be made of the weigelas. These should be pruned annually after flowering in June, cutting out old wood and leaving new shoots untouched.

Now to consider the second group, that is, those shrubs which flower on the current year's growth. This is a comparatively small group and for this very reason an important one. Shrubs in this group may as a general rule be pruned at any time during the dormant season although the period of flowering will be influenced to some extent by the time of pruning. Thus the buddleias of the *davidii* section and the caryopteris when pruned in the winter may flower a fortnight earlier than those pruned as growth is commencing in late Mar. The severity of the pruning can be adapted to suit the size and type of bush required. While the shrub is young and room is available for development, the young growths need only be shortened to half their length, but later as the bush attains more size, all young wood may be cut back to within a few buds of the base. In this way vigorous growth will be made and strong flower spikes produced. The same remarks apply to the late flowering hydrangea, *H. paniculata*, which when hard pruned in Apr. will produce its creamy-white panicles of flowers in late Aug., up to 10 in. in length. The foregoing shrubs cannot be too strongly recommended for a late summer display.

To conclude this section on pruning it may be well to emphasize again the importance of preserving and encouraging the full natural development of the tree or shrub. There is nothing more distressing to the plant lover or those of an artistic temperament, than the sight of a mutilated tree or shrub in the garden, and nothing can show more clearly the importance of selecting suitable material for planting. Even so, and despite every care, it does sometimes happen that a tree or shrub outgrows the space available to it. Should this occur, it is seldom that the remedy can be found in hard pruning; more often it is better that the offender should be sacrificed and a more suitable subject planted in its stead. Sometimes, however, it may be found possible to move such a plant to a more suitable site in the garden.

Transplanting trees and shrubs

The transplanting of a tree or shrub after it has been established in its present position for some years can often present a number of problems but within certain limits, and provided the job is tackled correctly, quite large specimens can be successfully moved.

Any shrub which has a good fibrous root system and can be transplanted with a good ball of soil adhering can be moved after several years of undisturbed growth subject only to the weight which can be transported. There are several points to be considered in carrying out this operation, but first comes the preparation for moving. In the case of very large or valuable specimens this preparatory work is most important and should be put in hand at least one season before the actual move. Trees with a spreading root system require most preparation and the procedure is as follows.

Having decided how large a ball of soil and roots can be moved, a trench should be taken out around the tree within this distance. Any roots that are roughly chopped through should be cut back cleanly and by working under the ball any downward growing tap roots should be severed. The trench should then be filled in with fine soil rammed in firm and well watered. If the tree is not too large it can be completely circled in one operation but, to allow a greater margin of safety with prized specimens, the work may be spread over two seasons. In any case following such preparation a growing season must elapse before the move takes place. The object of the whole process is to give the tree an initial check and encourage the formation of new fibrous roots nearer the stem which will assist re-establishment in a new position. At transplanting time the shrub having been dug round and undermined, the ball of soil should be wrapped in stout sacking or matting and tied round with strong cord. To prevent cutting in and root disturbance when the cords are tightened a few pieces of thin board around the ball will be found useful. To raise and transport the shrub the next step is provide two strong boards and two logs which can be used as rollers. The boards are worked under the ball and used as levers to lift the shrub from the hole and the rollers are then brought into use to move it to the new site. Rhododendrons, kalmias, some conifers and others with a similar root system lend themselves to this form of treatment.

The time for transplanting

The time for transplanting is governed by the type of plant, i.e. deciduous plants can be moved at any time from early Oct. to Mar. but, when dealing with large specimens, the operation is best performed in the early autumn just as the leaves are about to fall. At this season the soil is still sufficiently warm to allow some renewed root action before the plant becomes completely dormant and thus it will be more ready to grow away in the spring.

Evergreen trees or shrubs, with the exception of those referred to above, are more difficult to move than deciduous types. In particular, mention should be made of the laurels, hollies and evergreen oaks, all of which have strong, rambling roots with little fibre. With these the time of moving is very important and success is most likely to follow when the transplanting is done in early autumn, say late Sept., before inactivity sets in, or by choosing a suitable period in the late spring after the risk of drying east winds has passed and before the onset of drought conditions. Such an opportunity is most likely to occur during May.

Replanting and after care

When replanting, every care must again be taken. In preparing the hole you must ensure that it is of the correct width and depth before placing the tree or shrub in position. The aim should be to plant at the same depth as before and to make allowance for spreading out the roots without cramping. As the soil is returned, it should be finely broken down and worked well among the roots, firming well by treading or ramming as the filling in proceeds. The condition and nature of the soil will decide the amount of firming necessary, a heavy or moist soil requiring less treading than a lighter soil. The planting completed a thorough watering in should be given to settle the soil and bring it in close contact with the roots. Repeated watering is not advisable and only if the soil is drying out should water be given, when it should be enough to give a thorough soaking. A daily overhead spray is more beneficial than soil watering unless conditions are really dry.

To relieve the demands on a damaged root system some shortening back of the branches is often advisable, particularly with evergreens.

Staking

To prevent movement and dragging at the roots with newly planted trees or large shrubs staking is frequently necessary. Where a central stake is to be used it should be placed in position and driven well down into firm soil before the tree is planted, but with a large ball of roots this may not be practicable and in this case the stake should be well pointed in order to avoid unnecessary damage to the roots. There are now some admirable tree ties on the market and the cost of these is well worth while. Should home ties be used precautions against cutting in must be taken. A piece of sacking or rubber tubing around the stem will be found satisfactory for this purpose. The stem must also be prevented from rubbing against the stake and to avoid this the cord should be passed separately around both stake and tree stem and crossed in the centre. By this method the tree is held rigid a short distance from the stake. If there is any danger of the top of the stake causing damage this too may be bound round with sacking or rubber.

In cases where staking cannot be satisfactorily done by a central stake, such as with a large shrub, probably the best system is that of 'tent pegging'. This consists of driving in three short pegs at regular spacings around the shrub and at some distance from the base. From each of these a stout cord or wire is passed, fixed to a suitable branch and drawn tight, thus holding it secure in each direction. The pegs, before being driven in, should be notched on the under side to hold the cords.

There are other methods of staking such as the triangular, in which three stakes are placed wide at the base, drawn in and firmly strutted at the top, to which the tree can be centrally held free from danger of rubbing. The method used must be decided on the spot according to circumstances and needs. All such staked and tied plants must be periodically inspected to ensure that no cutting in is taking place or that no soil settlement has occurred causing the ties to drag. Staking may sometimes be unsightly and care should be taken to see that the stakes are as inconspicuous as possible and that the most suitable methods are employed.

Alphabetical List of Trees and Shrubs

ABELIA
A genus of evergreen and deciduous flowering shrubs requiring a sheltered corner or the protection of a wall with a south or south-west aspect. They are of moderately fast growth with a slender, semi-arching habit; foliage smooth, dark and shiny green; dainty funnel-shaped flowers produced singly or in groups in the leaf axils along the young shoots. Abelias like an open, well-drained loam with some peat added. Prune lightly after flowering to keep in shape. The late-flowering hybrid variety **grandiflora** may have half its shoots cut back to the base each year. Propagate by cuttings of young growth in Aug. inserted in pots or beds of sandy soil in a cold frame.

A. chinensis (deciduous), also from China and of the same dimensions. Flowers white, July–Oct.

A. floribunda (evergreen), a Mexican species 4 × 4 ft. Flowers rosy-red, June–July.

A. × grandiflora (evergreen), 8 × 8 ft. Flowers flesh-pink, July to Sept.

A. schumannii (evergreen), a Chinese species 4 × 4 ft. Flowers soft mauve-pink, June–Aug.

A. triflora (deciduous), a north-west Himalayan species 8 × 8 ft. Flowers pink-white, Aug.–Sept.

ABIES (*Silver Fir*)
A group of coniferous trees native to Europe, N. Africa, N. Asia and N. America, varying in height from 30 to 150 ft. and in spread from 20 to 70 ft. In a moist climate or high rainfall areas, fast-growing; in drier districts slow and sometimes unsatisfactory. Not suited to small gardens apart from the dwarf varieties **(A. balsamea nana).** No pruning required. Propagate by seeds sown in the open in spring; dwarf varieties by cuttings or grafts taken from leading shoots. May be attacked by aphids which can be controlled by spraying with white-oil emulsions.

A. balsamea (*Balsam Fir*), 40–60 ft. × 30–40 ft.

A. concolor (*Colorado Fir*), 60–70 ft. × 40–50 ft.

A. grandis (*Giant Fir*), 80–100 ft. × 60–80 ft.

A. nordmanniana (*Caucasian Fir*), 60–80 ft. × 60–80 ft.

ABUTILON (*Indian Mallow*)
A small genus of deciduous half-hardy shrubs of slender habit and quick growth. Those mentioned will succeed in the open in the warmer counties if given the protection of a south or west wall. An open, well-drained soil is essential. Propagate by cuttings of young wood taken in summer and placed in gentle warmth.

A. megapotamicum from Brazil, dimensions 8–10 ft. × 8–10 ft. Bell-shaped hanging flowers, yellow with red calyx, July–Oct. Should be planted on high ground to set off the beauty of the flowers. Hardy only in mild regions.

A. vitifolium, native of Chile, dimensions 10–12 ft. × 10–12 ft. Bell-shaped hanging flowers, deep mauve, July–Oct.

ACER (*Maple*)
A large genus of hardy deciduous trees grown for their decorative foliage and bark effects. They are of the easiest cultivation; the Japanese varieties need light shade to prevent leaf scorch, but others thrive in an open, sunny situation in any moist but well-drained soil. No pruning is required. Propagate coloured-leaved varieties by grafting on stocks of their own species, other varieties by cuttings inserted in cold frames in late summer.

A. ginnala, a large green-leaved species giving bright autumn colour; dimensions of 10–15 ft. × 10–15 ft.

A. griseum, noted for winter bark effect; 15–20 ft. × 12–15 ft. Prefers chalk soils.

A. japonicum aureum, sturdy, bushy, golden foliage, dimensions 8–12 ft. × 8–12 ft.

A. palmatum dissectum, fine-cut, light green foliage; 8–10 ft. × 9–10 ft.
A. p. d. atropurpureum, bronze-purple foliage; 6–8 ft. × 9–12 ft.
A. p. 'Osakazuki', has vivid autumn colour; 10–15 ft. × 10–15 ft.

AESCULUS (*Horse Chestnut, Buckeye*)
This genus contains some of our most beautiful flowering trees, most of them unfortunately too large for the smaller garden. They grow quickly and are of spreading, rounded habit. Cultivate in any ordinary soil in an open sunny situation. No pruning required other than to thin out overcrowded branches. Propagate by seeds sown in Mar., shrubby species by layering or grafting.
A. × carnea (*Pink Horse Chestnut*) makes a good lawn specimen where space is available; dimensions 35–50 ft. × 25–40 ft.; flowers pink, in terminal panicles, May–June. Variety **'briotii'** 30–50 ft. × 25–40 ft.; flowers rosy-crimson, May–June.
A. parviflora, valuable late-flowering shrub from south-east United States, of upright-spreading habit; 8–12 ft. × 12–18 ft.; white flowers, July–Aug. A good specimen for the lawn.
A. pavia (*Red Buckeye*), a somewhat rare shrubby species from southern United States; 8–12 ft. × 8–12 ft.; flowers deep reddish-pink when open (they frequently remain partially closed), early June.

AILANTHUS ALTISSIMA (GLANDULOSA) (*Tree of Heaven*)
A Chinese species with long palm-like leaves turning rich gold in the autumn. A fast-growing deciduous tree thriving in most districts (including towns); dimensions 50–80 ft. × 40–50 ft. Of upright habit, it can be maintained in shrub form by cutting to the ground in spring when it will produce leaves 3–4 ft. long. Cultivate in ordinary soil in an open, sunny situation. No pruning necessary unless treated as above. Can be propagated by root suckers placed in a frame in Aug.

AKEBIA
A small genus of climbing plants only two of which are hardy. Natives of China and Japan, they are best suited to a south-east or west aspect. Useful for arches and pergolas where they attach themselves by twining stems. Cultivate in ordinary fertile soil. Prune by cutting out unwanted growth in the spring. Propagate by cuttings of firm wood in gentle heat or by layering.
A. lobata. A deciduous tree which bears clusters of brownish flowers in Apr., followed by large purple fruits if flowers escape frost damage.
A. quinata. Evergreen in mild seasons only. Purplish, scented flowers, May.

ALDER. See *Alnus*

ALDER BUCKTHORN. See *Rhamnus*

ALMOND. See *Prunus*

ALNUS (*Alder*)
Deciduous catkin-bearing trees and shrubs. They thrive best in moist situations and can be very attractive by the waterside. All are best propagated by seed but some garden varieties may be grafted. Cuttings are uncertain of rooting.
A. glutinosa is not recommended for garden cultivation. Its variety **imperialis,** with deeply cut pinnate leaves, is more effective but of somewhat ungainly habit; it may reach a height of 40 ft. with a spread of 25 ft.
A. incana (*Grey Alder*), native to Europe, is a very hardy tree and useful for planting in cold wet places. There are several varieties of this species the best of which are: **aurea,** with golden leaves and shoots; **incisa** (*A. acuminata*) described as the handsomest of cut-leaved alders; **ramulis coccineis,** notable in the spring for its red twigs, buds and catkin scales. The rough dimensions of these trees are 40–60 ft. × 20–30 ft.

AMELANCHIER (*Snowy Mespilus*)
A genus of deciduous shrubs and small trees, natives of Europe, Asia and N. America. They are of graceful habit, bear pure white flowers in great profusion in early spring, and have beautifully coloured foliage in the autumn. Cultivate in an open sunny situation in light but moist

soil. Prune by thinning out when necessary, after flowering. Propagation by seeds or layers is best.

A. canadensis, a small, shapely tree with a rounded head; 20–30 ft. × 20–30 ft.; may also be successfully grown as a shrub. In Apr. it is a foaming mass of white flowers and in autumn a brilliant foliage effect.

A. × grandiflora, probably the finest amelanchier for garden decoration in the spring and also for brilliant autumn colour. Grow either as a small tree or in bush form.

A. ovalis vulgaris, a low, compact tree of 15–20 ft.

AMERICAN LAUREL. See *Kalmia*

AMERICAN MOUNTAIN ASH. See *Sorbus*

ANDROMEDA POLIFOLIA (*Bog Rosemary*)

A dwarf evergreen shrub only 12 in. or so in height, native to N. Europe and Britain, thriving in moist, peaty soil. Heathlike in character with urn-shaped, nodding, waxy pink flowers produced in May. May be grown in loamy, lime-free soil if ample moisture is provided. No pruning required. Propagation best carried out by division. See *Pieris.*

ARALIA CHINENSIS (A. ELATA) (*Chinese Angelica Tree*)

A hardy deciduous shrub generally seen at its best in milder coastal districts. Although it may grow up to 25 ft. high its habit of sending up suckers to form stout branches makes it a shrub. It has large pinnate leaves, the stems are well armed with spines, and the small whitish flowers produced in Aug. form a large panicle. There are two variegated forms cultivated, white and golden-edged foliage types, **albo-variegata** and **aureo-marginata** respectively. Cultivate in any ordinary well-drained soil. No pruning required. Propagation by means of small suckers, potted and established in warmth.

ARAUCARIA (*Chile Pine, Monkey Puzzle*)

Only one species of this coniferous tree, **A. imbricata,** is suitable for outdoor cultivation. Cultivate in an open position in well-drained loamy soil. No pruning required. Rather slow-growing, but reaches an eventual height of 40–70 ft. with a spread of 40–60 ft. and is therefore not recommended for smaller gardens. Propagate by seeds sown under glass.

ARBUTUS (*Strawberry Tree*)

A group of evergreen trees and shrubs, three of which are worthy of note for garden cultivation. Average dimensions 15–25 ft. × 15–20 ft. Grow in a warm, sunny and sheltered position on a moist, well-drained loam. Trim long shoots as required in Apr. to maintain shape. Propagate by seed sown in a frame. They are not easy to transplant and should be grown in pots until ready for permanent positions. Give slight protection until established.

A. × hybrida, of the same flowering and fruiting habits as **A. unedo,** but fruit smaller.

A. menziesii, native of California; white, scented flowers in May followed by orange-coloured fruits. This beautiful tree should be more widely planted.

A. unedo from S.W. Ireland and the Mediterranean regions. A shrubby, low-forking tree or shrub. Clusters of pinkish, pendent flowers produced from Oct. to Dec., the strawberry-like fruits which follow ripen the next autumn.

ARCTOSTAPHYLOS UVA-URSI (*Bearberry*)

A small, evergreen, trailing shrub with small, roundish leaves and native to the north temperate regions. Produces white flowers in Apr. and May. It inhabits peaty, moorland districts and therefore dislikes lime in the soil. Easily propagated from cuttings.

A. alpina (now included in the genus *Arctous*), native to Europe, including the mountains of North Scotland, has no particular merit as a flowering or fruiting plant but makes a pleasant low tuft of foliage which in most autumns turns a brilliant red.

ARISTOLOCHIA (*Birthwort*)

A small genus of deciduous, fast growing, climbing plants, adapted to any aspect and suitable for walls, arches and pergolas. They like a good loamy soil. Prune by thinning out as required in the spring. Propagate by division or by cuttings inserted in gentle warmth.

A. durior (sipho) (*Dutchman's Pipe*). The common name aptly describes the flowers which, opening in June, are yellow and brown, long, tubular and bent upwards. The large, bright green, heart-shaped leaves make this a striking foliage plant. This is the best known species and is a native of the eastern United States.

A. moupinensis, native of W. China, with large heart-shaped leaves, downy beneath; flowers produced in June are wide, tubular, yellowish green with purple markings.

ARUNDINARIA (*Bamboo*)

A genus of upright-growing, reed-like plants. All bamboos like a moist deep soil and should be planted in a position sheltered from north and east winds. Propagate in Apr. or May by means of division of the rootstock. They are slow to establish and should be given some shelter at first. Dead canes and any not required should be cut out in Apr. All bamboos are grown for their foliage. For convenience the following are listed under the Arundinaria, where a later classification is recognized this is given in brackets.

A. anceps (15 ft.), **A. auricoma** (*Pleioblastus viridistriatus*) (2 ft.), **A. fastuosa** (*Semiarundinaria fastuosa*) (20 ft.), **A. nitida** (*Sinarundinaria nitida*) (10 ft.), **A. palmata** (*Sasa senanensis*) (8 ft.), **A. simoni** (*Pleioblastus simonii*) (15 ft.), **A. veitchii** (*Sasa veitchii*) (1½–2 ft.)

ASH. See *Fraxinus*

AUCUBA (*Spotted Laurel*)

Asiatic evergreen shrubs. They grow to some 8 ft. high and are well suited to shady places and town gardens. Habit, bushy and spreading up to 7 ft.

A. japonica, variegated Japanese laurel. There are several slightly different forms of this species, e.g. **luteo-carpa** (*dentata fructu-alba*) with small leaves and yellowish fruits.

A. j. concolor (*viridis*), bright glossy green foliage.

A. picturata (*picta*) with green leaves conspicuously margined with yellow, and **salicifolia,** distinctive by reason of its narrow, sharply pointed leaves.

AZALEA (*Rhododendron*)

Following the older and still popular classification, azaleas are here treated separately although they are properly species of RHODODENDRON. Among the chief types are the **mollis** and **mollis sinensis,** which are deciduous with large, open flowers produced in May before the leaves expand. They may reach a height of some 6 ft. but are slow-growing. The Ghent and rustica hybrids (deciduous), flowering about ten days later than the above just as the leaves are opening, are sweetly scented, reach a height of 8 ft. or more, and many have brightly tinted foliage in the autumn.

There are a large number of hybrids which flower from May to June, dwarf and spreading in habit, with an average height of 3 ft. There are two fine strains known as the *Exbury* and *Knaphill* varieties, having been raised and selected on these establishments. The other group, often called Japanese azaleas, include the popular *Kurume* varieties. These are evergreen, in the general height range of 2½–4 ft. wide spreading from 4–6 ft., and flowering in Apr. and May—some lasting into June. There is probably a wider range of colours among the azaleas than among any other group of shrubby plants.

All the azaleas grow best in moist situations in semi-shade. Whilst liking peat, they succeed in any loamy lime-free soil. Pruning consists of shaping as required.

Propagate by means of layering in the summer or by cuttings taken just as the wood is ripening in July. A close frame or slight bottom heat provide the best means of rooting. The *mollis* and *sinensis* varieties are suited for grouping in shrub borders or in beds by themselves; the *Ghent* and *rustica* varieties for the thin woodland, and other types in beds or borders or on the rock garden. Good varieties of each group are: **mollis**—'Afterglow', bright rosy-red; 'Altaclarense', orange-yellow; 'Hugo Koster', orange-salmon; 'Mrs. L. J. Endtz', clear yellow. **Ghent** and **rustica** varieties—'Brazil', reddish-orange; 'Gloria

Mundi', vermilion; 'Pink Beauty', 'Vulcan', brick red.
Evergreen varieties—'Alice', salmon-red; 'John Cairns', blood-red; 'Naomi', rose-pink; 'Sakata', fiery-red. 'Hinomayo', salmon; 'Ima Shojo', bright red; 'Princess Maud', rose-pink, and many others. For the greenhouse **R. simsii** and varieties.
In a dry season azaleas may be attacked by thrips or red spider, and these may be controlled by spraying as soon as the pest is seen with a white-oil emulsion or liquid derris. The roots and lower stems may also be attacked by a bacterial disease known as crown gall. The plants should be examined on arrival and any galls removed with a sharp knife. This disease is a soil infection and, unless severe, is seldom damaging to the plant.

AZARA MICROPHYLLA

This is the hardiest of a small genus of evergreen plants from Chile and is useful for walls with a south or west aspect where it will furnish a large area. The flowers begin opening in Feb., have a vanilla-like fragrance, and although minute completely smother the branches. They are followed by small red fruits. The small leaves and frond-like arrangement of the branches give this shrub a most elegant appearance. Cultivate in ordinary fertile soil. Prune as required in Apr. to keep wall furnished. Propagate by cuttings of ripened wood in gentle warmth.

BACHELOR'S BUTTONS. See *Kerria*

BALSAM FIR. See *Abies*

BAMBOO. See *Arundinaria*

BAY LAUREL. See *Laurus*

BEAR BERRY. See *Vaccinium*

BEARBERRY. See *Arctostaphylos*

BEAUTY BUSH. See *Kolkwitzia*

BEECH. See *Fagus*

BERBERIDOPSIS CORALLINA

An evergreen climbing plant, native to Chile, with coral-red flowers produced from July to Sept. It should be given an east or west aspect and even then may not prove completely hardy except in mild districts. It requires a good deep, loamy soil and little pruning other than to keep the wall furnished. Propagate by cuttings of half-ripened wood in warmth or by layers.

BERBERIS

A large genus of evergreen and deciduous flowering shrubs, noted for their autumn foliage and fruits. Plant evergreens in Mar., Apr. or in the early autumn, and deciduous types from Nov. to Mar. in open, well-drained soil. Thin out growth to prevent overcrowding after flowering in the spring or in winter after fruiting. The species may be propagated by seeds and the hybrids, of which there are many, by cuttings or layers.
Some of the best species and varieties available are:
'Buccaneer', deciduous, of upright habit, orange-yellow flowers in July, followed by a heavy crop of large coral-red fruits and brilliant autumn foliage; dimensions 6–8 ft. × 5–7 ft.
B. darwinii, evergreen, with masses of orange-yellow flowers Apr.–May, followed by purplish-blue fruits; dimensions 8–9 ft. × 8–9 ft.
B. dictyophylla
deciduous, of graceful habit with long slender stems showing a whitish bark in the winter. The pale yellow flowers produced in May are followed by bright red fruits. It reaches a height of some 6 ft. with a spread of 5–6 ft.
B. × stenophylla, evergreen, bearing cascades of orange-yellow flowers in Apr. and May on gracefully arching branches; reaches a size of 8–10 ft. × 10–12 ft. This is one of our most striking flowering shrubs. 'Pirate King', deciduous, flowering in early July, orange-yellow, and especially recommended for its fiery-red fruits and brilliant autumn foliage; dimension 5–6 ft. × 5–6 ft.
B. thunbergii, deciduous, of note for its fresh green spring foliage and brilliant autumn colour which is unsurpassed by any other berberis, but not of special flowering merit. Broad

and bushy in habit; dimensions 6–8 ft. × 7–9 ft. **B. vulgaris** is attractive both in May when in blossom and later in the year when laden with coral-red berries.

BETULA (*Birch*)
Graceful deciduous trees, their chief garden value being in their elegant habit and silvery trunks. The birches thrive on the poorest of soils in any open sunny position. No pruning required. Propagate by seed or grafting.
B. maximowicziana, a native of Japan with larger leaves than any other species. The bark is smooth, at first orange-brown and later turning whitish-grey. Very hardy and quick-growing to a height of some 60 ft.
B. papyrifera (*Paper Birch*); this tree from N. America forms a rather thin, open head of semi-hanging branches. 60 ft. in height. The bark of the trunk is very white and peels away in thin, papery layers.
B. pendula (verrucosa) (*Silver Birch*), the well-known native species, of elegant drooping habit and silvery trunk; the best for normal purposes. Average height 40 ft. **B. pendula youngii** (*Young's Weeping Birch*), an extremely elegant tree very suitable for small gardens, of perfect weeping habit and slender growth; seldom exceeds 30 ft. in height.

BIGNONIA. See *Campsis*

BIRCH. See *Betula*

BIRTHWORT. See *Aristolochia*

BLACKBERRIES. See *Rubus*

BLADDER NUT. See *Staphylea*

BLADDER SENNA. See *Colutea*

BLUE BERRY. See *Vaccinium*

BLUE SPIRAEA. See *Caryopteris*

BOG ROSEMARY. See *Andromeda*

BOX. See *Buxus*

BRAMBLE. See *Rubus*

BROOM. See *Cytisus*

BROOM. See *Genista*

BRUCKENTHALIA SPICULIFOLIA
A dwarf evergreen shrub native to E. Europe and Asia Minor. Rarely exceeding 6–8 in. in height and therefore suitable for the rock garden. It is a member of the heath family and prefers a light peaty soil. The bell-shaped rose-pink flowers are borne in June and July.

BUCKEYE. See *Aesculus*

BUCKTHORN. See *Rhamnus*

BUDDLEIA
A genus of deciduous plants suitable for small gardens. Buddleias flourish in a deep, well-drained soil in sunny but sheltered situations. In many gardens they are overgrown and much neglected. All those of the **davidi** group should be hard pruned in Mar. by cutting the seasonal growths back to within a few inches of the old wood. **B. globosa** requires only that some of the flowered wood should be cut out when flowering is finished. **B. colvilei** also should be hard pruned in the spring. The buddleias root freely from cuttings taken in the late summer and placed in a cold frame.
B. alternifolia, a beautiful shrub or small tree for the lawn. Of pendulous habit and free flowering it makes a lovely picture in June when its soft purple flowers are open. This species, introduced from China, should be pruned after flowering by cutting out any flowered shoots that can be spared.
B. colvilei: unfortunately this species, from the Sikkim Himalayas, is too tender for outdoor cultivation except in the milder parts of the country, where it should be grown on a south wall. It is the largest flowering of all the buddleias, the pendulous terminal panicles produced in June being 8 in. long. The individual flowers are bell-shaped and rosy-crimson in colour.
B. davidi, from central and west China, has a number of fine varieties: 'Empire Blue', 'Fascination' (light pink) 'Royal Red' (purplish-red) and 'White Profusion'. These are of upright habit and if pruned as described will reach an average size of 6–7 ft. × 8–9 ft.
B. globosa, semi-evergreen, with sweet-

scented ball-like orange flowers May–June; dimensions 10–12 ft. × 10–12 ft.

BUPLEURUM FRUTICOSUM
An evergreen shrub some 4–5 ft. high with a spread of 5–6 ft., native of S. Europe, with an open, loose branching habit. It is only hardy in the milder districts or in sheltered positions. It has a long blooming season from July to Sept.; individual flowers small, yellow, in a terminal umbel 3–4 in. across. It is a good shrub for growing on chalk soils.

BUSH HONEYSUCKLE. See *Weigela*

BUTCHER'S BROOM. See *Ruscus*

BUXUS (*Box*)
Well-known evergreen shrubs or small trees, most accommodating in their requirements, being perfectly hardy and growing on any type of soil.

B. sempervirens (*Common Box*) will make a tree up to 20 ft. high and thrives well on chalk soils. Two varieties are worth noting: **B. s. elegantissima,** dwarfer in habit than the type and having silver striped leaves, and **B. s. handsworthii,** strong-growing up to 18 × 18 ft. Compact when young but spreading with age.

CALIFORNIAN LILAC. See *Ceanothus*

CALIFORNIAN MOCK ORANGE. See *Carpenteria*

CALLICARPA GIRALDIANA
A choice deciduous Chinese shrub forming a bush 5–6 ft. high and of upright growth, bearing purple flowers in July followed by masses of purple-blue fruits. The foliage turns a unique rosy-purple, making this a striking autumn plant. Requires a good soil and a sheltered situation. Propagate by cuttings in gentle warmth.

CALLUNA (*Scottish Ling, Heather*)
An evergreen shrub closely allied to the ericas. The species **C. vulgaris** is the shrub that spreads over so many acres of mountain, moor and common. There are many good cultivated varieties of which a selection is given below. Callunas thrive best on poor lime-free soil with peat added. They are most useful for mass planting and can also be used for grouping in beds or borders or on the rock garden. To keep the plants well furnished and neat, clip them over in Apr. before growth begins. Propagate by cuttings taken in July or Aug., inserted in sandy soil in a frame; or the roots may be divided in the autumn or spring. The flowering period is Aug. and Sept.

C. hammondii, a good white-flowering variety with bright green foliage; 'H. E. Beale', the best double-flowered calluna, with long spikes of mauve flowers (these two varieties are also roughly 3 × 2 ft.); 'Mullion', 2 × 3 ft., a free-blooming variety of spreading habit, with deep pink flowers; 'J. H. Hamilton', dwarfer in habit, 1½ × 2 ft., with rich double pink flowers.

C. vulgaris alportii, of upright habit, 3 × 2 ft. with crimson flowers; 'Barnett Anley', a compact erect-growing variety recently introduced, of similar dimensions to the above and producing 6-in. spikes of mauve-purple flowers.

CALYCANTHUS
A genus of N. American shrubs, deciduous in habit and with fragrant flowers. Cultivate in good fertile soil, well drained. Prune by shortening back the young growths after flowering. Best suited to wall culture and will succeed in any aspect, including north. Propagate by layers or cuttings.

C. floridus (*Carolina Allspice*), small reddish-purple flowers produced in June.

C. praecox. See *Chimonanthus praecox* (*fragrans*)

CAMELLIA
Beautiful evergreen shrubs more hardy than is generally thought. Given shelter from north and east winds and a light shade during hot summer days, even when not in flower they are most attractive evergreens. While they do not like lime in any quantity, they will grow well on soil with a pH range of 4·5 to 6·0, provided they are well supplied with humus. Established plants in particular benefit from an annual or biennial mulch of well-rotted manure. On

heavy soils a liberal quantity of peat or leaf-soil should be worked in prior to planting.

There are various methods of increasing stock of camellias. The species, where they produce seed, may be propagated by sowing the seed as soon as it is ripe in small pots filled with a peaty compost with silver sand added. The seed will germinate in the spring and grow fairly quickly. The young seedlings should be potted singly when very small, before the fleshy roots become entangled and broken while being handled. Apart from seed-sowing in the case of species, cuttings are the best means of propagation. The cuttings should be taken from healthy plants in late July. Select the current season's growth which is just beginning to ripen. Such shoots can usually be pulled off with a heel and require little or no trimming. Insert the cuttings around the edge of small pots and place in a close case with slight bottom heat, where they will root in about 8 to 10 weeks. It should be emphasized that the type of cutting has much to do with the time taken to root—if it is too hard several months may elapse before rooting. The method of leaf-bud cuttings has been dealt with in the chapter on propagation.

Camellias well grown in the open are seldom subject to attack by pest or disease. The occasional appearance of scale or caterpillar can be dealt with by an application of white-oil emulsion or liquid derris.

C. japonica 'Adolphe Audusson', semi-double red; **C. j. elegans,** pink splashed white, 'Lady Clare', semi-double rose-pink; **C. j. mathotiana rosea,** large double pink.

For Nov. flowering and growing on a north wall there are **C. sasanqua** 'Crimson King', 'Showa-no-sakae', double pink, and 'Toro-Noyo', single pink.

C. × williamsii var. 'J. C. Williams', clear pink, single; 'Donation', a beautiful large-flowered semi-double, soft pink; and 'Mary Christian'.

CAMPSIS (*Trumpet Flower*)

Deciduous climbers. Grow in good loamy soil. Prune in spring by cutting out unwanted growths. Propagate by cuttings of ripened wood in autumn placed in slight bottom heat.

C. grandiflora (*Scarlet Trumpet Vine*) from Japan, bearing pendent clusters of orange-scarlet flowers in Sept.

C. radicans (*North American Trumpet Flower*), orange-red flowers in Sept. Both these species should be given a south wall.

CANADA TEA. See *Gaultheria*

CARAGANA (*Pea Tree*)

Hardy deciduous shrubs, natives of Siberia. These are among the most adaptable of shrubs, thriving in any ordinary light soil on dry banks, in open positions. Little pruning is required other than the removal of dead wood. Propagate by seeds sown in the open or by layering. Dimensions 9 × 9 ft.

C. arborescens, yellow pea-like flowers in abundance in May and attractive fern-like foliage.

C. a. lorbergii, of graceful arching habit inferior to the type in flowering but remarkable in foliage, Can be cut back to old wood each spring to give improved habit.

CAROLINA ALLSPICE. See *Calycanthus*

CARPENTERIA CALIFORNICA (*Californian Mock Orange*)

An evergreen flowering shrub bearing a profusion of fragrant, pure white flowers with showy yellow stamens from July to Oct. Usually requires a sheltered position at the foot of a south-west or west wall where, given slight protection in severe weather, it will grow to a height of some 8 ft. Plant in good loamy soil. Prune out weak wood after flowering. Propagate by cuttings of soft wood in Apr. or May inserted in a close frame, or layer Aug.–Sept.

CARPINUS (*Hornbeam*)

Hardy deciduous trees which grow well in almost any soil type in open sunny positions. No pruning required. Propagate by seeds, or by grafting the varieties on to the common hornbeam.

C. betulus makes a tree with dimensions of 50 × 50 ft.

C. b. fastigiata (*pyramidalis*), an erect-branching tree, good for restricted spaces.
C. b. incisa has similar dimensions and deeply cut foliage.
C. b. pendula is an elegant weeping form.

CARYOPTERIS (*Blue Spiraea*)
Deciduous shrubs, native to China and Japan, with average dimensions of 4–5 ft. × 5–6 ft. Cultivate in light open soil in a sunny position. Prune young shoots to within a few inches of the old wood in Mar. Propagate by cuttings of soft wood taken in Apr.–May and inserted in a close frame, or by half-ripened shoots in Aug.
C. × clandonensis 'Kew Blue' is undoubtedly the best of the blue spiraeas; it is spreading and bushy in habit, and the rich blue flower spikes are produced in Sept. and Oct.
C. incana (*mastacanthus*) is a species with soft blue flowers, somewhat later-flowering than the above.
C. tangutica, violet-blue flowers in Aug. and Sept.

CASSINIA FULVIDA
An evergreen shrub native to New Zealand and the hardiest of a small genus. Yellowish foliage and a heath-like appearance. The flowers produced from July to Oct. are small, numerous and creamy-white. It forms a dense bush up to 5 ft. in height and about the same in spread. This shrub grows well in loamy or peaty soil, requires little pruning. Easily propagated by cuttings inserted in a close frame in late summer.

CATALPA BIGNONIOIDES (*Indian Bean Tree*)
A fine deciduous tree native to N. America, in habit low-forking and wide-spreading. Rarely reaches more than 10 ft. or so in height unless care is taken to take up a 'leader'. It has a spread of 30 ft. or more and will add character to any garden where space can be found for it. It bears large clusters of white flowers spotted with yellow and purple in July and Aug. There is a golden-leaved form, **C. b. aurea,** which is strikingly attractive. Catalpas appreciate generous soil treatment and an open sunny position not too exposed to wind. Little pruning is required. Propagation for the green-leaved form is best by seeds, for the golden form by cuttings of moderately firm wood inserted in gentle warmth in July or Aug.

CAUCASIAN FIR. See *Abies*

CEANOTHUS (*Californian Lilac*)
A genus of hardy and half-hardy evergreen deciduous shrubs native to N. America. In general the evergreen types may be regarded as half-hardy, the deciduous types as hardy. A warm well-drained soil is essential. The hardy deciduous varieties may be grown as bushes in the open, the less hardy evergreens being best on a wall facing south or west. Prune the later summer-flowering varieties in Apr. by cutting back the seasonal growth to within a few inches of the base. The spring and early summer flowering varieties should be pruned after flowering. Most varieties can be propagated by cuttings taken in July and Aug. and inserted in a close frame.
C. × burkwoodii (*evergreen*), deep blue flowers June to July.
C. dentatus, bright blue, May to June, **C. ×** 'Delight', rich blue flowers May. Deciduous varieties include **C. ×** 'Gloire de Versailles', powder blue, June–Oct., **C. ×** 'Henri Desfosse', deep violet, June to Oct., **C. ×** 'Topaz', rich blue, June to Oct. The last three varieties are of an average height of 10 ft. with a spread of 12 ft. when grown in shrub form. The first three are well suited for growing on walls with a south or west aspect.

CEDRUS (*Cedar*)
These trees grow up to 100 ft. in height, with a spread of 50–65 ft.
C. atlantica (*Mt. Atlas Cedar*), upright and spreading with green foliage.
C. a. glauca, with blue-green foliage.
C. deodara (*Deodar*), graceful drooping branches and soft green foliage.
C. libani (*Cedar of Lebanon*), a stately tree with horizontal spreading branches and green foliage. There are two dwarf cedars suitable for the rock garden, **C. libani pendula,** distinguished by its long needles and graceful habit, and **C. libani nana,** of rounded bushy habit. Both are slow-growing, reaching an eventual height

of some 6 ft., the former with a spread of 10 ft. and the latter of 6 ft.

CELASTRUS ORBICULATUS

A deciduous climbing plant. Suitable for any aspect and of value for its brilliant gold and scarlet fruits and yellow autumn foliage. No pruning is required other than as dictated by space. Seeds afford a ready means of propagation and a deep loamy soil will give the best results.

CERATOSTIGMA WILLMOTTIANUM

A deciduous shrub up to 4 ft. high from China, valuable for its late flowering—July to Oct. The terminal flower heads are a beautiful plumbago-blue. Its habit is upright, with a spread of about 4 ft. The woody stems frequently die to the base and should be cut hard back in late Mar. Any open situation in ordinary fertile soil suits this plant. It is easily propagated by cuttings of the young basal shoots taken as soon as they are available and inserted in a close frame.

CERCIS (*Judas Tree*)

A small genus of plants the best known of which is the S. European species **C. siliquastrum.** It forms a bushy low-branching tree up to 20 ft. in height with a spread of 18 ft. Its most distinguishing feature is its habit of producing flowers all along the old wood of branches and even the trunk. The blossoms are pea-like and open in May and June, making the tree a mass of rosy-purple. Transplanting should be done while the plants are quite small and is best carried out in May, since the fleshy roots are liable to decay if moved when dormant. A good loamy soil is appreciated. Propagation is by means of seed (usually imported). Prune only to maintain shape.

CERCIDIPHYLLUM JAPONICUM

A deciduous tree from China and Japan. In favourable positions it will grow up to 30 ft. high with a spread of 18 ft. The leaves, which are fine-textured and heart-shaped, turn a brilliant red in the autumn. It succeeds on any soil type but it is necessary that it should be planted in a sheltered position to preserve its autumn beauty.

CHAENOMELES (*Quince*) PLATE 8

A group of deciduous flowering shrubs from China and Japan. Ordinary fertile soil in semi-shade seems to suit these shrubs best. They may be planted in the open border, against a wall or to furnish a low balustrade. Pruning consists of thinning out the growths after flowering and spurring back young shoots to three or four basal buds. Cuttings of most varieties will root well in a close frame in the autumn.

The following are varieties of the species **C. japonica** and flower during Mar. and Apr. (average height 8–10 ft.): 'Boule de Feu' (rich red); 'Falconet Charlot' (deep pink); 'Hever Castle' (salmon-apricot); 'Rowallan Seedling' **(deep rosy-crimson). C. × 'Knaphill Scarlet'**, 7 ft., is one of the best varieties.

C. simonii, a rich blood-red form of low-spreading habit. $2\frac{1}{2} \times 4\frac{1}{2}$ ft.

CHAMAECYPARIS

One of the two related types of Cypress, the other coming under the **Cupressus** genus. A hybrid between them, **Cupresso-cyparis leylandii**, is now a popular choice for making a quick-growing hedge. To make a hedge it must be clipped once it has reached the desired height. **Chamaecyparis lawsoniana** (*Lawson's Cypress*) is a beautiful tree, the blue varieties **fletcheri** (10 ft.) and **ellwoodii** (a fine slow-growing form) being suitable for small gardens. There are a number of dwarf cultivars for the rock garden, such as **lutea nana**, a golden variety. Of the **Cupressus** species, **C. macrocarpa aurea** grows 15–20 ft. If used for hedging it must be well clipped. See also p. 111.

CHERRIES. See *Prunus*

CHIMONANTHUS PRAECOX (FRAGRANS) (*Winter Sweet*)

A deciduous wall shrub native to China. The flowers are produced on bare wood from Nov. to Mar.: they are greenish-yellow in colour and very fragrant. Prune early in Mar. by shortening back very strong shoots and removing weaker growths and any that may cause overcrowding. Cuttings are difficult to strike, so seeds and layers offer the best means of propagation.

CHIONANTHUS (*Fringe Tree*)
Deciduous shrubs or small trees. They like a moist soil of good quality and an open situation. Prune by thinning out as required after flowering. Propagate by seeds (imported) or by layers.

C. retusus, somewhat shorter but of more spreading habit, white flowers in erect panicles during June and July; 6–8 ft. × 8–10 ft.

C. virginicus, a shrub of good habit from N. America with large leaves up to 8 in. long and fragrant pure white flowers in June in loose, large panicles; dimensions 8–12 ft. × 10–12 ft.

CHOISYA TERNATA (*Mexican Mock Orange*)
A half-hardy evergreen shrub from Mexico bearing clusters of sweetly scented white flowers in May. Bushy and rounded in habit with dimensions of 8 × 8 ft. In mild coastal districts it succeeds in the open but elsewhere requires a sheltered position at the foot of a north, south or west wall. It prefers a rather light moist soil, requires no pruning. Propagated by hard-wood cuttings in a cold frame or short, half-ripened shoots in gentle warmth.

CINQUEFOIL. See *Potentilla*

CISTUS (*Rock Rose*)
Evergreen flowering shrubs not quite hardy in all districts. The cistus' succeed best on poor dry soils where they are less likely to succumb to frost. Little pruning is required, but to keep them well furnished some of the shoots should be pinched lightly as they grow. They can be propagated by seeds, or cuttings taken in the late summer and struck in mild heat.

C. × corbariensis, flowers white with yellow base, produced in June. Dimensions 3½ × 6 ft.

C. crispus, flowers purplish-red, in June and July. Dimensions 2½ × 3 ft.

C. × elma, extra large white flowers, June and July. Dimensions 5½ × 7 ft.

C. × purpureus, of bushy rounded habit, 5 × 6 ft. with deep pink flowers having a dark blotch in the centre; **C.** × 'Silver Pink', beautiful soft pink flowers in June and July. Dimensions 4 × 4 ft.

C. villosus creticus, large mauve-purple flowers and greyish foliage. Dimensions 4 × 4 ft.

CLADRASTIS SINENSIS (*Chinese Yellow Wood*)
A deciduous small tree growing to about 12 ft. high with a spread of some 12 ft. The fragrant blush white flowers are produced from June to Aug. in large terminal erect panicles, and the foliage is made up of several leaflets each about 4 in. long. A worth-while plant, requiring ordinary soil conditions and little or no pruning.

CLEMATIS PLATE 8
These are among the most useful of climbing plants. They can be used for a variety of purposes; as wall furnishing, on arches or pergolas, for tall pillars and tripods, or for rambling over mounds, tree stumps, etc. Perhaps the best-known species is **C. vitalba** (*Traveller's Joy*). Cultivation needs a soil of good texture, well prepared and efficiently drained. Direct sun on the roots is harmful and provision for shade should be made by a suitably placed dwarf shrub or by surface mulching. Kinking of the stem at planting time should be avoided. All varieties should be pruned back the spring following planting to about 9 in. from ground level. Pruning of established plants varies; large-flowered varieties of the **C. lanuginosa, C. × jackmannii** and **C. viticella** sections respond well if new growth is cut back annually to within a few buds of the base as soon as flowering is finished. The **C. florida** and **C. patens** varieties, which flower on short side shoots from the previous season's wood, should also be cut back to a good bud after flowering. The **C. alpina** and **C. montana** groups should be kept thinned out by cutting unwanted growths hard back in Aug. or in Feb. before growth starts. As there are numerous named varieties it is best for the reader to consult a good grower's catalogue.

CLERODENDRUM
Deciduous shrubs native to China and Japan. These shrubs should be given a sheltered position in a good loamy soil. Pruning consists of thinning out as required after flowering. Propagation is by means of seeds or cuttings of half-ripened shoots inserted in a close frame in July.

C. bungei (*C. foetidum*). Of soft woody growth

this species is killed to the ground each winter and throws new shoots in the spring to a height of 3–4 ft. The leaves are large and heart-shaped, and the flowers produced in Aug. and Sept. form dense corymbs of purplish-red. It has the drawback of suckering freely.

C. trichotomum is the most beautiful of the group, of sparse branching habit reaching 10 ft. in height × 9 ft. in spread; large dark green leaves and white flowers with red calyxes borne in clusters in the late summer and followed by turquoise berries.

C. fargesii, a vigorous shrub growing some 7 ft. tall and spreading to 6 ft. The fragrant white flowers produced in Aug. and Sept. are followed by dark blue fruits.

CLETHRA

A small genus of hardy deciduous shrubs. A good moist loam or a peaty soil is preferred by these plants. No pruning required. Propagate by cuttings of half-ripened shoots inserted in a close frame in June.

C. alnifolia (*Sweet Pepper*). Native to N.E. America and grows about 5 ft. high and spreading in habit up to 7 ft. The flowers, produced in Aug., are white and aromatic.

C. a. paniculata has larger flower spikes and **C. a. rosea** bears flowers pink in the bud, white when open.

C. barbinervis, a Japanese species growing to 6 ft. in height with a spread of the same size. The white flowers produced from July to Sept. are handsome and fragrant. This species is not as hardy as **C. alnifolia.**

COCKSPUR THORN. See *Crataegus*

COLORADO FIR. See *Abies*

COLUTEA ARBORESCENS (*Bladder Senna*)

A deciduous shrub from south-east Europe. Its yellow pea-like flowers are carried over a lengthy period from June to Sept. and are followed by inflated, bladder-like pods. In habit it is bushy and spreading with dimensions of 10 × 8 ft. It should be cut back lightly in Mar. Propagated by cuttings taken in Sept. and inserted in a cold frame. Any ordinary soil is suitable.

CONVOLVULUS CNEORUM

A small evergreen shrub native to S. Europe, in habit rounded with dimensions of $2\frac{1}{2} \times 2\frac{1}{2}$ ft. It has distinct silvery foliage and pale rose-coloured flowers produced from June to Sept. It requires a dry sunny position and is easily increased by cuttings taken at any time during the summer and inserted in a close frame.

CORNELIAN CHERRY. See *Cornus*

CORNUS (*Dogwood*)

Deciduous shrubs most of which are native to America. One species **C. sanguinea** is of little garden value. **C. alba** and its varieties, and **C. stolonifera** var. **flaviramea,** thrive best in moist soil by the water-side and should be cut to the ground each spring to encourage young shoots of value for the colour of their winter bark. The flowering species and their varieties grow well in ordinary soil and only require pruning to keep in shape. Propagation is by cuttings and layers.

C. alba and its varieties sibirica and s. variegata, and C. alba spaethii are all grown for bark and foliage.

C. florida rubra, a small bushy tree or shrub, dimensions 15 × 15 ft., with rosy red bracts and rich red autumn foliage.

C. kousa, conspicuous white bracts and fine autumn tints; same dimensions as the above.

C. nuttallii, the best of the cornels, with creamy white bracts and reaching a height of 30 ft. In the autumn it is a blaze of crimson and gold. Not easy to propagate.

The three flowering species and varieties mentioned are in flower during May and June.

C. mas (*Cornelian Cherry*) makes a small spreading tree of up to 20 ft. and produces masses of small yellow flowers on the bare wood in late Feb. and Mar.

COROKIA

Semi-evergreen flowering shrubs from New Zealand, needing ordinary fertile soil in a sheltered sunny position. Prune only to maintain shape. Propagate by cuttings of half-ripened wood in Aug. inserted in a close frame.

C. cotoneaster, a curious shrub with twisted,

entangled branches in bloom in May; flowers small and yellow, followed by red berries; average dimensions 5 × 5 ft.

C. virgata, also with peculiarly twisted stems, brownish in colour, and narrow leaves with a white reflex. The yellow flowers are followed by orange berries. Slightly more vigorous in habit than the above.

CORONILLA (*Crown Vetch, Scorpion Senna*)
Deciduous and evergreen, hardy and half-hardy flowering shrubs. The coronillas will succeed on poor dry soil, require little pruning. Propagated by hard-wood cuttings inserted in a cold frame in Aug. or Sept.

C. emeroides, native of south-east Europe with dainty pinnate foliage and yellow pea-like flowers produced from May to Aug.; dimensions 4–5 ft. × 5 ft.

C. emerus, a taller-growing shrub up to 8 ft. high with a spread of some 6 ft.; flowers yellow and red, freely produced in May. Native of central and southern Europe.

C. glauca, an evergreen species not sufficiently hardy for all districts, but succeeding well by a south wall where it will reach a height of 8 ft. or more. Its glaucous pinnate leaves and yellow flowers freely produced from May to Nov. make it an attractive shrub.

CORYLOPSIS
Hardy deciduous shrubs, natives of China and Japan, needing ordinary soil in a sheltered position to avoid damage from late spring frosts. Prune out weak wood after flowering. Propagate by layering in the summer.

C. pauciflora, a spreading shrub growing up to 4 ft. high. Yellow flowers.

C. spicata, brighter in colour than the preceding and with longer, drooping flower spikes —makes a wide-spreading bush up to 6 ft. high.

C. veitchiana, of rounded habit reaching 6–7 ft. in height. The young shoots are reddish, and the flowers fragrant with distinct red-brown anthers.

C. willmottiae, the tallest of the group, with dimensions of 10 × 8 ft.; the flowers are greenish-yellow and scented.

All produce their yellow flowers on bare branches in the early spring.

CORYLUS (*Hazel*)
Best known as fruiting shrubs (filberts and cobnuts), but some are recommended for their coloured leaves. The best of these is **C. maxima purpurea** whose leaves and catkins are a dark purple and give a striking effect where this colour is required. To get the best foliage effects the young shoots should be cut hard back in the spring. Ordinary fertile soil suits this shrub, and it will also grow well on chalk. It can be propagated by means of basal suckers. If allowed to develop freely it will make a large spreading shrub, but pruned as suggested can be kept to 10 × 8 ft.

COTONEASTER (*Rockspray*)
A genus of deciduous and evergreen shrubs and small trees. They vary greatly in habit from low, prostrate forms to erect shrubs, some with gracefully arching branches. Cultivation is easy as they are adapted to any soil or position. Pruning consists of thinning out as required, preferably in the late autumn or spring after fruiting. Cuttings of half-ripened shoots taken in July will root in slight bottom heat.

Two species of prostrate habit recommended for the rock garden are **C. adpressus** (*deciduous*) and **C. dammeri** (*evergreen*). The evergreen **C. microphyllus** is excellent for clothing a bank, while **C. horizontalis** (*deciduous*) very free-berrying and of flat-branching habit, is recommended for a low wall up to 4 ft. high. Of arching graceful habit, 10 × 10 ft., evergreen, and with grey-green foliage and fiery red fruits, **C. franchetii** is well worth considering, and the same can be said for **C. salicifolius rugosus,** which is rather more vigorous in habit. **C. simonsii,** of erect stiff growth, deserves mention because of its value for hedging. **C. integerrimus** although of little garden value is of interest as being the only species truly native to Britain. For a small tree of up to 25 ft. **C. frigidus** is recommended.

COTTON LAVENDER. See *Santolina*

COWBERRY. See *Vaccinium*

CRANBERRY. See *Oxycoccus*

CRATAEGUS (*Flowering Thorn, Hawthorn*)
An important genus of deciduous small flowering and fruiting trees. Crataegus' grow well on any soil, including chalk. No pruning required other than thinning out if overcrowded. The species can be raised from seed (after stratification) and named varieties by grafting on stocks of the parent species.

They are generally available as bush, half-standard and standard trees, average dimensions being 8 × 8 ft., 10 × 10 ft. and 18 × 15 ft. respectively. Their flowering period is May and June.

C. × '*Autumn Glory*', superb for fruiting and autumn foliage, white flowers.

C. × **carrierei** (*lavallei*), upright habit, large foliage and persistent orange-red fruits.

C. coccinea (*Scarlet Haw*) is a white-flowered species often confused with **C. mollis.** It differs from this species in that it is less vigorous —up to 20 ft. in height only—the leaves being smaller and wedge-shaped at the base, and the fruit pendulous and more persistent.

C. cordata (*phaenopyrum*) (*Washington Thorn*), making a rounded head and similar in flowering and fruiting to the above.

C. crus-galli (*Cockspur Thorn*), rather flat topped and spreading, noted for its long thorns, deep red fruits and brilliant autumn foliage.

'*Paul's Double Scarlet*' **(C. oxyacanthioides coccinea plena)** is popular for the rosy-red colour of its flowers.

C. punctata, one of the best of the American thorns, very free-flowering (white) and fruiting.

C. tanacetifolia (*Tansy-leaved Thorn*) is notable for its almost complete lack of spines. It is erect in habit up to 35 ft., and the young shoots are covered with a thick grey wool. The large white fragrant flowers appear in mid-June in clusters of six to eight and are followed by fruits of yellow suffused with red.

CROWBERRY. See *Empetrum*

CROWN VETCH. See *Coronilla*

CYTISUS (*Broom*)
These European plants fill an important place in garden shrubs. They are easy to grow, thrive on almost any well-drained soil, and are very attractive in flower. The plants like an open sunny situation. They should be planted from pots while quite small. They may be used in shrub groups, on banks or in the rockery. Species may be raised from seed and hybrids from cuttings taken in Aug. and dibbled in pots or beds of sandy soil in a cold frame. Any necessary pruning should be done after flowering.

The following of low prostrate habit are recommended for the rockery: **C. ardoinii** (*deep yellow*); **C.** × **kewensis** (cream); **C. purpureus** (rosy-purple). For general purposes 'Johnson's Crimson', 'Enchantress' (rose-pink) and 'C. E. Pearson' (apricot and carmine) are recommended among others.

C. **scoparius** (*Common Broom*), sometimes called **sarothamnus.** There are several varieties cultivated; among them 'Dorothy Walpole', rich velvety crimson, 'Firefly', yellow and crimson, and **fulgens,** with yellow wings and deep maroon keel, are worthy of note. Average dimensions of the above are 6 × 7 ft. All flower in May and June.

Of entirely different habit is the Moroccan species **C. battandieri.** It forms a large shrub of 10 × 10 ft. sending up vigorous shoots from the base. The bold trifoliate leaves are of a silvery appearance and the soft yellow flowers are sweetly scented.

DABOECIA CANTABRICA (*Poliofolia, Irish Heath*)
A hardy evergreen shrub native to western Europe. A lime-free or peaty soil is essential. No pruning required other than the removal of the dead flower spikes in the autumn. Propagate by cuttings in a cold frame in July or Aug.

D. cantabrica bears rosy-purple flowers from June to Oct. and its varieties **alba, atropurpurea** and **praegerae** have white, deep purple and rich pink flowers respectively. In habit they are bushy and spreading, 2 × 2 ft.

DAISY BUSHES. See *Olearia*

DAPHNE
A genus of deciduous and evergreen flowering shrubs the majority of which are native to

Europe. Several are sweetly scented. A good light loam seems to suit the majority. They like an open, sunny position but object to dryness at the root. Little pruning is necessary. Propagation is by seeds, cuttings and grafting.

D. burkwoodii, deciduous, carries soft mauve flowers in May and grows to 3 × 4 ft. **D.** × 'Somerset' is another deciduous hybrid with sweetly scented soft pink flowers in Apr.; dimensions 2½ × 2½ ft.

D. laureola (*Spurge Laurel*). The flowers are somewhat colourless—yellowish-green—and open in late Feb. A plant for the semi-shade, it is useful for the thin woodland rather than for the garden. Evergreen.

D. mezereum, deciduous, bears rosy-purple flowers in Feb. followed by red berries, and grows to 3 × 3 ft. There is a white-flowered form (var. **alba**) bearing yellow berries.

D. odora aurea marginata, 2½ × 4½ ft., evergreen, exquisitely scented, with flowers of reddish-purple from Feb. to Mar.

D. pontica, 3 × 2½ ft., evergreen, with yellowish-green flowers in Apr. and May.

D. retusa, evergreen, with fragrant white flowers in May and June, makes a close compact bush 3 × 5 ft.

DAVIDIA (*Chinese Ghost Tree*)

Hardy deciduous trees from China. They are of upright habit and reach a height of some 40 ft., or can be grown as large shrubs with dimensions of 20 × 15 ft. They need a good fertile soil in an open situation. No pruning necessary. Propagation by seeds or layers.

D. involucrata (*Dove Tree*) bears remarkable flowers with protruding red stamens in a rounded head about ¾ in. diameter, each head being subtended by two large creamy-white bracts giving a unique effect.

DENDROMECON RIGIDUM

A half-hardy Californian shrub with bright yellow poppy-like flowers borne from June to Sept. In the warmer counties, planted against a south or west wall and given slight protection in severe weather, it makes a magnificent sight and will reach a height of 10 ft. or more. Requires a good open soil, little pruning. Propagated by cuttings of moderately firm wood inserted in pots of very sandy soil placed in gentle warmth.

DESFONTAINEA SPINOSA

A holly-like evergreen flowering shrub, native to Chile and Peru, bearing trumpet-shaped, orange-scarlet waxy flowers from July to Oct. Makes a wonderful sight when in full bloom. It is of dense habit, slow-growing up to 5 × 5 ft., not hardy in all districts, and should be given a sheltered corner in semi-shade. A moist soil with some peat added is desirable. No pruning necessary. Propagation best by seed.

DEUTZIA PLATE 17

A genus of deciduous flowering shrubs native to China and Japan. Deutzias like a good loamy soil and plenty of moisture; the old wood should be thinned out after flowering, and cuttings of half-ripened shoots root readily if placed in slight warmth in July. Most species are in flower during late May and June.

D. × elegantissima, 5 × 5 ft., with rose-purple flowers on arching stems.

D. pulchra, hanging clusters of large white flowers; 6 × 7 ft.

D. × rosea carminea, of graceful arching habit, bearing soft pink flowers in abundance; 4 × 4 ft.

D. scabra var. **candidissima,** a tall-growing variety with pure white flowers; reaches 8 × 7 ft. 'Codsall Pink' is similar in habit but with rose-purple flowers.

DEWBERRY. See *Rubus*

DIERVILLA. See *Weigela*

DIOSPYROS

A genus of plants not well known. Only three species are really hardy, **D. armata, D. lotus** and **D. virginiana.** The last, also known as American Date Plum, is a handsome deciduous tree up to 60 ft. in height. The leaves are variable in size, from 2 to 5 in. long and 1 to 2 in. wide, oval or oblong in shape and pointed at the apex. Male and female flowers are separately produced; the female are solitary and yellowish white and larger than the male, which are reddish in colour. The tree is slightly tender when young but later perfectly hardy. A notable feature is the dark brown rugged bark and large, spreading branches.

DISANTHUS CERCIDIFOLIUS
Deciduous shrub from Japan. In habit it is slender and spreading, 8 × 8 ft. The flowers are small and dark purple in colour, and produced in Oct. In the autumn the heart-shaped leaves turn a fiery red. When young it may require slight protection, but after a few seasons it is quite hardy. It succeeds well in good loam with some peat added, requires little pruning. Propagated by hard-wood cuttings inserted in a cold frame in Sept.

DOGWOOD. See *Cornus*

DOVE TREE. See *Davidia*

DRIMYS WINTERI (*Winter's Bark*)
An evergreen small tree, native of Chile. It is of rapid growth up to 20 ft. and pyramidal in shape, with a lower spread of about 15 ft. The creamy-white flower clusters are produced in May and June. It has rhododendron-like foliage and the stems are reddish-coloured. In the milder coastal districts it makes a good shrub in the open but inland requires the protection of a south or west wall. A good loamy soil is suitable and propagation is by means of cuttings or layers. No pruning is necessary.

DUTCHMAN'S PIPE. See *Aristolochia*

ELAEAGNUS (*Oleaster, Wild Olive*)
A group of deciduous and evergreen shrubs grown for their foliage and fruits. These shrubs grow freely on any soil. Pruning consists of thinning out as required. Propagation is by hard-wood cuttings inserted in a frame in Sept. and Oct.
E. argentea (*commutata*), a striking species from N. America with silvery foliage, creamy-yellow fragrant flowers in great profusion in May, followed by large silvery fruits.
E. × ebbingei, glossy green foliage with grey reverse.
E. macrophylla, another native of Japan, the largest-leaved evergreen oleaster. The foliage is silvery-green and the young shoots silver-white. The flowers produced in clusters in Oct. and Nov. are also silver-white and are followed by red fruits.
E. multiflora (*longipes*), native of Japan, deciduous with silvery foliage and orange-red fruits.
E. pungens dicksonii has green leaves banded with gold and seldom reverts to green.
E. p. maculata (*p. aureo-variegata*) (*maculata*) has gold-edged leaves and is very attractive in the winter. All those mentioned except **E. argentea** are evergreen, the average dimensions being 7 × 9 ft.

ELDER See *Sambucus*

ELM. See *Ulmus*

EMPETRUM NIGRUM (*Crowberry*)
A dwarf evergreen shrub resembling those of the heath family and a native of Britain. It is a spreading wiry-stemmed plant some 12 in. high with small, narrow, crowded leaves. The minute greenish flowers produced in May and June are of separate sexes, the males and females usually being on different plants. This moorland plant is easy to grow and readily increased by cuttings.

ENKIANTHUS
Deciduous flowering shrubs from north-east Asia which thrive in a good deep loam with peat added. No pruning is required. Propagation is by seed or hard-wood cuttings inserted in a cold frame in Oct.
E. campanulatus grows to 6 × 5 ft., has greenish-yellow flowers edged with red in May, and richly coloured foliage in the autumn.
E. perulatus (*japonicus*), smaller-growing, 4 × 3 ft., with white flowers produced in Apr. and also brilliant autumn foliage.

ERICA (*Heath, Heather*)
A large genus of hardy flowering shrubs native to Europe. Ericas will thrive in any lime-free soil but generally appreciate the addition of some peat. The species *carnea* and its varieties, the *mediterranea* group, *darleyensis* and *cinerea*, will tolerate a lime soil. The only pruning necessary is to clip lightly over to remove dead flower heads. Propagation of most species is easy by cuttings about 1 in. long taken in July and Aug., inserted in pots of sandy peat, and

placed in slight bottom heat. Prick out into nursery beds when rooted and transfer to permanent positions when about 3 in. high.

E. arborea var. **alpina,** the tree heath, growing to 8 × 8 ft., with white, scented flowers in Mar. and Apr.

E. carnea (purple-pink) and its varieties 'Springwood White' and 'Springwood Pink', 'King George' (purplish-pink), 'Winter Beauty' (lilac), and others, flower from Nov. to Mar., are wide-spreading in habit and up to 10 in. in height.

E. ciliaris, of prostrate straggling habit, produces its urn-shaped flowers on erect terminal racemes from July to Sept.

E. cinerea 'C. D. Eason' (red), 9–12 in., 'Eden Valley' (lilac-pink), 9–12 in., and 'Rose Queen' (bright pink), 15 in., are also spreading and flower during June and July.

E. × darleyensis (rosy-red), 12–18 in. and of more upright habit, flowers from Nov. to Apr.

E. mackayi is usually regarded as a variety of the above.

E. mediterranea 'Silver Beads' (silvery-white), 15 in., and 'W. T. Rackcliff' (white), 15 in., flower in Feb. and Mar.

E. tetralix is a distinct species, bushy at the base with erect flowering stems up to 18 in. high produced from June to Oct. The varieties 'Con Underwood', crimson, and 'mollis', with frosted foliage effect and pure white flowers, are particularly recommended.

E. vagans, 'Mrs. D. F. Maxwell' (deep cerise) and 'St. Keverne' (bright pink), both of spreading habit and growing up to 18 in., flower from July to Sept.

ERINACEA PUNGENS (*Hedgehog Broom*)

An attractive shrub native to Spain and N. Africa. Thrives in a warm, well-drained soil. Propagate by seeds or cuttings. Pale purple-blue pea-shaped flowers, Apr. Grows to about 12 in.

ESCALLONIA (*Chilean Gum Tree*)

A genus of evergreen flowering shrubs native to S. America. As a group the escallonias are somewhat tender and in the coldest districts should be given the protection of a south or west wall. When they are grown in the open, the position should be sheltered but sunny. Ordinary fertile soil is suitable. Pruning consists of cutting out any old wood that can be spared after flowering. Propagation is by cuttings of half-ripened shoots taken in Aug. and inserted in pots of sandy soil in gentle warmth. 'Alice' (rosy-red), 'C. F. Ball' (rosy-crimson), 'Donard Seedling' (white-suffused pink), **E. × iveyi** (white) July–Sept., **E. × langleyensis,** rosy-carmine flowers and graceful arching habit, **E. macrantha sanguinea** (rich ruby-red), and 'Slieve Donard' (rose-pink). All average 8–10 ft. × 11 ft. They are of graceful arching habit with glossy green foliage and, except for **E. × iveyi,** bloom in June.

EUCALYPTUS

Evergreen shrubs or trees native to Australia and Tasmania. A deep, moist loam and a sheltered situation are needed for them. Propagation is by means of seed (when produced) sown in gentle warmth in early spring; no pruning required.

E. globulus can reach a height of 100 ft. or more. The foliage is glaucous blue-green and the flowers are borne in the leaf axils from Oct. to Dec.

E. gunnii is the hardiest of the eucalypti and will reach a height of some 80 ft. in this country. The oblong leaves are 4 to 6 in. long, glaucous green, and bear small clusters of flowers in the leaf axils from Oct. onwards.

EUCRYPHIA GLUTINOSA

A deciduous tree-like shrub, native of Chile. It bears large, pure white flowers with golden yellow stamens completely clothing the bush in July and Aug. The pinnate, rose-like leaves have beautiful autumn tints. It requires no pruning and must be propagated from seed. Its habit is low-branching and upright, slow-growing at first but reaching 16 × 12 ft.

There are two hybrid varieties worthy of note, both of them evergreen—**E. × nymansensis,** similar in flower to **E. glutinosa** but taller and more conical in habit, and **E. × intermedia** 'Rostrevor', 12 × 10 ft., white flowers with pink stamens. These varieties may be rooted from cuttings taken in July and placed in gentle warmth. Eucryphias should have a position sheltered from cold winds. They like a light loam or a peaty soil and thrive in western coastal districts.

EUONYMUS (*Spindle Tree*)
A group of shrubs grown for their autumn foliage and fruits. Plant in any ordinary garden soil in an open sunny situation. No pruning required other than to maintain shape. Propagate by seeds or cuttings.
E. alatus, native of China and Japan, of upright habit with 'winged' corky bark and feathery foliage that in autumn is uniquely pink-tinted; dimensions 7 × 9 ft.
E. europaeus 'Red Cascade' is one of the best fruiting varieties. Slightly taller-growing than the above, its arching branches are hung with large rosy-red fruits in autumn.
E. latifolius is of slender growth and makes a loose, spreading head. The pendent clusters of rich red fruits discharge their orange seeds in Sept.
E. yedoensis, native of Japan, has carmine-red fruits together with highly coloured autumn foliage; of about the same dimensions as 'Red Cascade'.

EXOCHORDA (*Pearl Bush*)
A small genus of deciduous shrubs from China, two of which are worth attention, **E. giraldii** and **E. grandiflora.** Both species bear pure white flowers in Apr. and May and have dimensions of about 8 × 8 ft. The young shoots of **giraldii** are pink in colour. Plant in good loamy soil in a sunny but sheltered position. Prune by thinning out the growths after flowering. Propagate by cuttings of half-ripened shoots in the late summer inserted in a cold frame.

FABIANA (*False Heath*)
Evergreen shrubs of heath-like appearance native to Chile. A light soil in a sheltered position is essential as these shrubs are a little tender. They require little pruning and late summer cuttings strike easily in gentle warmth.
F. imbricata, bearing tubular white flowers in profusion in June and growing to 5 × 4 ft.
F. violacea, of more dense, spreading habit and soft mauve flowers; growing to 3 × 3 ft.

FAGUS (*Beech*)
These trees are too well known to require description. They thrive on most soils including chalk. Propagation of the varieties is usually carried out by grafting.
F. sylvatica (*Common Beech*), and varieties **luteo-variegata** (*Golden Beech*), **cuprea** (*Copper Beech*), **laciniata** (*Fern-leaved Beech*), **pendula** (*Weeping Beech*) and **purpurea** (*Purple Beech*).

FALSE ACACIA. See *Robinia*

FALSE HEATH. See *Fabiana*

FATSIA JAPONICA (*Japanese Aralia*)
An evergreen shrub with bold foliage native to Japan. Grows to a height of 8–10 ft. with a spread of some 10 ft. with large creamy-white flowers in Oct. Although not completely hardy this shrub will succeed in a sheltered position and is excellent for town gardens. No pruning necessary. Two-inch pieces of stem inserted in pots and plunged in mild bottom heat will root from Sept. onwards. It requires a good fertile loam to produce its 12 × 16 in. leaves.

FIRETHORN. See *Pyracantha*

FLOWERING CRAB. See *Malus*

FLOWERING CURRANT. See *Ribes*

FLOWERING THORN. See *Crataegus*

FORSYTHIA (*Golden Bell Tree*)
PLATE 21
Hardy deciduous shrubs thriving in any soil in an open position. Thin out old wood after flowering and propagate by cuttings of half-ripened shoots inserted in a close frame in July.
F. × intermedia 'Lynwood', a free-blooming, large-flowered variety somewhat erect in habit but with semi-pendulous side shoots; dimensions 8 × 8 ft.
F. ovata, a Korean species of compact habit growing to 5 × 4 ft.
F. suspensa, a native of China, somewhat rambling habit and best placed on a wall in any aspect, where it will reach a height of 20 ft. or more. The variety **fortunei** is of stiffer habit, **F. s. decipiens** is very pendulous and excellent for a north wall.

F. viridissima, another native of China, is erect in habit and later to bloom. It seldom exceeds 5 ft. in height.

All the forsythias have yellow flowers opening from Feb. onwards to early Apr.

FOTHERGILLA

A small genus of deciduous shrubs from eastern N. America. They make medium-sized shrubs some 5 × 6 ft. The flowers produced in Apr. are creamy-white and feathery. The foliage, which is hazel-like, turns brilliant yellow and red in the autumn. A moist, sandy loam with peat is desirable. Cuttings root well in the late summer and little pruning is necessary.

F. major and **F. monticola,** both of which are suitable for small gardens.

FRAXINUS (*Ash*)

Too well known to need description. The variety **F. excelsior pendula** makes a good weeping specimen for the garden.

FREMONTIA CALIFORNICA

A semi-evergreen small tree from California. The young shoots are downy and the leaves a dull green. The large golden yellow flowers are produced singly on short stalks during June and July. It requires a sheltered position and is best given the protection of a south or west wall, where it will grow to a height of 20 ft. if required. Little pruning is necessary. Propagation is best carried out by seeds.

FRINGE TREE. See *Chionanthus*

FUCHSIA

In mild parts fuchsias make a good show in the late summer; they can also be grown in colder districts if given some winter protection. Plant in an open position in good soil. Do not cut down the growth in the autumn but protect the crown of the plant with a covering of light soil, leaf-mould or old ashes to a depth of 6 in. and cut back the old stems as required in the spring. Soft-wood cuttings root easily in pots of sandy soil in a close frame.

'Alice Hoffman' (carmine and white), 'Madame Cornelissen' (white and rose-carmine), 'Mrs. Popple' (carmine and violet), 'Ruth' (carmine and mauve), 'Tom Thumb' (violet and carmine) dwarf-growing, 15 × 24 in., **F. magellanica riccartonii** (red and purple) taller-growing—up to 8 ft.—and very suitable for a south or west wall. **F. m. gracilis** is a dainty shrub with slender arching branches bearing red and purple flowers.

GARRYA ELLIPTICA (*Californian Garrya*)

An evergreen shrub of vigorous quick-growing habit. It has small grey-green leaves and is noted for its clusters of soft jade-green catkins, which are at their best from Nov. to Feb. It may be grown as a shrub in the open if given a position sheltered from cold winds, but thrives best on a wall of any aspect. As a shrub its average dimensions are 8 × 8 ft., and on a wall it will reach a height of 12 ft. or more. It will grow in ordinary soil, requires little pruning, and will root from cuttings taken in the late summer and given a little warmth.

GAULTHERIA (*Canada Tea, Wintergreen, Shallon,* etc.)

A genus of dwarf evergreen shrubs spreading in habit and very suitable for ground cover or the rock garden. Gaultherias prefer a lime-free soil. Little pruning is necessary. Propagation is by seeds, division or layering.

G. miqueliana, native of Japan, low-spreading habit up to 12 in., profuse flowering (white) and berrying (also white).

G. procumbens, an excellent carpeter for the shade, wide-spreading, 6–9 in. in height, flowers pinkish-white in July and Aug., followed by red berries. The foliage also turns a reddish colour in the early winter.

G. shallon, from western N. America, has pinkish-white flowers in May and June succeeded by purplish-black fruits. It is taller-growing—up to 4 ft.—with an indefinite spread by means of underground suckers.

GENISTA (*Petty Whin, Broom*)

A large genus of shrubs which bear yellow pea-like flowers during the period May to July. Plant in an open sunny position and a light, dry soil. Most species need to be only lightly trimmed into shape after flowering. Where possible, seeds are the best means of propagation, since they give a longer-living plant, but cuttings of half-ripened shoots will root in a frame during Aug. The young plants should be potted and kept pinched to induce bushy growth, and planted out in the spring. The following are all deciduous.

G. aethnensis, a tall-growing species from Sicily, dimensions 15 × 15 ft. Should be staked to keep upright.

G. anglica is a 'needle furze' that can be quite striking when crowded with its yellow flowers in spring and early summer. It is deciduous, of prostrate habit and grows to about 18 in.

G. dalmatica (*sylvestris*), **a good species for** carpeting, 4–5 in. high, native of Dalmatia.

G. hispanica (*Spanish Broom*), of dense interlacing habit, bristly or spiny, growing to 3 × 3 ft.

G. lydia, native of E. Europe, pendulous habit, suitable for a dry wall or bank, dimensions 2½–3 ft. × 6–7 ft.

G. villarsii, another native of Dalmatia, dwarf compact habit, 15 × 24 in.

G. virgata (*Madeira Broom*) light graceful habit, very free-flowering, growing up to 12 × 12 ft. Stake to keep upright.

GERMANDER. See *Teucrium*

GIANT FIR. See *Abies*

GINKGO BILOBA (*Maidenhair Tree*)
An unusual and beautiful deciduous conifer with two-lobed green leaves resembling the Maidenhair Fern. In habit it is pyramidal with spraying branches. It is slow growing and although it may reach 60 × 30 ft. it is nevertheless quite suitable for the smaller garden and makes a good town garden tree. It is the only species of its genus and is probably a native of W. China. It likes a deep loamy soil and is propagated from seeds.

GLEDITSCHIA TRIACANTHOS
Deciduous small tree or shrub of erect habit and fern-like foliage, native of eastern N. America and Asia. Its flowers are not very attractive but it makes a good tree for the lawn, reaching dimensions of 30 × 20 ft. It may also be grown as a shrub, when it can be kept to 10 × 6 ft. The trunk and main branches are armed with spines. It likes a good loamy soil in a sunny position and is propagated by seed.

GOLDEN BELL TREE. See *Forsythia*

GOLDEN RAIN or CHAIN. See *Laburnum*

GORSE. See *Ulex*

GRAHAM'S SAGE. See *Salvia*

GRISELINIA LITTORALIS
An evergreen shrub from New Zealand and Chile, of rounded compact habit 6 × 6 ft. The flowers are insignificant but the foliage is a bright, shining green. A light, moist soil with some peat added is preferable. No pruning necessary. It is not hardy in all areas. Cuttings of half-ripened shoots root freely in gentle warmth.

GUELDER ROSE. See *Viburnum*

HALESIA CAROLINA (*Snowdrop Tree, Silver Bell Tree*)
A deciduous shrub from N. America, which deserves to be more widely cultivated. It is of wide-spreading habit, 15 × 20 ft., with bell-shaped white flowers all along the branches in May. It is slow-growing and may be planted in small gardens. It will succeed in ordinary garden soil, requires little pruning other than to prevent overcrowding. Can be raised from seed or by cuttings of hardwood taken in Oct.

HALIMIUM
Small-growing evergreen shrubs, dimensions of about 2½ × 4 ft. They are allied to the helianthemums and require the same treatment.

H. lasianthum, yellow flowers with purple blotch, and grey foliage.

H. l. var. **concolor,** pure yellow flowers.

H. ocymoides, brilliant yellow flowers with a zone of purple and black.

All the above are in bloom from May to July.

HAMAMELIS (*Wych Hazel*)
A small genus of valuable deciduous flowering shrubs native to China and Japan. All flower on bare branches from Dec. to Feb. Plant in sunny but sheltered position in a moist loam with peat added. Branches may be lightly

thinned out after flowering to prevent overcrowding. Propagate by seed or layer in the late summer.
H. japonica arborea, tree-like in habit, 10 × 10 ft. in size, with yellow flowers.
H. j. rubra, reddish flowers, and **H. j. zuccariniana,** with lemon-yellow flowers and of smaller growth—7 × 7 ft.
H. mollis is the best of this group, with fine large foliage and rich golden-yellow flowers. Average dimensions 14 × 14 ft.

HAWTHORN. See *Crataegus*

HAZEL. See *Corylus*

HEATHER. See *Calluna, Erica*

HEBE (*Formerly known as Veronica*)
Evergreen flowering shrubs from New Zealand requiring warm sheltered conditions in the colder counties. They need an open well-drained soil. No pruning necessary. Propagate by cuttings in a close frame in June and July.
H. gracillima, rounded in habit and one of the hardiest, with pearly-white flowers in June and July, 4 × 5 ft. 'Midsummer Beauty' bears long, lavender-purple flower spikes from July to Sept., 3 × 5 ft. 'Mrs. E. Tennant', a low-spreading variety with light violet flower spikes from July to Sept., 2½ × 4 ft.
H. pageana, a dwarf species of bushy habit 15 in. × 2½ ft., flowers pearly-white in June and July.
H. subalpina, another white-flowered variety with small apple-green leaves giving a good winter effect, 2½ × 3½ ft.
H. vernicosa, low and spreading, small glossy green leaves and soft lavender flowers borne in July and June, 2 × 2 ft.

HEDGEHOG BROOM. See *Erinacea*

HELIANTHEMUM (*Sun Rose*)
Beautiful dwarf evergreens native to Europe and Asia Minor. The helianthemums are sun-lovers and require open growing conditions on the rockery or in the forefront of borders. They should be moderately cut back after flowering and are easily rooted from cuttings taken in July or Aug. and placed in a cold frame.
H. nummularium, a species with crimped, yellow, brown-blotched flowers, has given rise to the following varieties—'Amy Baring' (orange), 'Bengal Rose' (rose-red), 'Ben Mhor' (orange, vermilion centre), 'Cerise Queen' (double, deep rose), 'Merstham Queen' (pale lemon) and 'Supreme' (large-flowered, rose-red), All are in flower from May to July and grow to about 12 × 24 in. There are many other good varieties available for the garden.

HEMP MALLOW. See *Hibiscus*

HIBISCUS (*Hemp Mallow, Rose Mallow, Musk Mallow,* etc.) PLATE 23
A late-flowering deciduous shrub, probably native to India and China. This shrub grows well in any good garden soil in an open sunny position. Little pruning is necessary, but where space is limited the plants may be cut back in Apr. Propagate by hardwood cuttings taken in Sept. and inserted in a close frame, or by layers.
The following are all varieties of the species **H. syriacus,** 'Coeleste' (single, deep blue), 'Hamabo' (single, pale blush), 'Mauve Queen' (single, mauve), 'Souvenir de Charles Breton' (double, soft lilac), 'Woodbridge' (large single, red). The single varieties are generally more satisfactory than the doubles as the flowers open more freely. All are of upright branching habit and grow to about 7–9 ft. × 7–9 ft., flowering during Aug. and Sept.

HIMALAYAN LABURNUM. See *Piptanthus*

HIPPOPHAE RHAMNOIDES (*Sea Buckthorn*)
A deciduous shrub native to Europe with narrow silvery leaves and very small flowers in Apr. followed by orange berries that colour early. Of open-branching habit when young, it becomes dense as it matures. This shrub grows freely on any soil and is frequently found on sand dunes on our western seaboard. The plants are uni-sexual and require the presence of both sexes to produce fruit. Average dimensions are 10 × 10 ft. Propagation is by seeds, suckers or layers.

HOHERIA GLABRATA (*Plagianthus lyallii*)
A native of New Zealand. It is slow-growing and of upright habit, reaching dimensions of 15 × 12 ft. It makes a useful wall shrub for a south aspect. The translucent-white flowers with golden stamens are open during July. A moist soil with peat added suits this shrub best. No pruning is necessary, and propagation is by hard-wood cuttings.

HOLLY. See *Ilex*

HONEYSUCKLE. See *Lonicera*

HORNBEAM. See *Carpinus*

HORSE CHESTNUT. See *Aesculus*

HYDRANGEA PLATE 26
Hardy and half-hardy deciduous flowering shrubs from Asia and N. America. The hardy group includes such species as **H. paniculata** and its varieties **floribunda** and **grandiflora.** They have dimensions of about 8 × 7 ft. and produce large panicles of creamy-white flowers in Aug. These species are among the most valuable of our late-flowering shrubs. They like a rich, moist soil and should be pruned in the spring.
H. quercifolia (*Oak-leaved*) needs a sheltered position, flowering from July to Sept. and growing to about 5 × 5 ft.
H. villosa has long, pointed grey-green leaves and flat flower heads composed of a centre disc of small light blue fertile flowers surrounded by larger, lavender male florets. The flowers are borne during Aug. and Sept. The other group **H. × macrophylla** (*Hortensia*), includes the well-known summer-flowering varieties among which are 'Hamburg' (deep pink), 'Kluis Superba' (deep pink), 'Mrs. Baardsee' (rosy-red), 'Parsival' (rosy-pink), 'Helge' (deep pink) and 'Westfalen' (red-crimson). The blue colour often seen in hydrangeas of this group is only induced by certain soils. **Attempts at artificial colouring by the use of alum are sometimes satisfactory.** This group likes a rich soil with peat added and a sheltered position. They should be pruned after flowering. Flower heads should be removed and weak stems cut out. No further pruning need be done except to induce stronger growth; then the stems may be cut back to within six buds of the old wood. The dimensions of the above varieties will vary from 3–6 ft. × 4–8 ft. according to the soil, district and treatment. Also included in the *macrophylla* group are the so-called 'Lacecaps' with their outer ring of large male flowers and central fertile flowers. The outer circle is usually of a deeper shade than the centre, giving a pleasing effect. Some varieties are 'Blue Wave', 'White Wave' and **lilacina.**
All hydrangeas root readily from cuttings in the late summer.

HYPERICUM (*St. John's Wort, Rose of Sharon*) PLATE 26
A genus of deciduous and evergreen flowering shrubs that produce their yellow flowers from June to Aug. Hypericums will grow in any soil type and need little pruning. Propagate easily by division and by cuttings taken in Aug.
H. calycinum, semi-evergreen with a low, spreading habit.
H. hookerianum, a tall-growing species from the Himalayas and Assam, is semi-evergreen and reaches a height of 6–8 ft. × 6 ft.
H. moserianum, deciduous, also of spreading habit, is slightly taller (up to 2 ft.) and the flowers have pink stamens.
H. patulum, deciduous, a Japanese species with dimensions of some 3 × 3 ft. The variety 'Gold Cup' is better than the type, of slightly larger dimensions and profuse flowering, the foliage being pink-tinted in the autumn. 'Hidcote' is also recommended for its large flowers and bushy habit of about 6 × 6 ft. **H. patulum** and its varieties should be hard pruned each spring.

ILEX (*Holly*) PLATE 27
A large genus of evergreen trees and shrubs growing well in sun or shade on almost any soil. The common holly should be raised from seed and the varieties from cuttings.
I. aquifolium (Common Holly); varieties worthy of note are **argentea marginata,** silver variegated and pyramidal in habit; 'Golden King', golden-edged leaves; 'Mme. Briot',

rich golden leaves; **hodginsii,** a vigorous large-leaved variety, and **polycarpa laevigata** (J. C. van Tol) with few spines and free-berrying. The last is good for hedges. 'Golden King', 'Mme. Briot' and **polycarpa laevigata** are less vigorous in habit with average dimensions of 10 × 10 ft.

INDIAN BEAN TREE. See *Catalpa*

INDIAN MALLOW. See *Abutilon*

INDIGOFERA GERARDIANA

A half-hardy deciduous shrub of the Himalayas. It bears purple pea-shaped flowers from July to early Sept. and has dainty foliage. It should be planted on a south, east or west wall in all but the mildest districts. It will reach a height of 6 ft. or more and spread to 9 ft. It requires a good well-drained soil and should be cut back fairly hard each Apr. May be propagated by cuttings of half-ripened shoots placed in gentle warmth in July or Aug. This shrub is worthy of wider planting.

IRISH HEATH. See *Daboecia*

JAPANESE ARALIA. See *Fatsia*

JASMINUM (*Jasmine*)

Evergreen or deciduous shrubs or climbers. Plant in any ordinary garden soil. Prune back after flowering and propagate by cuttings of ripened wood in the late summer.

J. humile revolutum, evergreen, a yellow-flowered species from the Himalayas. Plant on a wall with south or west aspect.

J. nudiflorum, deciduous, the yellow winter-flowering jasmine, blooming from Nov. to Feb. Plant on a wall of any aspect.

J. officinale, deciduous, the white summer-flowering jasmine in bloom from June to Aug.

JERUSALEM SAGE. See *Phlomis*

JEW'S MALLOW. See *Kerria*

JUDAS TREE. See *Cercis*

KALMIA (*American Laurel*) PLATE 29

A small genus of evergreen shrubs native to N. America. A peaty soil with moist conditions gives best results. Little pruning is necessary. Propagate by seed.

K. angustifolia, a shrub about 2 × 2 ft. with rosy-red flowers in June. The variety **rubra** is still smaller-growing with deeper-coloured flowers and is suitable for the rock garden.

K. latifolia (*Calico Bush*) carries bright pink flowers in terminal clusters during June and grows to 8 × 10 ft.

KERRIA JAPONICA (*Jew's Mallow*)

Native of China and Japan, grows to about 5 ft. and spreads indefinitely by underground suckers. It bears single yellow flowers during Apr. and May. The growths may be thinned out as necessary and division of the roots offers a ready means of propagation. There is also a double-flowered variety, **pleniflora** (*Bachelor's Buttons*), which is orange-yellow.

KOELREUTERIA PANICULATA

A deciduous tree from China, slow-growing in habit but finally reaching 30 × 25 ft. The small deep yellow flowers open in July and Aug. and are followed by pink triangular bladders containing the seed which together with the attractive foliage makes this a most striking tree. The foliage turns a bright yellow in the autumn. The tree likes a good deep soil and requires little pruning. Propagates readily from root cuttings and seed.

KOLKWITZIA AMABILIS (*Beauty Bush of America*)

A deciduous flowering shrub native to China. It reaches 7 × 7 ft. and carries clusters of urn-shaped flesh-pink flowers during May and June. It is of graceful arching habit and requires a good fertile soil. The old wood should be pruned back after flowering. Propagate from cuttings of firm wood in late summer.

LABRADOR TEA. See *Ledum*

LABURNUM (*Golden Rain, Golden Chain*) PLATE 33

Hardy deciduous trees bearing yellow flowers in May and June and growing to 30 × 25 ft. Laburnums grow well on any soil. **L. × vossii** is a selected form with extra long racemes of flowers. They should have all dead wood cut out in the winter. Propagated from seed.

L. adami (× *laburno cytisus*) is a tree of interest, being a graft hybrid between **L. vulgare** and **Cytisus purpureus**; it bears some yellow flowers, some purple and some intermediate. It makes a smaller tree of some 18 × 15 ft.

LAURUS NOBILIS (*Bay Laurel*)
An evergreen shrub native to the Mediterranean region. In cold districts it requires a sheltered position but will grow on most soil types in sun or shade. In habit it is close and compact with dimensions of 20 × 20 ft. or more; however, it stands clipping well and can be kept to smaller proportions. Propagate by cuttings inserted in a cold frame in Aug.

LAURUSTINUS. See *Viburnum*

LAVANDULA (*Lavender*)
Evergreen shrubs native to the Mediterranean region. Plant in ordinary garden soil in early autumn or spring. Clip over after flowering. Propagate by cuttings in Sept.
L. officinalis spica (*Common English or Mitcham Lavender*), 3½ × 3½ ft. 'Folgate', a dwarf form of the Munstead type. 'Gwendolyn Anley', a new variety of merit, somewhat later in flowering than most and of a delicate lavender shade tinged with pink, 1½ × 2 ft. 'Hidcote', one of the deepest-coloured lavenders (purple-blue) and one of the best, 1½ × 1½ ft. 'Twickle Purple', a semi-dwarf variety with long spikes of rich purple flowers, 2½ × 2½ ft. In the Dutch lavender the foliage is of silvery texture, the flowers of a light lavender colour, and the habit spreading, 3 × 5 ft.

LAVATERA OLBIA ROSEA (*Tree Mallow*)
A half-hardy evergreen flowering shrub bearing soft pink flowers from July to Oct. The foliage is grey-green, the dimensions some 5 × 6 ft. It must have protection while young and should be given a sheltered position. Little pruning is necessary.

LEDUM (*Labrador Tea*)
Small-growing evergreen shrubs that thrive in sun or shade in a lime-free soil with peat added. Plant in early autumn or spring. No pruning required. Propagate by cuttings taken in Sept.

L. groenlandicum (*latifolium*) (N. America), with white pink-tinged flowers, and **L. palustre** (Europe, Asia and N. America), pink-flowered. Both flower in Apr. and May and grow to about 20 in. × 2 ft.

LEIOPHYLLUM BUXIFOLIUM (*Sand Myrtle*)
A low-spreading evergreen up to 18 in. high, native of eastern N. America. It is very free-flowering, rose-pink in bud, opening to a lighter shade and blooming during May and June. It is well adapted to the rock garden, thrives in ordinary fertile soil and requires no pruning. Propagated by cuttings in Aug.

LEPTOSPERMUM
A small genus of evergreen shrubs native to Australia and New Zealand with fine heath-like foliage. They flower during June and July. They like a good loam with peat added and require little pruning. Propagate by cuttings in slight bottom heat in June.
L. scoparium is a white-flowered species; its varieties **chapmanii** and **nicholsii** are bright pink and rosy-red respectively. The flowers are small but profuse and the average dimensions are 6–8 ft. × 6–8 ft.

LEYCESTERIA FORMOSA
A deciduous flowering shrub from the Himalayas, upright in habit growing to 6 × 5 ft. In July and Aug. hanging clusters of pinkish-white flowers subtended by purplish-red bracts and followed by purplish berries. The olive-green bamboo-like stems are very attractive in the winter. It likes a well-drained but moist soil and will grow in the shade. Thin out old wood after flowering. Propagate by seed or cuttings taken in Oct. and inserted in a cold frame.

LIGUSTRUM (*Privet*)
With the exception of the common privet **(L. vulgare)**, which is a native of Europe, the ligustrums are all natives of China or Japan. All are evergreen. They thrive in ordinary soil. Propagate from cuttings inserted in the open during the autumn.

LILAC. See *Syringa*

LILY-OF-THE-VALLEY BUSH. See *Pieris*

LIPPIA CITRIODORA (syn. *Aloysia citriodora*)
This is the lemon-scented verbena and a good greenhouse shrub in colder regions but thrives on a sheltered wall in warmer areas. Prune in the spring to maintain a compact habit.

LIQUIDAMBAR STYRACIFLUA (*Sweet Gum*)
A deciduous tree from N. America noted for its brilliant autumn foliage. It is a somewhat slow-grower, but will reach dimensions of some 60 × 50 ft. It can be planted in small gardens for its pyramidal effect. In general appearance it is maple-like and it thrives in any ordinary garden soil.

LIRIODENDRON TULIPIFERA (*Tulip Tree*)
Another deciduous tree from N. America with dimensions of 70 × 45 ft. This tree, which must be regarded as too large for the small garden, has uniquely shaped leaves best described as saddle-shaped. It begins to flower when about 15 years old. Resembling a tulip in form, the flowers are greenish-white in colour and open in June and July.

LOCUST ACACIA. See *Robinia*

LOISELEURIA PROCUMBENS (*Mountain Azalea*)
This trailing shrub native to alpine heights is the only known species of its genus. The tufted growth is only a few inches high; the stems are thickly clothed with deep green leathery leaves with a whitish undersurface. The flowers are small and rosy-pink, appearing in clusters in May and June. This shrub thrives best in the cooler northern districts where it likes a peaty soil and a moist situation. No pruning is required. The trailing stems root freely of themselves.

LOMATIA FERRUGINEA
An evergreen shrub or small tree native to Chile. It can be safely planted in the milder coastal districts. This is an attractive plant with large fern-like leaves covered when young with a whitish down that on older leaves becomes a brown felt. It is erect in habit, becoming branched after a few years. Its ultimate height under favourable conditions will seldom exceed 25 ft.

LONICERA (*Honeysuckle*) PLATE 32
A genus consisting of both climbing and shrubby plants, evergreen and deciduous. Loniceras thrive in any ordinary garden soil. Pruning consists of cutting out unwanted growth after flowering. Propagation is by cuttings or layering.
Climbing species and varieties:
L. × americana (*italica*), deciduous, flowers scented, purplish-rose outside, apricot within, and blooming in June; aspect east, west or north.
L. caprifolium. Native to Europe and naturalized in some parts of Britain, this fragrant deciduous honeysuckle produces its yellowish flowers in June. The uppermost leaves are joined at the base, giving the appearance of a single leaf circling the stem, hence the plant's common name, perfoliate honeysuckle. 'Scarlet Trumpet' evergreen, with bright scarlet wax-like flowers from May to Sept., aspect south, west or east.
L. periclymenum (*Common Honeysuckle*). This is the honeysuckle so often seen wild in our hedgerows. It is very similar to **L. caprifolium** except that the upper leaves are never united. A good climber for a tall screen.
L. tragophylla, bright yellow flowers (not scented) produced in large clusters from June to Sept.; deciduous and will succeed in any aspect.
Shrubby species and varieties:
L. × purpusii, a winter-flowering hybrid of arching habit bearing creamy-white fragrant flowers in Jan. and Feb.; dimensions 8 × 8 ft.
L. syringantha, a Chinese species with pale lilac-scented flowers in May and June; 9 × 8 ft.
L. tatarica, variable in colour, the best forms being a deep reddish-pink, flowers in Apr.; 9 × 8 ft.
L. thibetica, an Asian species with very fragrant lilac-coloured flowers in May and June, spreading in habit; 6 × 10 ft.
L. xylosteum (*Fly Honeysuckle*). Native to Europe and some parts of south-east England, this is a bushy species up to 8 ft. high. The

flowers are a deep cream, unscented, appear from May onwards, and are followed by red berries which are conspicuous in Aug. All the above are deciduous.

LYCIUM CHINENSE (*Chinese Box Thorn*)
A deciduous wall plant that will succeed in any aspect. It is self-clinging and produces its purple flowers in May and June. These are followed by orange fruits that give a beautiful effect in the late summer and autumn. Somewhat rambling in habit, it is especially recommended for seaside gardens. Propagate by seeds, cuttings or layers.

MACLURA POMIFERA (*Osage Orange*)
Native to the United States where it is often used as a hedging plant, this tree, which will reach a height of 30 ft. or more, is seldom seen in this country. It is armed with 1-in.-long spines, the leaves are lanceolate up to 4 in. long, and the greenish flowers are borne in June. The sexes are produced on separate plants, the female flowers being quite insignificant. The fruit looks like a small orange but is not edible. The tree succeeds in any ordinary fertile soil and requires no pruning. May be propagated by seeds (when produced) or by layers and root-cuttings.

MAGNOLIA PLATE 35
Hardy and half-hardy deciduous and evergreen shrubs. The magnolias like a deep, well-drained loam with peat or leaf-soil added and an open sunny position. Little pruning is necessary. Propagation is by seeds, layering, cuttings or by grafting under glass in the spring.

M. denudata or **conspicua** (*Yulan Tree*), native to China, a low-branching deciduous shrub of spreading habit reaching 20 × 35 ft. but slow-growing. It bears white cup-shaped flowers in early Apr.

M. grandiflora, native to the southern United States, an evergreen tree of some 35 × 35 ft. frequently grown on a wall where it succeeds on a south or east aspect. It bears large glossy green leaves and globular white flowers up to 10 in. across intermittently from July to Sept. It is, however, often slow to flower. The variety 'Exmouth' is an improvement on the type.

M. liliflora is another good species.

M. macrophylla is not recommended for its flowering qualities but is remarkable for the large size of its leaves, which may measure as much as 30 in. long and 20 in. across. The flowers are large and fragrant but of a rather dull cream colour with a basal purple spot on each petal.

M. nigra is a dark-flowered variety of **M. × soulangiana.**

M. rustica var. **rubra** is similar in all respects to **M. lennei** but is of deeper colouring and less vigorous. (It is now more correctly listed as a variety of **M. × soulangiana.**)

M. sieboldii or **parviflora,** a native of Japan and Korea, is a deciduous species with white flowers and conspicuous crimson stamens produced from May to July; 18 × 15 ft.

M. × soulangiana perhaps the best known of the genus, comes from France and bears pink, shaded purple flowers in Apr. and May. It will reach dimensions of 25 × 35 ft., but is not fast-growing and can be used in most small gardens.

M. × soulangiana lennei has been described as the most beautiful of the hybrid magnolias. It bears large flowers, pink within and purple outside, during Apr. and May. Its deciduous habit is low-spreading and forking with dimensions of 20 × 25 ft., but it is sufficiently slow-growing to be planted in small gardens.

M. tripetala is called the Umbrella Tree because of its large decurving leaves some 20 in. long and 10 in. wide. This interesting magnolia is a native of the southern United States. It will reach a height of 25 ft. The creamy-white flowers up to 10 in. across opening in May and June have an unpleasant odour.

M. virginiana (M. glauca) (*Swamp Laurel*), a magnolia from the eastern United States. It makes a small tree or shrub, but in nature it will reach 45 ft. It has rich green foliage 4 in. long by 2 in. wide and fragrant flowers intermittently produced from June to Sept.; they are a creamy white colour and 2 to 3 in. across.

MAHONIA
Evergreen flowering shrubs related to the berberis. The mahonias grow well on most soils

and will tolerate shade. They can be propagated by seeds, cuttings, layers or by division. Little pruning is necessary.

M. aquifolium (*Holly-leaved Berberis*) is a native of western N. America. It bears erect golden-yellow racemes of flowers from Feb. to May, followed by purple berries; height 3–5 ft., spread indefinite.

M. a. undulata is of more upright habit and will reach a height of some 8 ft. and spread to 10 ft. It is of similar flowering habit to the above but has attractive crenelated foliage.

M. bealei is perhaps the best and boldest of the group, flowering during Feb. and Mar. when its long upright racemes are sweetly scented. In habit it is bushy and sturdy and its large, leathery foliage is most attractive. It may be allowed to develop freely to 7 × 12 ft., or can be kept compact by pruning.

MAIDENHAIR TREE. See *Ginkgo*

MALUS (*Flowering Crab*) PLATE 36

A genus of hardy deciduous trees formerly included under *Pyrus*. A good deep loamy soil suits these trees. Prune to keep an open shapely head. Propagate by grafting.

M. × atrosanguinea (rosy-crimson), **M. × lemoinei** (deep crimson, perplish-red foliage), 'Profusion' (rich deep crimson), 'Gibb's Golden Gage' (blush-pink flowers, egg-shaped yellow fruits). The above all grow to 20–25 ft. × 25–30 ft.

M. × purpurea (flowers rosy-crimson, foliage purplish-green).

M. × robusta (*Red Siberian Crab*), white flowers followed by bright red fruits. The last two varieties reach 30 × 35 ft. All flower during Apr. and May.

The Siberian Crab, **M. baccata,** and the Common Crab, **M. sylvestris,** are also worthy of note. Both are most effective in flower and fruit, the first white-flowered and the second pink-tinged. The fruit of the Siberian Crab is small and cherry-like and that of the Common Crab larger and yellow. Both fruits make an excellent preserve.

MAPLE. See *Acer*

MEDLAR. See *Mespilus*

MESPILUS GERMANICA (*Medlar*)

Although primarily a fruiting tree it is an interesting decorative tree when space will permit. Native to Europe it makes a tree about 18 ft. high with spreading, crooked branches. The leaves are 3 to 6 in. long, and downy, particularly on the under-surface. The white flowers produced in May are about 1 in. across, pink-tinged. Any ordinary soil is suitable for medlars. Prune only to keep a shapely head. If the fruit is wanted it should be left on the tree until late Oct. and stored until it appears in the first stages of decay; it is then ready for eating. More often the fruit is used for making jelly.

MEXICAN MOCK ORANGE. See *Choisya*

MOCK ORANGE. See *Philadelphus*

MONKEY PUZZLE. See *Araucaria*

MORUS NIGRA (*Common Mulberry*)

Native to Asia, in habit it is low-branching and wide-spreading, giving it a rugged appearance. It is slow growing and more suited to the southern counties than the north. Ordinary well-drained soil in an open situation is suitable. The minimum of pruning should be given, but spreading branches will need some form of support. Propagation may be effected by seed sown in gentle warmth in spring, cuttings of current year shoots from the upper part of the tree inserted in the late summer, layering in Sept., or grafting in Mar.

MOUNTAIN ASH. See *Sorbus*

MOUNTAIN AZALEA. See *Loiseleuria*

MULBERRY. See *Morus*

MUSK MALLOW. See *Hibiscus*

MYRTUS COMMUNIS (*Common Myrtle*)

A half-hardy evergreen shrub some 12 ft. high. The foliage is dark glossy green and fragrant when crushed. The small, white, scented flowers are produced singly in July and Aug. It must have a sheltered position, the protection of a wall giving the best chance of success. It makes a good cool greenhouse or tub plant. A well-drained loamy soil is suitable and cuttings root readily in gentle warmth.

NANDINA DOMESTICA
An evergreen shrub native to China. It is hardy only in the warm regions where it will grow to 8 × 3 ft. It requires shelter from strong winds and a good moist soil. In habit it is unbranched and erect, with long leaves that are tinted red when young and becomes purplish in the autumn. It bears an erect flowering panicle often 12 in. long and white with large golden-yellow anthers. It is difficult to propagate in this country, seed being seldom produced and cuttings being slow in rooting.

NUTTALLIA (OSMARONIA) CERASIFORMIS (*Osoberry*)
This deciduous shrub from California grows to a height of some 6 ft. The branches spring direct from a 'stool' at ground level, forming a dense thicket. The narrow leaves are about 3 in. long, smooth and thin-textured, greyish beneath. Male and female flowers, white in colour and ½ in. across, are borne on separate plants. The male plant is more showy than the female but the latter must be grown to get the purple, plum-like fruits. Its chief value as a garden plant lies in the fact that the flowers are produced on the bare branches in Mar. and Apr. Ordinary soil with some shade is preferred. Thin out shoots as required after flowering. Propagate by removing suckers from parent plant.

NYSSA SYLVATICA (*Tupelo Tree*)
A hardy deciduous tree from eastern N. America, but not often seen in cultivation here; the flowers have no particular merit, but the large leaves turn a brilliant crimson in the autumn.

OAK. See *Quercus*

OLEA EUROPAEA (*Olive*)
Native to S. Europe. A slow-growing evergreen tree of branching habit and reaching a height of about 30 ft., it has a characteristic rugged appearance. The narrow leaves are leathery in texture and the small white flowers bloom in July and Aug. Cultivate in ordinary fertile soil. Little pruning is required. Propagate by cuttings in sandy peat in the greenhouse in spring or autumn.

OLEARIA (*Daisy Bushes*)
Evergreen shrubs native to New Zealand. These will grow in any ordinary garden soil, and require little pruning. Propagated by cuttings inserted in a frame in Sept. and Oct.
O. gunniana is best suited to the milder counties; white flowers produced in early summer; 5 × 4 ft.
O. haastii produces masses of white daisy-like flowers in July and Aug., 6 × 7 ft.
O. macrodonta has attractive grey-green foliage and silvery-white flowers in June; 10 × 10 ft. This species does well on a south wall.

OLEASTER. See *Elaeagnus*

OLIVE. See *Olea*

OSAGE ORANGE. See *Maclura*

OSMANTHUS
A small genus of evergreen shrubs that succeed best in a light loam in sun or partial shade. No pruning is necessary. They may be propagated by cuttings taken in Sept. and inserted in a cold frame.
O. delavayi, a Chinese species growing to 8 × 10 ft. and bearing masses of scented white flowers during late July and Aug.
O. × fortunei, a Japanese hybrid with holly-like leaves and fragrant white flowers in the late summer and autumn; 6 × 6 ft.
O. ilicifolius var. **purpureus,** greenish-white flowers from Aug. to Oct. and bronze-tinted foliage, 7 × 6 ft.

OSMAREA BURKWOODII
A hybrid between **Osmanthus delavayi** and **Phillyrea decora** growing to 10 × 10 ft. It is a good evergreen shrub with olive-green foliage and scented white flowers during Apr. and May. Requirements and cultivation as for *Osmanthus*.

OSMARONIA CERASIFORMIS. See *Nuttallia cerasiformis*

OSOBERRY. See *Nuttallia*

OXYCOCCUS PALUSTRIS (*Cranberry*)
Correctly called **Vaccinium oxycoccus,** the cranberry is a dwarf evergreen inhabiting moist areas. The small red berries are used to make sauce, jam, jellies and pies. In the garden the plants can be grown on moist, poorly drained land of a peaty nature where they will form a dense interlaced mass. Propagation is easy by means of seed or layers.

OXYDENDRUM ARBOREUM (*Sorrel Tree*)
A beautiful deciduous late-flowering (July and Aug.) tree that deserves to be more widely grown. Native to eastern N. America, in tree form it will reach a height of 30 ft. but can be grown as a shrub of 8 ft. or so. The oblong leaves are up to 6 in. long, dark green, and under some conditions give red and gold autumn tints. The white bell-shaped flowers are borne on a loose panicle up to 10 in. long. As this tree belongs to the heath family it must be given a peaty soil. No pruning is required. Usually propagated by seeds.

PAPER BIRCH. See *Betula*

PARROTIA PERSICA (*Persian Witch Hazel*)
A deciduous flowering tree native to Persia. It flowers during Mar. and is inconspicuous apart from its red stamens. It is of value for its brilliant golden and crimson autumn tints. Although making a tree some 30 × 30 ft., by encouraging a low-branching habit it can be well adapted to the smaller garden.

PAULOWNIA TOMENTOSA (IMPERIALIS)
A deciduous flowering tree native to China. The flower buds form in the autumn and open the following May. They are blue-purple in colour. The tree may be grown in shrub form, when it will make a magnificent foliage specimen if cut to the base each spring. The leaves are up to 12 in. long and 6 in. wide, dark green above and greyish beneath. The dimensions of the tree are 30 × 30 ft. It will succeed on any good loam and is best propagated from seed.

PEA TREE. See *Caragana*

PEAR, WILD. See *Pyrus*

PEARL BUSH. See *Exochorda*

PERIWINKLE. See *Vinca*

PERNETTYA MUCRONATA
Evergreen flowering and fruiting shrubs native to S. America. A cool, moist situation in peaty loam suits these shrubs well. Thin out growths as required and expose fruits in the autumn by cutting back young shoots. Propagate by means of seeds or by taking off underground suckers. The male and female flowers are borne on separate plants and the two must be planted to ensure fruiting.
The following varietal names refer to the colour of the fruits: **alba,** 'Donard Pink', 'Donard White', **lilacina, rosea coccinea,** and **rubra lilacina.** These all grow to about 4 ft. in height and have an indefinite spread.

PEROVSKIA ATRIPLICIFOLIA
A deciduous semi-woody shrub from Afghanistan with average dimensions of 6 × 7 ft. It has grey-felted shoots and grey-green leaves. The powder-blue flowers are produced in Aug. and Sept. It should be given a warm sunny position in light, open soil and be pruned lightly in the spring by cutting back into firm wood. Easily propagated by cuttings taken in July.

PERSIAN WITCH HAZEL. See *Parrotia*

PETTY WHIN. See *Genista*

PHILADELPHUS (*Mock Orange*)
PLATES 36 and 44
Deciduous flowering shrubs popularly but erroneously known as 'syringa' (lilac). These shrubs will thrive in any ordinary garden soil in a sunny position. Prune after flowering by cutting out old or weak wood, giving preference to the young shoots springing from the base. Cuttings will root in a frame during July and Aug.
P. grandiflorus, a southern United States

species that received the Award of Garden Merit. It is tall-growing, up to 12 ft. or more, with large pure white flowers which blossom in July.

P. × 'Beauclerk', white; 6 × 6 ft. **P.** × 'Enchantment', double white, graceful arching habit, profuse flowering, 7 × 8 ft.

P. × **lemoinei erectus,** a small-foliaged and small-flowered variety with sweetly scented white flowers, 3½ × 4½ ft. **P.** × 'Manteau d'Hermine', another dwarf grower, similar to the last named.

P. microphyllus, a Colorado species small and dainty in all its parts. It has sweetly scented flowers and is especially recommended for small gardens. **P.** × 'Sybille', of bushy arching habit, very free-flowering, with purple-centred white flowers; 3 × 4 ft.

All the philadelphus flower during June and July, and are sweetly scented.

PHILESIA BUXIFOLIA

A dwarf evergreen shrub recommended for the warmer districts. It is a native of Chile and bears tubular, wax-like crimson flowers. It should be planted in a semi-shaded position in a good loam with peat added. It requires little pruning and can be propagated by division. It rarely exceeds 15 in. in height but when established can spread indefinitely.

PHILLYREA DECORA

A stiff-growing evergreen shrub of some 6 × 6 ft. native to the south-east coast of the Black Sea. The sage-green, willow-like leaves give it a distinctive appearance. It will grow in any soil or situation including shade, requires no pruning. Propagate by cuttings inserted in a frame in Sept.

PHLOMIS FRUTICOSA (*Jerusalem Sage*)

A shrubby evergreen with silvery foliage and yellow hooded flowers produced in the late summer. Grows to some 3½ × 3½ ft. An old-world plant of character, a native of southern Europe, this should be given a sheltered position. It requires no pruning other than shaping in Mar. Propagate by cuttings taken in the summer and inserted in a cold frame.

PHOTINIA (*Chinese Hawthorn*)

A small genus of deciduous and evergreen trees and shrubs of which **P. villosa** is the species most usually grown. Native to China, Japan and Korea, this shrub will grow to 9 × 14 ft. but can be kept smaller by pruning. It is of value for its rich autumn tints and produces flat heads of white flowers in May. Plant in ordinary garden soil. Prune as required in spring. Propagate by seed where possible, or by cuttings of half-ripened shoots in gentle warmth in Aug. or Sept.

PHYLLODOCE

A small genus of dwarf evergreen shrubs similar in habit and appearance to the heaths. Only one is noted here: **P. caerulea** (*Blue Menziesia*). This species grows to a height of some 10 in. and is native of Europe, Asia and N. America. It is an interesting plant for its bluish-purple flowers carried in clusters on slender stalks at the top of the branchlets. These are borne during June and July. A cool, moist root-run and peaty soil are essential. A surfacing of sphagnum moss is beneficial. Propagation is by means of cuttings about 1 in. long placed in sandy soil in slight bottom heat during July and Aug. Pots or pans are suitable for rooting the cuttings.

PIERIS (*Lily-of-the-Valley Bush*)

A small genus of evergreen shrubs all bearing creamy-white lily-of-the-valley-like flowers in early spring. A light, loamy soil with peat added is most suitable for these plants. No pruning is necessary. Propagate by layering in the late summer.

P. floribunda a native of the south-eastern United States of rounded, bushy habit and growing to about 5 × 5 ft.

P. formosa var. **forrestii,** a shrub native to Yunnan, with pink-tinted young foliage in the spring; rather stronger-growing—8 × 10 ft. **P. japonica,** a native of Japan, the earliest-flowering species (Feb.–Mar.), growing to 9 × 8 ft.

P. taiwanensis, a native of Formosa and probably the best of this group, with translucent red young foliage in the spring, of profuse flowering habit, average dimensions 7 × 8 ft.

PIPTANTHUS LABURNIFOLIUS NEPALENSIS (*Himalayan Laburnum*)
An evergreen shrub growing to 9 × 8 ft. and bearing yellow clusters of flowers in May and June. It requires a sheltered position in full sun and a well-drained soil of ordinary fertility. No pruning necessary. Propagation is by means of seeds, or cuttings of half-ripened wood inserted in a frame in the late summer.

PITTOSPORUM
A small group of evergreen shrubs of interest for their distinctive foliage and graceful habit. They grow quite freely in ordinary soil, require no pruning. Propagate by cuttings of half-ripened shoots in gentle warmth.
P. tenuifolium, a native of New Zealand, and its varieties 'Golden King', 'Jade Princess', **mayi** and 'Silver Queen' are recommended for their beautiful foliage effects. In **mayi** the young shoots are black, making a striking contrast to the pale green foliage.
P. tobira, a native of Japan and China, makes a good wall plant for any aspect other than north and has bright, laurel-like leaves and fragrant creamy-white flowers in early summer. In the south-west counties and sheltered coastal districts these shrubs make striking specimens with dimensions of some 15 × 12 ft. Elsewhere a sheltered position or the protection of a wall is necessary.

PLUMS. See *Prunus*

POLIFOLIA. See *Daboecia*

POMEGRANATE. See *Punica*

POPULUS (*Poplar*)
Deciduous trees for the most part too large for the smaller garden unless required for screening, in which case the species **P. trichocarpa** (*Black Cottonwood*) with its broad, long-pointed leaves and fragrant twigs is recommended. It is low-branching in habit and can be kept to the desired size by pruning.

POTENTILLA (*Cinquefoil*)
In this genus are included some very attractive small-growing deciduous shrubs. They bloom over a lengthy period from June to Oct., have attractive foliage and a pleasing outline of branch and twig. The potentillas will succeed in ordinary garden soil in an open position or in semi-shade. Pruning should be done in Mar.; the taller-growing varieties may be cut almost to ground level each year to maintain a neat, bushy habit. Cuttings of ripened shoots will root readily in a close frame in the autumn.
P. fruticosa, which may be found naturalized in the north of England, has produced many fine varieties of which the following may be mentioned—'Katherine Dykes', lemon-yellow, 5 × 5 ft.; 'Moonlight', silvery foliage, soft yellow flowers, 5 × 5 ft.; 'Mount Everest', white, 3½ × 3½ ft.; and **nana argentea,** a dwarf variety 1½ × 2 ft. with silvery foliage and buttercup-yellow flowers.
P. f. vilmoriniana, with creamy-white flowers and grey-green foliage, is one of the best and grows to 3 × 3 ft.

PRIVET. See *Ligustrum*

PRUNUS
A large genus of deciduous flowering trees and shrubs which includes the flowering almonds and peaches **(P. amygdalus),** cherries **(P. cerasus),** Bird cherries **(P. padus)** and the cherry laurels **(P. laurocerasus).** They appreciate a well-cultivated soil with a good lime content and should be sheltered from north and east winds. In general, any necessary pruning can be done either after flowering or in the autumn, by thinning out old wood and shaping as required. Propagation is usually carried out by grafting or budding.
Almonds and peaches—**P. tenella** 'Firehill', a beautiful shrub with a profusion of rosy-crimson flowers; grown in bush form it is about 3½ × 3½ ft.
P. persica 'Helen Borchers' is a bright double pink, and 'Windle Weeping' a pendulous form with double pink flowers. These all flower in Apr.
Flowering plums—**P. blireiana,** double pink, rosette-like flowers and coppery foliage, is of twiggy habit.
P. cerasifera nigra (*Pissardii nigra*) a dark red foliaged form with pink flowers in profusion. Both these varieties are very early

flowering (Feb.–Mar.), may be grown in bush or standard form, and are suitable for small gardens.

Flowering cherries—Of the large number of good varieties of flowering cherries the following, all varieties of **Prunus serrulata,** are among the best—'Accolade', a moderate grower with rich pink flowers; 'Kursar', pink; 'Okame', pink; 'Oku-miyako', large double white; 'Geraldine', a small-growing compact variety with double, deep pink flowers; 'Pandora', also of compact habit and a pleasing shade of pink, and 'Yae-Murasaki', of moderate growth and with semi-double, purplish-pink flowers. As standard trees the average dimensions of flowering cherries are 18–25 ft. Those noted as moderate growers are best suited to small gardens. The Bird Cherry **(Prunus padus)** in its double-flowered form **(flore plena)** is a fast-growing tree up to 25 × 25 ft. and is smothered with white flowers in drooping racemes in May and early June. More moderate in growth and with double rosetted flowers is **P. cerasus rhexii.** Among **Prunus laurocerasus** the variety 'Otto Luyken' will make a broad-spreading bush 5 × 8 ft. with dainty white flowers in Apr. **Prunus lusitanica** is the well-known Portugal Laurel. It may interest readers to note that the fruiting apricot, cherry, plum, the white bullace, the greengage, the damson, the nectarine, the peach and the wild sloe are all members of the prunus family.

PUNICA GRANATUM (*Pomegranate*)

Native to Persia, this beautiful tree about 20 ft. high can only be grown satisfactorily in the mildest districts. It bears bright scarlet flowers 1½ in. across from June to Sept. A sunny wall and a good loamy soil are recommended. Prune only as necessary for space limits. It can be raised from seeds or cuttings.

PYRACANTHA (*Firethorn*) PLATE 46

A group of hardy flowering and fruiting evergreens suitable for growing in the open or on walls of any aspect. Pyracanthas will grow on any ordinary garden soil and require little pruning beyond thinning out as necessary or spurring back young shoots when grown on walls. Propagate by seeds or cuttings of firm wood in the late summer.

P. atalantioides, a Chinese species good for wall planting, with deep red berries.

P. coccinea var. **lalandei,** a good garden form, produces brilliant red berries, and again is best on a wall.

P. rogersiana, a native of China, is perhaps best in its varietal form **flava,** which is of graceful arching habit and is very suitable for specimen planting, reaching dimensions of some 9 × 12 ft. and bearing cascades of orange-yellow berries in the autumn.

P. × watereri, another good specimen plant, is of dense twiggy habit and grows to 9 × 10 ft. In autumn it is completely covered with brilliant red fruits.

All the pyracanthas are a foam of white flowers in June.

PYRUS

Under this heading reference is made to the Wild Pear **(P. communis)** and the Cornish Pear **(P. c.** var. **cordata).** Regarding the former, it is doubtful whether any pear is truly wild in this country; those that appear to be so are most likely plants that have escaped from cultivation. The Cornish Pear, so called because it is seen only in Cornwall and parts of Devon, is in fact a form of **P. communis.** See also *Malus* and *Sorbus*.

QUERCUS (*Oak*)

There are several trees in this group notable for foliage effect, but they are all too large for the smaller garden. Note however should be made of **Q. coccinea,** the American Scarlet Oak, sometimes shown as **americana splendens.** Of all trees this probably gives the richest autumn effect, the leaves often being retained until late Nov. or early Dec. **Q. ilex** (*Holm Oak*) an evergreen if somewhat sombre is an outstanding evergreen of compact rounded habit.

QUINCE. See *Chaenomeles*

RHAMNUS CATHARTICA
(*Common Buckthorn*)

It is a native of Europe. The flowers are small and green and when they are followed by a heavy crop of black fruits the shrub can be quite striking in the autumn. Cultivated in any ordinary soil and propagated by seeds or layers.

R. frangula (*Alder Buckthorn*) is a deciduous shrub or small tree 15 ft. or more in height. An attractive fruiting small tree of rather loose habit. The glossy leaves and greenish-yellow flowers are followed by the fruits, which turn from green to red and finally to purple in the autumn.

RHODODENDRON

The rhododendrons rank high among hardy flowering shrubs. A great number of the species come from China and the Himalayas, but for general garden planting the hybrids take pride of place because of their greater show of flower. The old species **R. luteum** (*Azalea pontica*) should not, however, be overlooked for planting the thin woodland. A lime-free peaty soil suits rhododendrons best but they can be grown on most loam soils that have no appreciable lime content. Moisture is all-important. Semi-shaded positions give the best growth, but the roots of large trees should be avoided since these rob the soil of both moisture and nutrients. No pruning is necessary but all flower heads should be removed as they fade. Most of the hybrid varieties are propagated by grafting on the ponticum stock. Species can be raised from seed. There are hundreds of species and varieties. The few below are suitable to the small garden.

R. campylocarpum, up to 5 ft. of neat rounded habit and with yellow flowers in May.

R. cantabile, about $3\frac{1}{2} \times 3\frac{1}{2}$ ft. with deep violet flowers in Apr. and May.

R. hippophaeoides, of upright habit to about 4 ft. and with pale lavender flowers in late Apr.

R. impeditum, a dwarf species up to 18 in. covered with beautiful lavender-blue flowers during Apr. Varieties: 'Betty Wormald', large pink; 'Borde Hill', dark red; 'Cynthia', rosy-crimson; 'Mme. de Bruin', cerise red; 'Mrs. Holford', deep salmon, and 'Professor Hugo de Vries', large flowered clear pink. These are all mid-season flowering varieties and should thus escape late spring frosts.

RHODOTHAMNUS CHAMAECISTUS

A low-growing evergreen shrub seldom more than 12 in. high which makes a very attractive plant for the rock garden. It is a native of the Austrian Alps and enjoys a position fully exposed to the sun but with a cool, moist root-run; hence its suitability for a pocket between stones in the rock garden. It flowers during Apr., when it is covered with pale pink blossoms. The best method of propagation is by division of the rootstock.

RHUS

A genus of deciduous shrubs and small trees grown chiefly for their foliage effects. In common with other subjects whose chief feature is autumn foliage colour, they do not like a rich soil; however, with the 'sumach' section, if extra large foliage is desired, a well-cultivated and manured soil is essential. An open sunny position is desirable for these plants. Little pruning is necessary. Propagation is by seed, root cuttings and layers.

R. cotinoides (*Cotinus americanus*), a choice compact shrub giving brilliant orange-scarlet foliage effect in the autumn. During the summer the leaves are blue-green and makes a good foil to other plants, but the flowers are not spectacular. It is a native of the south-east United States and grows to 12 × 12 ft.

R. cotinus (*Cotinus coggygria*) (*Smoke Plant*), gets its popular name from the large terminal panicles, which bear no flowers but produce feathery, thread-like strands giving the plant a smoke-like appearance in the late summer. The foliage turns a brilliant yellow in the autumn. It is a native of Europe and of much the same size as the above. There are two varieties of **R. cotinus** worth noting—**foliis purpureis** with purple foliage and stems, and 'Royal Purple', which is probably the best purple-leaved shrub in this section.

R. glabra (*Smooth Sumach*) is a dwarf, compact species from the eastern United States. Of this species the variety *laciniata* is the best form, with handsome, deeply cut leaves turning a bright rich red in the autumn.

R. typhina (*Stag's Horn Sumach*) is again a

most striking foliage tree, with its fern-like fronds giving a bright red colour in the autumn. All the sumachs are of low-forking habit and produce their flowers in July and Aug. on a dense terminal panicle covered with reddish hairs. **R. glabra** reaches 6 × 9 ft. and **R. typhina** 10 × 12 ft.

RIBES (*Flowering Currant*)

The flowering currants in cultivation are varieties of the species **R. sanguineum,** a native of western N. America. Any ordinary garden soil suits these shrubs and they succeed in full sun or semi-shade. They need pruning only to maintain shape. Propagate by cuttings taken in the late summer.

The varieties 'China Rose', clear pink; 'King Edward VII', deep crimson; and 'Pulborough Scarlet', rich red, are good for all general planting and reach dimensions of about 8 × 8 ft. Mention may also be made of our native flowering currant, **R. alpinum,** which is quite a useful shrub for shady situations.

ROBINIA

A small genus of deciduous trees native to N. America. Their beautiful foliage and pea-shaped flowers make them one of the most ornamental of hardy trees. A soil of only moderate quality is best for all robinias since the brittleness of their wood and their susceptibility to wind damage is increased by a rich soil. No pruning other than shaping is needed. The species can all be propagated by seed; hybrid varieties by grafting on to roots of **R. pseudacacia** and placing in a warm greenhouse.

R. hispida (*Rose Acacia*) a shrub of some 8 ft. in height with large deep rose flowers in May; very showy.

R. kelseyi, to be grown as a small tree or shrub, is another rose-pink flowered species of great beauty. The flowers open in June and are followed by red seed pods.

R. pseudacacia (*False or Locust Acacia*) is a large tree up to 40 ft. in height. The handsome fern-like foliage and long racemes of white flowers in June are most attractive. The variety **inermis** (*Mop Headed Acacia*) is an improvement on the type and is recommended for small gardens. The variety **aurea** with golden foliage which in autumn turns a softer yellow, is very striking.

ROCK ROSE. See *Cistus*

ROCKSPRAY. See *Cotoneaster*

ROMNEYA

A genus of two semi-woody shrubs from California, commonly known as Californian Tree Poppy. A light, well-drained but fertile soil is essential to these shrubs. Plant (in Mar.) with great care, since they much resent root disturbance. Dead shoots and weak growths should be cut out in the spring.

R. coulteri, a beautiful plant with large glaucous green leaves and poppy-like, satin-white flowers with a mass of golden stamens from July to Oct. It is unfortunately not quite hardy and requires the protection of a wall or shelter from a near-by shrub. In winter it will repay further protection with straw or bracken. It is not a shrub to be propagated by the amateur as root cuttings are the only reliable means of increase.

R. trichocalyx, a shrub in all respects similar to the above, but it is of a hardier constitution and can be relied on in all but the coldest districts. If cut to the base in Apr. it will send up vigorous shoots to a height of some 6 ft. with an indefinite spread. It is slightly less vigorous than **R. coulteri** and can be increased by stem cuttings placed in bottom heat in the late summer.

The above two species are regarded as shrubs by some authorities, and herbaceous perennials by others. It is for this reason that the genus is also included in the flowering plants list.

ROSA PLATES 47–55

There are a number of rose species or, as they are frequently called, 'shrub roses', suitable for the smaller garden. They give magnificent displays in return for little trouble, are suited to many situations and purposes, and will withstand hard pruning where this is necessary because of limited space. Those given below are but a few suggestions; many other species and varieties can be used. All those mentioned are at the peak of blooming about mid-summer.

From the *Centifolia* section with their free, open habit the following are selected—'Blanche-fleur', white full flowers and somewhat coarse foliage; 5 × 3 ft. 'Bullata', a beautiful pink rose with large wrinkled foliage; 4 × 4 ft. 'Duc de Fitzjames', lilac-pink, a very effective flower; 6 × 5 ft. 'Fantin Latour', one of the best in this section with blush flowers and good foliage, and of sturdy, bushy habit; 6 × 5 ft. 'Unique Blanche', of compact habit and with red buds opening to white; 4 × 4 ft.

The *Gallicas* are of neat habit and although well provided with hairy bristles are practically thornless. The following are typical—'D'Agues-seau', full crimson flowers; 4 × 4 ft. 'Franco-furtana', rich pink, a high-quality rose; 3 × 3 ft. **officinalis** (*The Red Rose of Lancaster*), light crimson, semi-double flowers with conspicuous yellow stamens; 4 × 4 ft. 'Sissing-hurst Castle', dusky purple, flat semi-double flowers; 3 × 3 ft. The Damask roses give flowers loose in structure followed by long slender hips. Their growth is open and they offer a good selection of which the following are worth noting— 'Hebe's Lip', single flowers red in the bud opening to cream, offset by dark foliage; 4 × 3 ft. 'Ispahan', clear pink, double flowers borne over a longer period than most in this group; 5 × 4 ft. 'Mme. Hardy', probably the best white-flowered variety of all the old roses and with dark green foliage; 6 × 5 ft. 'Marie Louise', large mauve-tinted pink flowers, profuse blooming; 4 × 3 ft.

The popularity of old-fashioned roses justifies a few further notes on some of the older species from which many of the forms now in cultivation have been derived.

R. arvensis (*Field Rose*) is of tall, scrambling habit and bears scented white flowers from mid-summer to late Aug.

R. canina (*Dog Rose*) is familiar as a native of our hedgerows. It is a variable species of straggling habit, with white or pink flowers followed in most seasons by a profusion of bright red fruits.

R. gallica versicolor (R. mundi) a very old and attractive species worthy of a place in any garden. It makes a compact bush up to 4 ft. high and flowers from June to Sept.

R. pimpinellifolia resembles **R. spinosissima** (*Scots Briar*) and favours sand dunes in coastal districts where it colonizes in prickly thickets. The tiny flowers opening in May are creamy-white and scented, and are followed by shining black hips. A number of well-known varieties of this species are in cultivation.

R. rubiginosa (*Sweet Briar*) is correctly known as **R. eglanteria.** The chief features of this species are its aromatic foliage and the profusion of red hips succeeding the bright pink flowers. The Penzance varieties 'Amy Robsart', rich pink; 'Lady Penzance', copper yellow; and 'Lord Penzance', light yellow, are popular.

R. sempervirens (*Evergreen Rose*) is an old species of rambling habit and very hardy. Left to itself it will form a dense, attractive screen but it can be pruned after flowering if required to fit in with formal surroundings. The white flowers are slightly scented and the fruit is orange-red. It is a native of S. Europe and N. Africa.

R. villosa (*Downy Rose*) more correctly known as **R. pomifera,** is a native of Europe and W. Asia, being common in Scotland and north-west England. The flowers, pale pink or white, are similar to but rather smaller than those of **R. canina.** It is erect-growing up to 6 ft.

See also Chapter 10.

ROSE ACACIA. See *Robinia*

ROSE MALLOW. See *Hibiscus*

ROSE OF SHARON. See *Hypericum*

ROSEMARY. See *Rosmarinus*

ROSMARINUS OFFICINALIS
(*Rosemary*)

A shrubby evergreen native to Europe and Asia Minor. The flowers which are produced in May are pale blue and white, and the shrubs grow from 4 to 6 ft. in height with a spread of about the same. They should be lightly clipped over after flowering but not into old wood. They form a good dividing hedge in the garden. Cuttings of young shoots will root in a cold frame in the late summer. Any light, well-drained soil is suitable for their growth.

RUBUS (*Bramble*)
A large genus of hardy deciduous shrubs a number of which are of ornamental value in the garden. They like a good loamy soil and those of a semi-climbing habit need some means of support such as a stout pole. They may be used to furnish a screen or pergola, or, if provided with a few rough branches to scramble over, will form a picturesque mound or pyramid. Pruning treatment varies according to the species. **R. deliciosus** only needs an occasional cutting out of old wood; **R. biflorus** and **R. giraldianus** should have the stems of the previous year cut away in Aug. **R. odoratus** and **R. nutkanus,** which if left to themselves will form a thicket of growth, should be cut to the ground each spring; **R. thibetanus,** the stems of which flower and die in their second year, should have such stems cut out after flowering. Propagation, too, varies with the species, **R. odoratus** and **R. nutkanus,** which deteriorate if allowed to form too large a clump, are best lifted periodically and divided. Others may be 'tip' layered in the late summer.

R. biflorus is called the Whitewashed Bramble, because of its tall, wand-like canes which are particularly attractive in the winter when they are coated with their waxy white covering. This is a Himalayan species and bears white flowers in May. Its dimensions are about 9 × 6 ft.

R. caesius (*Dewberry*) is of no value for garden culture but is widely distributed on open lands. A deciduous shrub with slender creeping stems, it has fruits distinguished by the few large 'pips' of which they are composed.

R. deliciosus, the best of the flowering rubuses, bears large pure white flowers in May and June and is a native of the Rocky Mountains. It forms a large spreading bush up to 8 × 10 ft.

R. fruticosus is our common Blackberry, while **R. idaeus** is the name given to the wild Raspberry that was the forerunner of our garden varieties. It is found naturalized in woods and shady places.

R. giraldianus, a native of China, is similar in appearance and probably an improvement on the foregoing. It is more vigorous and arching in habit and needs plenty of space.

R. laciniatus (*Parsley-leaved Blackberry*) is aptly described by its common name 'parsley-leaved', which character distinguishes it from all other species. It is extensively grown for its fruit and is also of handsome appearance. A strong-growing member of this genus is the Loganberry, a hybrid between an American Blackberry and a Raspberry. The fruit is too acid for most tastes but makes a good preserve. Finally there is **R. saxatilis** (*Stone Bramble*). A dwarf grower, at most 18 in. high, and of slender habit, it resembles the Raspberry in appearance. The fruit is red, berry-like, and carried in clusters on slender stalks at the tips of the growths.

R. nutkanus from western N. America carries pure white flowers during July and Aug. followed by red fruits, and has five-lobed vine-like leaves. It will form a thick bush up to 8 ft.

R. thibetanus, from western China, is a striking foliage shrub with a low wide-spreading habit; dimensions 5 × 8 ft. The stems are covered with waxy-white bloom and the fern-like silver-grey leaves give a 'frosted' effect. The flowers are purplish in colour and appear in June. One hybrid may be mentioned—'Benenden', with large pure white flowers in May. It is of arching habit with dimensions of 7 × 9 ft., and is very graceful when in flower. In addition to the above ornamental species the genus rubus also includes a number of our well-known fruits, some cultivated, others to be found naturalized.

RUE. See *Ruta*

RUSCUS ACULEATUS (*Butcher's Broom*)
A hardy evergreen shrub native to Europe. Its chief value in the garden is that it grows well under the shade of trees. It is of some botanical interest in that the flowers (quite insignificant) are borne on the mid-rib of the 'leaf', which is in fact a modified flattened branch properly named a 'cladode'. It makes a compact bush about 3 ft. high.

RUTA GRAVEOLENS (*Rue*)
This evergeen shrub is a native of S. Europe.

From June to Aug. its dull yellow flowers contrast well with the glaucous-blue foliage. Of compact growth—3 × 3 ft.—it is suited to a number of positions, will grow in any soil, and should be lightly cut back each Apr. It is easily increased by cuttings. There is a selected form, 'Jackman's Blue', which is a considerable improvement on the type plant.

ST. JOHN'S WORT. See *Hypericum*

SALIX (*Willow*)
A large genus of hardy deciduous trees and shrubs of which several can be adapted for planting in the smaller garden. They are excellent for growing in moist conditions by the waterside, but succeed equally well in ordinary soils in open sunny positions, provided they do not dry out too severely. They also thrive in heavier soils. It is characteristic of the willows that whilst they are of rapid growth and root readily in the open ground from hardwood cuttings from Nov. to Mar., they do not transplant too well and should therefore be in permanent positions while quite young. Their chief garden value lies in three main features—a weeping habit, catkins in the spring and coloured winter bark. For the weeping habit the following are the most suitable for the smaller garden:

S. caprea pendula (*The Weeping Goat Willow or Palm*), a native of Europe and N. W. Asia, makes a good umbrella-like small specimen up to 8 ft. high and 7 ft. wide.

S. cinerea (*Grey Willow*) another native species closely related to the Goat Willow, of shrubby habit, 6 × 5 ft. The young wood is covered with a grey down and in Mar. and Apr. produces its silky inch-long catkins.

S. daphnoides (*Violet Willow*), a native of Europe, bears large pearly-grey catkins that show up well against the dark-coloured bark. It makes a small tree up to 15 × 10 ft.

S. matsudana var. **tortuosa** can be confidently recommended when space will allow. A native of China, it is fast-growing up to 35 × 20 ft. and its slender contorted young shoots make a fascinating picture in the winter.

S. purpurea pendula (*Weeping Purple Willow*), a native of Europe. When grafted on stems 8 to 10 ft. high it forms a wide-spreading head of pendulous branches with dimensions of about 20 × 25 ft.

S. vitellina (*Golden Willow*) and its red-barked counterpart, **S. v. britzensis,** are excellent. For best results they must be stooled to the ground each Apr., when they will send up long straight shoots that will take on a brilliant bark colour in the winter.

SALVIA GRAHAMII (*Graham's Sage*)
This evergreen sage from Mexico is quite hardy given the shelter of a south or west wall. Gives a continuous show of crimson sage-like flowers from June to Oct. It makes a spreading bush some 3 × 4 ft. and the leaves when crushed give a strong odour like that of the black currant. Late summer cuttings root freely in a cold frame.

SAMBUCUS (*Elder*)
A small genus of deciduous shrubs of which our native elder **(S. nigra)** is a well-known example. The elders like a moist, loamy soil. Pruning consists of thinning out the growth in spring. Propagation can be carried out by inserting half-ripened shoots (taken with a 'heel') in a frame in late summer or by hard-wood cuttings in the open ground in the early winter.

S. canadensis (*American Elder*) var. **maxima** is generally conceded the best elder. Its features are very large leaves often 15 in. long and almond-scented, white flowers borne in Aug. and Sept. It will form a large spreading bush up to 15 × 15 ft. and its vigour is increased by cutting to the ground each spring.

S. nigra aurea (*Golden-leaved Elder*) is a very striking foliage shrub of much the same dimensions as the foregoing.

S. racemosa (*Red-berried Elder*) is native to Europe. When seen at its best this is a handsome shrub, but unfortunately it does not always fruit to perfection in this country. The bright scarlet fruits ripen in June and July after the yellowish-white flowers. This elder grows up to 10 ft. in height and as much in width.

SAND MYRTLE. See *Leiophyllum*

SANTOLINA (*Cotton Lavender*)
Native to the Mediterranean region, this small

genus of shrubs has long been cultivated. To bring out the character of these plants they should be grown in poor soil in full sunshine, which gives sturdier growth and whiter foliage. Cuttings taken in July or Aug. root readily in a cold frame and the plants should be lightly clipped over in Sept. to maintain a bushy habit.
S. chamaecyparissus nana is the best form of this shrub, each shoot being densely clothed with small white-felted leaves that give the bush a frosted appearance.
S. neapolitana is similar to the above but the leaves are longer, and **S. virens** bears rich green foliage instead of silver.

SARCOCOCCA

A small genus of low-growing evergreen shrubs native to China. While growing well in any light soil these shrubs have a liking for peat. They are excellent shade plants and will withstand the drip of trees. The growth is renewed from the ground, giving them a spreading, bushy habit. Little pruning is required. Late summer cuttings will root in a close frame.
S. hookeriana digyna, a more vigorous species with dark green leaves and purplish-red shoots valuable for cut foliage in flower arrangement. It grows to some 5 ft. and spreads up to 7 ft.
S. humilis, a dense, compact species with narrow bluish-green foliage, good for grouping and ground cover; dimensions $2\frac{1}{2} \times 3\frac{1}{2}$ ft.
S. ruscifolia, an erect-growing shrub up to 3×3 ft., of neat habit and pleasing appearance. The small fragrant flowers borne in Feb. are whitish in colour and of little note.

SCARLET HAW. See *Crataegus*

SCORPION SENNA. See *Coronilla*

SCOTTISH LING. See *Calluna*

SEA BUCKTHORN. See *Hippophae*

SENECIO LAXIFOLIUS

A native of New Zealand, this evergreen low-growing shrub with grey foliage and of spreading habit is well worth growing. It bears bright yellow flowers in June and July which make a striking contrast to its grey, felted leaves. In height about 3 ft. and spreading up to 6 ft., it is ideal for furnishing a bank.
More hardy than the older species **S. greyii** it will succeed in any ordinary soil, requires no pruning and can be increased by cuttings inserted in a cold frame in the late summer.

SHALLON. See *Gaultheria*

SILVER BELL TREE. See *Halesia*

SILVER BIRCH. See *Betula*

SILVER FIR. See *Abies*

SKIMMIA

A small genus of evergreen shrubs native to China and Japan. Skimmias are grown chiefly for their winter fruits. They like a moist, loamy soil and thrive in semi-shade. No pruning is required, and summer cuttings root well in a cold frame.
S. japonica, a low-growing bush up to 3 ft. with a spread of some 5 ft. The male form of this species will assist the fruiting of both **S. reevesiana** and **S. × foremanii.** It bears scented spikes of cream-coloured flowers in May and June. It should be noted that **S. × foremanii** is an hermaphrodite form and will therefore fruit well when planted by itself.
S. reevesiana, a compact-habited shrub growing to about $2\frac{1}{2} \times 3$ ft. and with handsome red fruits in the winter. There is a male form of this species known as 'Bronze Knight' that is notable for the bronze flower heads carried throughout the winter.

SMOKE PLANT. See *Rhus*

SNOWBERRY. See *Symphoricarpos*

SNOWDROP TREE. See *Halesia*

SNOWY MESPILUS. See *Amelanchier*

SOLANUM

This genus has half-hardy deciduous climbing plants useful for planting on walls with a south or west aspect in all but the coldest districts. An open, well-drained soil is essential. Prune by cutting out unwanted and weak shoots in the early spring. Propagate by cuttings of young wood inserted in sandy soil with bottom heat.

S. crispum, a native of Chile, a fast-growing climber with large clusters of lavender blue potato-like flowers with yellow centres from July to Sept.

S. jasminoides, a native of Brazil, is of similar habit but of more slender growth and bears delicate pale blue flowers.

SOPHORA

Deciduous small trees or shrubs of attractive appearance. These plants like a good loamy soil in an open position. They require little pruning other than to prevent overcrowding of the branches. May be propagated by seeds or cuttings.

S. japonica makes a compact tree up to 40 ft. high and although somewhat slow-growing may spread up to 50 ft. with age. It is a native of China, has rich green pinnate leaves up to 10 in. long and bears creamy-white flowers in Sept. There is a pendulous form which if grafted on stems (of the type) about 12 ft. tall makes a picturesque lawn tree about 15 × 15 ft.

S. tetraptera is best grown as a low-branching shrub when it will reach about 8 × 8 ft. The foliage is smaller than that of **S. japonica** and the golden-yellow flowers are borne in pendulous racemes during Sept. This species is a native of New Zealand and Chile.

SORBUS

A genus of trees closely related to pyrus of value for their large clusters of white flowers in May and June, attractive foliage that takes on brilliant autumn tints and their red and yellow fruits. They are best propagated by seed and require no pruning.

S. americana (*American Mountain Ash*), a handsome tree forming a rounded head and growing to about 18 ft. high. It makes a striking picture in the autumn when laden with bright red fruits.

S. aria (*White-beam Tree*), a native tree with grey foliage (silver when young) and of vigorous upright habit to 30 × 30 ft. It bears red fruit. There are several forms of this species, notably **decaisniana** (*majestica*), a fine fruiting variety.

S. aucuparia (*Mountain Ash*) is widely spread over Europe. There are a number of good forms of this species such as **asplenifolia** with deeply cut leaves, and **fructu luteo,** a yellow-fruiting form.

S. conradinae from western China bears large clusters of orange-red fruits combined with orange and red-tinted foliage in the autumn. It makes a tree of some 25 × 25 ft.

S. domestica (*True Service Tree*), is a native of south and east Europe. Although inferior to the better forms of Mountain Ash it is noteworthy for its beautiful pinnate foliage and large creamy-white flowers. The fruits are of two forms—apple-shaped (var. **pomifera**), and pear-shaped (var. **pyrifera**). The tree will reach a height of some 40 ft.

S. hupehensis from China is of the same dimensions and bears white, pink-tinted berries with rich autumn foliage.

SORREL TREE. See *Oxydendrum*

SPANISH BROOM. See *Spartium*

SPARTIUM JUNCEUM (*Spanish Broom*)

A tall sparsely furnished evergreen shrub of rush-like appearance native to southern Europe. It thrives in the poorest of soils and is very showy when its yellow flowers are open from June to Sept. Long shoots may be cut back in Mar. Cuttings of young wood taken in July will root in a frame, or it may be increased by seed. Young plants should be grown in pots until planted in permanent positions, which should be open and sunny.

SPINDLE TREE. See *Euonymus*

SPIRAEA PLATE 58

The shrubby spiraeas constitute an important group of deciduous ornamental flowering plants. The species are widely spread over Europe, Asia and N. America. All the spiraeas like a good moist loam and an open sunny position. Propagation methods vary according to the species: those that produce basal suckers are easily increased by division, and others by means of cuttings of half-ripened wood taken during July and Aug., inserted in sandy soil, and placed in slight bottom heat, or by cuttings

of ripened shoots inserted in a cold frame in Sept.
Pruning with spiraeas is a 'must', and this also varies according to the species. This may be briefly stated as follows—those that flower in the early season on shoots of the previous year, such as **S. × arguta** and **S. thunbergii,** should be pruned after blooming by thinning out old and weak wood. No shortening back should be done. The later bloomers such as **S. douglasii, S. japonica** and **S. menziesii** may have unwanted wood cut out and young shoots shortened back in Mar. each year. The best varieties for the smaller garden include **S. × arguta,** 6 × 6 ft., **S. thunbergii,** 6 × 6 ft., and **S. × vanhoutteii,** 8 × 8 ft., all of graceful arching habit and bearing white flowers in the early spring. For later blooming there are **S. japonica** 'Anthony Waterer Improved', with flat heads of carmine-red flowers, **S. × margaritae,** flat heads of bright pink flowers, and **S. × billiardii triumphans,** deep rose flowers in erect panicles. All the above have dimensions of about 4 × 4 ft. and flower from June to Aug.
S. salicifolia (*Willow-leaved Spiraea*) is slender and erect in habit and grows to a height of about 5 ft. When well grown it will make a good show with its pink-tinted white flowers in June and July. It is useful for an odd corner where it will establish itself by means of suckering.

SPOTTED LAUREL. See *Aucuba*

SPURGE LAUREL. See *Daphne*

STAPHYLEA (*Bladder Nut*)
Hardy deciduous shrubs that will grow in ordinary soil in a sunny situation, need no pruning other than what is necessary to maintain shape. Can be increased easily by cuttings. Two species only need be noted, both producing white flowers in May and June: **S. colchica** with trifoliate leaves and the fruits contained in large, inflated capsules; dimensions about 6 × 7 ft. **S. pinnata,** with pinnate leaves, rather more vigorous in growth and with smaller seed capsules. The former is a native of the southern Caucasus, the latter of Europe.

STAUNTONIA HEXAPHYLLA
An evergreen climbing shrub suited only to mild districts, where it should be given a south or west wall for protection. It bears white fragrant flowers in June and July. It likes a light, well-drained soil. Any pruning necessary should be done in the spring. Propagation is by cuttings or layers.

STEPHANANDRA
A small genus of deciduous shrubs native to Japan. These shrubs are closely allied to the spiraeas and require the same growing conditions. Propagation is by cuttings or division, and pruning varies with the species.
S. incisa crispifolia, a compact, rounded bush about 4 × 5 ft., with fern-like foliage and small greenish-white flowers. The reddish-brown branches show up well in the winter. Little pruning is required.
S. tanakae, a shrub of slender growth and arching habit which has no flower value but brilliant autumn foliage and red winter stems. It makes a shrub of some 6 × 6 ft. and should be cut to the ground in Mar.

STEWARTIA (*Stuartia*)
Deciduous flowering shrubs. A light, warm soil with peat added and a sunny sheltered position are desirable. No pruning is required. Propagation is not easy; cuttings taken in late summer and inserted in very sandy soil in a close frame is the recommended method. Permanent planting should be done as soon as the young plants are well rooted.
S. malacodendron comes from the south-eastern United States, **S. ovata** (*S. pentagyna*) from the southern United States and **S. pseudo-camellia** from Japan. All carry beautiful creamy-white flowers with a boss of yellow or purple stamens during June and July and have average dimensions of 7 × 7 ft.

STORAX. See *Styrax*

STRANVAESIA
A small genus of evergreen small trees or shrubs, natives of China. A light, sandy loam suits these shrubs best. Little pruning is necessary. Propagation is by means of half-ripened wood placed in gentle warmth.

S. davidiana, of upright habit and slow growth to some 10 ft. under most conditions, although this may be exceeded in some localities. The white flowers are borne in June and July and are followed by handsome red fruits that last well into the winter, the older foliage also taking on brilliant colours.
S. undulata is of a low-spreading habit and will seldom exceed 6 ft. in height with a spread of 8 ft. It produces its white blossoms with great freedom in June and an abundant crop of red berries in the autumn. The foliage also turns red before falling.

STRAWBERRY TREE. See *Arbutus*

STYRAX (*Storax*)
Hardy deciduous shrubs or small trees. All the species of styrax need care until established. They should be planted in a sheltered position in a light soil to which some peat or leaf-soil has been added and the roots will later extend into the surrounding soil. They are beautiful flowering subjects and will repay the care bestowed on them. Pruning consists of thinning out any weak shoots in the autumn. Propagation is by means of cuttings or seed.
The four species mentioned all bear pure white flowers in June.
S. hemsleyana, a native of China, makes a small tree up to 15 × 15 ft. and carries its flowers on terminal racemes up to 6 in. long.
S. japonica, from Japan, slow-growing and less vigorous, will make a beautiful shrub of some 8 × 8 ft. The flowers borne from the leaf axils of short lateral shoots are on slender stalks, giving an attractive pendulous habit.
S. obassia, a large shrub up to 10 × 8 ft., is one of the most striking of flowering shrubs to come from Japan. The fragrant, waxy-white flowers are produced on terminal racemes up to 8 in. long. Its slow-growing habit makes it suitable for small gardens.
S. wilsonii is of branching, twiggy habit and grows to about 6 × 8 ft. Its flowering habit is similar to that of **S. japonica** and it begins to bloom while very small. This species comes from China.

SUMACH. See *Rhus*

SUN ROSE. See *Helianthemum*

SWEET GUM. See *Liquidambar*

SWEET PEPPER. See *Clethra*

SYMPHORICARPOS (*Snowberry*)
A small genus of deciduous shrubs. Grow in ordinary soil. No pruning required other than cutting out dead wood. Propagate by cuttings or division.
S. albus laevigatus (*S. racemosus*), a native of N. America, is the well-known snowberry. The insignificant flowers are borne in July and Aug. and are followed by the typical round white berries that last well into the winter. Average dimensions some 5 ft. spreading by means of suckers.
S. × chenaultii, a species of similar habit and dimensions but bearing rosy-purple berries.

SYRINGA (*Lilac*)
Hardy deciduous shrubs. For the best results the garden varieties of lilac should be given generous treatment. They will thrive in most garden soils provided they are well drained and manured; an annual mulch of well-decayed manure is also beneficial. It is important that seed formation should be prevented by the removal of the flower trusses as they fade, and at the same time weak and unwanted shoots may be cut out. Height may to some extent be regulated by a periodic cutting back of flowered shoots, but this will result in a reduction of flower spikes the following year. Unflowered shoots should never be cut back. Cuttings of ripened wood inserted in the open ground in Oct. will root, or layering may be done in June. As many of the finer varieties are grafted on stocks of the common species, all suckers should be regularly removed.
S. microphylla (sometimes called **S. palibiniana**), a miniature lilac from China of some 5 × 5 ft., with dainty lilac-coloured flower spikes in May.
S. persica (*Persian Lilac*), a native of Afghanistan, of dense, bushy and rounded habit and about 7 × 7 ft.; it bears typical small lilac flowers on a slender spike in May. This shrub should be more widely cultivated.

S. sweginzowii, from China, taller-growing —up to 10 ft.—and with long slender panicles of pale rosy-lilac in June.
S. villosa, also from China, of similar height and erect habit, very free-flowering, with large panicles of rosy-lilac in late May and June. This last species is particularly beautiful and is recommended with confidence for the small garden.
There are many good garden hybrids only a few of which can be mentioned here, those named being all May-flowering and varieties of **S. vulgaris.** Single varieties: 'Etna' (reddish-purple), 'Massena' (deep mauve), 'Souvenir de Louis Spath' (dark red). Double varieties: 'Katherine Havemeyer' (deep lavender), 'Madame Lemoine' (pure white), 'Paul Thirion' (rosy-red) (late flowering).

TAMARIX (*Tamarisk*)
Hardy deciduous shrubs native to S. and E. Europe. Ordinary dry soil in full sun suits these shrubs well. The summer-flowering species and varieties should be pruned hard back each Apr. to induce strong shoots with good flowers, and the early flowering **T. tetrandra** should be treated in the same way after flowering. Average dimensions (if hard pruned) are 7 × 6 ft. Cuttings of ripened wood inserted in the open ground in Oct. root freely.
T. pentandra—this species and its varieties 'Pink Cascade' and **rubra** are the best of the tamarisks. They are of graceful slender habit with feathery foliage and bloom profusely from July to Sept. The first two are a bright pink and the last a rosy-red.
T. tetrandra produces its bright pink flowers in May and June.

TANSY-LEAVED THORN. See *Crataegus*

TEUCRIUM FRUTICANS (*Germander*)
A grey-foliaged evergreen shrub native to S. Europe. A warm, sunny situation or the shelter of a wall is necessary for this shrub. No pruning is required. Propagate from cuttings of young shoots which root freely in a cold frame. The flowers, pale purple or lavender-coloured, are produced during June and July. Average dimensions are 3 × 4 ft.

TREE MALLOW. See *Lavatera*

TREE OF HEAVEN. See *Ailanthus*

TRUE SERVICE TREE. See *Sorbus*

TRUMPET FLOWER. See *Campsis*

TULIP TREE. See *Liriodendron*

TUPELO TREE. See *Nyssa*

ULEX (*Gorse*)
Evergreen shrubs native to Europe useful for poor soils and dry situations. They move badly and should be planted in permanent positions while young, preferably from pots. No pruning is necessary but they can be cut back when overgrown. Propagation is by cuttings inserted in a cold frame in Aug. or by seed sown in the spring.
U. europaeus var. **plenus** (*Double-flowered Gorse*), a slow-growing compact variety reaching some 5 × 5 ft. and flowering during Apr. and May. It must be planted on dry hungry soil to develop its full flowering habit.
U. gallii and **U. nanus** are both dwarf species species usually under 2 ft. in height and flowering during the late summer and autumn. These are suitable for the rock garden, giving a patch of colour when little else is blooming.

ULMUS (*Elm*)
Well-known deciduous trees succeeding in almost any soil and situation. The majority are too large for the average garden but two varieties of **U. glabra** (*Wych or Scotch Elm*) may be considered— **U. g. nana,** a dwarf type making a rounded bush of some 6 × 8 ft., and **U. g. pendula** (*Weeping Elm*), which when grafted on 12 ft. stems of the species makes an attractive specimen for any vantage point. It has an umbrella-like head and is easily kept to dimensions of some 15 × 18 ft.

VACCINIUM
A large genus of shrubs. They have a preference for a moist, light soil with peat added. Propagate by means of cuttings rooted under glass during the summer or by seeds sown as soon as ripe in the autumn.

V. arctostaphylos (*Bear Berry*), a deciduous shrub of some 6 × 5 ft. A native of the Caucasus, it has leaves up to 4 in. long and carries greenish-white bell-shaped flowers in June followed by purple berries in the autumn. The foliage also takes on purple and red tints.
V. corymbosum (*Blue Berry*) from eastern N. America is of similar dimensions to the above and forms a dense shrub. The flowers, which are produced in May, are pale pink or white followed by typical blue-black fruits. The foliage turns a beautiful shade of red before falling.
V. moupinense, a low-growing evergreen from China, is an attractive plant suitable for the rock garden, growing to about 18 × 24 in. The sturdy stems are crowded with small leaves and the reddish flowers are carried on short racemes towards the end of the shoots in May and June. The autumn fruits are purplish-black.
V. myrtillus (*Whortleberry*) is a dwarf shrub, one of the commonest inhabitants of moorlands and mountains in Britain. The small pale pink flowers produced in May are followed by black fruits which in the north have some market value. The shrub has a preference for the higher altitudes and can only be successfully cultivated in the north.
V. oxycoccus See *Oxycoccus*. **V. vitis-idaea** (*Cowberry*) is also known as red whortleberry'. This little evergreen is found in abundance on heath and moorland areas in this country. In habit it is neat and tufted with dark glossy foliage. The white or pinkish bell-shaped flowers open in May and June. The small red fruits have not the same value as those of **V. myrtillus,** but otherwise this is probably the best of the native species of **vaccinium.** Provided that it is planted in a dry, open position its creeping rootstock will speedily give good ground cover.

VERONICA (*Speedwell*). See *Hebe*

VIBURNUM PLATE 61

An important genus of deciduous shrubs adapted to most soils. Like the hydrangeas, several species of viburnum are composed of two types of flowers, the one showy but sterile **(V. opulus** var. **sterile)** and the other less conspicuous but complete with stamens and pistil and therefore fertile. By means of hybridization, an inflorescence consisting entirely of sterile flowers has been obtained in three species, thereby much increasing their beauty. Most viburnums are easy to grow, but they appreciate a good deep loam that does not dry out too readily. Any necessary pruning should be done after flowering. Most will root readily from cuttings of moderately firm wood inserted in a close frame during June and July.
V. × burkwoodii, of bushy arching habit up to 9 × 9 ft., producing large heads of fragrant white flowers in Apr.
V. carlesii, a native of Korea brought to this country from Japan, is a most desirable shrub for smaller gardens, making a shapely bush about 5 × 5 ft. The sweetly scented, white, flushed pink flowers are produced during late Apr. and May. In the warmer districts it prefers light shade and a moisture-holding soil.
V. fragrans, a native of China, is of tall upright habit, some 10 × 9 ft., and is one of the most attractive winter-flowering shrubs. Its white, pink-tinted flowers produced from Nov. to Feb. withstand quite severe frosts without injury. The young shoots and leaves are pink-tinted.
V. × juddii is strongly recommended for its free-flowering habit and good constitution. Its scented white flowers are open in late Apr. and May and its dimensions of some 5 × 6 ft. make it suitable for the smaller garden.
V. lantana (*Wayfaring Tree*). Although not of the same garden value as the other species it is a useful shrub for the thin woodland, where the white flower clusters in May followed by the purplish black fruits in the autumn can be quite effective. Seedling plants of this species are used as stocks on which to work the choicer varieties.
V. opulus (*Guelder Rose*), a native of Europe including Britain, is well worth growing. It is tall, up to 12 × 15 ft., and must be sited accordingly. The white blossoms opening during May and June are distinct from those of **V. opulus** var. **sterile** in that only the outer flowers of the cluster are sterile, hence the bright red berries with which the shrub is

adorned in the autumn. The foliage, too, turns a rich red before falling.

V. plicatum (from China), with its horizontal tiered habit, is a distinctive shrub. Many cultivars are grown including **grandiflorum**, with snowball-like flowers opening during May and June and carried in pairs all along the branches. It is an admirable shrub for planting on a wall on any aspect but north, and also makes a good specimen.

V. tinus (*Laurustinus*) is a well-known winter-flowering evergreen shrub growing 8 ft. or more and spreading up to 10 ft. It is a native of S. E. Europe and produces its white flowers from Dec. to Apr. There is a selected form that is more pink in bud than the type.

VINCA (*Periwinkle*)

These are dwarf evergreen shrubs useful for carpeting and furnishing banks. They will grow in any ordinary well-drained soil.

V. major, a strong-growing species native to Europe with a height of some 1½ ft. and of indefinite spread; bears purplish-blue flowers.

V. minor, also from Europe, is dwarfer in habit and has flowers of a softer blue. There are several varieties of this species—a white-flowering form, one with flowers of a brighter blue and a double-flowered purple variety. All flower from Mar. to early May.

VINES. See *Vitis*

VITIS (*Vine*)

A genus of deciduous climbing plants that includes the popular Virginia Creeper. Pruning consists of thinning out unwanted shoots in the spring and training as required. Most species will root from cuttings in a frame in Sept.

V. coignetiae, a native of Japan, is a strong-growing twining climber claimed to be the finest of all vines for the richness of its autumn colouring. It has large, bold foliage and looks well if planted to ramble through a tree. On a wall it should have a south or west aspect.

V. henryana (*Parthenocissus henryana*), a handsome self-clinging climber native to China, has purplish-green leaves with silver and white markings along the lines of the veins. The foliage turns red in autumn. Should have a south or west aspect.

V. heterophylla (*Ampelopsis brevipedunculata* var. *maximowiczii*), a native of China and Japan, should be planted on a south wall to give full effect to the turquoise-blue fruits that are the feature of this vine when it is established.

V. inconstans (*Parthenocissus tricuspidata*), also native to China and Japan, in the form known as 'Beverley Brook' is one of the best of the Virginian Creepers. It will grow on any aspect and is not so rampant as some. The autumn colour is a brilliant red.

V. quinquefolia (*Parthenocissus quinquefolia*) is the true, self-clinging Virginia Creeper. Again, it will grow in any aspect and the foliage turns brilliant scarlet in the autumn. It is a native of eastern N. America.

WASHINGTON THORN. See *Crataegus*

WEIGELA (*Bush Honeysuckle*)

Hardy deciduous shrubs thriving in sun or partial shade in almost any soil. Prune after flowering by cutting out weak and straggling wood. Propagate by cuttings of young wood inserted in a close frame in June and July.

'Bristol Ruby', red-flowering and of bushy habit, 8 × 8 ft. 'Descartes', of semi-arching habit and with crimson flowers; 8 × 8 ft. 'Feerie', of arching habit and with smaller and more dainty flowers of rose-pink freely borne; 8 × 8 ft. **W. vanhouttei**, a vigorous variety with flowers of two shades or bright pink; 8 × 8 ft. 'Eve Rathke', a dwarf variety 4 × 5 ft., with deep crimson flowers produced continuously from late May to Aug., recommended for small gardens. **W. styriaca**, a deep rose flowered variety of moderate vigour and semi-arching habit; 7 × 7 ft.

Often called diervillas, all the weigelas flower during May and June.

WHITE-BEAM TREE. See *Sorbus*

WHORTLEBERRY. See *Vaccinium*

WILD OLIVE. See *Elaeagnus*

WILLOWS. See *Salix*

WINTER GREEN. See *Gaultheria*

WINTER SWEET. See *Chimonanthus*

WINTER'S BARK. See *Drimys*

WISTERIA PLATE 62
A small genus of deciduous climbers invaluable for the beauty of their early summer flowers. They are most effective for many purposes, but any supports used must be strong enough to support their vigorous growth. They are not particular as to soil, but correct pruning is important. When young, unwanted shoots should be shortened back in the summer to two or three buds, tying in those required for extension. When established and fully trained, all current season's growth should be cut back in July to within four or five buds of the base. To propagate, layer young shoots in June.
W. floribunda, native to Japan, in its white form **(multijuga alba)** is the best white-flowered wisteria.
W. f. macrobotrys (*multijuga*) is not a pure species but a form of **floribunda** with long, drooping racemes up to 3 ft. in length of soft lavender flowers.
W. sinensis, a native of China with mauve flowers.
All wisterias flower during May and June.

WYCH HAZEL. See *Hamamelis*

YOUNG'S WEEPING BIRCH. See *Betula*

YUCCA PLATE 62
This small genus of plants is distinct in appearance from any other group of shrubs. Natives of N. and S. America, they are hardy in all but the coldest districts. Under favourable conditions the stem of some species may reach a height of 8 ft. or more; others remain dwarf. The long, narrow-pointed leaves give an exotic effect which, added to the stately appearance of the flower spikes, makes these plants of unique value in the garden. An open sandy soil in a fully exposed situation is essential. Propagation varies according to the habit of the species. Side shoots may be taken off, potted in sandy soil and stood in a cool greenhouse to root. Underground stems may be severed and they too will also form heads if placed in sandy soil. Any plant that may have grown too tall may have its head cut off a few inches below the rosette of leaves, and it will form roots when potted or boxed.
Y. filamentosa, of dwarf habit, producing side growths at the base; flower stem 5 ft. high with a loose panicle of pendulous, creamy-white flowers in July and Aug.
Y. gloriosa (*Adam's Needle*) will grow up to 8 ft. high and carries a head of glaucous green leaves 1½ to 2 ft. long. Flowering from July to Sept. the creamy-white blossoms are borne on a branched panicle often 5 ft. long by 1 ft. wide.
Y. recurvifolia is another tall-growing species with recurving foliage. The flower spike is somewhat shorter than that of **Y. gloriosa.** It is a graceful shrub and the species most frequently seen in town gardens, since it has a high resistance to atmospheric pollution.

ZENOBIA SPECIOSA
An evergreen ericaceous shrub native to the eastern United States. It blooms from June to Aug., bearing Lily-of-the-Valley-like flowers of a waxy whiteness. It likes a semi-shaded position in a well-drained peaty soil where it will reach a size of some 3 × 3 ft. No pruning is required. Propagation is by means of cuttings of young shoots inserted in a frame in June or by division in the early autumn.

CHAPTER FIFTEEN

General Principles of Fruit Cultivation

THERE are few gardeners who do not make some attempt at fruit growing, even if it is only with the so-called 'bargain' apple tree, of uncertain age and variety, bought at a local market. Somehow a garden does not seem complete without some fruit trees—even if they're only grown for shade! Nevertheless one must face up to the fact that compared with the commercial grower the average gardener is in a comparatively difficult position so far as pest and disease control is concerned. To get really first-class fruit these invaders have to be kept under close control, and that is not easy when neighbours, helpful as they may be, do not share the same horticultural enthusiasms, and are not prepared to wage the all-out war which is necessary. However, the newer spray materials are effective enough to give reasonable control of the few serious troubles while the others cause only superficial damage and can be borne with equanimity. The satisfaction of having really fresh fruit straight from the garden makes it easy to overlook a small pimple, or a patch of russet, which, while it may mar the beauty of the fruit bearing it, in no way impairs its flavour or dietetic value.

Situation

It is generally unwise to attempt to grow apricots, figs, grapes, peaches or nuts in a coldish climate, but all the fruits dealt with here can be grown in the open anywhere in a temperate situation with a reasonable chance of success. For apples and pears the ideal conditions are found where there is reasonable sun to give good colour to the fruit and to ripen the young wood at the end of the year, which is necessary to ensure a crop the following season. In colder situations it will be in good seasons only that these conditions will prevail and crops will consequently be rather uncertain, though this can be overcome to some extent by choosing particular varieties. In areas with a high humidity and consequent favourable conditions for the fungus causing scab, it is more difficult to produce clear-skinned fruit, but intrinsically the fruit is just as good, and the milder conditions prevailing have compensating advantages.

Local Conditions. So far as local conditions are concerned, the best position is one fully open to the sun and air, and preferably part-way up a slight slope facing south or west. The position must not be too exposed however. It is difficult to get well-shaped trees or bushes in such a position, but what is much worse is that bees are very loth to fly in districts in which strong winds persist during flowering time, and without bees there may be no pollination and no crop. If shelter is not already provided it is best to get it established before the trees are planted. Gooseberries and red currants are particularly liable to have branches blown out by strong winds. Even worse than high exposed positions are those which are known as frost-holes, or frost-pockets. These are low-lying places into which cold air drains from adjoining higher land, and which are consequently liable to early and late frosts. The greater the area of higher land which is feeding the frost-pocket with cold air, the more severe will the effect be, the worst position of all being where the garden forms the centre of a bowl, with the cold air coming in from all directions. In such a position it is best not to attempt fruit growing. In other positions it is sometimes possible to drain the cold air still lower, away from the fruit, by removing a hedge or other obstruction that is holding it up. In a 'frost-bowl' nothing can be done. In some seasons trees in a frost-pocket will bear no crop at all up to a sharply defined level, above which there may be a full crop, the dividing line being the height to which the frost rises at flowering time. Thus the lower-growing the plant, the more liable it is to be damaged, with strawberries being the most susceptible.

Soils for Fruit

Most fruits grow best on a slightly acid soil (see page 54), one with a pH of 5·5 to 6·5, but the top soil is not the most important factor where fruit growing is concerned. Having a good deep but well-drained sub-soil is more important. For tree fruits, particularly apples, good drainage is essential and if water lies for any time within 2 or 3 in. of the surface, the trees will suffer. If the sub-soil is shallow, as often happens on chalk or gravel, it is very difficult to grow fruit satisfactorily, because the roots quickly dry out. Chalk has the added disadvantage of making the iron in the soil unavailable to plants, which results in pale sickly foliage and poor crops, and it is best not to attempt bush fruits or strawberries on really chalky soils. Given a good sub-soil, the top soil can be heavy clay or light sand, so long as the trees or bushes receive the appropriate treatment to enable them to cope with any top soil shortcomings until their roots get down to the more congenial sub-soil. Nevertheless, a good medium loam as a top soil is an added advantage in getting the trees away to a good start, especially the shallow-rooting ones.

Forms of trees

Trees or bushes can be trained into almost any shape, but the commonest and most practical are the cordon, which is the most restricted form, the espalier, the fan, the pyramid and the bush, which are all of medium size, and the standard and half-standard which form the largest trees. See Fig. 17.

Rootstocks. Different varieties of any kind of fruit trees vary in their vigour, and while it is possible to obtain the degree of vigour needed by choosing a suitable variety, in very few cases would the trees be suitable in other respects. A much better control of vigour is obtained by budding or grafting a chosen variety on to another rootstock of the same or closely allied kind of fruit, and since there is a range of rootstocks for each kind of fruit, it is possible to choose one which will give the degree of vigour needed in each case. The method of budding and grafting is given in the chapter on propagation, but the best rootstock for each purpose is given under the individual fruits.

Cordons. A cordon consists of a single stem with fruiting spurs along its whole length. It may be grown vertically, horizontally, or at any angle between, but is generally most successful at an angle of 45 deg., as that ensures regular growth along its whole length. Cordons by their very nature need a permanent support of wire trellis, fence or wall.

Espaliers. An espalier is in effect a tree bearing a number of cordons. It can consist of a central vertical stem with the side branches trained horizontally, or the main stem can be stopped about 1 ft. from the ground and two or more branches taken up vertically. This latter form was previously known as a multiple cordon. The espalier needs similar support to a cordon, though usually of a more substantial nature as it makes a bigger tree. It is not a form suitable for stone fruits.

Fans. In this form the branches, of roughly equal vigour, radiate fanwise from a main stem stopped about 1 ft. above ground level. It is most suitable for stone fruits, red currants and gooseberries.

Pyramids. These can be grown on a stock which gives small trees of about 5 ft. high, known as dwarf pyramids, or on a stronger stock giving trees up to 9 ft. high. In both cases the main stem continues to its full height, the branches radiating from it getting shorter towards the top. It is a good type of tree for producing high-quality fruit, since all parts get adequate sunlight and air.

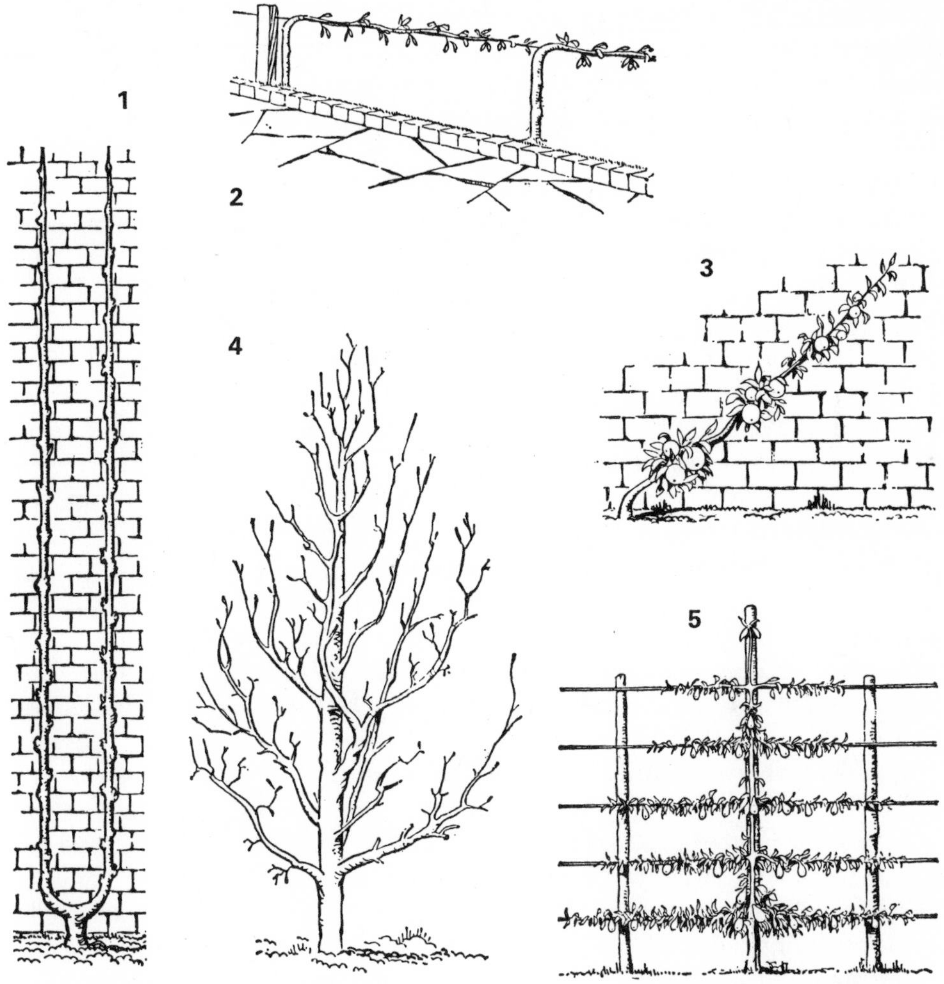

Fig. 17. Forms of trained fruit trees. 1, vertical cordon (double); 2, horizontal cordon (single); 3, diagonal cordon (single); 4, pyramid form; and 5, espalier (horizontal branched).

Open-centred trees. The open-centred bush tree is formed of a single main stem to a height of 2 to 3 ft., above which point three or four main branches spread out to form the framework of a cup-shaped tree with no central stem. The standard tree is like a bush, except that the main unbranched stem is continued to a height of from 5 to 7 ft., while a half-standard has a stem height of about 4 ft.

Planning the fruit garden

The first thing to decide is what fruits are to be grown, and this will largely be a matter of personal preference within the limitations of the site. In most cases it is best to decide what berried fruits are to be included, as their vigour is not complicated by the use of rootstocks, and the space that they will need can be easily reckoned. Then the tree-fruit requirements can be adjusted to the remaining available space by choosing the appropriate form of tree on the most suitable rootstock. Most gardeners like to include strawberries and black currants, but raspberries, which seem to be particularly troublesome to people with dentures, are often excluded. There is also only a limited use for red and white currants, so that generally one or two bushes are enough.

The distances between fruit trees and bushes varies and it is best to get this information from your nurseryman. Make sure you buy the right number of plants to fill the space allocated. When the bushes and trees are first put in at the correct distances they look very isolated, but they will quickly fill the space and will benefit from having sufficient room in which to develop freely. Even if there is adequate room for the larger type of tree, it may be felt that a larger number of smaller trees as cordons or dwarf pyramids will be preferable, in view of the fact that they come into fruit slightly earlier in their life and that they are more likely to produce top-quality fruit. It must be borne in mind, however, that the initial expense of the larger number of trees may be considerable, and that they must have regular attention.

The more vigorous bush or standard trees, once they have been formed to a reasonable shape, will survive a good deal of later neglect and come to little harm, but if cordons or dwarf pyramids are neglected they quickly get out of hand. So the amount of time which is likely to be available to look after them will have to be taken into consideration. Nevertheless, with the advantages that these smaller trees have, it is well worth while utilizing existing fences, walls, or other supports for cordons, and for having a few dwarf pyramids as a special interest.

Pollination. With tree fruits it is advisable to have at least two varieties of each sort, flowering at the same time, so that cross-pollination takes place. This is because many varieties, especially of pears and plums, are self-sterile; that is, they will not set fruit with their own pollen. In some cases the neighbour's trees will serve as pollinators, but it is best to be sure, and to plant one's own.

Birds. It is unwise to plant cherries in the open in a built-up area, because it is very unlikely that the birds will leave any to be picked. The only way to ensure a crop is to have them on a wall and net them when they start to colour. Even with soft fruits birds will take their share and in some districts a fruit cage is the only solution, in which case all the fruits to be netted must be arranged in as compact an area as possible to keep the cost of netting to a minimum. The cage is best formed of a permanent side framework of metal or wood, covered with $\frac{1}{2}$-in. mesh wire netting, the top being covered at fruiting time with fish netting. Wire netting over the top often causes injury to the plants through a fine deposit of zinc being washed down by rain, or if left in position in the winter may collapse under heavy snow and even bring the whole structure down. For the strawberry bed $1\frac{1}{2}$-in. square posts, driven in at intervals with 2 ft. out of the ground, and with strong wire stretched in each direction from their tops, gives a framework on which to rest fish netting for the fruiting season.

Layout. Do not combine fruit with vegetables, except possibly in the case of strawberries. Fruit needs quite different cultural and manurial treatment as well as specific spraying for disease control so that it is impracticable to combine the two successfully. If possible, fruits requiring the same manures should be put together. Dessert apples, gooseberries and strawberries want only limited amounts of nitrogen, whereas cooking apples, plums and bush and cane fruits want more, while black currants will take large amounts. Raspberries and gooseberries will tolerate moderate shade, whereas all other fruits like full sunshine.

Selection of trees

There are three main points to bear in mind in choosing fruit trees. They should be as young as is practicable, have good root systems and, except in the case of maidens, a good skeleton framework of branches. In general terms, the younger a plant is, the better will it stand transplanting. For trees, the ideal would be to buy them as maidens, that is 1 year old from budding and consisting of a single stem. Some amateurs, however, may prefer to let the nurseryman get the first main branches established, as he will be able to get them well-positioned, and this will mean that the tree will be 2 or 3 years old when bought. The shape of the mature tree will depend on the positioning of its main branches, and while the branches must be sturdy, they need not be imposingly large; a good root system will soon put extra vigour into them. Old thick-stemmed trees that are really the nurseryman's discards should be avoided. Bush fruit should be bought as 2-year-old bushes, except that raspberries will be 1-year-old canes and strawberries will be newly-rooted runners. As with all plants, the root system should be adequate with a good supply of fine fibrous roots. A tree with a fat stem-base, with thick fangs in place of roots, should go straight back to the seller or on to the bonfire.

Tree planting

Fruit trees can be planted at any time when they are dormant, that is from

Planting

Nov. to the end of Feb. Nov. planting is best because the soil is still warm and the roots make some growth before the winter. Planting can be continued into Mar., but it is generally unwise because cold drying winds are liable to set in at that time and these are very taxing for newly-planted trees. Ideal planting weather is dull, windless and with high humidity. The most important factor is the condition of the soil. It should be in a moderately moist, friable state, so that the soil crumbs work well in between the roots and so give them the maximum contact with the soil. If it is wet and pasty, all the roots will be sandwiched in one layer between the bottom of the hole and the replaced soil, and new root formation will be seriously hindered. If trees arrive when the soil is in a wet condition they should be 'heeled in' until it dries out. This simply means digging out a short length of trench in a sheltered part of the garden, large enough to accommodate the roots, and then laying the trees almost parallel with the ground and covering the roots with soil. If trees arrive during frost, when it is obviously unwise to plant even if it is possible, they are best left unpacked in a cool but frost-proof place until the frost breaks. Then soak the roots in water for a few hours before planting them or heeling them in. In planting, make the hole wide enough to take all the roots fully spread out, and of such a depth that the point of union between stock and scion will be 3 to 6 in. above ground level when filled in completely. It is best not to dig the holes until a short time before planting, otherwise the sides and bottom tend to cake and this makes it difficult for new roots to penetrate. The bottom of the hole should be slightly convex so that the roots can point downwards. If the soil is known to be short of potash or phosphate, suitable fertilizers can be added to correct this, but no nitrogen, either in the form of dung or artificials, should be applied at this stage. Damaged roots and long fibreless ones should be cut back. Good crumbly soil should be worked between the roots with a fork, or better still with the fingers.

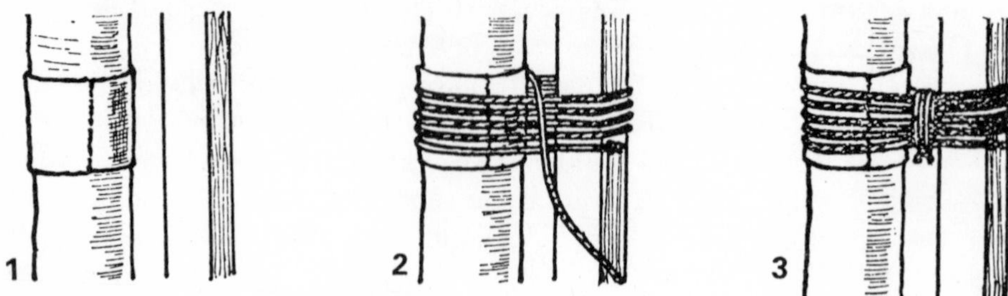

Fig 18. Three stages in securing a fruit tree to a stake using a strip of sacking to prevent chafing and damage to the bark.

Moving the tree sharply up and down for an inch or two will also help to work the soil between the roots, but care must be taken not to raise the tree permanently while doing this. When the roots are well covered, the replaced soil should be firmed by light treading, unless it is heavy or wet. Oblique cordons should be planted at the angle at which they are to be trained, and with the scion on the upper side to avoid breaking at the union.

Staking and tying

All trees must be given support in their early stages. For bush and standards, one strong stake, 2 to 3 in. in diameter and preferably of oak, ash, chestnut or of metal, should be driven in close to the tree, so that its top comes just below the tree crotch. This should be put in position at planting time, before the hole is filled in so as to avoid damage to the roots. In securing the tree to the stake precautions must be taken to prevent it chafing and damaging the bark. This is best done by using a manufactured tree tie such as can be bought at most horticultural shops, or by cutting a strip, up to 6 in. wide, of soft material such as thick woollen rag or sacking, or an old bicycle tyre, and wrapping it round the tree stem, and making the tie over that. It should be tied rigidly to the stake, so that there is no play in strong winds. The amount of 'give' in the padding will allow for stem growth for one season but not for longer, so ties should be loosened and renewed each year. This will also get rid of hibernating insects which tend to hide in the wrapping material. Pliable wire threaded through short lengths of ½-in. rubber hose also makes a good tie, crossing it over between tree and stake, and old bicycle tyres can be used similarly. Pyramid trees worked on very dwarfed stocks will need support all their lives. The best thing is to plant such trees in rows, so that support can be given them by two wires, at about 18 and 36 in. from the ground, stretched between posts.

Cordons. For cordons a strong wire fence is needed, with posts at 10 to 12 ft. intervals, and with stronger posts with straining bolts at the end to keep the wires taut. It is well worth while making a good job of this right at the start. The trees are usually taken to 6 ft. high, and the posts should be the same height. It is best to have three wires, with the bottom one 3 ft. from the ground, using gauge 10 for the top wire, but slightly thinner gauge for the lower wires. In the early stages at any rate it is best to fix strong bamboo canes to the wires by wiring, or tying with strong string, in the positions the trees are to occupy. The trees can then be tied to the canes with soft twine, which will not cut into the bark. Where canes are not used, the trees should be put on the leeward side of the wires so that they do not blow on to them and get chafed. The trees should not be continued along the top wire. Where trees are to be grown against walls, the wires should be at least 4 in. from the walls.

Management of tree fruits

Manuring. With trees planted in a reasonably fertile soil, no additional manure should be needed for at least a season, though a mulch over the root area will keep the soil cool and moist, and will help root action. An annual dressing of sulphate of potash at 1 oz. per sq. yd., and half that amount of superphosphate, is generally beneficial. If the leaves turn bluish-green towards autumn, with scorched edges, then still more potash is needed, while if they take on bright autumn tints of reddish purple, extra phosphate should be given. The amount of nitrogen to be applied will be decided by the vigour of the trees. Sufficient is needed to maintain active growth, but not so much that the wood formed is excessive or remains soft and unripened by the autumn. It should not be applied later than June. It will only be on poor soils that nitrogen will be needed at all in the first 2 or 3 years, but when the tree has settled down and is cropping, a dressing of sulphate of ammonia at 1 oz. per sq. yd. or its equivalent, in spring and repeated 2 months later, will be about the amount required.

Spraying. Control of specific pests and diseases is dealt with in Chapter 18. It is, however, possible to anticipate some of these troubles or to take them in one's stride, if a regular spraying programme is carried out. The following table sets out such a programme.

Stage of growth	*Month*	*Treatment*	*Troubles dealt with*
Dormant	Dec.–Jan.	Tar oil wash, or D.N.C.	Aphid, apple-sucker, and generally cleans up trees
Pink bud	Late Apr.	D.D.T. or lead-arsenate	Blossom weevil, and winter moth caterpillar
Petal-fall	Late May	Lime-sulphur + malathion or nicotine	Mildew, aphid, red-spider, and apple sawfly

In addition, monthly sprays with either malathion or nicotine are likely to be needed to keep down aphid coming in from surrounding gardens, and in humid areas these should have lime-sulphur or other fungicide added to control scab.

Fruit-thinning. In a good fruit year, much more fruit is set than the trees can hope to develop to a good size, and under those conditions some thinning is well worth while. It should, however, be deferred until mid-July, as in the first half of that month trees often do a lot of natural shedding of fruit, and if thinned before that a short crop can easily result. Young developing trees often set fruit which takes nourishment needed to build up the tree framework, and most of these fruits should be removed when quite young.

Frost prevention. While fruit trees generally are quite hardy, the flowers can be killed by 3 or 4 deg. of frost of even short duration. Snap frosts occurring at flowering time can often be countered by temporary cover put on at short notice. Such frosts almost always occur under still windless conditions, so that newspaper, muslin, old curtains, or similar material, laid over the plants will generally stay in position till the frost is past. It may look untidy for a few hours, but the benefit is reaped later in the season. Where blossoms are only slightly frozen they can sometimes be saved by covering them from the early morning sun, as it is the quick thawing which does most damage.

Training and pruning trees

Pruning is not an exact operation and it is impossible to lay down hard and fast rules for it. Varieties differ in their habit of growth, rootstocks affect the type of growth as well as the vigour, soil and weather have their effects, and pruning has to be adjusted to meet these variations. So it is only possible to state the general principles leaving the rest to the discretion of the pruner. The expert pruner does not blindly concern himself with making a tree conform to a given shape. If a tree tends to grow away from the shape he had in mind for it, he will adjust his ideas to what he thinks is best for that individual tree.

There are two stages in pruning. The first is the formation of a sound basic framework for the tree, generally with a definite shape in mind. The second is the maintenance of a balanced growth which will result in ample fruit buds and adequate wood growth, with the branches sufficiently spaced to let the sun and air get in in order to keep the tree healthy and to ripen up the fruit. Taking the different forms in which fruit trees can be grown, the procedure is as follows. The correct way to make a cut is shown in Fig. 19.

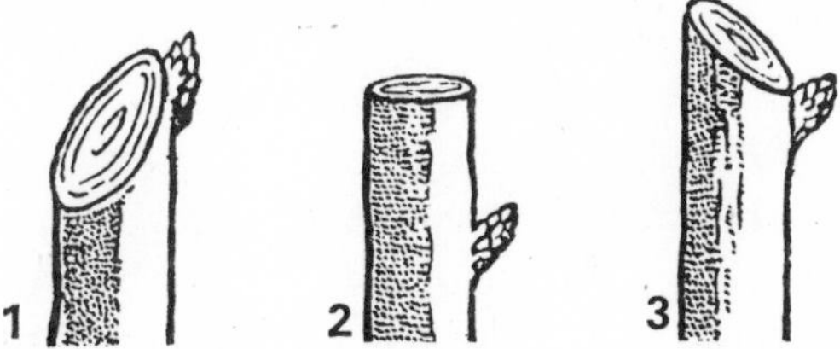

Fig. 19. 1 correct way of making a cut. 2 and 3 show how not *to make a cut. In 2 the cut is too far above the bud and in 3 the cut is incorrectly placed and runs into the bud.*

Cordons. For cordons maiden trees must be planted, though they may or may not have small lateral branches. If they do not reach their full length in one season, the main stem must be continued for a second year. Should the main stem bear a fruit bud at the end, it must be cut back to a wood bud in the winter, while if it is weak it should be cut back one-third of its length to induce greater vigour in a continuation shoot. Later on, to hasten the formation of fruit buds, summer pruning is practised. This involves cutting back all the firm, mature, lateral shoots to three or four buds, not counting any in the rosette of leaves at the base, in early July in the South, and about 14 days later in the North. Smaller shoots coming out from the lateral shoots should be cut back to one bud, and any soft immature shoots should be left until Sept. when they should be treated similarly. This concentrates the nourishment into the buds at the base of the shoot, and hastens their formation into fruit buds, and may take 2 or more years, during which time laterals arising must be pruned to one or two buds. Spurs may carry two or more fruit buds in young trees, and many more in older trees, in which case they may need to be thinned, or even taken out altogether to prevent the over crowding of the trees.

Espaliers. For a horizontal espalier a maiden is cut back about 18 in. from the ground in the winter. The top bud gives a shoot to continue the main stem vertically and the next two opposite buds form the first two horizontal branches. These branches should be trained at an angle of 45 deg. during the growing season to induce stronger growth, and taken down to the horizontal the following winter. Excessive growth of either shoot can be reduced by putting it at a lower angle. Other laterals on the main stem which are not needed for branches should be stopped at three or four leaves, and secondary shoots at one leaf, later removing them altogether. Each tier is formed in the same way in successive years, and each branch is pruned as if it was a cordon (see Figs. 17/5). The 'U' espalier starts off in the same way as the horizontal except that no central stem is taken upright. The first two branches are, however, brought down to the horizontal when about 18 in. long, and from that point trained vertically to form the two main arms, and are pruned as for cordons. Should they not send out sufficient laterals to form spurs, they should be cut back to induce the buds to break.

Fans. These can be formed by planting out a maiden tree, and cutting it back to a good bud about 2 ft. from the ground. All buds except the top three are then rubbed out. The resulting top shoot has to be pinched back to a few buds once or twice during the growing season to concentrate vigour into the two lower shoots, and then removed altogether the following winter. The two lower shoots should be trained at an angle of about 30 deg. from the horizontal, using canes secured

PLATE 47
'Blaze', a climbing rose.

PLATE 48

'Christian Dior', a hybrid tea rose.

PLATE 49

'Crimson Glory', a hybrid tea rose.

PLATE 50
'Firecracker', a floribunda rose.

PLATE 51
'Kordes Perfecta', a hybrid tea rose.

PLATE 52
'Ma Perkins', a floribunda rose.

PLATE 53
'Tally-Ho', a hybrid tea rose.

PLATE 54
'White Knight', a hybrid tea rose.

to the wires, and these form the two main arms of the fan from which the other shoots radiate. If one shoot is more vigorous than the other it can be checked by temporarily lowering it a little. The next winter cut back these two shoots one-third to one-half their length according to vigour, and then allow three strong and evenly-spaced shoots to develop on the top-side of each, and one on the under-side, rubbing out all other buds. The following winter these branches should then be cut back and stems taken from them, as was done with the two main branches the previous year. This is repeated each year until the whole area is covered with the branches spaced about 12 in. apart.

Pyramids. In the winter a maiden tree is cut back to a bud about 2 ft. from the ground, and the resulting shoot cut back the following winter to about half its length, but to a bud on the opposite side. This is repeated each successive winter, and in this way the central stem is kept upright. The lateral shoots which form the branches should be cut back a third of their length if strong growing and to half their length if weaker. Laterals from these branches must be shortened to three or four buds and sub-laterals to one bud, or removed altogether if too crowded (see Fig. 17/4). On dwarf pyramids summer pruning can be done as with cordons. Once the tree has settled down to fruiting, much less growth will be made and pruning will merely consist of keeping the branches well spaced.

Open-centred bush and standard trees. The pruning of these trees is very simple. The maiden stem is cut to a bud at the required height, and three or four of the resulting shoots which are well placed are selected to form the main branches. Those coming out at a wide angle are best, and for this reason the top one or two are often cut out, as they tend to be too upright. From then on pruning is aimed at building up a cup-shaped tree with well-spaced branches. Nothing in the way of detailed spur pruning need be attempted. It should always be remembered that hard pruning makes for more vigorous growth, so that where weak shoots need to be urged to grow stronger, they should be cut back to a few buds, but where vigour needs to be reduced, only the slightest cutting back should be done.

Root-pruning and ringing. In cases where trees are making excessive growth with few fruit buds, they can be checked by root-pruning. With a young tree it can be lifted and its main roots cut back, but with an older tree the work involves digging a trench about a yard from the stem, tunnelling below the tree and severing the roots (see Fig. 20). It is best to do one half one winter and the other the next. The considerable amount of work involved can be avoided in the case of apples and pears, however, as there is a much simpler operation which is quite safe and effective with them. This is bark ringing. It consists of taking out a complete ring of bark about $\frac{1}{4}$ in. wide for a tree of 3 in. diameter, up to the maximum of $\frac{1}{2}$ in.

wide for one double that size. It should be done at flowering time, when the bark will come away easily, and it should be covered with adhesive tape to encourage healing (see Fig. 20).

Harvesting

Soft fruit should be gathered when it is cool and dry. The best time is as early as possible in the morning after the dew is off, but before the sun has sufficient power to warm the fruit. Plums, too, should be picked dry. With apples and pears it is not so important so long as they can be spread out to dry soon after picking, but

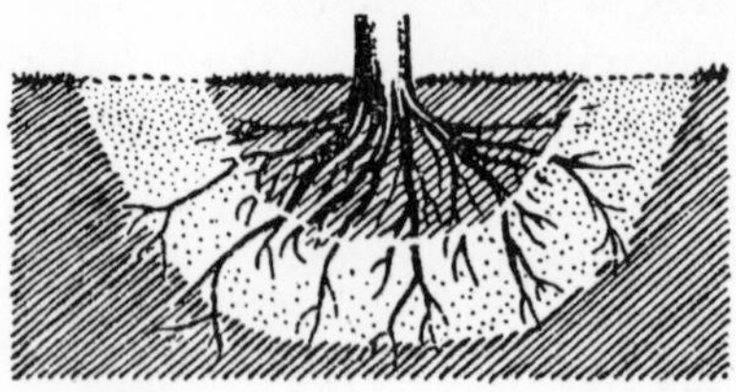

Fig. 20. Left, *side view section showing how roots should be pruned.* Below, *three stages in ringing a fruit tree and protecting the cut with adhesive tape.*

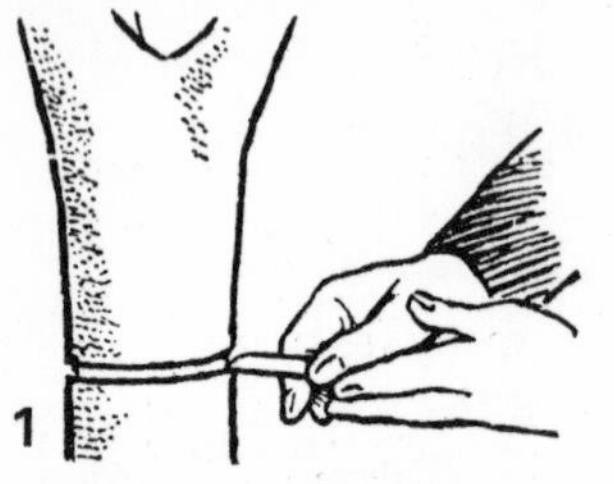

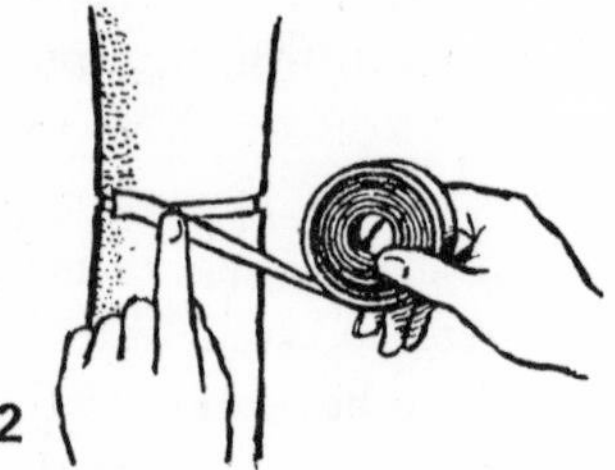

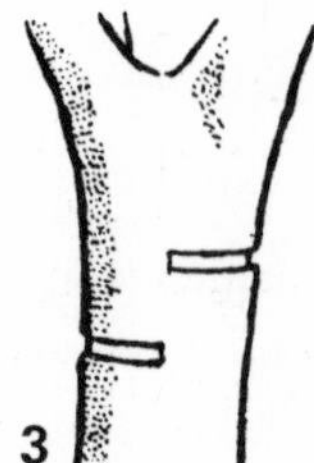

even so, varieties for long storage are best picked dry. Pick all fruit carefully and handle it as if it were eggs. Even hard fruit like apples will bruise easily, and though no damage may be visible at the time, its keeping quality will be affected. In picking do not grip the fruit with the finger-ends, but let the palm of the hand take the weight, then lift the fruit until it comes away easily.

CHAPTER SIXTEEN

The Practical Cultivation of Specific Fruits

THE general principles of fruit-growing have been given in the preceding chapter; this chapter is concerned with the essentially practical aspect of growing specific fruits.

Apples

Rootstocks. All nurserymen specializing in fruit trees give a choice of rootstocks on which their trees are worked. Most of the apple stocks now in use were raised at the East Malling Research Station, and their numbers are prefixed with 'M', or where raised in conjunction with the John Innes Horticultural Institution, by 'MM'. The rootstock most suitable for the very restricted type of tree, the small cordon or the dwarf pyramid, is the M.IX. It brings them into bearing quicker than any other stock, but it has a very restricted root system and consequently the trees worked on it have to be supported all their life. While M.IX is useful for its specialist purpose, a slightly more vigorous rootstock, but one which gives a small enough tree to be grown as a cordon, small pyramid or bush in the average garden, is the one that most practical gardeners will be looking for. The best for this purpose is MM.106., and it is particuarly good on sandy soil. M.VII is also very good, as it grows vigorously in its early years, but soon settles down to give good crops. For the larger bush tree with a 12 to 15 ft. spread, or for espaliers, the best stocks are MM.104., M.II, and MM.111., in that order of vigour, though there is not a lot of difference between them. MM.109 is a little more vigorous, and stands up to drought conditions better on a sandy soil. For very vigorous trees, which will generally be trained as standards or half-standards, and planted separately, the best stocks are M.XVI and M.XXV.

Pollination. Most varieties will pollinate any other variety, but 'Worcester

Pearmain' is probably the most effective for the purpose. There are a few varieties which are of limited value as pollinators. These include: 'Bramley's Seedling', 'Belle de Boskoop', 'Ribston Pippin', 'Blenheim Orange', 'Warner's King'.

Other varieties, including 'Beauty of Bath', 'Crawley Beauty' and 'Edward VII', are of little use as pollinators because most of their flowering period is outside that of most other varieties.

Varieties. There are over 2,000 varieties of apple in the National Fruit Trials alone, so that there is no dearth of varieties from which to choose. The difficulty is in getting down to a short list of those varieties likely to give the best results in a particular situation. The following lists are an attempt to do this, though many varieties of merit have perforce had to be left out. In choosing varieties account should be taken of any which do particularly well in the locality, even though they may not be included in the lists, for it may be found that a moderately good variety will, if local conditions suit it, be the equal of others more generally preferred.

Cooking varieties

Arthur Turner★ July–Oct. Good flavour and regular cropper. B/A.

Bramley's Seedling★ Nov.–Mar. Is the best keeping cooker and a heavy cropper if it misses frost damage, to which it is particularly subject. Is vigorous and spreading so requires little pruning. S/S, N/S, B.

Early Victoria July–Aug. Codlin type. A regular heavy cropper so fruit may need thinning. Upright habit. Reasonably tolerant of heavy soils. N/S.

Edward VII Dec.–Apr. Very good quality. Flowers late, so misses frost. Upright habit. C/G, S/S.

George Neal★ Sept.–Oct. An improvement on 'Grenadier'. Fruit large and crisp, and an excellent cooker. Regular cropper.

Howgate Wonder Dec.–Feb. Large flat apple, striped, and regular cropper.

Lane's Prince Albert★ Nov.–Jan. Reliable cropper. Fruit soft so needs careful handling. Prune fairly hard. Rather liable to mildew, but sulphur must not be used on it after flowering. N/S, C/G.

Monarch Oct.–Jan. Fruit soft so needs careful handling. Regular cropper and may need thinning. N/S.

Newton Wonder Dec.–Mar. Heavy cropper of excellent quality. Can be used for dessert late in season. Vigorous grower. B (strongly).

Rev. W. Wilks Sept–Dec. Bears very heavy crops. Cooks frothily. C/G.

Dessert varieties

Advance★ Aug. Of much better quality than the more usually grown 'Beauty of Bath', and only about a week later. Juicy, with a Cox's flavour. It has a good habit, but is not a heavy cropper. S/T, S/S.

Blenheim Orange Nov.–Jan. Excellent flavour and appearance. Growth is vigorous, but crops are light in the early years. S/S.

Charles Ross★ Oct. Large and attractive fruit of good quality. Thrives on chalky loam. N/S.

Cox's Orange Pippin Nov.–Dec. Unsurpassed quality. Is a difficult variety to grow even in mild conditions, and is only a moderate cropper. S/T, S/S. 'Crimson Cox' is inferior.

Egremont Russet★ Oct.–Dec. The best variety of russet apple. Fine flavour and a regular cropper. S/T, C/G.

Ellison's Orange Late Sept.–Oct. Looks like a Cox but has an aniseed flavour. Has only a short season. An easy variety to grow and a regular cropper. N/S, S/T, F/R, B.

Epicure Late Aug.–Sept. Good cropper of excellent flavour. Short season only. Spreading habit. S/S.

Fortune★ Sept.–Oct. Good quality and flavour, and moderately good cropper. Upright habit. N/S, S/T, S/S, B.

James Grieve★ Sept.–Oct. Very good flavour, but flesh tender so needs careful handling. Vigorous and upright, and easy to grow. N/S, S/T.

Orleans Reinette★ Nov.–Feb. A free cropper with fruit of excellent flavour.

Ribston Pippin Nov.–Dec. Regular cropper and of excellent flavour. B/A, S/S.

Sturmer Pippin Dec.–May. The best very late keeper. Leave on the tree as long as possible. Does well on most soils.

Sunset★ Nov.–Dec. Good quality of Cox's flavour, but fruit sometimes rather dull in appearance. Strong upright grower. B/A, S/T, S/S.

Superb Nov.–Jan. Good quality but rather dull appearance. Keeps well. Is rather an erratic cropper. Resistant to canker so suitable for heavier soils. Prune lightly. N/S, B.

Winston Dec.–Apr. A good cropper of fair quality.

Worcester Pearmain Sept.–Oct. Good colour and a regular cropper, but of moderate quality. Upright grower. N/S, F/R.

★ = Varieties of special merit.
S/T = Suitable for dwarf and trained trees.
S/S = Self-sterile, so needs a pollinator.
N/S = Does well in colder, northern regions.
B = Tends to biennial bearing, that is, fruiting only in alternate years.
F/R = Resistant to frost.
C/G = Compact grower, so particularly suitable for gardens.
B/A = Tree in blossom is particularly attractive.

Apricots

The apricot will ripen only in favoured spots, and even there will need a south- or west-facing wall. The soil must be of open texture and preferably of a chalky nature. The general treatment is the same as for the peach, to which it is nearly related. It differs in bearing fruit on spurs as well as on 1- and 2-year-old wood, so that unwanted laterals should be cut back to two buds instead of being removed altogether. Fruit-thinning need be less drastic than with the peach, the fruits being left at about 6 in. apart. All varieties are self-fertile. While trees in good situations will crop heavily, they are usually short-lived, often succumbing to 'die-back disease' for which there is no known cure. The best variety is 'Moor Park'.

Blackberries and hybrid berries

The cultivated blackberries crop heavily and have much finer fruits than the wild type, though not all varieties are of superior flavour. They will grow in any reasonable soil, preferring one with ample organic material in it, but tolerating even a very chalky one. They will grow in almost any position, enabling them to be used where most other crops would find it uncongenial. If too shaded, however, the fruit flavour will be poor. They are easily propagated by layering the tips of the new shoots in July, which can be severed from the parent plant and planted out the following spring. In planting mature plants the existing canes should be cut back to 6–9 in. from the ground. The fruit is borne mainly on 1-year-old wood, so pruning and training consists of cutting out old fruited canes and replacing them, fanwise, with the new shoots and removing any weak or surplus ones. Ample feeding is needed to maintain vigour, though 'Himalaya Giant' may be tamed a little by less generous treatment. Where trained to a wire trellis, three wires will be needed, at 2 ft., 3½ ft. and 5 ft. from the ground, though for 'Himalaya Giant' they will be better at 3 ft., 4½ ft., and 6 ft. Plants of most varieties should be 10 ft. to 12 ft. apart. If cane spot is troublesome, the fruiting canes should be trained on the lower wires and the new canes above them, so that the spores do not fall from the old canes on to the new. The best varieties are:

Himalaya Giant Very strong-growing, needing up to 20 ft. apart, with large fruit of only moderate flavour, and with vicious thorns. Ripens July.
Bedford Giant Ripens July.
John Innes Ripens Aug.–Sept.
Parsley-leaved Ripens Sept.

Loganberries

This is a hybrid, and is similar to the blackberry, but has dark red fruit of a more acid flavour. It is not so robust a grower, so sites exposed to severe frost or cold winds should be avoided. While it can be grown on a wide range of soils it does not like very chalky ones, or any of an extreme nature. Plants should be set at 8–10 ft. apart. To maintain good growth an annual application of 1 oz. each of a nitrogenous and potassic fertilizer should be given per sq. yd., and the same amount of superphosphate every third year. Other treatment is the same as for blackberries. In addition to the ordinary type of loganberry, there is the 'Merton Thornless', which crops equally heavily.

Other hybrid berries include: 'The Boysenberry', 'The Phenomenal Berry' and 'The Youngberry'. They need the same treatment as the above, but are generally inferior to them.

Blueberries

While the blueberry is not popular it can be successfully grown. The 'high bush' is the only suitable type, and good varieties are 'Berkley', 'Burlington' and 'Kengrape'. It needs an acid soil of pH 5·8 or below, and one that keeps moist even in the driest summers, but must also be well drained. A layer of peat at least 6 in. thick, overlaying ordinary soil, is most likely to supply these requirements. It will not thrive on high exposed places but needs a position at a lower altitude. Cross-pollination is desirable, so at least two varieties should be grown. Precautions will have to be taken against birds, which are very fond of the fruit.

Cherries

It is very doubtful if the growing of cherries in the open garden is worth while. In the form of tree needed for the open garden they take a long time to come into bearing, and even when they do start fruiting it is extremely difficult to prevent the birds taking most of the crop. By having trained trees, they can be brought into fruit more quickly, and can also be netted against the birds, and the flowers covered to protect them from frost. Even so, it is generally unwise to attempt cherries on a wall lower than 7 or 8 ft., as this would involve severe cutting to keep them in bounds, and would almost certainly lead to serious gumming. Unfortunately there are no really dwarfing rootstocks which can be used to restrict the vigour. Sweet cherries will have a spread of 20 to 24 ft., and sour cherries of 15 to 18 ft. Sweet cherries prefer walls facing south or west, but sour cherries will do well on any wall. The best form for trained trees is the fan.

Varieties. All the sweet cherries need cross-pollinating, but unfortunately all varieties do not cross-pollinate each other. The Morello is self-fertile, and will pollinate any other variety flowering at the same time. The following are good varieties and are listed with suitable combinations for pollinating.

	Season	*Pollinated by numbers*
Dessert		
1. Bigarreau Napoleon	Late July	5, 2, 6
2. Bradbourne Black	July	1, 4
3. Early Rivers	Mid-June	6, 7, 4
4. Merton Heart	Late June	3, 6
5. Roundel	Early July	1, 2
6. Waterloo	Late June	3, 4
Sour		
7. Morello	Aug.–Sept.	Self-fertile

Soil and Manuring. Cherries are rather fastidious so far as soil is concerned. It must have a fair amount of body in it, but must be deep and well drained, and preferably overlay a chalk sub-soil. They do not like heavy clays. With wall trees the vigour must be kept within bounds, so they should not be overfed. An annual mulch of well-decayed dung, plus 1 oz. of sulphate of potash and ½ oz. of super-phosphate per sq. yd. should be ample.

Pruning of established trees of sweet cherry should be done during the growing season. All laterals, except any needed as replacement branches, should be pinched back to four or five buds in July, and back to two or three buds in Sept. This helps the formation of spurs on which the sweet cherry fruits, as well as on younger wood. Surplus shoots and shoots growing towards the wall should also be removed in Sept. Sour cherries bear most of their fruit on the previous year's growth, so the shoots are not pinched back, but older branches should be cut back and replaced by younger growths. Young shoots can be left at from 4 to 6 in. apart.

Harvesting. For really rich flavour the fruit should be left on the tree until it is fully ripe. If the stalks do not part easily from the tree, cut them with scissors, as tearing them off may make wounds through which fungus disease may enter.

Cobnuts and filberts

In a filbert the outer husk extends beyond the end of the nut and enfolds it while in the cobnut it is much shorter. The soil should only be of moderate fertility, though not too hungry, and manuring must be done in moderation to avoid excessive growth. At least two varieties should be planted to ensure adequate pollination. Pruning should be delayed until early Mar. when the male catkins and female flowers can be seen, and sufficient left to give a good crop. They will be found mainly on rather weak lateral growths, and other shoots should be removed or cut back to two buds. Bushes can be allowed to grow naturally, merely thinning the branches occasionally, but they will then form big trees and the nuts will be smaller. Good varieties are: 'Pearson's Dwarf Prolific' (Cob), 'Kentish Cob' (Filbert), 'Cosford' (Cob).

Black currants

Black currants are the most accommodating of the bush fruits and will thrive on most soils, though the best results will be obtained on a deep free-rooting loam that keeps moist during the summer. While they will not tolerate really waterlogged conditions, they are less fastidious as to drainage than most fruits. They will also tolerate heavy dressings of farmyard manure which may be needed to bolster up a poorer soil, and which would upset the balanced growth of other fruits. Indeed, they are such gross feeders that a good dressing of farmyard manure, worked into the soil before planting, is desirable on all but the most fertile land. They do not like acid conditions, so where these exist a good dressing of lime should be given, though not at the same time as the manure. As black currants flower early in the year, they are particularly liable to injury from frost and cold winds, and suitable precautions must be taken against these.

Raising bushes. Propagation is by cuttings of mature shoots taken in Oct. or Nov., all the buds being left on, as the more shoots coming from below ground the better. The following winter the resulting shoots should be cut back to one or two buds, or to ground level. A further year's growth will result in bushes with up to a dozen shoots, and the next winter they should be put in their fruiting positions, as bushes older than 2 years do not grow away so well. Indeed, strong bushes can be planted out at 1 year, and will give equally good results. Plant deeply in order to get shoots from below ground, and cut down all shoots to ground level immediately after planting. There should be no suggestion of a 'leg' to the bush.

General care. Black currants send out a lot of surface roots, so once the root system is formed, deep hoeing or cultivating should be avoided. If a good thick mulch of farmyard manure can be given late each winter, it will keep down most of the weeds, and will go a long way to meet the plants' manurial needs. Additional food should be given each year in the form of 2 oz. of nitrogenous fertilizer, 2 oz. of sulphate of potash, and 1 oz. of superphosphate per bush when growth has got going in Mar. or Apr., doubling the amount of nitrogen if no farmyard manure has been given.

Pruning. After the initial cutting-down, all young shoots should be left intact, as it is on these that the fruit is borne. The only exception is with weak shoots, which should be cut hard back to induce stronger growth. If the bushes are growing well, little pruning will be needed for the first 2 or 3 years after planting, and after that, the aim should be to induce vigorous young shoots from as low down as possible by cutting out older moribund branches. Some varieties tend to become straggly as they get older, and with these the straggling branches must be removed to obtain a more upright bush.

Varieties. The following is a selection of good varieties.

Boskoop Giant The earliest, with large berries, but only a moderate cropper.

Laxton's Giant Almost as early as 'Boskoop', and has large exhibition berries. Not a heavy cropper.

Wellington XXX A good general-purpose variety, though of rather spreading habit. Second-early.

Blacksmith A good general-purpose variety, though it makes rather a large bush. Mid-season.

Baldwin Probably the best all-round variety, though it is the only 'temperamental' one, and will not thrive everywhere. A compact grower and regular cropper, though the berries are not impressively large. Rich in vitamin C. Mid-season.

Raven A regular heavy cropper, but makes a very big bush not suitable for small gardens. Mid-season.

Westwick Choice Very similar to Baldwin, and likely to succeed where that variety fails to do so.

Amos Black The latest fruiting. Upright grower. Moderate cropper.

Red and white currants

These require identical treatment, which is totally different from that needed by black currants. They are not fastidious as to soil, but do best of all on a light open one. Propagation is by 12-in. cuttings of well-ripened 1-year-old wood, of pencil thickness, taken in Oct., all buds other than the top three or four being removed to give a 6 in. leg. From this stage they can be trained as bush or as cordons. The fruit is borne mainly at the base of the previous year's shoots, so that a modified spur-pruning should be practised. This can include summer-pruning in July, followed by cutting back the laterals to two or three buds in the autumn.

Red currants are very sensitive to potash deficiency so an annual dressing of about 2 oz. per bush of sulphate of potash should be given, with other fertilizers to maintain growth. Muriate, or other chloride-containing potash salts must not be used.

The best varieties are:

Laxton's No. 1 The best all-round variety. A vigorous grower and heavy cropper. Wind-resistant. Early.

Red Lake Compact upright grower. Long trusses of large berries. Mid-season.

Wilson's Long-bunch Strong-growing and heavy cropper. Late.

Figs

Fig trees are quite hardy but a sheltered position with warm sunshine is needed to ripen the fruit. This generally calls for a warm wall. The soil must not be too rich, and in most cases it is necessary to restrict the root-run to induce fruiting. A cubic yard of soil will sustain a good tree, and this should be enclosed in brick or concrete sides, with the base packed with hard material which will allow drainage but deter root penetration. The soil can be given a reserve of nutrient by adding 8 oz. of coarse bone meal, and 4 to 5 lb. of mortar rubble or limestone. Training the tree merely consists in spreading the shoots fanwise as they grow, keeping them as evenly spaced as possible, but precise training is impracticable. The fruit is borne at the tips of well-ripened shoots made the previous summer, and is visible in embryo form in the autumn. The main pruning should be done in Mar., when sufficient of these fruiting shoots should be retained, and all surplus, weak or frost-damaged ones removed. In June it helps to swell the young fruits if the tips are pinched out of the fruiting shoots. This does, however, result in a lot more side-shoots developing lower down the tree, and these may have to be thinned out later. Frost damage can be reduced by protecting with straw or similar material secured over the tender shoots against wind, but it must be removed in good time in the spring. With the restricted root-run, watering may be needed in a dry summer, or the fruit may drop off, and a mulch will often help under these conditions. Manuring will not generally be needed as excess vigour must be avoided, but on occasion a dressing of a general fertilizer may be given to maintain adequate growth. The best varieties are 'Brown Turkey' and 'Brunswick'.

Gooseberries

Gooseberries need a fertile soil of open texture, and a good dressing of farmyard manure applied during digging operations will help them. They are also susceptible to potash deficiency, especially on light land, so a dressing of 2 oz. per sq. yd. of sulphate of potash worked into the top 3–4 in. of soil prior to planting is advisable. They can be grown in almost any form, except as standards. For 'rough' growing on poor soil the stool form where there is no leg, but shoots come up from the ground, is best, but this will not appeal to the tidy gardener. The best general-purpose form for the garden is the ordinary bush on a 6- to 8-in. leg, and this will give good size and quality fruit adequate for most needs. Where special dessert quality is desired, these bushes can be spur-pruned, and where suitable varieties are chosen, this will give smaller bushes which can be planted at 4 by 4 ft. instead of the usual 5 by 5 ft. They will also form cordons or espaliers, and in these forms can be planted against a north-facing wall to prolong the season. On a south wall they are rather too liable to severe attacks of red-spider.

Manuring. In planting see that no fresh dung is in contact with the roots. The best subsequent manuring programme is a good 1 in. thick mulch of farmyard manure or similar material in the early spring, plus about 1 oz. per sq. yd. of sulphate of potash. An alternative to this is a dressing of about 3 oz. per sq. yd. of a general fertilizer with a high potash and phosphate content. Care must be taken not to get the bushes over-vigorous or they will almost certainly be attacked by mildew, especially the variety 'Whinham's Industry', while too lush shoots are liable to be blown out by strong winds.

Training and Pruning. Propagation is by straight shoots of 1-year-old wood, about 12 in. long, taken just before all the leaves fall in the autumn. They should not be allowed to dry out between cutting off and planting. The soft tip should be cut off, and, except for the stool bush, all but the top three or four buds and spines removed, to give a clean leg of 6 to 8 in. The cuttings do not take root readily, so they should be given good conditions. The resulting growths can be pruned appropriate to the form of bush needed. After planting in their permanent positions the leaders should be cut back according to vigour, and side-shoots to a bud at about 1 in. from the base. Subsequently trained forms will be spur-pruned by cutting laterals back to two or three buds, and this can also be done on bushes, but for heavy crops of good-sized berries it is best to leave the laterals at six to eight buds, as fruit will be borne along these laterals as well as on spurs. Apart from this, branches should be thinned out if necessary to keep the bush open, and old branches and spurs removed and replaced by new shoots. Unripened shoot-tips, and any attacked by mildew, should be cut off and burned, also any shoots arising on the leg or from below ground, except in the case of stool bushes. A sprawling habit can be counteracted by cutting the straggling branches to upward-pointing buds. In cultivating care should be taken not to damage surface roots.

Varieties. These are not sharply divided between cooking and dessert, the general practice being to pick some berries from each bush when green for cooking, those remaining being used later for dessert. The following are good varieties:

Golden Drop Yellow. Small fruit of good flavour. A regular cropper.

Green Gem Yellow-green. A heavy cropper of good quality fruit.

Howard's Lancer Pale Green. A good general-purpose variety.

Leveller Green-yellow. The best dessert variety, but it needs really good soil conditions, spur-pruning and careful attention. Must not be sprayed with sulphur.

Whinham's Industry Red. A vigorous grower and a heavy cropper. Tolerates heavy soil.

Whitesmith Green-yellow. A good general-purpose variety.

Grapes

Grapes will ripen outdoors only in favoured positions, preferably on south- or west-facing walls, or on a warm southern slope. Excessive vigour delays ripening so much that the crop does not mature, so soil of only moderate fertility, but of open texture, must be chosen. For the same reason manuring must be kept to a minimum, except that well-timed applications given while the berries are swelling will increase the crop. Training is generally as cordons, planted at 4 ft. apart. Laterals are produced and these are stopped at two leaves beyond the flower-cluster, and secondary laterals at one leaf. Only one or two bunches should be taken off a vine in the first fruiting season, gradually increasing the number. These fruit-bearing laterals are cut back to one bud in the winter so that a spur system develops. If trained as horizontal espaliers, laterals should only be taken from the top side of the horizontal branches, and spaced at about 18 in. Much more informal training can also be quite successful with outdoor grapes; all that is needed being supports to keep the fruiting canes off the ground, these canes being replaced by new canes as they are formed. Indoor varieties are not suitable for outdoor cultivation. The following are suitable: *Brandt* Black; *Black Cluster* Black; *Royal Muscadine* Amber; *Grove End Sweetwater* White.

Thinning will need to be done for dessert berries. Birds are likely to be troublesome, and mildew will have to be combated.

Medlar

The medlar is easy to grow, as it thrives in almost any soil, and makes an attractive tree with its crooked picturesque habit. The training and treatment are the same as for the apple, except that medlars are not suitable for the trained forms of tree. The fruit is very much an acquired taste. It should be left on the tree until late Oct. or early Nov., and then stored in a cool place until it is 'bletted'; that is, until the flesh has become soft with incipient decay, when it is ready to eat.

Mulberry

The mulberry can be grown as a bush or standard, but in colder conditions it will need to be grown on a south- or west-facing wall. It likes a well-drained soil, and under good conditions will have a spread of 25–30 ft. Once the tree shape is obtained the only pruning needed will be a very occasional thinning out of the branches. It propagates readily by cuttings or layers from late summer onwards.

Peaches

Outdoor peaches can be grown as bush trees, at about 15 ft. apart, but it is rather a hazardous business. They prefer a light loam, slightly alkaline, but not a strongly chalky soil. The best rootstock is the Brompton. Once the tree-head is formed, pruning should be kept to a minimum, only thinning out crowded branches. The only way to be reasonably assured of crops outdoors, however, is by growing the trees on a south- or west-facing wall, and even then it will probably be necessary to protect the blossom from frost. Treatment for these walled trees is the same for those growing under glass, enough young shoots being trained in to replace the fruiting shoots, and the surplus shoots disbudded. For outdoors, early varieties must be used and among the best are: 'Duke of York', 'Hale's Early' and 'Peregrine', and the nectarines 'Early Rivers' and 'Lord Napier'.

Pears

The cultivation of pears is very similar to that of apples, but it requires rather more detailed attention. Pears need ample warm sunshine to ripen the fruits. So far as soil is concerned they are rather more tolerant of poor drainage than are apples, yet they are likely to suffer more from drought.

Forms of Tree. There is an old adage that 'Pears are planted for heirs', and that was true of trees on their own roots or worked on seedling pear rootstocks. On dwarfing stocks they will come into bearing as quickly as apples if they are grown as restricted trained trees to which they lend themselves very readily. They will succeed in any of the trained forms described in the preceding chapter, and as dwarf pyramids. There are only two rootstocks for pears, the quince for restricted or dwarf trees, and the seedling pear for the large standard trees. There are two varieties of quince, the 'Angers' (Malling A) and the 'Common Quince' (Malling B) which give trees of about equal vigour. Malling C Quince is not recommended. For large standard trees, or even for very large espaliers, the seedling pear stock must be used, but patience will be needed waiting for them to come into bearing. Certain varieties of pear do not make a good union with quince, and for these 'double working' must be practised; that is, a 'compatible' variety must first be worked on to the quince rootstock and the required 'incompatible' variety worked on to it the following season. The nurseryman has other, but more intricate ways of achieving this double-working with the object of avoiding the loss of a season.

Planting and after-care. As pears start into growth before apples they should be given priority for planting, but the method is the same. Special care must be taken to keep the union well above ground, because if the scion sends out roots this is likely to cause excessive vigour and so delay fruiting much more so than with apples. Pear trees on quince tend to make a lot of fruiting spurs at the expense of extension growth, especially when young, and more severe pruning is needed to counteract this. Older pear trees need to have some of the spurs cut out altogether and others shortened. For the same reason pears on quince stock need more nitrogen and less potash than do apples, in order to maintain adequate growth. A good general manuring programme would be to give the trees an annual mulch with farmyard manure or compost, plus a dressing of 1 oz. of a nitrogenous fertilizer, ½ oz. of sulphate of potash and ½ oz. of superphosphate per sq. yd in the spring. On trained trees and when good specimen fruits are needed, it is as well to thin out the fruits so that they are not touching when fully grown. This will be from one to three fruits per spur according to the fruit size of the variety. It should be done in June. Thinning is not generally necessary on bushes in the open.

Harvesting and Storing. Considerable experience is needed to harvest pears just at the right time, as it is unwise to go too much by the colour. Indeed, with the Sept. and early Oct. varieties, it is best to pick them 2 or 3 weeks before their season, at which time some of them may still be quite green. Others should be picked when they part easily from the tree if raised in the hand. Pears do not store well, and they need careful watching to see that they do not go 'sleepy'. A good storage temperature is around 45 deg. F. They should be brought into a warm room for a day or two at about 60 deg. F. to develop their bouquet.

Varieties. Since most pear varieties are unable to set fruit with their own pollen, at least two varieties must be planted to ensure cross-pollination. Most varieties will pollinate any other variety, except 'Beurré d'Amanlis' and 'Bristol Cross', which are useless for pollination, while 'Conference' will not pollinate 'Beurré d'Amanlis'. There are special cooking varieties such as 'Catillac' and 'Bellissime d'Hiver', but the general interest is in dessert varieties, of which the following is a selection:

Beurré Hardy Oct. Does especially well in the south-eastern countries.

*Bristol Cross** Sept.–Oct. Good flavour and appearance.

Conference Oct.–Nov. Self-fertile. A regular cropper and the best variety for bush trees in the open. Calabash-shaped fruits.

Doyenné du Comice Late Oct.–Nov. Needs a wall for best results. The finest flavoured pear, but not an easy one to grow.

Emile d'Heyst Oct.–Nov. A compact grower and regular cropper.

Louise Bonne of Jersey Oct. A regular heavy cropper.

*Packham's Triumph** Nov. A heavy cropper making a small compact tree.

*William's Bon Chrétien** Sept. The best early pear and a good cropper.

★ = Needs double-working.

Plums

While plums will not thrive in waterlogged soils, they are more tolerant of bad drainage than are apples. On poor soils they will make only little growth, damsons doing better than ordinary plums on such soils. As they flower early they are susceptible to frost damage, so the site for them must be chosen with care.

Forms of tree. The plum does not lend itself to undue restriction, and it is impracticable to train it in the form of cordons or dwarf pyramids. The espalier form also involves considerable cutting back, which in turn produces more vigour, so that the only successfully trained form is the fan. A high wall with ample spread is required for it, otherwise even in this form it will have to be cut more than it likes. For trees in the open the bush and half-standard are the best forms. Varieties with drooping habit, like 'Victoria' and 'Early Laxton', are best as half-standards.

Rootstocks. There are no really dwarfing rootstocks for plums, but the Common Plum gives the smallest trees and is best for walls and for garden trees generally. Unfortunately damsons and a few varieties of plums will not take on Common Plum, and the alternative for these is Common Mussel, though it is not quite such a good stock. For bigger trees for the large garden or orchard, the Brompton stock is best, except that Pershore is often grown on its own roots.

Manuring. Plums are gross feeders, so they must have ample nitrogen. It must, however, be given with discretion in the case of wall trees, otherwise they will become too vigorous. The best basis for the manuring programme is a good mulch annually, and it can be of fresher manure than would be safe for most crops. This will probably suffice for wall trees, but trees in the open should also have a dressing of 1 oz. of a nitrogenous fertilizer, ½ oz. of sulphate of potash and ½ oz. of superphosphate per sq. yd. each spring. Should potash-deficiency symptoms show, the main one being the drying-up of the leaf-edges, the potash should be stepped up a little. This is most likely on light soils.

Pruning. Bush or standard plums require comparatively little detailed pruning, and are better without it. Vigour can be controlled by suitable manuring. It is important not to make large cuts in plum trees during the winter, as that allows the entry of the silver leaf fungus, which is often fatal to susceptible varieties. Even the smaller cuts, such as those which have to be made in training the tree, are best made just before growth starts in the spring, rather than in the winter. On wall trees some pruning is unavoidable, and this should consist of pinching out the tips of young shoots at five or six buds, to be cut back later to two or three buds, except that as older branches become less fruitful they have to be replaced by young shoots from lower down the tree, and the pruning of these replacement shoots is left until the winter, when they are shortened back according to vigour. The plum fruits on 1-year-old, and also on older, wood.

Varieties. The self-fertile varieties can be planted alone and will give good crops. Some self-sterile varieties will pollinate other self-sterile varieties but some will not, and the best thing is to make sure by using a self-fertile variety as pollinator, as they are all efficient for that purpose. Early-flowering varieties cannot, however, be relied on to pollinate late-flowering ones and vice versa, as they may not be in flower together. The following is a selection of the best varieties, most of the cooking varieties being of good eating quality when fully ripe:

Cooking Varieties

Belle de Louvain Late Aug. Red-purple. An upright grower, but rather slow coming into bearing. S/F, L/F.

Czar Mid-Aug. Dark Blue. Not a top-quality plum, but the most regular and heavy cropper. A compact grower. S/F, M/F.

Early Laxton Late July. Yellow. A good cropper and excellent cooker. A rather straggly grower, but resistant to frost damage. E/F, P/S/F.

Marjorie's Seedling Sept.–Oct. Dark blue. Upright grower. S/F, L/F.

Merryweather Damson Being only of moderate vigour is the best garden damson. A heavy cropper of large fruit. S/F, M/F.

Pershore (Yellow Egg.) Late Aug. Probably the best cooker. Is resistant to silver leaf disease. S/F, L/F, T/T.

Victoria For cooking or dessert. Late Aug. Red. The most popular general-purpose plum. Rather liable to silver leaf disease. S/F, M/F.

Dessert Varieties

Cambridge Gage Green. Late Aug. A heavy cropper of greengage-flavoured fruit. Rather spreading habit. P/S/F, L/F.

Coe's Golden Drop Late Sept. Yellow, will keep 2 or 3 weeks after picking. S/S, E/F.

Comte d'Althanns Gage Deep red. Mid-Sept. S/S, E/F, T/T.

Denniston's Superb Yellow-green. Mid-Aug. A good 'doer', and regular cropper. S/F, E/F

Early Transparent Gage Golden-Yellow. Mid-August. A regular cropper. S/F, E/F, T/T.

Oullin's Golden Gage Early Aug. An upright grower. A little slow at coming into bearing. S/F, L/F.

S/F = Self-fertile
P/S/F = Partly self-fertile
S/S = Self-sterile
E/F = Early flowering
M/F = Mid-season flowering
L/F = Late flowering
T/T = Suitable for trained trees

Harvesting. For full flavour all plums need to be left until they are fully ripe, or almost over-ripe. This is not generally practicable because they have to be handled and possibly transported, and in the case of the gages because of their tendency to split if left on the trees. Most varieties, however, will keep and continue to ripen for at least a few days, especially if carefully wrapped in tissue paper.

Quince

This fruit is not grown as often as it deserves to be. It makes excellent jams and tarts and is a very attractive tree, especially when in flower or fruit. Unfortunately it is only in the warmer regions that it can be relied on to ripen its fruits. It is best grown as a bush or half-standard, and needs the same treatment as the pear to which it is closely related. The fruit should not be gathered until the end of Oct. unless severe frost threatens earlier. It should be stored in a cool frost-proof place, in a layer of straw and away from other fruits, or it may affect their flavour. The fruits will keep for 2 or 3 months under those conditions, and are ready for use when they turn yellow. The two best varieties are 'Pear-shaped' and 'Vranja', which also has pear-shaped fruits, but they are larger.

Raspberries

These will grow in any districts that are not excessively wet or dry. They like a deep moist soil, but will not tolerate faulty drainage, and this often rules out heavy soil. On the other hand, very light soils tend to dry out in the summer and this makes it very difficult to mature a good crop. Chalky soils are not suitable.

Planting. A good dressing of farmyard manure, around 1 cwt. to 15 sq. yd., should be worked into the soil during the preparation of the land. Raspberries must be assured of adequate potash, and if there is any likelihood of a shortage in the soil, about 2 oz. per sq. yd. should be worked into the top 6 in. Planting can be done at any time from Nov. to Mar. when the soil is workable. Comparatively small canes of about 2 to 3 ft. long, with plenty of fibrous roots on them form the best planting material, and should be planted reasonably deeply, at from 15 to 30 in. apart according to the freedom of suckering of the variety. The rows should run from north to south, and be at least 6 ft. apart. After planting cut down the canes to 9 in. from the ground.

After-care. The less root disturbance there is in the way of hoeing or other cultivation the better. Weeds are best kept down by a good annual mulch of farmyard manure or compost, applied in Feb. or Mar. This should be supplemented by 1 oz. of sulphate of potash per yard run, with about 1 oz. of superphosphate every third year. It is possible to grow raspberries without any artificial support by bending over the canes of one stool and tying the tops to the canes of the ones alongside, and so on along the row, but this is not really satisfactory. The best method is to have two wires, the lowest at 2 ft. from the ground, and another at 4 ft., or three wires at 18 in., 40 in. and 5 ft., for the taller varieties. The wires should be stretched between posts at about 20 ft. apart, but if posts and wire are stout enough they can be as far as 60 ft. apart.

Pruning. The canes which have fruited should be cut out as soon as fruiting is finished to allow the sun to get to the new canes to ripen them. These new canes should be tied in at about 6 in. apart, cutting out the surplus or weaker ones. In the spring any dead tips on the canes should be cut back to a good bud. Certain varieties, of which 'Lloyd George' is one, will fruit in the autumn if the young canes are cut right down in the early spring.

Varieties. Most of the older varieties of raspberry have gone out of cultivation because of deterioration of stocks due to virus infection, and care has to be taken to prevent the same thing happening with modern varieties. Some varieties, notably 'Norfok Giant', show the presence of virus disease in the leaves by numerous small yellow spots or small areas of uneven shape, but many varieties exhibit no visible symptoms until the general degeneration sets in. Care should therefore be taken to obtain stocks from a reliable source. The following are among the best varieties:

Lloyd George An excellent all-round variety having most of the virtues of a good raspberry. Unfortunately it is susceptible to virus disease, and is liable to degenerate rather quickly if grown close to other varieties, which may be carriers of the disease, and for that reason is best grown by itself. The best variety for autumn fruiting. Early.

Malling Exploit Vigorous and tends to make far too many canes. Early and of good appearance and flavour.

Malling Jewel A very good garden variety and makes an attractive picture when in fruit. Mid-season, and of fairly good flavour. Resists wind damage so is good for moderately exposed positions. Makes few canes, which are practically thornless, so must be planted closely.

Malling Promise One of the easiest varieties to grow, and of good general merit. It is very similar to 'Malling Exploit', though the fruit is probably of not quite such good flavour. Early.

Norfolk Giant An old variety, and of only moderate dessert quality but it is a heavy cropper and its fruit is attractive in appearance. It is a strong grower, making very tall canes. As it flowers late it is the variety most likely to miss damage by late frosts. Late.

Strawberries

Strawberries are particularly liable to blossom damage by spring frosts, so that frost-pockets should be avoided. Since early fruit is especially prized, a warm sheltered position, preferably on a south-facing slope, should be chosen for at least a few early plants. As some virus disease can be carried over from the debris of an old crop, it is best not to plant on the site of a recently discarded strawberry bed.

Soil. Strawberries will do reasonably well on most soils, except very chalky ones, but best results will be obtained on deep well-drained soils with plenty of organic matter in them. This will ensure that they do not dry out, which is one of the big dangers with this crop. Some varieties show a preference for a certain kind of soil, so it is worth while enquiring which varieties do particularly well in the district. In preparing the soil for planting, a good heavy dressing of farmyard manure should be worked into the soil. This is particularly valuable in that extreme care has to be taken later on in the plant's life not to give too much nitrogen, and an initial application in a slowly released form enables the plants to build themselves up during the first summer, with a small but steady supply available later. The soil should be reasonably consolidated before planting, as strawberries do not like a very loose, open soil.

Propagation. Unless strawberry plants are well isolated from other strawberries which may be diseased, it is unwise to save runners from them, as it will almost certainly mean starting off with diseased plants, and that is a very bad start. In such circumstances it pays to buy some new runners that have been grown in isolation. Where propagation is considered safe, do it by layering, and the first plant on each runner gives the best results. The pot method is best as the roots are not disturbed when the plants are planted out, but care must be taken to see that they do not dry out while in the pot. A stone placed on a runner will also keep it in position until it is rooted. The layering should be done as early as possible, to enable early planting to be carried out and the planting should be done as soon as the soil is in a suitable condition from mid-Sept. to mid-Nov. If not done by then it should be deferred to mid-Feb. Planting distances range from 12 to 18 in. between plants, and from 2 to 3 ft. between the rows, according to the variety and the fertility of the soil. Planting at the correct depth is important to ensure successful growth.

General attention. Spring-planted runners, or any autumn-planted ones which are at all unhappy, should have all the flower-trusses removed before the flowers open, so that they will not be made to produce a crop in their first season. The sacrifice will be more than repaid in subsequent crops. Summer care consists of keeping down weeds, but since a large proportion of the strawberry's roots are near the surface, this must be done with care, and the weeds removed when small. A severe attack of green-fly in Apr. is very common, and since it can cripple the plants, a sharp lookout must be kept for it and action taken. If an initial dressing of farmyard manure was given, little additional manure should be needed during the 3 or 4 years of the bed's life. If the plants appear to need some help, they can be mulched annually, or a nitrogenous fertilizer at up to 1 oz. per yd. of row but no more, can be given annually, plus the same amount of sulphate of potash. Too luxurious foliage often means virtually no crop. To keep the fruit clean, a layer of straw should be spread over the beds as soon as the fruits begin to swell, working it under the berries. Small bales of straw, weighing about $\frac{1}{3}$ cwt., will cover about 80 sq. yd. The bed will also have to be netted against birds. Towards the autumn the plants will begin to send out runners which should be cut off in order to concentrate the vigour into the crowns for the following year, unless they are needed for propagating.

Varieties. Among the very many varieties available, the following are generally the best:

Cambridge Favourite A very good second-early, though not happy on really heavy soils. Small foliage, so needs to be planted closely, and is useful for growing under cloches.

Cambridge Prizewinner Second-early. Very attractive fruit, but not quite such a heavy cropper as some. Good for early districts.

Redgauntlet Mid-season to late. Probably the best maincrop variety. A vigorous grower, and good quality fruit.

Royal Sovereign Of very high quality, and given good conditions it will crop heavily; under average conditions it is only a moderate cropper.

Talisman Mid-season to late. Fairly vigorous and a heavy cropper. Often gives a second crop in the autumn.

Cambridge Vigour This variety ripens very early, and crops very heavily in its first year, but in subsequent years it is later and gives a smaller crop. If planted early in the autumn it is worth treating as an annual, discarding it after the first crop.

Alpine Strawberries Such as 'Baron Solemacher', fruit from July to Oct. They are propagated by division or by seed, and like a soil rich in humus. Plant a foot apart each way.

Perpetual Strawberries Will tolerate a chalky soil better than will the ordinary type, and will crop from June to Oct. giving their heaviest crop the first season. Indeed, to maintain cropping they really need replanting each season, in a fertile soil. They do better in the warmer parts of the country. Varieties include 'Red Rich', 'Sans Rivale' and 'St. Claude'.

CHAPTER SEVENTEEN

Vegetables

THE value of fresh home-grown vegetables is well recognized and most gardeners know the urge to grow them. But comparatively few gardens provide all the conditions that are necessary for producing high-quality crops, and unless those conditions can be satisfied it is generally unwise to go in for vegetables. There is little point in struggling against circumstances that make it extremely difficult or even impossible to produce anything better than a third-rate crop when good vegetables can be bought in the shops at reasonable prices. But if the conditions are right then there is no doubt that the effort is well worth while, for first-quality vegetables straight from the garden are in a class entirely their own. Even so, the aim must always be to grow the best. Second-rate growth can perhaps be tolerated in a tree or a shrub but not in a vegetable; six good cauliflowers are always better and more economical than twelve or twenty poor ones and give the grower far more satisfaction.

Special requirements

Earlier chapters have shown that no plants will grow well unless the site and soil are suitable, there is enough properly-balanced plant food, sufficient but not too much water, and the cultivation and management are correct. This applies even more forcefully to vegetables since the aim is to produce heavy, high-quality crops.

It is essential to have a site that is open and unshaded yet well protected from the worst of the weather. The soil should ideally be a light loam, well drained, of good structure and high natural fertility, but the sandy and heavy loams will serve almost as well provided the necessary basic manuring or drainage is carried out. On all soils fertility and structure are of first importance and it is probable that these two, more than any other things, are the main keys to success. Commercial market-gardeners make a special study of their soil conditions, cultivations and timing, and use large quantities of both bulky and concentrated manures in order to ensure steady and continuous growth and private gardeners should follow this example. It should be remembered that vegetables consist of lush growth in the form of leaves, stems and roots and it is for this reason that they need heavier feeding, particularly with nitrogen, and require more frequent top dressing and watering than plants that are grown for their flowers or fruit.

New ground should always be double-dug and in large vegetable gardens it is good practice to double-dig a portion of the area every year, getting the job done in late autumn or early winter, particularly on the heavier types of soil. Generally no special tools or equipment that are not also needed in other parts of the garden are required, except a good line and one or two measuring sticks marked off in feet to ensure correct spacing between rows or plants. If, however, the area is large, a few additional tools will ease the work and a good store will be required (see Chapter 1). A triangular hoe is a convenient tool for taking out seed drills and an onion hoe, which is a short-handled swan-necked hoe and is best used kneeling down between the rows, will prove ideal for weeding and singling once a little practice has been put in. If potatoes are grown, a heavy draw hoe or a mattock will be found specially useful for earthing-up.

Since the whole art of producing vegetables is to keep the crops growing without any kind of check, it is essential for all the different jobs to be done at the optimum time and for each plant to have the best possible surroundings and treatment. Sowing should always be done thinly so as to avoid overcrowding, singling and transplanting must be done as soon as the plants and conditions are right, each plant must have its proper spacing, water and top dressing or liquid manure must be given when required, pests and diseases must be controlled as soon as they are seen and particular operations such as earthing-up or blanching must be correctly timed.

What to grow

In most gardens the area available is the main deciding factor. If it is limited the choice should be restricted to crops such as salads that do not require wide spacing and those such as early peas or broad beans, which occupy the ground for a short time and can be followed by a second crop such as leeks. Other crops to be chosen are those that give a heavy yield spread over a long period, such as French or runner beans, while the ones to avoid are those that take up a lot of room or occupy the ground for a long time, such as winter cauliflower, sprouts or potatoes, and can be bought at reasonable prices. The rule should be never to try to grow more than can be comfortably fitted in to the space available.

Rotations

Whether the area is small or large a cropping plan or rotation should be adopted.

The different groups of vegetables make different demands on the plant food in the soil and require different cultivation, and a well-timed arrangement of seasonal cropping will help to get the most out of a given area and ease the work, particularly sowing and planting. Pests and diseases will also be controlled to some extent because a regular change in cropping means that their favourite host plants are not grown on the same piece of ground year after year. But there is no need for the lengthy and intricate rotations that were commonly recommended up to a few years ago. A three-course rotation is generally suitable and is sufficiently elastic for most gardens. The space available should be divided into three and each plot cropped in turn in the following order: leguminous crops (peas and beans), brassicas (cabbage, etc.), root crops (carrots, parsnips). Under this arrangement the heavy-feeding brassicas that need plenty of nitrogen follow the nitrogen-fixing crops and time is given for the double-digging and manuring that brassicas enjoy, while the root crops have the benefit of the remains of the manures applied for the brassicas and do not therefore need any fresh bulky manure which often encourages the roots to fork. Early potatoes may be included with the roots but if main crop potatoes are to be grown they should form a fourth course and come between the leguminous and brassica crops. Runner beans and onions are the exceptions that can safely be grown on the same piece of ground for two or more successive years. Both require rich soil and a good position but beans should be placed carefully, generally north to south so that they do not shade adjoining crops.

Catch cropping

A well-planned rotation also helps to make the best use of the land by giving space for quick-growing 'catch' crops and allowing second crops to follow those that mature early in the season. Early carrots, lettuces or radishes may be sown between rows of beans or on the banks of a celery trench; early peas may be followed with spinach or spinach beet; summer cauliflower with lettuce for the autumn and early potatoes with winter cauliflower, sprouting broccoli or spring cabbage.

Varieties

The alphabetical list which follows gives details of the requirements of individual crops and recommends certain varieties. These varieties are those that are generally reliable in most districts but there are many others including some that are particularly suitable for specific areas. Advice can generally be obtained from local horticultural shops and societies.

ARTICHOKES

Three distinct kinds of artichokes are used as vegetables, each one belonging to a different botanical genus.

Chinese Artichoke or **Crosnes** (*Stachys tuberifera*) is not commonly grown. It produces white, round to oval tubers in strings tapering in size, which may be cooked or used raw in salads. Needs an acquired taste. Grows to about 18 in. high.

Soil Any good soil, preferably deep and well drained. Sunny.

Manuring Farmyard or compost if available.

Planting Mar.–Apr. Plant medium-sized tubers 6 in. deep and 9 in. apart in rows 1-1½ ft. apart.

Management Keep free of weeds. Water as necessary. Top dress in July, complete fertilizer 2 oz. per sq. yd.

Harvesting October onwards. Dig as required or store in boxes of sand. Undue exposure to light spoils the whiteness of the tubers.

Globe Artichoke (*Cynara scolymus*). Grown for the fleshy scales of its flower heads. It has been grown in Britain for 400 or 500 years, but has never attained the popularity it enjoys on the Continent. Foliage is ornamental.

Soil Deep, rich, medium loam. Sunny. Should be double-dug in autumn.

Manuring Farmyard manure or compost 10 lb. per sq. yd. at double-digging. Spring, use complete fertilizer 4 oz. per sq. yd. lightly forked in.

Planting Mar. Use suckers 9 in. high cut from established plants, with some root attached. Plant 2–3 ft. apart in rows 4 ft. apart. (Seed can also be used but the seeds do not come true and considerable variation results. The seed should be sown in Apr. or end of Mar., thinned to 6 in. and transplanted the following year.)

Management Keep free of weeds and water as necessary. Spring, mulch with farmyard or compost, top dress with complete fertilizer 4 oz. per sq. yd. Autumn, cut down stems and protect crowns with straw, bracken, etc.

Harvesting Disbud lateral flower heads as formed, or leave till about 1½ in. long when they can be eaten raw or fried. Terminal heads should be cut just before full development, while still closed or just about to open, but before any purple coloration appears. Cut with a 6-in. stem which prevents drying out. After fourth season, bed should be grubbed and replaced by a new bed planted the previous year.

Final year's cropping July, after cutting heads, cut stems down to 6 in. high, water well. Sept., tie growth into bunches, add a collar of brown paper or pack closely with straw. Earth up. Oct.-Nov., blanched shoots may be cut and used as cardoon (*q.v.*).

Varieties Green Globe, Purple Globe, Camus de Bretagne, Camus d'Angers.

Jerusalem Artichoke (*Helianthus tuberosus*). The well-known tuberous form.

Soil No special requirement. Does best on deep, rich, light loam.

Manuring Autumn. Farmyard manure or compost 10 lb. per sq. yd. (if available). Spring. Complete fertilizer 4 oz. per sq. yd.

Planting Feb.–Mar. Use tubers 1–2 in. long with 2–3 eyes, set 3–4 in. deep, 1–1½ ft. apart in rows 2–3 ft. apart.

Management Keep free of weeds. Rows should be earthed-up (not essential).

Harvesting October onwards. Lift as required or store in sand. (All tubers should be cleared, otherwise they will become 'weeds' in succeeding crop.)

Varieties New White, Fuseau.

Jerusalem artichokes can also be grown in a 'lazy way' by being left in the same position for several years, especially if they can have a separate, fairly well-isolated bed to themselves. Sufficient tubers must be left every season for propagation, but undue congestion or spreading must be watched. Size and quality of crop are not so good as when grown in new soil every year.

ASPARAGUS

Several species of the genus *Asparagus* are grown for decorative purposes, the best known being the various kinds of asparagus fern. *Asparagus officinalis* is used as a vegetable and has been grown in Britain for some 400 years, possibly longer. A hundred years ago the most renowned commercial growing area was Battersea. Unlike the majority of plants, the sexes are separate, the male plants giving the better and heavier crop. Unless seed is required, the female plants (distinguished by the berries they bear later in the season) should be discarded. Best grown in a warm situation protected from wind.

Soil Medium loam, deep, rich, well drained.

Preparation Double-dig in autumn with manure and form into beds 3–5 ft. wide and 6 in. above surface level.

Manuring Farmyard or compost 20 lb. per sq. yd. at double-digging.
(1) Just before planting time, fork in complete fertilizer 4 oz. per sq. yd. or
(2) Complete fertilizer 2 oz., plus 2 oz. guano or 2 oz. hoof and horn and 2 oz. bone meal.

Planting April. Use 2–3-year-old plants set 1 ft. apart in rows 1 ft.–1½ ft. apart, i.e. 3 rows to a 4-ft. bed, 4 to a 5-ft. bed. Plants can be bought, when males should be asked for, or raised from seed sown in Apr. in seed bed in drills 1 in. deep, 1 ft. apart, thinned to 9 in. Grow on for 2 years, select thickest, discard berry-bearing plants.

Management Cut no crop the first year after planting, nor until plants are over 3 years old. Lightly fork over beds at regular intervals, keep free of weeds, water as necessary. Autumn, cut off foliage when turning yellow and before berries shed seed which may produce undesirable seedlings. Add soil as necessary to make up height of bed. Mulch with farmyard manure or compost. Spring, fork over beds, removing any surplus mulch. Top dress with nitrate of soda 1 oz. per sq. yd. July, after cutting, top dress with complete fertilizer 4 oz., guano or hoof and horn 2 oz., salt 2 oz. per sq. yd. Beds should last 10–30 years.

Harvesting First year's cutting must be light. Use a sharp knife or a special 'asparagus' knife, pushing it down close to the stem so as to avoid injury to other developing stems, and cut obliquely about 3 in. below the surface. Cease cutting at end of June or early July.

Varieties Connover's Colossal, Martha Washington, Reading Giant, Argenteuil.

Forcing (1) In heated greenhouse or hotbed from Nov. to Feb. Temperature 60 deg. F. Use strong 4-year-old crowns, pack closely, cover with 3–4 in. sifted compost. Water as required. Discard crowns after forcing.
(2) On outdoor beds. Cover part or whole of bed with 2 in. compost in Nov. Place frame over in Jan., cover with mat and surround with fresh manure. Harvest Mar.–Apr. Then remove frame, scattering manure as protection from frost. Do not force in this way in successive years.
(3) Cloches. Cover plants in Jan. Harvest Apr.

AUBERGINE or EGG PLANT

(*Solanum melongena ovigerum*)

Increasing in popularity, especially for baking stuffed or frying in slices. Must be raised in heat and preferably grown on under glass, but will succeed out of doors if planted in a warm, protected, sunny position.

Soil Rich, light-medium.

Manuring Best given as regular liquid manuring.

Sowing Jan-Feb. 2–3 seeds in a 3- or 4-in. pot in heated greenhouse or hotbed. Temperature 60 deg. F. Select best plants and transfer to 6-in. pot.

Planting (1) Under glass. Plant out into large pots or boxes, in potting compost.
(2) In the open. Plant out June into well-sheltered, sunny position 2 ft. by 2 ft.

Management Pinch out growing point at 6–9 in. high. Hoe, mulch. Restrict fruits to 3 or 4 per plant. Syringe in hot weather. Stake when necessary.

Harvesting Gather when fully coloured.

Varieties Purple Long, White Long, Noire de Pekin (dark violet colour).

BEANS

The three most popular kinds of bean, the broad bean, the French (dwarf or kidney) bean and the runner bean have certain cultural requirements common to all. They are fairly heavy feeders, especially the runner bean, and, although able to obtain nitrogen from the air and store it in their roots they benefit from supplies given in the early stages of growth. For these reasons farmyard manure or compost should be given.

To grow high-quality crops, especially runners, trenches 1½ ft. wide and 1½–2 ft. deep should be dug, the manure placed in the bottom, covered with soil and allowed to settle before sowing.

Soil No special requirement, preferably deep, medium loam, well drained. Not acid. Broad beans will succeed on heavy soils, French beans prefer light soils.

Manuring Autumn or spring. (1) Farmyard manure or compost dug in or put into trenches 10 lb. per sq. yd. (More for runner beans if available.) At sowing time, superphosphate 2 oz., sulphate of potash 1 oz. raked in.

(2) If no farmyard manure or compost: (*a*) Bone meal 3 oz., sulphate of potash 1 oz., or (*b*) fish meal or meat meal 2 oz., superphosphate 1 oz., sulphate of potash 1 oz., or (*c*) hoof and horn 2 oz., superphosphate 2 oz., sulphate of potash 1 oz.

Sowing In double rows, seeds staggered 6–9 in. apart, 3 in. deep. Broad and French beans may also be sown in single rows. Broad beans. Nov.–Apr. Double rows 2½ ft. apart. French beans. Apr.–May. Double rows 2–2½ ft. apart. Runner beans. May–June. Double rows 4–6 ft. apart. Seeds may be sown in pairs. If both germinate remove the poorer plant. Also sow a few extra at the end of a row for transplanting into any gap. May also be sown in boxes for transplanting.

Broad Beans (*Vicia faba*)

Management Hoe regularly, drawing soil towards plants. Pinch out side-shoots as formed.

Harvesting Pick regularly as soon as pods fill but while seeds are still soft.

Varieties (1) Long-pod type: Seville, Aqua Dulce, Exhibition, Green Longpod.

(2) Broad-pod type: White Windsor, White Harlington, Green Windsor, Green Harlington

(3) Small-pod type: Royal Fan, Green Gem, The Sutton (dwarf)

The long-pods and broad-pods are divided into green- or white-seeded types, the long-pods being generally earlier and the broad-pods of better flavour.

French Beans (*Phaseolus vulgaris*)

Management Hoe regularly, drawing soil towards plants. Stake climbing types.

Harvesting Pick regularly. White-seeded varieties may be allowed to ripen for use as Haricots.

Varieties The Prince (early), Canadian Wonder, Masterpiece. Climbing: Earliest of All, Tender and True.

Forcing In heated greenhouse (using a climbing variety), hotbed or cold frame (using an early variety).

Runner Beans (*Phaseolus multiflorus*)

Management Hoe regularly drawing soil towards plants. If not staked pinch out growing points when plant is 18 in. high. (When so grown, rows need not be more than 3 ft. apart.) Syringe in dry weather during flowering.

Varieties Prizewinner, Best of All, Princeps (dwarf).

Asparagus Bean (*Dolichos sesquipedalis*). Bears cylindrical green pods, up to 24 in. long. Grown like runner beans.

Flageolet. A green-seeded type of French bean, the true Haricots Verts.

Varieties Green Gem, Green Flageolet.

Haricot (*Phaseolus vulgaris*). A type of French bean grown on to maturity for harvesting the ripe seeds. Grown as a French bean, but generally covered with cloches in Aug. to assist ripening, then hung up to dry out completely.

Varieties Comtesse de Chambord. (Dutch Brown may also be treated in this way.)

Lima Bean (*Phaseolus lunatus*). Not generally suited to Northern temperate conditions. Sow end May, pick end Aug. Requires warm sheltered position. (The ripe, dry seeds are the 'butter beans' of the shops.) There are both climbing and dwarf types, grown in the same way as runner or French beans.

Soya or **Soy Bean** (*Glycine hispida*). Sow May, ½ in. deep, thin to 9 in., rows 2 ft. apart. The small beans may be cooked green or after ripening as desired. Distinctive, oily flavour.

Stringless Bean. Types of French bean selected for the soft 'string' along the back of the pod. Generally less hardy.

Varieties Phenix Claudia, Refugee. (Masterpiece may also be used as a stringless bean.)

BEET, SEAKALE

Sometimes called **Silver Beet** or **Swiss Chard.** The white stalks and midrib of the leaf are used like seakale, the green part like spinach.

Soil No special requirement. Deep.

Manuring Farmyard manure or compost 10 lb. per sq. yd. Complete fertilizer 4 oz. per sq. yd. Liquid manure as required.

Sowing Apr.–May. Drills 12–18. in., thin to 9–12 in.

Harvesting Pull (not cut) leaves regularly.

BEET, SPINACH

Sometimes called Perpetual Spinach. Treat as for beet, adding farmyard manure if available.

Sowing Apr.–Aug. Thin to 9 in.

Harvesting Pull leaves regularly to encourage continuous new growth. Throw away large matured leaves.

BEETROOT

Derived from the wild beet (*Beta vulgaris*) of the coast.

Soil Deep light to medium loam, preferably manured with farmyard or compost the previous year. Rake down to fine tilth.

Manuring Complete fertilizer 4 oz. per sq. yd. Salt 2 oz. per sq. yd. may be added on light soils only.

Sowing Apr.–June. In succession, drills 1 ft. apart, 1 in. deep. Thin to 6–8 in. (The 'seed' is really a fruit containing 2–5 seeds and may be sown in the drill at 6 in. intervals, two 'seeds' together.) July, a late sowing may be tried.

Planting Transplant to fill any gaps (not always successful).

Management The aim is to grow the earliest sowings as quickly as possible. Hoe regularly but carefully. Never thin to more than 8 in. as large roots are not wanted.

Harvesting Pull early crop as required. Oct., lift main crop. Store.

Varieties Round type: Detroit, Globe, Crimson Ball. Long type: Cheltenham Green-top, Dells Crimson.

Frame Culture Early crops can be grown in cold frames or under cloches.

BORECOLE. See *Kale*

BROCCOLI

The word broccoli is commonly but wrongly used to include the winter-hardy types of cauliflower (*q.v.*). It should properly be confined to the sprouting broccoli, a branching type of cauliflower which produces a number of miniature heads on the ends of long stems and side-shoots, and matures in late winter and early spring.

Broccoli, Sprouting (*Brassica oleracea cymosa*)

Soil Grows well on most kinds except the lightest.

Manuring If following a well-manured crop, no farmyard manure necessary. Otherwise

(*a*) Farmyard manure or compost 10 lb. per sq. yd., or

(*b*) Bone meal 4 oz., hoof and horn, 2 oz., sulphate of potash 1 oz., per sq. yd. or

(*c*) Complete fertilizer 4 oz. at planting time.

Sowing Apr. to May in seed bed.

Planting June. Rows 2–2½ ft. apart, plants 2 ft. apart.

Management Top dress if required with nitrate of soda or sulphate of ammonia ½–1 oz. per sq. yd.

Harvesting Cut main stems first (when large enough) leaving side-shoots to grow for later cutting.

Varieties Purple Sprouting, White Sprouting.

Broccoli, Star. Treat as sprouting broccoli. Produces a number of small heads on one stem.

Broccoli, Calabrese or **Italian Green Sprouting.** Treat as sprouting broccoli; sow in spring, ready early autumn. Produces small green heads of excellent flavour.

BRUSSELS SPROUTS (*Brassica oleracea bullata gemmifera*)

To grow good sprouts it is essential to have a firm, rich soil and to give the crop a long growing season and plenty of space.

Soil Heavy and medium loams best. Very light or spongy peaty soils unsuitable. Preferably deeply dug and heavily manured for a previous crop. Not short of lime.

Manuring Farmyard manure or compost 20 lb. in autumn (if previous crop was not manured) Before planting out fork in
(*a*) Hoof and horn 2 oz.
Bone meal 4 oz.
Sulphate of potash 1 oz., or
(*b*) Complete fertilizer 4–6 oz.

Sowing In seed bed, thinly, either in Aug. to Sept. or Mar. Also in cold frame in Feb. pricked out in Mar.

Planting Mar.–June, 2–2½ ft. apart, rows 2½ ft. apart. Plant firmly (Catch-crops of radish and lettuce may be sown between the rows.)

Management Hoe regularly. Water as necessary. Remove decaying leaves. Top dress with potassic nitrate or failing that, nitrate of soda or sulphate of ammonia ½ oz. a fortnight after planting and a month later. Never top dress after June.

Harvesting Pick regularly, taking best sprouts only from all plants. Also pick off and throw away any very open 'blown' sprouts. At end of season (Feb.) the head or top of each plant may also be removed and used.

Varieties Early: Cambridge Special, Dwarf Gem, Triumph. Mid-season: Commando, Fillbasket, Wroxton. Late: Cambridge Late, Darlington, Exhibition.

CABBAGE (*Brassica oleracea capitata*)
With a proper selection of varieties cabbage can be had all the year round.

Soil Will grow well in almost any soil provided there is plenty of lime.

Manuring Farmyard manure or compost 20 lb. at digging, or hoof and horn 2 oz., bone meal 4 oz., sulphate of potash 1 oz. or complete fertilizer 4 oz. at planting time.

Sowing In seed bed, thinly. Mar.–Aug.

Planting Apr.–Oct. 1½–2 ft. apart, rows 2 ft. apart. (18 in. each way is sufficient for small types.)

Management Hoe regularly. Top dress with ½ oz. nitrate of soda or sulphate of ammonia as required. Do not top dress spring cabbage until growth begins in spring. Where spring greens and hearted cabbage are both desired the plants can be set out 18 in. apart, each alternate one being cut for greens, the others being left to heart up.

Cabbage, Chinese or **Petsai** (*Brassica cernua*). More like a Cos lettuce, with toothed, oblong, green leaves. Grows quickly and can be used as a catch-crop.

Sowing Apr.–July.

Planting Thin or transplant to 2 ft.

Management Water as necessary.

Cabbage, Colewort or **Collard.** A whiter, non-hearting type. Very hardy. Treat as cabbage.

Sowing Apr. in seed bed. May–July in permanent position, rows 18 in. apart.

Planting Transplant or thin to 1 ft. in rows.

Harvesting Cut before fully developed.

Varieties Hardy Green, Rosette.

Cabbage, Portuguese or **Couve Tronchuda** (*Brassica oleracea costata*). Treat as cabbage.

Sowing Feb. in heat, Mar. in cold frame and Apr. outside.

Planting Rows 2–3 ft. apart, plants 2 ft. apart.

Management Top dress with nitrate of soda ½ oz. or give liquid manure regularly.

Harvesting Midribs of leaves used as seakale, rest of leaf as cabbage. Flavour resembles seakale.

Cabbage, Red or **Pickling.** Treat as for cabbage.

Sowing Mar.–Apr.

Planting 2–3 ft. apart each way. May–June.

Varieties Red Drumhead, Niggerhead.

Cabbage, Savoy. Treat as for cabbage.

Sowing Late Mar.–early May.

Planting May–July. Rows 2–2½ ft., plants 2 ft. apart.

Management Do not top dress after July.

Harvesting Oct.–Mar.

Varieties Early: Dwarf Green, Best of All, Ormskirk Early. Mid-season: Autumn Green, Ormskirk Medium. Late: Ormskirk Late, Omega, Latest of All, Rearguard.

CAPSICUM (*Capsicum annuum*) Red or Yellow Pepper
Must be raised in heat and grown on under glass, but will succeed if planted out in a warm, protected, sunny position.

Sowing Feb.–Mar. in pots (2 seeds per pot) in-

CABBAGES—SEASONAL TABLE

Variety	*Type*	*Time for Sowing*	*Time for Planting out*	*Time for harvesting*
April Flower of Spring Harbinger Early Evesham Early Market	Spring greens or spring cabbage	Aug.	Sept.	Mar.–May
Golden Acre Primo Nonpareil	Summer	Mar.–Apr.	Apr.–June	June–Sept.
Winnigstadt Christmas Drumhead January King	Winter	May	June–July	Oct.–Jan.

heated greenhouse or hot-bed. Prick out into 3-in. pots.

Planting May. Put in 6-in. pots of rich potting compost. For outside planting, harden off and plant out in June into favoured position 2 ft. apart.

Management Water as required. Syringe in hot weather.

Harvesting Gather as soon as ripe, by end of Sept. before cold nights set in.

Chillies are the smaller type of capsicum often called Bird Peppers.

CARDOON (*Cynara cardunculus*)

Belongs to the same genus as the globe artichoke. Used in stews, soups and as salad.

Soil Deep, rich, medium loam. Best grown in trenches 1½ ft. deep and 1½ ft. wide.

Manuring Farmyard manure or compost 10 lb. in bottom of trench, covered with a little soil and complete fertilizer 2 oz.

Sowing Early Apr. in cold frame. Apr.–May in trench, 3 seeds together at 18-in. interval (may be staggered in a double row). Reduce seedlings to one.

Management Water freely as required, give liquid manure every fortnight. Sept., gather leaves together, tie loosely and add a collar of brown paper 6 in. wide. Oct., bank up with soil. Before either operation remove withered or yellow leaves.

Harvesting Commence gathering when blanched (end Oct.–Nov.). Protect with straw or bracken during winter or lift and store in a cool, dry place.

Varieties Spanish and Puvis (non-prickly), Tours (prickly).

CARROT (*Daucus carota*)

By the proper selection of varieties, careful storage and the use of a frame, carrots can be obtained in excellent condition all the year round.

Soil Light to medium (preferably sandy) loams. Deep and finely cultivated.

Manuring No farmyard manure or compost. Complete fertilizer 4 oz. at sowing time.

Sowing Mar.–July. Rows 1 ft. apart, 1 in. deep. Thin to 3–4 in. for early varieties, 6 in. for main-crop varieties. Sow thinly.

Management Hoe regularly. Thinning should be done in two operations, when soil is moist. If necessary water beforehand. Hoe afterwards. After each operation dust with B.H.C. or old soot to help reduce attacks by carrot fly.

Harvesting Pull early varieties as soon as ready. Store main crop.

Varieties Classed according to length of root: Short, Intermediate and Long.

CAULIFLOWER (*Brassica oleracea botrytis cauliflora*)

Cauliflowers may be had all the year round except in cold or exposed areas where the winter varieties are usually difficult to grow.

Soil Deep, rich, well supplied with lime. Medium to heavy loams best. Winter varieties dislike a loose or newly dug soil and should follow some early-maturing crop which was itself well cultivated, e.g. early potatoes.

Manuring At digging time:

(*a*) Farmyard manure or compost 20 lb., or

(*b*) Hoof and horn 2 oz.

Bone meal 4 oz.

Sulphate of potash 1 oz.

At planting time:

Complete fertilizer 4 oz. raked in.

If following a well-manured crop, winter varieties need not have farmyard manure. Summer varieties can have up to 30 lb. if available.

Sowing Jan.–May according to variety. In frame or seed bed, thinly.

Planting Mar.–July. 2–2½ ft. between plants in rows 2–2½ ft. apart. Plant firmly.

Management Hoe regularly. Top dress with nitrate of soda or sulphate of ammonia ½–1 oz. as required. Do not top dress winter varieties after Aug. as this may encourage soft growth incapable of standing hard weather. Water heavily in dry seasons.

Harvesting Mature heads not wanted for a day or two should be protected from hot sun or bad weather by bending a leaf over the curd or the whole plant may be lifted and hung upside down in a cool airy place. Winter varieties may be helped through a bad season by taking out a spadeful of soil on the north side of the stem, bending the whole plant over gently but firmly and holding it in position with more soil placed on top of the stem.

Frame culture Suitable varieties (All the Year Round or Pioneer) can be grown in hot-beds or cold frames to mature end of May to early June when there is often a gap in outdoor supplies.

Varieties See table on page 401

CARROTS—SEASONAL TABLE

Variety	*Type*	*Time for sowing*	*Site*	*Time for harvesting*
Amsterdam Forcing	Inter.	Jan.–Feb.	Hot-bed	May
		Feb.–Mar.	Cold frame	May–June
Scarlet Horn	Short	(1) Feb.–Mar.	Cold frame	May–June
Early Horn	,,		In the open	June–July
Favourite	,,			
Early Gem	,,	(2) Mar.–Apr.	In the open	Sept.
Ideal	Inter.			
Broadcast	,,	(3) July	In the open as catch-crop	Sept.
Early Nantes	,,			
Chantenay	Inter.	Apr.–May	In the open	Aug. onwards
James' Scarlet	,,			
St. Valery	Long			
Altrincham	,,			
Autumn King	,,			

SEASONAL TABLE

WINTER CAULIFLOWER

Variety	*Time for sowing*	*Time for planting out*	*Time for maturity*
Roscoff No. 1	Apr.	June–July	Nov.–Dec.
Early Feltham Early Roscoff	Apr.	June–July	Dec.–Jan.
Superb Early White Roscoff No. 2 Mid Feltham	Apr.–May	June–July	Jan.–Feb.
Snow White Roscoff No. 4	Apr.–May	July	Feb.–Mar.
Roscoff No. 5 Perfection Reading Giant	Apr.–May	July	Mar.–Apr.
Late Feltham Whitsuntide	Apr.–May	July	Apr.–May
Late Queen Rearguard	Apr.–May	July	May

SUMMER AND AUTUMN CAULIFLOWER

Variety	Time for sowing	Time for planting out	Time for maturity
Snowball Early London All the Year Round Harbinger	Sept. (winter in cold frame)	Mar.	June–July
Eclipse All the Year Round	Mar.	May	July–Aug.
Early Giant Orion Walcheren	Apr.	May–June	Aug.–Sept.
Majestic Autumn Giant Veitch's Self-Protecting Conquest	Apr.–May	June	Sept.–Nov.

The Roscoff varieties are less hardy and should not be grown in cold, exposed positions.

Cauliflower, Cape or **Cape Broccoli.** A small type of winter cauliflower hearting in Mar. and Apr. Treat as winter cauliflower.

CELERIAC or TURNIP-ROOTED CELERY (*Apium graveolens*)

A hardy easily-grown substitute for celery and used in the same ways, cooked or raw. The leaves and leaf-stalks can also be cooked.

Soil No special requirement. Deep, rich moist soils best.

Manuring (*a*) Farmyard manure or compost 10 lb. or

(*b*) Hoof and horn 2 oz., bone meal 4 oz., sulphate of potash 1 oz. or

(*c*) Complete fertilizer 4 oz.

Sowing Mar., in boxes in heated greenhouse, hot-bed or cold frame, pricked out and hardened off. Apr., outside in warm seed bed.

Planting May–June. Rows 1½ ft. apart, plants 1 ft. apart. Set plants at same level as they were growing in seed bed or box and do not earth up at all.

Management Hoe regularly, water freely when required. Top dress with liquid manure or nitrate of soda ½ oz. Remove any side-shoots or suckers.

Harvesting (1) May be left in the ground given some protection with straw, in winter.

(2) Lift Oct., remove all except central leaves. Store.

Varieties Giant Prague, Erfurt.

CELERY (*Apium graveolens*)

Derived from the wild celery found growing in marshy places, especially near the coast in many parts of the world, including Europe. To grow a first-quality crop demands a lot of attention; if this cannot be given the crop is generally disappointing. The necessary cultivation has an excellent effect upon the soil.

Soil Light to medium, rich, deep, well drained yet retentive of moisture. Lack of lime no disadvantage.

Preparation In early spring (or autumn on heavy soils) take out a trench 18 in. deep, 12 in. wide for a single row of plants or 18 in. wide for a double row. Place excavated soil in banks evenly on either side. Put 6–8 in. farmyard manure or compost in bottom of trench, treading it down firmly. Cover with the fine soil from banks and allow to settle naturally, to within 3 or 4 in. of surface level. Level remainder to form a flat bank on which catch-crops (radishes, lettuces) can be grown. Two or more trenches should be spaced 3–4 ft. apart. (The narrower trench for a single row of plants is easier for earthing-up later in the season.)

Sowing (*a*) Early Mar. in boxes in heated greenhouse or hot-bed 60 deg. F. Sow thinly. Prick out 3 in. apart into other boxes when large enough to handle. Harden off in cold frame.

(*b*) End Mar.–early Apr. As above, for later varieties. Prick out to 3 in.

(*c*) Apr. In the open in protected position or under cloches. Transplant to 3 in. Water as required.

Planting May–June. Plants 9 in. to 1 ft. apart, staggered for double rows. Water trench heavily two days before planting. Lift plants carefully from box or seed bed with good ball of soil. Plant at same level, not deeper.

Management Keep free of weeds and slugs, water as required. Give liquid manure every fortnight. Remove discoloured or diseased leaves. When 15 in. high, prepare for first earthing-up; remove any side growths and, holding all the leaves of a plant together with one hand, draw fine soil from the banks around each plant with the other hand or a hand fork. Give a second earthing-up at end of Aug. or early Sept. using a spade and tying each plant loosely with raffia or a rubber band which must be removed when the job is finished. In Oct. give the final earthing-up bringing soil up close to lower leaves. Always earth up when foliage is dry and never let soil run between the stems, or press it tightly against the plants. Collars of brown paper may be used to help blanching and keep soil away from the stems, but they sometimes encourage slugs and have then to be removed.

Harvesting Oct. onwards. After lifting always return soil to cover the next plant in the row.

Varieties White: Solid White, Giant White,

White Gem (dwarf).

Pink: Clayworth Prize Pink, Superb Pink.

Red: Standard Bearer, Giant Red.

(Celery may also be grown in beds, but earthing-up is then more difficult. This system is not recommended.)

Celery, Self-blanching. Although self-blanching, this type of celery is improved by some help to blanch the stems really white. Its main advantage is that it can be grown on the flat and does not therefore need so much labour.

Soil Deep, rich, moist but well drained.

Manuring Autumn or early spring, farmyard manure or compost 10–20 lb.

Sowing As for ordinary celery.

Planting June, 1 ft. apart in rows 18 in. apart.

Management Aug., straw may be placed around each plant or a paper collar used to help blanching. Water as required and give liquid manure every fortnight.

Harvesting Clear the crop before frosts set in.

Variety Doré, Golden Self-blanching.

CELTUCE or **CHINESE LETTUCE.** Treat as for summer lettuce

CHICORY (*Cichorium intybus*)

Special varieties of chicory have been raised for growing as salads. The varieties grown for producing roots to be used with coffee are not suitable.

Soil Deep, light to medium, preferably well manured for the previous crop.

Manuring Complete fertilizer 2–4 oz.

Sowing May–June in drills 1 ft. apart, thin to 9 in.

Management Nov. Lift and select best roots about 1 ft. long and with top diameters of not less than 2 in. or more than 3 in., trim off leaves and side-shoots. Store in a cool but frost-proof place. At intervals of a fortnight or so, place a few roots in deep boxes or pots of sand or fine soil. Crowns should be 1 in. above soil and 2–3 in. from each other. Water lightly and place in the dark (or cover the box or pot with another box or pot), temperature 50 deg. F. Can also be grown without heat, but must be kept free from frost.

Harvesting Forced growth of about 9 in. takes 4–6 weeks. Cut with a heel of root to preserve freshness and keep in dark till wanted so as to prevent greening.

Variety Witloof, Brussels Chicory

CHILI. See *Capsicum*

CHINESE LETTUCE. See *Celtuce*

COLEWORT. See *Cabbage*

CORN COB. See *Sweet Corn*

CORN SALAD or **LAMB'S LETTUCE** (*Valerianella olitoria*)

Soil Deep, rich.

Manuring Farmyard manure or compost 10 lb.

Sowing In succession Feb.–Aug. at intervals of 2 months, drills 1 ft. apart. Thin to 6 in.

Management Hoe regularly. Give some protection (straw), against frost.

Harvesting June onwards. When grown quickly the whole plant can be used, otherwise the leaves should be picked singly.

Varieties Large-leaved, Regence.

COUVE TRONCHUDA. See *Cabbage*

CRESS

There are several different kinds of cress belonging to separate botanical genera.

American or **Land Cress** (*Barbarea praecox*). Used as a substitute for water cress which it resembles in flavour.

Soil Moist but well drained.

Sowing Mar.–Sept. In drills 1 ft. apart, thin to 9 in.

Management Water freely as necessary. Pinch out growing point when plants are well established. Give some protection (cloche, straw or bracken) to late sowings in order to have winter supplies (or plants may be moved into cold frames).

Indian Cress (*Tropaeolum majus*). The common nasturtium. The leaves and flowers can be used in salads and the seeds as a substitute for capers.

Salad Cress (*Lepidium sativum*)

Sowing In frames Nov–Mar. or out of doors Mar. onwards. Mid-winter sowings should preferably have a little heat. Sow in succession, thickly and evenly, on surface of soil, in pans or boxes. Press gently with a flat board, and do not cover seed with soil. Water soil the previous day.

Management If further watering is necessary it must be done carefully to prevent soil splashing on to leaves. For this reason, even the outdoor-grown crops are best grown in boxes or pans so that heavy showers cause no splashing.

Harvesting Cut with scissors. Ready 10–14 days after sowing.

Varieties Curled, Plain. Golden or Australian Cress is a dwarf type with yellowish leaves.

Water Cress (*Rorippa spp.*) Successful growing requires a stream of clean water running over a clear, preferably gravelly bed, but reasonable crops can also be grown in shallow beds or trenches if liberally supplied with clear water.

Sowing Mar. in drills 1 ft. apart, thin to 6 in.

Planting Mar., using rooted pieces from old plants set 6 in. apart.

Management Give good and regular supplies of water. Remove flower-heads as formed. Gather regularly. Top dress 1 oz. superphosphate. Protect late supplies for winter.

Varieties Green, Brown.

CUCUMBER (*Cucumis sativus*)

Provided suitable varieties are chosen, cucumbers can be grown in three ways, in a heated greenhouse, on a hot-bed or in the open. The first method will give supplies during most of the year, the second over the whole of the summer and early autumn and the third in Aug. and Sept. The varieties requiring heat are best grown by themselves since they need a temperature and humidity much higher than is suitable for other greenhouse plants, or tomatoes. Cultivation in cold houses or frames is not always satisfactory and rarely leads to more than a light crop.

Soil For all methods a moist well-drained rich soil, well supplied with farmyard manure is essential.

In heated greenhouse. Temperature 70 deg. F., not less than 65 deg. F. at night nor rising to more than 85 deg. F. during day.

Sowing Oct.–June, in trays or pots. Prick out singly into 3½-in. pots, then pot on into 5-in. pots.

Planting Seedlings should be ready for planting out within 1–2 months of sowing. Set 2 ft. apart in beds at ground level or on staging. Beds should be prepared a week previously from 2 parts turfy loam and 1 part manure, well mixed together.

Management About 3 weeks after planting and thereafter at intervals when white roots appear on the surface of the bed, add a thin layer of mixed soil and manure. Top dress if required with ½ oz. bone meal and ½ oz. nitrate of potash. Dried blood can be added if plants appear backward. Only slight ventilation will normally be necessary as a regular thing. If day temperatures rise above 85 deg. F. full ventilation and possibly shading and damping as well will be required. Water frequently but beds must not become waterlogged. If blinds are not fitted, shade glass with proprietary shading or flour and water paste from beginning of May. The house should have wires running horizontally 9 in. apart and 1 ft. from the glass, with a cane running from the plant to the first wire. Stop main stem at roof-top and train laterals to wires, stopping these at second joint beyond where a fruit is formed. Pinch out male flowers to prevent pollination and formation of fruits with swollen ends containing seeds.

Varieties Conqueror, Telegraph, Rochford's Market, Butcher's Disease-resisting.

In heated frames or hot-beds. If the frame is heated artificially, beds must be prepared as in greenhouses. If a hot-bed is to be used it should be made as described in Chapter 8. The level of the surface should be about 12 in. from the glass. Temperature 65 deg. F. varying from 60 deg. F. at night to 80 deg. F. during day.

Sowing Mar. onwards. Seeds may be raised in frame or in heated greenhouse as above.

Planting Plants should be set 1 ft. from back of frame, one plant to a frame 3–4 ft. wide.

Management Watering, top dressing, ventilation and shading as for greenhouse crops. Train to give three or four main stems to run down the frame by pinching out after fourth leaf has been produced.

Varieties Conqueror, Telegraph, Tender and True, Butcher's Disease-resisting.

Ridge cucumbers and gherkins

Sowing Apr. in greenhouse or frame, May in cold frame or under cloche.

Planting End May–June, 3–4 ft. apart on ridges formed by filling a trench 6–9 in. deep with manure and covering with loamy soil mixed with compost.

Management Pinch out growing point when 6–7 leaves have formed. Leave male flowers on. Water regularly, about 3 days a week. Top dress or give liquid manure every fortnight. Mulch round with compost.

Harvesting Gather as soon as ready and as often as possible.

Varieties Cheltenham, Long Green, Stockwood, King of the Ridge. For Gherkins: Short Prickly.

EGG PLANT. See *Aubergine*

ENDIVE (*Cichorium endivia*)

A most valuable salad capable of taking the place of lettuce during the winter. It can be obtained all the year round but the summer crops tend to run to seed in a dry season unless carefully grown.

Soil Light to medium, deep, moist.

Manuring (*a*) Farmyard manure or compost 20 lb. or

(*b*) Hoof and horn 2 oz., bone meal 4 oz., sulphate of potash 1 oz.

Sowing June to Aug., in drills 1 in. deep, 1 ft. apart. Thin to 1 ft. Germination may be slow and watering necessary. Can be transplanted, but this is not always satisfactory. Early supplies may be obtained by sowing in frames in Apr.–May.

Management Hoe and water as necessary. When nearly full grown plants must be blanched by tying or preferably by covering with an inverted flower pot with the hole filled in or a small box. Late sown plants for winter use can be lifted and blanched in a darkened frame. Blanching takes 10–14 days, up to 3 weeks in winter. Blanched plants do not keep for long so a few only should be done at a time. They should always be dry when blanching begins.

Varieties (1) With curled divided leaves: Green Curled, Moss Curled, Staghorn.

(2) With broader undivided leaves (Batavian endive) Round-leaved Batavian.

GHERKINS. See *Cucumber*

GOOD KING HENRY or MERCURY (*Chenopodium bonus-henricus*)

Formerly quite popular but now little grown. Its shoots can be used as asparagus and its leaves as spinach. Perennial.

Soil Deep, rich, fairly dry.

Sowing Apr. In drills 1 ft. apart. Thin to 1 ft. Sow thinly.

Management At end of first season, cover with 4–5 in. leaf-mould or old compost.

Harvesting Cut lightly the following season, using a knife as for asparagus. Do not cut before Apr. or after June.

GOURDS (*Cucurbita spp.*)

These, like marrows, pumpkins and squashes belong to the genus *Cucurbita* which comprises both edible and ornamental species. Some have distinct and pleasant flavours and can be used in the same way as marrows. All are grown in the same general way. When several species are grown together, cross-pollination may readily occur; if seed is saved it is unlikely to breed true.

Soil Deep, rich, moist but well drained.

Manuring Farmyard manure or compost placed under the soil where the plant is to be set, forming a slight mound.

Sowing Apr., in boxes or pots in frame or greenhouse, preferably with gentle heat. 50 deg. F. Harden off.

Planting May–June. (Early plants should be protected by cloches.)

Management Water freely and give liquid manure as necessary. Climbing varieties must have some support, e.g. trellis, pergola or strong branches. Trailing kinds can be pinched back if they tend to get out of hand. Large kinds which can produce fruits weighing 1 cwt. or more must be provided with strong nets.

Harvesting Cut as soon as large enough to handle. Some fruits may also be left to grow on for harvesting when ripe and storing for winter use.

Varieties (Edible) Gourds and Pumpkins: Custard, Golden Crook-neck, Table Queen Squashes: Banana, Golden Hubbard, Ohio

KALE

Although they are not in the front rank of green vegetables, the kales are especially valuable because they will grow on most soils and are so hardy that they generally survive the most severe winters and so provide greens when there is the greatest scarcity. There are two distinct types, the true kales sometimes called borecole, and the rape kales. Each belongs to a separate species and requires different management.

True Kales (*Brassica oleracea acephala*)

Soil Most kinds suitable. Best is fairly rich, medium to heavy loam.

Manuring Farmyard manure or compost 10 lb., or complete fertilizer 2 oz.

Sowing Apr.–May in seed bed.

Planting May–June, rows 2 ft. apart, plants 2 ft. apart.

Management Hoe regularly. Top dress if required but do not give any nitrogen late in the season as this will encourage soft growth which may fail in the winter.

Harvesting Should be regarded as a reserve and left as long as possible, using other less-hardy vegetables first. After taking first crop of leaves, the tops may be used and side-shoots will develop for further use.

Varieties Scotch or Curled Kale, Cottager's (less curled), Russian Kale (or Chou de Russie), Thousand-headed. Variegated Kales (red to purplish in colour) are more ornamental and although not wholly suitable for cooking can be so used and generally boil green. There is also a perennial kale propagated by cuttings taken in Mar.–Apr.

Rape Kales (*Brassica napus*). These are grown in the same way as true kales, except that being plants of later maturity they must not be sown so early, otherwise the foliage is too soft to withstand the winter.

Sowing Not before July. In drills 2 ft. apart in permanent position. Thin to 2 ft.

Varieties Asparagus Kale, Hungry Gap, Siberian.

KOHL-RABI (*Brassica oleracea caulorapa*)

Also known as knol-kohl or turnip cabbage. Used principally as a substitute for turnips in areas where a hardier and more drought-resistant crop is required.

Soil Most kinds are suitable, even if fairly dry.

Manuring Only poor soil needs manuring. Hoof and horn 1 oz., bone meal 2 oz., sulphate of potash ½ oz.

Sowing Apr.–June, in seed bed or in permanent position. Rows 1–1½ ft. apart.

Planting **Plant out or thin to 9 in. May–July.**

Management Hoe and water as necessary. Fill up any gaps, as the aim is not to grow the roots too large.

Harvesting May be stored or left in ground.

Varieties Small Top Green, Early White, Early Purple.

LAMB'S LETTUCE. See *Corn Salad*

LEEK (*Allium porrum*)

One of the oldest vegetables, dating back to the time of ancient Egypt. A wild form occurs in most parts of Europe. Very hardy and therefore very useful in cold or exposed gardens.

Soil Deep rich loam, well drained. Very light or very heavy soils are unsuitable.

Manuring Farmyard manure or compost 20 lb.

Sowing Feb. under glass for early crops, pricked out and hardened off. Mar. in the open in seed bed for main crops. Sow thinly.

Planting May for early crops; May–June for main crops. If roots or leaves of seedlings are very long they can be trimmed shorter quite safely. On the flat: 9 in. apart, rows 12–18 in. apart. The best way is to make holes 3 in. in diameter, 9 in. deep with a dibber. Drop in a seedling and water it in, but not filling up the hole with soil. In trenches: 12–18 in. wide and 2 ft. apart, prepared as for celery. Plants 9 in. apart.

Management Hoe and give liquid manure regularly. Never let the plants get dry. Top dress once or twice with 1 oz. bone meal or 1 oz. superphosphate and ½ oz. sulphate of potash.

Blanching For a crop grown in trenches earth up as for celery. For crops on the flat growing in holes, soil should be drawn up towards the the end of the season. For crops on the flat, not grown in holes, regular earthing-up or paper collars will be necessary.

Harvesting Lift as required from Nov. to Mar. Specially fine roots can be stored in sand.

Varieties The Lyon, Musselburgh, Prizetaker, Royal Favourite.

Leek, Perpetual. A continental form, producing side growths often of a bulbous nature, which may be planted to produce a crop the following year.

Leek, Sand or **Rocambole.** A different and perennial species of the same genus, grown for the bulbs which form at the top and base of the stem. The bulbs are dried and stored, and used as substitutes for garlic. Management is the same as for shallots.

Planting Feb.–Mar. The bulbs are planted 2 in. deep and 9 in. apart in rows 1 ft. apart.

LETTUCE (*Lactuca sativa*)

Probably the oldest of the salad vegetables. Supplies can be obtained all the year round, between May and Oct. from outdoor crops and Nov. to Apr. from glass-grown crops. It is most important to choose varieties suitable for each season and method of cultivation.

Outdoor crops

Soil Medium to light, rich. Not deficient in lime.

Manuring Farmyard manure or compost 20 lb. dug in in autumn or for a previous crop.

Sowing Mar.–Oct. in succession at intervals of 2–3 weeks. Early sowings can be transplanted but it is generally better (and essential for later sowings) to sow in their permanent positions and thin to 6–12 in. according to size of variety.

Planting When transplanting plant firmly and not too deeply.

Management Hoe regularly. Water as required during summer. Top dress after singling with complete fertilizer 2 oz. or, if farmyard manure was given, with ½ oz. sulphate of ammonia. At end of Oct. select best of hearted plants and transplant carefully into cold frame for use during Nov.

Under glass. In heated greenhouse or hot-bed.

Sowing Sow in seed bed out of doors end of Aug. to Oct. Prick out and protect latest sowings with cloches.

Planting Plant in house or hot-bed end of Sept. to Jan. 9–12 in. apart.

In cold house or cold frame

Sowing Sow in seed bed out of doors Oct. Prick out and protect with cloches.

Planting Plant in house or frame Feb. onwards. 9–12 in. apart.

Management under glass Watering is most important. Soil must be kept moist but never wet. After transplanting watering is not generally needed for a fortnight or so. Then weekly is usually sufficient. Water with can held close to soil, not overhead. Ventilate freely on all suitable days.

Note: Seed can also be sown in cold frames in Oct. and from Feb. onwards, for growing on or planting out of doors end of Mar. onwards.

Varieties For sowing in the open in spring and summer: Improved Trocadero, Feltham King, Favourite, All the Year Round, Tom Thumb, Webb's Wonderful. For sowing in autumn in cold frames, sheltered border or under cloches: May Queen, Improved Trocadero, Feltham King, Majestic, Cheshunt Early Ball. For sowing in autumn for wintering in the open: Arctic King, Imperial, Winter Crop. For heated greenhouse or hot-bed: Cheshunt Early Giant, Premier.

Lettuce, Cos. The Cos lettuce grows taller than cabbage lettuce and in a conical shape, and when well grown is generally crisper. Most modern varieties are self-blanching, but the older ones require tying; the leaves should be held loosely together and tied with raffia or a rubber band, a little above the middle point, about 10–14 days before being wanted.

Varieties For sowing in autumn and planting out in spring: Lobjoit's Dark Green, Prince of Wales. (Should be protected with cloches or in cold frame during winter.) For sowing in autumn and wintering in the open: Winter Density. For sowing in the open in spring and summer: Lobjoit's Dark Green, Superb

White. For sowing in frames Jan.–Feb. and planting out in Mar. for early supplies: Little Gem, Early Perfection.

Lettuce, Cutting. This is a third type, more or less intermediate between the cabbage and the Cos types. The leaves form a rosette rather than a heart and when these are cut a fresh growth develops. Cutting lettuces are grown on the continent and in America, the leaves being cooked as a vegetable as well as being used in salads.

MARROWS (*Cucurbita pepo*)

Marrows are grown in much the same way as gourds. They are divided into two types, trailing or bush, and can be trained to grow on a fence or grown on open ground, or a compost heap. Male and female flowers are produced separately.

Soil Deep, rich, well-drained but moist. A little shade is no handicap.

Manuring Farmyard manure or compost 20 lb. or placed in forkfuls under the soil to form a small mound on which plants are set. Complete fertilizer 2 oz.

Sowing Apr. 1–2 seeds in a pot, in gentle heat or cold frame, or out of doors in early May preferably in warm border or under cloche. Prick out and harden off when two rough leaves have formed.

Planting End May–June 4 ft. apart. Protect with cloche for first few days.

Management Water regularly but not excessively. Roots must never become dry. Trailing kinds must be kept within bounds by training and stopping by pinching out as required. Give liquid manure every fortnight as soon as fruits begin to set. Hoe and mulch. If fruits form but fail to set, pollination should be helped (especially in early stages) by dusting pollen from a male flower on to a female flower, using a soft (preferably camel-hair) brush or by picking a male flower, turning back the petals, putting into a female flower and leaving it there.

Harvesting Cut when young, about 9 in. long to ensure continued cropping. Large matured marrows can be stored for winter use.

Varieties Trailing: Long White, Long Green, Moore's Cream, Table Dainty. Bush: Tender and True (green), White Bush, Green Bush, Superlative (green), Courgette.

Marrows can also be grown in a heated greenhouse (60 deg. F.–65 deg. F.). Sow in pots in Jan. plant out in Feb. Use a trailing type and train up purlin post or strong stake. Pollinate by hand.

MUSHROOMS (*Psalliota campestris*)

The mushroom belongs to a class of fungi called *Basidiomycetes*, which in its turn belongs to one of the main divisions of the vegetable kingdom and botanically is far removed from the division containing the green-coloured flowering vegetables of the kitchen garden. While its structure, form and method of growth and its cultural requirements are different, it ranks as one of the most popular 'vegetables' of the day, and provided its particular demands can be satisfied it is easy to grow, although the preparatory work is heavy and exacting. Attention to hygiene is most essential; lack of it is probably the main reason why a first crop so often seems to be blessed with beginner's luck and because of some unchecked pest or disease, seldom reaches that level again. Unless, therefore, the necessary time, care and facilities can be provided the private gardener should hesitate before growing this crop.

Mushrooms can be grown in the open for cropping from summer to autumn or in sheds, cellars, greenhouses or frames for cropping from late summer to winter or, if heat is available, until spring. In all cases high-quality spawn, manure and casing (or covering) soil are essential. Being a fungus, the crop cannot be grown from seeds or plants but must be produced from spawn which is a pure culture obtained under controlled sterilized conditions. This will give rise to the mycelium or fine root-threads forming the vegetative part from which fructifications (mushrooms) arise.

In sheds, cellars, greenhouses, frames These must be clean, dry, free from draughts and either dark or well shaded. If necessary they must be disinfected, preferably with formalin, before use. Temperature should never exceed 70 deg. F. or fall below 50 deg. F. so that for all-the-year-round cropping good insulation by means of thick or double walls is essential and heating must be available. Walls should be of brick, stone, wood or asbestos with an inner lining forming an air-space or containing a layer of sawdust, cork or aluminium foil, and roofs should be of asbestos or tiles and preferably flat, although some slight slope should be given to drain off condensation. Floors too should be level. The crop should be grown on flat beds, not more than 4 ft. wide, made up on the ground or on shelves (in tiers if room). Boxes or trays may also be used. All shelving should be movable for easy cleaning and disinfection. Ventilation must be provided and any windows fitted with movable shutters. Glasshouses must be shaded and insulated with mats or covers of straw, or beds may be made under the staging with mats or heavy sacking hung in front. Frames must have a depth of at least 20 in. and should be of brick or turf or, if wood, should have a surrounding wall of straw. Lights must be shaded and covered by mats or straw.

Preparation Fresh, strawy horse manure should be stacked (under cover in winter). Add 2–3 in. clean fresh loam. In 10 days or so when temperature reaches 150 deg. F. turn the stack, outsides to inside and top to bottom. Add a sprinkling of gypsum and a little water if the whole is not moist. When temperature again reaches 150 deg. F. turn once more. Repeat 2–3 times. (1 ton manure will make 36 sq. ft. of flat bed or 12 ft. of outdoor ridge beds.)

Making the beds Fill the beds with compost made as above, tread down lightly but evenly to 8 or 10 in. deep. Put on heat if available. Ventilate freely for 2 days. Then close up shed, fumigate with burning sulphur or hydrocyanic acid gas (poison) or dust with pyrethrum or derris. Open up next day.

Spawning When bed temperature steadies at 70 deg. F. put in spawn broken up to size of walnuts, 1 in. deep, 9 in. apart.

Casing In 10–12 days white threads of mycelum should appear. Beds must then be covered with 1½–2 in. of casing soil. This should be dug from heavy or clay loam, taking second spit, and breaking up to small lumps about pea-size. It should be moist enough to bind together when put on the bed. Thereafter water beds lightly if necessary to keep them moist. Ventilate enough to keep air fresh.

Harvesting 6–8 weeks after spawning. Gather by twisting, not cutting. When stump has dried up, remove and fill hole with soil. Cropping season lasts 8–15 weeks, yield 1–3 lb. per square foot. When finished remove bed for manuring outdoor soil. Clean, scrape and sterilize building, tools and equipment.

Varieties White, Brown.

Ridge beds in the open

Beds are made on level, well-drained soil, 2½ ft. high, 2½ ft. wide at base tapering to about 6 in. at apex. Make up with manure composted as above, tread and pat into shape. Cover with 4 in. straw. When temperature falls to 70 deg. F. remove straw, add spawn and replace straw. When ready for casing, remove straw, add soil and replace straw adding more to give 6 in. in summer and 12 in. in winter. Finally cover with tarpaulin, mats or thick sacking, pegged down.

MUSTARD

The mustard used as salad may be grown from seeds of the black mustard (*Brassica nigra*), white mustard (*B. alba*) or common rape (*B. napus*). The first two species are also used for producing seed from which table mustard is prepared or for digging in as green manure when the crop reaches the flowering stage. Mustard seedlings are 'cold'; it is cress which is 'hot'.

Cultivation is the same as for cress, but since mustard germinates more quickly seed should be sown 3 days later than the cress if the two are required for cutting at the same time.

Mustard, Chinese. Two other members of the brassicae, *B. juncea* and *B. japonica*, are sometimes grown to produce a substitute for spring greens.

Soil Rich, deep, moist but well drained.

Manuring Preferably the previous crop should have received farmyard manure or compost. Failing this, bone meal 2 oz., hoof and horn

1 oz., sulphate of potash ½ oz. or complete fertilizer 4 oz.

Sow Mar. onwards, in succession, in rows 1 ft. apart. Thin to 6 in.

Harvesting Pull larger leaves from the base as produced.

ONIONS (*Allium cepa*)

One of the oldest vegetables dating back at least to the days of the Egyptian Pharaohs and originating probably from the wild species found in various parts of Asia. The crop is often regarded as one of the most difficult to grow, but, except in very wet areas or on very heavy land, there should be no great difficulty provided the soil is suitable, the right varieties are chosen, the management is correct and storage is available. If freedom from pests and disease can be maintained the crop may be grown on the same plot for several years in succession and it is often well worth while spending a good deal of time and work in bringing an unsuitable soil to the right texture. The crop can be grown from seed, from plants raised under glass or from 'sets'. The seed may be sown in early spring or autumn, spring generally giving the better results.

Soil Rich, deep, medium loam in sunny open position. Well drained. Heavy or light soils must be improved with manure or compost and sand or clay. Double-digging is essential on most soils.

Manuring Farmyard manure or compost 20 lb. dug in in autumn followed by surface dressing of 4 oz. bone meal and 2 oz. sulphate of potash.

Sowing Under glass: Jan. in boxes, preferably in gentle heat. Prick out 2–3 in. apart, harden off for planting out in Apr.

In the open: in drills 1 ft. apart, ½ in. deep, Feb.–Mar, thinly; Aug.–early Sept., fairly thickly. After sowing firm soil by treading or light rolling.

Thin to 2 in., then to 6 in. Final thinning should not be done before end of Apr. (Thinnings can be used as 'spring' onions.)

Planting 'sets' Mar. 6 in. apart in rows 1 ft. apart. (Sets or small bulbs should preferably be bought, although they can, with care, be raised from seed sown in fairly poor ground the previous May and not thinned, the object being to produce bulbs not more than ½ in. to ¾ in. in diameter. Keep such plants growing slowly; water as required but do not feed. Defer lifting until Sept.; store in a cool, dry, airy place until following Mar.)

Management A fine, deep but firm tilth is essential. Several rakings will be necessary. At last raking add a good dressing of soot, or of dried powdered poultry manure, hoof and horn or guano 2 oz. When seedlings appear start hoeing and dusting lightly with old soot every 7–10 days. First thinning to 2 in. should be done as soon as possible, finally thinning to 6 in. Transplant to fill up any gaps. Glass-raised plants should be planted with a good ball of soil and put in at proper level. Never draw soil up to plants. Feed with liquid manure every fortnight. Water regularly in dry weather.

Harvesting Aug. When tops begin to colour, the bulbs should be eased partly out of the ground with a fork. Sept. Tops can be bent over with a wooden rake or pole, and when yellow and dry, bulbs should be pulled, preferably on a fine day. Leave in rows for a few days, then bring into cool, dry, airy place. Rub off loose skin and stems. Store in ropes, sticks or on trays. Always handle carefully.

Varieties For spring sowing: White Spanish, Ailsa Craig, James' Keeping, Bedfordshire Champion, Up-to-Date. For spring or autumn sowing: A.1, Giant Zittau, Improved Reading. For autumn sowing: Giant Rocca.

Onions, Pickling. Medium-sized bulbs of the main crop can be used for pickling but it is far better to grow one of the special varieties of an oval shape and with white skin.

Treat as for the main crop, sowing fairly thickly in Apr. ½ in. to 1 in. deep, thinning to not more than 2 in.

Varieties White Queen, Small Paris Silverskin, Covent Garden Pickling.

Onion, Egyptian or **Tree.** Produces a bulb at the base and smaller bulbs on the stems. Requires sunny open position, but will succeed on a soil less rich than that needed for the common onion.

Planting Mar.–Apr. Plant bulbs 2–3 in. deep and

6 in. apart in rows 1 ft. apart. Smallest bulbs can be used to produce salad onions. Manage and store as for common onions. Supporting stakes may be required.

Onion, Potato. Somewhat similar to shallots.

Planting Jan.–Mar. Plant bulbs 6 in. apart in rows 1 ft. apart, tips just above surface. Manage and store as for common onions.

Onion, Salad or **Spring**

Soil Rich, deep, light-medium loam, preferably well manured for a previous crop.

Manuring Hoof and horn 2 oz. raked in just before sowing.

Sowing Aug. and Feb.–Mar. In rows 1 ft. apart, ½ in. deep.

Management Hoe regularly. Water if required in very dry weather.

Harvesting Pull as required. Large plants may be left to produce bulb onions for early use, but are not suitable for storing.

Varieties White Lisbon, White Portugal.

Onion, Welsh. A perennial, evergreen type resembling clusters of spring onions. Best propagated by division in spring but can also be raised from seed sown in July or Aug.

Planting 9 in. apart in rows 1 ft. apart.

ORACH. See *Spinach*

OXALIS

A few species of this genus are sometimes grown for their tubers. *Oxalis deppei* is the one most usually chosen. The tubers are round to oval about 1½ in. thick and are cooked in the same way as potatoes and usually eaten with veal.

Soil Deep, rich, medium to light loam.

Manuring Farmyard or compost 20 lb.

Planting May. 1 ft. apart in rows 2 ft. apart.

Management Hoe regularly to obtain good tilth. Earth up as for potatoes, adding top dressing of complete fertilizer 2 oz.

Harvesting Lift in Oct.–Nov. and store.

PARSLEY

Parsley, Hamburg or **Turnip-rooted.** Sometimes grown as a substitute for parsnips, having a similar root. The top is like parsley. Treat as for parsnips.

Sowing Feb.–Apr., in rows 1 ft. apart. Thin to 9 in.

Harvesting Oct. Should be stored but may also be left in the ground.

Parsley, Neapolitan or **Celery-leaved.** Used as a substitute for celery and grown and blanched in the same way.

Sowing Mar.–Apr.

PARSNIP (*Peucedanum sativum*)

One of the oldest vegetables, used in earlier times as the main vegetable dish until superseded by the potato.

Soil Deep, rich, light to medium loam, free of stones. Preferably one that was well manured for the previous crop. Should be double-dug in early autumn.

Manuring Bone meal 2 oz., sulphate of potash 1 oz., raked in just before sowing.

Sowing Feb.–Mar., thinly or in groups of 3–4 seeds 12 in. apart and 1 in. deep. Rows 18 in. apart. In stony soil or to obtain long roots, 3–4 seeds may be sown on top of holes made with a crow-bar and filled with sifted soil. In all cases final thinning should leave plants 9–12 in. apart.

Management Hoe regularly.

Harvesting Roots not generally mature until Nov. Should be left in the ground and dug as required. Protect with straw if weather is severe. Roots remaining at the end of the winter should be lifted before second season's growth begins and can be stored for a short time.

Varieties Tender and True, Hollow Crown, Student. For shallow soils a short or turnip-rooted variety is better; Offenham, Turnip-rooted.

PEAS (*Pisum sativum*)

It is probable that in early times peas were harvested in the mature state and used only for 'pea porridge' or 'pottage', since there are no references to fresh green peas until well into the sixteenth century. But during the last 150 years the various forms, types and colours have been well recognized and considerable selection and hybridization have been carried out and the number of varieties is now very great, making exact classification extremely difficult. There are, however, two main groups, the round-seeded and the wrinkle-seeded. The former are generally earlier and hardier and are often dwarf-growing, while the latter are better flavoured and usually give a heavier crop.

Soil Most types except the very heavy or very light are suitable. Must be moist, but well drained and not short of lime. Preferably a deep, rich loam, double-dug in autumn.

Manuring Farmyard manure or compost 20 lb. in autumn. Complete fertilizer 4 oz., or bone meal 2 oz., hoof and horn 1 oz., and sulphate of potash 1 oz. raked in just before sowing.

Sowing Jan.–Mar. for early crops. (A sowing may also be tried in Nov.) Mar.–May for second early and main crops. May–July for late crops. Sow 2½–3 in. deep in broad flat drills 6 in. wide, setting peas 2–3 in. apart. Rows should be 2 ft. apart for dwarf varieties, 3–4 ft. for medium-height varieties and 4 ft. or more for tall varieties. Cover with pea-guards to protect from birds. Under glass: in pots or boxes in cold frame from Nov.–Jan. Ventilate freely. Can also be sown in gentle heat (not over 50 deg. F.) in Jan. Harden off. Plant out in March, 6–9 in. apart. Under cloches Nov.–Feb.

Management Provide sticks as soon as possible on each side of the row, 4 in. away from the side. Sticks should be vertical or incline outwards; they must not slope inwards. Trim the tops to the height of the variety and use the cut tips between the bases of the sticks. Large-mesh wire or cord-netting may also be used. Hoe regularly, bringing soil up slightly towards the plants. Water if required. Protect from birds with black cotton or fish netting.

Harvesting Pick regularly and frequently. Pods should not be allowed to mature unless a seed crop is desired.

Varieties (Figures denote height in feet.)

Early: Meteor 1½, Little Marvel 1½–2, Kelvedon Wonder 1½, The Pilot 3, Early Bird 3, Early Giant 3½. For sowing in Jan. under cloches, Feltham First.

Second Early: British Lion 3, Dwarf Defiance 2½, Gradus 3, Onward 2½, The Lincoln 2½, Phenomenon 2.

Main Crop: Alderman 5, Senator 3, Kelvedon Peerless 3½.

Late Crop: Gladstone 4, Autocrat 4, Invicta 4, or an early quick-maturing variety like Little Marvel, Kelvedon Wonder, for sowing in June or July.

For autumn sowing: Meteor, British Lion.

Pea, Asparagus (*Tetragonolobus purpureus*). A hardy annual belonging to a genus different from that of the garden pea. It is of bushy habit, up to 1½ ft. high and bears reddish-brown flowers and small pods which are rectangular in section and born singly or in pairs in the leaf-axils. The pods are cooked whole.

Soil Most kinds suitable if rich or well manured.

Sowing Mar.–Apr. ½ in. deep in drills 2 ft. apart. Thin to 1 ft.

Management Hoe regularly. Water in dry weather. Support with twigs if necessary.

Harvesting Gather pods while still tender (about half-grown).

Pea, Sugar or **Mangetout.** This is of the same genus as the garden pea and is grown in the same way. The pods are used sliced like French or runner beans and should be picked while still tender as soon as the peas can be felt to be forming. Sow Apr.–May. Both dwarf and tall types are available.

PETSAI. See *Cabbage*

PORTUGAL CABBAGE. See *Cabbage*

POTATO (*Solanum tuberosum*)

Although Sir Walter Raleigh is popularly credited with the introduction of potatoes into England, there is little historical justification and Drake or Grenville or any of the sixteenth-century settlers who returned from the New World may be given the honour just as easily. What is known is that the new plant reached Spain early in the century and that long after it had spread across Europe, it was regarded as being of little value and only gradually became a food for the poorest in the land. It was not until the nineteenth century that the real value of the crop was recognized.

The gardener has certain great advantages over the farmer; he can grow the best-flavoured varieties which are often too tender or uneconomic for field cultivation, he can harvest early potatoes as a luxury as soon as they are big enough to use and, if he has room, can still grow the heavy yielding main crops which are normally grown in the fields, and comprise varieties which will store through the winter until new potatoes come round again.

Soil Most types are suitable except wet heavy clay which also makes planting and lifting difficult. Best is a deep well-drained light to medium loam, not too rich in lime. Position should not be shaded as this encourages blight. Should be double-dug in autumn or for previous crop.

Manuring Farmyard manure or compost 20 lb. applied at planting time or in autumn Complete fertilizer 4 oz. or bone meal 3 oz., hoof and horn 1 oz., and sulphate of potash 1 oz. raked in before planting. Avoid salt or chloride (muriate) of potash. Lime must not be applied before planting as this encourages skin scab. Top dress as required.

Planting Early varieties: Feb. to Mar., 12 in. apart in rows 20 to 24 in. apart. Main crop. Mar. to early May, 15 to 18 in. apart in rows 24 to 27 in. apart. These distances may be increased where there is plenty of space or the crop is being grown as a cleaning crop to improve neglected land. Tubers may be planted 4 to 5 in. deep in trenches or in holes made with a spade or dibber. Trenches are best especially where manure is to be applied at planting time. Seed should be of certified stock and sprouted in boxes or trays in a well-lighted frost-proof place.

Management All cultivation must be done with the object of maintaining a loose friable soil and creating a deep tilth for easy earthing-up. Trenches should be made 6 in. wide, 5 in. deep. Put in manure, sprinkle on fertilizer and just a little fine soil. Place tubers in position, eye up, handling sprouted ones carefully. Cover with soil, forming slight ridge. Hoe between rows. If frost threatens when foliage appears protect with straw, polythene, light brushwood or even soil. When about 6 in. high give first earthing-up, almost covering foliage, afterwards forking or hoeing well between rows. About 3 weeks later give second earthing-up, making ridges as wide as possible but coming close up to stems at the top. Before each earthing-up top dress carefully between rows with complete fertilizer 2 oz. Watch for blight and spray as soon as the first signs are seen or disease is known to be in the district.

Under glass Early crops can be forced in cold or heated frames or houses or on hot-beds. Sprouted tubers with sprouts reduced to two for each tuber should be planted in pots or boxes, leaving space for compost to be added in place of earthing-up. Ventilate freely. Water lightly but regularly.

Harvesting Earlies can be lifted as soon as crop is worth having.
Main crops must not be lifted until haulm has matured. Store in clamps or in a cool, dark frost-proof store (see Chapter 1).

Varieties Several hundred distinct varieties have been raised and grown at different times. Nearly fifty are still popular. The following are selected as being generally suitable for garden cultivation.

Early

Arran Pilot* Kidney, white. Heavy cropper, second quality.

Di Vernon* Oval, long, splashed blue purple. High quality.

Duke of York Kidney, white. Yellow flesh. Suitable for forcing.

Edzell Blue* Flat round, purple. Late early of good quality.

Epicure Round, white. Good quality. Deep Eyes.

Home Guard* Oval, white. Good quality if used early.

Ulster Premier* Kidney, white with round red eyes. Good quality.

Second early

Dunbar Rover* Oval, white. Good quality.

Eclipse Oval, white.

Great Scot* Round, white, Heavy cropper.

Main crop

Arran Peak* Oval, white. Heavy cropper.

Arran Victory* Round, purple skin. Good quality, good keeper.

Dr. McIntosh* Kidney, white, Heavy cropper.

Golden Wonder* Kidney, white. Excellent quality. Needs careful growing.

King Edward VII Kidney, white splashed pink. Good quality.

Majestic* Kidney, white. Heavy cropper, good keeper.

(Under the Wart Disease of Potatoes Order only immune varieties may be planted in infected land and all potatoes sold for planting must have been certified for the purpose and the certificate number must be given to the purchaser. The highest qualities of seed bear the prefixes S.S. or A. The country of origin and the size must also be stated.)

* Immune from wart disease

Potato, Salad. Certain varieties, generally producing long cylindrical tubers with coloured flesh and retaining the flavour of new potatoes are suitable for use in salads. They are grown in the same way as the main crops. Yields are usually smaller.

Varieties Pink Fir Apple, pink with yellow flesh. Congo, black-purple skin and flesh.

RADISH (*Raphanus sativus*)

The secret of radish growing is to grow the crop quickly, otherwise they are stringy and hot to the taste. If hot-beds and frames are available supplies can be had all the year round, but always the sowings should be made in succession and each sowing should be small. In the open the crop should be treated as a catch-crop and sown between rows of slower-growing crops or on the banks of celery trenches.

Soil A finely-raked, deep, moist, but well-drained soil is best. It should not have been freshly manured.

Manuring As a general rule, none required.

Sowing Thinly, $\frac{1}{2}$ in. deep in drills 12 in. apart. Can also be broadcast. Firm after sowing. Thin any thick bunches. In the open: Mar.–Sept. and in favoured protected positions Dec.–Feb. Under glass: Dec.–Feb. in gentle heat 50 deg. F. Feb.–Mar. in cold frames. May be sown among other crops, e.g. lettuce.

Management Hoe and water as required. Earliest sowings will need protection in cold weather with cloches, straw, bracken or mats.

Harvesting Begin pulling as soon as possible. Never use old or slow-growing roots.

Varieties For outdoor sowing: French Breakfast (oval), Scarlet Globe, Sparkler (round), Wood's Long Frame, Icicle (long).

For hot-beds and frames: French Breakfast Forcing (oval), Red Short-top Forcing (round).

(There is also a winter type producing larger roots for storing over the winter. Sow in July–Aug., rows 1 ft. apart, thin to 9 in. The flesh is generally hard and should be sliced for use in salads.

Varieties Black Spanish, Chinese Rose.)

RAMPION (*Campanula rapunculus*)

A biennial with white fleshy roots which should be peeled thinly for use in salads or cooking like turnips. Leaves also used in salads.

Soil Rich, fairly light. Partial shade.

Sowing May–June (not earlier as plants easily bolt). Seeds are very small. Sow thinly in drills 1 ft. apart. Thin to 6 in.

Management Hoe and water as required.

Harvesting Ready from Nov. Lift as required or put into store.

RHUBARB (*Rheum rhaponticum*)

One of the oldest cultivated plants, rhubarb can be traced back to the China of 3000 B.C. Until about 150 years ago it was grown exclusively for the medicinal properties of its roots, but with the introduction of modern varieties it has attained the stage where it is often classed as a fruit.

Soil Most types are suitable but a rich, deep, medium to light loam is best. Not shaded. (Too often poor results are due to the crop being grown in 'any old corner'.) Double-dig in autumn.

Manuring Farmyard manure or compost 20 lb. or bone meal 4 oz., hoof and horn 2 oz., sulphate of potash 1 oz.

Sowing Can be raised from seed sown in Mar. in a frame preferably with gentle heat, but seeds generally do not breed true. Prick out and transplant in the open and plant in permanent position the following Mar.

Planting Established roots are divided and planted out in Mar., 3 to 4 ft. apart each way. Crown should be just above surface.

Management Hoe and water freely. No stems should be pulled the first year. Cut off any flower stems. Every autumn mulch with manure or compost or give 2 oz. of fish or meat meal to each plant in July. Some of the roots should be lifted after 5 or 6 years, divided and fresh plantings made in succession.

Harvesting Pull lightly in second year and subsequently do not pull too much from any one root.

Forcing In gentle heat 55 deg. F. From Nov. onwards 3- or 4-year-old roots can be lifted in succession. Pack closely in darkened glasshouse, shed or hot-bed.

In the open: In Jan.–Feb. forcing pots or large boxes can be placed over roots and covered with manure.

Varieties Hawke's Champagne, Dawe's Champion, Linnaeus, Prince Albert, Victoria. Most suitable for forcing: Prince Albert, Victoria.

ROCAMBOLE. See *Leek*

SALSIFY or **VEGETABLE OYSTER** (*Tragopogon porrifolius*)

Soil Deep, moist, medium to light, sandy loam. Preferably manured for previous crop.

Manuring Complete fertilizer 4 oz. or bone meal 3 oz., hoof and horn 1 oz., sulphate of potash 1 oz.

Sowing Apr. 1 in. deep in drills 1–1½ ft. apart. Thin to 9 in. On stony soil make holes with a crowbar as for carrots or parsnips.

Management Hoe regularly. Water in dry weather.

Harvesting Lift roots as required or put into store. If left in the ground chards or tender young shoots can be taken the following Mar. or Apr., green or blanched. Handle roots carefully.

SCORZONERA

One species of this genus (*S. hispanica*) can be grown and used in the same way as salsify. It is not of high quality and the roots have black skin although the flesh is white.

SEAKALE (*Crambe maritima*)

Soil Deep, rich, light to heavy loams with good lime content. Open, sunny position.

Manuring Farmyard manure or compost 20 lb. double-dug in autumn. Complete fertilizer 4 oz. or bone meal 4 oz., hoof and horn 2 oz., muriate of potash 2 oz. (or sulphate of potash 1 oz.).

Sowing Mar.–Apr. in seed bed. Drills 1 ft. apart 1 in. deep. Thin to 6 in. or transplant. Following Mar., lift, trim off tops to just below crown and plant in permanent position.

Planting The usual method of propagation is to take cuttings or thongs from established roots when being lifted and trimmed for forcing in Nov. onwards. Select straight side growths about the thickness of a pencil. Trim to 6 in. long, cutting top level and lower end on the slant so as to indicate which is the right way up for planting. Tie the cuttings in a bundle and stand in fine earth or damp sand, covering them 2–3 in. deep. In Mar. take up cuttings, rub off all weak eyes, and plant 15 in. apart in rows 1½ ft. apart, if the roots are to be lifted for forcing indoors. If forcing is to be done in the soil by means of forcing pots, plant in clumps 2–3 ft. apart consisting of 3 to 4 cuttings set about 4 in. apart.

Management Both seedlings and planted-out cuttings should be hoed regularly. Water as required and top dress twice during summer with ½ oz. nitrate of soda or give liquid manure. On light soils top dress with salt 4 oz. Remove any flower stems. Oct., trim off foliage.

Forcing In sheds, greenhouse or frame: All light must be excluded. Temperature should be 50 deg. F.–55 deg. F. Not over 60 deg. F. Roots must be lifted, trimmed and packed together with 2 in. space between in a mixture of compost or old hot-bed manure with a little sand or fine soil. Water lightly and cover with 3 in. fine soil or short straw. Roots may also be packed in boxes and covered with inverted boxes. In the open: (*a*) Seakale pots or large pots or drainpipes (made light-proof) can be put over the plants from Nov. onwards and surrounded with long manure, short straw or leaves. (*b*) Roots can be earthed up when soil is fairly dry, to a height of 9 in. Roots forced in heat are of no use afterwards, and a new crop from cuttings must be raised each year. Roots forced in the ground can be left down for many years, provided a good mulch of manure is given after removing the pots or soil.

Harvesting Forcing with heat should give a crop in 3 weeks; without heat in 4–5 weeks and earthing-up about 3 months. Cut when growth is 6–8 in. high, taking off a strip of root which helps to prevent the shoots drying.

Varieties Lily White.

SHALLOTS (*Allium ascalonicum*)

The main requirements of shallots are similar to those of onions, except that they will grow on a wider range of soil and need not be so liberally fed. It is generally sufficient if the previous crop was well manured. Shallots can be raised from seed, but this is not always satisfactory owing to variation or bolting. The better way is to plant small bulbs.

Planting Feb.–Mar., the earlier the better. Clean bulbs of all loose scales or leaves and plant by pressing into soil fairly firmly with about half the bulb above ground, 4–6 in. apart in rows 1 ft. apart. Firm down as necessary if bulbs get displaced before rooting.

Management Hoe regularly and when leaves begin to turn yellow and wither, draw soil lightly away from roots. Lift, allow to dry and store under same conditions as onions. Each bulb should make 4 or 5 bulbs during growth.

Varieties Jersey (or Dutch or Russian) Shallot, True Red, True Yellow.

SKIRRET (*Sium sisarum*)

Grown for its tuberous roots which are produced in bunches and used in the same way as salsify. Can be propagated by root cuttings taken in Mar. or Apr. in the same way as for seakale, but the more usual way is by seeds.

Soil Deep, medium or light loam. Not freshly manured.

Sowing Apr., in drills 1 ft. apart, 1 in. deep. Thin to 9 in.

Management Hoe and water freely in dry weather.

Harvesting Sept. onwards. Lift as required.

SPINACH (*Spinacia oleracea*)

There are two types of true spinach, the round or summer spinach and the winter or prickly spinach. Other plants belonging to quite different genera are also widely used in place of spinach, and are included under this heading.

Soil Deep, medium to light loam best. Light, dry soils unsuitable for the summer crops.

Manuring Bone meal 4 oz., hoof and horn 2 oz., sulphate of potash 1 oz.

Sowing End of Feb. or early Mar. onwards, in fortnightly succession. 1 in. deep in drills 1 ft. apart. Thin to 6–9 in. Sow winter type from Aug. to end of Sept. Thin to 4–6 in.

Management Everything must be done to grow the summer crop quickly otherwise it invariably runs to seed. It makes a very useful catch-crop for sowing between slower-growing crops. Hoe regularly, water as required, mulch and feed with liquid manure. Top dress with ½ oz. nitrate of soda. In dry weather water soil before sowing and soak seed for 12–24 hours. For winter sowing a lighter, drier soil can be used. Heavy wet soils are unsuitable unless raised beds are made so that excess moisture can drain away. Cloches are very useful. In severe winters cover with straw, bracken, etc.

Harvesting Gather largest leaves first. Do not pull winter crops too heavily.

Varieties Summer: Giant Lettuce-leaved, Longstanding Round, Victoria.

Winter: Longstanding Prickly, New Giant-leaved.

Spinach, Mountain or **Orach** (*Atriplex hortensis*). A decorative plant with green or red foliage, growing about 4 ft. high, succeeds on nearly all soils, but prefers a deep, moist, rich loam.

Sowing Mar.–May in succession in rows 2 ft. apart. Thin to 18 in.

Management Pinch out flower stems when forming. Hoe regularly. Support if necessary.

Harvesting Pick regularly, otherwise bolting invariably occurs.

Spinach, New Zealand (*Tetragonia expansa*). Will grow well on nearly all soils and does not bolt in dry seasons.

PLATE 55
'Yellow Pinocchio', a floribunda rose.

PLATE 56
SALPIGLOSSIS. There are several strains of this annual, all in a wide range of rich brilliant colours.

PLATE 57
SALVIA. The hardy and half-hardy species are good for borders or beds. All have showy spikes of nettle-like flowers.

PLATE 58

SPIRAEA. The shrub shown above is 'Anthony Waterer' a variety of the species S. japonica, and flowers June to August.

PLATE 59
TULIP. This photograph demonstrates clearly the attractiveness of tulips in borders and beds.

PLATE 60

VIOLA (Pansy). These well-loved flowers are derived from V. tricolor. There are three main groups of varieties: "bedding" varieties, "giant or trimardeau" varieties and "winter-flowering" varieties. There are a number of named varieties in each group, all in a wide range of colours.

PLATE 61
VIBURNUM. This is the species V. tomentosum plicatum, a native of China, with a graceful habit and masses of snowball-like white flowers.

PLATE 62
Right, YUCCA. This is a truly unique plant for the garden. The average height of this shrub is 8 ft., but there is a dwarf species (Y. filamentosa) about 5 ft. The flower spike of the former is about 5 ft. The Yucca thrives in town gardens because of its resistance to atmospheric pollution. Below, WISTERIA. These shrubs can be trained to pergolas or screens or as standard weeping trees (specimens shown here). All flower during May and June.

Manuring As for true spinach.
Sowing (1) Mar. in gentle heat or frame. Prick out, and plant out in May.
(2) End of Mar.–Apr. out of doors, preferably under cloches.
Planting Plant 2 ft. apart in rows 3 ft. apart.
Management Hoe and water freely.
Harvesting Gather young shoots whole to encourage further branching.

Spinach, Perpetual or **Spinach Beet.** See *Beet.*

Spinach, Seakale or **Swiss Chard.** See *Beet.*

SQUASHES. See *Gourds*

SWEDE (*Brassica rapa*)

A close relative of the turnip but with a distinct flavour and type of flesh. It is extremely hardy and should be grown and treated in the same way as the winter crop of turnips, except that the most suitable sowing time is May–June.
Varieties Purple Top, Bronze Top.

SWEET CORN, CORN-ON-THE COB or SUGAR CORN (*Zea mays*)

Only the varieties specially selected and bred for garden cultivation should be grown. The common varieties of maize are quite unsuitable.
Soil Most kinds are suitable except very heavy or very light. Preferably manured for a previous crop. Sunny open position.
Manuring Bone meal 4 oz., hoof and horn 2 oz., sulphate of potash 1 oz. applied just before sowing.
Sowing Apr.–May, preferably under cloches. Drills $1\frac{1}{2}$ in. deep, 2 ft. apart. Space seeds 9–12 in. apart. Rows arranged in a square block rather than one or two long drills assist in pollination.
Planting Seeds may also be sown under glass in early Apr. for transplanting, but often severe checks occur.
Management Hoe regularly. Water freely. Support stems if necessary.
Harvesting It is most essential to harvest at the right stage of growth. About 3–4 weeks from time of flowering the 'silks' will begin to wither and the grain can be tested. The protecting green sheath should be pulled back and one or two grains pressed with the thumb nail. The contents should spurt out and have the consistency of cream. If watery the grain is not quite ripe, if doughy it is over-ripe and will be tough. Cut or pull off gently. Use at once as the cobs dry quickly.
Varieties Canada Cross (early), John Innes Hybrid, Golden Bantam.

TOMATO (*Lycopersicon esculentum*)

Not much more than 100 years ago the tomato was regarded in Europe as being of little or no value. It had been introduced from S. America in the sixteenth century, but was grown chiefly as a curiosity until Joseph Paxton opened the modern era of commercial glasshouses and gave the crop a suitable environment.

Tomatoes are properly a glasshouse crop. They can also be grown out of doors, but are then subject to climatic effects which may seriously reduce quality or encourage certain diseases, so that except in favoured localities results are often disappointing. Raising the crop from seed is not difficult, but unless the private gardener has the facilities of a heated greenhouse or frame and has gained the necessary experience it is usually better to buy plants ready for setting out. He can then be more certain of getting tomatoes ripe in good time. But it is essential to buy from a reliable source and so ensure strong steadily-grown plants that have not been unduly hurried and are free from disease.

Whether the crop is to be grown in a greenhouse in beds at ground level or in large pots, boxes or beds on the staging, in frames, or in the open with or without cloches, certain general rules must be observed. All seed boxes and pots must be cleaned, washed and sterilized and the soil in greenhouses renewed or sterilized at least every 5 years or so, in order to control soil-borne diseases.
Soil Most types are suitable provided they are deeply dug and well drained. Fibrous loam is best. Must not be short of lime.
Manuring Farmyard manure or compost 20 lb. at digging. Bone meal 6 oz., hoof and horn 4 oz., sulphate of potash 2 oz. forked or mixed in before planting.

Production in heated greenhouse or hot-bed 60 deg. F.

Sowing Feb.–Mar. Sow thinly in sterilized pots, pans or boxes filled with John Innes seed compost or sterilized home-made compost. (For very early crops sow Dec.–Jan.) When first pair of rough leaves appear, prick out into 3-in. pots. Handle gently. Keep close to glass. Ventilate whenever possible. Keep soil just moist; never over-water. Use only water at house temperature. (Apr.–May. Harden off plants for planting in cold houses or out of doors.)

Planting Mar. to Apr. Plant out into bed or border of house or on staging, 15–18 in. apart. If in more than one row, rows should be 2–3 ft. apart. Tap plants out of pots gently, keeping ball of soil intact. Water lightly.

Training Plants must be trained up canes or preferably up fillis string running from the roof wires of the house to pegs or other wires at soil level. Pinch out side-shoots and gently twist fillis round the growing stem or tie to cane with raffia.

Management Two to three weeks after planting remove leaves below bottom flower-truss, to provide air space. Water only lightly until second truss is setting. Thereafter water liberally once a week. To help flowers to set, damp with a fine overhead spray once or twice a week, preferably in the morning, or brush over flowers with camel-hair brush or tap stems with a finger every day. Every fortnight top dress before watering with a good tomato fertilizer or 1–2 oz. of the following mixture: superphosphate 4 oz., sulphate of potash 2 oz. and sulphate of ammonia 1 oz. As each successive truss forms give ½ oz. nitrate of potash or dried blood. When plants reach the top of the wires stop by pinching out the growing point.

Ventilation and temperature Night temperature should be kept up to 60 deg. F. Day temperature must not exceed 80 deg. F. and full ventilation and shading may be necessary. In general ventilate whenever possible, if only to a small extent. In dull weather keep temperature low, otherwise soft growth will result.

In cold house

Planting Apr.–May. 15–18 in. apart in rows 2–3 ft. apart.

Management Do not spray overhead except on very hot days. Top dress with half the quantities recommended for heated houses. Otherwise treat the same. The plants can be allowed to grow higher up into the roof. Ventilate as much as possible.

In cold frame

Treat as for cold house, training plant along a stout stake running almost horizontally. Stop at fourth truss.

In the open

Planting End of May. 18 in. apart, rows 2½ ft. apart. Give strong stake for support.

Management Water only when required, as it is better to rely on rain and mulching. Stop at 3 ft. high. Use cloches for early protection and for ripening. Late crops can be grown by sowing seed in the open in a favoured position in Apr., under cloches.

Harvesting Pick by turning the fruit upwards and backwards so that the stem breaks at the joint, leaving the calyx attached to the fruit. In the open, pick when beginning to turn red to avoid bird damage, and pick all the crop by end. of Sept., bring indoors or put on a shelf in the greenhouse to finish ripening.

Varieties Under glass: Ailsa Craig, E.S.I., Hertford Cross, Market King, Stonor's Exhibition, Stonor's Moneymaker, Potentate, Ware Cross.

In the open: Amateur, Harbinger, Hundredfold, Early Market, Market King, Moneymaker.

Varieties having yellow fruits: Golden Queen, Orange Sunrise.

TURNIP (*Brassica rapa*)

By using the newer varieties which are more tender and palatable than the older ones, turnips may be had all the year round either as roots or as tops.

Soil Medium to light loams, moist but well drained. Not short of lime. Preferably one that was well manured for a previous crop.

Manuring Bone meal 4 oz., hoof and horn 2 oz.,

sulphate of potash 1 oz., or complete fertilizer 4 oz. forked in before sowing.

Sowing In mild hot-bed or cold frame: End Jan. onwards, between lettuce or other frame crop or by themselves. Sow 1 in. deep, 4–6 in. apart. In the open: Mar.–Apr. for early crop in favoured position. Apr.–May for summer crop. July–Aug. for autumn and winter. Aug.–Sept. for tops in spring. Drills 1 in. deep, 1 ft. apart. Thin early crops to 6–9 in., later crops 9–12 in. Tops are not thinned.

Management Hoe regularly. Water in dry weather. Small sowings can often be sown as catch-crops.

Harvesting Early crops should be pulled as soon as ready. Late crops can be used as required or stored.

Varieties Under glass: Early White Frame, Red Milan, White Milan.

In the open: Early: White Milan, Early Snowball, Golden Ball. Main crop: Manchester Market, Red Globe. For tops: Greentop White.

CHAPTER EIGHTEEN

Diseases and Pests

THE harm done to garden plants by diseases and pests varies from season to season but even in the lightest years the damage over the whole country is very considerable. Epidemics are by no means rare and it is common to hear a particular year referred to as 'a bad blight year' or 'a bad aphis year' but even when conditions seem to be favourable for plant growth there is always some damage or some reduction in quantity or quality and the gardener consequently suffers disappointment, particularly if he has spent much time and money on good cultivation, seeds, plants and manures. To avoid or at least to reduce such disappointment, it is necessary to be able to recognize the more common pests and diseases, to know something about their control and, above all, to be ready to act at the first and best opportunity.

Warning

Some of the most efficient of the modern sprays or dusts are unfortunately not suitable for use in private gardens and are therefore not mentioned in this book. They are safe on farms and market gardens, where experienced men wear special protective clothing and know how to handle them and how to guard against the danger of wind-drift, but they are totally unsuitable for use in a residential area with its children and domestic pets and where fruit, flowers and vegetables are grown together in a small area and there is always the risk of damage to plants in a neighbouring garden.

There can be only one rule. No spray, dust, bait or fumigant should ever be regarded as 'safe' in a garden. Many are harmless, but they should all be treated the same and handled with the greatest care.

When not being used, they should be stored out of the reach of children and preferably locked away. Empty tins and bottles should never be left lying about. After use all utensils, sprayers, cans, spoons, mixing rods, etc., should be washed thoroughly and preferably not used for other purposes. Cans, etc., used for hormone weed-killers should never be used for spraying for pests or diseases. The maker's instructions should be followed precisely and the stated concentration never exceeded. Any warning given that the material is unsuitable for certain crops should be carefully observed. (For example BHC will taint many edible crops, malathion will damage sweet peas and certain other plants and some greenhouse fumigants are fatal to particular genera.) Insecticides should not be applied to fruit or ornamental trees when the blossom is open owing to the danger to bees and other pollinating insects, winter sprays should be used only in the dormant season and replaced by spring sprays if vegetables or other evergreens are growing under the trees and no edible crops should be treated when nearing their harvesting times. Chemicals should not be used where they may contaminate a pond or stream containing fish. DDT is no longer recommended for general garden use.

All spraying or dusting should be done in calm weather so as to avoid any drift on to adjacent plants or gardens.

ANTS (*Formicoideae*)
Although causing little direct damage apart from the hills they make, ants are undesirable in a garden because they may invade the house and also assist in spreading aphids which they seek for the 'honey-dew' excreted. They frequently 'nurse' the aphids and carry them from one plant to another, so extending the pest which may be carrying a virus disease. Damage may also be caused in greenhouses and frames and among delicate seedlings out of doors by the ants tunnelling among the tiny roots which are, so to speak, left in mid-air to wither or fail to develop. Destroy nests with boiling water, liquid derris, paraffin, sodium cyanide or a proprietary ant-killer. Any difficulty in discovering the nests can usually be overcome by sprinkling a little sugar around the most popular haunts and watching the ants carry it away to their home.

APHIDS (*Aphididae*)
These are the well-known green-fly or blackfly which attack a wide range of outdoor and glasshouse plants, trees and shrubs. The colour of the many different species varies from green, black or reddish to almost white or bluish. The body is plump, semi-transparent, winged or wingless and often exudes a sticky honey-dew which is attractive to ants or forms a medium on which sooty moulds grow, further spoiling the appearance of the plant. The woolly aphis or American blight commonly seen on apple trees exudes a white fluffy covering. There are several generations in one season mostly producing living young and finishing up with eggs which form the winter stage. All are sucking insects and may therefore carry virus diseases.

Attacks usually start on the undersides of the leaves or on the tips of shoots but may also occur on the roots of a number of plants. Leaf-curling, malformation and discoloration follow, interfering with normal growth. Once leaf-curling starts spraying becomes difficult; early action is therefore essential. Spray or dust with BHC, malathion, nicotine, derris or pyrethrum, making sure that the insects themselves are covered. Or apply a systemic insecticide, which acts through the plant tissue. In greenhouses BHC or nicotine smoke fumes may also be used, and on fruit trees a winter egg-killing spray may be applied. The root forms are best controlled by pulling up the root stumps as soon as possible and burning those infested.

APPLE and PEAR SCAB

Two species of fungi are concerned, *Venturia inaequalis* and *V. pirina* each confined to its own host. Infection can occur at any time during the growing season, the winter stage being passed under the bark or on fallen leaves.

As the leaves develop, dark olive-green patches appear and later become brownish or black. Blister-like swellings and cracks occur on the shoots. Later the fruits are attacked, the skin becoming cracked or covered with scattered dark or black spots. Diseased material should be collected and burned, and the trees sprayed with lime-sulphur at the following stages of growth:

(1) When the flower buds are fully developed but still green, lime-sulphur 1 gal. to 40 gal. of water.

(2) When the flower buds are showing pink but have not opened, lime-sulphur 1 gal. to 50 gal. of water.

(3) When most of the petals have fallen, lime-sulphur 1 gal. to 100 gal. of water.

As far as possible, the sprayings should be spaced at intervals of 14 days, and on no account must heavier concentrations be used otherwise damage will be done to some varieties such as Cox's Orange Pippin and Lanes Prince Albert apples and Doyenne du Comice pears. For these a captan spray is recommended.

APPLE and PEAR SUCKER (*Psylla* spp.)

Small flattened or crab-like yellowish insects are often seen around the developing blossoms and young leaves where they cause puckering and withering. They excrete a sticky fluid and white waxy threads. Later they become greenish and when adult have wings. Small, oval, creamy eggs are laid in the autumn on the fruit spurs. In severe attacks the flower buds die or fail to bear fruit and the tree may look as though it had been damaged by frost. The best control is obtained by routine spraying with a winter wash. If this has been missed, spray in spring just before the blossoms burst, with BHC or malathion.

The pest also occurs on box trees.

BIG BUD

This is the common, descriptive name for the damage caused by the black currant gall mite (*Cecidophyopsis ribis*) which is minute, just too small to be visible to the naked eye, and often causes serious damage to black currants. It may also act as a carrier of virus diseases. Red and white currants and gooseberries are occasionally attacked.

The mites live in the buds which swell to about twice the normal size and fail to open normally, or dry up and shrivel. On a small scale hand-picking of all infested buds if done in good time will reduce attacks, but the best control is by spraying with lime-sulphur (1% solution) when the flower buds show purple but are not yet open. The mites are then exposed as they begin to move to fresh buds. In severe cases the bushes should be grubbed and burned and replaced by healthy stock.

Other gall mites occur on hazel, yew and a few other plants but generally the damage is slight.

BLACK SPOT OF ROSES (*Diplocarpon rosae*)

This disease which may lead to complete defoliation is serious in certain parts of the country only. Round, black or purplish-black spots appear on the leaves of roses and occasionally on the stems from June onwards and later develop a yellow edging. A captan or thiram spray should be applied regularly every 2 to 3 weeks and since the fungus overwinters on the fallen leaves, these and any affected shoots should be collected and burned. Some varieties are more susceptible than others.

BOOTLACE FUNGUS. See Root Rot

BORING INSECTS, BARK BEETLES

Species of *Scolytidae* may cause damage to a number of fruit and ornamental trees and shrubs by tunnelling into the wood. Usually the attacks are confined to trees that are not growing happily and the cause should therefore be remedied. Pruning cuts should be painted and all prunings, dead branches, etc. burned.

Other kinds of boring insects occur on a number of plants. The yellowish-white caterpillars of the leopard moth which grow to 2 in. long tunnel into the shoots and branches of many fruit and ornamental trees causing wilting and dieback; the creamy-white larvae of the currant clearwing and the currant shoot borer and the pinkish larvae of the raspberry moth burrow into the young shoots and several others bore into conifers and other trees. Generally little harm results if a good watch is kept and all affected parts are cut off and burned as soon as they are seen.

CABBAGE CATERPILLARS

These are the well-known larvae of the various cabbage white butterflies (*Pieris spp.*) and of the cabbage moth (*Mamestra brassicae*) commonly found on brassicas and many other cruciferous plants. The eggs are laid in clusters on the leaves and the larvae eat ragged holes and spoil the crop with their excreta. Spraying with derris is effective but it must be done while the larvae are young and before they eat into the heart of the cabbage and become protected by the leaves.

CABBAGE ROOT FLY (*Delia brassicae*)

An ashy-grey fly about $\frac{1}{4}$ in. long resembling a small house fly, may attack brassicas, particularly cabbages and cauliflowers.

Young plants begin to look blue, wilt and stop growing, and if dug up may show legless maggots about $\frac{1}{3}$ in. long gnawing or tunnelling into the root or the stem. Infested plants should be destroyed and calomel dust sprinkled around the stem of other plants in a ring about 1 in. wide. Any later planted crops should be similarly treated at planting time.

Another species *D. antiqua* attacks the bulbs of onions and may be controlled in the same way.

CANKER

The word canker is customarily used for any kind of wound that is surrounded or covered by a callus or swollen tissue. It may be due to mechanical injuries, certain fungi, bacteria or pests.

Mechanical injuries, including pruning cuts, will usually heal naturally provided no infection enters. Broken branches should therefore be pared smooth and pruning cuts made cleanly and all larger cut surfaces covered with grafting wax or a white lead paint. Pests such as woolly aphis must be controlled.

Cankers caused by fungi may occur on fruit trees, some ornamentals including roses, certain greenhouse plants such as cucumbers and brassicas. Many different fungi are concerned. The **Fruit Tree Canker** (*Nectria galligena*) causes depressed areas in the bark, generally extending to form a ragged wound, often encircling the branch or twig and showing whitish pustules followed by small, round red bodies. **Coral Spot** (*Nectria cinnabarina*) occurs on many ornamentals, forest and fruit trees and is sometimes serious on red currants when the branches suddenly wilt and die. Pinkish or red pustules appear on the dead wood and contain the spores that will spread further infection, invariably through wounds in healthy trees. Other fungi may cause a basal canker on roses, plums and cherries and still others may cause dark-coloured cankers on the stems of roses. In all these cases the remedy is to cut out the affected branches and burn the material. In severe attacks the wisest plan is to grub and destroy the plant, and since the disease seems to be most common on wet soils, drainage should be considered. Canker on vegetables is not common but may be found in the northern counties. It is caused by yet another fungus, *Phoma lingam*, which attacks the cabbage family particularly broccoli, turnips and swedes, causing typical cankers on the stems at ground level or on the roots, brown or purple at first then becoming black. Grey spots also appear on the leaves which may wilt and in turnips and swedes, brownish splits appear on the roots which usually rot in the soil or in store with a brown, dry rot. Here again, all infected material should be burned.

Canker of Parsnips is a physiological disorder, not due to any specific fungus. Cracks appear on the top part of the root, generally of a brownish-black colour. Fungi may then gain entry and set up rotting. It is most common in a wet autumn and on wet soils deficient in lime or potash or having excess of nitrogen.

Bacterial Canker (*Pseudomonas mors-prunorum*) may be a serious disease on plums and cherries particularly in young trees. If the canker appears on the main stem the tree generally dies but if it occurs only on the branches the tree may survive for a year or two and even recover. Infected leaves show pale spots which later become brown, the dead tissue falling out and leaving a 'shot-hole' appearance. The disease is difficult to control and when it is present the wisest course is to grub and burn.

CAPSID BUGS (*Lygus spp.*)

The species comprise active green to reddish-brown insects about ⅓ in. long which damage a number of plants including trees and shrubs.

The insects suck the sap like aphids, leaving a number of rusty pin-prick holes. In severe attacks appreciable areas of the leaf die. They also cause rough scars on the surface of fruits and may so damage the growing point of trees and plants that poor or distorted growth results. Use BHC, dimethoate or malathion, covering also the soil around the plants as the insects readily drop off when disturbed. Clean up weeds and hedges where the insects hibernate.

CARROT FLY (*Psila rosae*)

The small almost colourless maggots burrow into the roots, giving a rusty appearance and causing a wilt of the foliage. In badly infested areas, seed should be sown late, end of May to June, so as to avoid the first generation. Sow thinly to reduce thinning which bruises the seedlings and sets free the smell of carrots which attracts the flies. After thinning firm down the soil around the remaining plants. Keep hedges tidy and free from weeds which provide shelter for the flies. Dust with BHC along the rows at fortnightly intervals up to end of June, not any later.

Parsnips and celery may also be attacked.

CATS

Those which belong to other people are of course the ones that do the damage. They often take a regular path through a garden, gradually trampling down some plants. On a warm day they will roll in a fine newly sown seed bed and when they bring their friends to play a great deal of damage can be done.

The cats should be driven off whenever seen and protection given to crops by wire-netting or other covers. The old-fashioned remedy of sinking jam jars containing ammonia in the track of the cat-paths is sometimes worth trying. Frames and cloches should be kept away from walls from which cats may jump, since the animals seem unable to avoid them on very dark nights. Where there are rats or mice in the garden, shed or greenhouse, a cat can do far more good than harm.

CENTIPEDES. See Millepedes

CHAFER BEETLES

There are four species, cockchafer or May bug, summer chafer or June bug, garden chafer and rose chafer, the first three being the most common. The adult beetles of the first two fly in the evenings often at dusk, the other two during the day. They vary from ½ to 1 in. long and have hard, yellowish-brown to reddish-brown wing cases except the rose chafer which has green. The adults feed on the leaves of trees, shrubs and some plants; the grubs which are fleshy, white, characteristically curved and have brown heads, feed on the roots of many plants. They take from 1 to 4 years to reach maturity when they may measure up to nearly 2 in. long and often occur as epidemics, especially in wooded or heathland areas.

Attacked plants suddenly wilt and on being dug up a chafer grub is often found. The fine roots are usually eaten away and larger roots cut through. Collect and destroy during digging and other cultivations. Weed-free soil discourages egg-laying. On lawns, roll thoroughly.

CLUB ROOT or 'FINGER-AND-TOE' (*Plasmodiophora brassicae*)

Affects a large number of cruciferous plants which include the cabbage family, turnips, radishes, mustard and many flowers and weeds, causing the well-known swellings on the roots or on the stems at ground level. The swellings are generally solid or when they begin to decay become soft and slimy and are therefore distinct from the swellings of the gall weevil which are hollow and often show the maggot inside when cut across. Affected plants, particularly seedlings, look blue and become stunted. The fungus can remain in the soil for several years. Keep up the lime content of the soil and space susceptible plants as far apart as possible in the rotation. Seedlings should be raised in soil which has been sterilized or is known to be free from infection. Before planting out, the plants should be dipped in a paste made of calomel and water or calomel dust may be sprinkled in the dibber holes. Plants bought in should be most carefully examined.

COCKROACHES and CRICKETS
These may sometimes be serious in greenhouses eating seeds, seedlings, foliage and flowers. They shelter in any rubbish so the house should be kept clean. BHC dust is effective.

CODLING MOTH (*Lydia pomonella*)
This is a common pest of apples, including the ornamental species, and also occurs on pears, quince and walnut. The larva eats into the core and when fully fed burrows its way out, leaving a characteristic hole with no 'frass' showing. (Compare with sawfly on apples.) As the larva hibernates in cracks in the bark or in rubbish on the ground, general tidiness is essential. Trees with rough, moss-covered bark should be sprayed with tar oil in winter. In bad attacks malathion or fenetrothion should be sprayed on to the blossoms 14 days after petal-fall.

CROWN GALL (*Bacterium tumefaciens*)
Attacks a large number of plants, trees and shrubs causing swellings on the roots or stems generally at ground level. The galls are usually rounded, although of irregular shape, soft and white at first, becoming hard and brownish later. The size varies from that of a pea up to 2 or 3 in. across. The disease is more common on wet soils and probably enters through wounds, but rarely seems to affect growth as much as might be expected. Diseased plants should not be used for propagation.

A somewhat similar disease known as **Leafy Gall** is often confused with crown gall, but it is caused by a different bacterium (*B. fascians*) and produces a number of crowded malformed shoots at the base of the stems, giving a cauliflower appearance to the growth. Many plants are susceptible and all found to be infected should be burned.

CUCKOO SPIT
The small pale greenish-yellow larva of the frog hoppers (*Cercopidae*) attacks many cultivated and wild plants sucking the sap and surrounding itself with a white froth.

The small patches of the 'cuckoo-spit' are generally found towards the tops of the shoots and while they sometimes cause malformation the effects are usually not serious. In light attacks the larvae may be crushed or picked off; in heavy attacks the plants should be sprayed with malathion, BHC or dimethoate, spraying forcibly in order to penetrate the froth.

DAMPING OFF or SEEDLING BLIGHT
Many fungi of which the most common are certain species of *Phytophthora* and *Pythium* attack seedlings at ground level and cause a collapse of the stem. A wide range of plants is affected. Good growing and general hygiene are necessary. Affected plants should be sprayed with a proprietary captan or copper spray and under glass ventilation should be increased and moisture reduced. Seedlings should always be grown in sterilized soil or compost.

DOGS
Strange dogs should be driven away (the hissing sound generally answers), but the gardener's own dog (being of high intelligence) can easily be trained to keep to the paths and never get on to the beds or cause damage in the garden. A patient, quiet 'get off' or some word not resembling any other order will quickly have results, provided it is always used and no transgression is allowed to pass unchecked.

EARTHWORMS
Earthworms are entirely beneficial. Their burrowing helps to drain and aerate the soil and

they pull down large quantities of decaying vegetable matter for their food. It is only on lawns that their casts are undesirable and here, regular brushing is generally sufficient to maintain a good appearance. If the number of casts is excessive the lawn should be dressed with a proprietary worm-killer or watered with potassium permanganate, ¾ oz. to 1 gal. of water for every sq. yd.

EARWIGS

Earwigs feed at night and hide during the day under leaves, rubbish or stones or in canes or boxes. They are usually most troublesome on greenhouse plants but also attack many others out of doors, eating holes in the leaves and flowers and giving the plant a ragged appearance. Dead leaves and rubbish should be cleared up and plants sprayed or dusted with BHC. Large numbers of them may be entrapped in pieces of sacking or corrugated paper laid on the soil or in pots loosely filled with straw and set up on canes or stakes. The traps should be shaken out every day over a bowl of paraffin or insecticide.

EELWORMS

There are a number of different species and strains, many of them causing serious damage to cultivated plants. As a rule each one keeps to its specific host plant or group of plants (including weeds) and even if the host is removed may still exist in the soil in the form of dormant cysts for 3 or more years. All are minute, the largest being just visible to the naked eye.

The stem and bulb eelworm causes stunted or malformed growth in a wide range of herbaceous and bulbous plants. The leaves are often discoloured, narrow and twisted, the stems split or wiry-looking and the flowers malformed or broken. Leaf eelworms attack a number of flowering plants including many grown under glass and one species is particularly destructive to chrysanthemums causing the leaves to turn brown or black and drop off, and the buds and flowers to be blind or distorted. Root eelworms attack many vegetables and flowering plants, one species being particularly damaging to cruciferous plants, another to certain leguminous plants and a third to potatoes which may sometimes be so seriously infested that little or no crop is obtained and the females can then be seen on the roots as minute whitish to brown spherical bodies. The root-knot eelworms attack a wide variety of plant hosts particularly tomatoes, cucumbers and flowers grown under glass, generally causing galls on the roots.

There is no one method of control that will eradicate all the different species. Hot-water treatment and soil sterilization are effectively employed on a commercial scale but the equipment required and the precautions that have to be taken generally make them impracticable or uneconomic in a small private garden. But much can be done to reduce infestation or at least to prevent it getting worse. The general rules of hygiene should be carefully followed, weeds and rubbish should be removed, pots and seed boxes cleaned and sterilized, prepared seed and potting composts should be used and the soil in greenhouse borders should be sterilized or replaced from a tested source. All plants bought in should be purchased from reliable sources only. Susceptible crops should not be planted in infested soil for 3 and preferably 5 years and in the vegetable garden a long rotation should be strictly followed.

FINGER-AND-TOE. See Club Root

FIRE BLIGHT (*Erwinia amylovora*)

This bacterial disease was first recorded in England in 1958, and is serious on pears, particularly the variety Laxton's Suberb but less damaging on hawthorn, certain cotoneasters, pyracantha, mountain ash and a few others. The leaves wilt and turn brown but hang on the tree as though damaged by fire, and the branch and less often the whole tree dies. Infection is probably carried by pollinating insects but no research has been carried out and little is known beyond the experience of other countries, such as America and New Zealand. The disease is notifiable to the Ministry of Agriculture and no control should be attempted except under statutory directions.

FLEA BEETLES (*Phyllotreta spp.*)

There are several species, varying in colour

from blue-black to black usually with a yellow stripe on each wing-case. All are about $\frac{1}{10}$ in. long and are often difficult to see since they jump away when disturbed. They attack a wide range of plants, principally brassicas, beetroot and wallflowers in the seedling stages. Severe damage may be caused, the leaves being eaten right away or showing many small holes as well as larger eaten areas. The plants look unhappy and blue. The beetles hibernate in rubbish and hedgerows, so a clean and tidy garden in the winter is essential. Spray or dust with BHC as soon as the new seedlings appear and every 10 to 14 days afterwards as necessary.

FRUIT TREE BROWN ROT

(*Sclerotinia fructigena*)

This disease causes the well-known brown decay of many kinds of fruit. Whitish, yellow or grey pustules appear, generally in rings and the infected fruits either fall or shrivel and remain on the trees into winter in a mummified state. The disease may also be seen on stored apples and pears. Since the diseased fruits act as the source of infection in the following year, they should be collected carefully and burned.

FRUIT TREE CATERPILLARS

A large number of different caterpillars cause varying degrees of damage to the buds and leaves of fruit and ornamental trees and shrubs but are perhaps most serious on fruit because they may severely reduce the crop. Among the most important are the winter moths which feed on the young leaves and developing blossom, the magpie moth often found on currants and gooseberries, the lackey, ermine and other moths whose caterpillars spin 'tents' while feeding on fruit, forest and ornamental trees. Egg-killing sprays may be used in winter on deciduous trees or derris applied in spring. Tents may be burned out and the wingless winter moths trapped on grease bands put round the tree trunks.

HONEY FUNGUS. See Root Rot

INK DISEASE OF IRISES (*Mystrosporium adustum*)

This occurs on bulbous irises particularly on *Iris reticulata* and causes black spots on the leaves and bulbs. There is no reliable cure. The bulbs should be dug up and those severely affected should be burned.

Slightly infected bulbs may be saved by cleaning off all infected material.

LAWN DISEASES AND PESTS

The commonest diseases are the **Snow Mould** (*Fusarium nivale*) causing diseased patches which slowly increase in size and in moist weather display a white growth, **Dollar Spot** (*Sclerotinia homeocarpa*) which kills the grass in small patches or spots and **Red Thread** (*Corticium fuciforme*) which mainly affects the fescue grasses, causing scattered patches of pink-coloured leaves. The well-known **Fairy Rings** may be due to a number of different fungi and apart from being unsightly may leave dead patches in the centre of the rings as the fungi advance outwards. All these diseases can be controlled by spraying but usually several applications are necessary and since the materials are not suitable for mixing on a small garden scale the wisest plan is to choose a proprietary lawn fungicide.

Damage by insects is generally due to attacks by the common root-eating pests such as leather jackets, wireworms, etc., and spraying or dusting with BHC is usually effective. As a general rule, however, pests and to a lesser extent, diseases are not serious in lawns that are well kept and where the soil is in good condition.

LEAF AND STEM GALLS

Several different kinds of galls or swellings may occur on the leaves or stems of a fairly wide range of plants, trees and shrubs. They are caused by various species of gall-wasps, gall-midges or gall-mites, the larvae of which feed in the plant and set up some reaction in the tissues, resulting in a swelling. Generally little harm is done and it is sufficient to cut off and burn the galled tissues, but on black currants serious effects may occur (see *Big Bud*) and on glasshouse chrysanthemums the spike-like galls of the chrysanthemum gall midge may appear on the upper surface of the leaves or less commonly on the stems and flowers, severe attacks leading to distortion of the buds and blooms. Weekly spraying with BHC or nicotine will then be required. Outdoor chrysanthemums are rarely attacked.

LEAF HOPPERS

Several species of small, slender, active insects may often be seen running or jumping among the leaves of roses, fruit and other trees and among many flowering plants and vegetables grown under glass or out of doors. They feed on the sap causing distinctive mottling or irregular yellowish areas. If seriously bad spray with malathion wetting both sides of the leaves and the soil underneath.

LEAF-MINERS

The larvae of many different species of moths, weevils and flies are loosely but conveniently classed as 'leaf-miners'. They attack a wide range of plants, among them apples, roses, shrubs, herbaceous plants and vegetables. Chrysanthemums, cineraria, azalea, celery and beetroot are probably the most important. The carnation fly begins as a leaf-miner but continues by burrowing into the shoots.

The larvae live on the tissue of the leaf between the upper and lower surfaces, generally making serpentine tunnels or mines as they move along. Weeds must be kept down since many of them can act as host plants. On a small scale the larvae can be crushed in their mines with the finger and thumb or affected leaves can be picked off and burned. A quick-acting top dressing can be applied to help the crop along and soot can be dusted over to repel the egg-laying adults. On a larger scale or when the attack is severe the plants should be sprayed well with malathion or BHC. Smokes may be used under glass.

LEAF SPOTS

Several different fungi cause spotting on the leaves of a wide range of plants. Usually the spots are round, varying in colour from white to yellowish, brown or reddish-brown, with the margins a different colour from the centres. Sometimes the spots also occur on the stems. Generally no harm is done apart from spoiling the appearance of the plants as in strawberries or chrysanthemums, but on currants severe defoliation may occur and on celery growth may be seriously affected. In severe cases Bordeaux Mixture or a proprietary copper fungicide should be used and with celery, where the disease is carried by the seed, supplies should be bought from reliable sources only.

Some leaf-spotting fungi also affect the fruits. A species of *Colletotrichum* may cause brown sunken areas on the pods of French and less commonly runner beans, and another species may produce decayed areas on cucumbers, which may also show gummy areas caused by a species of *Cladosporium*. In these cases careful growing and strict hygiene are the best controls. A sulphur spray may be used on cucumbers.

LEATHER JACKETS (*Tipula spp.*)

These are the well-known dirty-brown to greyish-black legless grubs of the daddy long-legs or crane fly. They are 1–1½ in. long with a tough leathery skin and feed on the roots of a large range of plants, causing a sudden wilting among small or young plants. If an attacked plant is dug up a grub can sometimes be seen, but more often it will be found at the next plant in the row. The damage done resembles that caused by other kinds of soil pests (see *Surface Caterpillars*) and is most common after breaking up old or neglected turf. Regular hoeing and cleaning up is generally sufficient but in severe attacks BHC should be forked into the soil.

MEALY BUGS

Somewhat similar to scale insects but with a soft white woolly covering, mealy bugs are mainly a pest of greenhouses where they may attack fruit such as vines or peaches and a wide range of flowering plants. Their feeding causes the leaves to turn yellow and fall and their excretion of 'honeydew' favours the development of sooty moulds. They may also be found on the roots, particularly of pot plants, and occasionally occur out of doors on certain flowering shrubs. Spray with malathion or nicotine. Small outbreaks may be dealt with by brushing with the insecticide.

MIDGES

In addition to the gall-forming midges (see *Leaf and Stem Galls*) several species of small flies (*Diptera*) cause varying kinds of damage on a number of different plants. Among the more important are the **Black Currant Midge** which causes the young leaves of the shoots to become curled, twisted and blackened, and the **Swede Midge** which damages the growing point of many brassicas, both being controlled by spraying with BHC during May and June. The **Pea Midge** which attacks the blooms and terminal shoots is not easily controlled but rarely appears on early varieties. The **Pear Midge** larvae feed inside young fruits which become swollen and distorted and are best controlled by spraying with BHC during the early 'white-bud' stage. The **Pear Leaf-curling Midge** causes the leaves to curl upwards and shrivel with the margins usually meeting and requires a BHC spray during May and June. In all these cases reasonable control on a small scale can usually be gained by collecting and burning attacked fruits, leaves or stems and by regular cultivation to destroy pupae in the soil.

MILDEWS

The mildews which occur on a great number of trees, shrubs and plants are caused by many different species of fungi but for practical purposes may be broadly divided into two types: the 'powdery' mildews where the fungi live on the surface of the foliage, spoiling the appearance rather than causing serious harm, and the 'downy' mildews, which are more deep-seated, live within the tissues and as a rule are far more serious since they cause decay. Powdery mildews are found on roses, vines, apples, gooseberries, marrows, turnips, strawberries, chrysanthemums, asters, calendulas and many other plants, particularly in the seedling stage. Downy mildews appear on brassica seedlings, lettuce, onions, spinach, vines, wallflowers, stocks, etc.

The powdery mildews are generally more conspicuous and produce a whitish to greyish powdery effect on the foliage while the downy mildews cause yellowish patches on the leaves often with a greyish or purplish downy growth on the underside. For powdery mildews remove badly-infected shoots and dust with sulphur. For downy mildews remove all infected plants and shoots and spray with Bordeaux Mixture or dust with a copper-lime dust. In both cases, avoid overcrowding and under glass give ample ventilation and reduce humidity.

MILLEPEDES

These must not be confused with centipedes which are beneficial and feed on various insects, small slugs and snails. Centipedes have only one pair of legs to each body segment, whereas millepedes have two; they run away when disturbed, but millepedes generally curl up. There are two common species of centipedes, one flat and brown in colour, the other cylindrical, slender and yellow. Millepedes are mostly shorter, from ½ to 1 in. long, and according to species are black with white legs, yellowish-white with red to purple spots, or purplish-white to dull brown with a flat body somewhat resembling a centipede but the segments are much more distinct.

Millepedes feed on a variety of vegetable matter, and are frequently found eating tissue already damaged in some other way. In large numbers they affect growth and damage seedlings. Eradication is probably impossible, and in most years general hygiene and good cultivation are a sufficient check. When large numbers occur they may be trapped by placing just under soil-level pieces of potato or carrot, marking and examining them every 2 or 3 days, or BHC dust may be lightly forked in.

MITES

In addition to the gall-mites (see under *Big Bud*) and the red spiders, several other mites attack many different kinds of plants, causing damage other than that described under leaf galls. The **Broad Mite** causes the leaves of many different kinds of greenhouse plants to curl and become brittle but is usually controlled by sulphur dust; the **Pear Leaf Blister Mite** causes yellowish or brownish raised pustules on the leaves of pear and certain ornamentals and lime-sulphur sprays may be necessary, and the **Spruce Mite** causes bronzing on many conifers and in severe attacks malathion should be used. The **Bulb Mite** which is whitish, round and large enough to be seen may be found on many different kinds of bulbs but is generally secondary to some previous damage and its control therefore is obvious. But the **Bulb**

Scale Mite which causes yellowish or reddish-brown streaks on the inner scales in the neck of many bulbs and the **Strawberry Mite** which causes a puckering of the leaves, can be controlled only by hot-water treatment which is beyond the capacity of small gardens and the wisest plan is to grub and buy afresh from a reputable source.

MOULDS

For gardening purposes moulds may be divided into two main groups, the saprophytic moulds which live on dead and decaying vegetable or animal matter and the parasitic moulds which attack living plants. Both groups are encouraged by damp airless conditions. Saprophytic moulds, among them certain of the *Penicillium* species, may be found on fruit, vegetables or bulbs stored under poor conditions or damaged in handling and the preventive measures are consequently obvious and simple. The sooty moulds referred to under aphids, mealy bugs and scale insects are entirely superficial and while they do not cause damage themselves, they may spoil appearances. Here again, the remedy is to get rid of the pest depositing the honeydew on which the moulds live.

Grey Mould is the most important of the parasitic group. It is caused by *Botrytis cinerea* and is often known as botrytis. It attacks a wide range of plants but as a rule is serious only on outdoor plants in wet seasons or on glass-grown plants when humidity is too high, ventilation poor or temperatures too low. A grey furry mould develops and may be found on seedlings, cuttings, vegetables, flowers, vines and other fruit under glass, ripe strawberries and raspberries in the open, sweet peas, lettuce, forced rhubarb and many others. Other species of *Botrytis* also cause diseases which do not resemble the typical grey mould, such as **Chocolate Spot** of beans, **Die-back** of gooseberries, **Tulip Fire**, etc., or play a part in storage diseases such as **Neck Rot** of onions. (For *Tomato Leaf Mould* see under *Tomatoes.*)

MUSHROOM MOULDS

The plaster moulds of which there are two, the white (*Monilia fimicola*) and the brown (*Papulaspora byssina*) are not usually serious and may be kept in check by hygienic growing. The former appears as a white powder on the surface of the bed at spawning time; the latter is often seen on the compost as a white fluff which later turns brown. But the true white mould (*Mycogone perniciosa*) may completely cover the young growth with a thick vigorous white mould and ruin the crop. Strict cleanliness is essential. On appearance all infected material must be burnt and after cropping the house and all boxes, shelves and trays must be disinfected with formalin.

NARCISSUS FLIES

There are three species which attack narcissus and less commonly certain other bulbs. The larvae burrow into the bulbs and eat away the centre.

Bulbs which show weak or distorted growth in spring should be lifted. If soft they will probably contain one larva of the large narcissus fly (*Merodon equestris*) or several of the smaller flies (*Eumerus spp.*) and should be burned. In bad attacks BHC dust should be regularly applied every fortnight from end-Apr. to end-June. At planting time bulbs should be pressed gently and those which feel soft and springy should be discarded.

NUTRITIONAL DISEASES

This term is used to cover a wide range of non-parasitic disorders which are due mainly to the lack of some essential food element and lead to unnatural or malformed growth. Among the most common are:

Leaf scorch which is due to a deficiency of potassium and produces poor colour in the leaves, the tips or margins turning brown and frequently dying.

Chlorosis which is due to excess of lime or deficiency of iron or manganese and reduces the green colour of leaves and shoots. Deficiency of magnesium will also cause chlorosis together with premature defoliation.

Boron deficiency causes varying types of malformation of tissue in many different plants and has been responsible for a number of descriptive names such as brown heart in turnips, hollow stem in cauliflowers or corky core in apples.

Molybdenum deficiency affects the growing point of certain brassicas and lettuce and produces the well-known whip-tail of cauliflowers.

(see also Chapter 4 Nutrition.)

ONION SMUT (*Urocystis cepulae*)
Attacks onions, leeks, shallots and chives, causing dark, greyish stripes on the leaves followed by masses of black spores. The disease is usually fatal to seedlings, and since it remains in the soil for many years is difficult to control. Further cropping should only be contemplated if an area of clean soil can be found.

PARSNIP CANKER. See Canker

PEA MOTH (*Laspeyresia nigricana*)
This small dull greyish-brown moth about ¼ in. long, appears from mid-June to mid-Aug. fluttering over peas that are then in flower or pod. The caterpillars eat into the pods and cause the damage which is so well known. In susceptible areas damage can be avoided by sowing early and late crops only and missing out mid-season varieties. Regular hoeing between the rows will help to destroy the larvae which pupate in the soil. The use of carbaryl gives a fair but not complete control.

PEACH LEAF CURL (*Taphrina deformans*)
Sometimes called **Peach Leaf Blister,** this disease may attack peaches, nectarines, almonds and occasionally other species of *Prunus*.

The leaves become swollen, curled or malformed, look blistered and change to a reddish colour. The flowers and fruits may sometimes be affected. Spray with lime sulphur or Bordeaux Mixture as soon as the buds begin to swell, generally about the middle of Feb.

POTATO BLACKLEG (*Bacterium phytophthorum*)
May appear from June onwards, usually on a few plants only and not spread over the whole crop. Infected plants look yellowish and stunted and the base of the stem goes black and begins to rot. The tubers may become infected and will then rot in the soil or in store. The disease can be carried on the seed. Infected plants should be removed and burned and the tubers sorted over carefully when lifting and storing. Do not save seed from an infected crop.

POTATO BLIGHT (*Phytophthora infestans*)
This disease which is endemic and can spread over appreciable distances, may cause serious losses, especially in warm, moist summers when infection spreads rapidly. The damage done to the leaves prevents a normal yield being obtained and leads to infection of the tubers.

Patches appear on the leaves, generally near the edges at first, brown to black on top and greyish underneath. From these, spores may be washed down through the soil to the tubers where the disease produces the well-known brownish colour on the flesh under the skin. The infected tubers may rot in store. As soon as it is known that the disease has appeared in the district or the first sight is seen on the leaves, the crop must be sprayed with Bordeaux Mixture or a proprietary copper spray and the spraying must be repeated every fortnight as necessary. Dusts may also be used (as often as once a week in a wet season). At lifting time the haulm should first be cut off and burned and only sound tubers should be put into store and none saved for seed.

POTATO TUBER DISEASES
In addition to blight, a number of other diseases cause trouble on the tubers. The more important are:

(1) **Common Scab** (*Actinomyces scabies*). This disease, which is not usually serious, causes the well-known rough, dry, scabby patches on the skin of potatoes. Sometimes the patches are deep and sunken, but generally they are only skin deep and are removed in peeling. The importance of the disease is that it spoils the appearance of the tubers.

Common scab is worst on dry, gravelly or overlimed soils and can be reduced by good dressings of farmyard manure or compost. Lime should never be applied to a potato crop.

(2) **Corky** or **Powdery Scab** (*Spongospora subterranea*). Also causes scabby areas on the skin of potato tubers, but they are at first raised swellings and not sunken like common scab. Later the swellings break, resembling a canker,

and in severe attacks the tubers are distorted. It is a less common but more serious disease than common scab and remains in the soil for many years, but can be reduced by spacing the crop as far apart in the rotation as possible. Seed from an infected crop should never be used.

(3) **Dry Rot** (*Fusarium caeruleum*). Infected tubers shrink and shrivel, the decaying part generally wrinkling and showing white or pinkish pustules. Early varieties are the more susceptible and the disease is most noticeable during storage or just before planting. Diseased seed should never be planted since even a slight infection may be progressive and result in 'misses' in the rows. Tubers in store should be examined regularly and before planting. Burn those infected. In severe cases wash down the store, boxes and trays with formalin. Always handle tubers carefully as the fungus generally enters through wounds.

(4) **Gangrene** (*Phoma foveata*). This disease is becoming more common. It generally shows as a small depression which gradually extends until the whole tuber shrinks and decays. It is sometimes mistaken for dry rot but never shows the characteristic wrinkling and pustules of that disease. The remedial measures are, however, the same.

(5) **Skin Spot** (*Oospora pustulans*). Sometimes occurs on potatoes in store causing small pimples or spots, but as these are only skin-deep little harm results. The disease is however serious if it attacks the eyes of seed potatoes. These should not be planted.

(6) **Wart Disease** (*Synchytrium endobioticum*). Sometimes called black scab, causes crinkled warts on the tubers and sometimes on the stems at ground level. Infected tubers may rot or turn black if cooked. The disease remains in the soil for an indefinite period. Under the Wart Disease of Potatoes Order, outbreaks must be notified to the Ministry of Agriculture and Fisheries, and only immune varieties may be planted in infected soil.

(7) **Others.** A number of other diseases cause rotting in the tubers but most of them occur only under unfavourable conditions. **Watery Wound Rot** (*Pythium ultimum*) may occur if the potatoes are carelessly damaged at lifting time, the fungus entering the wounds and causing a wet soft rot, the affected tissue turning black when exposed to the air. A bacterial **Soft Rot** (*B. carotovorum*) having its own characteristic smell, may develop in tubers stored under damp conditions or put into store when wet. Other troubles may arise from physiological causes; certain soils appear to produce spotting or discoloration of the flesh, particularly the aptly named **Internal Rust Spot** the cause of which is not known. **Second Growth** resulting from heavy rains following a dry spell during the growing season often produces tubers that are cracked, malformed, hollow or occasionally translucent at the heel end, a condition known as **Jelly End Rot. Black Heart** is due to overheating or lack of ventilation in store and frost damage may cause browning or complete collapse according to the degree of freezing. Slightly frosted seed potatoes may appear unharmed yet the eyes may be dead.

RABBITS

The only sure remedy is to enclose the garden with 1-in.-mesh wire netting 3 ft. high and buried 18 in. below ground level with the lower edge curving outwards. Some success can be achieved with the old-fashioned remedy of laying down a line of fish manure around the boundaries of the garden. This acts as a repellent and can later be forked into the soil; it should be renewed after heavy rain.

RASPBERRY BEETLE (*Byturus tomentosus*)

Yellowish larvae attack the buds and flowers and burrow into the fruits, causing the well-known 'maggoty raspberries'. Loganberries and blackberries are also attacked. Severe infestation will render the crop useless and even slight attacks spoil the appearance of the fruit.

The larvae are not always noticed until they are found inside the fruit when it is too late to spray, but they give warning that control will be essential the following year. Spray or dust with derris 10 days after flowering and again 12–14 days later.

RATS AND MICE

These probably do most damage to fruit and vegetables in store, but often eat crops in the open garden. Mice will, for example, quickly destroy a row of newly sown peas once they have made a start, and if this happens, the seed for subsequent sowings should be coated in a mixture of paraffin and red lead made to the consistency of cream.

Poison baits and traps may be used, but they must be so placed that no harm can come to domestic animals. Warfarin gives excellent results, so does a good 'hunting' cat.

RED SPIDER MITES

Three different species are important in gardens, the **Glasshouse Red Spider** (*Tetranychus telarius*) which attacks many fruit, vegetable and flowering plants grown under glass, the **Fruit Tree Red Spider** (*Panonychus ulmi*) found out of doors principally on apples, pears and plums and the **Gooseberry Red Spider** (*Bryobia ribis*) which is fairly common and occurs also on alpines, hawthorn and a few other plants.

The mites are small, just visible, and are usually greenish-grey to pink, becoming reddish as they mature. They feed mainly on the undersides of the leaves and usually spin a fine webbing which acts as a protection. The leaves lose colour, become dry and yellow at first, but later take on a rusty appearance with varying degrees of bronzing or silvering. Deciduous trees should be sprayed in winter with a petroleum wash to destroy the eggs or in spring with malathion or derris. Under glass fumigate with azobenzene or spray regularly with malathion or derris.

RHODODENDRON BUG (*Stephanitis rhododendri*)

The adult insect is about $\frac{1}{6}$ in. long, shiny and black with netted wings, and its larvae feed on the leaves which become spotted with rusty-looking spots on the underside and mottled on the upper surface. BHC should be sprayed on to the undersides of the leaves about mid-June and again 2–3 weeks later. After severe attacks all shoots should be cut back in Mar. and burned.

ROOT ROT (*Armillaria mellea*)

Often called **Bootlace Fungus** or **Honey Fungus,** this disease attacks a wide range of trees and shrubs and occasionally some herbaceous plants, and may cause serious losses. It normally lives on the dead wood of old stumps or roots and sends out black, shiny cord-like strands or 'boot-laces' to infect near-by healthy trees. The first signs are usually a wilting and dying of the leaves followed by decay of the trunk or main stem at ground level where the fungus shows as white sheets or fan-like growths under the bark. In the autumn the toadstool stage may appear in the form of honey-coloured caps with brown scales and yellowish stems. The only remedy is to grub and burn affected material taking care to pick out all the roots and old stumps or stakes. In a hedge, the trees adjoining the affected trees, though apparently healthy, should also be grubbed. The soil should then be dressed heavily with lime and dug deeply or, if practicable, replaced with new soil or treated with a 2% solution of formalin. Fruit trees and bushes, ornamental and hedge trees, particularly privet, are all liable to attack.

ROTS

The direct cause of rotting is not always easy or even possible to determine. It may be a disease itself or it may be that some mechanical injury, attack by pest or bad growing conditions have allowed secondary organisms to enter and produce decay. Many bacterial rots occur in this way and most of them result in a wet, slimy rot, generally black and often quick-acting so that rotting is appreciable by the time it is noticed. The wisest plan in all such cases is to burn the affected material and to grow a different kind of plant in the position. Rots caused by fungi are usually more easy to detect because some stage of the fungus growth can generally be seen, either in the form of mycelium or as fruiting or spore-bearing growths, and the necessary control measures may then be taken. But in all cases careful growing, common-sense hygiene and the destruction of affected material will go far to reduce or even eradicate infection.

RUSTS

A large number of different fungi are concerned, many being specific to one species of plant or even to certain parts of the plant. Many too require a secondary host for the completion of their life cycle, certain stages in the growth of cineraria rust for example, being spent on the Scots pine and of gooseberry rust on certain sedges. Many flowering plants and vegetables are attacked and the usual symptoms are small brown, reddish or orange-coloured spots on the foliage often giving a dry, rusty appearance. The spots contain the spores which may sometimes be released as a dust when the plant is shaken. Defoliation is common and in severe attacks death may follow. General hygiene and good, careful growing are usually a sufficient control on a number of plants, particularly if the first infected leaves are removed and burned, but in severe attacks spraying with a copper fungicide may be necessary. With antirrhinums resistant varieties may be used and with mint infected beds should be destroyed and replaced with healthy stock.

SAWFLIES and SLUGWORMS
There are two main groups, one in which the larvae vary in colour from whitish to green or black, have up to ten pairs of legs and are often called false caterpillars, and the other, the true **Slugworms,** which resemble small, shiny black slugs up to ½ in. long. Their habits vary widely; the **Apple** and **Plum Sawflies** eat into the fruits causing ribbon-like scars and exuding a dirty brown frass, the **Rose Sawflies** roll the leaves together or bore into the shoots, the **Gooseberry Sawfly** may cause severe defoliation and others cause leaf damage to geums, irises, spiraeas, solomon's seal, black currants, etc. The **Slugworms** may skeletonize the leaves of pears, cherries or roses. In spite of the varying types of damage, control measures are similar. Since pupation generally occurs in the soil, regular cultivation will destroy large numbers of them, but in severe attacks BHC sprays should be applied.

SCALE INSECTS (*Coccidae*)
There are many different species, varying in colour and shape, but all are what may be called 'stationary pests'. When young the larvae move about on the host-plant, but later they develop a protective covering, which may be hard or soft, under which they live by sucking the sap from the plant. These scales often appear to be stuck hard on to the plant. Some species attack outdoor plants including fruit trees, forest trees and ornamental trees and shrubs, others are found on a wide range of greenhouse plants, particularly vines, figs, ferns, orchids and palms. In numbers, scale insects can be very serious.

Many species excrete a honeydew which falls on to other leaves and often becomes covered with a 'sooty mould', and ants are frequently present, attracted by this honeydew. Tender plants should be sponged with nicotine wash. Single scales should be prised off gently. In more serious cases nicotine or malathion should be sprayed on and deciduous trees sprayed with tar oil in winter. Greenhouses should be fumigated when possible.

SILVER LEAF (*Stereum purpureum*)
This disease which may be serious on plums, particularly Victorias, also occurs on apples, poplars, Portugal laurel, cherries, thorns and peaches. The fungus invades the branches and interferes with the normal growth of the leaves by allowing air to enter between the top and bottom surfaces, so producing the characteristic silvery or leaden sheen.

In addition dead branches or twigs are usually present and on these the infectious fruiting stage of the fungus may often be seen in the form of purplish, bracket-shaped growths. All dead wood should be cut out and burned, and all cut surfaces covered with white lead paint or grafting wax, the work being done preferably in late spring and early summer when natural healing is quickest. There is no need to cut out the silvered foliage as this is not the infectious stage and trees infected in this way only will often recover.

SLUGS and SNAILS
These cause enormous damage, much of it never visible. There are several species, some feeding at or below ground level, others well above this level, sometimes shredding leaves and even eating flowers. Feeding is done mostly at night or during still, moist evenings. Slugs feed all the year round except during very cold weather, snails hibernate, generally in groups, in hedges, under rocks or at the base of a wall.

Control measures must be kept up without

ceasing. Baits or sprays containing metaldehyde are the most successful and are best used on a mild, moist evening, preferably after a dry spell. Many excellent proprietary brands are available.

SPRINGTAILS (*Collembola spp.*)

Small wingless jumping insects, varying in colour from dirty-white or grey to brown or black, frequently seen in manure. Most of the species are harmless as they feed on decaying vegetable matter, but they often invade damaged roots or bulbs. They prefer moist conditions and are commonest on wet soils or in ill-kept greenhouses where they may attack seedlings, orchids and other plants. They may also be serious pests in mushroom houses.

As the insects like moist conditions and thrive on decaying matter general cleanliness is the best treatment. Houses should be kept clean, stems and leaves should not be left on the floors to wither and decompose, and outside, wet soils should be drained. In severe cases spray or dust with BHC.

SURFACE CATERPILLARS or CUTWORMS

These are the larvae of several different kinds of moths. They feed at night and shelter among leaves, stones, thick grass or weeds during the day. The colour is generally grey to black and blends with the soil.

Seedlings and young plants suddenly wilt through being eaten or sometimes cut right through at ground level. The caterpillars should be collected by hand or affected plants dusted with BHC.

SYMPHYLIDS

These are small and active with twelve pairs of legs and generally feed on decaying vegetable matter. One species which is white and grows to about ¼ in. long is sometimes a serious pest in greenhouses where it feeds on the roots of many different plants, causing the leaves to wilt and turn yellow. BHC dust may be worked into the soil or a solution watered in.

THRIPS or THUNDER FLIES

There are many species attacking a wide range of plants both out of doors and in greenhouses. The adults are small, about $\frac{1}{16}$ in. long, and generally black or brown. Some species help to spread certain virus diseases, particularly spotted wilt (see under *Virus Diseases*).

Thrips feed by scraping away the surface and sucking the sap, causing mottled, bleached areas which are particularly noticeable on the pods of peas and beans. In severe attacks spray with BHC, malathion or nicotine. Under glass smokes may be used.

TOMATO BLIGHT

This may be serious on outdoor tomatoes but rarely occurs under glass. It is caused by the same fungus disease (*Phytophthora infestans*) as attacks potatoes and the control measures are the same.

TOMATO LEAF MOULD

(*Cladosporium fulvum*)

A common and often serious disease of tomatoes grown under glass. Yellowish spots appear on the upper surface of the leaves generally in June or July, with a brownish-green mould on the under surface. The leaves shrivel and die. The fungus spreads most rapidly in a warm humid atmosphere. Ample ventilation must therefore always be given as a preventive measure and at the first sign of infection, must be increased. Overhead spraying should be stopped and watering reduced to the safe minimum. If the disease persists all infected leaves should be removed and burnt and the plants sprayed with a proprietary thiram or copper spray every one or two weeks. At the end of the season the house should be cleaned by spraying with formaldehyde. Certain varieties are resistant.

Grey mould (see under *Moulds*) may also attack the unripe fruits and less often the stems of tomatoes, particularly when night temperatures are too low. Diseased plants and fruits should be removed and night temperatures raised.

TOMATO ROOT ROTS

Species of *Pythium*, *Phytophthora* and other fungi may cause rotting of the roots of both outdoor and glass-grown tomatoes. The attacks generally occur in the early stages of growth and the first symptoms are usually some stunting or varying degree of wilting. The roots will show decay or rotting. Infected plants should be destroyed. In the open, tomatoes should not be grown again on the same piece of land and under glass the soil in beds should be renewed or sterilized.

TOMATO STEM ROT (*Didymella lycopersici*)
The plants wilt suddenly and a dark-coloured canker can be seen at ground level. The fruit turns black and rots. Remove and burn infected plants, together with the soil immediately surrounding the stems. Under glass, the house and soil should be sterilized; in the open tomatoes should not be grown on the same piece of soil for several years. All stakes, benches, pots, etc., must be washed and houses including pathways sprayed with formaldehyde and the soil sterilized.

TOMATO VIRUSES AND OTHER DISORDERS
Tomatoes seem to have more than a normal share of virus diseases (see this page) among them **Spotted Wilt** which is rare under glass but more common out of doors where it may seriously affect growth. The young leaves show a distinctive bronzing, usually curl downwards and wilt. Infection is spread by thrips and probably occurs when the seedlings are raised under glass with other ornamental plants of which many kinds are susceptible to the disease. Affected plants should be destroyed and thrips controlled.

Various other troubles occur, most of them commonly known by descriptive names. **Blossom Drop** and **Blossom End Rot** are due to inadequate or irregular watering. **Cracking** of the fruit is due to over-watering and is common out of doors in wet summers. **Blotchy Ripening** and **Greenback** are due to poor growing conditions, often to a deficiency of potash; **Dropsy** or **Oedema** causing greyish blister-like swellings on the undersides of the leaves is due to hot, humid conditions and lack of ventilation, and **Dry Set** causing small misshapen fruit is due to poor pollination and may be reduced by over head syringing.

TORTRIX MOTHS (*Tortricidae*)
There are a number of species which attack a wide range of plants in various ways. The larvae appear in spring, most of them active and having the characteristic of wriggling backwards when disturbed or hanging from the leaf by a thread.

The larvae feed on the leaves, shoots or buds, most of them rolling or spinning the leaves together. They are common on oak trees. In apples the surface of the fruit may also be scarred, in some herbaceous plants the buds or flowers may be eaten, and in some shrubs the centre of the shoot may be eaten out. The larvae may be crushed in the rolled leaves. In severe attacks malathion or BHC spray or dust should be used as soon as possible (in the case of apples a few days before the blossom opens), and before rolling has become general.

TULIP FIRE (*Botrytis tulipae*)
This disease is often serious in wet seasons. Greyish spots and streaks occur on the leaves and flowers causing decay, and the tips of the leaves become brown and scorched. The bulbs should be lifted at the end of the season and all unsound ones destroyed. Tulips should not be planted in the same soil for at least 3 years.

VIRUS DISEASES
This group of diseases may be found on a wide range of plants, trees and shrubs and while some may seem to do little harm, the majority are serious and every effort must be made to get rid of them. All are carried in the sap and so are frequently spread by sucking insects or other means of contact or by vegetative propagation of infected plants. Some plants or even some varieties of plants may carry a virus disease yet show little or no symptom, but nevertheless can act as the source of infection for others.

The general symptoms are an unhappy, staring or stunted appearance and a malformation or discoloration of the foliage or flowers.

Mosaic produces a typical mottling of the leaves often with some yellowing or vein-clearing and decay of tissue and occurs on a number of different plants including potatoes, certain other vegetables, apples, raspberries, dahlias and many other herbaceous plants, freesias and other bulbous plants. Other forms of leaf-marking or distortion also occur, such as pale stripes in narcissus, spots or rings on carnations, or rolling of the margins in potatoes (leaf roll), yellowing of the margins or a general puckering in strawberries or the development of leafy outgrowths or enations as in tomatoes or sweet peas.

Other viruses cause distortions or colour changes in the flowers, such as 'breaking' in tulips and chrysanthemums, and still others such as the spotted wilt virus may begin as streak-like markings and end in causing the plant to wilt and die as in cinerarias, tomatoes and many others.

There is no garden cure for these diseases. Infected plants should be destroyed, insects, particularly aphids, should be rigorously controlled, only healthy plants should be used for propagation and all bought-in plants including potatoes, bulbs, cuttings, etc., should be purchased from reliable sources. New techniques such as strict roguing, heat therapy and tip-culture which demand meticulous attention and special skill or equipment are now being practised by a number of nurserymen and enable them to offer virus-tested or certified stocks of many different kinds of plants, including chrysanthemums, potatoes and fruit.

Plants are often said to have 'reverted', 'gone wild' or 'degenerated' and while there may occasionally be a true genetical breakdown or the 'wild' plants may originate from seed shed by a more beautiful but less vigorous parent which becomes crowded out, the condition is frequently due to virus diseases. The terms should be avoided, although reversion in black currants has come to be accepted as the everyday name for virus infection.

WASPS

In most gardens wasps are simply a nuisance, but if fruit is grown serious damage can be done both out of doors and under glass. The problem is generally finding the nests which too often, are some distance away on other property, but if the search is successful a proprietary wasp destroyer will be effective. If the nest cannot be found some relief can be obtained by using the old-fashioned method of hanging narrow-necked bottles of syrup or sweetened beer on or around the trees.

WATER PLANTS

These suffer more from pests than diseases. Aphids are often troublesome and the brownish-black larvae of the **Water Lily Beetle** (*Galerucella nymphaeae*) may attack the leaves and blooms of lilies. Pyrethrum or nicotine sprays may be used for aphids and lead arsenate for the beetles but if there are fish in the pool the best control is to submerge the plants for a day or two so that the fish can clear the pests away. Derris must not be used because it is highly poisonous to fish.

Leaf spot may occur on lilies and a species of *Phytophthora* may cause serious rotting of the stems. Affected parts should be removed and if no success follows, copper sulphate should be applied at the rate of 2½ oz. to every 10,000 gal. of water in the pool. The cubic capacity must be calculated carefully and the correct quantity of copper sulphate put in a small sack and drawn over the water until dissolved.

WEEVILS

These are types of beetle distinguished by their snout-like heads and legless grubs. There are several important species varying in colour, some with pretty sheen, stripes or bands but mostly grey or brown to black, about ⅓ in. long. The adults generally hide by day and feed at night, eating the tissues of many trees, bushes and plants. Some species eat notches out of the leaves, particularly of peas and beans, or roll them up to form a tube in which the larvae live and feed, others form rounded galls on the roots particularly of cruciferous plants, the damage resembling club root (page 424), while still others attack twigs, buds or flowers as in apples and strawberries, the apple blossom weevil causing the well-known 'capped' blossoms. The bark of young trees is often attacked. The vine weevil may become a serious pest both out of doors and under glass, particularly on alpines and plants in pots, and the grubs may often be seen on the roots if the plants are knocked out of their pots. In addition to the visible damage the plants may also show a poor colour and look unhappy.

The adults may be trapped in pieces of sacking or corrugated paper. The grubs may be picked off the roots of pot plants, the plants being repotted in fresh or sterilized soil to which BHC dust has been added (8 oz. per bushel of soil). For general purposes a BHC spray or dust should be used, applying it to the soil as well as the plants since many of the species have the habit of dropping to the ground when disturbed.

WHITE FLIES

There are three important species:

(1) **Cabbage White Fly** (*Aleurodes brassicae*), which is a small white moth-like fly often found on brassica crops, particularly in the south or in warm, sheltered gardens. The eggs and the flat, oval and scale-like larvae appear on the undersides of the leaves, but cause little damage to the plant, although sometimes the crop is spoilt by the 'honeydew' exuded, and by the flies getting into sprouts or hearts. All old stems should be composted as soon as possible and the lower leaves of infested crops pulled off and burnt. The flies may be attacked with carbaryl or malathion. They are extremely difficult to hit.

(2) **Greenhouse White Fly** (*Trialeurodes vaporariorum*), which is similar in appearance but is found only on greenhouse plants. It cannot survive the winter out of doors.

The larvae suck the sap causing the leaves to lose colour and look spotted. The flies fly readily when disturbed. Fumigate or spray with malathion, taking care to wet the undersides of the leaves.

(3) **Rhododendron White Fly** (*Dialeurodes chittendein*), which occurs mainly in the south and often encourages quantities of sooty moulds on the foliage. The adults are particularly active during June and July and the larvae feed mainly from Aug. to Apr. Spray with dimethoate or malathion at fortnightly intervals.

WHITE ROT OF ONIONS (*Sclerotium cepivorum*)

This is a common disease causing the leaves of onions and leeks to turn yellow and wilt and the base of the bulbs to become covered with a whitish growth which later produces black bodies about the size of a pin's head. Diseased material should be burned and no onions grown on the same soil for several years. Calomel dust applied along drills at seed sowing is a preventive.

WILTS

There are three main causes of wilting among plants. One may be the natural reaction to lack of moisture and is often purely temporary as when a plant wilts on a hot summer day and recovers in the cool of the evening. The second is due to attack by certain voracious insects such as leather jackets or cockchafers and is generally sudden and fatal. The third is caused by disease organisms of which the most important are certain species of *Verticillium*, *Fusarium* and *Sclerotinia* fungi, and the spotted wilt virus.

The fungal wilts may occur on a wide range of outdoor plants such as asters and dahlias and of glass-grown plants such as tomatoes, cucumbers, chrysanthemums or carnations. Usually the symptoms appear first in the lower leaves which wilt and turn yellow, followed by a collapse of the stem due to the fungus attacking the water-conducting tissue. If the stem is cut downwards it will show a brown discoloration. Blossom wilts are sometimes serious in fruit trees, the blossoms turning brown and giving the tree a scorched appearance. In all cases the simplest remedy is to remove and burn diseased tissue or the whole plant, and under glass, to raise the temperature and sterilize the soil.

WIREWORMS

These are the well-known slow-moving, shiny, yellowish-brown grubs common to most soils, particularly when turf has been newly broken up. The grubs are the larvae of the click beetles which are brown to black, ½ in. long and often 'skip' with a click when disturbed. The larvae vary in length, taking some 5 years to reach their mature length of ¾ in. They feed on the roots and stems of most plants and also burrow into bulbs, potatoes and other roots. They do not generally affect the growth of established plants•

but seedlings and small or young plants may wilt and die. Thorough cultivation and tidiness are usually sufficient to keep them in check, but if necessary the soil may be dusted with BHC or pieces of potato or carrot may be set just below the surface of the soil, marked and lifted every two or three days when the wireworms may be shaken out and destroyed.

WOODLICE or PILL BUGS

Although woodlice normally feed on decaying vegetable matter, particularly decaying wood, they may also attack the stems and leaves of plants both in the open and under glass and sometimes feed on vegetables in store. Generally tidiness keeps them in check but it may be necessary to dust with BHC or carbaryl.

Index

Index

Index

Index

Index